The *BIG IDEA*
COMPANION for
PREACHING
and
TEACHING

The *BIG IDEA*
COMPANION for
PREACHING
and
TEACHING

A Guide from Genesis to Revelation

Edited by
Matthew D. Kim and Scott M. Gibson

B
Baker Academic
a division of Baker Publishing Group
Grand Rapids, Michigan

© 2021 by Matthew D. Kim and Scott M. Gibson

Published by Baker Academic
a division of Baker Publishing Group
PO Box 6287, Grand Rapids, MI 49516-6287
www.bakeracademic.com

Printed in the United States of America

Library of Congress Cataloging-in-Publication Data
Names: Kim, Matthew D., 1977– editor. | Gibson, Scott M., 1957– editor.
Title: The big idea companion for preaching and teaching : a guide from Genesis to Revelation / edited by Matthew D. Kim and Scott M. Gibson.
Description: Grand Rapids, Michigan : Baker Academic, a division of Baker Publishing Group, [2021] | Includes index.
Identifiers: LCCN 2020031998 | ISBN 9781540961792 (cloth)
Subjects: LCSH: Bible—Homiletical use.
Classification: LCC BS534.5 .B547 2021 | DDC 220.6/1—dc23
LC record available at https://lccn.loc.gov/2020031998

21 22 23 24 25 26 27   7 6 5 4 3 2 1

In keeping with biblical principles of creation stewardship, Baker Publishing Group advocates the responsible use of our natural resources. As a member of the Green Press Initiative, our company uses recycled paper when possible. The text paper of this book is composed in part of post-consumer waste.

To preachers and teachers of God's Word
who disciple Christians through faithful proclamation

Contents

THE NEW TESTAMENT

Acknowledgments

We would like to thank each of the contributors who helped make this resource what it is—a comprehensive volume that seeks to encourage, equip, and energize pastors, preachers, teachers, and all God's people. Thank you for your friendship and partnership in the gospel and for sharing your knowledge on how to effectively preach and teach from this wide array of biblical books and genres.

We are also grateful for the superb team at Baker Publishing Group, especially Robert Hosack and Julie Zahm, for shepherding this large project from start to finish. Thank you for continuing to value the place of faithful preaching and teaching of God's Word. Thank you to Dan Gregory for compiling the indexes.

Last, we could not appreciate enough our wives, Sarah Kim and Rhonda Gibson, for their generosity of time and sacrifice that enables us to pursue scholarship. We know how much you also treasure the salience of effective proclamation and teaching of Scripture, and we love you for that. Thank you for all that you do so that we can work on *yet another* book project. We love you and thank God for you.

Introduction

MATTHEW D. KIM

Preparing a sermon or a Bible-study lesson can be daunting. Have you ever wished that you had a trusted conversation partner for determining the main idea or big idea of each book of the Bible? Have you wondered what the big idea is for the passages in Scripture on which you're preaching and teaching each week? It's not always easy or even convenient to ask someone for assistance. Studying the Bible can be a lonely and challenging venture for all believers in Christ, including preachers and teachers.

Well, you need not look any further. That elusive help is in your hands. Welcome to *The Big Idea Companion for Preaching and Teaching*. Written by leading evangelical homileticians, teachers of preaching, and experienced pastors, this book provides a concise resource for you—whether you are a pastor, teacher, or layperson—to check your understanding and interpretation of a particular Bible book or passage. But more than just handing you a catalog of big ideas, we want you to study the passages on your own and become confident that you can determine the main ideas of biblical texts in the privacy of your study or as you work together in groups.

This book is based on the late Haddon W. Robinson's big idea philosophy from his textbook *Biblical Preaching*. In it you will get an insider's view of the process of determining the main idea of a passage in its context (i.e., subject, complement, exegetical idea, and homiletical idea). In addition, for each book of the Bible you will have quick access to several features: (1) a brief introduction to the big idea of the entire book, (2) tips on how to divide the book into preaching and teaching pericopes, (3) guidance on difficult passages and

1

verses, (4) cultural perspectives to facilitate faithful application, and (5) recommended resources for interpreting, preaching, and teaching each book.

The Big Idea Companion for Preaching and Teaching will guide you in your hermeneutics, homiletics, and teaching of biblical texts. While we do not claim to have the sole voice on correctly interpreting any of these passages, our hope is simply to walk alongside you in this journey and act as that coveted conversation partner for you. As you'll soon find out, the overall framework for each book of the Bible, as mentioned above, will be the same. However, each author has a distinctive process for determining and wording the main ideas. We didn't want cookie-cutter chapters that taste exactly the same. Rather, we wanted each contributor's preaching and teaching voice to be read and received in a natural way. In addition, due to space limitations, the contributors may not cover every verse or pericope in their respective Bible books. As you engage in intentional and faithful study of Scripture, we ask you to pray that the Holy Spirit will lead you to *his* interpretation. The contributors to this handbook are fallible, imperfect people. Every time we read the Bible we are also submitting ourselves to the authority of God and to the authority of Scripture.

Our Christian culture is in a time of crisis—some might say apathy, despondency, or even upheaval. The very act of preaching is on a precarious slope. Too often, preachers and teachers are concerned more about their own image and popularity than they are about their integrity and faithfulness. Our hope and prayer in putting together this volume is to play a small role in assisting your daily and weekly preparation. Open up this volume whenever you feel stuck on the meaning of a given text or simply want to check your understanding with others. Depending on your needs, it can also be used as a mini-commentary to provide additional historical, grammatical, literary, and cultural context.

We believe in the faithful interpretation, proclamation, and teaching of God's Word as do you. This is our desire because we believe in the church. We believe that God is faithful to use us in this salient work of building his kingdom. May you preach and teach the Word with excellence, passion, and excitement—to the glory of God and the edification of God's people. Now, let's get to some big ideas.

THE OLD TESTAMENT

Genesis

CASEY C. BARTON

The Big Idea of Genesis

Genesis narrates our origins as God's people. The book traces humanity's story with God from its origin in God's spoken word that initiates and completes creation. The story moves through our first ancestors' disobedience to God and their consequent exile from God's presence. Once outside God's garden, humanity immediately finds itself mired in sin. Murder, shame, and immorality begin to abound in the story of God's once perfect world. From the first moments after Adam and Eve's entanglement with the serpent who led them astray, however, Genesis records God's work to bring about a reconciliation with his creation and to give his blessing to the world. The story follows the flow of God's covenant promise and blessing through his chosen servants, Abraham, Isaac, and Jacob. Jacob's family is preserved through God's gracious salvation of Jacob's son Joseph, and they will become the people of God's promise, Israel. Genesis is a book of beginnings, tracing the origin of God's people back to God's word.[1]

SUBJECT: What story does the book of Genesis tell God's people about their origins?

COMPLEMENT: That from the beginning, with creation broken by sin, they are a people created by God's word of promise and blessing to bring God's word of promise and blessing to all people, which will heal and reconcile creation with God in the end.

---

1. For a more complete and quite accessible introduction to Genesis, see Tremper Longman III, *Genesis*, The Story of God Bible Commentary (Grand Rapids: Zondervan, 2016), 1–25.

EXEGETICAL IDEA: The book of Genesis tells God's people the story of their origins, that from the beginning, with creation broken by sin, they are a people created by God's word of promise and blessing to bring God's word of promise and blessing to all people, which will heal and reconcile creation with God in the end.

HOMILETICAL IDEA: God's story begins with promises of his presence with his people for the world.

Selecting Preaching and Teaching Passages in Genesis

Genesis is the first portion of the larger literary unit that includes Exodus, Leviticus, Numbers, and Deuteronomy—the Pentateuch. The book is composed of four broad narrative arcs that focus on God's presence and promise with the central characters of the story. The narratives that make up these larger sections detail God's particular history with his people as he forms them through covenant, promise, and blessing, and as he judges sin and wickedness both in his own people and in the world. Selection of preaching passages should take into account the pericope's place in these larger narratives.

The first of these arcs is the prehistory of God's people, from creation through the flood and on to the introduction of Abram (chaps. 1–11). Here the story is told of God's good creation spoiled by the sin of the first people that he made to steward it. From the fall, God's gracious presence travels alongside the spread of sin in the world. Even with God's cleansing of the earth with a flood, sin remains in the generation of Noah's sons (9:18–28). Sin stubbornly will not go away. Two paths begin to emerge—the path overgrown with sin and choking most of creation, and a path of promise graciously given to Abram and his descendants (though even this path has its fair share of sin along the way).

God's promises are formalized as we are introduced to Abram (soon to be Abraham) and the all-important covenant that God makes with him (chaps. 12–25). The arc of Abraham is a story of God making promises to one man for the blessing of all people, and that one man struggling in faith and obedience to believe and live the promises of God when they are nearly impossible for him to believe. The son born out of God's covenant promise, Isaac, inherits that promise from Abraham and in turn passes it to his son.

The next generation of God's covenant promises working their way into the world comes through the narrative arc of Jacob (chaps. 25–36), the deceptive younger brother who both steals the blessing and is given it by God. Jacob's story, like Abraham's (Jacob will also get a new name), is one of emerging faith in the fulfillment of promises that Jacob may not be able to fully see or understand but that he will grab and hold on to for dear life (32:22–32).

A final set of stories focus on Jacob's son, Joseph, and are told for the sake of Jacob's entire family (chaps. 37–50). Joseph's story recalls how God preserved the people that he had created and blessed to be the bearers of his covenant blessing to the world. It is given to show God's providential work in bringing the people of Israel to Egypt, saving them from famine and building them into a nation. This sets the stage for the central redemptive act of God in the Old Testament when he brings his people out of Egypt in Exodus, keeping yet another promise (46:2–5).

Selecting specific texts for preaching within these larger sections will be a matter of tracing narrative beginnings and endings, seeking the central idea in each as it functions within the whole.[2]

Getting the Subject, Complement, Exegetical Idea, and Homiletical Idea

Genesis 1:1–2:3

SUBJECT: What does the author of Genesis say is the origin of the cosmos and everything in it?

COMPLEMENT: God speaking all things into existence, forming and filling it all out of nothing.

EXEGETICAL IDEA: The author of Genesis says that the origin of the cosmos and everything in it was God speaking all things into existence, forming and filling it all out of nothing.

HOMILETICAL IDEA: God spoke, forming and filling all of creation out of nothing.

Genesis 2:4–25

SUBJECT: What does the author say is the origin and original state of humanity?

COMPLEMENT: God created man and woman as innocent and perfect complements, stewards of his good creation.

---

2. Commentators outline Genesis in varying ways for both exposition and preaching. For alternative structural outlines, see Longman, *Genesis*; Walter Brueggemann, *Genesis*, Interpretation (Louisville: John Knox, 1982); or R. Kent Hughes, *Genesis: Beginning and Blessing* (Wheaton: Crossway, 2004).

EXEGETICAL IDEA: The author says that the origin and original state of humanity is that God created man and woman as innocent and perfect complements, stewards of his good creation.

HOMILETICAL IDEA: God created us to be the perfect caretakers of his creation.

Genesis 3

SUBJECT: How does the author say humanity lost the innocence with which it was created?

COMPLEMENT: Through disobedience to God, which brought a curse on creation and separation from God.

EXEGETICAL IDEA: The author says that humanity lost the innocence with which it was created through disobedience to God, bringing about a curse on creation and separation from God.

HOMILETICAL IDEA: Sin leaves its scars when we allow it into God's world.

Genesis 4:1–16

SUBJECT: What does the author say happened in the generation after the fall?

COMPLEMENT: Sin began to dominate as Cain murdered his brother Abel.

EXEGETICAL IDEA: The author says that, in the first generation after the fall, sin began to dominate as Cain murdered his brother Abel.

HOMILETICAL IDEA: Sin overwhelms with violent force.

Genesis 4:17–5:32

SUBJECT: What does the author's juxtaposition of Cain's and Seth's lines reveal about humanity after the fall?

COMPLEMENT: Humanity's path was split as Cain's family pursued sin and vengeance while Seth's family pursued God's relief from the curse.

EXEGETICAL IDEA: The author's juxtaposition of Cain's and Seth's lines reveals that, after the fall, humanity's path split as Cain's family pursued sin and vengeance while Seth's family pursued God's relief from the curse.

HOMILETICAL IDEA: After the fall our paths diverge, leading us either toward God or farther away.

Genesis 6:1–9:17

SUBJECT: How does the author say God responded to wickedness overtaking humanity and the whole creation?

COMPLEMENT: By bringing a flood to cleanse creation, saving for himself a small remnant for a new creation.

EXEGETICAL IDEA: The author says God responded to wickedness overtaking humanity and the whole creation by bringing a flood to cleanse creation, saving for himself a small remnant for a new creation.

HOMILETICAL IDEA: God's way is to make all things new.

Genesis 9:18-28

SUBJECT: How does the author say sin persisted in the first generation after the flood?

COMPLEMENT: Noah's son Ham dishonored his father, bringing a curse on his son Canaan's line and a blessing on the families of his brothers Shem and Japheth.

EXEGETICAL IDEA: The author says sin persisted in the first generation after the flood when Noah's son Ham dishonored his father, bringing a curse on his son Canaan's line and a blessing on the families of his brothers Shem and Japheth.

HOMILETICAL IDEA: God makes all things new, and sin still pushes back.

Genesis 10-11

SUBJECT: How does the author present the development of nations and languages from the time of Noah to Abram?

COMPLEMENT: By recounting that humanity's problem with sin was magnified rather than overcome through coordinated human effort, and in God's judgment and grace God divided the people into nations and languages, tracing his plan to and through Abram.

EXEGETICAL IDEA: The author presents the development of nations and languages from the time of Noah to Abram by recounting that humanity's problem with sin was magnified rather than overcome through coordinated human effort, and in God's judgment and grace God divided the people into nations and languages, tracing his plan to and through Abram.

HOMILETICAL IDEA: The path to God must follow his story, not ours.

Genesis 12:1-9

SUBJECT: What does the author say about the covenant God made with Abram?

COMPLEMENT: That Abram would leave all he had and God would make him a great nation, give him a great name, and bless him and the world through him.

EXEGETICAL IDEA: The author says that in the covenant God made with Abram, Abram would leave all he had and God would make him a great nation, give him a great name, and bless him and the world through him.

HOMILETICAL IDEA: God's people are created with a promise, and its blessing remains today.

Genesis 12:10-13:18

SUBJECT: What does the author reveal about God's treatment of Abram in these stories of his wandering?

COMPLEMENT: That God rescued him from harm and promised to bless him in the land.

EXEGETICAL IDEA: In these stories of Abram's journeying, the author reveals about God's treatment of Abram that God rescued him from harm and promised to bless him in the land.

HOMILETICAL IDEA: God cares for the bearers of his promise.

Genesis 14

SUBJECT: How does the author say God reinforced his covenant with Abram at the end of the battle in which he rescued Lot?

COMPLEMENT: Through the blessing of Melchizedek, king of Salem and priest of God Most High.

EXEGETICAL IDEA: The author says God reinforced his covenant with Abram at the end of the battle in which he rescued Lot through the blessing of Melchizedek, king of Salem and priest of God Most High.

HOMILETICAL IDEA: God's blessing appears in surprising places.

Genesis 15

SUBJECT: How does the author say God answered Abram's fear over the covenant's delayed fulfillment?

COMPLEMENT: By guaranteeing the covenant promises with God's own self in a self-curse ritual.

EXEGETICAL IDEA: The author says God answered Abram's fear over the covenant's delayed fulfillment by guaranteeing the covenant promises with God's own self in a self-curse ritual.

HOMILETICAL IDEA: God's promises rest on God's shoulders.

Genesis 16

SUBJECT: How does the author say God treated Hagar when she was used by Sarai and Abram to seek the fulfillment of the covenant promises on their own, apart from God?

COMPLEMENT: God found, heard, and saw her in her abuse and blessed her with a son who would become a great nation who would stand in hostile relationship with other nations.

EXEGETICAL IDEA: The author says that when Hagar was used by Sarai and Abram to seek the fulfillment of the covenant promises on their own, apart from God, God found, heard, and saw her in her abuse and blessed her with a son who would become a great nation who would stand in hostile relationship with other nations.

HOMILETICAL IDEA: God's love comes to those abandoned by God's people.

Genesis 17

SUBJECT: What does the author say about God establishing the line and sign of his covenant with Abraham and his descendants?

COMPLEMENT: That God's covenant would flow through Isaac's line with circumcision as the covenant's sign.

EXEGETICAL IDEA: The author says about God establishing the line and sign of his covenant with Abraham and his descendants that God's covenant would flow through Isaac's line with circumcision as the covenant's sign.

HOMILETICAL IDEA: God has set his people apart, then and now.

Genesis 18:1-15

SUBJECT: How does the author say God confirmed the covenant to Sarah?

COMPLEMENT: With a personal visit by God and his emissaries, in which he read Sarah's heart and affirmed the imminent fulfillment of the promise of a son.

EXEGETICAL IDEA: The author says God confirmed the covenant to Sarah with a personal visit by God and his emissaries, in which he read Sarah's heart and affirmed the imminent fulfillment of the promise of a son.

HOMILETICAL IDEA: The impossible won't prevent God's promises from prevailing.

Genesis 18:16–19:38

SUBJECT: How does the author say sin persisted through the age of God's covenant with Abraham?

COMPLEMENT: The citizens of the cities of Sodom and Gomorrah practiced egregious sin, such as asserting power through forcible rape, bringing God's destructive judgment on them even while, for Abraham's sake, God saved Lot's family, whose descendants would be the result of further sexual sin and become enemies of Abraham's descendants throughout their story.

EXEGETICAL IDEA: The author says sin persisted in the age of God's covenant with Abraham as the citizens of the cities of Sodom and Gomorrah practiced egregious sin, such as asserting power through forcible rape, bringing God's destructive judgment on them even while, for Abraham's sake, God saved Lot's family, whose descendants would be the result of further sexual sin and become enemies of Abraham's descendants throughout their story.

HOMILETICAL IDEA: God's mercy emerges even as his judgment ensues.

Genesis 20

SUBJECT: How does the author say God responded to Abraham's habitual sin of lying about his marriage to Sarah, putting her and the covenant in danger?

COMPLEMENT: In preserving the covenant promise by preventing Abimelech from taking Sarah for himself.

EXEGETICAL IDEA: The author says God responded to Abraham's habitual sin of lying about his marriage to Sarah, putting her and the covenant in danger, in preserving the covenant promise by preventing Abimelech from taking Sarah for himself.

HOMILETICAL IDEA: God's promise won't be derailed by our sin.

Genesis 21:1–21

SUBJECT: What does the author say about the status of Abraham's two sons in relation to God's covenant?

COMPLEMENT: That Isaac was the long-awaited and impossibly conceived child of God's covenant promise, while Ishmael would not inherit God's promise and was driven away, though cared for by God.

EXEGETICAL IDEA: The author says about the status of Abraham's two sons in relation to God's covenant that Isaac was the long-awaited and impossibly conceived child of God's covenant promise, while Ishmael would not inherit God's promise and was driven away, though cared for by God.

HOMILETICAL IDEA: God's promise follows God's story.

Genesis 21:22-34

SUBJECT: What does the author say Abraham's oath with Abimelech revealed about God's covenant with Abraham?

COMPLEMENT: That while God's blessing would remain on Abraham despite his previous dishonesty, he must deal honestly with his neighbors in the land, becoming a blessing to them.

EXEGETICAL IDEA: The author says that Abraham's oath with Abimelech revealed about God's covenant with Abraham that while God's blessing would remain on Abraham despite his previous dishonesty, he must deal honestly with his neighbors in the land, becoming a blessing to them.

HOMILETICAL IDEA: God's promise must change who and how we are in the world.

Genesis 22

SUBJECT: What does the author say was Abraham's response to God's test of his faithfulness by asking him to sacrifice Isaac?

COMPLEMENT: Abraham displayed the maturity of his faith in God's promises by obeying without question, to which God reaffirmed the covenant promise through Isaac.

EXEGETICAL IDEA: The author says Abraham's response to God's test of his faithfulness by asking him to sacrifice Isaac was to display the maturity of his faith in God's promises by obeying without question, to which God reaffirmed the covenant promise through Isaac.

HOMILETICAL IDEA: Only Jesus provides the sacrifice that brings us life.

Genesis 23:1–25:18

SUBJECT: How does the author say Abraham's part in God's story was concluded?

COMPLEMENT: After Sarah's death and burial, Abraham ensured the continuation of the covenant line by finding Isaac a wife and passing on all he had to Isaac before he died.

EXEGETICAL IDEA: The author says Abraham's part in God's story was concluded when, after Sarah's death and burial, Abraham ensured the continuation of the covenant line by finding Isaac a wife and passing on all he had to Isaac before he died.

HOMILETICAL IDEA: God's promise lives past our part in his story.

Genesis 25:19–34

SUBJECT: How does the author trace the path of God's covenant promises at the beginning of the story of Isaac and his sons?

COMPLEMENT: By revealing that God chose the younger Jacob to inherit the covenant rather than the older Esau, who sold and despised his birthright.

EXEGETICAL IDEA: The author traces the path of God's covenant promises at the beginning of the story of Isaac and his sons by revealing that God chose the younger Jacob to inherit the covenant rather than the older Esau, who sold and despised his birthright.

HOMILETICAL IDEA: God's promises flow in his own ways.

Genesis 26

SUBJECT: How does the author describe the beginning of God's fulfillment of covenant promises to Isaac?

COMPLEMENT: By showing that, for the sake of Abraham's obedience, God blessed Isaac with wealth and prosperity and elevated his status among the peoples.

EXEGETICAL IDEA: The author describes the beginning of God's fulfillment of covenant promises to Isaac by showing that, for the sake of Abraham's obedience, God blessed Isaac with wealth and prosperity and elevated his status among the peoples.

HOMILETICAL IDEA: God fulfills his promises from generation to generation.

Genesis 27:1–28:9

SUBJECT: Who does the author say is the recipient of Isaac's blessing and God's covenant promises?

COMPLEMENT: Jacob, who deceived his father and yet was chosen by God from his birth.

EXEGETICAL IDEA: The author says the recipient of Isaac's blessing and God's covenant promises was Jacob, who deceived his father and yet was chosen by God from his birth.

HOMILETICAL IDEA: God sees his way through our deception to fulfill his promises.

Genesis 28:10–22

SUBJECT: How does the author say God confirmed the passing of covenant promises to Jacob?

COMPLEMENT: By coming to him in a dream in which he showed himself to Jacob and made to him the promises he made to Abraham, to which Jacob responded with a vow of faithfulness.

EXEGETICAL IDEA: The author says God confirmed the passing of covenant promises to Jacob by coming to him in a dream in which he showed himself to Jacob and made to him the promises he made to Abraham, to which Jacob responded with a vow of faithfulness.

HOMILETICAL IDEA: God's promises span heaven and earth to bring his children home.

Genesis 29–31

SUBJECT: How does the author say God preserved and progressed the story of his covenant through Jacob's raucous time in exile?

COMPLEMENT: By providing him children who would carry the story on.

EXEGETICAL IDEA: The author says God preserved and progressed the story of his covenant through Jacob's raucous time in exile by providing him children who would carry the story on.

HOMILETICAL IDEA: God's promises endure through the craziest times.

Genesis 32:1–33:17

SUBJECT: How does the author say Jacob was both changed and remained the same in his two meetings as he returned to the promised land fearing Esau's wrath?

COMPLEMENT: In his meeting with and defeat by God, Jacob was changed as he was reborn, newly named Israel and blessed though crippled, after which he found reconciliation with Esau as the new Israel and remained a deceiver when he lied again to his brother.

EXEGETICAL IDEA: The author says Jacob was both changed and remained the same in his two meetings as he returned to the promised land fearing Esau's wrath when, in his meeting with and defeat by God, Jacob was changed as he was reborn, newly named Israel and blessed though crippled, after which he found reconciliation with Esau as the new Israel and remained a deceiver when he lied again to his brother.

HOMILETICAL IDEA: Magnificently defeated, we are being made new.[3]

Genesis 33:18-34:31

SUBJECT: What does the author say Israel's sons did to Shechem and his people when he raped their sister Dinah?

COMPLEMENT: They used the sacred symbol of God's covenant, circumcision, to exact a violent and brutal revenge for personal satisfaction and economic gain.

EXEGETICAL IDEA: The author says that when Shechem raped their sister Dinah, Jacob's sons used the sacred symbol of God's covenant, circumcision, to exact a violent and brutal revenge on Shechem and his people for personal satisfaction and economic gain.

HOMILETICAL IDEA: In humanity's sin we turn God's blessings into inhumane weapons of violence.

Genesis 35:1-36:43

SUBJECT: How does the author affirm the lineage along which God's covenant would travel?

COMPLEMENT: By recounting Jacob's and Esau's lines, highlighting Jacob's blessing by God at Bethel.

EXEGETICAL IDEA: The author affirms the lineage along which God's covenant would travel by recounting Jacob's and Esau's lines, highlighting Jacob's blessing by God at Bethel.

HOMILETICAL IDEA: God's promises follow God's story.

---

3. The phrase "magnificent defeat" for the story of Jacob wrestling with God comes from Frederick Buechner, *The Magnificent Defeat* (San Francisco: Harper, 1985).

Genesis 37:1-11

SUBJECT: What does the author indicate about Joseph as he introduces the story of Jacob's sons?

COMPLEMENT: Joseph was Jacob's favored son, whose dreams reveal that he would rule over his older brothers.

EXEGETICAL IDEA: As he introduces the story of Jacob's sons, the author indicates that Joseph was Jacob's favored son, whose dreams revealed that he would rule over his older brothers.

HOMILETICAL IDEA: God's promises fulfilled are our grandest dreams come true.

Genesis 37:12-36

SUBJECT: How does the author say Joseph's life was spared when his brothers determined to kill him because of their father's favoritism and the implications of his dreams?

COMPLEMENT: Instead of killing him, they sold him into slavery, which brought him to Egypt.

EXEGETICAL IDEA: The author says Joseph's life was spared when his brothers determined to kill him because of their father's favoritism and the implications of his dreams when, instead of killing him, they sold him into slavery, which brought him to Egypt.

HOMILETICAL IDEA: God's promise rolls right over whatever barriers we put in its way.

Genesis 38

SUBJECT: Why does the author say Judah regarded Tamar as more righteous than himself?

COMPLEMENT: Because his self-serving preservation revealed his denial of her justice.

EXEGETICAL IDEA: The author says Judah regarded Tamar as more righteous than himself because his self-serving preservation revealed his denial of her justice.

HOMILETICAL IDEA: Denying justice to those it is owed distances us from God's righteousness.

Genesis 39

SUBJECT: Why does the author say Joseph was able to prosper in Egypt despite being a slave who was falsely accused of rape and imprisoned?

COMPLEMENT: Because the Lord was with him and brought him success.

EXEGETICAL IDEA: The author says Joseph was able to prosper in Egypt despite being a slave who was falsely accused of rape and imprisoned because the Lord was with him and brought him success.

HOMILETICAL IDEA: Even when the deck is stacked against God's people, God's presence preserves them.

Genesis 40-41

SUBJECT: How does the author say God prospered Joseph in Egypt?

COMPLEMENT: By giving him the gift of interpreting dreams, which put him into favor with Pharaoh, who made him second in command over all Egypt in the time leading up to and during a great famine.

EXEGETICAL IDEA: The author says God prospered Joseph in Egypt by giving him the gift of interpreting dreams, which put him into favor with Pharaoh, who made him second in command over all Egypt in the time leading up to and during a great famine.

HOMILETICAL IDEA: God gifts us to play our part in his big story.

Genesis 42-45

SUBJECT: In this extended story of Joseph's reconciliation with his brothers, what does the author say had been God's ultimate purpose in bringing Joseph to Egypt?

COMPLEMENT: To preserve the lives of the family of Israel, and by extension the promises of God's covenant with them.

EXEGETICAL IDEA: In this extended story of Joseph's reconciliation with his brothers, the author says God's ultimate purpose in bringing Joseph to Egypt had been to preserve the lives of the family of Israel, and by extension the promises of God's covenant with them.

HOMILETICAL IDEA: Through good and bad, God tells his story to preserve his promises.

Genesis 46-47

SUBJECT: What assurance does the author say Jacob had from God as Joseph settled his family in Egypt?

COMPLEMENT: That God would go with him, prosper his family, and bring him back.

EXEGETICAL IDEA: The author says that as Joseph settled his family in Egypt, Jacob had the assurance that God would go with him, prosper his family, and bring him back.

HOMILETICAL IDEA: God joins us as we play our role in the story he's telling.

Genesis 48:1-50:14

SUBJECT: What does the author say Jacob did for his family at the end of his life?

COMPLEMENT: He bestowed on the whole of his family blessings appropriate for each one individually, passing God's covenant blessing on to his descendants.

EXEGETICAL IDEA: The author says that at the end of Jacob's life he bestowed on the whole of his family blessings appropriate for each one individually, passing God's covenant blessing on to his descendants.

HOMILETICAL IDEA: God's promises live past our part in his story.

Genesis 50:15-26

SUBJECT: What messages does the author say Joseph gave to his brothers before he dies?

COMPLEMENT: All that had happened had been from God, who would fulfill his promise to bring them out of Egypt and into the land promised to their fathers.

EXEGETICAL IDEA: The author says the messages Joseph gave to his brothers before he dies are that all that had happened had been from God, who would fulfill his promise to bring them out of Egypt and into the land promised to their fathers.

HOMILETICAL IDEA: Looking back at God's faithfulness encourages us for the road stretched out ahead.

Difficult Passages/Verses

A number of difficulties await the preacher approaching the book of Genesis. First, some of the book's stories have a fantastical quality, and the preacher will benefit from understanding the literary nature of Genesis when shaping his or her interpretation and proclamation of these stories. Second, the story unfolds into scenes that are seemingly incongruous with our vision of God, of God's people, and of the interaction between the two, and the preacher can be left not quite knowing what to say.

We don't have to wait around long in the pages of Genesis before we recognize the fantastical nature of the story of our beginnings. From the outset we are faced with realities that seem apart from our own experiences of the world. Herein lies a world where God breathes into lumps of dirt (2:7), snakes speak (3:1), God walks in the garden (3:8) and wrestles with men (32:24), and God speaks creation into existence (1:3) and speaks to those he's chosen to hear him (46:3–4). The world revealed in these pages makes its claim to be the very same world in which we live. When proclaiming Genesis as God's story, the preacher must be able to bring the creative world of Genesis into focus for the congregation that lives in that same world today.

Recognizing that the literary genre of Genesis is *theological* or *sacred history* is helpful.[4] The book is centrally a historical narrative, making real claims about a real past. However, it is not history that seeks only to recount facts, figures, dates, people, and locations. Genesis narrates events, and those events all have their origin and significance in the relationship of God's real and actual interaction with humanity. The author is centrally concerned about the work and action of God in the world. In this sense, the author often uses figurative or nonliteral language to recount and present events and realities that literally happened. The point here is that Genesis was not intended to function as history in the same way a twenty-first-century history book recounts history. Sidney Greidanus notes about Hebrew historical narratives that they "are like stained-glass windows which artistically reveal the significance of certain facts from a specific faith perspective."[5] Genesis recounts the events of God with God's people through a theological lens. God himself is fantastical and creative. That his story is also fantastical and creative shouldn't give us much pause.

A second set of difficulties arises when the text presents stories that strike modern ears as particularly unethical or violent, that reveal God's people as immoral and yet heroes of the faith, or that present actions of God that are simply difficult to understand.

When God gives Abraham circumcision as a sign of the covenant, he commands that all males be circumcised, including those "born in your house or bought with your money" (17:12 ESV). Does God here condone slavery? Or does God merely acknowledge its reality? Why doesn't God condemn it

---

4. Longman discusses the genre and style of Genesis as theological history. See Longman, *Genesis*, 7–10.

5. Sidney Greidanus, *The Modern Preacher and the Ancient Text* (Grand Rapids: Eerdmans, 1988), 196. Greidanus's discussion of Hebrew narrative on the whole is helpful; see 188–227.

outright? The preacher should be ready to address questions such as these inside and outside the church.

Some stories are simply violent and shocking. What are we to make of Shechem's rape of Dinah in chapter 34?[6] The story is at once disorienting and infuriating. Shechem rapes Dinah, and yet we are told that he loves her and wants to marry her. Her father and brothers negotiate her marriage to her rapist with his father, and in the story she is given no voice in the matter. In the end, Jacob's sons weaponize the sign of the covenant blessing of God, circumcision, to gain a tactical advantage in their plan to slaughter not just Shechem but also all the men of the city and to plunder what was left. How should the preacher address such a violent scene? Telling this story in the pulpit will take wisdom to not say too little and distill the power of the offense, and to not say too much, exploiting Dinah once again for homiletical spectacle, still not able to speak her own story. In any case, the story is God's and we cannot ignore it.

Other times the story's heroes act very unheroically. In chapter 16 Abram and Sarai use their servant Hagar as a surrogate for Sarai in an attempt to force the fulfillment of God's promise rather than having patient faith that God will be faithful. Too often preachers skip or gloss over these stories of unvarnished abuse. Here, the patriarch is guilty of using Hagar as a sexual servant and then allowing his wife to abuse her. It is important to acknowledge that God's people are flawed, even if God and his covenant are not. It is notable here that God cares for those whom God's people have abandoned. That is a powerful story to tell today, calling God's people to repentance and preaching hope to those who have found themselves unwelcome among them.

Among these stories that are difficult to hear, there are also the stories in which we cannot fathom the action of God on the stage. These may have to do with the utter scope and destruction of God's judgment, such as in the flood (chaps. 6–9) or the judgment of Sodom and Gomorrah (chaps. 18–19). God's people today are not accustomed to interacting with God as judge. Central among these stories, however, must be God's test of Abraham's faith by asking him to sacrifice his son Isaac, the son of the promise, as a burnt offering to God (chap. 22), a story that can cause logical dissonance in the reader. While this story is incredibly important to the whole of Genesis, and for understanding the sacrifice of Christ later in God's story, it can be equally difficult to interpret, understand, and preach. On the one hand, it is hard to think of God as asking for a human sacrifice, when we know that elsewhere in Scripture he abhors the practice (Lev. 18:21; Deut. 18:10). On the other

---

6. With the NIV, Longman translates Shechem's offense in 34:2 as rape. See Longman, *Genesis*, 426–35.

hand, it is nearly as horrible to think of Abraham's willingness to comply. The preacher must keep the focus on the overarching themes of Genesis—the faithfulness of God to his covenant promises, the creation of a covenant people for himself—to lead the congregation in hearing God's Word here. It is helpful to remember that we preach these stories in the context of the gospel of Christ.

Cultural Perspectives and Application

In this space I will focus on just two observations of application: Genesis gives us a story about origins, and that story shows us that God will not abandon his people.

In recent years at-home DNA tests have become increasingly popular for consumers looking to connect with others and connect to their roots. At the end of 2018 more than twenty-six million people had added their DNA samples to databases through companies such as Ancestry and 23andMe. Researchers extrapolate that number to be more than one hundred million by the beginning of 2021.[7] One way to interpret this phenomenon is to say that people are longing to connect to their history, to discover their origins, and new technology is making it easier and more accessible to do so. At the center of the human experience there is a sense in which we long to be connected to something larger than ourselves.

Genesis tells this story of our origins. It gives us the history that we are longing for. We have our origins in the very word of God spoken into nothing to bring about something good, beautiful, lovely, and loved. Genesis tells us that we are something good. We are the ones whom God loves. We are the inheritors of the story of God pursuing his creation, despite our sin, through Sodoms and Shechems, deceptions and famines, promises and blessings down through the generations of God's people. In the death and resurrection and reign of Christ, we are connected to this story of the beginning of God's people because in Christ we are God's people. Genesis begins the story of how God loved us so much that he wouldn't let us go. Proclaiming this story can help people connect to that bigger story that all of those DNA tests promise but cannot deliver in remotely the same way.

Another pervasive experience of contemporary living is abandonment. Children experience abandonment when they don't receive the love or care

---

7. Antonio Regalado, "More Than 26 Million People Have Taken an At-Home Ancestry Test," *MIT Technology Review*, February 11, 2019, https://www.technologyreview.com/s/612880/more-than-26-million-people-have-taken-an-at-home-ancestry-test.

from a parent that should be given to them. These fears and feelings can follow individuals through the entirety of their lives, possibly casting a shadow over every relationship they will ever have. Marriages that end in divorce often carry feelings of abandonment by one or both partners. It is striking that so many relationships in our world that are supposed to be marked with love, care, and stability end in infidelity, apathy, and abandonment of the other.

Genesis tells us another story, though. Throughout the narrative we are confronted with a God who simply will not abandon those he loves. At times in the story it seems as if humanity is trying to get God to abandon us as we persist in taking God's good creation and using it for selfish or violent ends. And yet through it all God is relentless in his faithfulness to his covenant promises, unyielding in his pursuit of the redemption of humanity. God has been faithful to his creation throughout history, working to remove the sin that separates us from him. In the beginning God created the heavens and the earth, and he created us good in the midst of it all. In Christ, he is re-creating the world the way it was meant to be from the beginning, restoring the garden, and he will not leave us or let us get away from him until the story is finished (Rev. 22:1–5).

This is good news to preach.

RECOMMENDED RESOURCES

Arnold, Bill T. *Encountering the Book of Genesis*. Encountering Biblical Studies. Grand Rapids: Baker Academic, 1998.

Brueggemann, Walter. *Genesis*. Interpretation. Louisville: John Knox, 1982.

Longman, Tremper, III. *Genesis*. The Story of God Bible Commentary. Grand Rapids: Zondervan, 2016.

Exodus

NATHANIEL M. WRIGHT

The Big Idea of Exodus

The book of Exodus is thematically central to the Bible. In it we learn not only that God is faithful to his promises but also that he exercises unmatched power in the affairs of human history in order to save his people and fulfill those promises. Further, the initial revelation of the Ten Commandments and additional precepts of instruction form the basis of the Bible's moral vision—all founded on the saving love of the Lord.

SUBJECT: What did the Lord do when Israel was enslaved in Egypt?

COMPLEMENT: As he had promised, the Lord rescued Israel from slavery, judging Pharaoh and the gods of Egypt, giving Israel his covenant at Sinai, and remaining faithful to his promise to dwell among the people of Israel.

EXEGETICAL IDEA: When Israel was enslaved in Egypt, the Lord rescued Israel as he had promised, judging Pharaoh and the gods of Egypt, giving his covenant at Sinai, and remaining faithful to his promise to dwell among the people of Israel.

HOMILETICAL IDEA: God is faithful to his promises and delivers his people.

Selecting Preaching and Teaching Passages in Exodus

The first half of Exodus breaks relatively easily into pericopes that follow historical accounts. Preachers should remember that though Exodus is chronological in a general sense, the text does at times favor thematic development over a strict historical sequencing. The defeat of the Amalekites, for example, is mentioned next to the appointing of the seventy elders, and Hebrew verbal parallels emphasize the similarity between the two episodes: in both cases Moses chooses others to help him. This kind of structuring of Exodus allows preachers the opportunity to preach on longer sections of text with one big idea, rather than focusing simply on the "and this happened after that" analysis that sometimes can occur within extended narratives. Look for themes woven throughout the events, not only at the events themselves.

The second half of Exodus differs in form and pace from the first half, as sections of law are interspersed with lengthy descriptions of tabernacle materials and instructions. These sections are not without helpful big ideas but must be approached with special attention to how contemporary hearers will remain interested.

The reader of Exodus discovers several literary genres throughout the book, ranging from relatively simple narratives to recipes for anointing oil and holy incense. It is the overarching theme of God delivering Israel and making them his people, particularly by dwelling among them, that links together and gives thematic context to these various parts of the book and their corresponding literary forms. When in doubt, stick to those big themes and all will be well.

Getting the Subject, Complement, Exegetical Idea, and Homiletical Idea

Exodus 1

SUBJECT: How did Israel become enslaved in Egypt?

COMPLEMENT: A new pharaoh, who did not know about Joseph, came to power and enslaved Israel.

EXEGETICAL IDEA: Israel was enslaved in Egypt when a new pharaoh, who did not know about Joseph, came to power and enslaved them.

HOMILETICAL IDEA: Sometimes the world turns against God's people.

Exodus 2:1–10

SUBJECT: How did Moses survive Pharaoh's edict to kill all newborn Hebrew boys?

COMPLEMENT: His mother placed him in the Nile River in a basket, where Pharaoh's daughter found him.

EXEGETICAL IDEA: Moses survived Pharaoh's edict to kill all newborn Hebrew boys because his mother placed him in the Nile River in a basket, where Pharaoh's daughter found him.

HOMILETICAL IDEA: Fear Pharaoh, but fear God more.

Exodus 2:11–25

SUBJECT: As God remembered his promise during Israel's slavery, what happened to Moses and to Israel?

COMPLEMENT: Moses killed an Egyptian, fled Egypt, and married a Midianite, while the Israelites cried out to God in their suffering.

EXEGETICAL IDEA: As God remembered his promise during Israel's slavery, Moses killed an Egyptian, fled Egypt, and married a Midianite, while the Israelites cried out to God in their suffering.

HOMILETICAL IDEA: God remembers his promises, even when circumstances seem to say otherwise.

Exodus 3:1–4:17

SUBJECT: How did God call Moses to lead Israel out of Egypt?

COMPLEMENT: God appeared to him, outlined his task, and answered his objections.

EXEGETICAL IDEA: God called Moses to lead Israel out of Egypt by appearing to him, outlining his task, and answering his objections.

HOMILETICAL IDEA: Whom God call, he equips.

Exodus 4:18–26

SUBJECT: After Moses had set out for Egypt in obedience to God, why did God seek to kill him?

COMPLEMENT: God sought to kill Moses because his son was not circumcised, and Zipporah intervened to save Moses's life.

EXEGETICAL IDEA: After Moses had set out for Egypt in obedience to God, God sought to kill Moses because his son was not circumcised, and Zipporah intervened to save Moses's life.

HOMILETICAL IDEA: Full obedience to God's call affects our families.

Exodus 4:27–5:5

SUBJECT: What happened when Moses and Aaron obeyed God and returned to Egypt?

COMPLEMENT: The Israelites believed their message and worshiped God, but Pharaoh rejected their message and accused them.

EXEGETICAL IDEA: When Moses and Aaron obeyed God and returned to Egypt, the Israelites believed their message and worshiped God, but Pharaoh rejected their message and accused them.

HOMILETICAL IDEA: Obey God even when some join and others accuse.

Exodus 5:6–6:12

SUBJECT: What happened when Pharaoh required bricks without straw?

COMPLEMENT: The Israelites were beaten, Moses conveyed their complaints to God, and God restated his promise of deliverance.

EXEGETICAL IDEA: When Pharaoh required bricks without straw, the Israelites were beaten, Moses conveyed their complaints to God, and God restated his promise of deliverance.

HOMILETICAL IDEA: In hardship, God sticks to his same promises.

Exodus 6:13–7:7

SUBJECT: Who were Moses and Aaron?

COMPLEMENT: They were Israelite brothers whom the Lord used as God's prophet to Pharaoh, in order to bring Israel out of slavery.

EXEGETICAL IDEA: Moses and Aaron were Israelite brothers whom the Lord used as God's prophet to Pharaoh, in order to bring Israel out of slavery.

HOMILETICAL IDEA: God uses ordinary people for his extraordinary plans.

Exodus 7:8–11:10

SUBJECT: What was Pharaoh's response when God struck Egypt with increasingly destructive plagues?

COMPLEMENT: Pharaoh repeatedly hardened his heart and did not let Israel go.

EXEGETICAL IDEA: When God struck Egypt with increasingly destructive plagues, Pharaoh repeatedly hardened his heart and did not let Israel go.

HOMILETICAL IDEA: It may take a few more plagues, but God will get you out.

Exodus 12:1-30

SUBJECT: How was Israel to respond to God's promise to strike down the firstborn of Egypt?

COMPLEMENT: They were to observe the Passover meal on that night and the Feast of Unleavened Bread in perpetuity every year thereafter.

EXEGETICAL IDEA: Israel was to respond to God's promise to strike down the firstborn of Egypt by observing the Passover meal on that night and the Feast of Unleavened Bread in perpetuity every year thereafter.

HOMILETICAL IDEA: Observe God's Passover in Christ and remember it thereafter in the Lord's Supper.

Exodus 12:31-13:16

SUBJECT: How did it come about that the Israelites left Egypt, and how is it to be remembered?

COMPLEMENT: After the tenth plague, Pharaoh agreed to let the Israelites go, and Moses instructed the Israelites to avoid eating yeast, to consecrate their firstborn sons to the Lord, and to specifically tell their children why and what they are remembering.

EXEGETICAL IDEA: It came about that after the tenth plague, Pharaoh agreed to let the Israelites go, and Moses instructed the Israelites to avoid eating yeast, to consecrate their firstborn sons to the Lord, and to specifically tell their children why and what they are remembering.

HOMILETICAL IDEA: God's deliverance truly happened, so tell your children.

Exodus 13:17-14:31

SUBJECT: How did Israel escape when Pharaoh pursued them with chariots?

COMPLEMENT: The Lord opened the Red Sea for Israel, but the water flowed back and covered Pharaoh and his army.

EXEGETICAL IDEA: Israel escaped when Pharaoh pursued them with chariots by the Lord opening the Red Sea for Israel, but the water flowed back and covered Pharaoh and his army.

HOMILETICAL IDEA: When all hope seems lost, God fights for his people.

Exodus 15:1-21

SUBJECT: What did Moses, Miriam, and the Israelites sing after the Lord saved them from Pharaoh at the Red Sea?

COMPLEMENT: They sang that God was highly exalted, that he had defeated Pharaoh, that he would continue to love and guide Israel, and that he would plant them in the promised land.

EXEGETICAL IDEA: After the Lord saved them from Pharaoh at the Red Sea, Moses, Miriam, and the Israelites sang that God was highly exalted, that he had defeated Pharaoh, that he would continue to love and guide Israel, and that he would plant them in the promised land.

HOMILETICAL IDEA: God has worked salvation, so praise him and know that he will be with us to fulfill the rest of his promises.

Exodus 15:22–17:7

SUBJECT: How did the Lord test Israel so that they would rely on his provision rather than grumble?

COMPLEMENT: He sweetened the waters at Mara, rained down manna and quail, and made water flow from the rock at Rephidim.

EXEGETICAL IDEA: The Lord tested Israel by sweetening the waters at Mara, raining down manna and quail, and making water flow from the rock at Rephidim so that they would rely on his provision rather than grumble.

HOMILETICAL IDEA: Don't grumble, but trust God.

Exodus 17:8–18:27

SUBJECT: How did Moses work to defeat the Amalekites as well as judge between disputes of the Israelites?

COMPLEMENT: He chose others from among Israel who knew God's commandments to help him.

EXEGETICAL IDEA: To defeat the Amalekites and to judge between disputes of the Israelites, Moses chose others from among Israel who knew God's commandments to help him.

HOMILETICAL IDEA: Choose people who know God's Word to help you.

Exodus 19:1–20:21

SUBJECT: What happened at Mount Sinai when Moses returned there with Israel?

COMPLEMENT: Moses mediated the covenant between the Lord and Israel, that Israel would be God's treasured possession and a kingdom of priests as they acknowledged his holiness and obeyed his commands.

EXEGETICAL IDEA: At Mount Sinai when Moses returned there with Israel, Moses mediated the covenant between the Lord and Israel, that Israel would be God's treasured possession and a kingdom of priests as they acknowledged his holiness and obeyed his commands.

HOMILETICAL IDEA: You belong to a holy God, so back away and obey.

Exodus 20:22–23:19

SUBJECT: What initial commands did God give Israel at Sinai through Moses?

COMPLEMENT: Israel was to be different than the other nations in their treatment of servants, in their punishments for wrongdoing, in their social and family responsibilities, and in observing Sabbaths and festivals.

EXEGETICAL IDEA: At Sinai, God commanded Israel through Moses to be different than the other nations in their treatment of servants, in their punishments for wrongdoing, in their social and family responsibilities, and in observing Sabbaths and festivals.

HOMILETICAL IDEA: God expects his people to be different.

Exodus 23:20–24:18

SUBJECT: How was the Sinai covenant ratified?

COMPLEMENT: Moses built an altar at the base of Mount Sinai and read the book of the covenant to the people, and the people agreed; after this, he sprinkled them with blood, and the elders of Israel ascended Sinai and ate in the presence of God, and then he ascended to the summit and entered God's glory.

EXEGETICAL IDEA: The Sinai covenant was ratified by Moses building an altar at the base of Mount Sinai and reading the book of the covenant to the people, and the people agreeing; after this, he sprinkled them with blood, and the elders of Israel ascended Sinai and ate in the presence of God; and then he ascended to the summit and entered God's glory.

HOMILETICAL IDEA: God has made a covenant with you and you have eaten in his presence, so wait for Christ's return.

Exodus 25:10–28:43; 30:1–10, 17–38; 35:4–29; 36:8–39:31

SUBJECT: Why was the tabernacle built to such precise specifications?

COMPLEMENT: In order for the Lord to dwell in Israel's midst, the tabernacle was to be congruent with what Moses saw on the mountain.

EXEGETICAL IDEA: The tabernacle was built to such precise specifications because in order for the Lord to dwell in Israel's midst, the tabernacle was to be congruent with what Moses saw on the mountain.

HOMILETICAL IDEA: God's plan for holiness in our lives is detailed and specific, so don't skip the small stuff.

Exodus 31:1-11; 35:30-36:7

SUBJECT: Who did God appoint to make the tabernacle and all of its furniture and special materials?

COMPLEMENT: Bezalel and Oholiab, men of Israel with special skills of craftsmanship and the Spirit of God, were to make everything he commanded Moses.

EXEGETICAL IDEA: God appointed Bezalel and Oholiab, men of Israel with special skills of craftsmanship and the Spirit of God, to make the tabernacle and all its furniture and special materials.

HOMILETICAL IDEA: God appoints and gifts humans to build his beautiful house.

Exodus 31:12-17; 35:1-3

SUBJECT: Why was Israel to observe the Sabbath on pain of death, both during the building of the tabernacle and thereafter?

COMPLEMENT: The Sabbath is holy to Israel, and by observing it they would know that the Lord makes Israel holy.

EXEGETICAL IDEA: Israel was to observe the Sabbath on pain of death, both during the building of the tabernacle and thereafter, because the Sabbath was holy to Israel, and by observing it they would know that the Lord makes Israel holy.

HOMILETICAL IDEA: Stop for worship or risk forgetting God.

Exodus 31:18-33:6

SUBJECT: Though they had just seen Moses and heard the Lord's voice, what great sin did Israel commit, and what were its results?

COMPLEMENT: Israel worshiped a golden calf, breaking their covenant with God; only after bloodshed and intercession did the Lord not forsake Israel.

EXEGETICAL IDEA: Though they had just seen Moses and heard the Lord's voice, Israel worshiped a golden calf, breaking their covenant with God; only after bloodshed and intercession did the Lord not forsake Israel.

HOMILETICAL IDEA: When God's people sin, the problems aren't easily solved.

Exodus 33:7-11; 34:28-35

SUBJECT: Why did Moses wear a veil over his face?

COMPLEMENT: Moses's face glowed when he met with the Lord.

EXEGETICAL IDEA: Moses wore a veil over his face because his face glowed after he met with the Lord.

HOMILETICAL IDEA: We are changed when we meet the Lord.

Exodus 33:12-34:27

SUBJECT: When Moses interceded for Israel after their sin, how did the Lord respond?

COMPLEMENT: God renewed his covenant promises to be with them and gave them laws once again.

EXEGETICAL IDEA: When Moses interceded for Israel after their sin, God renewed his covenant promises to be with them and gave them laws once again.

HOMILETICAL IDEA: Sometimes we need an intercessor.

Exodus 39:1-31

SUBJECT: Why was Israel to ordain its priests?

COMPLEMENT: So the Lord would dwell among the Israelites and they would know that he is the Lord who brought them out of Egypt.

EXEGETICAL IDEA: Israel was to ordain its priests so the Lord would dwell among the Israelites and they would know that he is the Lord who brought them out of Egypt.

HOMILETICAL IDEA: Church leaders show us that God really saves.

Exodus 39:32-40:38

SUBJECT: After the tabernacle was completed and set up and the priests were consecrated according to God's commands, what occurred?

COMPLEMENT: The glory of the Lord filled the tabernacle, and God dwelt among Israel during all of Israel's travels.

EXEGETICAL IDEA: After the tabernacle was completed and set up and the priests were consecrated according to God's commands, the glory of the Lord filled the tabernacle, and God dwelt among Israel during all of Israel's travels.

HOMILETICAL IDEA: God dwells in the church when we build it in obedience.

Difficult Passages/Verses

Exodus presents several challenging passages and concepts. The circumcision narrative (4:24–26) presents several interpretive challenges; this passage has long been labeled one of the most obscure in the Torah. Moses has just obeyed God and set off for Egypt, yet he nearly loses his life because God "sought to kill him." The fact that Zipporah's quick action of circumcising Gershom saves Moses from death implies that Moses had incurred the divine wrath by neglecting to circumcise his own son. While obeying God's call to rescue Abraham's descendants, Moses now is confronted with his own lack of adherence to the Abrahamic covenant. Zipporah's foresight not only saves Moses but may also hint at her own faith in the God of Moses's fathers. She is the third woman in Exodus—and the second foreign woman—who saves Moses's life. Interpreters are divided concerning the significance of touching Moses's feet with the foreskin, though it may somehow anticipate and parallel the Passover ritual whereby the Destroyer will pass over those houses with blood on the lintel. Regardless of how precisely these details are understood, the thrust of the passage is that Moses, through his wife's action, becomes fully integrated within his Israelite identity and dedicated to his divine calling.

Relatedly, contemporary hearers may balk at how often Exodus presents death as the result of disobeying or resisting God, even for the firstborn son of every Egyptian family. The careful preacher does not need to overexplain this but can simply state that Scripture communicates clearly that God is holy and that all life in creation is accountable and subject to God's will. One might mention that Scripture also states that when all things are considered at the end of time, our questions about fairness or justice will be satisfied utterly.

One final note: because the events and laws of Exodus figure prominently throughout the rest of Scripture, understanding first how those events and laws fit into the fabric of Exodus will enable listeners to better understand and interpret the entire Bible. Care must be taken, however, to allow the text of Exodus to speak for itself before it is drawn into those larger discussions of Christ, the new exodus of the cross, the new covenant, and so on. Exodus itself is inspired Scripture for the church today.

Cultural Perspectives and Application

Several points of information concerning ancient culture can help clarify Exodus as a book.

First, a large portion of the literary structure of Exodus is similar to ancient international contracts known as suzerain-vassal treaties. These treaties were written agreements between two nations; one nation—the suzerain—was more powerful and therefore demanded tribute and obedience from the other, or vassal, nation. In return, the vassal nation would receive protection and other benefits of relationship with the suzerain. While it is not essential for all Christians to be aware of this basic literary structure that seems to undergird Exodus, mindfulness of suzerain-vassal treaty dynamics may help preachers emphasize that, for example, the golden calf incident was not one sin among many but a rejection of the covenant stipulations that God had just spoken from Sinai, and therefore a breaking of the treaty altogether. The remainder of the book—including God's passing before Moses and agreeing to go with the people, and finally God's choosing to dwell in the tabernacle that Israel had set up for him—is therefore the result of the sheer mercy of the Lord.

A second point of cultural awareness helps clarify the law texts in Exodus. Many law texts from ancient Near Eastern traditions contain similar lists of prohibitions. Whereas a contemporary reader of these texts might think them random and uncoordinated, the ancient mind received such lists differently. Douglas Stuart comments, "Ancient people were expected to be able to ex- trapolate from what the sampling of laws did say to the *general* behavior that the laws in their totality pointed toward. . . . Likewise, judges were expected to extrapolate from the wording provided in the laws that did exist to *all other* circumstances, and not to be foiled in their jurisprudence by any such concepts as 'technicalities' or 'loopholes.'"[1] The insight here relevant for the contemporary preacher is that the lists of stipulations sketch general images of how God intended Israelite society to be; in other words, summarizing these laws and restating them as positive principles is possible, helpful, and even expected by the nature of the laws themselves.

Finally, a brief word regarding repetition. The text of Exodus, like other written accounts of its day, uses verbatim repetition to indicate specific obe- dience to divine commands. God says for Moses to do or say specific things, and then Moses does and says exactly those specific things; this results in, for example, many of the details of the tabernacle's construction being recorded

---

1. Douglas Stuart, "Preaching from the Law," in *Preaching the Old Testament*, ed. Scott M. Gibson (Grand Rapids: Baker Books, 2006), 95.

two times in Exodus. Whereas some commentators have suggested that such repetition resulted from mistaken copies of the book of Exodus, such analyses overlook other ancient texts wherein the same pattern is used. The repetition pattern emphasizes the obedience of the one performing the tasks stipulated. Exodus thus presents the construction of the tabernacle as a significant act of obedience, not only by Moses but also by Bezalel, Oholiab, the other craftspeople, and indeed all Israel.

RECOMMENDED RESOURCES

Beale, G. K., and D. A. Carson. *Commentary on the New Testament Use of the Old Testament*. Grand Rapids: Baker Academic, 2007.

Cassuto, Umberto Moshe David. *A Commentary on the Book of Exodus*. Translated by Israel Abrahams. Jerusalem: Varda, 2005.

Childs, Brevard. *Exodus: A Critical, Theological Commentary*. Louisville: Westminster John Knox, 1974.

Leviticus

BRUCE W. FONG

The Big Idea of Leviticus

Leviticus is a book about the holiness of God and how Israel may have a relationship with this holy God and live out this holiness among themselves and other nations. The laws are part of the overall covenant that God made with his people, Israel. These laws have to do with the relationship that Israel is to have with God. In the context of the Old Testament, Leviticus comes as Israel is camped at the bottom of Mount Sinai and as God gives his covenant to them to bear his likeness. The sacrifices provide opportunity to present a gift of worship to God and to note a relationship with God, and they perform a function of healing when the relationship is broken—atonement.

SUBJECT: How is Israel given the precise prescription to recognize the holiness of God?

COMPLEMENT: With laws of dutiful worship, that although unworthy they can be his people—acceptable, holy—to bear his likeness with loving compassion.

EXEGETICAL IDEA: Israel is given the precise prescription to recognize the holiness of God with laws of dutiful worship, that although unworthy they can be his people—acceptable, holy—to bear his likeness with loving compassion.

HOMILETICAL IDEA: Although unworthy, we are called to be holy like God, to show his likeness to others.

Selecting Preaching and Teaching Passages in Leviticus

Leviticus may be preached as one sermon, as noted in the big idea for the entire book, or it may be split into two parts—chapters 1–16 (the Levitical Code) and chapters 17–27 (the Holiness Code). The first sermon would engage the way that God's holiness is communicated in the regulations for people and priests as directly related to the tabernacle. The second sermon would explore the charge "Be holy because I, the LORD your God, am holy" (19:2) as expressed in the various laws for a person's relationship with God and others.

Of course, a single sermon would not be able to explicate the minute details of each of the laws contained in the book, but the emphasis on the holiness of God is repeated throughout the book, underscoring the importance of any generation's need to recognize who God is and the call to live a life in relationship with him that honors him and loves others with the same covenant love.

Getting the Subject, Complement, Exegetical Idea, and Homiletical Idea

Leviticus 1-7

SUBJECT: How are the five offerings to be understood by the Israelites as they worship their holy God?

COMPLEMENT: As symbolic meals with God as their holy host who forgives them of their sin.

EXEGETICAL IDEA: The five offerings are to be understood by the Israelites as they worship their holy God as symbolic meals with God as their holy host who forgives them of their sin.

HOMILETICAL IDEA: God is our holy host as we celebrate the Supper.

Leviticus 8-10

SUBJECT: What does the Lord require of those who serve him in their holy assignment as priests?

COMPLEMENT: To follow obediently what the Lord requires in worship; otherwise, there are consequences.

EXEGETICAL IDEA: The Lord requires those who serve him in their holy assignment as priests to follow obediently what the Lord requires in worship; otherwise, there are consequences.

HOMILETICAL IDEA: Our holy God requires wholehearted obedience in worship.

Leviticus 11-16

SUBJECT: What does it mean to be clean or unclean before a holy God?

COMPLEMENT: Clean means being acceptable to God in worship, and unclean means being unacceptable to God and banished from his presence, underscoring that on special days like the Day of Atonement, only people cleansed from their sin—holy people—are able to worship a holy God.

EXEGETICAL IDEA: To be clean before a holy God means being acceptable to God in worship, and to be unclean means being unacceptable to God and banished from his presence, underscoring that on special days like the Day of Atonement, only people cleansed from their sin—holy people—are able to worship a holy God.

HOMILETICAL IDEA: A holy God gives us holy hope to worship him because of a holy Christ.

Leviticus 17-25

SUBJECT: How is the holiness of God demonstrated in the lives of his covenant people?

COMPLEMENT: By personal and social holiness in daily life, by following holy religious observance, and by recognizing the consequences of not following God's holy call, but also with the provision of forgiveness and rest as found in the Sabbath and celebrations.

EXEGETICAL IDEA: The holiness of God is demonstrated in the lives of his covenant people by personal and social holiness in daily life, by following holy religious observance, and by recognizing the consequences of not following God's holy call, but also with the provision of forgiveness and rest as found in the Sabbath and celebrations.

HOMILETICAL IDEA: Be holy for I am holy, says the Lord.

Leviticus 26

SUBJECT: What is the outcome for Israel of keeping the covenant or not keeping it with their holy God?

COMPLEMENT: There will be either blessings or curses dispensed by the Lord.

EXEGETICAL IDEA: The outcome for Israel of keeping the covenant or not keeping it with their holy God is that there will be either blessings or curses dispensed by the Lord.

HOMILETICAL IDEA: Wholly following God brings blessings, but cursing him through disobedience brings curses.

Leviticus 27

SUBJECT: What is the purpose of the laws of redemption?

COMPLEMENT: To demonstrate that all that Israel has is the Lord's, even to the slightest detail, for all is his and he is holy.

EXEGETICAL IDEA: The purpose of the laws of redemption is to demonstrate that all that Israel has is the Lord's, even to the slightest detail, for all is his and he is holy.

HOMILETICAL IDEA: All that we are and ever hope to be is the Lord's.

Difficult Passages/Verses

Several themes and related passages need an expositor's consideration when unfolding this remarkable book. First, the theme of holiness is central to Leviticus: "Be holy, because I am holy" (11:44). Clearly, Moses intended to communicate that holiness is both possible and sustainable (20:8; 21:15, 23; 22:9–32). Modern readers and fledgling theologians may have strong doubts about whether this spiritual condition can actually be met apart from Christ. Not only is extensive lifestyle adjustment necessary but it is also too intricate to be achievable for the average Hebrew. If the system was too complicated to be realistic, then what good was it if, in fact, it was impossible?[1]

A study of Leviticus clearly reveals that the difficulty of this book from a homiletical perspective is not the challenge of exegesis of any particular verses. Rather, it is the theological transition from application in the ancient world to pertinence in the modern day. The modern preacher must be committed to exposition of the theological bridge between the distant original intent of the book and the modern lives of Christians who are in pursuit of righteousness.

Over time a preacher develops strong convictions with a constant building of theology. With the beginning of each new exposition, the preacher's theology is adjusted and deepened. Eventually, that system of theology becomes the grid through which the preacher senses the divine intention to apply the meaning of Scripture. Theology does not impose itself on the interpretation of Scripture, but it sorts out the way in which Scripture challenges a

---

1. Kenneth G. Hanna, *From Moses to Malachi: Exploring the Old Testament* (Bloomington, IN: CrossBooks, 2014), 70.

Christian to confess, adjust, change, or reset personal priorities by the power of the Spirit.

It will also be important for the preacher to set Leviticus into the context of the Pentateuch. This maligned and "boring" book does not stand alone. Instead, it must be seen in its clear relationship to Exodus. The second book of the Bible traces the historical departure from bondage in Egypt. The Hebrew people's being led by Moses out of the bondage and into divine promise is a powerful message. After the Hebrew people are released, they must rearrange their priorities to enter into an intimate relationship with God. That reentry is not self-sustaining after an initial start. Rather, it is a connection that requires constant attention. The maintenance of the connection between a people and God is required because of the problem of sin. Temptation and disobedience become regular threats to righteous living. Leviticus provides the procedure for the nation of Israel to nurture its relationship with God. This procedure may at first appear to be onerous, demanding, picky, and burdensome. However, it is effective and rewarding, and it offers specific guidance through the ministry of the Levitical priests. That helpful assistance is paralleled by modern-day ministers, pastors, and elders.

Cultural Perspectives and Application

How do Christians apply the book of Leviticus to their lives? After all, it was given to Israel as part of the "handbook" (Pentateuch) on how to stay faithful to God when they entered the promised land. Where Israel was traveling to was populated with people who believed in many gods. Their immoral behavior would be a temptation for Israel. The Pentateuch would keep the Hebrews morally straight if they lived obedient lives.

At first blush it seems that this ancient book is pertinent only to an ancient people in an ancient land. Many Christians who embark on their first foray into reading the Bible in a year fall victim to the book of Leviticus. The details of practices not germane to modern lives easily cause many to lose interest in reading, let alone applying this book to their lives.

As mentioned, it is helpful to note the connection between Exodus and Leviticus. Exodus is about a people being redeemed, purchased, and brought close to God. Leviticus is about a people being sanctified, learning how to live with their new identity as God's people, and being guided in how to maintain and stay close to God.

The prescriptive nature of Leviticus and its ancient-history context do not remove the book from being pertinent to modern-day believers. Instead,

God reveals his desire and instructions for Israel to both gain and preserve a righteous relationship with him. God's values have not changed over time. He does not change. Today, with a redemptive relationship with the Savior, Jesus Christ, a righteous life has all the sacrificial requirements completely fulfilled by Christ's sacrifice on the cross; nevertheless, nurturing a growing intimacy with God requires a believer's constant attention. Today we can discern and convey a theological application of what is learned from Leviticus.

RECOMMENDED RESOURCES

Hanna, Kenneth G. *From Moses to Malachi: Exploring the Old Testament*. Bloomington, IN: CrossBooks, 2014.

Lindsey, Duane. "Leviticus." In *The Bible Knowledge Commentary: Law*, edited by John F. Walvoord and Roy B. Zuck, 163–214. Colorado Springs: David C. Cook, 2018.

The NET Bible: Full Notes Edition. Nashville: Thomas Nelson, 2019.

Numbers

SID BUZZELL

The book of Numbers, in a combination of narrative, law, and genealogy, records Israel's forty-year journey from Sinai to the borders of Canaan with their various rebellions against God.

SUBJECT: What did the author of Numbers want Israel to learn from the book?

COMPLEMENT: In spite of Israel's numerous rebellions against God, he never abandoned his covenant with them.

EXEGETICAL IDEA: The author of Numbers wanted Israel to learn from the book that in spite of Israel's numerous rebellions, God never abandoned his covenant with them.

HOMILETICAL IDEA: Even though God promises to discipline us for our good when we disobey him, he will never abandon us.

Selecting Preaching and Teaching Passages in Numbers

Numbers divides into three sections: Israel at Sinai (1:1–10:10), Israel in the wilderness (10:11–25:18), and preparation of Israel's next generation to enter Canaan (26:1–36:13). But the text of Numbers is notoriously difficult to navigate. R. Dennis Cole says, "The Book of Numbers perhaps has been neglected in evangelical circles because of a seeming lack of coherence and overall meaning and purpose."[1] The seemingly random mixture of law, narrative, and genealogical lists in the book makes it difficult to connect sequences of chapters into coherent teaching/preaching segments.

Getting the Subject, Complement, Exegetical Idea, and Homiletical Idea

Numbers 1-2

SUBJECT: How did God prepare Israel for their journey to Canaan?

COMPLEMENT: By numbering their military strength, identifying the Levites to care for the tabernacle, and placing his own presence in the center of their camp.

EXEGETICAL IDEA: God prepared Israel for their journey to Canaan by numbering their military strength, identifying the Levites to care for the tabernacle, and placing his own presence in the center of their camp.

HOMILETICAL IDEA: God equips the church to prosper by assuring us of his presence, by gifting us to minister to one another, and by establishing his presence through the Holy Spirit.

Numbers 3-5

SUBJECT: How did God intend to nourish holiness among his people Israel?

COMPLEMENT: He ordained Aaron and the Levites to care for Israel's spiritual health.

EXEGETICAL IDEA: God intended to nourish holiness among his people Israel by ordaining Aaron and the Levites to care for Israel's spiritual health.

HOMILETICAL IDEA: God uses believers as his priests to minister in specific ways as he ordains and equips us through his spiritual gifts.

Numbers 6:1-21

SUBJECT: Could non-Levites commit themselves to God for an intense spiritual relationship?

COMPLEMENT: God established the Nazirite vows to provide any Israelite the opportunity to enjoy an intense spiritual relationship with him.

EXEGETICAL IDEA: Non-Levites could commit themselves to God for an intense spiritual relationship because God established the Nazirite vows to provide

---

1. R. Dennis Cole, *Numbers*, The New American Commentary (Nashville: Broadman & Holman, 2000), 36.

any Israelite the opportunity to enjoy an intense spiritual relationship with him.

HOMILETICAL IDEA: God urges all believers to present themselves to him as a living and holy sacrifice.

Numbers 6:22-27

SUBJECT: How did God use and honor his ordained priests for more than administering the daily religious practices?

COMPLEMENT: By ordaining them to place his personal blessing on Israel's people and by putting his name on them.

EXEGETICAL IDEA: God used and honored his ordained priests for more than administering the daily religious practices by ordaining them to place his personal blessing on Israel's people and by putting his name on them.

HOMILETICAL IDEA: As God's ordained priests, we have the honor to place his personal blessing on one another.

Numbers 7-8

SUBJECT: How did God prepare Israel's people to worship him?

COMPLEMENT: By allowing Israelites to participate in building and furnishing an anointed place to worship him, and ordaining and cleansing Levites as their worship leaders.

EXEGETICAL IDEA: God prepared Israel's people to worship him by allowing Israel's people to participate in building and furnishing an anointed place to worship him, and ordaining and cleansing the Levites to lead them in their worship.

HOMILETICAL IDEA: Take corporate worship seriously enough to prepare an anointed place to worship God and seek purified ministers to lead us in our corporate worship.

Numbers 9-10

SUBJECT: How did God plan to successfully lead Israel from Sinai to Canaan?

COMPLEMENT: By reminding them of his previous care for them (9:1–14), by providing visible and audible directions for them to follow (9:15–10:10), and by assuring them of his presence (10:11–36).

EXEGETICAL IDEA: God planned to successfully lead Israel from Sinai to Canaan by reminding them of his previous care for them, by providing visible and audible directions for them to follow, and by assuring them of his presence.

HOMILETICAL IDEA: God leads us by reminding us of his previous faithfulness, revealing his moral will in the Scriptures, and providing his Holy Spirit to direct and encourage us.

Numbers 11

SUBJECT: How did God respond to Israel's first wave of complaints against him and his leaders?

COMPLEMENT: By supporting Moses, his appointed leader, by answering his prayers, assuring him of his faithful presence, providing additional leaders to support him, and performing a miracle to strengthen his challenged faith.

EXEGETICAL IDEA: God responded to Israel's first wave of complaints against him and his leaders by supporting Moses, his appointed leader, by answering his prayers, assuring him of his faithful presence, providing additional leaders to support him, and performing a miracle to strengthen his challenged faith.

HOMILETICAL IDEA: When God's people rebel against him and his servant leaders, he will faithfully minister to those who seek his help.

Numbers 12

SUBJECT: How did God respond to Aaron and Miriam's complaint against Moses as God's spokesperson?

COMPLEMENT: God exalted Moses before them by praising him for his faithful service as God's chosen spokesperson and by answering his prayer on Miriam's behalf.

EXEGETICAL IDEA: God responded to Aaron and Miriam's complaint against Moses as God's spokesperson by exalting Moses before them by praising him for his faithful service as God's chosen spokesperson and by answering his prayer on Miriam's behalf.

HOMILETICAL IDEA: When people challenge God's ministers, their strongest defenses are their record of faithfulness to God and the fruit of their ministry.

Numbers 13-15

SUBJECT: How did God respond to Israel's refusal to enter Canaan because they lacked faith in his promises to give them Canaan as their own land?

COMPLEMENT: By condemning them to die in the Sinai wilderness but assured them that he had made provision for their children to enter the land and prosper in it.

EXEGETICAL IDEA: God responded to Israel's refusal to enter Canaan because they lacked faith in his promises to give them Canaan as their own land by condemning them to die in the Sinai wilderness but assuring them that he had made provision for their children to enter the land and prosper in it.

HOMILETICAL IDEA: When we disobey God, he disciplines us with the consequences of our disobedience but continues to reassure us of his covenanted presence and love.

Numbers 14:1-45

SUBJECT: What did Moses, Aaron, Joshua, and Caleb, Israel's godly leaders, do when Israel refused to obey God?

COMPLEMENT: They passionately reasoned with Israel, asked God to forgive their refusal to repent, and continued to provide strong, godly leadership for them.

EXEGETICAL IDEA: When Israel refused to obey God, Moses, Aaron, Joshua, and Caleb, Israel's godly leaders, passionately reasoned with Israel, asked God to forgive their refusal to repent, and continued to provide strong, godly leadership for them.

HOMILETICAL IDEA: When God's people fail to follow him, they demonstrate the need for godly leaders to pray for them and to model strong spiritual leadership for them.

Numbers 15

SUBJECT: How did God relate to Israel on a day-to-day basis?

COMPLEMENT: By being intimately involved in every aspect of Israel's life, instructing them to acknowledge his presence and commanding sacrifices to atone for their failure to do so.

EXEGETICAL IDEA: God related to Israel on a day-to-day basis by being intimately involved in every aspect of Israel's life, instructing them to acknowledge his presence and commanding sacrifices to atone for their failure to do so.

HOMILETICAL IDEA: Christians cultivate a sense of God's constant presence and participation in our life even as we confess our failure to acknowledge him.

Numbers 16-19

SUBJECT: What did God do when Israel challenged his order of spiritual leadership for them and attempted to function as his priests?

COMPLEMENT: God judged them and strongly reaffirmed Aaron's priesthood and its essential role in Israel's relationship with him.

EXEGETICAL IDEA: When Israel challenged his order of spiritual leadership for them and attempted to function as his priests, God judged them and strongly reaffirmed Aaron's priesthood and its essential role in Israel's relationship with him.

HOMILETICAL IDEA: When people challenge the church's role and function, our greatest response is to *demonstrate* the unique contribution our local church is making through its faithful pursuit of the Great Commission.

Numbers 20:1-22:1

SUBJECT: What happened to Moses when he failed to honor God by striking the rock at Meribah?

COMPLEMENT: God severely disciplined him but forgave him and continued to answer his prayers and to guide and protect Israel through his leadership.

EXEGETICAL IDEA: When Moses failed to honor God by striking the rock at Meribah, God severely disciplined him but forgave him and continued to answer his prayers and to guide and protect Israel through his leadership.

HOMILETICAL IDEA: Because of his sovereign grace, God can continue to minister through a disobedient but repentant person whom he has forgiven and disciplined.

Numbers 22:2-25:18

SUBJECT: Why was Balaam successful when he attempted to induce God to curse Israel?

COMPLEMENT: Balaam was successful because when God blessed Israel in response to Balaam's efforts to curse it, Balaam found another way to curse Israel.

EXEGETICAL IDEA: When Balaam attempted to induce God to curse Israel, he was successful because when God blessed Israel in response to Balaam's efforts to curse it, Balaam found another way to curse Israel.

HOMILETICAL IDEA: God protects his children from Satan's power to seduce us but doesn't violate our power to choose our own means of destruction.

Numbers 26-30

SUBJECT: How did God prepare Israel's next generation to succeed spiritually in Canaan?

COMPLEMENT: By reminding them of their tribal heritage and reconnecting them to the laws and ceremonies that distinguished them as his holy, chosen nation.

EXEGETICAL IDEA: God prepared Israel's next generation to succeed spiritually in Canaan by reminding them of their tribal heritage and reconnecting them to the laws and ceremonies that distinguished them as his holy, chosen nation.

HOMILETICAL IDEA: God reminds us of our heritage as his redeemed people by giving us access to his Word and by ordaining sacred ceremonies for our corporate worship.

Numbers 27:1-11; 36

SUBJECT: How did God protect unmarried and/or widowed women from losing their allotted inheritance, since in Israel's laws sons inherited the family's land?

COMPLEMENT: God added a commandment to ensure that where there was no son, a daughter would inherit her family's land.

EXEGETICAL IDEA: God protected unmarried and/or widowed women from losing their allotted inheritance, since in Israel's laws sons inherited the family's land, by adding a commandment to ensure that where there was no son, a daughter would inherit her family's land.

HOMILETICAL IDEA: God's laws of love and justice address the needs of all his children.

Numbers 27:12-23

SUBJECT: How did Joshua's commission to lead Israel differ from Moses's commission?

COMPLEMENT: Although Moses took direction directly from God and gave instructions to Aaron, Joshua would hear God's directions for Israel from Eleazar the high priest, through whom God would speak.

EXEGETICAL IDEA: Joshua's commission to lead Israel differed from Moses's commission because although Moses took direction directly from God and gave instructions to Aaron, Joshua would hear God's directions for Israel from Eleazar the high priest, through whom God would speak.

HOMILETICAL IDEA: Leaders are wise to seek advice from other godly people and not assume God will speak to them as he did to Moses.

■ *Numbers 28–29*

SUBJECT: What was God's plan to keep Israel involved in their covenant relationship with him?

COMPLEMENT: To command Israel to celebrate regularly scheduled feasts and sacrifices that involved conscious effort to communicate with and celebrate their relationship with him.

EXEGETICAL IDEA: God's plan to keep Israel involved in their covenant relationship with him was to command Israel to celebrate regularly scheduled feasts and sacrifices that involved conscious effort to communicate with and celebrate their relationship with him.

HOMILETICAL IDEA: Christians are well served by meaningfully and seriously participating in our regularly scheduled corporate worship services.

■ *Numbers 30*

SUBJECT: How did God protect Israel's women and children from making unwise vows?

COMPLEMENT: By putting safeguards on their ability to make vows neither they nor their fathers or husbands could fulfill.

EXEGETICAL IDEA: God protected Israel's women and children from making unwise vows by putting safeguards on their ability to make vows neither they nor their fathers or husbands could fulfill.

HOMILETICAL IDEA: God provides wise and experienced men and women who can guide us in making critical decisions, and it is foolish not to consult with them before making "vows" that may be unwise.

Numbers 31–36

SUBJECT: How did God prepare Israel's new generation to succeed politically in Canaan?

COMPLEMENT: By reminding Israel of his protection and provision and gave them laws to guide and protect a just and fair distribution of their new land.

EXEGETICAL IDEA: God prepared Israel's new generation to succeed politically in Canaan by reminding Israel of his protection and provision and by giving them laws to guide and protect a just and fair distribution of their new land.

HOMILETICAL IDEA: God teaches us in his Word that the church is Christ's unified body of people and provides clear instructions about how we should relate to one another.

▣ Numbers 31

SUBJECT: Why did God command Israel to completely destroy the Midianites?

COMPLEMENT: Because they had seduced Israel to worship Baal and there was a danger they might do so again.

EXEGETICAL IDEA: God commanded Israel to completely destroy the Midianites because they had seduced Israel to worship Baal and there was a danger they might do so again.

HOMILETICAL IDEA: God jealously guards his children's holiness and commands us to separate ourselves from people and things that tempt us to sin.

Difficult Passages/Verses

Gordon Wenham points out a difficulty related to the organization of the book of Numbers, asking, "How is the order, or disorder, of the material to be explained?"[2] The relationship between some of its chapters is difficult to define and so makes identifying clear preaching/teaching passages difficult. Many of our teaching segments will have to include multiple chapters.

A number of chronological references are scattered throughout Numbers. Identifying these references and coordinating them (some are out of chronological sequence) makes our teaching and preaching of these passages less confusing and more interesting.

Connecting Numbers with Exodus, Leviticus, and Deuteronomy

Because of both chronology and repetition of laws and narrative, it's important in our preparation to cross-reference passages in Numbers with those in Exodus, Leviticus, and Deuteronomy that contain similar material.

Numbers 5:11-31

This passage presents a harsh way for a man to treat his wife, and in an egalitarian culture some will undoubtedly note that there is no commensurate process for a wife who suspects an adulterous husband. Be prepared to discuss the

---

2. Gordon Wenham, *Numbers*, Tyndale Old Testament Commentaries (Downers Grove, IL: InterVarsity, 2008), 16.

vastly different role of women in the ancient Near Eastern culture. While the law may appear unjust in today's culture, it was God's commanded procedure for Israel. Jacob Milgrom explains that the ritual actually "provides the priestly legislator with an accepted practice by which he could remove the jurisdiction over and punishment of the unapprehended adulteress from human hands and thereby guarantee that she would not be put to death."[3] So in a male-dominant culture, the law protected a wife from a jealous or otherwise enraged or dissatisfied husband who inaccurately suspected, or outright falsely accused, his wife of adultery and sentenced her to death.

Numbers 13-15

When we present this text, it is important to identify the difference between forgiveness and consequences. Even though God condemned Israel to die in the wilderness as a *consequence* of their rebellion, he did forgive them and continued to lead and interact with them. When Moses prayed, asking God to forgive Israel, God responded, "I have forgiven them. . . . Nevertheless . . ." (14:19–21).

Numbers 14:10-23

God responded to Moses's request to spare Israel (14:20) after God announced his intention to destroy them (14:11–12). This is one of three incidents in Numbers where God reversed a stated intention (see also 16:20–24; 22:12–20). None of these texts explains why God made a statement he would later change. While it's important to address the fact of God relenting, it's also important that our listeners understand that we are giving an explanation based on human reasoning and not on any divinely revealed explanation in the biblical text.

Numbers 20

Moses and Aaron's severe discipline for striking the rock at Meribah seems unjust. It may be because God holds his leaders to a higher standard or that there is more to the story than the brief narrative reveals, or other explanations. But if we "explain" the harsh sentence, it is crucial to inform listeners that the explanation is given nowhere in the text and we are only guessing at why.

Numbers 21-25

Balaam is a strange character and is treated inconsistently in commentaries—some honoring and others condemning him. R. Dennis Cole writes, "Balaam

---

3. Jacob Milgrom, *Numbers*, JPS Torah Commentary (Philadelphia: Jewish Publication Society, 1990), 350.

is a rebellious instrument of God, a paradoxical and oxymoronic character himself in the story."⁴ Although he spoke on God's behalf, he was not a traditional prophet. He is condemned in numerous Bible passages as morally and ethically unfit (Num. 31:7–8, 15–54; Deut. 23:3–6; Josh. 13:22; 24:9–10; Neh. 13:1–3; Mic. 6:5; 2 Pet. 2:15–16; Jude 11; Rev. 2:14). Wenham refers to Balaam as "this numb-skulled, money-grubbing heathen seer" who was inspired by God to vision Israel's future.⁵ Take time to form your own opinion of this complex and confusing character. Because he was responsible for Israel's moral failure recorded in chapter 25 (Num. 31:15–16; Rev. 2:14), consider including the chapter as part of the Balaam/Balak pericope.

Numbers 22:1-34
This section records God's reversal in his responses to Balaam's request. After forbidding him to go, God allowed him to do so with the restriction that he speak only what God instructed him to say. Milgrom, in answering the question of why God allowed Balaam to go, says that one realistic answer might be that without the change we would have neither the tale nor the oracle. He referenced the rabbis' assessment that "in this tale is the source of the doctrine of human responsibility and free will." We learn from this that "if one comes to defile himself, he is given . . . the opportunity."⁶

Cultural Perspectives and Application

The question of application is a bit complex in Numbers because of the various genres the book contains. We can draw principles from some of the legal material, but, as Ephesians (and other New Testament books) teaches us, we no longer practice the ceremonial laws. The narrative sections of Numbers too are rich in principles we can apply, but they don't always have one-to-one universal application between Israel's wilderness journey and contemporary Christians' daily experiences.

There are, however, some applications we can make from Numbers:

- Obey the clearly stated will of God presented in the Bible (14:1–45).
- Pray for the Holy Spirit's guidance when God doesn't provide clear direction in his Word (27:21).

4. Cole, *Numbers*, 365.
5. Wenham, *Numbers*, 185.
6. Milgrom, *Numbers*, 188.

- Support our ministry leaders when they are faithfully engaged in God's work (12:1–16).
- Reflect on God's faithfulness in our past to strengthen our trust in him for our future (9:1–4).
- Protect ourselves from sin by removing tempting influences from our life (25:1–9).
- Develop a consistent and lively prayer life, trusting that God does respond to prayer (14:11–19).
- Don't equate sin's consequences with a lack of God's forgiveness (14:20–22).

RECOMMENDED RESOURCES

Cole, R. Dennis. *Numbers*. The New American Commentary. Dallas: Broadman & Holman, 2000.

Milgrom, Jacob. *Numbers*. JPS Torah Commentary. Philadelphia: Jewish Publication Society, 1990.

Wenham, Gordon. *Numbers*. Tyndale Old Testament Commentaries. Downers Grove, IL: InterVarsity, 2008.

Deuteronomy

PATRICIA M. BATTEN

The Big Idea of Deuteronomy

The book of Deuteronomy, written by Moses, is a covenant renewal intended to prepare the people to enter the promised land after thirty-eight years of wandering in the wilderness.

SUBJECT: How does Moses prepare the Israelites to enter the promised land?

COMPLEMENT: By renewing the covenant with them and reminding them that their obedience demonstrates a response of love to God's saving love for them.

EXEGETICAL IDEA: Moses prepares the Israelites to enter the promised land by renewing the covenant with them and reminding them that their obedience demonstrates a response of love to God's saving love for them.

HOMILETICAL IDEA: When we obey God, we remember his love and covenant blessings.

Selecting Preaching and Teaching Passages in Deuteronomy

Deuteronomy is a book of thirty-four chapters consisting of Moses's farewell addresses within the framework of a covenant renewal. Since much of the information in Deuteronomy is repetitive, preachers will benefit from combining chapters and/or related material.

Getting the Subject, Complement, Exegetical Idea, and Homiletical Idea

Deuteronomy 1-3

SUBJECT: Why does Moses review the Israelites' past?

COMPLEMENT: Because by knowing their past, they can avoid the sins/disobedience of their fathers (predecessors).

EXEGETICAL IDEA: Moses reviews the Israelites' past because, by knowing their past, they can avoid the sins/disobedience of their fathers (predecessors).

HOMILETICAL IDEA: Knowing the past helps us live for God in the future.

Deuteronomy 1:19-46

SUBJECT: Why do the Israelites fail at Kadesh-Barnea?

COMPLEMENT: Because they have forgotten what God had done.

EXEGETICAL IDEA: The Israelites fail at Kadesh-Barnea because they have forgotten what God had done.

HOMILETICAL IDEA: Remembering God's faithfulness in the past will give us courage to face the future.

Deuteronomy 2:24-3:11

SUBJECT: What do the Israelites learn, unlike their fathers, in their defeat of Sihon and Og?

COMPLEMENT: To trust God even when the giants are big and the walls are tall.

EXEGETICAL IDEA: In their defeat of Sihon and Og, the Israelites learn, unlike their fathers before them, to trust God even when the giants are big and the walls are tall.

HOMILETICAL IDEA: Have courage and trust God in adversity.

Deuteronomy 4:1-14

SUBJECT: What does Moses tell the Israelites concerning the decrees and laws that he is about to teach them?

COMPLEMENT: To carefully obey them and to teach future generations so that they will not forget, and so that the nations will see how God has given them wisdom and understanding.

EXEGETICAL IDEA: Moses tells the Israelites to carefully obey the decrees and laws that he is about to teach them, and to teach future generations so that they will not forget, and so that the nations will see how God has given them wisdom and understanding.

HOMILETICAL IDEA: When we obey God's Word and teach future generations to do so, we have an impact on the world around us.

Deuteronomy 4:15-31

SUBJECT: What does Moses say will happen to the Israelites if they turn to other gods?

COMPLEMENT: They will be scattered, but God will have mercy on them if they return to him with all their heart and soul.

EXEGETICAL IDEA: Moses says the Israelites will be scattered if they turn to other gods, but God will have mercy on them if they return to him with all their heart and soul.

HOMILETICAL IDEA: God has mercy on sinful people who return to him.

Deuteronomy 4:32-49

SUBJECT: What does God want the Israelites to remember?

COMPLEMENT: That he has done great deeds for them, to remember that the Lord is God and there is no other, and to keep his decrees and commands so that generations will be blessed.

EXEGETICAL IDEA: God wants the Israelites to remember that he has done great deeds for them, to remember that the Lord is God and there is no other, and to keep his decrees and commands so that generations will be blessed.

HOMILETICAL IDEA: The Lord is God so remember what he has done, and do as he says so future generations will be blessed.

Deuteronomy 5

SUBJECT: Why does Moses reiterate the Decalogue for the new generation about to enter the promised land?

COMPLEMENT: To remind them of their covenant responsibilities toward the one true God who saved them and to remind them of their responsibilities toward others.

EXEGETICAL IDEA: Moses reiterates the Decalogue for the new generation about to enter the promised land to remind them of their covenant responsibilities toward the one true God who saved them and to remind them of their responsibilities toward others.

HOMILETICAL IDEA: When we know who God is and how he has saved us, we can't help but love him and love others.

Deuteronomy 6

SUBJECT: What are the implications of the confession of faith that God is the one true God?

COMPLEMENT: To love God with heart, soul, and mind and to teach this truth to future generations.

EXEGETICAL IDEA: The implications of the confession of faith that God is the one true God are to love God with heart, soul, and mind and to teach this truth to future generations.

HOMILETICAL IDEA: If we want to teach the next generation, then we need to know who God is and love him with everything we've got.

Deuteronomy 7

SUBJECT: Why are the Israelites to obey God's command to totally destroy the nations he was driving out before them?

COMPLEMENT: Because as God's loved, chosen people (not because of anything they had done) they are to be set apart for God's glory, while the Canaanites are set apart for destruction because of their steadfast and violent opposition to God and because they will turn the Israelites to worship other gods.

EXEGETICAL IDEA: The Israelites are to obey God's command to totally destroy the nations he is driving out before them because as God's loved, chosen people they must be set apart for God's glory, while the Canaanites are set apart for destruction because of their steadfast, violent opposition to God and because they will turn the Israelites to worship other gods.

HOMILETICAL IDEA: God relentlessly protects and preserves his treasured possession.

Deuteronomy 8-11

SUBJECT: How does Moses prepare the new generation of Israelites for the promised land?

COMPLEMENT: By reminding them of their forty years in the desert that served to test and humble them in order to reveal their hearts for God.

EXEGETICAL IDEA: Moses prepares the new generation of Israelites for the promised land by reminding them of their forty years in the desert that served to test and humble them in order to reveal their hearts for God.

HOMILETICAL IDEA: Our hearts for God are revealed when we're humbled and tested.

Deuteronomy 12-13

SUBJECT: What does Moses tell the people about worship?

COMPLEMENT: They are to be set apart in their worship and worship God alone.

EXEGETICAL IDEA: Regarding worship, Moses tells the people they are to be set apart in their worship and worship God alone.

HOMILETICAL IDEA: How we worship reveals what we think about who we worship.

Deuteronomy 14:1-16:17

SUBJECT: What does Moses say are the marks of the worshiping community?

COMPLEMENT: Holy, generous, trusting, and celebratory.[1]

EXEGETICAL IDEA: Moses says the worshiping community are to be holy, generous, trusting, and celebratory.

HOMILETICAL IDEA: Our worship pleases God when we are holy, generous, trusting, and celebratory.

Deuteronomy 16:18-18:8

SUBJECT: How does Moses prepare the people entering the promised land for governance in that land?

COMPLEMENT: By organizing government among judges, godly kings, priests, and Levites (spiritual leaders).

EXEGETICAL IDEA: Moses prepares the people entering the promised land for governance in that land by organizing government among judges, godly kings, priests, and Levites.

HOMILETICAL IDEA: Governing God's way means governing to please God by being just to others and obedient to him.

1. Warren W. Wiersbe, *Be Equipped*, The BE Commentary Series (Colorado Springs: David C. Cook, 1999), chap. 6.

Deuteronomy 19:1-21:14

SUBJECT: What do the laws about manslaughter, war, and murder tell the people entering the promised land?

COMPLEMENT: God values human life because people are made in his image.

EXEGETICAL IDEA: The laws about manslaughter, war, and murder tell the people entering the promised land that God values human life because people are made in his image.

HOMILETICAL IDEA: We should value all people because God values them.

Deuteronomy 21:1-9

SUBJECT: According to Moses, how does God say the land must be atoned for when blood is shed by murder?

COMPLEMENT: Through the blood of an innocent sacrifice.

EXEGETICAL IDEA: According to Moses, God says the land must be atoned for when blood is shed by murder through the blood of an innocent sacrifice.

HOMILETICAL IDEA: Sin can be forgiven only through the blood of Jesus, the perfect sacrifice.

Deuteronomy 21:15-25:19

SUBJECT: Why does Moses reiterate various laws related to relationships to prepare the people to enter and live as God's chosen people in the promised land?

COMPLEMENT: To reveal God's heart for obedience, holiness, and justice for all.

EXEGETICAL IDEA: Moses reveals God's heart for obedience, holiness, and justice for all when he reiterates various laws related to relationships in order to prepare the people to enter and live as God's chosen people in the promised land.

HOMILETICAL IDEA: God's heart for his worshiping community is for obedience, holiness, and justice for all.

Deuteronomy 26:1-15

SUBJECT: What does Moses say the Israelites are to do with the first fruits of the land upon entering the promised land?

COMPLEMENT: Give them back to God and acknowledge God's continued provision for his people by recounting the events of the exodus, then give to those in need.

EXEGETICAL IDEA: Moses says the Israelites are to give back to God the first fruits of the land upon entering the promised land and acknowledge God's continued provision for his people by recounting the events of the exodus, then give to those in need.

HOMILETICAL IDEA: We give back to God with gratitude for his provision in saving us (through Jesus Christ), and we give back to others.

Deuteronomy 26:16–28:14

SUBJECT: What does Moses say are the implications of disobedience/obedience to the law as God's people?

COMPLEMENT: Disobedience results in judgment and obedience in blessing, glory to God, and witness to other nations.

EXEGETICAL IDEA: Moses says that as God's people the implication of disobedience is judgment and the implications of obedience are blessing, glory to God, and witness to other nations.

HOMILETICAL IDEA: The law *uncovers* our sin, but Christ *covers* our sin.

Deuteronomy 28:15–68

SUBJECT: What is the nature of the judgments God promises to send on his people when they disobey?

COMPLEMENT: They will affect every area of life.

EXEGETICAL IDEA: The nature of the judgments God promises to send on his people when they disobey is that they will affect every area of life.

HOMILETICAL IDEA: Our sin is deep, but God's grace is deeper.

Deuteronomy 29

SUBJECT: How does Moses reaffirm the covenant with the people?

COMPLEMENT: By reminding them of God's mighty acts among them, encouraging them to obey the law, and warning them of the implications of disobedience.

EXEGETICAL IDEA: Moses reaffirms the covenant with the people by reminding them of God's mighty acts among them, encouraging them to obey the law, and warning them of the implications of disobedience.

HOMILETICAL IDEA: Remembering how God has saved us (new covenant through Jesus) will turn our hearts toward obedience.

Deuteronomy 30:1-10

SUBJECT: After disobedience and return from exile, how will God ensure his people love him and live?

COMPLEMENT: By circumcising their hearts.

EXEGETICAL IDEA: After disobedience and return from exile, God will ensure his people love him and live by circumcising their hearts.

HOMILETICAL IDEA: Changed lives come through changed hearts.

Deuteronomy 30:11-20

SUBJECT: What is the choice that Moses puts before the Israelites?

COMPLEMENT: Life through obedience or death through disobedience.

EXEGETICAL IDEA: The choice that Moses puts before the Israelites is life through obedience or death through disobedience.

HOMILETICAL IDEA: Choose life through Jesus and God will give you a heart that honors him.

Deuteronomy 31:1-13

SUBJECT: Who does God say will lead Israel and cross the Jordan into the promised land?

COMPLEMENT: Through the person of Joshua so the Israelites can trust God.

EXEGETICAL IDEA: God says that he will lead Israel and cross the Jordan into the promised land through the person of Joshua so the Israelites can trust God.

HOMILETICAL IDEA: God leads his people, so we can trust in him.

Deuteronomy 31:14-32:47

SUBJECT: Why does Moses teach the Israelites a song before they enter the promised land?

COMPLEMENT: To plant God's Word in their hearts and minds so they wouldn't forget who he is and how he has saved them.

EXEGETICAL IDEA: Moses teaches the Israelites a song before they enter the promised land in order to plant God's Word in their hearts and minds so they wouldn't forget who he is and how he has saved them.

HOMILETICAL IDEA: God's Word is life.

Deuteronomy 32-34

SUBJECT: How is Moses unlike any other prophet in Israel?

COMPLEMENT: He knew the Lord face to face and performed awesome deeds in the sight of all Israel.

EXEGETICAL IDEA: Moses is unlike any other prophet in Israel because he knew the Lord face to face and performed awesome deeds in the sight of all Israel.

HOMILETICAL IDEA: The life of God's servant points to God's Son.

Difficult Passages/Verses

Deuteronomy is a challenging book to preach because it was written long ago and far away. We are new-covenant people trying to understand the old covenant and how the two relate. A modern audience might find many verses and chapters not only confusing but also downright disturbing. Deuteronomy 2:34 describes the defeat of Sihon, king of Heshbon. Moses reminds the Israelites, "At that time we took all his towns and completely destroyed them—men, women and children. We left no survivors." The modern reader cringes on reading *women and children*, and the preacher cannot ignore it.

Chapter 7 deals with the complete elimination of nations residing in the promised land. A misapplication of that passage could lead down a treacherous path where listeners might surmise that people who don't believe what *they* believe are worthless to God or that they deserve to be harmed or even annihilated. Those verses yield all sorts of homiletical and pastoral questions. Solid exegesis as well as careful application is absolutely crucial.

A knowledge of the religious and cultural background of the Canaanites is imperative. Their religious practices were deplorable by any standard and included practices such as child sacrifice, religious prostitution, and divination.

An understanding of other Bible references that shed light on the difficult passages in Deuteronomy is also a task of the preacher. The prophecy given by God to Abraham in Genesis yields important information regarding chapter 7 of Deuteronomy. It reveals God's extreme patience in judgment in Genesis 15:13–16.

The Israelites were informed, in no uncertain terms, that they were not inheriting the promised land as a result of their obedience or exceptional character traits. Rather, Moses makes it crystal clear that the righteousness of the Israelites has absolutely nothing to do with the dispossession of the nations in Deuteronomy 9:4–6.

In Deuteronomy 25:17–19 Moses tells the people to remember ("Do not forget!") what the Amalekites did to them as they were leaving Egypt and they were weary and worn out.

From the pew, Moses's words seem over the top. This is not how we teach our children, and it certainly doesn't sound like Jesus when he says, "Love your enemies." Preachers have to deal with the text and avoid a tendency to soften it.

Some scholars view the Amalekites as a people who were actively at work to destroy God's people and God's plan to bless the entire world through the Israelites. Walter Kaiser writes, "Some commentators note that the Amalekites were not merely plundering or disputing who owned what territories; they were attacking God's chosen people to discredit the living God." Some even see a possible connection to Haman (possibly an Amalekite) in the book of Esther, where he demonstrates a deep-seated hatred for the Jewish people and pulls together a wicked plot to annihilate God's people. His plot of destruction stemmed from a centuries-old hatred of God's people and an evil desire to destroy God's treasured possession. Kaiser notes of Haman, "His actions then would ultimately reveal this nation's deep hatred for God, manifested toward the people through whom God had chosen to bless the whole world."[2]

The consideration that God limited the destruction to nations that resided *in* the promised land must be taken into account. Other nations were left alone, and Moses went to great pains to avoid conflict with neighboring nations. God made gracious provisions for the descendants of Esau and Lot. See, for example, Deuteronomy 2:4–6, 9.

The preacher must look at difficult passages in light of the larger context of Deuteronomy and God's provision and grace. These passages can be stumbling blocks for our parishioners. We need to handle them carefully and faithfully.

Chapters 14–26 deal with specific laws regarding life in the promised land. My three sons were surprised by 21:18–21, in which a mother and father are obligated to take their rebellious son to the city gate to be stoned in order to purge the evil among the nation. I couldn't help but wonder how many parents actually *did* that. (I warned my boys it was a good reminder to take Isaiah 5:22 seriously: "Woe to those who are heroes at drinking wine and champions at mixing drinks.")

Preaching these passages requires movement up the ladder of abstraction where our big ideas might be more general in nature. We must work to make

2. Walter C. Kaiser Jr. et al., *Hard Sayings of the Bible* (Downers Grove, IL: InterVarsity, 1996), 207.

sure we distinguish between necessary implications and possible implications in our applications.

Finally, as Christians we read Deuteronomy and the renewal of the covenant through the lens of the new covenant of Jesus Christ. Do we deal strictly with the text as it was understood by the Israelites entering the promised land? (What did the author say to the original audience?) Do we make applications according to the new covenant? Do we read the text not as the original audience heard it but as we hear it as people of the new covenant? Do we navigate both? How do we avoid a moralistic preaching approach? When studying Deuteronomy, preachers have to take Jesus's words seriously in the Sermon on the Mount in Matthew 5:17: "Do not think that I have come to abolish the Law or the Prophets; I have not come to abolish them but to fulfill them." These are all issues and questions with which the preacher must wrestle.

Cultural Perspectives and Application

Deuteronomy was an important book for the Jewish people and for Jesus in particular. It's likely that the first Scripture Jesus memorized as a young boy was from Deuteronomy, chapter 6. He quoted from the book as an adult when he was tempted in the wilderness. When answering the question of an expert in the law, Jesus turned back to his first lessons as a toddler by responding from Deuteronomy 6: "Love the Lord your God with all your heart and with all your soul and with all your strength and with all your mind" (Mark 12:30; cf. Deut. 6:4–5). In his book *Our Father Abraham*, Marvin Wilson describes Deuteronomy in Jesus's day as the most widely "circulated and popular book of the Pentateuch."

> We know that Deuteronomy carried this broad influence for two main reasons: (1) The New Testament has more quotations from Deuteronomy than from any other book of Moses. (2) Among the Dead Sea Scrolls at Qumran, more separate copies of the scroll of Deuteronomy were found than of any other Mosaic writing. But the importance of the book of Deuteronomy is not limited to the early childhood of Jesus and others from his period. As an adult, Jesus, at the beginning of his ministry, quotes three times from this book in mustering spiritual support in response to the three temptations of Satan (Matt. 4:1–11).[3]

---

3. Marvin Wilson, *Our Father Abraham: Jewish Roots of the Christian Faith* (Grand Rapids: Eerdmans, 1989), 123.

Covenant

Deuteronomy is a covenant-renewal document, composed of a number of farewell addresses given by Moses to the people as they prepared to enter the promised land. The book resembles the structure of ancient Near Eastern suzerain-vassal treaties. These types of covenants described the relationship between a great king (suzerain) and one of his subject kings (vassal). Subject kings were required to demonstrate total obedience and loyalty to the suzerain. In the Bible, covenants are initiated by God.

Covenant is a strange concept for modern listeners, but certainly there are parallels in our modern world, and as Christians we are familiar with the new covenant in Jesus Christ. How does a preacher speak into a culture that sometimes lacks a certain gravitas when it comes to keeping contracts? We often take the breaking of a contract lightly when we want to avoid duty, obligation, or responsibility. But breaking a contract always comes at a cost.

The Israelites did not and could not keep the covenant. Moses knew this would be the case because the Lord told him before he died: "You are going to rest with your ancestors, and these people will soon prostitute themselves to the foreign gods of the land they are entering. They will forsake me and break the covenant I made with them. And in that day I will become angry with them and forsake them; I will hide my face from them, and they will be destroyed" (Deut. 31:16–17). Moses often uses three words to describe the Israelites: stubborn/stiff-necked (9:6, 13; 10:16; 31:27), unbelieving (1:32; 9:21; 28:66), and rebellious (1:26, 43; 9:7, 23–24; 21:18, 20; 31:27). Clearly, the Israelites needed a change of heart.

Moses knew that a day would come in which God would indeed change their hearts: "The Lord your God will circumcise your hearts and the hearts of your descendants, so that you may love him with all your heart and with all your soul, and live" (30:6). Moses, the mediator of the old covenant, looked forward to the new covenant in Jesus Christ.

One God

Throughout the book of Deuteronomy, Moses reminds the Israelites that God is the only God and that he saved them by his mighty hand. The Decalogue begins, "I am the Lord your God, who brought you out of Egypt, out of the land of slavery" (5:6) The first two commandments deal with God as the only God: "You shall have no other gods before me" and "You shall not make for yourself an image in the form of anything in heaven above or on the earth beneath or in the waters below" (5:7–8).

Surrounded by polytheistic nations, the concept of one God was somewhat foreign to the Israelites. Deuteronomy teaches us that Yahweh and Yahweh alone was/is God. It's true that much of our contemporary culture shudders at that claim when proclaimed from the pulpit. It was a serious confession to make back then, and it's a serious, even shocking, confession to make today: there is only one God and that God is Yahweh. As preachers, might we help our congregations make such a bold confession today?

Idols

The idea that people routinely worshiped idols—usually carved stone—is alien to many parishioners living in the Western world. But it may not be as foreign as we think. An idol is anything that we treasure more than God. We may think it can help us, save us, or make us happy or stable or loved. But in the end, only God is to be worshiped. By talking about idols as a modern issue, preachers will bridge the gap between the world of the Old Testament and the present day.

The Shema (Deut. 6:4-9)

The idea that *God is the only God* cannot be overstated. It forms the basis of Israel's confession of faith, known as the Shema.[4] The Shema stands as the centerpiece of Deuteronomy. Many Jews still recite the Shema two times per day: "when you lie down and when you get up" (6:7). It's been referred to as a summary of the Ten Commandments, and the Ten Commandments a summary of the entire law. "The Decalogue (or Ten Commandments) of Deut. 5:6–21 (Exod. 20:2–17) embodies the great principles of covenant relationship that outline the nature and character of God and spell out Israel's responsibilities to him. It is thus an encapsulation or distillation of the entire corpus of covenant text. The passage at hand is a further refinement of that great relational truth, an adumbration of an adumbration, as it were. It is the expression of the essence of all of God's person and purposes in sixteen words of Hebrew text."[5]

To understand the Shema is to see the heart of God for his people: God's faithful love. Preachers sometimes get lost in the Deuteronomy labyrinth of

---

4. As the Shema developed, it came to include three passages from the law of Moses. The first (Deut. 6:4–9) proclaims God's oneness (v. 4) and calls Israel to love him and obey his commandments (vv. 5–9). The second (Deut. 11:13–21) details the rewards promised for obeying these commandments and the punishments for disobeying them. The third (Num. 15:37–41) sets forth the law concerning tassels on the garments as a reminder to keep "all the commandments of the Lord" (v. 39). See Wilson, *Our Father Abraham*, 123.

5. Eugene H. Merrill, *Deuteronomy*, The New American Commentary (Nashville: Broadman & Holman, 1994), 162.

laws. But obedience has always been in response to God's love, which he demonstrated through his mighty saving acts and his calling of this undeserving people his "treasured possession." See, for instance, Deuteronomy 7:6–9.

Expositors must be careful to remember that God's grace undergirds the covenant. His love precedes his laws, and his love is expressed through his laws. Our love for the one and only God is demonstrated in obedience to the law—an impossible task on our own strength.

Imagination as an Exegetical Tool

Wise preachers will spend time trying to imagine what it would have felt like for this new generation to stand at the edge of the promised land. They had known only wilderness wandering. Now they were preparing to settle down. In what ways might a modern audience identify with those men, women, and children from so long ago? What did it feel like to be set apart by God as his treasured possession? How is that related to the church today? What was it like to experience his mighty acts? How did parents feel about teaching God's law to their children—overwhelmed, not up to the task, excited? What do all the laws reveal about the giver of the law? When we ponder such questions, our applications will be more natural than forced.

RECOMMENDED RESOURCES

Kaiser, Walter C., Jr., et al. *Hard Sayings of the Bible.* Downers Grove, IL: InterVarsity, 1996.

Merrill, Eugene H. *Deuteronomy.* The New American Commentary. Nashville: Broadman & Holman, 1994.

Wiersbe, Warren W. *Be Equipped.* The BE Commentary Series. Colorado Springs: David C. Cook, 1999.

Wilson, Marvin. *Our Father Abraham: Jewish Roots of the Christian Faith.* Grand Rapids: Eerdmans, 1989.

Joshua

CHRIS RAPPAZINI

The Big Idea of Joshua

After the death of Moses, God appoints a new leader, Joshua, to fulfill his promise made to the people of Israel by having Joshua lead them into the promised land, fight in many battles, and eventually distribute the land and resources to the twelve tribes of Abraham's descendants.

SUBJECT: How does the author describe the Lord's fulfilled promise of providing land to Abraham's descendants?

COMPLEMENT: Through the appointment of Joshua to lead the Israelites across the Jordan River and into battle, and the parceling out of territories to the twelve tribes of Israel.

EXEGETICAL IDEA: The author describes the Lord's fulfilled promise of providing land to Abraham's descendants through the appointment of Joshua to lead the Israelites across the Jordan River and into battle, and the parceling out of territories to the twelve tribes of Israel.

HOMILETICAL IDEA: Keep your courage because the Lord keeps his promises.

Selecting Preaching and Teaching Passages in Joshua

The book of Joshua records the Lord leading his people into the promised land as he promised Abraham (Gen. 15:18–21; 26:3), promised Isaac's son Jacob (Gen. 28:13), and explained the promise in further detail to Moses (Exod. 32:31). This book of courage, conquest, providence, and provision can be broken down into four major units with several sections in each unit. While most congregations may be familiar with some of the beginning narratives of the book, it might be fruitful for the preacher to cover the entire book in a three- to four-month series.

Many people who have been in the church world for some time most likely have heard the stories of Rahab and the spies or the walls of Jericho falling down, but perhaps they have learned them in isolation from the more complete picture of God fulfilling his promise to the Israelites. The first two units of the book address Israel's entrance and struggle with their new occupancy in the land that the Lord promised. Each unit could be separated by the various scenes (e.g., conversations, encounters, battles, etc.) taking place. The third unit describes the distribution of the land and may seem unnecessary to the modern reader, but it is extremely important for the twelve tribes of Israel. The final unit contains Joshua's last words to the people of Israel as they go their separate ways.

The following is a suggested strategy for preaching through the book of Joshua in eighteen weeks.

Unit 1: Joshua Takes Charge (Chaps. 1–5)

1. Joshua is called to be strong and courageous (1:1–18)
2. Joshua's spies are helped by Rahab (2:1–24)
3. The Israelites cross the Jordan into the promised land (3:1–4:24)
4. Circumcision at Gilgal (5:1–12)
5. Joshua's encounter with the commander of the army of the Lord (5:13–15)

Unit 2: The Israelites versus the God-haters (Chaps. 6–12)

6. The miracle at Jericho (6:1–27)
7. The sin and consequence of Achan (7:1–26)
8. Ai is demolished and the covenant is reborn (8:1–35)
9. The deception of the Gibeonites and the clemency of Joshua (9:1–27)
10. The Lord of lights fights for Israel (10:1–15)
11. The conquest continues to the south and north (10:16–12:24)

Unit 3: Distribution of Land (Chaps. 13–22)

12. Division of land (13:1–19:51)
13. Cities of refuge (20:1–9)

14. God fulfills his promises (21:1–45)

15. The eastern tribes return to their homeland (22:1–34)

Unit 4: Joshua's Final Remarks (Chaps. 23–24)

16. Joshua's last words to his leaders (23:1–16)

17. Restoring the covenant at Shechem (24:1–27)

18. Joshua's final resting place (24:28–33)

Getting the Subject, Complement, Exegetical Idea, and Homiletical Idea

Joshua 1

SUBJECT: How does the author say the Lord will fulfill his promise of land to the Israelites after his servant Moses dies?

COMPLEMENT: By calling on Joshua to be strong and courageous, to lead the people of Israel in taking possession of the promised land, and to teach them how to obey the law that was given to Moses, for God will be with them wherever they go.

EXEGETICAL IDEA: The author says the Lord will fulfill his promise of land to the Israelites after his servant Moses dies by calling on Joshua to be strong and courageous, to lead the people of Israel in taking possession of the promised land, and to teach them how to obey the law that was given to Moses, for God will be with them wherever they go.

HOMILETICAL IDEA: Good leaders are godly leaders.

Joshua 2

SUBJECT: What does the author reveal about the Lord's reputation through the story of Rahab the prostitute?

COMPLEMENT: The reputation of the Lord has reached neighboring nations, and while many people are preparing to fight the Lord, a few people confess the Lord's rule and reign.

EXEGETICAL IDEA: The author reveals through the story of Rahab the prostitute that the reputation of the Lord has reached neighboring nations, and while many people are preparing to fight the Lord, a few people confess the Lord's rule and reign.

HOMILETICAL IDEA: Instead of fighting God, let God fight for you.

Joshua 3-4

SUBJECT: Why does God tell Joshua to command the priests and the ark of the covenant to go first when crossing the Jordan River?

COMPLEMENT: To demonstrate that God is going before Joshua and the Israelites, just like he went before Moses and the previous generation.

EXEGETICAL IDEA: God tells Joshua to command the priests and the ark of the covenant to go first when crossing the Jordan River to demonstrate that God is going before Joshua and the Israelites, just as he went before Moses and the previous generation.

HOMILETICAL IDEA: God is going before us as he has gone before people like us.

Joshua 5:1-12

SUBJECT: Why is the Lord's first command to Joshua and the Israelite men after crossing the Jordan River to circumcise themselves and celebrate Passover?

COMPLEMENT: So that they will remember their past and also look forward to their future as a nation with a land to call their own.

EXEGETICAL IDEA: The Lord's first command to Joshua and the Israelite men after crossing the Jordan River is to circumcise themselves and celebrate Passover so that they will remember their past and also look forward to their future as a nation with a land to call their own.

HOMILETICAL IDEA: Sometimes it is important to look back while looking forward.

Joshua 5:13-15

SUBJECT: What message does the Lord send Joshua before Joshua enters Jericho?

COMPLEMENT: The Lord is the supreme, holy warrior and he will ultimately lead his people.

EXEGETICAL IDEA: The message the Lord sends to Joshua before Joshua enters Jericho is that the Lord is the supreme, holy warrior and that he will ultimately lead his people.

HOMILETICAL IDEA: Our God is a holy warrior.

Joshua 6

SUBJECT: How does the author say Joshua and the inexperienced Israelite army penetrate Jericho's massive walls and conquer the city that God had delivered to them?

COMPLEMENT: By listening and obeying the Lord's strict commands.

EXEGETICAL IDEA: The author says Joshua and the inexperienced Israelite army penetrate Jericho's massive walls and conquer the city that God had delivered to them by listening and obeying the Lord's strict commands.

HOMILETICAL IDEA: Listen carefully to God for deliverance in your life.

Joshua 7

SUBJECT: What does the author say is a result of Achan's act of unfaithfulness, deception, and disobedience?

COMPLEMENT: The Lord's anger burns against the Israelites, leading to their defeat at Ai and calamity being brought on Achan and his family.

EXEGETICAL IDEA: The author says that as a result of Achan's act of unfaithfulness, deception, and disobedience the Lord's anger burns against the Israelites, leading to their defeat at Ai and calamity being brought on Achan and his family.

HOMILETICAL IDEA: One's sinful actions can have consequences for many.

Joshua 8

SUBJECT: How does the Lord respond to Joshua and the Israelites after they confront Achan's sin?

COMPLEMENT: By leading them in victory over the people of Ai and recommences his covenant with his people following Joshua's burnt offering and renewed commitment to the book of the law of Moses.

EXEGETICAL IDEA: The Lord responds to Joshua and the Israelites after they confront Achan's sin by leading them in victory over the people of Ai and recommencing his covenant with his people following Joshua's burnt offering and renewed commitment to the book of the law of Moses.

HOMILETICAL IDEA: A renewed covenant is offered to a new type of person.

Joshua 9

SUBJECT: Why do Joshua and the leaders of Israel keep their oath to the Gibeonites even though they were deceived?

COMPLEMENT: Because the Lord keeps his promises despite the failures of Israel.

EXEGETICAL IDEA: Joshua and the leaders of Israel keep their oath to the Gibeonites, even though they were deceived, because the Lord keeps his promises despite the failures of Israel.

HOMILETICAL IDEA: God keeps his promises, and so should we.

Joshua 10:1-15

SUBJECT: When the Amorite kings join forces against the Gibeonites and Joshua receives a call for help, how does the Lord use Joshua?

COMPLEMENT: To come to the Gibeonites' defense through miracles such as making the sun stand still and hurling down large hailstones.

EXEGETICAL IDEA: When the Amorite kings join forces against the Gibeonites and Joshua receives a call for help, the Lord uses Joshua to come to the Gibeonites' defense through miracles such as making the sun stand still and hurling down large hailstones.

HOMILETICAL IDEA: The Lord of lights fights for us.

Joshua 10:16-12:24

SUBJECT: Why does the author say Joshua and the Israelites could continue to conquer the unjust cities and kings in the promised land?

COMPLEMENT: Because all but one city does not make a peace treaty with Israel, so the Lord hardens their hearts and helps Joshua and his army defeat anyone who stands against him so that the Lord's promise of giving the Israelites land will be fulfilled.

EXEGETICAL IDEA: The author says Joshua and the Israelites could continue to conquer the unjust cities and kings in the promised land because all but one city does not make a peace treaty with Israel, so the Lord hardens their hearts and helps Joshua and his army defeat anyone who stands against him so that the Lord's promise of giving the Israelites land will be fulfilled.

HOMILETICAL IDEA: God seeks justice in order to fulfill his promises.

Joshua 13-19

SUBJECT: Why does the author include lists and boundary lines regarding the allotment and distribution of the conquered land?

COMPLEMENT: To demonstrate the detail with which the Lord fulfills his prom-ise to Abraham and his descendants.

EXEGETICAL IDEA: The author includes lists and boundary lines regarding the allotment and distribution of the conquered land to demonstrate the detail with which the Lord fulfills his promise to Abraham and his descendants.

HOMILETICAL IDEA: God doesn't look past the details.

Joshua 20

SUBJECT: Why does the Lord tell Joshua to set up a city of refuge?

COMPLEMENT: Because an unjust shedding of blood would be in contradiction to God, his character, and the purpose of the promised land.

EXEGETICAL IDEA: The Lord tells Joshua to set up a city of refuge because an unjust shedding of blood would be in contradiction to God, his character, and the purpose of the promised land.

HOMILETICAL IDEA: There is safety and security under God's protection.

Joshua 21

SUBJECT: How does the author conclude the distribution of the land?

COMPLEMENT: By announcing that the Lord has fulfilled all of his promises and granted rest for the people of Israel on every side.

EXEGETICAL IDEA: The author concludes the distribution of the land by an-nouncing that the Lord has fulfilled all of his promises and granted rest for the people of Israel on every side.

HOMILETICAL IDEA: Many of God's promises end in rest.

Joshua 22

SUBJECT: What happens after the Reubenites, the Gadites, and the half-tribe of Manasseh go home and build an imposing altar by the Jordan River?

COMPLEMENT: Phinehas, an Israelite priest, warns them of the consequences of defiling the Lord, and the eastern tribes quickly repent and avoid bloodshed.

EXEGETICAL IDEA: After the Reubenites, the Gadites, and the half-tribe of Manasseh go home and build an imposing altar by the Jordan River, Phine-has, an Israelite priest, warns them of the consequences of defiling the Lord, and the eastern tribes quickly repent and avoid bloodshed.

HOMILETICAL IDEA: God quickly accepts those who repent.

Joshua 23

SUBJECT: What does Joshua tell the elders, leaders, judges, and officials in his second to last farewell address?

COMPLEMENT: That blessings will come if they obey all that is in the book of the law of Moses and that they are not to associate with the nations that remain, but if they break the law or associate with other nations, God will bring divine justice on them and exile them from the land.

EXEGETICAL IDEA: Joshua tells the elders, leaders, judges, and officials in his second to last farewell address that blessings will come if they obey all that is in the book of the law of Moses and that they are not to associate with the nations that remain, but if they break the law or associate with other nations, God will bring divine justice on them and exile them from the land.

HOMILETICAL IDEA: Remaining faithful to God is a lifelong pursuit.

Joshua 24:1-27

SUBJECT: After reminding the Israelite elders, leaders, judges, and officials about the Lord's promises and deliverance out of Egypt, what does Joshua challenge the people to do?

COMPLEMENT: To make a covenant to serve God and only God.

EXEGETICAL IDEA: After reminding the Israelite elders, leaders, judges, and officials about the Lord's promises and deliverance out of Egypt, Joshua challenges the people to make a covenant to serve God and only God.

HOMILETICAL IDEA: Serve God and nothing else.

Joshua 24:28-33

SUBJECT: Why does the author record the final resting places of Joshua, Joseph, and Eleazar?

COMPLEMENT: To remind the readers that God continues to use people after their death to bring glory to himself.

EXEGETICAL IDEA: The author records the final resting places of Joshua, Joseph, and Eleazar to remind the readers that God continues to use people after their death to bring glory to himself.

HOMILETICAL IDEA: The life we lead shapes the legacy we leave.

Difficult Passages/Verses

When one first reads the book of Joshua, it is hard not to be shocked by and squeamish at the amount of death and destruction found within its pages. Historian John Bright somewhat jokingly writes, "You simply cannot preach from this book, and you ought not to teach it to children. Shield our gentle ears from violence such as this."[1] Large sections of Joshua have difficult passages of conquest and killing. The preacher could avoid the book altogether, but perhaps a better option is to tackle these challenging issues up front and honestly.

The total destruction of cities and kings, particularly in the middle portion of the book (Josh. 6, 8, and 10–12), is puzzling to understand at first. The violence can be overwhelming and bothersome to Christians and completely offensive to skeptics. Many may be wondering, Doesn't Jesus say to love your enemies? Why would God command genocide? Why is the God of the Old Testament so different from the God of the New Testament?

It is important to remind listeners that the people God delivered into the hands of the Israelites were morally corrupt and practiced child sacrifice. The author of Joshua does not go into detail about the opposing nation's utter sinfulness and rebellion against God, but this is where extrabiblical resources and study will be helpful to explain that those whom the Israelites conquered were God-haters and extremely evil. It is also helpful to communicate to listeners that God sometimes speaks hyperbolically when he says to "completely destroy" and "leave no survivors." When Joshua describes the distribution of the land in chapters 13–19, some of the cities are still populated, meaning that not everyone was annihilated. God uses this hyperbolic language to communicate that one either serves God or not. This marks a unique time in the history of the Israelites that demonstrates that there is no middle ground as they begin their nation in the promised land.

The killing of Achan and his family in Joshua 7 is another difficult passage to preach from because of the seemingly extreme consequences of Achan's sin. Many would agree that Achan deserved to be punished because of his deception and disobedience, but was the brutal death penalty of being stoned and the burning of his remains really necessary? In addition, it seems purely evil to include his family in the sentencing (7:25). However, it is important to remember that Achan's sin, as well as most likely the approval from his family, cost the lives of many who died at Ai. Therefore, God was teaching

---

1. John Bright, *The Authority of the Old Testament* (Grand Rapids: Baker, 1975), 243.

his people that in order to inherit the land and be his people, they needed to trust him and be obedient to his ways. This scenario, like that of Rahab and her family, also shows that both destruction and salvation can come through one person (i.e., sin/death through Adam and salvation through Jesus; see Rom. 5:12–21).

A large section of the book covers the distribution of the land (Josh. 13:1–19:51). At first glance, this may not seem too controversial, but readers may feel uncomfortable with God's promise of material success. This idea of nationalism and colonialism may be misused and misunderstood by people in the majority West. The exhortations of total devotion to the nation of Israel may need to be fully explained in light of the New Testament and one's cultural context.

Cultural Perspectives and Application

The book of Joshua takes its readers on an exhilarating journey of God fulfilling his promise to a people who are on a quest for a place to dwell after decades in the wilderness and centuries in slavery. While today's readers may not be on a bloody conquest to take over another's land, several important truths in the book of Joshua are extremely applicable for today.

At first it may seem that the God of Joshua is a different or perhaps even a polar opposite God from the one expressed as the gentle, loving Messiah in the New Testament. However, it is vital to remember that the God of Joshua and the Israelites is the same God as in the first century, as well as the twenty-first century. His truths, character, and attributes never change. Therefore, it is important for the preacher to remind listeners of this certainty throughout the sermon series.

A big takeaway for the twenty-first-century listener is that God fulfills his promises. The driving force behind the events found in the book of Joshua is the Lord's promise of land to Abraham and his descendants. While it may seem today that God is distant or absent or just doesn't care about the person in the pew, Joshua reminds readers that God is deeply concerned with the people who share a covenant with him. God makes numerous promises to today's Christians that are vital for their everyday walk with him. Promises such as the free gift of salvation (Eph. 2:8–9), comfort in trials (2 Cor. 1:3–4), power from on high (Acts 1:8), and Jesus's imminent return (John 14:2–3) are often forgotten as believers monotonously go through life. It is significant for today's listener to know that God is still alive and active and that he keeps his promises.

The fulfillment of God's promise is a sheer act of the unconditional grace of God. The Israelites did nothing on their own to be the chosen recipients of God's promise. Because they are receivers of his grace, the Lord demands their obedience and exclusive devotion in return. For instance, some of those commands were to destroy cities, to pillage the lands, to make public spectacles of killings, to deny the temptation to take the possessions, and at times not to associate with some from other nations. The Lord had his reasons for these commands, which will need to be addressed, and today's listener will also need explanation for some of the commands God gives to us. Ultimately, the character of the believer is always on display before God, and recipients of grace are called to be faithful in the midst of a world that hates God.

Another key takeaway from this book is the leadership of Joshua. From the very beginning we see the reality and vulnerability of Joshua with his lack of confidence that he can fill the shoes (or sandals, rather) of Israel's most recent leader, Moses. Today's world is full of leaders. Books, movies, magazines, conferences, and the news engulf us with leadership. However, the Israelites were in slavery for centuries and learned leadership only from their captors or their deliverer, Moses. The book of Joshua shows us a different type of leader. He combines success and faithfulness with disappointment and failure. In his commentary, J. Gordon Harris writes, "Joshua's leadership shows that leaders can act decisively, prepare well, be unprepared, make mistakes, be manipulated, and compromise outside of God's will."[2] This wide array of leadership abilities and shortcomings can help listeners identify with the character of Joshua and see themselves in the narrative in many ways.

RECOMMENDED RESOURCES

Hess, Richard S. *Joshua: An Introduction and Commentary*. Tyndale Old Testament Commentaries. Downers Grove, IL: InterVarsity, 2008.

Howard, David M. *Joshua*. The New American Commentary. Nashville: Broadman & Holman, 1998.

Woudstra, Marten H. *The Book of Joshua*. The New International Commentary on the New Testament. Grand Rapids: Eerdmans, 1981.

2. J. Gordon Harris, *Joshua, Judges, Ruth*, New International Biblical Commentary (Peabody, MA: Hendrickson, 2000), 11.

Judges

GREGORY K. HOLLIFIELD

The Big Idea of Judges

Judges—named for the charismatic protagonists whose military exploits and personal failings feature prominently in the book—is a theologically framed record of Israel's history for the period stretching from the death of Joshua to the rise of the monarchy.

SUBJECT: Why didn't Israel ever fully possess the land that God promised to their ancestors?

COMPLEMENT: "Because of the apostasy that followed the death of Joshua and continued in spite of all Yahweh's efforts to reclaim Israel from it."[1]

EXEGETICAL IDEA: Israel never fully possessed the land God promised to their ancestors "because of the apostasy that followed the death of Joshua and continued in spite of all Yahweh's efforts to reclaim Israel from it."

HOMILETICAL IDEA: Ungodly compromise in the absence of godly leadership produces a downward spiral to destruction.

Selecting Preaching and Teaching Passages in Judges

The book of Judges documents Israel's overall downward spiral and lack of godly leadership during the period under consideration. The reasons for this spiral are introduced in 1:1–3:6, the book's introduction, and illustrated in gruesome detail in 17:1–21:25, the book's epilogue. In between, 3:7–16:31, one can trace the spiral as it unravels across the accounts of Israel's judges.

1. Barry G. Webb, *The Book of Judges*, The New International Commentary on the Old Testament (Grand Rapids: Eerdmans, 2012), 33–34.

The author's reason for structuring his record as he does is seen to be for a theological assessment of the nation during this period rather than a bald chronological recounting of Israel's leaders and their deeds.

Once the preacher understands why the book is structured as it is, he or she is in a better position to divide the book for exposition. The book's introduction can be treated as a whole or divided into halves, with part one (1:1–2:5) tracing Israel's social fragmentation and part two (2:6–3:6) its religious deterioration.[2] While fourteen noteworthy characters appear in the book's middle section, two of them are paired with their more recognizable colleagues (Barak with Deborah; Abimelech with Gideon), and six of them are mentioned only in passing (Shamgar, Tola, Jair, Ibzan, Elon, and Abdon). That leaves six judges, each of whom the preacher might devote one or more messages. The epilogue, given its length and the questions it raises, will require no less than two messages (17:1–18:31; 19:1–21:25).

Getting the Subject, Complement, Exegetical Idea, and Homiletical Idea

Judges 1:1-2:5

Introduction, Part 1—Social Fragmentation

SUBJECT: Who was to lead Israel in its fight against the inhabitants of Canaan (hereafter, Canaanites)?

COMPLEMENT: God appointed the tribe of Judah to lead, but the other tribes failed to follow even Judah's flawed example by compromising with the Canaanites.

EXEGETICAL IDEA: God appointed the tribe of Judah to lead Israel in its fight against the Canaanites, but the other tribes failed to follow even Judah's flawed example by compromising with the Canaanites.

HOMILETICAL IDEA: The way of those who fail to follow godly leadership is beset with thorns and snares.

Judges 2:6-3:6

Introduction, Part 2—Religious Deterioration

SUBJECT: What were the consequences of Israel's neglect to pass on its faith to the generation following Joshua's?

2. The tags "social fragmentation" and "religious deterioration" as applied to the introduction's two parts and in reverse order to the book's epilogue are taken from Dennis Olson, "The Book of Judges," in *The New Interpreter's Bible*, vol. 2 (Nashville: Abingdon, 1998), 863, as cited by Webb, *Book of Judges*, 32.

COMPLEMENT: Israel underwent a repetitious cycle of idolatry, judgment, supplication, and temporary deliverance.

EXEGETICAL IDEA: The consequences of Israel's neglect to pass on its faith to the generation following Joshua's resulted in a repetitious cycle of idolatry, judgment, supplication, and temporary deliverance.

HOMILETICAL IDEA: The apostasy of a family or nation is always only one generation away.

Judges 3:7-11

■ *The Judgeship of Othniel*

SUBJECT: Who was Othniel?

COMPLEMENT: He was Caleb's nephew, affiliated with the tribe of Judah, and the exemplary judge who, by the Lord's Spirit, delivered Israel from the king of Mesopotamia's oppression.

EXEGETICAL IDEA: Othniel was Caleb's nephew, affiliated with the tribe of Judah, and the exemplary judge who, by the Lord's Spirit, delivered Israel from the king of Mesopotamia's oppression.

HOMILETICAL IDEA: We need exemplary, Spirit-filled leaders to guide us.

Judges 3:12-31

■ *The Judgeship of Ehud (and Shamgar)*

SUBJECT: Who were Ehud and Shamgar?

COMPLEMENT: They were inauspicious men (Ehud—a trickster; Shamgar—an unheralded "nobody") with inauspicious weapons (Ehud—a dagger and a lie; Shamgar—an oxgoad) who delivered Israel from a Moabite confederation (Ehud) and six hundred Philistines (Shamgar).

EXEGETICAL IDEA: Ehud and Shamgar were inauspicious men (Ehud—a trickster; Shamgar—an unheralded "nobody") with inauspicious weapons (Ehud—a dagger and a lie; Shamgar—an oxgoad) who delivered Israel from a Moabite confederation (Ehud) and six hundred Philistines (Shamgar).

HOMILETICAL IDEA: God often uses flawed people with flimsy means to achieve his desired ends.

Judges 4

■ *The Judgeship of Barak (Assisted by Deborah)*

SUBJECT: Who was Barak?

COMPLEMENT: He was the fearful Israelite leader who refused to obey God's call until he was accompanied by Deborah onto the battlefield, and who was assisted by Jael in vanquishing Sisera, thus forfeiting the honor that would have been his.

EXEGETICAL IDEA: Barak was the fearful Israelite leader who refused to obey God's call until he was accompanied by Deborah onto the battlefield, and who was assisted by Jael in vanquishing Sisera, thus forfeiting the honor that would have been his.

HOMILETICAL IDEA: Each of us will be recognized and rewarded according to the faith we alone demonstrate.

Judges 5

■ *Deborah's Song*

SUBJECT: Who is honored in Deborah's song of victory over Sisera and his forces?

COMPLEMENT: The leaders who led by following the Lord (Deborah; Barak, barely; the heavens personified; Jael) and the people who offered themselves willingly (with a few notable exceptions).

EXEGETICAL IDEA: Honor in Deborah's song of victory over Sisera and his forces goes to the leaders who led by following the Lord (Deborah; Barak, barely; the heavens personified; Jael) and the people who offered themselves willingly (with a few notable exceptions).

HOMILETICAL IDEA: Those who join God in his endeavors will enjoy with God the blessings of victory.

Judges 6-7

■ *The Judgeship of Gideon: The Rise of Gideon*

SUBJECT: Who was Gideon in the beginning?

COMPLEMENT: He was that thrice reluctant Israelite leader who, with a contingent of three hundred men armed only with trumpets and torches, delivered his people from Midianite oppression.

EXEGETICAL IDEA: In the beginning Gideon was that thrice reluctant Israelite leader who, with a contingent of three hundred men armed only with trumpets and torches, delivered his people from Midianite oppression.

HOMILETICAL IDEA: God's ability to use us far surpasses our confidence in his ability to use us.

Judges 8

■ *The Judgeship of Gideon: The Downfall of Gideon*

SUBJECT: How were Gideon's leadership and legacy marred?

COMPLEMENT: Both were marred by a vindictive (8:1–21) and vain (8:22–28) spirit, fully incarnated by his son Abimelech.

EXEGETICAL IDEA: Gideon's leadership and legacy were marred by a vindictive and vain spirit, fully incarnated by his son Abimelech.

HOMILETICAL IDEA: Our vindictiveness and vanity will prove to be a snare to those who follow us.

Judges 9:1-10:5

■ *Gideon's Son: Abimelech (and Tola and Jair)*

SUBJECT: Who was Abimelech?

COMPLEMENT: He was a son of Gideon whose self-contrived leadership resulted in the deaths of his brothers, his subjects, and himself.

EXEGETICAL IDEA: Abimelech was a son of Gideon whose self-contrived leadership resulted in the deaths of his brothers, his subjects, and himself.

HOMILETICAL IDEA: Self-contrived leadership is ultimately self-destructive leadership.

Judges 10:6-18

■ *God Refuses to Deliver*

SUBJECT: Why did the Lord refuse to deliver Israel from the Ammonite-Philistine coalition, despite Israel's purported repentance?

COMPLEMENT: Because of the Lord's impatience with Israel's persistent and rampant idolatry.

EXEGETICAL IDEA: The Lord refused to deliver Israel from the Ammonite-Philistine coalition, despite Israel's purported repentance because of his impatience with Israel's persistent and rampant idolatry.

HOMILETICAL IDEA: God's patience wears thin with persistent idolatry.

Judges 11-12

■ *The Judgeship of Jephthah (and Ibzan, Elon, and Abdon)*

SUBJECT: Who was Jephthah?

COMPLEMENT: He was the Gileadite son of a prostitute (11:1–3) who was appointed by his clansmen to lead in their war against the Ammonites (11:4–11 [see 10:6–18]) and who attempted to manipulate the Lord into giving him the victory (11:12–33), no matter the cost or consequence (11:34–12:7).

EXEGETICAL IDEA: Jephthah was the Gileadite son of a prostitute who was appointed by his clansmen to lead in their war against the Ammonites and who attempted to manipulate the Lord into giving him the victory, no matter the cost or consequence.

HOMILETICAL IDEA: Tragedy is sure to follow when those who should submit to God try instead to manipulate him.

Judges 13

■ *The Judgeship of Samson: The Rise of Samson*

SUBJECT: Who was Samson in the beginning?

COMPLEMENT: He was a Nazirite whom God gave to a childless Israelite couple to begin saving his people from the Philistines.

EXEGETICAL IDEA: In the beginning Samson was a Nazirite whom God gave to a childless couple to begin saving his people from the Philistines.

HOMILETICAL IDEA: Without us even thinking to ask for him, God in his grace has sent the Savior we so desperately need.

Judges 14-16

■ *The Judgeship of Samson: The Downfall of Samson*

SUBJECT: Who was Samson in the end?

COMPLEMENT: He was an enigmatic and tragic Israelite loner whose repeated clashes with the Philistines and eventual death as their slave resulted from his own selfish perspective and self-pleasing ways.

EXEGETICAL IDEA: In the end Samson was an enigmatic and tragic Israelite loner whose repeated clashes with the Philistines and eventual death as their slave resulted from his own selfish perspective and self-pleasing ways.

HOMILETICAL IDEA: There is a way that appears right to each of us, but it is a dead end.

Judges 17-18

Epilogue, Part 1–Religious Deterioration: The Gods of the Godless

SUBJECT: How did the tribe of Dan descend into idolatry?

COMPLEMENT: It all started around Ephraim/Shiloh (home to the shrine of the Lord), in the days when Israel had no recognized king, with a thieving son, a quasi-religious mother, a restless Levite, and a dissatisfied/disobedient tribe (17:1–18:2), leading to robbery, threats, slaughter, and, soon enough, tribe-wide idolatry (18:3–31).

EXEGETICAL IDEA: The tribe of Dan's descent into idolatry all started around Ephraim/Shiloh (home to the shrine of the Lord), in the days when Israel had no recognized king, with a thieving son, a quasi-religious mother, a restless Levite, and a dissatisfied/disobedient tribe, leading to robbery, threats, slaughter, and, soon enough, tribe-wide idolatry.

HOMILETICAL IDEA: As goes the worship of the home, so goes the worship of a people.

Judges 19

Epilogue, Part 2.1–Social Fragmentation: The Plight of the Powerless

SUBJECT: How was the Levite's concubine treated by the powerful men in her life?

COMPLEMENT: She was exploited, ignored, handed over, raped, murdered, and dismembered.

EXEGETICAL IDEA: The Levite's concubine was exploited, ignored, handed over, raped, murdered, and dismembered by the powerful men in her life.

HOMILETICAL IDEA: In the absence of godly leadership, the powerless suffer most.

Judges 20-21

Epilogue, Part 2.2–Social Fragmentation: The Chaos of the Kingless

SUBJECT: How did the tribe of Benjamin nearly become extinct?

COMPLEMENT: It all started around Ephraim/Shiloh (home to the shrine of the Lord), in the days when Israel had no recognized king, with a powerless concubine, her treacherous Levite master/husband (who eventually sacrificed her), an Israelite city with elements as wicked as Sodom, and a dismembered corpse (19:1–30), leading to revenge, civil war, and near tribicide (20:1–48), followed by cruel measures in an attempt to rescue the situation (21:1–25).

EXEGETICAL IDEA: The tribe of Benjamin's near extinction all started around Ephraim/Shiloh (home to the shrine of the Lord), in the days when Israel had no recognized king, with a powerless concubine, her treacherous Levite master/husband (who eventually sacrificed her), an Israelite city with elements as wicked as Sodom, and a dismembered corpse, leading to revenge, civil war, and near tribicide, followed by cruel measures in an attempt to rescue the situation.

HOMILETICAL IDEA: As goes the welfare of the home, so goes the welfare of a people.

Difficult Passages/Verses

Judges is a deceptively simple book to read. Simple, because it divides easily into three parts: introduction (1:1–3:6), the stories of various judges (3:7–16:31), and epilogue (17:1–21:25). Those stories are developed with only slight, but significant, variations following a repeated pattern: (1) the Israelites do evil in the sight of the Lord, (2) the Lord sells them into the hands of their enemies, (3) the Israelites cry out to the Lord, and (4) the Lord raises up a deliverer. The author is even careful to state clearly how long each judge ruled. Simple! That's undoubtedly a major reason why Judges, among the Old Testament's historical books, "has perhaps received the least attention in the history of interpretation."[3]

But let the reader beware! Judges is a *deceptively* simple book. The term "judges" is itself misleading for modern readers, who would naturally take it to mean the presiding officers in a court of law. Instead, the term as it is used here refers to military chieftains who led pockets of Israelites against their oppressors.

Please note: the judges led only *local* pockets of their people, usually members of their own tribe, not the entire nation. For this reason, the years that each judge ruled can't be laid down end to end and then added up to arrive at the duration of the entire period. Some of the judges were contemporaries, serving at the same times but in separate locales.

Readers who take the book to be nothing more than a straightforward history of the period will miss the book's subtly encoded messages. First,

---

3. J. Alan Groves, "Judges," in *Dictionary for Theological Interpretation of the Bible*, ed. Kevin J. Vanhoozer (Grand Rapids: Baker Academic, 2005), 410.

there's the not so subtly stated refrain, "In those days there was no king in Israel. Everyone did what was right in his own eyes" (17:6; 18:1; 19:1; 21:25 ESV). The author intends for his words to be taken as more than a historical marker or his personal assessment of the nation's morality. Rather, after having recounted the temporary deliverances wrought by the judges with each one followed by the people's persistent return to sin, the refrain is meant to point to Israel's need for a "God-fearing, covenant-keeping king, who would help the people themselves keep covenant."[4] Second, and related to that, the author subtly implies that the king whom Israel needs will come from the tribe of Judah (portrayed favorably from the beginning [1:2–20]) and no other (because the other tribes, most notably Benjamin [throughout the book], failed to trust God and take their allotted inheritance). Who came from the tribe of Judah? David. Who came from the tribe of Benjamin? Saul. So it would appear the author is promoting a Davidic, as opposed to Saulide, kingship.

Judges *is* deceptively simple, as can be seen now, and occasionally difficult. The preacher will need wisdom when handling God's call for the genocide of the Canaanites; the deceptive dealings of Ehud (3:19–20) and others; the wisdom of laying out a fleece as Gideon does (6:36–40); the inexplicable inconsistencies of the judges themselves, Moses's own grandson, and other religious figures (8:22–28; 18:30–31; 19:1–30); Jephthah's notorious vow (11:29–40); Samson's enigmatic life and inability to see through Delilah's deception (13:1–16:31); and the graphic nature of certain passages (e.g., 19:1–30).

Cultural Perspectives and Application

The preacher must be clear in connecting God's command to drive out the Canaanites with God's concern for Israel's covenantal fidelity. That is to say, his command wasn't born from racist motives but from his desire for a faithful relationship. Israel's failure to drive the Canaanites from its borders lay at the heart of its unfaithfulness. Leaving those peoples in the land exposed Israel to the godless ways and idol gods of those whom it was meant to dislodge. Before long, Israel was looking to its pagan neighbors for cues on how to live in their shared land and, eventually, to their gods for the blessing of their land.

Why Israel failed to dislodge the Canaanites had a great deal to do with *when* it failed—beginning after the death of Joshua's generation. That generation's failure to pass on an intimate knowledge of their God (2:10) proved disastrous then, just as it will for any family or nation that neglects the evangelization and discipleship of its children and youth.

4. Groves, "Judges," 413.

No one is an island unto oneself. We are influenced by and influence one another, if by no other means than example. In that sense, we are all leaders. The questions we each must ask are: What kind of leader am I? Am I an exemplary leader like Othniel, a duplicitous leader like Ehud, a fear-paralyzed leader like Barak, a prideful leader like Gideon, a manipulative leader like Jephthah, or a selfish leader like Samson? Am I willing to use whatever I have in service to God, like Shamgar with an oxgoad and Jael with a tent peg, or do I use those things to garner power for myself, like Abimelech? Am I willing to take the risk of stepping out of the place society assigns me to do the unimaginable, like Deborah, or to labor faithfully with little fanfare wherever God has situated me, like Tola, Jair, Ibzan, Elon, and Abdon?

God's appointment, anointing, and use of a leader are no sure sign of his approval of all that leader is or does. Several of Israel's judges were deeply flawed and their methods for carrying out God's work less than laudable. As *leaders*, we must keep ourselves in the uncomfortable glare of the Spirit's searchlight, refusing to allow the public spotlight to blind us to our own flaws and constant need of grace. As *followers*, we should remember Paul's exhortation to follow him (or our leaders), but only as he (or they) follows Christ (1 Cor. 11:1).

Ungodly compromise is always ruinous. Always. With each passing generation the Israelites became more and more like the Canaanites among them, as evidenced poignantly in the judgeship of Samson and the book's two epilogues. Godly leadership—a king—from the tribe of Judah was sorely needed to lead the people to love God and obey his Word. David? Actually, one greater than David. His heir, Jesus of Nazareth!

RECOMMENDED RESOURCES

Fee, Gordon D., and Douglas Stuart. *How to Read the Bible Book by Book*. Grand Rapids: Zondervan, 2002.

Kuruvilla, Abraham. *Judges: A Theological Commentary for Preachers*. Eugene, OR: Cascade Books, 2017.

Ruth

PATRICIA M. BATTEN

The Big Idea of Ruth

In the midst of dark times, Ruth, a foreigner, demonstrates what it means to be a true Israelite as God uses her to fill the empty Naomi, her mother-in-law.

SUBJECT: How does God fill Naomi?

COMPLEMENT: Through the selfless acts of love of the Moabitess Ruth and Boaz.

EXEGETICAL IDEA: God fills Naomi through the selfless acts of love of the Moabitess Ruth and Boaz.

HOMILETICAL IDEA: Sometimes God fills us through committed people.

Selecting Preaching and Teaching Passages in Ruth

A preacher could preach one sermon on the book of Ruth or split the book into four or five separate sermons.

Getting the Subject, Complement, Exegetical Idea, and Homiletical Idea

Ruth 1:1–5

SUBJECT: Why do Elimelech and Naomi leave Israel for Moab?

COMPLEMENT: Because they don't trust the provision of God in the midst of a famine and they believe they'll be filled in Moab.

EXEGETICAL IDEA: Elimelech and Naomi leave Israel for Moab because they don't trust the provision of God in the midst of a famine and they believe they'll be filled in Moab.

HOMILETICAL IDEA: Trust in God's provision wherever you are.

Ruth 1:6-22

SUBJECT: How does Naomi return to Israel?

COMPLEMENT: Emptied of her husband and sons but filled by a loyal daughter-in-law.

EXEGETICAL IDEA: Naomi returns to Israel emptied of her husband and sons but filled by a loyal daughter-in-law.

HOMILETICAL IDEA: When we walk with God, we walk with others, and God uses that to fill emptiness.

Ruth 2

SUBJECT: How does God show kindness to Naomi and Ruth?

COMPLEMENT: By providing a safe place for Ruth to glean through the kindness of Boaz.

EXEGETICAL IDEA: God shows kindness to Naomi and Ruth by providing a safe place for Ruth to glean through the kindness of Boaz.

HOMILETICAL IDEA: God's kindness is demonstrated through the kindness of others.

Ruth 3

SUBJECT: How does God provide protection for Ruth and Naomi?

COMPLEMENT: Through the love of Boaz. (A "male protector" was crucial in that culture.)

EXEGETICAL IDEA: God provides protection for Ruth and Naomi through the love of Boaz.

HOMILETICAL IDEA: God acts in the interests of his people.

Ruth 4

SUBJECT: How is Naomi's emptiness filled?

COMPLEMENT: By God's loving hand, which provides a child and a future royal line.

EXEGETICAL IDEA: Naomi's emptiness is filled by God's loving hand, which provides a child and a future royal line.

HOMILETICAL IDEA: God lovingly provides for us by filling our emptiness.

Difficult Passages/Verses

One of the most challenging mysteries in Ruth concerns why Naomi sends Ruth to visit Boaz late at night. This seems like unseemly behavior even for non-Jewish people such as the Moabites. It would be improper for a woman in the ancient Near East to visit a man in a manner that could be so easily misinterpreted. Did Naomi put Ruth at risk since she did not know Boaz's character? The preacher or teacher must properly assess the biblical situation and decide what details to include and how to explain this questionable action.

Cultural Perspectives and Application

First, the concept of the kinsman-redeemer must be explored and explained to a modern audience. The purpose of the kinsman-redeemer is explained in Leviticus 25: "In the case of an Israelite man's death in which he fails to leave behind a son, the brother of the deceased man is commanded to take his widow as wife and both redeem the land and provide a son to carry on the deceased father's name."[1]

Second, the Israelites have strayed from God's covenant. Famine, for example, was one of the prescribed results of disobedience to the covenant. The idea that Ruth, a foreigner, upholds covenant living more than many Israelites should be fleshed out from the pulpit. What can we learn from this stranger? Does she have a right to God's blessing even though she's a foreigner? The genealogy that ends the book serves as a resounding yes. That list of progeny can also be fleshed out and extended beyond David to the ultimate kinsman-redeemer, Jesus.

1. Stephanie Van Eyk, "The Ultimate Kinsman-Redeemer," Ligonier Ministries, June 5, 2013, https://www.ligonier.org/blog/ultimate-kinsman-redeemer.

─────── **RECOMMENDED RESOURCES** ───────

Block, Daniel. *Judges and Ruth*. The New American Commentary.
Nashville: Broadman & Holman, 1999.

Wiersbe, Warren W. *Be Committed*. The BE Commentary Series.
Colorado Springs: David C. Cook, 2008.

1 Samuel

J. KENT EDWARDS

The Big Idea of 1 Samuel

The books of Samuel were written to help God's people know how to make the decision that will determine their destiny: Who will be our leader?

SUBJECT: What determined the relative effectiveness of the various leaders of Judah and Israel?

COMPLEMENT: The depth of each leader's relationship with God.

EXEGETICAL IDEA: What determined the relative effectiveness of the various leaders of Judah and Israel was the depth of each leader's relationship with God.

HOMILETICAL IDEA: What determines our ability to lead God's people is the depth of our relationship with God.

Understanding Narrative Literature

God wrote the Scriptures to communicate to all of his people, not just the scholarly community. I believe that the ordinary person, with the help of the Holy Spirit, is capable of understanding the main ideas of the Bible. But while a PhD is *not* a prerequisite for biblical interpretation, a basic understanding of the various types of literature found in Scripture is necessary.

Fortunately, the majority of Scripture was written in narrative, and people everywhere have an intuitive understanding of stories. Stories commonly share these two characteristics: conflict and characters.

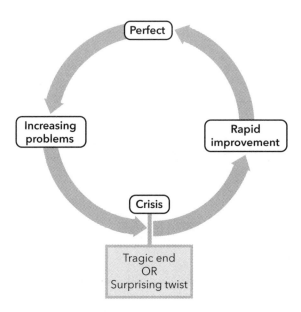

Figure by J. Kent Edwards. An earlier version of this figure can be found in J. Kent Edwards, *Effective First-Person Biblical Preaching: The Steps from Text to Narrative Sermon* (Grand Rapids: Zondervan, 2005), 43. Used by permission.

Conflict. Stories typically revolve around a problem that increases from one scene to the next until the tension climaxes either in a tragedy or an unexpected comedy.[1] The first question an interpreter should be asking is, What's the problem? The second question is, When does the problem resolve? When readers understand the beginning and end of a narrative's tension, they have discovered the beginning and end of the story. They have discovered a natural unit of Scripture, and this is a prerequisite for locating the author's big idea.

Characters. All stories feature individuals who experience the conflict of the story. While many people may be mentioned in a narrative, readers need to identify two key individuals: the protagonist and the antagonist.

The protagonist is the character in the story who makes the decisions that drive the story forward. Their choices move the plot and determine whether the story is a comedy or a tragedy. Protagonists will embody the big idea of the story. They are a living demonstration of what the narrator is telling the reader not to do (tragedies) or what the reader should do (comedies). Protagonists can be morally good or bad, but their decisions drive the story

---

1. While a comedy in a literary sense can involve humor, it primarily conveys an expectation of a happy outcome or positive resolution of the conflict.

forward and demonstrate the implicit truth of the story. God can be but is often not the protagonist of biblical stories.

The antagonist is the person or group of people who are opposed to the protagonist. They can be bigger and stronger than the protagonist (e.g., David versus Goliath), or they can be a much larger group (e.g., Philistine armies). Sometimes the antagonist is internal (e.g., self-doubt or pride), and it is not unusual for God to be the antagonist.

The remaining people in the story are secondary to the main idea. They are included to give us greater insight into the protagonist and the conflict the protagonist is facing. Readers shouldn't let the minor characters deflect their attention. The protagonist embodies the truth of the passage. The story is about the protagonist!

Locating the Big Idea of a Story

The point of the story is revealed by the protagonist at the moment of maximum conflict. This is when the story either ends in a tragedy or unexpectedly twists back up to perfection.

Unlike many epistle passages, stories have only one point. Every story contains a single primary truth, and that truth is embodied by the protagonist. For this reason, the protagonist is always prominently mentioned in the subject of the exegetical idea. Stories are about their protagonist.

The Challenge of Stories

Unlike epistles, biblical narratives don't discuss truth; they display the truth in the lives of the characters. The truth of stories is almost always implied and rarely explicitly stated. The careful reader will often *feel* the weight of the biblical truth in the emotion of the story. The effective interpreter will emotionally put themselves in the sandals of the protagonist and reexperience the protagonist's story. When a big idea coherently connects all the details of a natural unit of Scripture, eureka! Now we have an idea worth preaching!

Be aware, not all the stories in Scripture are simple comedies and tragedies. God's creativity can be seen in the varied ways that the narrator tells his stories. And I have often found that the scene that is most troublesome to understand becomes the key to a correct and profound understanding of the entire story. I will point out these creative story shapes as we walk through Samuel together.

Sticky Statements

These short, pithy statements crystalize and memorialize the big idea in listeners' minds. To preserve tension, these are typically used at the very end of a sermon.

Overview of 1 and 2 Samuel

A quick read of the books of Samuel reveals the dominant characters, and the theme of leadership quickly emerges. We begin with Eli and soon realize that he is a bad leader who is replaced by Samuel, who is a wonderful leader for Israel. The next major characters are Saul and David, and the bad-good theme is repeated, although David rapidly declines in effectiveness after his affair with Bathsheba.

The narrator treats us to an inside look into the character of these men and the ramifications of the decisions they make. As a result, we gain tremendous insight into the possibilities and pitfalls of leadership—and how the fate of the men and women of Israel was inexorably tied to the quality of their leader. Good leaders lead to good times. Bad leaders lead to bad times.

Selecting Preaching and Teaching Passages in 1 Samuel

While this chapter and the next outline the natural units and big ideas of 1 and 2 Samuel, do not assume that every natural unit must be preached individually. While preachers should begin Bible book–based sermon series with a clear understanding of the book's overall flow of thought, when that is achieved a simple question needs to be asked: "How important is the topic of this book to the spiritual health of my congregation?" Your answer will determine whether you take either a focused or broad approach to preaching that book. Let me explain.

Since the topic of 1 and 2 Samuel is leadership, if leadership is a critical issue for your listeners, you may want to adopt a focused strategy and preach all twenty-six natural units of 1 and 2 Samuel. However, if the issue of leadership is not urgent, you could take a broad approach and preach the nine larger sections outlined in the Samuel chapters.

1. How God Selects Leaders (1 Samuel 1–4:1a)
2. The Difference Godly Leadership Makes (1 Samuel 4:1b–7:17)
3. The Challenges of Leadership Transition (1 Samuel 8–12)
4. The Leader's Achilles' Heel (1 Samuel 13–15)
5. How God Develops His Leaders (1 Samuel 16–31)
6. The Challenge of Being the Leader (2 Samuel 1–5:5)
7. How to Succeed as a Leader (2 Samuel 5:6–10:19)
8. The Decline of a Leader (2 Samuel 11:1–20:25)
9. Never Forget! (2 Samuel 21–24)

Or, if the situation warrants, you could broaden the natural unit even more to include all 1 and 2 Samuel and preach it in a single sermon. If you chose this option, you could use the overarching idea: "What determines our ability to lead God's people is the depth of our relationship with God." The decision of which passages to preach is up to you. Like a family doctor, you must determine the best treatment for the people God has placed under your care.

Getting the Subject, Complement, Exegetical Idea, and Homiletical Idea

HOW GOD SELECTS LEADERS

1 Samuel 1:1–2:11

This is Samuel's origin story and is somewhat unusual for a Bible story in that the protagonist is a woman and the story ends with a prayer in which Hannah expresses the final condition of her soul.

While reading this story, linger over the early scenes. Visualize the terrible home life she has had to endure—for decades. Hers is a polygamous marriage, sharing a home with a bitter, vindictive co-wife, and suffering the ache and humiliation of barrenness. To make matters worse, her husband thinks that his love will compensate for the love of a child (it doesn't) and that he will make her feel better with an extra helping of meat. Divorce is not an option. Her distress is so great that she weeps continually and has stopped eating. As we read slowly, we become afraid that Hannah might consider suicide. But then Hannah goes to the temple.

The most puzzling scene is 1 Samuel 1:9–11, Hannah's vow. Here she promises that if God gives her a son, she will give him back to God. That's puzzling because at the end of the day, she will still be childless. So why does Hannah make this vow? Because when she makes that vow, she declares to God that there is something she wants more than a child. What is it she wants?

The reader must understand that in Jewish society children were correctly seen as a blessing from God while barrenness was interpreted as evidence that a woman was cursed by God. Childlessness meant that a woman had been rejected by God. No wonder it was grounds for divorce.

Prior to making her vow, Hannah wanted a son more than anything else in life. Making a vow to give her son back to the Lord means that she now wants something else more than a baby. She wants confirmation that God loved her.

In this scene Hannah shifts her ultimate desire in life. Now, more than anything else, she wants to experience acceptance, love, and intimacy with God. The vow is the twist in the story. After this vow, Hannah's attitude changes,

God opens her womb, and as soon as Samuel is weaned, she takes him to the temple and goes home without him. Think how hard that would be. Yet Hannah does this because she wants God more than anything else in life. Read her prayer and see if the first commandment had not been tattooed on her heart.

SUBJECT: When does Hannah escape the horror of her home life?

COMPLEMENT: When she desires God over everything else.

EXEGETICAL IDEA: Hannah escapes the horror of her home life when she desires God over everything else.

HOMILETICAL IDEA:[2]

> Subject: When will we enjoy the life that God wants us to have?
>
> Complement: When we want God more than anything.
>
> Sticky Statement: If all we want in life is God, then we will have everything we want in life.

It's worth noting that Samuel, one of Israel's most effective leaders, was the child of a woman who developed a passionate relationship with God. Surprised?

1 Samuel 2:12–4:1a

This narrative is more complicated. As you read this passage, you will likely be confused about the story's structure and find it difficult to identify the protagonist. Why? Because this story is actually a combination of two stories with two protagonists. Each story is dealing with the same topic, but one is a tragedy and the other is a comedy. Confused? Let's dive in.

In the first scene (2:12–17) Eli is introduced. Eli holds a twofold office: high priest at the central sanctuary of Shiloh, and judge of Israel (4:11). Eli's leadership positions help create tension because his sons, who serve as priests, are wicked men. After the narrator declares and demonstrates the gross sins of Hophni and Phinehas, he declares, "The sin of the young men was very great in the LORD's sight, for they were treating the LORD's offering with contempt" (2:17).

This is a huge problem for Eli because Leviticus 22:9 states, "The priests are to perform my service so that they do not become guilty and die for treating it with contempt." The penalty his sons deserve for their sins is death, but what father would want to execute his own sons? And he cannot let someone

---

2. I offer a second subject and complement to determine the homiletical idea/sticky statement.

else decide their fate because he is Israel's high priest and judge. What will Eli do? We see Eli's fateful decision in 2:22–25, when he gives his sons a good, firm lecture but fails to execute them.

God's response to his decision to honor family over God is swift and terrible. In 2:27–36 a man of God delivers God's commentary on Eli's choice: "Those who honor me I will honor, but those who despise me will be disdained" (v. 30). Eli's decision to honor family over God leads God to pronounce a death sentence on the family. A family that despises God cannot lead the people of God.

Eli's story is a tragedy, and its meaning is clear.

SUBJECT: Why is Eli removed as leader of Israel?

COMPLEMENT: Because he fails to punish his sons as God required.

EXEGETICAL IDEA: Eli is removed as leader of Israel because he fails to punish his sons as God required.

HOMILETICAL IDEA:

> Subject: Why would God remove us as leaders of his people?
>
> Complement: We fail to give God our ultimate allegiance (even over family).
>
> Sticky Statement: God removes leaders who fail to give him full allegiance.

The reader will note that intertwined with Eli's story is Samuel's story. In 2:18–21 the narrator abruptly describes how Samuel was raised from infancy by Eli. While Samuel appears in the midst of Eli's narrative in 2:26, Samuel is clearly the protagonist of a separate but parallel story in chapter 3.

In 3:1–10 God wakes up Samuel, and Samuel wakes up Eli three times before Eli realizes that God has a message for Samuel. The fourth time the Lord comes in person to give him a message. What was this message? In 3:11–14 God simply summarizes the man of God's message given back in 2:27–36! So why wake up both Samuel and Eli in the middle of the night to tell Samuel a message that everyone already knew?

This becomes more confusing when we read that Samuel is afraid to tell Eli the vision, implying that Samuel did not sleep all night. Why would Samuel be afraid to tell Eli what he already knew?

The answer is revealed in 3:16 when Eli calls to him, "Samuel, my son." Eli is not just Samuel's priest; Eli is his *adopted father*. No son wants to give his father the bad news that God's judgment is irrevocable. As a loving son, Samuel must have been tempted to lie or sugarcoat God's message. But he doesn't. In verse 18 we learn that Samuel tells Eli everything.

The tension of Samuel's story is the same as Eli's. Would Samuel honor family over God or God over family? This is a test of Samuel's ultimate priority. And Samuel passes where Eli failed.

Samuel's story is a comedy, as revealed in the final scene, because after Samuel's priorities are revealed, he rises and replaces Eli as Israel's leader.

SUBJECT: Why is Samuel selected as leader of Israel?

COMPLEMENT: Because Samuel is willing to tell his adopted father the difficult news God gave him.

EXEGETICAL IDEA: Samuel is selected as leader of Israel because Samuel is willing to tell his adopted father the difficult news God gave him.

HOMILETICAL IDEA:

Subject: Would God consider you as a leader of his people?

Complement: Only if you give God your ultimate allegiance (even over family).

Sticky Statement: What you do with God determines what God does with you.

The big ideas of these two stories are opposite sides of the same coin; they are communicating the same message. While both ideas are required to understand this passage, I suggest using the positive expression of the idea when preaching.

THE DIFFERENCE GODLY LEADERSHIP MAKES

In chapters 4–7 the importance of good leadership is displayed in a problem-solution format.

The problem is presented in a battle with the Philistines. After losing four thousand soldiers in an initial battle, the elders of Israel suggest that the ark of the covenant be brought to the battlefield "so that he may go with us and save us from the hand of our enemies" (4:3). Israel disrespects God by bringing his ark to the battlefield. They believe that since God would not allow his ark to be captured, victory is assured. When God refuses to be manipulated, their strategy fails. God allows the Philistines to capture the ark, and Israel loses thirty thousand more soldiers as well as Hophni, Phinehas, and Eli.

The Philistine leaders who capture the ark also face a problem that taught them the importance of honoring the Lord. In chapters 5 and 6 the Philistine leaders attempt to use God's ark as a propaganda tool. The resulting religious humiliation and physical pain that the Philistines suffer ends only when their leaders respectfully send the ark back to Israel with a guilt offering.

In the story's final scene (6:19–7:1), after the ark returned to Israel, God strikes down some of the men of the Israelite town Beth Shemesh because they disrespected God by looking into the ark. The story ends as a tragedy after the people ask, "Who can stand in the presence of the LORD, this holy God?" The nation will fail unless they have a leader who can answer that question.

1 Samuel 4:1b–7:1

SUBJECT: What do the Israelite and Philistine leaders discover when they attempt to use the ark of the covenant for their benefit?

COMPLEMENT: Their actions have led to great suffering for their people.

EXEGETICAL IDEA: Israelite and Philistine leaders discover when they attempt to use the ark of the covenant for their benefit that their actions have led to great suffering for their people.

HOMILETICAL IDEA:

Subject: What happens when leaders disrespect God by trying to use him to accomplish their own agendas?

Complement: Disaster will follow as God frustrates their plans.

Sticky Statement: Thy kingdom come, not my kingdom come!

In stark contrast to the previous story, Samuel honors God by leading Israel into a corporate confession of sin. Then, in response to Samuel's prayers, God supernaturally enables Israel to win a great victory, Samuel is established as the nation's leader, and Israel enjoys a wonderful period of peace.

1 Samuel 7:2–17

SUBJECT: What happens when Samuel focuses Israel on restoring their filial relationship to the Lord as the Philistines are coming to attack them?

COMPLEMENT: The thunder God sends provides Israel with a great victory that establishes Samuel as one of Israel's greatest leaders.

EXEGETICAL IDEA: When Samuel focuses Israel on restoring their filial relationship to the Lord as the Philistines are coming to attack them, the thunder God sends provides Israel with a great victory that establishes Samuel as one of Israel's greatest leaders.

HOMILETICAL IDEA:

Subject: What can happen when leaders' primary agendas are to strengthen their follower's relationship with God?

Complement: Those leaders can be a catalyst for their followers to enjoy God's blessing.

Sticky Statement: A leader's motives matter.

Although I have separated 1 Samuel 4–7 into two sections, since both stories deal with a leader's motivation they could be preached as a single sermon. If you prefer to preach the larger natural unit, consider the following unifying idea.

HOMILETICAL IDEA:

Subject: Why is it so important for a leader's agenda to echo God's agenda?

Complement: Because God's blessing can be enjoyed only when God's people walk in God's footsteps.

Sticky Statement: Matching our personal agenda with God's agenda is the secret sauce of successful leaders.

THE CHALLENGES OF LEADERSHIP TRANSITION

It is not easy to replace a successful spiritual leader. This time of transition is fraught with danger, and mistakes are easily made. Here are some of them.

Challenge 1: What criteria should we use to select a leader?

1 Samuel 8

The tragedy of this passage is that Israel, God's unique people, wants to be like everyone else. And when God clearly warns them of the danger of their decision, they disregard his counsel and insist on their own leadership model. The reader knows that the kings of Israel will lead Israel into generations of heartache, but the people refuse to listen to Samuel. And the sobering truth is that God will not stop us from making poor choices or living a life far below what he wants for us.

SUBJECT: What happens when Israel insists on choosing a king as their next leader like all the other nations?

COMPLEMENT: God warns Israel of the dire consequences of this decision but ultimately grants their request.

EXEGETICAL IDEA: When Israel insists on choosing a king as their next leader like all the other nations, God warns Israel of the dire consequences of this decision but ultimately grants their request.

HOMILETICAL IDEA:

> Subject: What happens when God's people insist on using secular criteria to select their leaders?
>
> Complement: God warns us with Scripture but will allow us to make bad decisions.
>
> Sticky Statement: God gives us freedom—the freedom to fail.

Challenge 2: Who is the leader's best friend?

1 Samuel 9:1–11:13

Although Saul is an impressive-looking young man (9:2), few people thought God would select him for a role as important as king. For one thing, he is a Benjamite (9:21). The tribe of Benjamin has a history of gross immorality and has been viewed with such disdain that the other tribes will not intermarry with them (Judg. 19–21). Not a good start for a political leader! In addition, Saul has no leadership experience and suffers from a poor self-image (10:22). How can a man like this succeed in this critical leadership role?

SUBJECT: How does God help Saul succeed as king of Israel?

COMPLEMENT: By giving him everything he needs to succeed: he gives him personal information that could only have come from God; he has Samuel give Saul the seat of and food of honor, speak with him on the roof, anoint him, and inform him of future personal events; he changes his heart, gives him the Holy Spirit, provides public confirmation of his divine appointment when selected by lot, and gives him an important early victory over the Ammonites.

EXEGETICAL IDEA: God helps Saul succeed as king of Israel by giving him everything he needs to succeed: he gives him personal information that could only have come from God; he has Samuel give Saul the seat of and food of honor, speak with him on the roof, anoint him, and inform him of future personal events; he changes his heart, gives him the Holy Spirit, provides public confirmation of his divine appointment when selected by lot, and gives him an important early victory over the Ammonites.

HOMILETICAL IDEA:

> Subject: How does God help the leaders he chooses to succeed?
>
> Complement: God provides them with all the resources they need to thrive in their important role.
>
> Sticky Statement: Take the job because when God calls us, he equips us.

Challenge 3: Effective leadership requires more than just a good leader.

1 Samuel 11:14–12:25

SUBJECT: What advice does Samuel give to all Israel as they celebrate Saul's confirmation as king?

COMPLEMENT: To remain faithful, because the success of Israel has always been tied to Israel's faithfulness to the God who has been faithful to them.

EXEGETICAL IDEA: The advice Samuel gives to all Israel as they celebrate Saul's confirmation as king is to remain faithful, because the success of Israel has always been tied to Israel's faithfulness to the God who has been faithful to them.

HOMILETICAL IDEA:

> Subject: What do God's people need to remember?
>
> Complement: Their success is entirely dependent on their faithfulness to the Lord.
>
> Sticky Statement: We can't do it alone.

THE LEADER'S ACHILLES' HEEL

In chapters 13–15 King Saul's star falls as quickly as it rose. It is stunning and frightening to see how a leader who has been divinely chosen and equipped to serve God's people can so quickly lose both his ability and authority to lead. How can leadership be lost?

1 Samuel 13–14

The literary form of this passage is somewhat complicated. It begins with a single tragic story in chapter 13. Verses 1–15 give us the moral background for what is to come. Here we discover Saul's desire for approval from his followers. The poor self-image the narrator hints at in 10:22 seems to have grown into a deep-seated need for the approval of his followers. Saul's Achilles' heel is his pride. We see this in 13:3–4 when Saul lies to the nation by claiming Jonathan's victory as his own. And we see it in 13:5–12 when Samuel is late and Saul sees his men begin to scatter. In an attempt to preserve his reputation, he unlawfully takes the initiative and offers the burnt offering. Saul values the approval of the people above the approval of God.

In the following stories we see the effect that pride has on Saul's leadership abilities. First Samuel 13:16–22 describes a dire military situation between the Philistines and Israel. This leads to two intertwined stories in chapter 14, one a comedy and the other a tragedy. In one of the stories, Jonathan is the protagonist. He, with virtually no resources, leads his young armor-bearer in a two-man, one-sword attack against a well-fortified Philistine outpost located at the top of a cliff. Jonathan attempts the impossible in faith that God will respond, and God responds with an earthquake that throws the Philistines into a panic.

While Jonathan is defeating the enemy almost singlehandedly, Saul sits paralyzed under a pomegranate tree surrounded by six hundred men who have no orders (14:2). With the battle well under way, Saul's lookouts finally see what is happening off in the distance. What is Saul's reaction? Rather than running to join the fight, he takes a roll call to see who is going to get credit for the win (14:16–17). When Saul finally arrives at the battlefield, the outcome is clear and Saul is irrelevant. For a leader with a pride issue, this is a problem.

How does Saul insert himself into the situation? By declaring, "Cursed be anyone who eats food before . . . I have avenged myself on my enemies" (14:24). This is one of the worst orders ever given on a battlefield. Saul's command seriously hindered Israel's war effort in a transparent attempt to draw attention to himself. Saul is so concerned about his reputation that when he hears that Jonathan, unaware of this order, has eaten some honey, he almost kills his son in anger.

This is a case study in leadership. Two leaders are placed in the identical difficult situation, but while Jonathan's success exceeds everyone's expectation, Saul is a spectacular failure. Why? Saul is defeated by his pride. When leaders become preoccupied with people's opinions, they become unable to act with the bold faith demonstrated by Jonathan. Leaders who are not willing to risk their reputations by acting with bold faith lose their ability to lead.

When we combine the backstory of chapter 13 with the intertwined stories of Saul and Jonathan in chapter 14, the following idea emerges:

SUBJECT: How does Saul lose the ability to lead Israel into battle with the courage he demonstrated earlier at Jabesh Gilead?

COMPLEMENT: Because his concern for his reputation prevents him from acting with the bold faith that Jonathan displayed.

EXEGETICAL IDEA: Saul loses the ability to lead Israel into battle with the courage he demonstrated earlier at Jabesh Gilead because his concern for his reputation prevents him from acting with the bold faith that Jonathan displayed.

HOMILETICAL IDEA:

> Subject: How could we lose our ability to effectively lead God's people?
>
> Complement: When our concern for our reputations makes us so risk averse that we cannot move forward with bold faith.
>
> Sticky Statement: Whose smile are we looking for?

1 Samuel 15

In this passage, God runs out of patience with Saul. While Saul's disobedience in chapter 13 resulted in a shortening of his reign, here God strips him of his authority. His anointing is lifted. Why? Because Saul's pride led to willful disobedience; his denial of wrongdoing and the attempt to excuse his failure as a sign of worship disqualify him as a leader of God's people. This passage is a fulfillment of Samuel's warning in chapter 13. The irony of this tragic story is that even after Saul admits his sin in verse 24, his pride causes him to beg Samuel in verse 30 to make him look better in front of the elders by walking back with him. The sin that cost him his kingship remained after his insincere repentance.

SUBJECT: What happens when Saul's desire for his soldiers' approval causes him to repeatedly defend his refusal to obey God's clear instruction to destroy the Amalekites?

COMPLEMENT: God rejects Saul as king of Israel.

EXEGETICAL IDEA: When Saul's desire for his soldiers' approval causes him to repeatedly defend his refusal to obey God's clear instruction to destroy the Amalekites, God rejects Saul as king of Israel.

HOMILETICAL IDEA:

> Subject: What will happen if leaders desire to please their followers more than their God?
>
> Complement: God will remove them from leadership.
>
> Sticky Statement: Leaders cannot follow two masters.

HOW GOD DEVELOPS HIS LEADERS

In chapters 16–31 the narrator shows us how Saul's pride slowly leads to his death and to disaster for the people he leads. Interwoven with Saul's tragic story are glimpses of David's development as a leader.

1 Samuel 16-17

Since God said that he was grieved that he made Saul king (15:10–11), we wonder what criteria God will use when he selects Saul's replacement. If Saul is the wrong kind of leader, who is the right one? The answer is found in the two separate but complementary stories found in chapters 16 and 17.

In chapter 16 Samuel comes to Bethlehem to anoint the next king and requests that Jesse bring his sons to the upcoming sacrifice. When Samuel sees the oldest son, Eliab, he is so impressed that he assumes he will be the next king. "But the LORD said to Samuel, 'Do not consider his appearance or his height, for I have rejected him. The LORD does not look at the things people look at. People look at the outward appearance, but the LORD looks at the heart'" (16:7). Surprisingly, it was the youngest son, David, whom God chose to be anointed as king. Why?

Two questions begin to surface for the careful reader. First, the reader wants to know what was so unique about David's heart? What was it about David's heart that qualified him to be king? It would be helpful to know the criteria God uses to select leaders for his people.

A second question arises from the chronological discrepancy between these chapters. Chapter 16 concludes with David becoming Saul's personal harp player and then one of Saul's favorite armor-bearers. Saul is so impressed with David that he sends a letter to Jesse requesting that David remain in his service. But if Saul and David enjoy a close relationship in chapter 16, why in chapter 17, after David famously kills Goliath, do Abner and Saul not know David's name? And since Saul wrote a personal letter to Jesse in chapter 16, why in 17:58 does Saul ask him who his father is?

To properly understand the relationship between these two stories, the reader must note that the narrator deliberately tells these stories in non-chronological order. Why? Because chapter 17 explains the attribute of David's heart that qualified him to lead Israel. It is the answer to the question raised in chapter 16. The narrator puts these stories in reverse order to make his point.

In chapter 17 we read that Goliath is from Gath. Gath is a leading Philistine city that occupies land that God promised to Israel. But Gath's military strength and the giants that inhabit it are so formidable that even Joshua was unable to conquer it. In fact, Israel so fears the giants of Gath that in chapter 17 David is the only person in all Israel willing to fight Goliath. Only David is willing to act in bold faith because of the promise of Scripture that the land belongs to Israel. He is so confident of God's Word that he is willing to put his life and the fate of the nation on the line. And God is true to his Word.

SUBJECT: Why does God anoint David to replace Saul as the next king of Israel?

COMPLEMENT: Because by fighting Goliath David demonstrates his belief in God's promise that Israel could conquer Gath.

EXEGETICAL IDEA: God anoints David to replace Saul as the next king of Israel because by fighting Goliath David demonstrates his belief in God's promise that Israel could conquer Gath.

HOMILETICAL IDEA:

Subject: Would God consider you as a leader of his people?

Complement: Only if your confidence in God's Word enables you to make courageous faith-filled decisions for his kingdom.

Sticky Statement: Boldly go where only God can take you.

1 Samuel 18-20

In this tragic story we see how Saul's desperate attempts to destroy his rival backfire. The more Saul tries to hurt David, the more he hurts himself.

SUBJECT: What happens when Saul's desire to remain king leads to repeated efforts to kill David?

COMPLEMENT: David's popularity increases, while Saul loses the loyalty of Michal and Jonathan.

EXEGETICAL IDEA: When Saul's desire to remain king leads to repeated efforts to kill David, David's popularity increases, while Saul loses the loyalty of Michal and Jonathan.

HOMILETICAL IDEA:

Subject: What happens when leaders try to hold on to power by attacking their rivals?

Complement: Their plans will always backfire.

Sticky Statement: When our pride makes us want a rival to fail, we are lost.

1 Samuel 21-23

In these chapters we have two contrasting stories, one negative and the other positive. These narratives communicate the same idea from a different perspective. Let's look at these stories first individually and then collectively.

▦ *1 Samuel 21-22*

SUBJECT: What happens when David decides to lie to the priest of Nob?

COMPLEMENT: The priests and entire town of Nob are executed, and David is forced into exile.

EXEGETICAL IDEA: When David decides to lie to the priest of Nob, the priests and entire town of Nob are executed, and David is forced into exile.

▦ *1 Samuel 23*

SUBJECT: What happens when David inquires of the Lord when making decisions?

COMPLEMENT: God not only helps David save the city of Keilah but also frustrates Saul's attempts to capture him.

EXEGETICAL IDEA: When David inquires of the Lord when making decisions, God not only helps David save the city of Keilah but also frustrates Saul's attempts to capture him.

When we combine these two separate stories, we create a single homiletical idea.

HOMILETICAL IDEA:

Subject: What will happen when we make decisions based on God's Word rather than relying on our wits?

Complement: Our ministries will flourish.

Sticky Statement: "There is a way that appears to be right, but in the end it leads to death" (Prov. 14:12).

In the next two stories we see how David responds to injustice. The first story deals with injustice from an authority over us, while the second focuses on unjust treatment from someone under our authority. Both stories are comedies.

1 Samuel 24

SUBJECT: What happens when David refuses to take advantage of the opportunity to kill King Saul as Saul is trying to kill David?

COMPLEMENT: Saul returns home after publicly acknowledging David's righteousness.

EXEGETICAL IDEA: When David refuses to take advantage of the opportunity to kill King Saul as Saul is trying to kill David, Saul returns home after publicly acknowledging David's righteousness.

HOMILETICAL IDEA:

Subject: What can happen when we choose not to attack authority figures who persecute us?

Complement: We strengthen our position as the contrast in character becomes clear to everyone.

Sticky Statement: When we fight fire with fire, everyone gets burned.

1 Samuel 25

SUBJECT: What happens when David listens to Abigail's advice not to respond to Nabal's insults with bloodshed?

COMPLEMENT: Not only does the Lord kill Nabal, but David marries Abigail.

EXEGETICAL IDEA: When David listens to Abigail's advice not to respond to Nabal's insults with bloodshed, not only does the Lord kill Nabal, but David marries Abigail.

HOMILETICAL IDEA:

Subject: What happens when we refuse to strike back when we are disrespected by those we have served well?

Complement: We allow God to right the wrong we've suffered.

Sticky Statement: "Will not the Judge of all the earth do right?" (Gen. 18:25). Let him!

1 Samuel 26–31

In this large section, chapter 26 serves as a prologue to the two stories that follow: the story of David's comedic rise toward the throne and the tragedy of Saul's self-destruction. In these chapters the narrator illustrates how leaders are rewarded for their righteousness.

Chapter 26 is very similar to David and Saul's encounter in the cave back in chapter 24. Once again Saul is trying, unjustly, to murder David. And once again David righteously refuses to take advantage of the opportunity to murder Saul. What is notable about chapter 26 is David's assertion in 26:23–24:

> The LORD rewards everyone for their righteousness and faithfulness. The LORD delivered you into my hands today, but I would not lay a hand on the LORD's anointed. As surely as I valued your life today, so may the LORD value my life and deliver me from all trouble.

Saul then replies to David, "May you be blessed, David my son; you will do great things and surely triumph" (26:25). As we will soon see, Saul's prediction will come to pass. What rewards will these men reap as a reward for their respective levels of righteousness?

David's story begins in chapter 27 with his surprising success in hiding from Saul when he takes his men and their families to live near Gath. It is also surprising in chapter 29 to see how the internal politics of the Philistine rulers allow David to avoid joining his Philistine host's war against Israel (28:1–2; 29:1–11). This saves David from the impossible situation of being part of the devastating Philistine attack on Israel described in chapter 31. In chapter 30, it is surprising that David is able to find the Amalekite army who has destroyed the homes and captured the families of David's men in their absence. Even better, when David defeats the Amalekites, he not only recovers all the goods and family members; he also takes possession of much additional treasure that the Amalekites had captured from previous raids on other towns. With this additional booty, David is able to give generously to those Israelites who could not join them in battle and give presents to the elders of Judah. These gifts are politically strategic and will facilitate David's rise to the throne. In these chapters God is sovereignly creating these "surprising" moments. These moments are David's rewards for his righteousness. God clearly values David's life and is delivering him from all trouble.

SUBJECT: How does God reward David for his righteousness?

COMPLEMENT: By giving David the resources he needs to become the king God wants him to be.

EXEGETICAL IDEA: God rewards David for his righteousness by giving David the resources he needs to become the king God wants him to be.

Although Saul's story also begins in chapter 27, it takes a radically different path. With the Philistine armies approaching, Saul consults with the witch of Endor and asks her to call up Samuel. Samuel's message is to remind him of the reward he will receive for his lack of righteousness. In chapter 31 God will remove Saul from his position of leadership by death. As a result of Saul's sin, God will not value Saul's life or deliver him from all trouble.

SUBJECT: How does God reward Saul for his lack of righteousness?

COMPLEMENT: By removing him from office during Israel's loss to the Philistine army.

EXEGETICAL IDEA: God rewards Saul for his lack of righteousness by removing him from office during Israel's loss to the Philistine army.

When the exegetical ideas of David's story and Saul's story are seen in contrast, a single homiletical idea emerges.

HOMILETICAL IDEA:

Subject: How important is a leader's righteousness?

Complement: While God actively helps his righteous leaders, he removes the unrighteous.

Sticky Statement: God is a better friend than an enemy.

First Samuel 31 is such a powerful, tragic, and relevant passage for our day that after preaching chapters 26–31 as one sermon, I enjoy coming back and preaching 31 as a stand-alone sermon. It is noteworthy in this chapter that Saul commits suicide to avoid being abused by the Philistines. Yet after his death the Philistines abuse his body and reputation very badly. Taking his own life does not solve his problems. But the key to this sad short story is found in the last scene, verses 11–13. The men of Jabesh Gilead who risked their lives to stop the Philistines from abusing Saul's body are citizens of the city that Saul rescued in chapter 11. What is more, in Judges 21 we discover that the people of Jabesh Gilead are Saul's relatives. They are family.

If these brave members of Saul's family are willing to risk their lives by coming deep into Philistine territory to save his body from abuse, would they not have come earlier to save his life? Yes, Saul had lost the throne, but he didn't have to lose his life. I believe that Saul's Jabesh Gilead family would have come to his rescue if only he had asked. As Christians we have been adopted into the family of God. We have brothers and sisters in Christ who are willing to come to our aid if we ask.

Not only does suicide not solve our problems but it is also unnecessary. We can always call on family for help!

■ *1 Samuel 31*

SUBJECT: Why is Saul's suicide on Mount Gilboa so tragic?

COMPLEMENT: Because it is unnecessary: the men of Jabesh Gilead who come to his aid in death would have done so in life.

EXEGETICAL IDEA: Saul's suicide on Mount Gilboa is so tragic because it is unnecessary: the men of Jabesh Gilead who come to his aid in death would have done so in life.

HOMILETICAL IDEA:

Subject: Why is suicide so tragic?

Complement: Because it is unnecessary: our brothers and sisters in Christ will come to our aid if we ask.

Sticky Statement: Seek help from your family in Christ!

Difficult Passages/Verses

One of the reasons narrative passages can be challenging to preach is their genre. Perhaps because of our theological education, many preachers prefer to think deductively and systematically. But biblical narrators don't communicate that way. Their stories communicate truth implicitly rather than explicitly. They display truth in action instead of describing it with words. This concretized theology requires a new hermeneutic. It forces us to read narratives as stories and develop the skill of identifying subtle literary clues and recognizing how the author is using them to communicate their big idea.

Since developing expertise in literary exegesis is as challenging as it is important, the author has, on occasion, added additional commentary to provide insight into the narrator's subtle strategies (e.g., 1 Sam. 1:1–2:11; 1 Sam. 13–14). Readers are encouraged to read these portions slowly with open Bibles and minds.

An additional difficulty preachers face when interpreting longer narratives is the influence that separate stories have on each other. Narrators sometimes choose to use early stories of epic literature to inform later narratives. Careful preachers will pay attention to the unspoken interplay of these stories. One example of interconnected stories is Saul's help of Jabesh-Gilead in 1 Samuel 11 and the irony of Jabesh-Gilead's postmortem help to Saul in 1 Samuel 31. Another is the narrator's connection of David's betrayal of Uriah and Bathsheba in 2 Samuel 11 to the irony of Ahithophel's betrayal of David in 2 Samuel 16.

A further challenge in preaching these narratives is the significant gap that exists between ancient Israel and contemporary listeners. Israel was a minor nation-state trying to survive and thrive in a lawless militaristic age. The brutality frequently referenced in the books of Samuel can be jarring to contemporary listeners and prevent people from receiving the big idea of the passage. You cannot, for example, preach 1 Samuel 15 without dealing with the problem of God commanding Saul to initiate a campaign of genocide against the Amalekites.

Cultural Perspectives and Application

A preacher's knowledge of the cultural differences that exist between ancient Israel and twenty-first-century preachers can significantly improve the effectiveness of their communication. For example, in 1 Samuel 16:11, when Samuel came to Bethlehem to anoint Israel's next king, he paused and "asked Jesse, 'Are these all the sons you have?' *There is still the youngest,*' Jesse answered. 'He is tending the sheep.' Samuel said, 'Send for him; we will not sit down until he arrives.'"

Preachers should note the subtle clues the narrator provides in the text, and ask, "Why did the narrator put this detail in the text? Why does the narrator provide a seemingly unimportant birth order detail?" The answer is often culture. Here the detail reflects the ancient eastern cultural priority placed on family birth order. Failure to note this cultural reference would prevent the interpreter from appreciating the shock of the ancient reader when David, the eighth-born son of Jesse, was anointed king instead of Eliab, the firstborn son.

Also, in 2 Samuel 11:3–4a, we read that David "sent someone to find out about her. The man said, '*She is Bathsheba, the daughter of Eliam and the wife of Uriah the Hittite.*' Then David sent messengers to get her. She came to him, and he slept with her." Here the narrator emphasizes that Bathsheba was the wife of Uriah—one of David's mighty men. Only the preacher who understands military culture will grasp the enormous impact David's sin with Bathsheba would have on Israel's army. Within a military culture, it is a grievous offense for a commanding officer to send a subordinate on a mission and use their absence to take sexual advantage of their spouse. If knowledge of the officer's betrayal becomes known, the trust and respect of their soldiers would be lost. Knowledge of military culture heightens the tension of this narrative.

When preachers attempt to apply biblical narratives, several challenges emerge. One of these is relevance. While the writer of Samuel focuses on the leadership of God's people, there may be occasions when preachers want to apply a passage outside that context. While this can be done, preachers need to carefully take the homiletical idea up the ladder of abstraction without altering the content. An example from 1 Samuel 4:1–7:1 follows:

Subject: What happens when leaders disrespect God by trying to use him to accomplish their own agendas?

Complement: Disaster follows as God frustrates their plans.

Subject: What happens if we try to use God to accomplish our personal agenda?

Complement: We discover that it won't work.

The second challenge with narrative application is the temptation to universalize a narrative's events. The point of a biblical story is not what happened but why it happened. Priority needs to be placed on the idea revealed by the story and care taken not to guarantee that God will do for our listeners exactly what he did in the lives of the biblical characters.

Just because Hannah's radical commitment to the Lord in 1 Samuel 1 resulted in her ability to have a child, this doesn't mean the passage provides a universal cure for barrenness. Nor does the great faith that Jonathan demonstrated in 1 Samuel 14 guarantee we will always win wars. And I'm confident that you will never be anointed as king of Israel like David. God does not promise to replicate the narratives of the past, but he does reveal his eternal character in them. That's why we preach ideas.

RECOMMENDED RESOURCE

Baldwin, Joyce G. *1 and 2 Samuel*. Tyndale Old Testament Commentaries. Downers Grove, IL: InterVarsity, 1988.

2 Samuel

J. KENT EDWARDS

The Big Idea of 2 Samuel

See the discussion in 1 Samuel.

Selecting Preaching and Teaching Passages in 2 Samuel

See the discussion in 1 Samuel.

Getting the Subject, Complement, Exegetical Idea, and Homiletical Idea

THE CHALLENGE OF BEING THE LEADER

As we begin 2 Samuel, we enter a new phase of David's life. With the death of Saul, David begins the challenging task of being recognized as king of a united Israel. In 2 Samuel David is no longer preparing for a significant leadership role. Now he must begin acting as a senior leader of God's people. Not an easy task.

2 Samuel 1:1–5:5

This large natural unit is quite complicated. The unit is bookended with similar stories. In chapter 1 an Amalekite comes to David claiming to have killed Saul. Although we know this is not true, David does not know this. How does David respond when a powerless foreigner claims to have committed murder? David justly condemns him to death.

In chapter 4 two foreigners murder Saul's son Ish-Bosheth (the only potential rival to David's ascension to the throne) and bring his severed head to David as a trophy. David references his previous punishment of a murder in chapter 1 and orders the just execution of the two murderers.

These two bookend stories stand in sharp contrast to the decision David makes in between. In chapter 2 David is quickly appointed as king over Judah, and David begins the difficult task of assuming the position Saul enjoyed: becoming king over all the tribes of Israel.

The commander of Saul's army, Abner, has aspirations for power and makes Saul's surviving son, Ish-Bosheth, a puppet king. It is not long before conflict breaks out between Abner and David's military commander, Joab. Abner and Joab stage a wrestling match that quickly evolves into a battle. As the battle rages, Abner kills Joab's brother, Asahel. The text is clear that Abner kills in self-defense, in the context of war, and only after Abner gives at least two warnings.

In chapter 3 David's power is growing, and Abner comes to David and agrees to use his influence to give Israel to David. When Joab realizes that Abner is gaining David's favor, he secretly arranges a private meeting with Abner. We read, "Joab took him aside into an inner chamber, as if to speak with him privately. And there, to avenge the blood of his brother Asahel, Joab stabbed him in the stomach, and he died" (3:27).

This is murder. A murder that makes things politically difficult for David. On the one hand, David has to honor Abner. If he doesn't, he risks alienating the house of Saul. On the other hand, Joab is a powerful man in Judah, and if David alienates him, he could lose his power base. How David handles this situation will determine whether he will ever become king of a united Israel. David makes a decision that would haunt him the rest of his life.

In 3:28–37 David puts on a great public show of grief over Abner's death in order to gain political support, but he chooses not to punish Joab for murder. Why? He says to his men in verses 38–39: "Do you not realize that a commander and a great man has fallen in Israel this day? And today, though I am the anointed king, I am weak, and these sons of Zeruiah are too strong for me. May the LORD repay the evildoer according to his evil deeds!"

David has no problem punishing people for murder when there is no political price to pay. But David is not willing to risk his political future to punish Joab. He allows a known murderer to escape justice. The scary thing about this story is that it ends in 5:1–5 with all the tribes coming to David and anointing him as king over all Israel. David's moral compromise accomplishes his goal.

SUBJECT: When does David fail to act justly by punishing Joab for his murder of Abner?

COMPLEMENT: When doing so could jeopardize his opportunity to become king of Israel.

EXEGETICAL IDEA: David fails to act justly by punishing Joab for his murder of Abner when doing so could jeopardize his opportunity to become king of Israel.

HOMILETICAL IDEA:[1]

Subject: When will we leaders be tempted to make grave moral compromises?

Complement: When political consequences could put our leadership ambitions at risk.

Sticky Statement: Doing what's right is easy when it's easy.

HOW TO SUCCEED AS A LEADER

2 Samuel 5:6–6:23

In this comedic passage we see Israel beginning to thrive under David's leadership. As David listens to God and follows his direction, Israel's enemies are being defeated. Since David knows that God's blessing is critical to his success, he wants God's ark inside Jerusalem, his new capital city. He first attempts to retrieve the ark with a large crowd and great celebration, but things go bad quickly when God strikes Uzzah down for irreverently touching the ark. David, now afraid of God, leaves the ark at Obed-edom's home for three months as he thinks about what he did wrong.

When David returns, he does things differently. This time David treats God's ark with respect. He doesn't place the ark on a cart but has it carried by hand as God had commanded. David is so excited that the ark and its blessings are coming to Jerusalem that he takes off his kingly robes, puts on a simple linen ephod, and dances before the Lord. No king of the day would have thought of dancing like this. It was *very* undignified for any adult, but especially the king. No wonder Michal, the daughter of Saul, despises David when she sees this. Her father's pride made him very concerned about his reputation, and he would never have acted this way. But David is not concerned about his public image. He wants the people's attention to be focused on the Lord, not him. He wants God to receive the glory and honor. Not him.

---

1. I offer a second subject and complement to determine the homiletical idea/sticky statement.

SUBJECT: When is successful King David able to enjoy the blessings of having the ark of God in the city of David?

COMPLEMENT: When he publicly humbles himself by dancing before the Lord, wearing a linen ephod.

EXEGETICAL IDEA: Successful King David is able to enjoy the blessings of having the ark of God in the city of David when he publicly humbles himself by dancing before the Lord, wearing a linen ephod.

HOMILETICAL IDEA:

Subject: When can leaders enjoy God's blessing on their ministry?

Complement: When they publicly deflect all the glory for their success to the Lord.

Sticky Statement: The secret to success is to give God glory.

2 Samuel 7

In this comedic story we see another demonstration of David's humility in the way that he responds to God's declaration that his request to build God's temple has been refused. That honor will go to David's son. As difficult as this news must have been to hear and understand, David does not resist.

SUBJECT: How does David respond to God's refusal to allow him to build a temple?

COMPLEMENT: By gratefully accepting the role that God has for him.

EXEGETICAL IDEA: David responds to God's refusal to allow him to build a temple by gratefully accepting the role that God has for him.

HOMILETICAL IDEA:

Subject: How should we respond when God's plans for our ministry don't mesh with ours?

Complement: By gratefully accepting the role God wants us to play.

Sticky Statement: Stay in your lane!

2 Samuel 8-10

This natural unit is a comedy that describes perhaps the best period of David's reign. The reason David is enjoying tremendous military and financial success is that he is "doing what was just and right for all his people" (8:15). This is demonstrated in his generous treatment of Jonathan's son Mephibosheth in chapter 9, as well as his kindness to Hanun the Ammonite in chapter 10.

SUBJECT: How can David consistently enjoy God's blessing on his leadership of Israel?

COMPLEMENT: By consistently doing "what was just and right for all his people."

EXEGETICAL IDEA: David can consistently enjoy God's blessing on his leadership of Israel by consistently doing "what was just and right for all his people."

HOMILETICAL IDEA:

Subject: How can we expect God's favor as we lead God's people?

Complement: By consistently treating those we lead with the highest moral standards.

Sticky Statement: Leading God's people well means following the Golden Rule.

THE DECLINE OF A LEADER

2 Samuel 11–12

Different periods of life present different temptations. Here David succumbs to the two temptations that come with the success often achieved later in life. The first temptation of success is to use the power that accompanies high office to take advantage of others. This story begins with David, one of the most successful leaders in Israel's history, abusing his position as king by coercing Bathsheba into submitting to him sexually.

A second temptation that accompanies success is a willingness to do whatever it takes to preserve the success that has been achieved. The idea that status and significance could be lost after having worked so hard to attain both is too great. So the first thought is to deny any wrongdoing, cover up the iniquity, and attack those who would expose the act. This describes David's cascading sins after learning he has impregnated Bathsheba.

David realizes that his sin, if exposed, could cost him the support of his military. Bathsheba's husband, Uriah, is one of his mighty men (2 Sam. 23:39). If the military learns that David has sent his men to war and then has taken advantage of their absence to coerce one of his men's wives, his most trusted warriors could easily turn against him.

What is more, 2 Samuel 11:3 indicates that Bathsheba's father is Eliam, while 2 Samuel 23:34 tells us that Eliam's father was Ahithophel, David's most valued adviser. If Ahithophel learns how David has abused his power to take sexual advantage of his granddaughter, Ahithophel could (and does) become a powerful enemy.

And if the people of Israel learn that David is not the righteous leader they need him to be for God to continue to bless them, the nation will turn against him. In short, the enormous cost of his night with Bathsheba leads David into an increasingly serious descent into sin in a desperate attempt to escape the consequences of his actions. This passage shows the horrific consequences that occur when leaders attempt to cover up their sin.[2]

When Nathan confronts David and announces God's punishment, David confesses. But while God forgives David, he is clear that David's child will die as a consequence of David's sin. What follows, however, is a strange scene in which David spends a week desperately fasting and pleading for God to spare his child's life. David's actions are so intense that when the child does die, the servants are afraid to tell him for fear that "he may do something desperate" (12:18).

In 2 Samuel 12:21, however, the servants are shocked that when the baby does die, David doesn't grieve. Instead he gets up and goes back to life as normal. Why? "While the child was still alive," David says, "I fasted and wept. I thought, 'Who knows? The LORD may be gracious to me and let the child live.' But now that he is dead, why should I go on fasting? Can I bring him back again?" (12:22–23). David does not grieve as parents normally do, because his week of fasting is not a sign of love for his child but is another failed attempt to escape the consequence of his actions.

While David does go out to war and wins a battle in the final scene of chapter 12, he does so as a much-diminished leader. His secret sins have been made public, and the consequences are coming. Since God forgave David, this story is not a tragedy. But neither is it a comedy.

SUBJECT: What happens when David desperately attempts to escape the consequences of his sin with Bathsheba?

COMPLEMENT: He discovers that he cannot.

EXEGETICAL IDEA: When David desperately attempts to escape the consequences of his sin with Bathsheba, he discovers that he cannot.

HOMILETICAL IDEA:

Subject: What will happen when we try to escape the consequences of our sin?

Complement: We will discover that we can't.

Sticky Statement: Forgiveness can come with consequences.

---

2. It's worth noting that since David had allowed Joab to escape punishment for murder in 2 Samuel 3, Joab was a willing coconspirator in Uriah's murder.

2 Samuel 13:1-14:24

This passage outlines the tragic consequences that David's sin has on his family. In 2 Samuel 13, Amnon, imitating his father's sexual abuse of Bathsheba, rapes his half-sister Tamar. In 2 Samuel 14, David, undoubtedly seeing himself in the actions of his son, fails to punish Amnon. This encourages Absalom to imitate his father's murder of Uriah by taking justice into his own hands, murdering Amnon and fleeing the country. While Absalom is eventually allowed to return home to Jerusalem, the relationship between David and Absalom is permanently ruptured.

SUBJECT: What happens to David's family after his sin with Bathsheba?

COMPLEMENT: David's sons repeat his sins.

EXEGETICAL IDEA: What happens to David's family after his sin with Bathsheba is that David's sons repeat his sins.

HOMILETICAL IDEA:

Subject: What impact does our sin have on our families?

Complement: All too often our children not only see our sins but also echo our sins.

Sticky Statement: Sin is more than personal because it's generational.

2 Samuel 14:25-20:26

This is the account of how David's sin hurt his kingdom (the consequence David was trying to avoid by covering up his sin with Bathsheba), even though he is able to reclaim his throne.

The contrast between the narrator's descriptions of Absalom and David in this story is striking. Absalom is shown to be vain (14:25–26), a bully (14:28–32), and a liar (14:33). What is more, Absalom makes a practice of publicly slandering his father and making promises he cannot keep (15:1–6). Absalom also practices fake religiosity to advance his cause, launches a secret rebellion against his father and recruits Ahithophel, David's trusted counselor (15:7–12), and disgraces his father by publicly sleeping with David's concubines on the roof of the palace (16:20–22).

David is portrayed in a far different light. Here David is seen as an older, chastened man who humbly accepts the consequences of his sin as he leaves Jerusalem (15:25–26, 30; 16:5–14), refuses to try to manipulate God for his own ends (15:25–26), and prays to the Lord for help (15:31).

Absalom and David are two men striving for the privilege of leading God's people but demonstrating a very different morality in the process. What difference does righteousness make? David begins to receive many unsolicited offers of assistance. These include offers from the Gittites (15:19–22), Zadok and Abiathar (15:27–29), Hushai the Arkite (15:32–37), and Mephibosheth's steward, Ziba (16:1–4; see also 2 Sam. 9).

Absalom's rebellion falters. Hushai counters Ahithophel's advice on how to defeat David (17:1–13) by appealing to Absalom's pride. Absalom listens: "For the LORD had determined to frustrate the good advice of Ahithophel in order to bring disaster on Absalom" (17:14). When David's allies inform him of Absalom's military strategy, David's troops defeat Absalom's forces and Absalom is killed by Joab while hanging in humiliation from a tree by his hair.

While David returns to Jerusalem as king, he is in deep grief from the death of Absalom (18:19–19:8), reigns over a newly divided kingdom (20:1–2), and has diminished authority. This is shown by Joab's blatant disregard for David's wishes. Joab not only kills Absalom against David's clear command to the contrary (18:4–18) but after David promises Amasa—Absalom's former military commander—that he will replace Joab as commander of David's army (19:11–15), Joab also murders Amasa and takes the role of commander for himself (chap. 20).

SUBJECT: What happens when David's acceptance of the consequences of his sin with Bathsheba causes him to humbly put his role as a leader in God's hands?

COMPLEMENT: God restores David as king, but the kingdom has been fractured by open insubordination.

EXEGETICAL IDEA: When David's acceptance of the consequences of his sin with Bathsheba causes him to humbly put his role as a leader in God's hands, God restores David as king, but the kingdom has been fractured by open insubordination.

HOMILETICAL IDEA:

Subject: What happens when fallen leaders humbly place their future in God's hands?

Complement: While God may use them again, the people they lead will never enjoy the future they could have.

Sticky Statement: When leaders sin, pain reaches beyond their family to God's family.

CONCLUSION

The final three stories of this book do not chronologically continue the story of David. These are episodes arranged by the narrator to summarize the major thrust of the entire book.

2 Samuel 21:1-14

This is a simple comedic story that contains a familiar but important message.

SUBJECT: Why is Israel suffering from a three-year drought?

COMPLEMENT: Because Saul's sin against the Gibeonites needs to be atoned for.

EXEGETICAL IDEA: Israel suffers from a three-year drought because Saul's sin against the Gibeonites needs to be atoned for.

HOMILETICAL IDEA:

  Subject: Why do God's people sometimes struggle?

  Complement: Because of the sins of their leaders.

  Sticky Statement: Listen up leaders: your sin is significant![3]

2 Samuel 21:15-23:51

This natural unit is a combination of two passages of different genres. This results in two separate exegetical ideas that will be combined into a single homiletical idea.

With 2 Sam. 21:15–22 serving as a reminder of David's military prowess, in chapter 22 David reflects in song on the reason for his battlefield success. This gives us our first exegetical idea:

SUBJECT: How is David able to thrive against overwhelming odds?

COMPLEMENT: Because God is his deliverer.

---

3. While 2 Samuel 23:1–7 is not located immediately beside this narrative, the last words of David resonate with this story by emphasizing the positive side of the same truth. The sin of a leader harms the people of God, but
> when one rules over people in righteousness,
>   when he rules in the fear of God,
> he is like the light of morning at sunrise
>   on a cloudless morning,
> like the brightness after rain
>   that brings grass from the earth. (23:3–4)
I would use 2 Samuel 23:1–7 in the conclusion of the message.

Second Samuel 21:15–22 and 23:8–39 are not classic narrative literature. Instead these are semi-narrative lists of the "mighty men" who fought beside David. The lists contain names and some of the exploits of strong, skilled warriors whose bravery enables David to succeed as a leader. This passage outlines the significant battlefield contributions made by the men who fought with him and gives us our second exegetical idea:

SUBJECT: How is David able to defeat his enemies?

COMPLEMENT: With the assistance of his mighty men.

When we combine the ideas of these two passages, the following idea emerges.

SUBJECT: How is David able to succeed as a leader?

COMPLEMENT: With the help of the Lord and his mighty men.

EXEGETICAL IDEA: David is able to succeed as a leader with the help of the Lord and his mighty men.

HOMILETICAL IDEA:

Subject: How can you succeed as a leader of God's people?

Complement: Only with God's favor and the assistance of the people he gives you.

Sticky Statement: It's not all about you!

2 Samuel 24

In a day when censuses are common and all modern armed forces know the number of personnel they have in uniform, we may wonder why counting soldiers would be a sin. But time and again we have seen in the books of Samuel that God's leaders are not victorious because of the size of their armies. The secret of success is the blessing of God. As David says in 2 Samuel 22:28–30,

> You save the humble,
>> but your eyes are on the haughty to bring them low.
> You, LORD, are my lamp;
>> the LORD turns my darkness into light.
> With your help I can advance against a troop;
>> with my God I can scale a wall.

David's request for a census is rooted in arrogance and a lack of faith in God. At this moment he is trusting in the size of his army rather than the strength of his God.

SUBJECT: What happens when David angers God by counting his fighting men?

COMPLEMENT: Israel suffers until David makes a costly sacrifice to the Lord.

EXEGETICAL IDEA: When David angers God by counting his fighting men, Israel suffers until David makes a costly sacrifice to the Lord.

HOMILETICAL IDEA:

Subject: What happens when leaders rely on their own resources to accomplish God's assignments?

Complement: The people suffer until their leaders truly repent.

Sticky Statement: We cannot accomplish God's purposes with our own resources.

Difficult Passages/Verses

See the discussion in 1 Samuel.

Cultural Perspectives and Application

See the discussion in 1 Samuel.

RECOMMENDED RESOURCE

Baldwin, Joyce G. *1 and 2 Samuel*. Tyndale Old Testament Commentaries. Downers Grove, IL: InterVarsity, 1988.

1 Kings

STEVEN D. MATHEWSON

The Big Idea of 1 Kings

The book of 1 Kings provides a theological history of the reigns of Israel's and Judah's kings from Solomon to Ahab.[1] The story line is tragic, descending from the glory of Solomon's kingdom into a divided kingdom marked by idolatry and instability. First and Second Kings were originally one book. It was divided into two books because its length increased substantially when translated from Hebrew into Greek (the Septuagint). Therefore, the books of 1 and 2 Kings have a single idea.

SUBJECT: Why do Israel and Judah end up in captivity?

COMPLEMENT: Because their kings led them into idolatry and rebellion against God.

EXEGETICAL IDEA: Israel and Judah end up in captivity because their kings led them into idolatry and rebellion against God.

HOMILETICAL IDEA: The result of idolatry and rebellion against God is spiritual bondage.

A related theme, which emerges at the end of the entire book (1 and 2 Kings), is the need for a new Davidic king to lead God's people out of captivity.

---

1. King David, of course, appears in 1 Kings 1–2. But David is on his deathbed by this time, and his role is solely to confirm his son Solomon as his successor. Similarly, the final two kings appearing in 1 Kings are Jehoshaphat (Judah) and Ahaziah (Israel). However, Ahab is the final major character in the book. His story runs from the end of chapter 16 through most of chapter 22. The story of Ahaziah, the final king mentioned in 1 Kings, begins the book of 2 Kings.

Selecting Preaching and Teaching Passages in 1 Kings

Faithful preaching and teaching of narrative texts generally require the selection of longer textual units—often an entire chapter or even multiple chapters together. This reflects the need to preach an entire story (or episode). Typically, Old Testament narratives contain four plot elements, just like stories from other times and cultures.[2] They begin with *exposition*, a literary term for the information that sets up a story. The exposition section can be as short as one verse or as long as several verses. It provides information about the characters (names, traits, physical appearance, relationships) or about the geographical and historical setting. The second element in a narrative plot is the *crisis*. This is the complication or conflict in a story. The crisis may be a single event or a series of events. The third element is the *resolution*. Here the plot descends rapidly from its climax to a solution to the original crisis. Of course, the narratives in the Old Testament defy neat and tidy classification. Often there is a series of crises and resolutions with the tension rising and falling a few times before final resolution occurs. This resolution can take the form of a happy ending (a comedy in literary terms) or a sad ending (a tragedy). The ending of a story is often signaled by the characters returning home. Some stories have an additional plot element called a *conclusion* or *denouement*. This separate element sums up the outcome of a story and its influence on the characters. A preaching unit, then, must contain a complete story in which a crisis is resolved.

But how can preachers cover a long chapter or multiple chapters in a thirty-minute sermon? The key is to summarize sections of the narrative while reading only key verses or sections of text. This means focusing on verses or sections of text containing dialogue (speech) or narrator statements that provide privileged information unknown to the characters.[3]

Some preachers and teachers may wish to focus on the Solomon story (chaps. 1–11) or the story of Elijah (chaps. 17–19, 21). However, there is an advantage to feeling the cumulative weight of the book's developing message by preaching all the way through it in sixteen messages or lessons (see below). This becomes even more feasible by dividing it into two parts: a ten-part series on chapters 1–16, eventually followed by a six-part series on chapters 17–22. See the next chapter on 2 Kings for preaching the Elijah-Elisha narratives together.

2. See Steven D. Mathewson, *The Art of Preaching Old Testament Narrative* (Grand Rapids: Baker Academic, 2002), 44–47.
3. According to Robert Alter, in biblical narrative "dialogue is made to carry a large part of the freight of meaning." See *The Art of Biblical Narrative* (New York: Basic Books, 1981), 37.

Getting the Subject, Complement, Exegetical Idea, and Homiletical Idea

1 Kings 1-2

SUBJECT: How does the Lord establish Solomon's rule?

COMPLEMENT: By working through and triumphing over the questionable "wisdom" of Solomon, as counseled by his father David, in eliminating the political threats to his throne.

EXEGETICAL IDEA: The Lord establishes Solomon's rule by working through and triumphing over the questionable "wisdom" of Solomon, as counseled by his father David, in eliminating the political threats to his throne.

HOMILETICAL IDEA: God accomplishes his purposes even though his servants act in morally suspect ways.[4]

1 Kings 3

SUBJECT: What will it take for Solomon to rule with wisdom and discernment?

COMPLEMENT: A heart that listens to the Torah.

EXEGETICAL IDEA: Solomon's ability to rule with wisdom and discernment requires a heart that listens to the Torah.

HOMILETICAL IDEA: Leading with wisdom and discernment requires a heart that listens to God's Word. Or: The greatest gift we can ask from God is the gift of a listening heart.

1 Kings 4-5

SUBJECT: What kind of conditions does Solomon's wisdom create in his kingdom?

COMPLEMENT: Peace and rest.

EXEGETICAL IDEA: Solomon's wisdom creates conditions of peace and rest in his kingdom.

HOMILETICAL IDEA: People flourish when godly wisdom is present.

1 Kings 6-7

SUBJECT: What will it take for Solomon and Israel to experience God's presence?

---

4. See "Difficult Passages/Verses" below for a discussion of the morally questionable actions of Solomon in consolidating his kingdom and for another possible homiletical idea.

COMPLEMENT: Covenant faithfulness, not merely the magnificent temple Solomon built.

EXEGETICAL IDEA: Solomon and Israel can experience God's presence through covenant faithfulness, not merely the magnificent temple Solomon built.

HOMILETICAL IDEA: The requirement for experiencing God's presence is faithfulness to his covenant.

1 Kings 8-9

SUBJECT: How can Israel continue to experience God's presence?

COMPLEMENT: By not abandoning him to serve other gods.

EXEGETICAL IDEA: Israel can continue to experience God's presence by not abandoning him to serve other gods.

HOMILETICAL IDEA: God's people can experience his ongoing presence by not abandoning him to serve idols.

1 Kings 10

SUBJECT: Why does God give wisdom, wealth, and influence to Solomon?

COMPLEMENT: So he can execute justice and righteousness.

EXEGETICAL IDEA: God gives wisdom, wealth, and influence to Solomon so he can execute justice and righteousness.

HOMILETICAL IDEA: God gives us wisdom, wealth, and influence to execute justice, not to serve ourselves.

1 Kings 11

SUBJECT: What is the result of Solomon's divided heart?

COMPLEMENT: A divided kingdom.

EXEGETICAL IDEA: The result of Solomon's divided heart is a divided kingdom.

HOMILETICAL IDEA: A divided heart leads to a broken life.

1 Kings 12

SUBJECT: How does God handle the failures of Rehoboam and Jeroboam?

COMPLEMENT: By working through them to accomplish his will.

EXEGETICAL IDEA: God handles the failures of Rehoboam and Jeroboam by working through them to accomplish his will.

HOMILETICAL IDEA: God works through his people's failures to accomplish his will.

1 Kings 13-14

SUBJECT: What is the result when kings and prophets disobey God's law?

COMPLEMENT: God's judgment.

EXEGETICAL IDEA: Disobedience to God's law by kings and prophets results in God's judgment.

HOMILETICAL IDEA: Disobedience to God's law results in God's judgment—no matter who we are.

1 Kings 15-16

SUBJECT: What is the cost of kings whose hearts are not fully devoted to the Lord?

COMPLEMENT: An unstable kingdom.

EXEGETICAL IDEA: The cost of kings whose hearts are not fully devoted to the Lord is an unstable kingdom.

HOMILETICAL IDEA: When the hearts of God's people are not fully devoted to him, the result is instability in the family of God.[5]

1 Kings 17

SUBJECT: Why can the people of Israel trust God's Word through Elijah?

COMPLEMENT: Because God is powerful enough to sustain the life of a widow and her son and to raise the widow's son from death to life.

EXEGETICAL IDEA: The people of Israel can trust God's Word through Elijah because God is powerful enough to sustain the life of a widow and her son and to raise the widow's son from death to life.

HOMILETICAL IDEA: We can trust God's Word because he is powerful enough to sustain and restore life.

---

5. There is another way to understand the big idea of chapters 15–16. The exegetical idea could be that God is still at work fulfilling his Word when the hearts of Israel's and Judah's kings are not fully devoted to him, even though he takes years to do so. The homiletical idea could be that God is still at work fulfilling his Word in the worst of times, even though he takes years to do so. This emphasis on the "slowness of God" is apparent in 15:29–30 and in 16:12–13, 34. Because God's Word in these instances is a word of judgment, the homiletical idea could also be: God brings about the judgment he promises, even though he takes his time.

1 Kings 18

SUBJECT: Why does the Lord deserve the complete loyalty of Israel?

COMPLEMENT: Because Baal is powerless and the Lord alone is all-powerful over the forces of nature.

EXEGETICAL IDEA: The Lord deserves the complete loyalty of Israel because Baal is powerless and the Lord alone is all-powerful over the forces of nature.

HOMILETICAL IDEA: The Lord deserves our complete loyalty because he alone is the all-powerful God.[6]

1 Kings 19

SUBJECT: Why does God tell Elijah not to give up on his prophetic mission?

COMPLEMENT: Because there are still seven thousand in Israel who have not given their allegiance to Baal.

EXEGETICAL IDEA: God tells Elijah not to give up on his prophetic mission because there are still seven thousand in Israel who have not given their allegiance to Baal.

HOMILETICAL IDEA: Don't give up too soon because the mission of God is making more progress than we realize.[7]

1 Kings 20

SUBJECT: What is the consequence of Ahab's failure to obey God by putting to death Ben-Hadad, the pagan king of Aram?

COMPLEMENT: God's promise of Ahab's death.

EXEGETICAL IDEA: Ahab's failure to obey God by putting to death Ben-Hadad, the pagan king of Aram, leads to God's promise of Ahab's death.

HOMILETICAL IDEA: When we fail to obey God's command to kill sinful desires, we set ourselves up for destruction.[8]

1 Kings 21

SUBJECT: What is the result of King Ahab's greed for Naboth's vineyard?

---

6. Preachers may need to use the personal name of God, Yahweh (translated "LORD" in our English versions), in narratives like this to highlight the superiority of the God of Israel (Yahweh) over the storm god of the Canaanites (Baal).

7. See "Difficult Passages/Verses" below for a discussion of Elijah's emotional state when he fled from Jezebel.

8. See "Difficult Passages/Verses" below for a discussion of how the exegetical idea of this passage leads to this homiletical idea.

COMPLEMENT: Queen Jezebel's treacherous plot against Naboth and his wrongful execution.

EXEGETICAL IDEA: King Ahab's greed for Naboth's vineyard leads to Queen Jezebel's treacherous plot against Naboth and his wrongful execution.

HOMILETICAL IDEA: Injustice happens when God's people worship greed instead of God.[9]

1 Kings 22

SUBJECT: What is the result of Ahab's efforts to resist the prophet Micaiah's words and to disguise himself in battle?

COMPLEMENT: God still brings about his promised judgment of Ahab.

EXEGETICAL IDEA: The result of Ahab's efforts to resist the prophet Micaiah's words and to disguise himself in battle is that God brings about his promised judgment of Ahab.

HOMILETICAL IDEA: God will bring about his promised judgment despite human attempts to deny or escape it.

Difficult Passages/Verses

1 Kings 1–2

A couple of debatable issues occur in this narrative. First, had David really promised Solomon his throne (1 Kings 1:13)? There is no record of this in 2 Samuel, including Solomon's birth narrative where we are told that "the LORD loved him" (2 Sam. 12:24). Robert Alter observes, "Perhaps David actually made a private vow to Bathsheba promising that Solomon would succeed him." However, it is possible that "Nathan the man of God has invented the vow and enlists Bathsheba's help in persuading the doddering David that he actually made this commitment."[10] Second, there is debate as to whether Solomon went too far in removing political threats from his kingdom. His father, David, counseled him to deal with Joab "according to your wisdom, but do not let his gray head go down to the grave in peace" (1 Kings 2:6). So Solomon had Joab killed, claiming that it would "clear me and my whole family of the guilt of the innocent blood that Joab shed" (2:31). However,

---

9. Some preachers may wish to focus the big idea on the final scene—Ahab's humility before God and God's gracious response (21:27–29). However, since the bulk of the narrative deals with Ahab's greed and its outcome, it seems best to focus on the humility theme as the appropriate application of the proposed homiletical idea.

10. Robert Alter, *The Hebrew Bible*, vol. 2, *Prophets* (New York: Norton, 2019), 435n13.

Solomon shows grace to Shimei and allows him to live as long as he stays put in Jerusalem (2:36–38). Solomon has him executed only when he violates his oath and leaves Jerusalem (2:39–46). In both instances, Solomon views the executions as the Lord's repayment of wrongdoing (Shimei in 2:23, Joab in 2:44). The result is the establishment of Solomon's kingdom (2:46)—but according to what kind of wisdom? This is why the big idea proposed for 1 Kings 1–2 speaks of morally suspect ways. Preachers and teachers who view Solomon's actions more positively may prefer the following homiletical idea: God accomplishes his purposes even though his servants face difficult leadership challenges.

1 Kings 3:16–28

Some listeners will find the story of the two prostitutes who claim to be the mother of the same baby rather disturbing. After listening to their dispute, Solomon says, "Cut the living child in two and give half to one and half to the other" (3:25). It is not difficult to show listeners that this is a ruse designed to identify the real mother. However, there are some important observations to make when preaching or teaching this narrative. First, by taking the case of two prostitutes, Solomon demonstrates his commitment to carrying out justice (see 3:28) even for the lowest and most disadvantaged members of society. Second, this situation illustrates the difficulty highlighted by Solomon's words in Proverbs 18:17: "In a lawsuit the first to speak seems right, until someone comes forward and cross-examines." Third, it's worth noting that while Solomon's "old wisdom" led him to use the sword in questionable ways (see 1 Kings 2), his new wisdom leads him in a more constructive way. He still uses the sword, but only as a threat designed to achieve justice.[11] Finally, this narrative functions as confirmation that Solomon has really received wisdom from God. It is a reminder that what we need to navigate life's challenges is not more intelligence but rather a wise and discerning heart (3:12). For new-covenant believers, the source of our wisdom is Jesus himself. He is the one who is greater than Solomon (Matt. 12:42), and in Jesus all the treasures of wisdom and knowledge are hidden (Col. 2:3).

1 Kings 19

Preachers and teachers often portray Elijah's flight from Queen Jezebel as the result of cowardice and sheer panic. After all, 19:3 reads: "Elijah was afraid

---

11. Iain W. Provan, *1 and 2 Kings*, Understanding the Bible Commentary Series (1995; repr., Grand Rapids: Baker Books, 2012), 52.

and ran for his life." However, Ronald Allen argues, "Elijah was broken, but he was not afraid."[12] The Masoretic Text reads "saw," while the Septuagint and several Hebrew manuscripts read "feared." The difference is only a single vowel—and remember that Hebrew was originally written without vowel markers. It's possible, then, that Elijah flees for his life because he sees Jezebel's unrepentant spirit and realizes that revival is not going to break out in Israel. Believing that his mission has been a failure, he asks the Lord to take his life (19:4). Regardless of how much fear was involved, preachers and teachers will want to focus on this larger concern: Elijah's belief that his mission has failed and that he is the only one left who is zealous for the Lord God Almighty (19:14).

1 Kings 20

Whenever we preach from an Old Testament text, we must examine how the theological message applies to new-covenant believers who are united with Christ. This task is more difficult in passages like 1 Kings 20, which deal with *herem*—the Hebrew word for "devoted things" that are to be destroyed rather than used for profit (see Josh. 6:17–18; 7:1, 11–13). In 1 Kings 20:42 the Lord rebukes King Ahab for setting free Ben-Hadad, a "man of *herem*" (NIV, "a man I had determined should die"). The key to applying this narrative is to understand how "holy war"—the destruction of people and objects considered *herem*—finds its fulfillment in Jesus Christ. Whereas God's people in the Old Testament waged war against human opponents, his people in the New Testament fight against everything that sets itself up against the knowledge of God. This means fighting against the world, the flesh, and the devil and his forces (see 2 Cor. 10:3–5; Eph. 6:10–18). For this reason, it is advisable to move from "putting to death Ben-Hadad" in the exegetical idea to "kill sinful desires" in the homiletical idea of 1 Kings 20. This reflects the command in Colossians 3:5 to "put to death, therefore, whatever belongs to your earthly nature: sexual immorality, impurity, lust, evil desires and greed, which is idolatry."

Cultural Perspectives and Application

Interpreting and applying the book of 1 Kings (and 2 Kings) requires some knowledge of its historical-cultural backdrop. The narratives make more sense when we understand the way kings in the ancient Near East consolidated

12. Ronald B. Allen, "Elijah the Broken Prophet," *Journal of the Evangelical Theological Society* 22, no. 3 (September 1979): 201.

power (see 1 Kings 1–2), the importance and role of temples (see 1 Kings 5–8), and the temptation of idolatry (see, e.g., 1 Kings 11:1–8; 12:25–33).

Contemporary listeners may not think of themselves as idolaters. After all, we do not bow down to figurines on our fireplace mantles or statues that stand in our gardens. Yet the apostle Paul refers to greed as idolatry in Colossians 3:5. Thus we must help listeners see that idols are substitutes for God. Idolatry today is subtle and devious because we can easily take God's gifts—family, career, athletics, education—and look to them for the satisfaction and security that only God provides. As the hymn-writer Robert Robinson says in his hymn "Come Thou Fount," we as God's people are "prone to wander" and "prone to leave the God we love." The consequences are disastrous. As Iain Provan notes, "The worship of something *other* than God inevitably leads to some kind of mistreatment of fellow-mortals in the *eyes* of God."[13] Ahab's greed for Naboth's vineyard is a case in point (1 Kings 21).

One of the expressions of idolatry in Israel was worship at "high places." These shrines were as prolific in the ancient world as fast-food restaurants and gas stations are in American culture today. The high places were located in the hills, mountains, or valleys. Some of them were open-air sites located under a large tree, while others were roofed houses. They were a threat to the worship of God because they often contained objects used in pagan worship: sacred pillars, Asherah poles, and carved images of false gods. Deuteronomy 12:2–5 calls for Israel to destroy these places and instead worship God at a central place God chooses.

The narratives beginning in 1 Kings 18 need to be read against the backdrop of Baal worship. Baal was the storm god worshiped by Israel's neighbors to the north. They believed he controlled rain, thunder, and lightning. Thus the fertility of the land depended on Baal sending rain. Even the self-mutilation by the prophets of Baal in 1 Kings 18:28 reflects the mourning of Baal's death in the Baal myth, a text discovered at ancient Ugarit. Baal supposedly descended yearly to the underworld, where he was held powerless until the growing season began. This helps us make sense of Elijah's taunt about Baal sleeping and needing to be awakened, unable to return from his annual imprisonment (18:27).

There is encouragement, though, for God's people—then and now. Throughout 1 Kings we see God display his amazing grace. Surprisingly, Ahab receives it in response to humble repentance (21:29). God even shows grace when kings lack wholehearted devotion to him, doing so for the sake of King David (11:9–13 and 15:1–5).

---

13. Provan, *1 and 2 Kings*, 12.

RECOMMENDED RESOURCES

Alter, Robert. "1 Kings." In *Prophets*, vol. 2 of *The Hebrew Bible: A Translation with Commentary*, 433–527. New York: Norton, 2019.

Leithart, Peter. *1 & 2 Kings*. Brazos Theological Commentary on the Bible. Grand Rapids: Brazos, 2006.

Provan, Iain W. *1 and 2 Kings*. Understanding the Bible Commentary Series. 1995. Reprint, Grand Rapids: Baker Books, 2012.

Wray Beal, Lissa M. *1 & 2 Kings*. Apollos Old Testament Commentary. Downers Grove, IL: InterVarsity, 2014.

2 Kings

STEVEN D. MATHEWSON

The Big Idea of 2 Kings

The book of 2 Kings continues the theological history of the reigns of Israel's and Judah's kings that began in 1 Kings. Originally one book, Kings was divided into two books because its length increased substantially when translated from Hebrew into Greek (the Septuagint). The time period of 2 Kings spans the reign of Ahaziah (Israel) to the reign of Zedekiah (Judah). By the end of the book, both the Northern Kingdom of Israel and the Southern Kingdom of Judah have fallen. Israel fell to Assyria in 722 BC (2 Kings 17:3–7), and Judah fell to Babylon in 586 BC (2 Kings 25:1–26).

There is a glimmer of hope, though, at the end of the tragic story line. In 2 Kings 25:27–30 Jehoiachin—the second to last king of Judah—is released after thirty-seven years of imprisonment. The Babylonian king speaks kindly to Jehoiachin, gives him a seat of honor, lets him eat at the king's table, and gives him a regular allowance for the rest of his life. This provides a subtle hint that the story is not over and that God's people have a reason to hope for better days. Perhaps the entire nation will receive this kind of favor. It is clear that God's people need a Davidic king who has the strength and godly integrity that their previous kings lacked.

Here again is the big idea for the entire book of Kings (both 1 and 2 Kings):

SUBJECT: Why do Israel and Judah end up in captivity?

COMPLEMENT: Because their kings led them into idolatry and rebellion against God.

EXEGETICAL IDEA: Israel and Judah end up in captivity because their kings led them into idolatry and rebellion against God.

HOMILETICAL IDEA: The result of idolatry and rebellion against God is spiritual bondage.

Selecting Preaching and Teaching Passages in 2 Kings

Faithful preaching and teaching of narrative texts generally require the selection of longer textual units—often an entire chapter or even multiple chapters together. This reflects the need to preach an entire story (or episode), complete with a crisis and a resolution.

One approach to preaching 2 Kings is to work through it in eighteen messages or lessons (see below). This helps listeners feel the cumulative weight of the book's developing message and the self-destruction of the two kingdoms.

Another option is to preach a fourteen-part series on the Elijah-Elisha narratives. The narratives challenge God's people to worship him exclusively and obey him fully because of his greatness. God showed his stunning power through both prophets. Here is a breakdown of the fourteen narratives:

- 1 Kings 17, 18, 19, 21
- 2 Kings 1; 2; 3; 4; 5; 6:1–23; 6:24–7:20; 8; 9–10; 13

Getting the Subject, Complement, Exegetical Idea, and Homiletical Idea

2 Kings 1

SUBJECT: Why is it foolish for Ahaziah to live as if there is no God in Israel when he is recovering from a serious injury?

COMPLEMENT: Because his consultation with the god of Ekron has doomed him to no recovery.

EXEGETICAL IDEA: It is foolish for Ahaziah to live as if there is no God in Israel when he is recovering from a serious injury because his consultation with the god of Ekron has doomed him to no recovery.

HOMILETICAL IDEA: It is foolish to live as if there is no God because without him we have no future.

2 Kings 2

SUBJECT: How does the passage of leadership from Elijah to Elisha affect God's plan to create a treasured, holy people who display his greatness?

COMPLEMENT: It does not derail the plan.

EXEGETICAL IDEA: The passage of leadership from Elijah to Elisha does not derail God's plan to create a treasured, holy people who display his greatness.[1]

HOMILETICAL IDEA: The passage of great spiritual leaders does not derail God's plan to create a treasured, holy people who display his greatness.

2 Kings 3

SUBJECT: What is the result of Israel's limited obedience to God?

COMPLEMENT: A limited victory over Moab.

EXEGETICAL IDEA: Israel's limited obedience to God results in a limited victory over Moab.[2]

HOMILETICAL IDEA: Limited obedience to God leads to limited victory in life.

2 Kings 4

SUBJECT: What does God do through Elisha when people are threatened by poverty, death, harmful stew, and a meager supply of food?

COMPLEMENT: He sustains and restores life.

EXEGETICAL IDEA: When people are threatened by poverty, death, harmful stew, and a meager supply of food, God, through Elisha, sustains and restores life.

HOMILETICAL IDEA: No matter how dark life becomes, God's life-giving power is still at work.

2 Kings 5

SUBJECT: Why does Naaman finally receive God's grace while Gehazi receives God's judgment?

COMPLEMENT: Naaman shows humility while Gehazi acts out of greed.

---

1. The exegetical key to understanding this bizarre, complex chapter is Elisha's route from Gilgal to Bethel to Jericho to crossing the Jordan. This is a reverse tracing of Joshua's conquest. Thus by reenacting the conquest, Elisha ("God saves") establishes himself as the new Joshua—a successor to Elijah even as Joshua was the successor to Moses. The language of creating "a treasured, holy people who showcase his greatness" comes from passages like Deuteronomy 7:6 that establish God's vision for bringing his people into the land. See "Difficult Passages/Verses" below for the bizarre episode in 2:23–25, where Elisha calls down a curse on some boys who call him "baldy" and end up getting mauled by bears.

2. The outcome in 3:27 (Israel was forced to withdraw because of the furious fighting of the Moabites) can be traced to the situation in 3:2–3 (Joram, Israel's king, was not as evil as his father, Ahab, and mother, Jezebel, yet he continued in idolatry). Only Jehoshaphat, Judah's king, took the word of the Lord seriously (3:12). Joram simply wanted his own plans affirmed.

EXEGETICAL IDEA: Naaman receives God's grace once he shows humility, while Gehazi receives God's judgment because of his greed.

HOMILETICAL IDEA: God shows grace to those who are humble and content.

2 Kings 6:1-23

SUBJECT: How does Elisha respond to a lost ax head (a smaller problem) and to being surrounded by the Aramean army (a much larger problem)?

COMPLEMENT: He relies on the power of God to overcome both circumstances.

EXEGETICAL IDEA: Elisha responds to a lost ax head (a smaller problem) and to being surrounded by the Aramean army (a much larger problem) by relying on the power of God to overcome both circumstances.

HOMILETICAL IDEA: God's power is greater than the impossible situations we face.[3]

2 Kings 6:24-7:20

SUBJECT: How does God save Israel from the Aramean siege of Samaria?

COMPLEMENT: By scaring away the Aramean army and by using four lepers who discover the army's abandoned camp to share the good news with the desperate Israelites, who then plunder the camp.

EXEGETICAL IDEA: God saves Israel from the Aramean siege of Samaria by scaring away the Aramean army and by using four lepers who discover the army's abandoned camp to share the good news with the desperate Israelites, who then plunder the camp.

HOMILETICAL IDEA: God saves by pouring out his grace on desperate sinners who respond in faith to the good news.

2 Kings 8

SUBJECT: What is the effect of God's prophetic word to the Shunammite woman, to Hazael, and to Jeroboam?[4]

COMPLEMENT: It shapes the destiny of the Shunammite woman and the nations of Israel and Judah.

---

3. This idea, of course, needs to be nuanced theologically. While God's power is greater than our impossible situations, the way he uses his power is not always predictable. His power is tethered to his purposes. Sometimes God does not display his power in the ways for which we pray. Even at the end of this narrative, Elisha extends God's mercy to the captured Arameans, allowing them to live for another day.

4. The promise of God to which 2 Kings 8:19 refers—"to maintain a lamp for David and his descendants forever"—was made by God in his words to Jeroboam in 1 Kings 11:36.

EXEGETICAL IDEA: God's prophetic word to the Shunammite woman, to Hazael, and to Jeroboam shapes the destiny of the Shunammite woman and the nations of Israel and Judah.

HOMILETICAL IDEA: God's Word shapes the history of individuals and of nations.

2 Kings 9–10

SUBJECT: How does God respond to the house of Ahab for its sin and to the house of Jehu for doing what is right in God's eyes?

COMPLEMENT: God finally brings judgment on the former while honoring the latter.

EXEGETICAL IDEA: God responds to the house of Ahab for its sin and to the house of Jehu for doing what is right in God's eyes by finally bringing judgment on the former while honoring the latter.[5]

HOMILETICAL IDEA: God makes evildoers face payday someday for their evil deeds while honoring those who do what is right in his eyes.

2 Kings 11

SUBJECT: How is God's promise that David would have a descendant on the throne affected by Athaliah's attempt to destroy the entire royal family?

COMPLEMENT: It is not thwarted.

EXEGETICAL IDEA: God's promise that David would have a descendant on the throne is not thwarted by Athaliah's attempt to destroy the entire royal family.

HOMILETICAL IDEA: God's purposes will not be thwarted by evildoers.

2 Kings 12

SUBJECT: What positive legacy does the reign of Joash leave for the nation of Judah?

COMPLEMENT: The restoration of pure temple worship.

EXEGETICAL IDEA: The positive legacy left by the reign of Joash over Judah is the restoration of pure temple worship.

---

5. However, a sermon or lesson on these chapters should not portray Jehu as an untainted hero. The end of the narrative notes that Jehu "was not careful to keep the law of the LORD, the God of Israel, with all his heart. He did not turn away from the sins of Jeroboam, which he had caused Israel to commit" (10:31).

HOMILETICAL IDEA: One of the greatest legacies a leader can leave for God's people is the restoration of pure worship.

2 Kings 13-14[6]

SUBJECT: What is the only hope for Israel and Judah as they suffer under their sin?

COMPLEMENT: God's grace and compassion.

EXEGETICAL IDEA: The only hope for Israel and Judah as they suffer under their sin is God's grace and compassion.[7]

HOMILETICAL IDEA: The only hope for those who suffer under their sin is God's grace and compassion.

2 Kings 15-17[8]

SUBJECT: How does God judge the Northern Kingdom of Israel for abandoning him for idols?

COMPLEMENT: By sending them away from his presence into exile in Assyria.[9]

EXEGETICAL IDEA: God judges the Northern Kingdom of Israel for abandoning him for idols by sending them away from his presence into exile in Assyria.

HOMILETICAL IDEA: God judges those who abandon him for idols by withholding his presence.

2 Kings 18-19

SUBJECT: Why should Hezekiah trust God to deliver the nation of Judah from the Assyrian threat?

COMPLEMENT: Because God has supreme power over the strongest of enemies and is true to his promises.

---

6. The final episode about Elisha in the narrative of Kings could serve as a preaching text—especially in a series on Elijah and Elisha. A homiletical idea for 2 Kings 13:14–21 could be: "Our hope in the worst of times is in God's power to raise his people to new life." See the comments in "Difficult Passages/Verses" below.

7. See especially 2 Kings 13:23; 14:26–27.

8. The focus of this sermon or lesson will be chapter 17. Chapters 15–16 set up chapter 17 by cataloging the various failures of the kings of both Israel and Judah. Since these failures have been repeatedly exposed in 2 Kings, it may be best to summarize these chapters briefly (before concentrating on chap. 17), rather than devoting a separate sermon to them.

9. Notice the three mentions of this narrative of the loss of God's presence—that is, God removed them "from his face"—in 17:18, 20, and 23. See the comments in "Cultural Perspectives and Application" below.

EXEGETICAL IDEA: Hezekiah should trust God to deliver the nation of Judah from the Assyrian threat because God has supreme power over the strongest of enemies and is true to his promises.

HOMILETICAL IDEA: Trust God in the face of opposition because of his supreme power and faithfulness to his promises.

2 Kings 20

SUBJECT: What is God able to do in the face of Hezekiah's illness and the impending Babylonian captivity?

COMPLEMENT: Extend Hezekiah's life and the life of the nation of Judah.

EXEGETICAL IDEA: In the face of Hezekiah's illness and the impending Babylonian captivity, God is able to extend Hezekiah's life and the life of the nation of Judah

HOMILETICAL IDEA: God is able to extend life in the face of impending death.[10]

2 Kings 21

SUBJECT: What is the result of Manasseh's turn from God to idols?

COMPLEMENT: It leads him to shed innocent blood and thus arouse the anger of God.

EXEGETICAL IDEA: Manasseh's turn from God to idols leads him to shed innocent blood and thus arouse the anger of God.

HOMILETICAL IDEA: People who turn from God to idols end up abusing others and thereby arousing God's anger.

2 Kings 22:1–23:30

SUBJECT: How does Josiah respond to the book of the law?

COMPLEMENT: By turning to God with all of his heart, soul, and strength.

EXEGETICAL IDEA: Josiah responds to the book of the law by turning to God with all of his heart, soul, and strength.

HOMILETICAL IDEA: The proper response to God's Word is to turn to God with wholehearted devotion.

---

10. This homiletical idea comes from Lissa M. Wray Beal, *1 & 2 Kings*, Apollos Old Testament Commentary (Downers Grove, IL: InterVarsity, 2014), 484.

2 Kings 23:31–25:30

SUBJECT: What hope does Jehoiachin's release from prison and elevation to honor provide to the destroyed, exiled nation of Judah?

COMPLEMENT: That God will restore them.

EXEGETICAL IDEA: Jehoiachin's release from prison and elevation to honor provides hope to the destroyed, exiled nation of Judah that God will restore them.

HOMILETICAL IDEA: The grace of God provides hope that God will restore his people who suffer the consequences of their sin.

Difficult Passages/Verses

2 Kings 2:23–25

This brief episode is a notoriously difficult one to preach and teach. It sounds as if Elisha was a grumpy old man who responded violently to the rude insults of some boys who kept saying, "Get out of here, baldy!" However, these "boys" may have been in their teens, or even in their twenties, given the way this word (*na'ar*) is used elsewhere in the Hebrew Bible.[11] The modifier "small" (*qaton*) may refer to insignificance rather than to age. Even if "small" refers to "small of stature," it does not necessarily follow that these were eight- or nine-year-old boys. Furthermore, we should view Elisha not as a grumpy old man outraged over a personal insult but as a prophet of God who curses them for their rejection of God. These boys or young men were typical of a nation that "mocked God's messengers, despised his words and scoffed at his prophets" (2 Chron. 36:16).[12] Obviously, the bear mauling is not God's standard operating procedure. But it serves as a stark reminder—like the deaths of Nadab and Abihu in Leviticus 10:1–3 or Ananias and Sapphira in Acts 5:1–11—that God is utterly holy and does not tolerate rebellion and sin. At any rate, it is consistent with God's warning that he would send wild animals against his people if they refused to listen to him (Lev. 26:21–22).

---

11. The term is used in reference to Joseph at seventeen years of age (Gen. 37:2) and of Absalom by his father, David (2 Sam. 14:21 and 18:5), when Absalom was old enough to try to take the throne from his father.

12. Paul R. House, *1, 2 Kings*, The New American Commentary (Nashville: Broadman & Holman, 1995), 260.

2 Kings 6:1-7

The story of the rescue of the floating ax head may strike some readers as trivial. Yet it is a reminder that God cares about small needs as well as big ones (see Matt. 10:29–31). Besides, this need may be bigger than we realize. Iron was expensive, and the ax was borrowed. So it's possible that Elisha's miracle (making the iron float on the water so it could be retrieved) spared the borrower from a debt he might not have been able to pay to the ax's owner.

2 Kings 13:14-21

There are at least two odd details in the final story in Kings about the prophet Elisha. First, it seems a bit extreme for Elisha to command the king of Israel to strike the ground with his arrows and then get angry when the king stops after three times instead of striking it five or six times (13:18–19). However, Elisha sees in this symbolic action a halfhearted response by the king. As a result, the victory over the Arameans would only be partial. Second, what are we to make of the man who is hastily thrown into Elisha's grave when a band of Moabite raiders is spotted? This may well be a symbol—a real-life parable—of God's people being thrown out of his sight into exile (see 17:20). The unexpected resurrection of the dead man points to God raising his people to new life—something he had done through the prophet Elisha. The story, then, anticipates God raising the nation to life, both through the return from exile and ultimately at the resurrection at the end of time.

Cultural Perspectives and Application

One cultural phenomenon necessary for understanding 2 Kings is siege warfare. There are two sieges laid against Samaria—one by the Arameans (6:24–7:20) and a second by the Assyrians, which led to the captivity and exile of the Northern Kingdom of Israel (17:5–6/18:9). In Judah, God prevents the Babylonians under Sennacherib from laying siege to Jerusalem (19:32). Later, though, Babylonian king Nebuchadnezzar lays siege to Jerusalem and forces the surrender of Jehoiachin, king of Judah (24:10). Nebuchadnezzar eventually returns to Jerusalem and keeps it under siege for over a year and a half before breaking through it and capturing Judah's king, Zedekiah, and destroying the city and its temple (25:1–21). In siege warfare, an army surrounds a city and waits for those held up inside to surrender before they run out of food and water. As a result, famines occur, causing everything from inflation to cannibalism (see 2 Kings 6:24–29). Meanwhile, the attacking army does more than wait for a city to surrender. They do everything they can "to penetrate the walls using surprise, deception, ladders, tunnels, or very often breaches."[13] They attempt breaches by using siege engines. These are leather-covered wooden boxes on wheels that protect soldiers who swing a battering ram mounted on a frame. Usually, these siege engines had towers to protect archers who provided cover fire, shooting arrows at the defenders on top of the city wall.[14] Sometimes the attacking army constructed siege ramps to make it easier to wheel them up close to the city wall.[15]

Idolatry continues to be a problem in 2 Kings (see the comments in "Cultural Perspectives and Application" in the chapter on 1 Kings), and the later narratives bring out some of its more striking consequences. First, idolatry results in the loss of God's presence. When Israel finally falls to the Assyrians, the narrator tells us three times that God removed his people "from his face"—in 17:18, 20, and 23. God allows Nebuchadnezzar to invade the land of Judah and make Jehoiakim his vassal to accomplish the same purpose—that is, to remove his people "from his face" (24:3). This is fully accomplished when the city falls under the rule of Zedekiah (24:20). The Bible is the story of God rescuing his people and restoring them to life in his presence. So this is a tragic moment in the Bible's story line. To lose God's presence is to lose intimacy with the one who provides his people with joy (Ps. 16:11), comfort (Ps. 23:4), protection (Ps. 46:1), and contentment (Heb. 13:5–6).

A second tragic result of idolatry is abuse. People who turn to idolatry end up abusing others. We already saw this in 1 Kings 21 where King Ahab's greed for Naboth's vineyard leads to Queen Jezebel's treacherous plot against Naboth and his wrongful execution. Such tragedy happens again in 2 Kings 21 with King Manasseh shedding so much innocent blood "that he filled Jerusalem from end to end" (v. 16). Today, the rampant practices of bullying, sexual harassment, sexual abuse, and various forms of violence can be traced back to idolatry—trying to find ultimate satisfaction or security in anything and everything other than God. Idolizing money, sex, and power will lead to the mistreatment of others.

Finally, the juxtaposition of the Hezekiah and Manasseh narratives (2 Kings 19–21), as well as the narratives of Josiah and the last five kings of Judah (2 Kings 22–25), reminds us how quickly God's people can become ignorant of Scripture. God's people are "never more than a generation or two from apostasy and oblivion. Only grace is a sufficient hedge."[16]

---

13. Boyd Seevers, *Warfare in the Old Testament* (Grand Rapids: Kregel Academic, 2013), 244.
14. Seevers, *Warfare in the Old Testament*, 234.
15. Seevers, *Warfare in the Old Testament*, 268.
16. D. A. Carson, *For the Love of God*, vol. 1 (Wheaton: Crossway, 1998), November 9 entry.

─── **RECOMMENDED RESOURCES** ───

Alter, Robert. "2 Kings." In *Prophets*, vol. 2 of *The Hebrew Bible: A Translation with Commentary*, 529–613. New York: Norton, 2019.

Leithart, Peter. *1 & 2 Kings*. Brazos Theological Commentary on the Bible. Grand Rapids: Brazos, 2006.

Provan, Iain W. *1 and 2 Kings*. Understanding the Bible Commentary Series. 1995. Reprint, Grand Rapids: Baker Books, 2012.

Wray Beal, Lissa M. *1 & 2 Kings*. Apollos Old Testament Commentary. Downers Grove, IL: InterVarsity, 2014.

1 Chronicles

GREGORY K. HOLLIFIELD

The Big Idea of 1 Chronicles

First Chronicles is a theologically driven, highly selective history of the unified Jewish nation, culminating in the reign of David and centered on his preparations for the temple's construction.

SUBJECT: How should the postexilic Jews have viewed themselves following God's chastisement of their nation and their subsequent return to what was left of their once proud state?

COMPLEMENT: As the people of God for whom God's promises, particularly to David, still held.

EXEGETICAL IDEA: The postexilic Jews should have viewed themselves, following God's chastisement of their nation and their subsequent return to what was left of their once proud state, as the people of God for whom God's promises, particularly to David, still held.

HOMILETICAL IDEA: God's gracious promises still hold for those who worship him in spirit and in truth.

Selecting Preaching and Teaching Passages in 1 Chronicles

The Chronicles, like the books of Samuel and Kings, were originally one scroll but later divided by the translators of the Septuagint into two books. The chronicler basically retells the same history as covered in Samuel and Kings but with a different emphasis and purpose. Those earlier books were written to remind the Jews living in exile how their disobedience to the prophetic word had resulted in their captivity. While not denying that fact, the chronicler emphasizes instead that God's promises to David (as found in 1 Chron. 17) still held. David's throne would stand forever. Moreover, the temple that David's son Solomon later built, as stipulated in God's covenant with David, was not only central to the nation's identity; its condition and their worship therein were a reflection of their relationship to God. They should therefore appreciate all that their restored temple stood for and seek and serve their merciful God, who awaited their response and heard their prayers.[1] This was the chronicler's purpose.

The unity of "all Israel" is touched on often in the Chronicles and is accounted for in the genealogical history from Adam to the returned exiles found in chapters 1–9. Israel was its best and truest self when united under God's man and worshiping at his appointed place.

As Saul did nothing to contribute to the building of God's house, he is passed over after only one chapter (chap. 10). The reign of David, on the other hand, fills the rest of the book (chaps. 11–29). From his conquest of Jerusalem, where the temple would eventually stand (11:4–9), to his transportation of the ark to Jerusalem (chaps. 13–16), and from God's covenant with him (chap. 17) to his own efforts to clear the land of Israel's enemies, order his empire, and collect the materials Solomon would need to build the temple (chaps. 18–29), David is portrayed as that ideal king whose heart was fixed on God.

Despite the chronicler's favorable portrait of David, his failings were well known, even then. David wasn't perfect. Preachers should beware of placing the monarch on too high a pedestal. At the same time, his dedication to God, as manifested in his commitment to God's house, stands as a model for all.

A chapter-by-chapter analysis of 1 Chronicles is all but impossible. The first nine chapters should be viewed from a mile high with attention to the following: the prevailing themes of Israel's special place in the sweep of human history; the disproportionate attention paid to David, his extended family, and those tribes that sided with him; the role the Levites played in keeping Israel connected to its past and to its God; and the beleaguered returnees from Babylonian exile who wondered what the future held.

What little is said about the death of Saul and his sons (10:1–14) is haunting when one considers how differently things might have turned out if Israel's first royal family had followed God as David did. David's saga (11:1–29:30) is much more encouraging. Regardless of how many sections into which the book is

---

1. Mark A. Throntveit, "Chronicles, Books of," in *Dictionary for Theological Interpretation of the Bible*, ed. Kevin J. Vanhoozer (Grand Rapids: Baker Academic, 2005), 110.

divided for preaching and teaching purposes, hearers should be constantly reminded of the big picture—Jerusalem, ark, land, materials, and people all being readied for the building of God's house.

Getting the Subject, Complement, Exegetical Idea, and Homiletical Idea

1 Chronicles 1–9

SUBJECT: What was the chronicler telling the returnees from Babylonian exile through his recounting of the genealogies in chapters 1–9?

COMPLEMENT: Israel's history was of key importance to all human history and key to Israel's history was the house of David and the Levites.

EXEGETICAL IDEA: The chronicler was telling the returnees from Babylonian exile through his recounting of the genealogies in chapters 1–9 that Israel's history was of key importance to all human history and that key to Israel's history was the house of David and the Levites.

HOMILETICAL IDEA: At the center of history stands a Jewish throne and temple.

1 Chronicles 10

SUBJECT: Why did Saul and his sons come to an ignominious end—one that led to the Philistines taking over some of Israel's cities and displaying Saul's armor and head in Dagon's temple and resulted in the kingdom being turned over to David?

COMPLEMENT: It was because of Saul's breach of faith in not keeping the Lord's commands and seeking guidance from a medium rather than the Lord.

EXEGETICAL IDEA: Saul and his sons came to an ignominious end—one that led to the Philistines taking over some of Israel's cities and displaying Saul's armor and head in Dagon's temple and resulted in the kingdom being turned over to David—because of Saul's breach of faith in not keeping the Lord's commands and seeking guidance from a medium rather than the Lord.

HOMILETICAL IDEA: Breaches of faith bring about ignominious ends.

1 Chronicles 11–12[2]

SUBJECT: Who supported the anointing of David as God's chosen king over Israel?

2. David's first act as king in the taking of Jerusalem from the Jebusites (11:4–9) demonstrated what type of leader he was and secured the city where the temple would later stand. The exploits of the warriors who followed him (11:10–12:37) attest to the depth of devotion

COMPLEMENT: The elders, warriors, and "all Israel."

EXEGETICAL IDEA: The elders, warriors, and "all Israel" supported the anointing of David as God's chosen king over Israel.

HOMILETICAL IDEA: Now or later (Phil. 2:9–11), all of us will recognize as King the one whom God has appointed.

1 Chronicles 13-14

SUBJECT: Why did the Lord "break out" against Uzzah (13:11) and later the Philistines (14:11)?

COMPLEMENT: Because the Lord wasn't consulted or obeyed in the case of Uzzah but was consulted and obeyed after the Philistines raided Israel.

EXEGETICAL IDEA: The Lord broke out against Uzzah and later the Philistines because he wasn't consulted or obeyed in the case of Uzzah but was consulted and obeyed after the Philistines raided Israel.

HOMILETICAL IDEA: The breaks go against us when we fail to consult with and obey God.

1 Chronicles 15:1-16:42[3]

SUBJECT: Why did David lead Israel to transport the ark of the covenant to Jerusalem in the manner he did, with rejoicing along the way and at the end?

COMPLEMENT: To praise the Lord for all he had done for Israel.

EXEGETICAL IDEA: David led Israel to transport the ark of the covenant to Jerusalem in the manner he did, with rejoicing along the way and at the end, to praise the Lord for all he had done for Israel.

HOMILETICAL IDEA: "Enter his gates with thanksgiving and his courts with praise; give thanks to him and praise his name. For the LORD is good and his love endures forever; his faithfulness continues through all generations" (Ps. 100:4–5).

---

he inspired. Sermons might be derived from both of these pericopes but should be delivered as supplements to the main story line if one is preaching through 1 Chronicles sequentially.

3. David's transportation of the ark might be covered in one sermon or two. The natural dividing point is 15:1. Even if divided in half, the preacher would be wise to deliver an additional supplemental sermon based solely on David's psalm of praise in 16:8–36, drawn from Pss. 96:1–13; 105:1–15; and 106:1, 47–48. "These Psalms stress the Lord's deliverance of Israel especially when Israel was small and weak. These words would have been very encouraging for the small, struggling postexilic audience of 1–2 Chronicles." J. Daniel Hays, "1–2 Chronicles: Focusing on the Davidic Promise and Worship in the Temple," in *The Baker Illustrated Bible Handbook*, ed. J. Daniel Hays and J. Scott Duvall (Grand Rapids: Baker Books, 2011), 217.

1 Chronicles 16:43-17:27

SUBJECT: How did God respond to David's desire to build him a house?

COMPLEMENT: By promising to provide Israel a secure home and to build David's house by eternally establishing the throne of David's son who himself would eventually build God's house, thereby prompting David's thanksgiving and praise.

EXEGETICAL IDEA: God responded to David's desire to build him a house by promising to provide Israel a secure home and to build David's house by eternally establishing the throne of David's son who himself would eventually build God's house, thereby prompting David's thanksgiving and praise.

HOMILETICAL IDEA: A faithful home is blessed with and by an eternal throne.

1 Chronicles 18-20

SUBJECT: What was the immediate aftermath of God's covenant with David?

COMPLEMENT: "After this" (ESV) or "in the course of time" (NIV in 18:1; 19:1; 20:4) the Lord gave David victory everywhere he turned (18:6, 13b)—beginning and ending with the Philistines at Gath (18:1; 20:4-8).[4]

EXEGETICAL IDEA: The immediate aftermath of God's covenant with David was that "after this" or "in the course of time" the Lord gave David victory everywhere he turned—beginning and ending with the Philistines at Gath.

HOMILETICAL IDEA: The battles are ours to wage, but God gives the victory.

---

4. The chronicler's repeated use of "after this" signals that all of David's battlefield victories should be viewed together as a follow-up to God's earlier promise to provide Israel with a secure home by subduing its enemies (17:9-10). This section of the Chronicles taken as a whole portrays David as both a man of war/bloodshed, which disqualified him from being the builder of God's house (22:8), and a collector of precious materials that Solomon would later use to build that house (18:7-8, 10; 20:2).

It is interesting to see how David's kind intentions toward Hanun of the Ammonites in the wake of his father's death were misconstrued by the Ammonite nobles as an act of espionage in preparation for war. Their reaction and the reprisals that followed (19:1-9) could be a case study in itself.

Joab's defeat of Rabbah but David's own claim of the defeated monarch's crown (20:1-2) and David's family's and his servants' intertwined history with the giants of Gath (20:4-8) are equally as interesting. The former evokes thoughts of that day when the saints will cast their hard-earned crowns at the feet of their King, and the latter reminds us that God's people will always have giants to face. Clearly though, that's not what the chronicler intended to convey, so it's best to take all of 18:1-20:8 together as the beginning of God's fulfillment of his covenant with David.

1 Chronicles 21:1–22:1

SUBJECT: How did the Lord's house come to be situated on the mount where the threshing floor of Araunah the Jebusite formerly stood?

COMPLEMENT: David's sin in numbering Israel's fighting men resulted in the angel of the Lord ravaging Israel until God stayed his hand at Araunah's floor and then commanded David to build an altar there, which David did after purchasing the site.

EXEGETICAL IDEA: The Lord's house came to be situated on the mount where the threshing floor of Araunah the Jebusite formerly stood after David's sin in numbering Israel's fighting men resulted in the angel of the Lord ravaging Israel until God stayed his hand at Araunah's floor and then commanded David to build an altar there, which David did after purchasing the site.

HOMILETICAL IDEA: God's house stands as a perpetual monument to his justice and mercy.

1 Chronicles 22:2–19

SUBJECT: What preparations did David make for the construction of God's house after purchasing the site of Araunah's threshing floor?

COMPLEMENT: He amassed precious metals and cedar timbers, charged Solomon to build it while praying for him, and commanded Israel's leaders to assist Solomon.

EXEGETICAL IDEA: David prepared for the construction of God's house after purchasing the site of Araunah's threshing floor by amassing precious metals and cedar timbers, charging Solomon to build it while praying for him, and commanding Israel's leaders to assist Solomon.

HOMILETICAL IDEA: To support the building of God's house is both our privilege and our duty.

1 Chronicles 23–27

SUBJECT: Whom did David charge with the leadership of Israel and God's house when he was old and full of days?

COMPLEMENT: Solomon, the Levites (whom he organized for work in the Lord's house as attendants to the descendants of Aaron, as musicians, as gatekeepers, as treasurers, and as other officers and judges), military commanders, and tribal leaders.

EXEGETICAL IDEA: When David was old and full of days, he charged Solomon, the Levites (whom he organized as attendants to the descendants of Aaron, as musicians, as gatekeepers, as treasurers, and as other officers and judges), military commanders, and tribal leaders with the leadership of Israel and the temple.

HOMILETICAL IDEA: God is a God of decency and order who is to be worshiped and served in decency and order.

1 Chronicles 28:1-29:9

SUBJECT: How did David present to Solomon and the assembly of Israel the task that lay ahead in the construction of the Lord's house?

COMPLEMENT: As (1) his heart's desire that was denied him because of his bloody past but graciously assigned by God to Solomon his son, whose throne would endure forever if he persisted in obedience to God's commands (28:1–10), (2) a project whose plans were given to him by God (28:11–19), and (3) a great work for which David had gathered tremendous sums of wealth and to which he asked the people to contribute of their own free will (28:11–18; 29:1–9).

EXEGETICAL IDEA: David presented to Solomon and the assembly of Israel the task that lay ahead in the construction of the Lord's house as (1) his heart's desire that was denied him because of his bloody past but graciously assigned by God to Solomon his son, whose throne would endure forever if he persisted in obedience to God's commands, (2) a project whose plans were given to him by God, and (3) a great work for which David had gathered tremendous sums of wealth and to which he asked the people to contribute of their own free will.

HOMILETICAL IDEA: We should not take for granted the sacrifices that others have made for sake of the Lord's house.

1 Chronicles 29:10-22a

SUBJECT: How did David assess the offerings that he and the people presented to God for the building of his house?

COMPLEMENT: As coming from God's own sovereign, gracious hand and as pleasing to him because they were presented from sincere hearts.

EXEGETICAL IDEA: David assessed the offerings that he and the people presented to God for the building of his house as coming from God's own sovereign, gracious hand and as pleasing to him because they were presented from sincere hearts.

HOMILETICAL IDEA: God receives gladly what we give humbly, freely, and wholeheartedly.

1 Chronicles 29:22b-30

SUBJECT: What was the state of Israel at the time of David's death?

COMPLEMENT: All Israel was united behind King Solomon, God bestowed majesty on Solomon unlike any king before him in Israel, and David died "at a good age, full of days, riches, and honor" (29:28 ESV).

EXEGETICAL IDEA: The state of Israel at the time of David's death was that all Israel was united behind King Solomon, God bestowed majesty on Solomon unlike any king before him in Israel, and David "died at a good age, full of days, riches, and honor" (29:28 ESV).

HOMILETICAL IDEA: Shalom is God's gift to us when our hearts are at peace with him.

Difficult Passages/Verses

The difficulties of preaching from the Chronicles are many. To begin with, there are all those lists! A preacher will want to handle them with care, looking at only brief selections at a time and focusing on the better-known names and events in those lists.

Speaking of names, what's their significance? According to scholars, family lists serve several purposes: "to demonstrate the legitimacy of a person or family's claim to a particular role or rank . . . to preserve the purity of the chosen people and/or its priesthood . . . [and] to affirm the continuity of the people of God despite expulsion from the Promised Land."[5] Hearers will appreciate the genealogies more if they understand why they're recorded.

How to pronounce all those names is another difficulty the teacher faces. Once again, the safest route is to be selective about which names to read and then to practice pronouncing them aloud before stepping into the pulpit. If you stumble, do your best and move on to the next name on the list. It's doubtful anyone else in the congregation will catch your slip, much less have a better idea of how to pronounce it! That's not to say you should handle

---

5. Larry Richards, *The Bible Reader's Companion*, quoted by Charles R. Swindoll, *Insight's Old Testament Handbook* (Plano, TX: IFL Publishing, 2009), 54.

the names in Scripture disrespectfully. After all, they are in the Bible, and there's a chance you'll meet some of those folks in heaven one day. Just do your best. You'll be fine.

The chronicler shows a penchant for using speeches, prophecies, and prayers rather than extended narratives to report history. The temptation we face is to go back to Samuel and Kings to fill out those bits of the history left untold by the chronicler himself. Beware of that temptation! The writers of Samuel and Kings had their own theological agendas. To pull their texts into your exposition of Chronicles may do more harm than good by confusing the point the chronicler was trying to make when he wrote what he wrote and omitted what he omitted.

Included in the pericope-by-pericope analyses above are a handful of suggestions on how a preacher might supplement his or her exposition of 1 Chronicles by digging more deeply into intriguing texts (like 11:10–25) and pericopes that contain quotations or summaries of other parts of Scripture (like 16:8–36). The best way to do this would be to preach through the story line of 1 Chronicles on Sunday mornings and then to return to those chosen excerpts on Sunday or Wednesday nights.

Thankfully, few events in 1 Chronicles are difficult to fathom, the exceptions being in chapters 13 and 21. To take these in reverse order, the chronicler reports in chapter 21, "Satan stood against Israel and incited David to number Israel" (v. 1 ESV), and "God was displeased with this thing" (v. 7 ESV). Recalling that one whole book of the Pentateuch is called Numbers and that there are other places in Chronicles where people and objects are seemingly counted without satanic influence or divine disapproval, one must ask what was wrong with David conducting a census of his own people. Moreover, why was Joab so quick to realize it was a problem whereas David didn't (vv. 3–4)? Was it a sign of David's misplaced faith (in the number of his troops versus faith in his God), an indicator of pride in David's heart, or something else entirely? The chronicler doesn't say.

If God's reaction to David's census of Israel appears to be an overreaction to our modern eyes, how much more so is God's striking down of Uzzah, who, with the best of intentions in our view, stuck out his hand to steady the ark of the covenant when it nearly fell off the ox cart on which it was being carried (13:9–10)? Wasn't David to blame for that inappropriate mode of transportation? Why did God punish Uzzah?

The consequences of David's census and Uzzah's touch were both swift and severe. Both point toward an uncomfortable spotlight on the wrath of God. God's wrath receives little play nowadays, replaced almost entirely in our sermons and songs with a celebration of his love. While it's undoubtedly and thankfully true that "God so loved the world," it's equally true that he's a God with whom we trifle at our own peril. To paraphrase C. S. Lewis in *The Chronicles of Narnia*, he is a good lion, but he is not tame.

Perhaps the greatest difficulty in reading, teaching, or preaching through 1 Chronicles is the risk of missing the forest for the trees. All the genealogical and other detailed lists in the book can obscure its basic story line if one doesn't read the record first with a wide-angle lens and then more closely with a telephoto lens.

The big picture in 1 Chronicles focuses on God's covenant with David and David's preparations for the construction of God's house. It's a picture the chronicler paints in bright colors to be hung on the walls of his readers' hearts, reminding them of who they were and the hopeful future that was still theirs.

Within this big picture are lots and lots of people—some well-known to history, some barely known, and others practically unknown, except to God. While we find it nearly impossible not to lose sight of all but the major actors in the grand narrative of history, the Lord remembers the name of each and every one of us, and the names of our parents and grandparents too! Nothing we do—no matter how small, how misunderstood, or how well intended but wrongheaded—ever escapes his attention.

Cultural Perspectives and Application

The average American pays little attention to the past and may know even less about his or her own family's history. That's changing for millions of people as they turn to a handful of ancestry websites that are helping them trace their roots. They're discovering that genealogies aren't necessarily boring after all. The genealogies in 1 Chronicles 1–9 will become meaningful to today's hearers once they understand why the chronicler recorded them for his postexilic audience and appreciate how they remain relevant to God's people still.

Like Israel after the exile, we believers are prone to taking lightly our own spiritual heritage. We forget who we are. Not seeing our promised King sitting on a visible throne while the world around us remains in ruins, we go to his house week in and week out feeling defeated and cut off from the world he promised. The chronicler reminds us that God's house stands as a perpetual monument to his mercy and that God's promise to David still stands. Just as his postexilic readers had to take it on faith that David's son would one day come to retake his throne, so we await our King's return. On that day when the new Jerusalem—our King's throne room and temple—descends to earth, we will wear his name clearly and proudly (Rev. 22:4). Then none will doubt that he is our God and we are his people (Rev. 21:3).

When the Lord punished David for numbering Israel and struck down Uzzah for touching the ark, those punishments were direct, immediate, and retributive. When God punishes sin directly, he gets personally involved—as when he confounded the languages at Babel after examining the workers' tower there (Gen. 11), and when he rained down fire and brimstone from heaven after determining that the wicked report he'd received on those twin cities was true (Gen. 19). When God punishes sin indirectly, he sits back and lets us get what's coming to us—as when the sexually immoral person contracts a sexually transmitted disease. In such instances, the seed of punishment is in the fruit of the sin. As with a strawberry or banana, one can't eat the fruit without also ingesting the seed.

Whether administered directly or indirectly, God intends for his punishments to serve at least one of three purposes, if not a combination of the three. His punishments serve a retributive purpose when they inflict pain by giving the transgressor his or her due for violating one of God's laws. His punishments are meant to be remedial when they're sent to correct the sinner's behavior. Sometimes, for the sake of onlookers, the Lord punishes disobedient people as a warning not to pursue their course of action. Such punishments are intended to be deterrents.[6] The two punishments administered in 1 Chronicles 13 and 21, and the many others recorded in 2 Chronicles, are of the immediate and retributive varieties. Today's hearers should be made aware of these and the other ways that God punishes sin.

RECOMMENDED RESOURCES

Fee, Gordon D., and Douglas Stuart. *How to Read the Bible Book by Book*. Grand Rapids: Zondervan, 2002.

Hays, J. Daniel, and J. Scott Duvall, eds. *The Baker Illustrated Bible Handbook*. Grand Rapids: Baker Books, 2011.

Vanhoozer, Kevin J., ed. *Dictionary for Theological Interpretation of the Bible*. Grand Rapids: Baker Academic, 2005.

---

6. Millard J. Erickson, *Christian Theology*, 2nd ed. (Grand Rapids: Baker, 1998), 626–28.

2 Chronicles

PAUL A. HOFFMAN

The Big Idea of 2 Chronicles

Second Chronicles presents a hopeful narrative, intended to bolster and inspire the postexilic Jews toward fully restoring the temple and city of Jerusalem. Two intertwined themes prevail throughout: David's kingdom and the temple. God demonstrates his loyal love to the royal line of David when King Solomon builds the temple. After this halcyon period, the book depicts the rise and fall of nineteen kings, culminating in God's disciplining his chosen people for their unrelenting wickedness (2 Chron. 36:15–21). Second Chronicles, however, concludes with a redemptive trajectory: God "moved the heart of Cyrus king of Persia" (2 Chron. 36:22) to catalyze the rebuilding of the temple and release the exiles to return home.

SUBJECT: What message does the chronicler tell God's broken and discouraged people after the destruction of Jerusalem and their exile?

COMPLEMENT: Despite their failures, God remains faithful to David's kingdom because "he is good; [and] his love endures forever" (2 Chron. 5:13).

EXEGETICAL IDEA: The message the chronicler tells God's broken and discouraged people after the destruction of Jerusalem and their exile is that despite their failures, God remains faithful to David's kingdom because "he is good; [and] his love endures forever."

HOMILETICAL IDEA: Despite the failures of his people, God remains faithful because "he is good; [and] his love endures forever."

Selecting Preaching and Teaching Passages in 2 Chronicles

When interpreting Old Testament narratives, a keen expositor understands each story contains "three levels": "The *top level* is that of the whole universal plan of God. . . . The *middle level* center[s] on Israel. . . . Then there is the *bottom level*. Here are found all the hundreds of *individual* narratives that make up the other two levels."[1]

As far as 2 Chronicles is concerned, it is vital to continually recall its overarching goal: "to provide the postexilic community with hope and a desperately needed sense of identity and direction."[2] With that in mind, Gordon Fee offers a broad outline that gives historical and thematic clarity:

2 Chronicles 1–9   The United Monarchy: The Story of Solomon

2 Chronicles 10–36   The Divided Monarchy: The Davidic Dynasty[3]

As one studies 2 Chronicles 1–9, it is important to note "the one essential point—faithfulness to the temple as the place of true worship." Furthermore, the second section of 2 Chronicles (chaps. 10–36) places "special emphasis on God's direct intervention for blessing and judgment on the basis of either of the kings' 'seeking' or 'humbling themselves before' Yahweh or of their 'abandoning' or 'forsaking' Yahweh."[4]

Regarding choosing texts to preach and teach from, the interpreter can reasonably utilize the topic headings presented in the NIV. To simplify, I consolidate the fifty-one headings from the NIV into thirty pericopes, according to each topic, story, or king. They are delineated in the next section.

Getting the Subject, Complement, Exegetical Idea, and Homiletical Idea

2 Chronicles 1

SUBJECT: What is the result of Solomon asking God for wisdom to lead Israel?

COMPLEMENT: God grants him wisdom to lead Israel along with wealth, possessions, and honor.

---

1. Gordon D. Fee and Douglas Stuart, *How to Read the Bible for All Its Worth*, 2nd ed. (Grand Rapids: Zondervan, 1993), 79.

2. David A. Dorsey, *The Literary Structure of the Old Testament* (Grand Rapids: Baker, 1999), 145.

3. Gordon D. Fee and Douglas Stuart, *How to Read the Bible Book by Book* (Grand Rapids: Zondervan, 2002), 104–5.

4. Fee and Stuart, *How to Read the Bible Book by Book*, 105.

EXEGETICAL IDEA: The result of Solomon asking God for wisdom to lead Israel is that God grants him wisdom along with wealth, possessions, and honor.

HOMILETICAL IDEA: God honors leaders who seek to honor him.

2 Chronicles 2:1–5:1

SUBJECT: Why does Solomon invest significant time, attention, and resources to build the temple?

COMPLEMENT: Because "God is greater than all other gods" (2:5).

EXEGETICAL IDEA: Solomon invests significant time, attention, and resources to building the temple because "God is greater than all other gods" (2:5).

HOMILETICAL IDEA: Our God is worthy of our best time, attention, and resources because he is greater than all other gods.

2 Chronicles 5:2–6:11

SUBJECT: As the ark is brought into the temple, what does Solomon praise the Lord for?

COMPLEMENT: Keeping his promise to David.

EXEGETICAL IDEA: As the ark is brought into the temple, Solomon praises the Lord for keeping his promise to David.

HOMILETICAL IDEA: Praise the Lord for keeping his promises.

2 Chronicles 6:12–7:10

SUBJECT: What does Solomon pray for as he dedicates the temple?

COMPLEMENT: That the Lord will listen to the prayers of his people and foreigners coming from the temple and respond with forgiveness, justice, and salvation.

EXEGETICAL IDEA: As he dedicates the temple, Solomon prays that the Lord will listen to the prayers of his people and foreigners coming from the temple and respond with forgiveness, justice, and salvation.

HOMILETICAL IDEA: The Lord listens to our prayers and responds with forgiveness, justice, and salvation.

2 Chronicles 7:11–22

SUBJECT: What does the Lord tell Solomon?

COMPLEMENT: That he will respond to humility, earnest prayer, and repentance but will punish disobedience and idolatry.

EXEGETICAL IDEA: The Lord tells Solomon that he will respond to humility, prayer, and repentance but will punish disobedience and idolatry.

HOMILETICAL IDEA: The Lord responds to humility, earnest prayer, and repentance but punishes disobedience and idolatry.

2 Chronicles 8-9

SUBJECT: What is the consequence of Solomon fastidiously caring for the temple and meeting the requirements of the sacrificial system?

COMPLEMENT: God makes him famous and "greater in riches and wisdom than all the other kings of the earth" (9:22).

EXEGETICAL IDEA: The consequence of Solomon fastidiously caring for the temple and meeting the requirements of the sacrificial system is that God makes him famous and "greater in riches and wisdom than all the other kings of the earth" (9:22).

HOMILETICAL IDEA: God promotes those who worship him properly.

2 Chronicles 10-11

SUBJECT: What is the outcome of King Rehoboam rejecting the advice of his father's elders and responding harshly to the people's request for lighter labor?

COMPLEMENT: Ten of the tribes rebel against his rulership, which divides the kingdom.

EXEGETICAL IDEA: The outcome of King Rehoboam rejecting the advice of his father's elders and responding harshly to the people's request for lighter labor is that ten of the tribes rebel against his rulership, which divides the kingdom.

HOMILETICAL IDEA: Foolish and harsh leadership brings rebellion and division.

2 Chronicles 12

SUBJECT: What happens when Rehoboam and the people are unfaithful to the Lord, abandon the law, and serve the kings of other lands?

COMPLEMENT: The Lord intends to destroy them unless the king and leaders humble themselves, but instead the Lord responds by allowing a lesser punishment: the plundering of the temple and palace.

EXEGETICAL IDEA: When Rehoboam and the people are unfaithful to the Lord, abandon the law, and serve the kings of other lands, the Lord intends to destroy them unless the king and leaders humble themselves, but the Lord responds by allowing a lesser punishment: the plundering of the temple and the palace.

HOMILETICAL IDEA: While the Lord punishes unfaithfulness, he responds to humility and repentance.

2 Chronicles 13:1–14:1

SUBJECT: How is it that Abijah's army defeats Jeroboam's superior army?

COMPLEMENT: "They relied on the LORD" (13:18) and so God "routed Jeroboam" (13:15).

EXEGETICAL IDEA: Abijah's army defeats Jeroboam's superior army because "they relied on the LORD" (13:18) and so God "routed Jeroboam" (13:15).

HOMILETICAL IDEA: God grants triumph to those who rely on him.

2 Chronicles 14:2–15

SUBJECT: What does King Asa's relationship with the Lord demonstrate?

COMPLEMENT: Those who rely on the God who "help[s] the powerless against the mighty" (14:11) will receive rest and victory.

EXEGETICAL IDEA: King Asa's relationship with the Lord demonstrates that those who rely on the God who "help[s] the powerless against the mighty" (14:11) will receive rest and victory.

HOMILETICAL IDEA: Trust in the God who helps the powerless against the mighty, and you will receive rest and victory.

2 Chronicles 15

SUBJECT: What do Asa's reforms indicate?

COMPLEMENT: The Lord "reward[s]" (15:7) those whose hearts are "fully committed" (15:17) to him.

EXEGETICAL IDEA: Asa's reforms indicate that the Lord "reward[s]" (15:7) those whose hearts are "fully committed" (15:17) to him.

HOMILETICAL IDEA: The Lord rewards those whose hearts are fully committed to him.

2 Chronicles 16

SUBJECT: What is the lesson gleaned from Asa's failure?

COMPLEMENT: The Lord strengthens those solely dependent on him but weakens the self-dependent.

EXEGETICAL IDEA: The lesson gleaned from Asa's failure is the Lord strengthens those solely dependent on him but weakens the self-dependent.

HOMILETICAL IDEA: The Lord strengthens those solely dependent on him but weakens the self-dependent.

2 Chronicles 17

SUBJECT: How does the chronicler describe the onset of Jehoshaphat's reign?

COMPLEMENT: As a period in which the Lord gives him wealth, honor, and power because he obeys God's commands and ensures they are taught throughout Judah.

EXEGETICAL IDEA: The chronicler describes the onset of Jehoshaphat's reign as a period in which the Lord gives him wealth, honor, and power because he obeys God's commands and ensures they are taught throughout Judah.

HOMILETICAL IDEA: The Lord "establish[es]" (17:5) those who obey his commands and teach them to others.

2 Chronicles 18:1-19:3; 20:31-21:3[5]

SUBJECT: Why does the Lord express displeasure with Jehoshaphat?

COMPLEMENT: Because he forms alliances with two wicked kings and fails to remove the high places.

EXEGETICAL IDEA: The Lord expresses displeasure with Jehoshaphat because he forms alliances with two wicked kings and fails to remove the high places.

HOMILETICAL IDEA: The Lord disapproves of unholy alliances and incomplete obedience.

2 Chronicles 19:4-20:30

SUBJECT: After his sinful alliance with Ahab, how does Jehoshaphat recover?

COMPLEMENT: By appointing judges to institute justice and proclaims a fast when Moab and Ammon wage war against Judah.

EXEGETICAL IDEA: After his sinful alliance with Ahab, Jehoshaphat recovers by appointing judges to institute justice and proclaims a fast when Moab and Ammon wage war against Judah.

HOMILETICAL IDEA: The Lord delivers those who practice justice and submission.

5. Chapters 18–21 are divided thematically: sections 18:1–19:3 and 20:31–21:3 describe two major failures committed by Jehoshaphat, while 19:4–20:30 depicts two successes. Even the best, most devoted kings had mixed records when serving the Lord.

2 Chronicles 21:4–20

SUBJECT: How is Jehoram's evil kingship defined?

COMPLEMENT: Jehoram murders his brothers and leads the people to prostitute themselves to false gods, so the Lord strikes him through rebellion, war, familial loss, and a painful and dishonorable death.

EXEGETICAL IDEA: Jehoram's evil kingship is defined by his murdering his brothers and leading the people to prostitute themselves to false gods, so the Lord strikes him through rebellion, war, familial loss, and a painful and dishonorable death.

HOMILETICAL IDEA: The Lord opposes and dishonors violence and idolatry.

2 Chronicles 22–23[6]

SUBJECT: How does the Lord respond to Ahaziah's wicked reign?

COMPLEMENT: By keeping his promise and preserves the descendants of David through the courageous actions of Jehosheba and Jehoiada.

EXEGETICAL IDEA: The Lord responds to Ahaziah's wicked reign by keeping his promise and preserving the descendants of David through the courageous actions of Jehosheba and Jehoiada.

HOMILETICAL IDEA: The Lord keeps his promises through the courageous actions of a few faithful followers.

2 Chronicles 24

SUBJECT: How does the death of Jehoiada change the direction of Joash's rule?

COMPLEMENT: Under Jehoida's guidance, Joash restores the temple and proper worship; however, after Jehoida's death Joash forsakes the Lord and abandons the temple.

EXEGETICAL IDEA: The death of Jehoida changes the direction of Joash's rule in that under Jehoida's guidance Joash restores the temple and proper worship; however, after Jehoida's death Joash forsakes the Lord and abandons the temple.

HOMILETICAL IDEA: Reformation is a fragile enterprise as sometimes one factor will cause its disintegration.

---

6. Chapters 22 and 23 are combined because of the shared theme of God's faithful and providential action. Second Chronicles 22:10–12 acts as a bridge connecting the two chapters.

2 Chronicles 25

SUBJECT: What causes the downfall and death of Amaziah?

COMPLEMENT: His idol worship and arrogance.

EXEGETICAL IDEA: Amaziah's downfall and death are caused by his idol worship and arrogance.

HOMILETICAL IDEA: "Before a downfall the heart is haughty" (Prov. 18:12).

2 Chronicles 26

SUBJECT: What causes the downfall of Uzziah?

COMPLEMENT: His pride and unfaithfulness.

EXEGETICAL IDEA: Uzziah's downfall is caused by his pride and unfaithfulness.

HOMILETICAL IDEA: "Pride [as well as unfaithfulness] goes before destruction" (Prov. 16:18).

2 Chronicles 27

SUBJECT: How does the chronicler summarize the rulership of Jotham?

COMPLEMENT: By stating, "Jotham grew powerful because he walked steadfastly before the LORD his God" (27:6).

EXEGETICAL IDEA: The chronicler summarizes the rulership of Jotham by stating, "Jotham grew powerful because he walked steadfastly before the LORD his God" (27:6).

HOMILETICAL IDEA: The Lord empowers those who walk steadfastly before him.

2 Chronicles 28

SUBJECT: What is the final analysis regarding the reign of King Ahaz?

COMPLEMENT: "The LORD humbled Judah" because Ahaz "promoted wickedness" (28:19), including unprecedented idolatry, child sacrifice, and closing the temple.

EXEGETICAL IDEA: The final analysis regarding the reign of King Ahaz is "the LORD humbled Judah" because Ahaz "promoted wickedness" (28:19), including unprecedented idolatry, child sacrifice, and closing the temple.

HOMILETICAL IDEA: The Lord humbles those who promote wickedness.

2 Chronicles 29-31

SUBJECT: Upon becoming king, what changes does Hezekiah enact and what are the results?

COMPLEMENT: Hezekiah reopens and purifies the temple, restores the priesthood, and reinstitutes the festivals, including Passover, resulting in a vital spiritual and societal reformation.

EXEGETICAL IDEA: Upon becoming king, Hezekiah enacts the following changes: he reopens and purifies the temple, restores the priesthood, and reinstitutes the festivals, including Passover, resulting in a vital spiritual and societal reformation.

HOMILETICAL IDEA: When God's people reprioritize proper worship and obedience to his Word, God sends renewal and reformation to them.

2 Chronicles 32:1-23

SUBJECT: How does Hezekiah face the threat of Sennacherib?

COMPLEMENT: By praying to the Lord, the "greater power" who "fight[s] our battles" (32:7–8), and God annihilates the Assyrian army.

EXEGETICAL IDEA: Hezekiah faces the threat of Sennacherib by praying to the Lord, "the greater power" who "fight[s] our battles" (32:7–8), and God annihilates the Assyrian army.

HOMILETICAL IDEA: When facing danger, pray to the Lord, the "greater power" who "fights our battles," and he will deliver you.

2 Chronicles 32:24-33

SUBJECT: What happens when Hezekiah becomes prideful and ungrateful?

COMPLEMENT: God's holy anger comes against him and the people until they repent.

EXEGETICAL IDEA: When Hezekiah becomes prideful and ungrateful, God's holy anger comes against him and the people until they repent.

HOMILETICAL IDEA: Even mature Christians can fall into pride and ingratitude, so remember: "God opposes the proud but shows favor to the humble" (James 4:6).

2 Chronicles 33:1-20

SUBJECT: What is the final analysis regarding Manasseh's reign?

COMPLEMENT: Although he starts as the most evil king in Judah's history, when God disciplines Manasseh, he repents so deeply that God restores him and changes his priorities.

EXEGETICAL IDEA: The final analysis regarding Manasseh's reign is that although he starts as the most evil king in Judah's history, when God disciplines him, he repents so deeply that God restores him and changes his priorities.

HOMILETICAL IDEA: No person is ever so evil that God cannot change and restore them for his service.

2 Chronicles 33:21-25

SUBJECT: How does Amon differ from his father Manasseh?

COMPLEMENT: He refuses to humble himself before the Lord and is assassinated by his officials.

EXEGETICAL IDEA: Amon differs from his father Manasseh in that he refuses to humble himself before the Lord and is assassinated by his officials.

HOMILETICAL IDEA: Those who refuse to humble themselves before the Lord receive what they deserve.

2 Chronicles 34-35

SUBJECT: Why does the prophet Jeremiah "commemorate Josiah" (35:25)?

COMPLEMENT: For faithfully seeking God like his ancestor David and for leading a vital reformation in which he purifies the temple, promotes reading the law and obeying it, and reinstitutes the Passover.

EXEGETICAL IDEA: The prophet Jeremiah "commemorate[s] Josiah" (35:25) for faithfully seeking God like his ancestor David and for leading a vital reformation in which he purifies the temple, promotes reading the law and obeying it, and reinstitutes the Passover.

HOMILETICAL IDEA: God honors faithful followers who prioritize pure worship, the study and obedience of God's Word, and the blood of the lamb.

2 Chronicles 36:1-14

SUBJECT: What are the common threads running through Judah's final four kings?

COMPLEMENT: They are "evil," enemy kings depose them and take them captive, and the temple is plundered under their watch.

EXEGETICAL IDEA: The common threads running through Judah's final four kings are that they are "evil," enemy kings depose them and take them captive, and the temple is plundered under their watch.

HOMILETICAL IDEA: Evil leaders suffer the repercussions of their ways.

2 Chronicles 36:15-23

SUBJECT: How does 2 Chronicles conclude?

COMPLEMENT: It concludes with judgment and hope: because of Judah's wickedness, God sends the Babylonians to destroy the temple and Jerusalem; however, the Lord preserves a remnant in exile and moves Cyrus to proclaim the rebuilding of the temple.

EXEGETICAL IDEA: Second Chronicles concludes with judgment and hope: because of Judah's wickedness, God sends the Babylonians to destroy the temple and Jerusalem; however, the Lord preserves a remnant in exile and moves Cyrus to proclaim the rebuilding of the temple.

HOMILETICAL IDEA: "Though [the Lord] brings grief, he will show compassion, so great is his unfailing love" (Lam. 3:32).

Difficult Passages/Verses

When approaching 2 Chronicles, the expositor will consider three potential challenges. The first is reconciling the differences between 1 and 2 Kings and 1 and 2 Chronicles. Although these books recount the same historical events, the book of Kings furnishes a more bleak assessment regarding the disintegration of Israel and Judah than does the book of Chronicles.[7] For instance, Kings gives pronounced emphasis to the ministries of the prophets Elijah and Elisha (see 1 Kings 17 through 2 Kings 8), whereas 2 Chronicles mentions Elijah once (21:12) and Elisha not at all.

Second, the New Testament appears to interact very little with 2 Chronicles. Due in large part to its descriptions of Solomon's temple, 2 Chronicles 1–9 are referenced or alluded to in the book of Revelation around a dozen times. Furthermore, Jesus cites "the Queen of the South" (i.e., the queen of Sheba in 2 Chron. 9:1) as one who will judge the Pharisees and teachers of the law because they failed to recognize the greatness of Jesus, who is "greater than Solomon" (Matt. 12:42; Luke 11:31). Otherwise, in general, the expositor

7. See Fee and Stuart, *How to Read the Bible Book by Book*, 92–98.

has very little material to draw from when it comes to incorporating the New Testament as a lens to interpret 2 Chronicles.[8]

Finally, the teacher must be cautious when handling texts that indicate God rewards a king's faithfulness with "great wealth" (such as Solomon, Jehoshaphat, Uzziah, and Hezekiah). There are many pastors espousing the so-called prosperity gospel: that God will necessarily bless those who adhere to biblical principles like "tithing" or "sowing one's seeds." On the contrary, covenant obedience does not automatically require or compel the Lord to bless a king. Biblical narratives are meant to be more descriptive than prescriptive and thus offer patterns rather than ironclad promises.

As far as specific passages are concerned, the following may prove confusing and so call for careful exegesis and precise explanation.

2 Chronicles 18:1–19:3

Micaiah's prophesy is perplexing. Why would the Lord, while sitting in his throne room, invite a spirit to "entice" King Ahab (18:18–19)? And what does it mean that the Lord "put a deceiving spirit in the mouths of these prophets" (18:22)?

2 Chronicles 19:4–20:30

This narrative is fascinating and multilayered. After "proclaim[ing] a fast for all Judah" (20:3), Jehoshaphat "appointed men to sing to the LORD and to praise him . . . as they went out at the head of the army. . . . As they began to sing and praise, the LORD set ambushes" and defeated Judah's invading enemies (20:21–22). This story merits deep reflection regarding the potency and role of worship.

2 Chronicles 28:1–4 and 33:1–6

The chronicler relates how the kings Ahaz and Manasseh engage in the horrific pagan practice of child sacrifice, killing their own children "in the fire" to supplicate and appease their false gods.

2 Chronicles 33:6

King Manasseh not only sacrificed his children but also "practiced divination and witchcraft, sought omens, and consulted mediums and spiritists." The preacher would be wise to explain the meaning of these activities and

8. Scholars call this hermeneutical approach the *sensus plenior*, which means "fuller sense/meaning." Some Old Testament texts (e.g., Psalms, Deuteronomy) find their fulfillment in the New Testament in the coming of Jesus Christ. See Fee and Stuart, *How to Read the Bible for All Its Worth*, 183–85.

warn his or her audience regarding the dangers of witchcraft and the occult, which are demonic.

Cultural Perspectives and Application

Second Chronicles gives significant weight to the importance of the temple, sacrificial system, and priesthood (Levites). God requires his people to worship and serve him alone with purity and propriety. People from Western cultures often struggle to comprehend crucial concepts delineated in 2 Chronicles, such as animal sacrifice; the sacredness of particular locations; ritual purity; God's glorious, holy, and manifest presence; and pagan idolatry, to name a few. The expositor will be sensitive to this dynamic and take care in explaining these historical and cultural themes. Nevertheless, thankfully, the book of Hebrews declares that Jesus Christ is our great high priest (Heb. 4–5, 8) and perfect sacrifice who covers our sins and makes us holy, once and for all (Heb. 9–10). Consequently, Christians are "being built into a spiritual house to be a holy priesthood, offering spiritual sacrifices acceptable to God through Jesus Christ" (1 Pet. 2:5). However, this does not mean Christians should ignore proper worship as Jesus taught: "God is spirit, and his worshipers must worship in the Spirit and in truth" (John 4:24).

Another concept 2 Chronicles presents, which confronts our twenty-first-century sensibilities, is how governmental structures and godly/ungodly leadership promote or detract from the health of a society. While Judah existed as a theocracy (a government organized under the kingship, covenant, and laws of God), modern Western societies are more democratic in nature. That is, they are run by and for the people rather than (explicitly) by and for God. And while some laws have been animated and shaped by biblical ideas, as mostly human constructs, constitutions do not carry the authority of the Holy Scriptures. Indeed, the Bible does convey principles of leadership and governance that are God-honoring and contribute to the common good and flourishing (the Hebrew word frequently used is *shalom*) of human societies. Christians and non-Christians alike would benefit from studying and reflecting on both the good and the bad examples presented in 2 Chronicles.

Third, some Christians in late-modern societies struggle to grasp (or even resist) the idea that one person can affect the fate of the many. How is it that one king, ruler, or leader can cause the rise and fall of countless (presumably) innocent subjects? In other words, why must so many suffer for the sins and failures of one leader or cohort of officials? This brings to bear the biblical idea of "federal headship," which is laid out in Romans: "Sin entered the world through one man [Adam] . . . and in this way death came to all people, because all sinned. . . . [But] how much more did God's grace and the gift that came by the grace of the one man, Jesus Christ, overflow to the many!" (Rom. 5:12, 15). John Stott explains that all sinned this way: "There can be only one explanation. All died because all sinned in and through Adam, the representative or federal head of the human race."[9]

In addition, human beings—both leaders and followers—are more interconnected and therefore more mutually influencing than we understand. This means to a certain extent that when it comes to social/communal/national sins, everyone is complicit and can oftentimes occupy multiple roles simultaneously, including victim, perpetrator, and beneficiary.[10]

To summarize, this historical book poses numerous applications:

- God is faithful and gracious despite human sinfulness and failure.
- God disciplines his people when they commit persistent and unrepentant idolatry (see also Heb. 12).
- God commands his people to pray, worship, and serve him wholeheartedly in accordance with his Holy Scriptures.
- God's covenant with King David is an everlasting covenant. While it has been fulfilled in the coming of Jesus Christ, God nonetheless has not abandoned his beloved people (see also Rom. 11).
- Ultimately, the failure of Judah's kings gestures to the sinless and holy King of kings, Jesus Christ. Embedded inside their evil reigns is the seed of the gospel.

RECOMMENDED RESOURCES

Dorsey, David A. *The Literary Structure of the Old Testament.* Grand Rapids: Baker, 1999.

Fee, Gordon D., and Douglas Stuart. *How to Read the Bible Book by Book.* Grand Rapids: Zondervan, 2002.

See also recommendations for 1 Chronicles.

---

9. John Stott, *The Message of Romans: God's Good News for the World* (Downers Grove, IL: IVP Academic, 2001), 152.

10. See James E. Beitler III, *Seasoned Speech: Rhetoric in the Life of the Church* (Downers Grove, IL: IVP Academic, 2019), 128–60.

Ezra

TIMOTHY BUSHFIELD

The Big Idea of Ezra

Ezra is the story of God's redeeming work bringing his people out of exile and back to the promised land. What first appears as geographical relocation, Ezra is the story of God calling a people back into relationship with him and concludes by anticipating an even greater redemption that is yet to come.

SUBJECT: What does the book of Ezra teach about the relationship between God and his people in Ezra's day?

COMPLEMENT: God keeps his promises from generation to generation, and he redeems his people so that they might enjoy a relationship with him.

EXEGETICAL IDEA: The book of Ezra teaches that God keeps his promises from generation to generation by redeeming his people so that they might enjoy a relationship with him.

HOMILETICAL IDEA: God has promised to redeem, and he'll keep that promise.

Selecting Preaching and Teaching Passages in Ezra

For Ezra, "renewal" is a useful concept on which the entire preaching series can be built. The book can be preached almost chapter by chapter from beginning to end. There are a few places where it will be helpful to introduce additional texts from other biblical books to fill out the narrative. A first sermon would benefit from including Jeremiah 29, as the prophet is mentioned in these opening verses of Ezra. This will help frame the book within its geopolitical as well as its redemptive history. It is also suggested below that chapters 5 and 6 be taken together as an extended narrative of opposition to the rebuilding of the temple, with the added recommendation of including Haggai 1 to shed light on the people's hearts during those years of dormancy. Chapters 7 and 8 can be taken together as the introduction to Ezra and his ministry in Jerusalem, connecting them with Nehemiah 8 to round out a concrete example of what his ministry looked like. Overall, the biblical material is already arranged in preachable units. Following these recommendations, the book of Ezra can be effectively preached across nine weeks.

Getting the Subject, Complement, Exegetical Idea, and Homiletical Idea

Ezra 1:1-4

SUBJECT: How does God fulfill his promise to his people?

COMPLEMENT: By inaugurating a great renewal among his people, restoring them from captivity, and calling them back to a relationship with himself.

EXEGETICAL IDEA: God fulfills his promise by inaugurating a great renewal among his people, restoring them from captivity, and calling them back to a relationship with himself.

HOMILETICAL IDEA: Even in the darkness, there is always hope because the Lord keeps his promises.

Ezra 1:5-11

SUBJECT: What does God reveal about life with him as he orchestrates the rebuilding of the temple?

COMPLEMENT: That God himself is both the agent of renewal and the goal of renewal.

EXEGETICAL IDEA: As God orchestrates the rebuilding of the temple, he reveals himself as both the agent of renewal and the goal of renewal.

HOMILETICAL IDEA: Renewal itself is not the goal; rather, life with God is the goal.

Ezra 2

SUBJECT: What does God reveal about himself through the census?

COMPLEMENT: That God knows and loves his people by name, preserving them from generation to generation, yet he also has standards of holiness for his people.

EXEGETICAL IDEA: God reveals about himself through the census that he knows and loves his people by name, preserving them from generation to generation, while also reminding them of standards of holiness.

HOMILETICAL IDEA: God welcomes us by name but invites us on his terms.[1]

Ezra 3

SUBJECT: What does the beginning of a renewed relationship with God look like before the foundations of the temple are even laid?

COMPLEMENT: God's people begin with worship right in the midst of their fear and in the midst of the ruins of their ancestral home.

EXEGETICAL IDEA: At the beginning of a renewed relationship with God and before the foundations of the temple are even laid, God's people begin with worship right in the midst of their fear and in the midst of the ruins of their ancestral home.

HOMILETICAL IDEA: In the midst of fear and rubble, renewal begins with worship.

Ezra 4

SUBJECT: What obstacles do God's people face as they attempt to rebuild the temple?

COMPLEMENT: God's people face covert and overt opposition to the rebuilding of the temple and the reestablishment of life with God.

EXEGETICAL IDEA: The obstacles God's people face as they attempted to rebuild the temple are covert and overt opposition to reestablishment of life with God.

HOMILETICAL IDEA: If you're seeking renewal, expect opposition.

Ezra 5–6

SUBJECT: What is the result of the opposition faced by God's people as they are trying to rebuild the temple?

COMPLEMENT: Even though there is a great delay, work on the temple resumes in God's own time when God's people focus on him once again.

---

1. The census begins with a beautiful picture of God knowing each tribe and family and person, emphasizing continuity with the preexilic community and God's personal knowledge of his people. Toward the end of the chapter, however, the documentation requirements for leadership remind us of God's holiness and the necessity of living according to his law.

EXEGETICAL IDEA: The result of the opposition faced by God's people as they tried to rebuild the temple is that even though there is a great delay, work on the temple resumes in God's own time when God's people focus on him once again.

HOMILETICAL IDEA: Stay focused on the Lord, because renewal happens according to God's timetable, not ours.[2]

Ezra 7-8[3]

SUBJECT: What is Ezra's commission before God and the people as he finally shows up in the story?

COMPLEMENT: To study and observe the law of the Lord and to teach God's decrees and laws in Israel.

EXEGETICAL IDEA: Ezra's commission before God and the people as he finally shows up in the story is to study and observe the law of the Lord and to teach God's decrees and laws in Israel.

HOMILETICAL IDEA: Renewal invites us to study and obey the Law of God—not as a prerequisite for God's redemption, but in response to it.

Ezra 9

SUBJECT: How do God's people respond in light of Ezra's arrival and teaching of God's law?

COMPLEMENT: They become aware of their sin, so they humble themselves before the Lord in confession and repentance.

EXEGETICAL IDEA: In light of Ezra's arrival and teaching of God's law, God's people become aware of their sin and humble themselves before the Lord in confession and repentance.

HOMILETICAL IDEA: Confession is God's gift to a renewed people to help us continue in a relationship with him.

---

2. Bringing in Haggai 1 allows a congregation to see that it was not just external circumstances that prevented ongoing construction on the temple; the hearts of the people had drifted from the Lord, and so he sends Haggai to reset their priorities and refocus them on him and his glory.

3. Taking Ezra 7 and 8 together from a thematic point of view allows us to introduce Ezra and his ministry among God's people as the main idea of this text. Bringing Nehemiah 8 into this discussion provides a practical example of his ministry.

Ezra 10[4]

SUBJECT: What does the people's situation reveal about God's great redemptive story (even though we don't know if their response to their sin was appropriate)?

COMPLEMENT: That even as a renewed people they still struggle with sin, and that no amount of human effort or wisdom can mitigate this broken relationship with God.

EXEGETICAL IDEA: The people's situation reveals about God's great redemptive story (even though we don't know if their response to their sin was appropriate) that even as a renewed people they still struggle with sin, and that no amount of human effort or wisdom can mitigate this broken relationship with God.

HOMILETICAL IDEA: A better renewal is needed and a better renewal is coming.

Difficult Passages/Verses

An initial difficulty when preaching Ezra is determining Ezra's relationship to the book of Nehemiah. Hebrew tradition, in agreement with the oldest versions of the Septuagint, present Ezra and Nehemiah as a single book. But Nehemiah 1:1 signals the beginning of a new document; both English and Hebrew Bibles today present them as two separate books. As a preacher, you will have to decide whether you will preach Ezra on its own or as part of a series covering both Ezra and Nehemiah. The present work approaches Ezra as separate from, yet closely related to, the book of Nehemiah.

A second difficulty relates to chronology. In places Ezra has rearranged some material away from a strict historical time line. For example, work on the temple ceases in the mid-530s BC, and yet Ezra 4 attributes the reason for this stoppage to a letter sent by opponents to King Artaxerxes I—who doesn't take the throne for roughly seventy years. In some places, the dates of the events in Ezra are specific ("in the second month of the second year" [3:8]), while other times identifiers are remarkably vague ("after these things had been done" [9:1]). Ezra should be read with the understanding that the

---

4. See "Difficult Passages/Verses" below for a discussion of the approach to this text. The present work neither affirms nor condemns the decision for mass divorce; rather, it understands this national divorce event as the community-crippling effects of sin, pointing them—even at the end of a beautiful story of renewal—to their need for an even greater redemption, accomplished by Jesus at the cross.

author transposed some events in order to present a theological story rather than a strictly chronological one.

The final chapters of this book are also difficult to teach. Ezra 9–10 recount the people's realization of their sin (marrying foreign wives) and the people's proposed solution (divorce all their foreign wives). While the text does demonstrate that some measure of discernment was applied on a case-by-case basis (10:16–17), there is a conspicuous absence of God's direct agency in these chapters. The book begins with unambiguous clarity that it is the Lord who moves in the hearts of people according to his will (1:1 and 1:5). But in these final chapters of the book, God is silent. Should we affirm the decision to divorce their wives for the sake of obedience to the law, or should we present this divorce solution as the people trying to solve the problem of their own sin? The cultural distance that separates our day from theirs is significant, and direct one-to-one application needs to be avoided. Presented above is a third alternative for interpreting these chapters—namely, that sometimes there are no good solutions when dealing with the very real consequences of sin. In this situation, what seems most clear is that the people's own wisdom and efforts are insufficient to redeem themselves. The book ends not with joyful repentance and purity, but with the mess of sin tearing a community apart and the obvious and desperate need for a better solution to human sinfulness. Seen through this lens, the book of Ezra ends by pointing to the need for Jesus and an ever better redemption to come as God redeems his people from sin and death once and for all. Now that is something we can preach!

Cultural Perspectives and Application

Viewed through the lens of renewal as presented above, the book of Ezra is directly applicable to life in our culture. Christians throughout the ages have struggled through times of feeling alienated from God, either because of their sin or through some period of perceived estrangement like a dark night of the soul, as described by St. John of the Cross. The lessons from the book of Ezra bring deep wisdom by presenting renewal as a process—one without quick fixes that automatically bring us nearer to God. Ezra teaches that renewal is God's initiative, and ours is only to respond to the divine invitation. As with God's people in Ezra's day, we often begin our journey in the midst of fear and rubble; we too will face opposition and delay; we too will become aware of our sin and our need for holiness. Ultimately, we too will come face to face with our need for God to ultimately redeem us from our sin through Christ precisely so that we might enjoy a renewed relationship with him.

Ezra is an extraordinary and relevant book to teach to the modern and postmodern church. However, care should be taken when seeking dynamic equivalence to our own cultural context. Our pining for renewal cannot compare to an entire people living in bondage in a foreign country. Ezra presents a second exodus for God's people, in many ways mirroring the first, while also being a foretaste of the ultimate exodus from sin in Christ. Preaching Ezra should be done with an awareness that "feeling distant from God this week" is significantly different from living in exile because of the sin of an entire people. Comparisons can be made, but one-to-one parallels should be avoided by moving up the ladder of abstraction when bridging to our day.

Last, Ezra 9–10 present a special challenge for application. When teaching Ezra in my church, conversations were quick to arise about whether Ezra provides biblical justification for divorcing unbelieving spouses. Care must be taken to clearly explain the differences between a national spiritual identity as an ethnic group in the time before Jesus came and the contemporary transethnic scope of the gospel as illuminated by Jesus and Paul. Far from justifying divorce, Jesus calls us to be a covenant-affirming and covenant-keeping people who remain faithful even beyond what seems to make sense to an unbelieving world. Paul provides additional specific counsel regarding our sexuality and marriage. Taking Ezra 9–10 as presented above (see "Difficult Passages/ Verses") can help diffuse some of the tension these chapters may create. But it may be necessary, depending on a church's specific needs, to complement these final chapters of Ezra with some topical teaching on biblical marriage and divorce to clarify any confusion that might arise. While a few sentences in a sermon along these lines may alleviate the majority of concerns, some people may need additional pastoral care and clarity on the Bible's overall teaching on this subject.

RECOMMENDED RESOURCES

Allen, Leslie C., and Timothy S. Laniak. *Ezra, Nehemiah, Esther.* Understanding the Bible Commentary Series. Grand Rapids: Baker Books, 2003.

Breneman, Mervin. *Ezra, Nehemiah, Esther: An Exegetical and Theological Exposition of Holy Scripture.* The New American Commentary. Nashville: Broadman & Holman, 1993.

Kidner, Derek. *Ezra and Nehemiah.* Tyndale Old Testament Commentaries. Downers Grove, IL: InterVarsity, 1979.

Nehemiah

MATTHEW D. KIM

The Big Idea of Nehemiah

The book of Nehemiah (meaning "the Lord comforts") is a story of God's faithfulness to the nation of Israel (approximately 445 BC) in spite of their disobedience and sins as they return from exile to the city of Jerusalem. It narrates Nehemiah's journey of leadership (from cupbearer to the king turned governor) through opposition and conflict, the eventual rebuilding of the wall in Jerusalem, and the Israelites' communal life together afterward.

The book records Nehemiah's tender heart toward God and God's people, and his sacrificial efforts to care for them during a volatile time of corruption, opposition, and challenging circumstances. Nehemiah is an example of a godly leader who is attuned to the spirit of God, led by the mission of God, and proactive to meet the physical and spiritual conditions of God's people.

SUBJECT: What is the book of Nehemiah about?

COMPLEMENT: It recounts the history of exilic Israelites' resettlement of Jerusalem led by Nehemiah, who brings God's community together through rebuilding the wall and gates and reforming worship.

EXEGETICAL IDEA: The book of Nehemiah recounts the history of exilic Israelites' resettlement of Jerusalem led by Nehemiah, who brings God's community together through rebuilding the wall and gates and reforming worship.

HOMILETICAL IDEA: Trust the Lord and worship him in all circumstances and in all places.

Selecting Preaching and Teaching Passages in Nehemiah

Much like Ezra, Nehemiah is rather straightforward in terms of determining preaching and teaching pericopes—that is, for the most part, you can teach or preach this book chapter by chapter. In the past I have preached through the entire book in twelve sermons by combining chapters 7 and 8 into one sermon. Depending on one's interpretation and discretion, chapter 7 can serve as a hinge chapter that could be preached with either chapter 6 or chapter 8. You might also see fit to preach chapter 6 through 7:3 as one unit of thought and then preach the genealogical record from 7:4–7:73 as its own sermon passage. In addition, it makes sense to preach Nehemiah 11:1–12:26 as one text as it relates to the descendants of Judah and Benjamin who settled in Jerusalem in addition to the Levites and the priests. Preaching in such a chapter-by-chapter fashion provides a straightforward three-month sermon or Bible study series. You may also deem that chapter 7 deserves its own sermon or Bible study. With this in mind, I have included the big idea process for chapter 7 as a stand-alone passage. What could complicate this structure is whether (as Timothy Bushfield mentions in the chapter on Ezra) the preacher chooses to connect Nehemiah with any portion of Ezra.

Getting the Subject, Complement, Exegetical Idea, and Homiletical Idea

Nehemiah 1

SUBJECT: What does Nehemiah pray to the Lord for on behalf of the Israelites who are returning to Jerusalem from exile?

COMPLEMENT: He praises God for who he is, confesses his personal sins and the corporate sins of the Israelites, and asks God for help in speaking to the king.

EXEGETICAL IDEA: In his prayers to the Lord on behalf of the Israelites who are returning to Jerusalem from exile, Nehemiah praises God for who he is, confesses his personal sins and the corporate sins of the Israelites, and asks God for help in speaking to the king.

HOMILETICAL IDEA: In times of trouble, praise God, confess your sins, and seek his wisdom.

Nehemiah 2

SUBJECT: What does Nehemiah ask of King Artaxerxes?

COMPLEMENT: For safety and for provisions to rebuild the wall in Jerusalem, where Nehemiah faces persecution.

EXEGETICAL IDEA: Nehemiah asks King Artaxerxes for safety and for provisions to rebuild the wall in Jerusalem, where he faces persecution.

HOMILETICAL IDEA: When persecution comes, trust in the God who makes improbable provisions.

Nehemiah 3

SUBJECT: How does the author explain the process of rebuilding the wall in Jerusalem?

COMPLEMENT: By naming all the skilled individuals who played a specific role in its reconstruction.

EXEGETICAL IDEA: The author explains the process of rebuilding the wall in Jerusalem by naming all the skilled individuals who played a specific role in its reconstruction.

HOMILETICAL IDEA: Everyone plays a part in building the community of God.

Nehemiah 4

SUBJECT: How do Nehemiah and the Israelites respond to Sanballat and others' opposition to rebuilding the wall?

COMPLEMENT: They pray and trust in God, who will fight their battles.

EXEGETICAL IDEA: Nehemiah and the Israelites respond to Sanballat and others' opposition to rebuilding the wall by praying and trusting in God, who will fight their battles.

HOMILETICAL IDEA: Trust in the God who fights for us and who can do what we cannot do.

Nehemiah 5[1]

SUBJECT: What do Nehemiah's actions show about how he views the lowest persons in society in difficult economic times?

COMPLEMENT: He values them as God's people and cares generously for their needs.

EXEGETICAL IDEA: Nehemiah's actions show that he values the lowest persons in society in difficult economic times as God's people and cares generously for their needs.

---

1. You can find the same big idea process in my sample sermon "Revere God by Remembering Others" in Matthew D. Kim, *Preaching with Cultural Intelligence: Understanding the People Who Hear Our Sermons* (Grand Rapids: Baker Academic, 2017), 231.

HOMILETICAL IDEA: Out of reverence for God, care for others and God will remember you.

Nehemiah 6

SUBJECT: How does Nehemiah respond to his enemies' persistent plot to stop the Jewish people's work and to intimidate them?

COMPLEMENT: By praying to God that he would strengthen his hands to complete God's mission to rebuild the wall and to remember the evil of his enemies.

EXEGETICAL IDEA: Nehemiah responds to his enemies' persistent plot to stop the Jewish people's work and to intimidate them by praying to God that he would strengthen his hands to complete God's mission to rebuild the wall and to remember the evil of his enemies.

HOMILETICAL IDEA: Persistence and prayer complete God's calling on our lives.

Nehemiah 7:1-73a

SUBJECT: What does Nehemiah do after completing the wall?

COMPLEMENT: He appoints godly leaders to be in charge over Jerusalem and helps them settle into their new community.

EXEGETICAL IDEA: Nehemiah, after completing the wall, appoints godly leaders to be in charge over Jerusalem and helps them settle into their new community.

HOMILETICAL IDEA: Every place needs godly leaders.

Nehemiah 7:73b-8:18

SUBJECT: How do the Israelites react to Ezra's reading of the law in corporate worship?

COMPLEMENT: They initially weep and later celebrate God's faithfulness with joy and obey God's command to live in booths.

EXEGETICAL IDEA: The Israelites react to Ezra's reading of the law in corporate worship by initially weeping and later celebrating God's faithfulness with joy and obeying his commands to live in booths.

HOMILETICAL IDEA: The Word of God brings joy and obedience to those who respond in faith.

Nehemiah 9:1–37

SUBJECT: What is the confession the Israelites make to God in their prayers?

COMPLEMENT: That God is worthy of praise and that he has been faithful, compassionate, and just throughout the generations and even in allowing their present difficult circumstances because of their continued rebellion, idolatry, and sin.

EXEGETICAL IDEA: The confession the Israelites make to God in their prayers is that God is worthy of praise and that he has been faithful, compassionate, and just throughout the generations and even in allowing their present difficult circumstances because of their continued rebellion, idolatry, and sin.

HOMILETICAL IDEA: Confess all your sins to the Lord, for he is faithful and just even in allowing times of trouble.

Nehemiah 9:38–10:39

SUBJECT: What is the agreement that the Israelite leaders, Levites, and members of the community make to God?

COMPLEMENT: To bind themselves with a curse and an oath to follow the law of God given through Moses and to obey carefully all the commands, regulations, and decrees of the Lord.

EXEGETICAL IDEA: The agreement that the Israelite leaders, Levites, and members of the community make to God is to bind themselves with a curse and an oath to follow the law of God given through Moses and to obey carefully all the commands, regulations, and decrees of the Lord.

HOMILETICAL IDEA: Pledge yourselves today to obey the Word of the Lord.

Nehemiah 11:1–12:26

SUBJECT: Who does God send to resettle in the city of Jerusalem?

COMPLEMENT: One out of ten Israelites (cast by lots), including priests, Levites, temple servants, and descendants of Judah and Benjamin who are called to fulfill civilian or spiritual responsibilities.

EXEGETICAL IDEA: God sends to resettle in the city of Jerusalem one out of ten Israelites (cast by lots), including priests, Levites, temple servants, and descendants of Judah and Benjamin who are called to fulfill civilian or spiritual responsibilities.

HOMILETICAL IDEA: Wherever God places you, be prepared for God-given responsibilities.

Nehemiah 12:27-47

SUBJECT: How do the Levites and the citizens dedicate the wall of Jerusalem?

COMPLEMENT: By celebrating God's faithfulness with joy through purification and song and by giving to the Lord's work.

EXEGETICAL IDEA: The Levites and citizens dedicate the wall of Jerusalem by celebrating God's faithfulness with joy through purification and song and by giving to the Lord's work.

HOMILETICAL IDEA: Celebrate joyfully with purity, singing, and giving to the God who has done great things for you.

Nehemiah 13

SUBJECT: What does Nehemiah ask the Lord for as he makes his difficult final reforms?

COMPLEMENT: That he will remember him with favor.

EXEGETICAL IDEA: As he makes his difficult final reforms, Nehemiah asks the Lord to remember him with favor.

HOMILETICAL IDEA: Live a life of faithfulness because God remembers faithful lives.

Difficult Passages/Verses

One of the challenges in preaching historical narratives, particularly ones that are connected to other books, is in knowing how much or how little to include by way of biblical background. More specifically, how much of Nehemiah's story should interact with the book of Ezra? It's clear in certain passages that Ezra's character is central to the narrative, such as in Nehemiah 7:73b–8:18. Chronologically, one also needs to discern when to refer to Ezra's account to provide accuracy as well as the appropriate details.

A second difficulty with Nehemiah regards the general history and records of all the new residents in the book. As with genealogies, how much study must a preacher and teacher put in with respect to these names? What is the added value of digging up information about these priests and other inhabitants? What might one gain from closer examination of the myriad names throughout Nehemiah? Select character/name studies may help listeners and students gain a fuller picture of the entire narrative: King Artaxerxes, Sanballat the Horonite, Tobiah the Ammonite, Gesham the Arab, Eliashib the high priest, and Nebuchadnezzar king of Babylon to name a few.

Cultural Perspectives and Application

At a high level, the book of Nehemiah is rather daunting with regard to the enormity of historical and cultural contexts that an effective preacher or teacher will take the time to understand in order to interpret and communicate its truths. It is not simply Nehemiah's story of Jewish resettlement and the rebuilding of the wall and gates in the land of Jerusalem. Beyond Jewish exilic and postexilic cultures, the astute preacher will take the extra step to explore other biblical geographic locations and cultures mentioned in Nehemiah (and even Ezra), such as Persia, Babylon, Egypt, Trans-Euphrates, Hauran or Horon, fifth-century Samaria, Ammon, and the district of Keilah among many others, as well as becoming familiar with names of people, including Sanballat, and named landmarks like Jeshanah Gate, Valley Gate, Dung Gate, and Fountain Gate. It would be easy to overlook the specificity of the author's details for the overarching narrative, which of course needs to be properly communicated as well.

Applying any historical book can be challenging as the interpreter must weigh whether the narrative is merely descriptive or prescriptive or both. While certain elements of biblical narratives are more context specific, there are some parallel applications for today's hearers.

One of the universal themes that the author accentuates throughout the book is Nehemiah's shepherding and compassionate heart, even as a government official. In Nehemiah 1:4 it's clear that Nehemiah's burden for the exiles in trouble returning from Babylonian captivity is both intense and empathetic. His weeping over them leads to a tenderhearted prayer to the Lord on their behalf.

A second applicational characteristic that one might emulate is Nehemiah's corporate identity rather than individualistic mindset. He identifies with the exilic masses and puts himself in their situation, leading them in confession for their wickedness and disobedience (Neh. 1:7). Here is an example of a godly leader who resembles what Paul speaks of in looking out not just for personal interests but also for the interests of the entire group (Phil. 2:4) and doing so even with a spirit of joy (Neh. 8:10).

A third core application comes in the form of Nehemiah's deep trust in God. Throughout the book, he prays to the Lord for guidance, strength, and power. At every juncture in leading God's people, Nehemiah displays confidence in the Lord that is commendable and worthy of imitation.

RECOMMENDED RESOURCES

Boice, James Montgomery. *Nehemiah: An Expositional Commentary*. Grand Rapids: Baker Books, 2006.

Kidner, Derek. *Ezra and Nehemiah*. Tyndale Old Testament Commentaries. Downers Grove, IL: InterVarsity, 2009.

Petter, Donna, and Thomas D. Petter. *Ezra, Nehemiah*. The NIV Application Commentary. Grand Rapids: Zondervan, 2021.

Esther

SCOTT M. GIBSON

The Big Idea of Esther

The book of Esther is unusual in that it "contains neither the divine name *Yahweh* nor *'elohim*, the Hebrew noun meaning *God*," and its only connection to the Old Testament is that the story it tells involves Jewish people following the decree of Cyrus in 539 BC, allowing Jews to return to Jerusalem from exile in Babylon.[1]

The story is told in typical Hebrew style with characters acting and speaking and the story given without explanation or even interpretation. As Karen Jobes notes, "The astute reader sees a disquieting moral ambiguity, at best, in the way Esther and Mordecai are portrayed."[2] Yet this narrative of God's providential deliverance is a miniature painting of the wider landscape of God's dealing with his covenantal people.

The story of Esther is a story of providence, a narrative of God's redemptive work, moving history toward redemption in Christ.

SUBJECT: What does the story of Esther demonstrate?

COMPLEMENT: God's providential provision of protecting and prospering his people, moving all the while to redemption through the promised Messiah.

---

1. Karen H. Jobes, *Esther*, The NIV Application Commentary (Grand Rapids: Zondervan, 1999), 19.
2. Jobes, *Esther*, 20.

EXEGETICAL IDEA: The story of Esther demonstrates God's providential provision of protecting and prospering his people, moving all the while to redemption through the promised Messiah.

HOMILETICAL IDEA: God's hands are on history, making the way for the Messiah.

Selecting Preaching and Teaching Passages in Esther

Since the book of Esther is a ten-chapter narrative, it does not seem to be easily divided into smaller preachable units. A preaching series that moves from chapter to chapter may break the flow of the story. Above is a suggested one-sermon approach to preaching Esther, reflecting the overall idea of the book. One may choose a different approach.

Getting the Subject, Complement, Exegetical Idea, and Homiletical Idea

See above.

Difficult Passages/Verses

Perhaps the most disturbing element in the narrative is the moral ambiguity of the characters, particularly Esther and Mordecai. Esther hides her ethnicity and her religious convictions until much later in the story—which is a violation of the Torah (2:10)—following the advice of her uncle, Mordecai. She is part of a harem and eventually loses her virginity as an unmarried woman to a gentile (2:15–18). She does not act on protecting her people until Mordecai urges her to do so (chap. 4). When victory over Haman is celebrated, she extends the slaughter for another day so that Haman's sons may be hung on the gallows, slaughtering three hundred more gentiles (9:13–17).

In addition, Mordecai refuses to recognize Haman's position, which catapulted him to replace Haman. But there appears to be no reason why Mordecai did not bow to Haman (3:5; 5:9). His conversation with Esther about "such a time as this" could be seen as a veiled threat to reveal her identity as a Jew (4:12–14).

Throughout the narrative is the backdrop of sensuality and ruthlessness; neither are explained nor commented on in the story itself. The careful reader will want to take into consideration the nature and function of Hebrew literature of this period.

Cultural Perspectives and Application

In light of this ambiguity, the exegete will want to keep in mind biblical history. Mordecai the Jew (a Benjaminite) is pitted against Haman an Agagite (another way of saying Amalekite)—both peoples sworn enemies of the other. The Jews are spared from annihilation, another way of saying holy war. The wars of Saul and Kish (1 Sam. 15) are reminiscent in this narrative, especially chapters 9–10.

Application of this text urges the preacher to help listeners see the doctrine of providence in action, for God is present in every turn of the narrative.

RECOMMENDED RESOURCES

Duguid, Iain M. *Esther and Ruth*. Reformed Expository Commentary. Phillipsburg, NJ: P&R, 2005.

Firth, David G. *The Message of Esther: God Present but Unseen*. The Bible Speaks Today. Downers Grove, IL: InterVarsity, 2010.

Jobes, Karen H. *Esther*. The NIV Application Commentary. Grand Rapids: Zondervan, 1999.

Phillips, Elaine A. "Esther." In *Ezra, Nehemiah, Esther*, edited by Tremper Longman III and David E. Garland, 569–674. The Expositor's Bible Commentary. Grand Rapids: Zondervan, 2010.

Job

KEN SHIGEMATSU

The book of Job is regarded as one of the great literary treasures of the world. In the first verse we read, "There was a man in the land of Uz whose name was Job, and that man was blameless and upright" (1:1 ESV). An ancient person would have heard these opening words the way we hear "Once upon a time" or "In a galaxy far, far away." We are invited into a story. While the Bible itself affirms Job as a historical figure (Ezra 14:14; James 5:11), the book's author desires that we hear God speak to us through the medium of story and poetry.

The timeless quality of Job complements the other books of Wisdom literature in the Bible. While Proverbs shows us how God's wisdom tends to work in everyday life and Ecclesiastes displays the exceptions to the rule, the book of Job explores wisdom in the midst of painful and confusing circumstances. By guiding us through Job's experiences, the author calls us to pursue questions about God in a broken world that don't always make sense. The book of Job invites our pain, anger, questions, and doubts. Rather than providing simplistic answers, it invites us to learn through our greatest suffering that God is the only answer to our most challenging questions.

Ultimately, both the book and the character of Job point us to the greater Job: the one truly innocent sufferer, who endured not only physical agony and social ostracization but also bore our sin upon himself, so that we who deserve to suffer the consequences of our sin might experience forgiveness, redemption, and restoration.

SUBJECT: How, in a world where even godly people suffer, can readers of Job understand the nature of God's character?

COMPLEMENT: That God is all-powerful and good.

EXEGETICAL IDEA: In a world where even godly people suffer, readers of Job can understand the nature of God's character: that God is all-powerful and good.

HOMILETICAL IDEA: Even in pain we can trust God's power and providence.

Selecting Preaching and Teaching Passages in Job

The book of Job contains forty-two chapters, but for the sake of coherence and concision—as many of the themes repeat especially in the cycle of speeches—Job can be preached in five (or fewer) sermons. Only selected passages will be discussed within the chapter ranges in the section that follows.

The book of Job has three main parts: prologue, dialogue, and epilogue. The dialogue contains five cycles of poetic conversations between Job and his friends and then Job and God.

Getting the Subject, Complement, Exegetical Idea, and Homiletical Idea

Job 1–2

This sermon could introduce Job as an upright, righteous person (1:1–3) who experiences catastrophic loss (1:13–2:8). The message would focus on how suffering enables Job (and us) to demonstrate that we love God for God's sake, not because knowing God benefits us (1:20–22). A subtheme of the sermon could be that there are no simple answers to the problem of suffering (in Job's case, Satan is involved; 1:6–2:7). This message could also show how even people of genuine faith experience deep anguish and mourning (1:20).

SUBJECT: What opportunity does suffering offer people?

COMPLEMENT: To show that they love God for God's sake, not because God benefits them.

EXEGETICAL IDEA: Suffering offers people the opportunity to show that they love God for God's sake, not because God benefits them.

HOMILETICAL IDEA: In our suffering, we can show that we love God for God's sake, not because of what we get from God.

Job 3-31

This sermon could cover the speeches of Job's friends from Job 4–31. It could discuss how Job exerts superhuman spiritual strength by praising God in the midst of his devastating calamities (1:20–21), but then begins to cry out, "Why? Why? Why?" and curses the day he was born (Job 3). A preacher could then explain how Job's friends are right in visiting him in the midst of his troubles and acknowledging his pain through their presence and tears (2:11–13). The takeaway here is that we should not avoid people who are suffering, but instead be present to them, acknowledge their pain and serve them in ways that provide support, such as listening or providing a meal. Finally, a preacher could take a selection from the speeches of Eliphaz, Bildad, and Zophar and demonstrate how, when they speak into Job's suffering, they offer simplistic and unhelpful answers, such as asserting that the innocent always prosper and evil people always perish (4:7–9).

SUBJECT: How do Job's friends respond to his suffering?

COMPLEMENT: By offering presence and tears and then simplistic and unhelpful answers.

EXEGETICAL IDEA: Job's friends respond to his suffering by offering presence and tears and then simplistic and unhelpful answers.

HOMILETICAL IDEA: When people suffer, offer your presence and your tears—not simplistic answers.

Job 32-37

This sermon could cover selections of Elihu's speech (Job 32–37). While he repeats some of the same arguments as Job's three friends, who contend that the innocent prosper and evil people suffer, he seems to offer a more enlightened perspective. Job contests the speeches of Eliphaz, Bildad, and Zophar but not Elihu's speech. At the end of the book of Job, God looks back over Job's suffering and rebukes his three friends Eliphaz, Bildad, and Zophar but does not rebuke Elihu. While Elihu's words are not flawless, one could preach a sermon on his discussion of how God speaks to us and refines us through suffering (33:14–19; 36:15).

SUBJECT: How does Elihu respond to Job?

COMPLEMENT: By repeating some of the same simplistic arguments as Job's three friends, but he offers a more enlightened perspective of how God speaks to humanity and refines people through suffering.

EXEGETICAL IDEA: Elihu responds to Job's suffering by repeating some of the same simplistic arguments as Job's three friends, but he offers a more enlightened perspective of how God speaks to humanity and refines people through suffering.

HOMILETICAL IDEA: God can reveal himself and refine us through suffering.

Job 38–42

This sermon focuses on God breaking his silence through two speeches. In God's first speech, he asks over fifty questions and demonstrates his understanding of and control over the universe, and by contrast how much Job (and we) do not know. In God's second speech, he focuses on his power over chaotic, powerful creatures such as Behemoth and Leviathan. These creatures likely not only represent the hippopotamus and the crocodile, respectively, but are also symbols of cosmic evil. God has power over cosmic evil. God does not answer Job's questions or those of his friends, but instead gives his presence. While Job likely still has questions about his suffering and why there is evil in the world, when he "sees" God, Job also experiences a certain level of peace and repents of his accusations that God is unjust (42:5–6). In a way that dovetails with Proverbs, the book of Job affirms that the fear of the Lord is the beginning of wisdom (Job 28:28; Prov. 9:10).

SUBJECT: How does God reveal himself to Job?

COMPLEMENT: God shows his wisdom and power through a series of questions that Job cannot answer and by demonstrating his power over cosmic evil.

EXEGETICAL IDEA: God reveals himself to Job by showing his wisdom and power through a series of questions that Job cannot answer and by demonstrating his power over cosmic evil.

HOMILETICAL IDEA: God's wisdom is beyond our understanding, and his power is greater than cosmic evil.

Job 42

This sermon would focus on the epilogue of the book of Job, affirming that the God who speaks to Job from the storm controls the universe (Job 38–41). In addition, the preacher could draw on the book of Revelation and affirm that the slain lamb is on the throne of the universe (Rev. 5:6). While we see in both Job's life and in the book of Revelation that there is great suffering in the world, some of which is caused by Satan, we also see that God is ultimately in control. The slain lamb shows us that God has vanquished Satan (Col. 2:13–15); though he is still active, he is a defeated foe on a leash. Job's restoration, which includes his being given children and receiving even greater material prosperity, also shows us that God is gracious and good. While we may not experience the same kind of tangible, visible prosperity at the end of our lives as Job did, we will experience a final redemption and restoration in the world to come—a place where there are no more tears, death, mourning, crying, or pain (Rev. 21:4).

SUBJECT: How does God finally provide for Job?

COMPLEMENT: By giving him children, restoring his material prosperity, and vindicating him in the eyes of his detractors.

EXEGETICAL IDEA: God finally provides for Job by giving him children, restoring his material prosperity, and vindicating him in the eyes of his detractors.

HOMILETICAL IDEA: God is good and, in this life or the next, will redeem our suffering and provide complete restoration.

Difficult Passages/Verses

Does God Control the Universe?

The book of Job makes it clear that God is all-powerful and in control of the universe. God is the one who laid the earth's foundations (38:4) and set the constellations in place (9:9; 38:32). God alone establishes the boundaries of the seas (38:8–11) and makes the eagle fly at his command (39:27). God also controls Behemoth (40:15–24) and Leviathan (41:1–34), which likely symbolize cosmic spiritual evil. It is also clear that while Satan is given some freedom, God is ultimately in control. Satan is on a leash (1:6–12; 2:1–6).

Why Is Satan Allowed to Be Active in the World?

There is debate as to whether Satan, literally "the satan" (1:6) or "the accuser," is the devil or an angelic member of the heavenly court. The inclusion of the definite article before "satan" might preclude the idea that this is a proper name. Part of the reason Job is allowed to be tested is so he can demonstrate his integrity before God. As mentioned, however, the interaction between God and the accuser demonstrates God's sovereignty and control over each part of Job's and our lives—the bad and the good.

Are We Allowed to Doubt and Complain to God?

In the book of Job, we see Job complaining about his lot and accusing God (Job 3; 21:4; 23:3–6; 40:8). Yet at the end of the book of Job we see he is deemed (relatively) innocent and vindicated (42:7–8). Grumbling is a sin and distances us from God—for example, when the Israelites complain about their life in the wilderness (Num. 16:31–35; 21:6–7). However, there is a kind of lament that is directed toward God and can lead us closer to him. David's complaints and brutal honesty before God (Pss. 13, 22), as well as Job's ultimately, create a bridge of conversation to God, and God responds (Ps. 22:2–4; Job 38–42).

How Do We Live Wisely in the Midst of Suffering and Brokenness?

The book of Job shows us that there are purposes to suffering we may not be aware of (1:6–12; 2:1–6). It is also clear that our suffering is not necessarily the result of our sin (42:7–9). Job's "friends" are often wrong in their content and tone, but occasionally they are correct. Job's friend Eliphaz speaks truth when he asserts that suffering can be used by God to discipline us (5:17; cf. Heb. 12:5–6). Elihu also rightly contends that God delivers the afflicted by their affliction and speaks to us in our suffering (36:15). We also see that God will ultimately redeem our suffering—if not in this life, certainly in the world to come (42:7–17). In the book of James (5:10–11) we are called to follow the example of Job's patience and live with hope, seeing what the Lord finally brought about in his life. Scripture affirms in Job and other places that God redeems our suffering (Rom. 5:3–5; 8:28–30; 1 Pet. 4:12–19; Rev. 21:4).

Does God Care When We Suffer?

Job doesn't understand why he is suffering. He feels that God does not care and is not aware of his affliction (Job 3; 23:1–6). When we suffer, we can feel as though God does not see us or care. But in Job's situation this is not the case. He did not know he was on "center stage" before God and that God was on his side (1:6–12). The life and death of Jesus also shout an emphatic "Yes!" to the question "Does God care when we suffer?" Jesus is not indifferent to our suffering; Jesus experienced suffering firsthand during his earthly lifetime (Heb. 4:15), and on the cross he experienced affliction like none of us will have to endure. In Revelation, John says that after he saw heaven coming to earth, a voice called out saying, "He will wipe away every tear from their eyes, and death shall be no more, neither shall there be mourning, nor crying, nor pain anymore, for the former things have passed away" (21:4 ESV). We also know that Jesus cares because when he returns, he will remove our suffering.

Cultural Perspectives and Application

What applications can we draw from this ancient but timeless book of Job?

There are no easy answers to suffering. The book of Job refutes a karmic understanding of life where we always get what we deserve. Our lives are not as simple as a mathematical formula in which we are at the center.

Job's three friends express their thoughts with great poetry and some truth, but generally provide overly simplistic applications. Their presence in silence with tears is exemplary, but their explanations for why Job is suffering actually hurt him. How do we walk (and not walk) with others through suffering?

Consider and speak to the actual pain and challenges that people in your congregation are experiencing: loss of a loved one, wayward children, infertility, financial stress, health concerns, social isolation, a difficult relationship, unwanted singleness, pain from childhood memories, depression, mental illness, addiction, identity issues, inability to find a job, and so on.

Remember that wisdom is found in God alone. While we understand some things, there is much we don't understand. Our relationship with God may be analogous to a dog's relationship with its master—only our ability to understand God may be more than a million times more limited than our dog's ability to understand us! True wisdom comes from the fear of the Lord.

God is on the throne of the universe. God is good. God intends good for us, and our story ultimately, though not necessarily during our lifetime on this earth, has a good ending.

--- RECOMMENDED RESOURCES ---

Andersen, Francis I. *Job*. Tyndale Old Testament Commentaries. Downers Grove, IL: IVP Academic, 2008.

Longman, Tremper, III. *Job*. Baker Commentary on the Old Testament Wisdom and Psalms. Grand Rapids: Baker Academic, 2012.

Rohr, Richard. *Job and the Mystery of Suffering: Spiritual Reflections*. New York: Crossroad, 1998.

The Bible Project (https://bibleproject.com/explore/job) offers two videos and three podcast episodes on Job that are helpful for preachers seeking a quick and easy entry into the book's structure and themes.

Psalms

KENNETH LANGLEY

The Big Idea of Psalms

It is hard to summarize so long and varied a book in one sentence, but the following reflects scholarly consensus that praise and lament are the two main movements in Psalms.

SUBJECT: How do these songs and prayers of the Psalter help God's people fittingly worship him?

COMPLEMENT: They give words of wholehearted praise and honest, reverent lament.

EXEGETICAL IDEA: The songs and prayers of the Psalter help God's people fittingly worship him by supplying words of wholehearted praise and honest, reverent lament.

HOMILETICAL IDEA: God's people worship him with wholehearted praise and honest, reverent lament.

Other candidates for the big idea of Psalms have been proposed. Some believe that every psalm is ultimately about Christ, so the exegetical idea should include reference to him. Some note that kingship dominates the collection; therefore, arguably, "the LORD reigns" is the exegetical idea. Others believe that wisdom is even more prominent than kingship; perhaps the subject of the Psalter is wisdom? The exegetical idea suggested above is broad enough to include these theological themes and has this advantage: it addresses not only what psalms *say* but also what they *do*.

Selecting Preaching and Teaching Passages in Psalms

Few will spend three years preaching straight through the Psalter. More likely, we'll use individual psalms for special occasions (funerals, communal celebrations and dedications, laments when tragedy strikes) or for brief series (psalms of the Lord's kingship, psalms of ascent, penitential psalms for Lent or Communion Sundays). A summer sermon series on Psalms allows continuity with variety; since each sermon can stand alone, vacationers don't miss essential context.

Evidence of intentional editorial arrangement will encourage some preachers to handle groups of psalms sequentially. But these poems can legitimately serve as stand-alone sermon texts without reference to neighboring psalms.

There's no universally accepted system for classifying psalms, and some fit more than one type (a royal psalm or Zion song is also a hymn, a wisdom psalm a lament, etc.). Here you will find suggestions for preaching and teaching laments (Pss. 3, 13, 14, 22, 41, 42, 51, 83, 90, 130, 137, 142), hymns and thanksgivings (Pss. 8, 18, 19, 30, 32, 65, 67, 84, 87, 100, 103, 107, 117, 150), wisdom psalms (Pss. 1, 119, 73, 90, 128, 133, 139), royal psalms and songs of the Lord's kingship (Pss. 2, 72, 97, 98, 99, 110), and others less easily classified. Two imprecatory psalms are included (Pss. 83, 137). Avoid the temptation to preach only the happy psalms: in an age in which celebration seems to be the only permissible mode of worship, we need to recover the legitimacy of lament.

Getting the Subject, Complement, Exegetical Idea, and Homiletical Idea

Psalm 1

The exegetical idea is shaped by the location and function of Psalm 1 as introduction to the collection. The homiletical idea is shaped by imagery: listeners should shrink from a wasted chaff life and long for God to "make me a tree."

SUBJECT: What are the two types of people encountered in Psalms?

COMPLEMENT: The wicked (chaff) and the righteous (trees).

EXEGETICAL IDEA: The two types of people encountered in the Psalms are the wicked (chaff) and the righteous (trees).

HOMILETICAL IDEA: There are two kinds of people in the world: tree people and chaff people.

Psalm 2

We "overhear" God's dismissive laughter, his warning to the rebels, and his words to his Son, and we're encouraged. One sermon on Psalm 2 is titled "The Contagious Serenity of God's Laughter."

SUBJECT: How shall God's people live in a world where the powerful disdain God's Anointed?

COMPLEMENT: With confidence that God who laughs at their resistance still rules.

EXEGETICAL IDEA: God's people can live in a world where the powerful disdain God's Anointed with confidence that God who laughs at their resistance still rules.

HOMILETICAL IDEA: God is not threatened or thrown by earthly powers, and neither are we who trust his Son.

Psalm 3

This is the first of many laments asking protection from enemies. But these prayers are not all the same; don't preach them all the same! This one, uniquely, invites us to sleep, trusting God to handle our numerous troubles.

SUBJECT: How can God's servant face the threats and taunts of multiple enemies?

COMPLEMENT: With confidence that God hears, sustains, and delivers.

EXEGETICAL IDEA: God's servant can face the threats and taunts of multiple enemies with confidence because God hears, sustains, and delivers.

HOMILETICAL IDEA: Even when surrounded by troubles, we can sleep like a log because God sustains us.

Psalm 5

One distinctive shaping this homiletical idea differently from that of other psalms is the longer than usual opening appeal for a hearing, which concludes with a resolution to wait.

SUBJECT: What does the psalmist want God to do about the wicked and the righteous?

COMPLEMENT: To bring down the wicked and to protect the righteous and grant them joy.

EXEGETICAL IDEA: The psalmist wants God to deal with the wicked and protect righteous people and grant them joy.

HOMILETICAL IDEA: We ask God to deal with evil and to protect us; then we wait in expectation.

Psalm 8

God is majestic, of course, but surprisingly, so are humans. We have a noble and humbling role as rulers and stewards of his creation. This psalm almost begs for application to ecological responsibility and connection to Christ (Heb. 2).

SUBJECT: How is the majesty of God seen?

COMPLEMENT: In his creation and in his granting humans responsibility for his creation.

EXEGETICAL IDEA: The majesty of God is seen in his creation and in his granting humans responsibility for his creation.

HOMILETICAL IDEA: The majesty of God is reflected in the majesty of humans, his appointed lords and stewards of creation.

Psalm 11

Stay put! You might want to run away and hide. Well-meaning friends (or are they enemies?) may counsel you to do so. But with God as refuge, you can confidently stand your ground.

SUBJECT: How does David resist the temptation and counsel to flee from trouble?

COMPLEMENT: By taking refuge in his just and all-seeing God.

EXEGETICAL IDEA: David resists the temptation and counsel to flee from trouble by taking refuge in his just and all-seeing God.

HOMILETICAL IDEA: When tempted and counseled to run away, stay put in God your refuge.

Psalm 12

The sins most commonly mentioned in Psalms are sins of the lips. God's people are expected to speak truly and, as here, petition God for protection from ungodly speech.

SUBJECT: For what problem does David want help from God?

COMPLEMENT: The lying, flattering, boastful, malignant speech of the wicked.

EXEGETICAL IDEA: The problem David needs God's help with is protection from the lying, flattering, boastful, malignant speech of the wicked.[1]

HOMILETICAL IDEA: God, deliver us and our culture from the devastating effects of ungodly speech.

Psalm 13

The big idea suggested here summarizes not the text's affirmations (the poem consists mostly of questions and petition) but its thrust or intention. Psalm 13 models reverent lament; the sermon lets listeners know they can do the same.

SUBJECT: How does David handle long waiting for deliverance from trouble?

COMPLEMENT: By pleading honestly and earnestly with God.

EXEGETICAL IDEA: David handles long waiting for deliverance by pleading honestly and earnestly with God.

HOMILETICAL IDEA: If it seems God is taking a long time to meet your need, tell him so.

Psalm 14

Bad guys are everywhere, frustrating and devouring God's people. But (by faith, v. 5) we can see them overwhelmed (already or in the future?) by dread of God.

SUBJECT: When surrounded by evil, what can the righteous do?

COMPLEMENT: Realize it's the evildoers who should be scared and rejoice in the presence and salvation of God.

EXEGETICAL IDEA: When surrounded by evil, the righteous can realize it's the evildoers who should be scared and rejoice in the presence and salvation of God.

HOMILETICAL IDEA: The bad guys are the ones who should be scared, so rejoice in your salvation.

Psalm 15

Psalm 15 does not teach works righteousness but does insist (and the sermon must insist) that those who by grace have a relationship with God will, in some degree, manifest God-honoring character. Let the big idea do its

---

1. Here and elsewhere, "David" in the exegetical idea does not imply a definitive judgment that he is the author.

convicting work; then proclaim mercy in the closing prayer, hymn, or Lord's Table.

SUBJECT: Who may dwell with God?

COMPLEMENT: Only the blameless in word and deed.

EXEGETICAL IDEA: Only the blameless in word and deed may dwell with God.

HOMILETICAL IDEA: God welcomes into relationship with him only the blameless in word and deed.

Psalm 16

New Testament usage indicates that the soaring claims of this psalm apply even more perfectly to David's Greater Son than to the poet himself. David is fully satisfied in God, fully devoted to God, secure for this life and the next.

SUBJECT: Why is David not shaken, even at the prospect of dying?

COMPLEMENT: He trusts and prizes God for time and eternity.

EXEGETICAL IDEA: David is not shaken, even by the prospect of dying, because he trusts and prizes God for time and eternity.

HOMILETICAL IDEA: Trust God, prize God, and nothing will shake you.

Psalm 18

What holds together the testimony, assertions, and petitions of this long psalm? God is a rock! Make this image prominent in the sermon. Then sing some "rock" songs. "Faith" is a better word here than "trust," because we know David was not righteous by works but by faith, and because verse 25 uses the vocabulary of faithfulness.

SUBJECT: How is David able to survive desperate situations with integrity?

COMPLEMENT: By faith in God, his rock.

EXEGETICAL IDEA: David is able to survive desperate situations with integrity by faith in God his rock.

HOMILETICAL IDEA: God is a rock!

Psalm 19

This psalm is a beautiful lyric celebrating God's self-disclosure in the heavens and in his law/statutes. What we see there makes us long to live blamelessly before our awesome Creator-Redeemer. This one is a joy to preach. And it gives us in the last verse a fitting prayer for any time we preach.

SUBJECT: Where does God reveal himself to human eyes?

COMPLEMENT: In the heavens and in his Word.

EXEGETICAL IDEA: God reveals himself to human eyes in the heavens and in his Word.

HOMILETICAL IDEA: Meet God in these two books: the sky and the Scriptures.

Psalm 22

Pain and praise alternate in this lament, but praise gets the last word. All the world, even future generations (including those who hear the sermon), will honor God for how he responds to his people's afflictions (including the innocent suffering of Jesus).

SUBJECT: How does David voice his experience of Godforsakenness?

COMPLEMENT: By recognizing that God has not hidden his face.

EXEGETICAL IDEA: David voices his experience of Godforsakenness by recognizing God has not hidden his face from his servant.

HOMILETICAL IDEA: God has not forsaken us.

Psalm 24

God is not confined to a box or tent (vv. 1–2), and no one is worthy to have him live with them (vv. 3–6), but if a great and gracious God is at our gate, what do we do? We let him in (vv. 7–10)!

SUBJECT: What should God's people do when God condescends to dwell with them?

COMPLEMENT: Open their city and their hearts and let him in.

EXEGETICAL IDEA: When God condescends to come dwell with his people, they should open their city and their hearts and let him in.

HOMILETICAL IDEA: When the King is at the gate, let him in.

Psalm 27

"One thing I ask." David's troubles include war (v. 3), slander (v. 12), maybe even betrayal by his own parents (v. 10), but he remains confident that God is with him. And this is all he asks for. The preacher can echo David and cast the big idea as testimony.

SUBJECT: What sustains David in trouble?

COMPLEMENT: Confidence in God, and that is all he needs or wants.

EXEGETICAL IDEA: In times of trouble David is sustained by confidence in God, and that is all he needs or wants.

HOMILETICAL IDEA: All I need, all I want, is God.

Psalm 29

In an awesome, literal storm the powerful voice of God is heard. Heaven's hosts cry, "Glory!" And the King, serenely enthroned above the tumult, blesses his people with peace.

SUBJECT: What prompts angels and God's people to glorify him in the storm?

COMPLEMENT: The powerful voice of God and the peace he grants.

EXEGETICAL IDEA: Angels and God's people glorify him in the storm for his powerful voice and the peace he grants.

HOMILETICAL IDEA: Glorify God for his powerful voice and the peace he grants in the storm.

Psalm 30

David testifies to a time God lifted him from unspecified depths. The sermon can retell one or more similar situations and assure listeners that "joy comes with the morning."

SUBJECT: What does David testify to learning when God lifts him from the depths?

COMPLEMENT: The darkness doesn't last, and rejoicing comes in the morning.

EXEGETICAL IDEA: David testifies to learning that when God lifts him from the depths the darkness doesn't last, and rejoicing comes in the morning.

HOMILETICAL IDEA: Weeping may remain for a night, but joy comes in the morning!

Psalm 32

Don't be stubborn. Learn from David what a relief it is to confess sin and know the joy of forgiveness. The sermon can flesh out the misery of unconfessed sin and the sense of relief David felt. Note the "cover" vocabulary of verses 1 and 5.

SUBJECT: What does David learn from his experience of confession and forgiveness?

COMPLEMENT: Covering sin leads to misery, but confession leads to rejoicing.

EXEGETICAL IDEA: David learns from his experience of confession and forgiveness that covering sin leads to misery, but confession leads to rejoicing.

HOMILETICAL IDEA: Happy are those who don't cover up sin but let God cover it up.

Psalm 41

David's illness is made more painful by his enemies' gloating and his friend's betrayal. Jesus knows what that is like (John 13:18). Though a sinner, David is a man of integrity; as such, he looks to God for healing, forgiveness, and vindication.

SUBJECT: What does David do when sick, harassed, and betrayed?

COMPLEMENT: He trusts God for healing, forgiveness, and vindication.

EXEGETICAL IDEA: When David is sick, harassed, and betrayed, he trusts God for healing, forgiveness, and vindication.

HOMILETICAL IDEA: When afflicted by illness and other people, keep your integrity and trust God for healing, forgiveness, and vindication.

Psalm 42

Sometimes the big idea captures not just what the writer says but what he *does* with what he says. Here, speaking about spiritual depression, both what the poet says and the fact and manner of his saying it are instructive. Note his refrain. Consider preaching Psalms 42 and 43 together.

SUBJECT: What does the psalmist do when God seems far away?

COMPLEMENT: He speaks honestly both to God and to himself.

EXEGETICAL IDEA: When God seems far away, the psalmist speaks honestly to God and to himself.

HOMILETICAL IDEA: When God seems far away, it's time for an honest talk with him—and with yourself.

Psalm 51

This is the best-known penitential psalm. What David longs for is not only forgiveness but also restored joy, after which he'll testify publicly of God's goodness. There's no reason to doubt or ignore the superscription of this poem that links it to the Bathsheba affair.

SUBJECT: What does David do when convicted of his adultery with Bathsheba?

COMPLEMENT: He pleads with God for forgiveness and renewal, leading to testimony.

EXEGETICAL IDEA: When convicted of his adultery with Bathsheba, David pleads with God for forgiveness and renewal, leading to testimony.

HOMILETICAL IDEA: Forgiveness and restored joy in God can be yours for the asking.

Psalm 65

This poem turns, somewhat surprisingly, from praising God for salvation to celebrating his providence over creation (particularly agriculture). Both need to find their way into the big idea. Watch for other places in the Psalter where creation themes make a surprising appearance.

SUBJECT: Why is praise due God from the people of Zion?

COMPLEMENT: He has rescued them and provides for them.

EXEGETICAL IDEA: Praise is due God from the people of Zion because he has delivered them and provides for them.

HOMILETICAL IDEA: Let's give God the praise due him for his powerful deliverance and abundant provision.

Psalm 67

Poetics make this psalm's main point unmistakable: it comes in the middle (a chiastic structure), has three lines (every other verse has two), and is bracketed by a refrain. The poem begins and ends hoping God will bless us, but that blessing is tied to his intentions for *all* peoples.

SUBJECT: What is learned here about God blessing all peoples?

COMPLEMENT: It's inseparable from the joy and praise of the nations.

EXEGETICAL IDEA: God's blessing all peoples is inseparable from the joy and praise of the nations.

HOMILETICAL IDEA: God, bless us—and all the nations!

Psalm 72

We don't have a king to pray for, but like Israel we long for good government. We'll get it at the return of Christ (the sermon's conclusion might express this longing), but till then here's a model for what we pray and labor for.

SUBJECT: What kind of king does this psalm ask God for?

COMPLEMENT: One who is just, stable, and successful and defends the vulnerable.

EXEGETICAL IDEA: The kind of king this psalm asks for is one who is just, stable, successful and who defends the vulnerable.

HOMILETICAL IDEA: God, grant us good government—and come, Lord Jesus!

Psalm 73

Here's long-range perspective to keep us from envying the prosperous wicked. That perspective comes to the poet in a flash of insight in God's house.

SUBJECT: Why does the poet think faithfulness to God is in vain, and what changes his mind?

COMPLEMENT: He envies the prosperous wicked but then realizes that God, his treasure, will bring them to ruin.

EXEGETICAL IDEA: The poet thinks faithfulness to God is in vain because he envies the prosperous wicked, but then he realizes that God, his treasure, will bring them to ruin.

HOMILETICAL IDEA: When good things happen to bad people, see things long-term and keep God as your all-satisfying treasure.

Psalm 78

This long psalm tells a sad story with a happy conclusion. God did so much for them, but (the key word!) they turned away again and again. But (again!) he remains faithful: he gives them David (and, we know now, David's Greater Son).

SUBJECT: What is Israel's story?

COMPLEMENT: God does them good; they keep rebelling, but he gives them David.

EXEGETICAL IDEA: Israel's story shows that God does them good; they rebel, but he gives them David.

HOMILETICAL IDEA: Despite Israel's failures and ours, God gives us a Great King.

Psalm 83

This is not the most disturbing of the imprecatory psalms, but it does illustrate the motivation of those who pray like this.

SUBJECT: Why does Israel pray for the destruction of enemies?

COMPLEMENT: Not only for their own protection but also so all people will revere God.

EXEGETICAL IDEA: Israel prays for the destruction of enemies not only for their own protection but also so all people will revere God.

HOMILETICAL IDEA: We may pray for God to destroy evil, not primarily for our sake but for his.

Psalm 84

Echo this poem's longing for God in vocabulary, tone, music, and the wording of the big idea. This is the only psalm to use "blessed" three times: blessed are those who live at the sanctuary, those on pilgrimage, and *all* who trust the Lord Almighty.

SUBJECT: What experience is modeled and evoked in this hymn?

COMPLEMENT: Longing for God's presence.

EXEGETICAL IDEA: The experience modeled and evoked in this hymn is longing for God's presence.

HOMILETICAL IDEA: Lord, I want to be where you are, in your dwelling place forever.

Psalm 87

One of several psalms displaying God's missionary heart, this song envisions God rejoicing as he records some surprising names in his book. The psalm may be especially applicable to congregations in changing communities, where some of the names on their rolls are new and different.

SUBJECT: Who will God include in his "Registry of the Redeemed"?

COMPLEMENT: Gentiles, even enemies.

EXEGETICAL IDEA: God includes in his "Registry of the Redeemed" even Israel's enemies.

HOMILETICAL IDEA: Rejoice with God over these surprising birth announcements.

Psalm 90

Verse 12 voices our appropriate response when we realize our all-too-brief lives are in the hands of a God who is not happy about our sin.

SUBJECT: How should mortals, sinners whose lives are in God's hands, pray?

COMPLEMENT: With consideration of the brevity of life and asking for wisdom and mercy.

EXEGETICAL IDEA: Mortals, sinners whose lives are in God's hands, should pray with consideration of the brevity of life and ask for wisdom and mercy.

HOMILETICAL IDEA: Lord, help us count our days and make our days count.

Psalm 91

This psalm of trust is so straightforward the homiletical idea almost writes itself. The difficulty is that it may seem to overpromise. The preacher needs to sound its robust promises yet remind listeners that it is poetry, not some kind of contract.

SUBJECT: What can harm the one who trusts in God?

COMPLEMENT: Nothing.

EXEGETICAL IDEA: Nothing can harm the one who trusts in God.

HOMILETICAL IDEA: Nothing can harm the one who trusts in God.

Psalm 97

This is one of those psalms that say quite clearly how to respond to their message: those who love the Lord should rejoice in his reign and hate evil. Reverent fear is not spelled out but implied in verses 2–7. The homiletical idea supplies a four-point sermon outline.

SUBJECT: How should Israel, like all people, respond to God's reign?

COMPLEMENT: With reverence, rejoicing, and hatred of evil.

EXEGETICAL IDEA: Israel, and all people, should respond to God's reign with rejoicing, reverence, and hatred of evil.

HOMILETICAL IDEA: God reigns so rejoice; fear him and hate evil.

Psalm 98

This is another psalm that leaves no doubt about what we're to do and why.
This one (the source for the hymn "Joy to the World") commands us to join
all creation in song, "for he has done marvelous things" (v. 1). This would
make a good Christmas text; follow the sermon with the carol.

SUBJECT: How and why should all people join creation in praising God?

COMPLEMENT: Sing joyfully for his marvelous deeds.

EXEGETICAL IDEA: All people should join creation in praising God, singing joyfully for his marvelous deeds.

HOMILETICAL IDEA: With all creation, let's sing for joy for God's marvelous
deeds.

Psalm 99

The verbs in this psalm are summed up by "worship." Reasons are summed
up by "he is holy." This vocabulary makes it easy to identify the poem's big
idea (here stated in two short sentences for variety). "He is holy" also marks
refrains and provides a clear outline.

SUBJECT: Why does the psalmist say that all people, especially Israel, should
worship the King?

COMPLEMENT: Because he is holy.

EXEGETICAL IDEA: The psalmist says that all people, especially Israel, should
worship the King because he is holy.

HOMILETICAL IDEA: Worship the King for he is holy.

Psalm 100

Consider stating the big idea as an imperative or invitation. The indicative
"We should . . ." means the same thing, but it gets old if used every week.
Also, consider using the words of the text itself when stating the idea; in this
case the word "gladness" is an obvious choice.

SUBJECT: Why are those who belong to God invited to worship with gladness?

COMPLEMENT: God is good and God loves them.

EXEGETICAL IDEA: Those who belong to God are invited to worship him with gladness because he's good and he loves them.

HOMILETICAL IDEA: Worship God gladly because he's good and he loves us.

Psalm 103

This psalm is a familiar, upbeat praise song. What distinguishes it from similar hymns is the call to "forget not."

SUBJECT: Why should everyone everywhere praise the Lord?

COMPLEMENT: Because of his manifold gifts, deeds, and loving character.

EXEGETICAL IDEA: Everyone everywhere should praise the Lord for his manifold gifts, deeds, and loving character.

HOMILETICAL IDEA: Praise the Lord and forget not all his benefits!

Psalm 107

This psalm offers five scenarios in which God comes through for his people. Develop each with imaginative retellings and similar contemporary situations. The expected refrain of thanks is missing at the end: preacher and congregation can supply it as a fitting exclamation point for the sermon.

SUBJECT: How does God demonstrate his unfailing love in this psalm?

COMPLEMENT: By rescuing people from varied perils.

EXEGETICAL IDEA: In this psalm God demonstrates his unfailing love by rescuing people from varied perils.

HOMILETICAL IDEA: Through many dangers, toils, and snares, trust God to rescue you and thank him for his unfailing love.

Psalm 110

Jesus and his apostles view David as a prophet who spoke here of no ordinary descendant. Exposition can begin with the ancient setting but will soon make the New Testament-authorized move to Christ.

SUBJECT: What does David prophesy about God's chosen King?

COMPLEMENT: God will crush his enemies, extend his rule, and make him priest as well as monarch.

EXEGETICAL IDEA: David prophesies about God's chosen King that this King will crush his enemies, extend his rule, and be a priest as well as a monarch.

HOMILETICAL IDEA: Honor our King and Priest, whose victorious rule is ensured by God.

Psalms 111–12

These poems are paired, linked by acrostic structure and thematic similarities. Together their big idea differs from that of two separate sermons. Psalm 111 says what God is like, Psalm 112 what the God-fearing person is like: they're like God! The last verse of 111 is the literary-theological link.

SUBJECT: What is the God-fearing person like?

COMPLEMENT: God.

EXEGETICAL IDEA: The God-fearing person is like God.

HOMILETICAL IDEA: The God-fearing person is like God.

Psalm 117

In *Biblical Preaching*, Haddon Robinson uses this psalm (the "little giant" of the Psalter) as an example of texts with an uncomplicated subject and complement.[2]

SUBJECT: Why should everybody praise the Lord?

COMPLEMENT: Because his love is great and his faithfulness is eternal.

EXEGETICAL IDEA: Everyone should praise the Lord because his love is great and his faithfulness is eternal.

HOMILETICAL IDEA: Praise the Lord for his great love and everlasting faithfulness.

Psalm 119

All but two lines of this giant acrostic piece extol the Word of God. A sermon might select verses representing various situations and needs addressed, or unpack the meaning of "ordinances," "statutes, "law," and so on.

SUBJECT: What does this long acrostic poem teach about God's Word?

COMPLEMENT: It comprehensively addresses all human needs and situations.

---

2. See Haddon W. Robinson, *Biblical Preaching: The Development and Delivery of Expository Messages* (Grand Rapids: Baker Academic, 2014), 23.

EXEGETICAL IDEA: This long acrostic poem teaches that God's Word comprehensively addresses all human needs and situations.

HOMILETICAL IDEA: God's Word speaks to all life from A to Z.

Psalm 128

Israel valued family more than many Christians do. But we have something to learn from this and the preceding psalm about the value God places on family.

SUBJECT: How does the poet image God's blessing on those who fear him?

COMPLEMENT: In terms of a large family, long life, and seeing one's grandchildren.

EXEGETICAL IDEA: The poet images God's blessing on those who fear him in terms of a large family, long life, and seeing one's grandchildren.

HOMILETICAL IDEA: Thank God for the blessing of children and grandchildren!

Psalm 130

"The depths" (v. 1) are usually the poet's circumstances; here the problem is his own sin and God's frown. The mercy he requests is not deliverance from bad guys but restored joy.

SUBJECT: What does the psalmist do when he is not experiencing God's smile on his life?

COMPLEMENT: He resolves to trust and to wait for light to dawn again.

EXEGETICAL IDEA: When the psalmist is not experiencing God's smile on his life, he resolves to keep trusting, waiting for light to dawn again.

HOMILETICAL IDEA: Wait for the Lord and wait for the morning.

Psalm 131

David, warrior-king, type-A mover and shaker is, in God's grip, like a child, a *weaned* child, old enough to consciously choose to leave in God's hands what belongs there.

SUBJECT: How does the poet picture trust in God?

COMPLEMENT: As a weaned child, secure in his mother's arms.

EXEGETICAL IDEA: The poet pictures trust in God as a weaned child, secure in his mother's arms.

HOMILETICAL IDEA: Like a trusting toddler, leave in God's hands what belongs there.

Psalm 133

This uncomplicated psalm makes its point by word pictures familiar to David's first hearers but not to ours. We may need more contemporary illustrations of unity. And we may choose to state the homiletical idea as a prayer.

SUBJECT: Why does the psalmist commend and picture unity?

COMPLEMENT: God chooses to richly bless unity.

EXEGETICAL IDEA: The psalmist commends and pictures unity because God chooses to richly bless unity.

HOMILETICAL IDEA: God, make us one!

Psalm 137

Don't skip or allegorize this psalm: God put it here for some reason. If we can't endorse the appalling sentiment of the last line (which asks God to do what Isaiah said God would do), we can still learn something about honest lament.

SUBJECT: How can Israel respond to horrific oppression?

COMPLEMENT: Grieve honestly, remember Jerusalem, and appeal to God to judge rightly.

EXEGETICAL IDEA: Israel can respond to horrific oppression by grieving honestly, remembering Jerusalem, and appealing to God to judge rightly.

HOMILETICAL IDEA: In extreme distress, grieve honestly, remember Jerusalem, and trust God to judge rightly.

Psalm 139

Four stanzas portray God as the all-seeing, the all-present, the all-creative, the all-holy. God is awesome; let the sermon be delivered with a sense of awe. Let congregational music and prayer echo the final two verses.

SUBJECT: How does David respond to God's knowledge and presence?

COMPLEMENT: With awe and a desire to live in agreement with God.

EXEGETICAL IDEA: David responds to God's intimate knowledge and presence with awe and a desire to live in agreement with God.

HOMILETICAL IDEA: God, you're awesome, so help us live in agreement with you.

Psalm 142

Laments may sound much the same, but if we pay attention to details and not just their similar form and subject matter, we'll see that their subjects and big ideas do vary. In this prayer David's troubles are made worse by the sense that he's *alone*.

SUBJECT: Who can David turn to when he is alone in his trouble?

COMPLEMENT: God, his refuge.

EXEGETICAL IDEA: When David is alone in his trouble, he can turn to God as his refuge.

HOMILETICAL IDEA: We're never truly alone if God is our refuge.

Psalm 150

Preach this exuberant conclusion to the Psalter early in the service, then lead the congregation in accepting its invitation. The text's mood is preserved if the homiletical idea drops the word "should" and issues a warm, compelling imperative. A four-movement outline follows: Where? Everywhere. Why? For everything he is and does. How? With everything we have. Who? Everyone.

SUBJECT: Who should praise God?

COMPLEMENT: Everyone everywhere, for what he is and does, and wholeheartedly.

EXEGETICAL IDEA: Everyone everywhere should praise the Lord wholeheartedly for what he is and does.

HOMILETICAL IDEA: Everyone everywhere, praise God with everything we have, for everything he is and does!

Difficult Passages/Verses

Some say that Psalms are speech *to* God, not *from* God, so they should be prayed or sung but not preached. Wrong! Pastorally wise, imaginatively rich, beautifully crafted—if these poems aren't suitable preaching texts, what is?

But this literature does present some challenges. The Psalter includes obscure geographic and literary references (some would add "mythological" references). The terseness of Hebrew parallelism presents some ambiguity (maybe, in places, intentional ambiguity). Preachers have to decide whether "of David" always entails Davidic authorship. Dating most of the psalms with certainty is impossible. Scholars differ on whether the collection is more like an anthology or a book that tells a story, and if so, what story? Other difficulties could be mentioned, but four in particular present a challenge for expositors.

First, psalms, even didactic psalms, are poetry. Affect, image, and aesthetics loom large and should not be neglected in the pulpit. Boiling off these features of poetry to preach only the paraphrasable contents dishonors the Spirit who gave these texts as poetry and cheats listeners out of part of their Spirit-intended impact. In some psalms it's hard to identify a single big idea; what holds the poem together is not an overarching idea but an image, mood, or motif. Acrostic psalms achieve unity by a structure that does not survive translation; finding one comprehensive idea in these texts is hard. Although this chapter suggests exegetical and homiletical ideas, sermons on these poems must communicate more than ideas. Sometimes imagery and emotion will be at least as prominent as the propositional contents. The kind of analysis we do with epistles will not serve when identifying the thrust of a poem.

Second, many psalms sound alike: vocabulary, imagery, and structure are repeated. But this doesn't mean that the homiletical ideas of, say, ten lament psalms will be identical: each has its own contribution to make, and sermons on psalms should not all sound the same. If we pay close attention to imagery and emotional tone in these texts, not just the ideas they express, we'll be able to re-present them in all their particularity and richness. Consider using the words of the psalm itself for the big idea (see, for example, the discussions of Pss. 30 and 32).

Third, how do we preach Christ from Psalms? Some (like Ps. 110) are clearly messianic. Others might legitimately connect to Christ but don't make this connection the main point or neglect the original meaning and referents in order to make a beeline for Jesus and Calvary.

Fourth, without doubt, the most difficult psalms to preach are the imprecations (like Pss. 109 and 137, though "curses" can be found in many other places). Should we who follow the one who said "love your enemies" pray like this? For some, the answer is obvious. But a case can be made for careful, theologically nuanced appropriation of these problematic texts by the church and its preachers.[3]

Cultural Perspectives and Application

These hymns and prayers were ancient Israel's, but they're ours too. Like Israel, we enjoy a covenant relationship with the gracious King revealed and

3. See Daniel Michael Nehrbass, *Praying Curses* (Eugene, OR: Pickwick, 2013).

worshiped in Psalms. Like Israel, we praise God for who he is and what he's done. We too bring our pain and perplexity to God in honest, reverent lament. We too need the wisdom, hope, joy, rebuke, and consolation expressed here. We too need to learn how to pray. For many psalms, background circumstances are uncertain. This is actually a boon to preachers: these texts can fit a variety of situations. Preachers should have no trouble—most of the time—applying psalms to contemporary congregations.

Most of the time. Some psalms express love for Jerusalem or temple; we feel something like this for the church, but it's not exactly the same. Some psalms picture blessing as material, agricultural, and military success; what does God's favor look like for New Testament believers? Some extol or pray for the king; should Christian appropriation of these psalms focus on King Jesus, on human government, or both?

What about psalms that mention enemies? Don't trivialize these agonized prayers by equating the psalmists' enemies with neighbors who blast their radios or classmates who mock us for attending church. If our lives or livelihoods aren't threatened, it's better to relate these psalms to demonic enemies or to the persecution of our brothers and sisters around the world.

Western Christians can be quite individualistic in their Bible reading, asking, How does this apply to *me*? Look for corporate applications too: How does this psalm address *us*, our church and the global church?

Some psalms seem to make unrealistic, sweeping promises: "No harm will overtake you" (Ps. 91:10). Really? Be careful not to overpromise; remind listeners that this is poetry, not a contract.

And because we're dealing with poetry, we'll appeal to listeners' emotion, imagination, and aesthetic sense.

- *Emotion.* Learn to exegete feelings, not just ideas. Is this lament a scream or a moan? Is the mood angry or weary? Identify emotion in a text as precisely as you identify ideas.
- *Imagination.* Don't make passing reference to imagery so you can move on to explaining and theologizing. Don't turn the picture of God as rock into abstractions like dependability or strength; preach "God is a rock."
- *Aesthetics.* The psalmists crafted artistic literature, so let's commend the beauty of these texts and the vision they cast. Listeners should think not only "I see this is true" or "So that's how it applies" but also "What a beautiful way to live!"

Don't forget that psalms are prayers and songs—worship texts. Pray and sing your sermon text; use it as a call to worship or benediction. Word your big idea as an invitation to praise. Help your people make psalms their worship language. Cultivate a love for the Psalms and their Lord. In *Reflections on the Psalms*, C. S. Lewis said the best thing the Psalms did for him was express the same delight in God that made David dance.

RECOMMENDED RESOURCES

For a good introduction to Psalms:

Anderson, Bernhard W. *Out of the Depths: The Psalms Speak for Us Today*. 3rd ed. Louisville: Westminster John Knox, 2000.

Resources focused specifically on how to preach and teach psalms:

Ash, Christopher. *Teaching Psalms: From Text to Message*. 2 vols. Fearn, UK: Christian Focus, 2017–18.

Futato, Mark D. *Interpreting the Psalms: An Exegetical Handbook*. Grand Rapids: Kregel, 2007.

Mays, James L. *Preaching and Teaching the Psalms*. Louisville: Westminster John Knox, 2006.

McCann, J. Clinton, and James C. Howell. *Preaching the Psalms*. Nashville: Abingdon, 2001.

Nehrbass, Daniel Michael. *Praying Curses*. Eugene, OR: Pickwick, 2013.

Proverbs

STEVEN D. MATHEWSON

The Big Idea of Proverbs

The book of Proverbs offers its readers the gift of wisdom. The word "wisdom" in the Old Testament is actually the term "skill." It can refer to the skill of garment makers, craftsmen, goldsmiths, sailors, and even professional mourners. In Proverbs, wisdom is the skill of living life in a God-honoring way that adapts to how God made life work. Proverbs argues for the superiority of wisdom over folly (Prov. 1–9) and then explains what the lifestyle of wisdom looks like (Prov. 10–31). Here is the big idea for the entire book:

SUBJECT: What is the result of living wisely?

COMPLEMENT: Success rather than ruin in God's world.

EXEGETICAL IDEA: The result of living wisely is success rather than ruin in God's world.

HOMILETICAL IDEA: Wisdom produces people who succeed in God's world.

Selecting Preaching and Teaching Passages in Proverbs

Proverbs 1–9 is relatively preacher-friendly. These chapters contain a series of "sermonettes" designed to convince the reader to follow a lifestyle of wisdom rather than a lifestyle of folly. The invitations are personified by two women: Lady Wisdom and Madam Folly.

However, all "homiletical hell" breaks loose in chapters 10–31. Most of these chapters contain sayings that appear as if they were drawn one by one from a hat. Here we encounter a debate. Some Old Testament scholars believe the proverbs in chapters 10–29 simply appear in random order.[1] This requires a careful search for sayings that speak to a particular topic. Although God's Spirit could have guided the writers to use a more accessible format (e.g., placing all the sayings on anger in chap. 10, all the sayings on wealth in chap. 11, etc.), the scattering of these sayings forces us to search for wisdom. The search resembles mining for silver (see 2:4) rather than picking up rocks from the surface. Other scholars see a more skillful composition in these chapters rather than a haphazard collection.[2] Still others take a more mediating position, arguing for "thematic clustering" (where two or more sayings are grouped by topic or catchword) but dismissing larger complex structures.[3]

What, then, is a preacher or teacher to do with chapters 10–29? The big ideas given below will reflect both approaches. It is possible to preach blocks of consecutive verses (e.g., 25:1–15 and 26:16–28) as long as one recognizes that the big idea will be a bit more general in its sweep. This is not a problem, though, because a big idea is not a sermon. The treasure is still in the individual sayings. In this case, the big idea distills the teaching of the text into a summary statement that provides a framework for all the individual sayings. There are also five big ideas below that develop topics. These big ideas are based on collecting the various problems that address a particular topic like conflict, speech, wealth, decision-making, or parenting.

Preaching through the entire book of Proverbs requires forty-one sermons (based on the big ideas given below). This consists of eleven sermons on chapters 1–9 and thirty sermons on chapters 10–31. Preachers and teachers might break this up into a two-part (chaps. 1–9 and 10–31) or a three-part (chaps. 1–9, 10–22a, and 22b–31) series. Of course, it might be useful to select some representative texts from each section to provide an overview of Proverbs in eight to twelve weeks.

Another option is to handle the material in chapters 10–29 topically (as in the five final examples below) and preach/teach on five to ten topics. Whatever the approach, preachers and teachers can use the big ideas below as a starting point for sermons and lessons on this tremendous book of wisdom.

1. Tremper Longman III, *Proverbs*, Baker Commentary on the Old Testament Wisdom and Psalms (Grand Rapids: Baker Academic, 2006), 40.

2. See Bruce K. Waltke's two-volume commentary for perhaps the most detailed and most compelling exploration of the editorial structuring of Proverbs 10–29: *The Book of Proverbs*, The New International Commentary on the Old Testament (Grand Rapids: Eerdmans, 2004–5), especially 1:9–28.

3. Michael V. Fox, *Proverbs 10–31*, Anchor Yale Bible (New Haven: Yale University Press, 2009), 478–82.

Getting the Subject, Complement, Exegetical Idea, and Homiletical Idea

Proverbs 1:1-7

SUBJECT: What kind of person does wisdom equip one to become?

COMPLEMENT: A successful person (vv. 1–3a, 4–6), an ethically good person (v. 3b), and a God-fearing person (v. 7).

EXEGETICAL IDEA: Wisdom equips one to become a successful person, an ethically good person, and a God-fearing person.

HOMILETICAL IDEA: Wisdom is good for producing successful, good, and godly people.[4]

Proverbs 1:8-33

SUBJECT: What happens to those who reject wisdom for a life of folly?

COMPLEMENT: They end up destroying their lives.

EXEGETICAL IDEA: Those who reject wisdom for a life of folly end up destroying their lives.

HOMILETICAL IDEA: The cost of rejecting wisdom is self-destruction.

Proverbs 2

SUBJECT: What benefits does one receive for pursuing wisdom?

COMPLEMENT: The knowledge of God (vv. 5–8), a moral compass (vv. 9–15), protection from immorality (vv. 16–19), and a stable life (vv. 20–22).

EXEGETICAL IDEA: The benefits one receives for pursuing wisdom are the knowledge of God, a moral compass, protection from immorality, and a stable life.

HOMILETICAL IDEA: The pursuit of wisdom leads to God and the good life he wants for us.

Proverbs 3:1-12

SUBJECT: What rewards does wisdom provide?

COMPLEMENT: Peace (vv. 1–2), favor (vv. 3–4), success (vv. 5–6), healing (vv. 7–8), prosperity (vv. 9–10), and loving discipline (vv. 11–12).

EXEGETICAL IDEA: The rewards that wisdom provides are peace, favor, success, healing, prosperity, and loving discipline.

HOMILETICAL IDEA: God makes sure that people who live wisely live well.

---

4. Another way to state the homiletical idea is this: The way to improve the quality of your life is to acquire the skill of living it in a God-honoring way.

Proverbs 3:18-35

SUBJECT: How should one live in light of the blessing and security wisdom provides?

COMPLEMENT: By doing good to one's neighbor (vv. 27–30) and not envying fools (vv. 31–35).

EXEGETICAL IDEA: The way to live in light of the blessing and security wisdom provides is by doing good to one's neighbor and not envying fools.

HOMILETICAL IDEA: Wisdom's gifts compel us to do good to others.

Proverbs 4

SUBJECT: What does a wise father teach his son to do with wisdom?

COMPLEMENT: Acquire it (vv. 5–9), treasure it (vv. 10–19), and protect it (vv. 20–27).

EXEGETICAL IDEA: A wise father teaches his son to acquire, treasure, and protect wisdom.

HOMILETICAL IDEA: Wise fathers teach their children to acquire, treasure, and protect wisdom.

Proverbs 5

SUBJECT: How does a young man honor God in the way he satisfies his sexual desires?

COMPLEMENT: He gets intoxicated solely on the love of his wife.

EXEGETICAL IDEA: A young man honors God in the way he satisfies his sexual desires by getting intoxicated solely on the love of his wife.

HOMILETICAL IDEA: God-honoring people look only to their spouses for sexual satisfaction.

Proverbs 6

SUBJECT: What destructive lifestyles does wisdom help to avoid?

COMPLEMENT: Indebtedness (vv. 1–5), laziness (vv. 6–11), worthlessness (vv. 12–15), dissension (vv. 16–19), and adultery (vv. 20–35).

EXEGETICAL IDEA: Wisdom helps to avoid the destructive lifestyles of indebtedness, laziness, worthlessness, dissension, and adultery.

HOMILETICAL IDEA: Wisdom helps to avoid destructive lifestyles.

Proverbs 7

SUBJECT: Why should a young man avoid the house of Madam Folly?

COMPLEMENT: Because it is a highway to the grave.

EXEGETICAL IDEA: A young man should avoid the house of Madam Folly because it is a highway to the grave.

HOMILETICAL IDEA: It is wise to resist the lure of a foolish lifestyle because it leads to death.[5]

Proverbs 8

SUBJECT: What do people gain from accepting what Lady Wisdom offers?

COMPLEMENT: The blessings of life and favor.

EXEGETICAL IDEA: People who accept what Lady Wisdom offers gain the blessings of life and favor.

HOMILETICAL IDEA: Those who embrace God's gift of wisdom receive his gifts of life and favor.

Proverbs 9

SUBJECT: Whose invitation provides the best possible life?

COMPLEMENT: The invitation of Lady Wisdom, not Madam Folly.

EXEGETICAL IDEA: The invitation that provides the best possible life comes from Lady Wisdom, not Madam Folly.

HOMILETICAL IDEA: We will find the best way to live in wisdom, not folly.

Proverbs 10:1-16

SUBJECT: What is the difference between a wise and a foolish son?

COMPLEMENT: In the way they use their wealth (vv. 2–5, 15–16) and their words (vv. 6–14).

EXEGETICAL IDEA: The difference between a wise and a foolish son is in the way they use their wealth and their words.

HOMILETICAL IDEA: The difference between the wise and foolish is in how they use their wealth and their words.

---

5. To keep the vivid imagery in the homiletical idea, state it this way: It is wise to avoid the house of Madam Folly because it is a highway to death.

Proverbs 10:17-32

SUBJECT: Where do foolish and righteous lifestyles lead?

COMPLEMENT: To perversion and ruin for the foolish, but to joy and security for the righteous.

EXEGETICAL IDEA: The foolish lifestyle leads to perversion and ruin, but the righteous lifestyle leads to joy and security.

HOMILETICAL IDEA: The pathway to joy and security is through a righteous lifestyle.

Proverbs 11

SUBJECT: Where is security found?

COMPLEMENT: In honesty (vv. 1–2), in righteousness (vv. 3–8), in wise speech (vv. 9–15), and in generosity (vv. 16–31).

EXEGETICAL IDEA: Security is found in honesty, in righteousness, in wise speech, and in generosity.

HOMILETICAL IDEA: We can create a secure life through honesty, integrity, wise speech, and generosity.

Proverbs 12

SUBJECT: Who experiences the good life?

COMPLEMENT: Those who are wise in their speech (vv. 1–14) and deeds (vv. 15–28).

EXEGETICAL IDEA: Those who experience the good life are wise in their speech and deeds.

HOMILETICAL IDEA: Living the good life requires wise speech and deeds.

Proverbs 13

SUBJECT: How can a person eat what is materially good?

COMPLEMENT: By pursuing morally good teaching and behavior.

EXEGETICAL IDEA: A person can eat what is materially good by pursuing morally good teaching and behavior.

HOMILETICAL IDEA: If we want to eat good things, we need an appetite for good teaching and behavior.[6]

6. This big idea zeroes in on vv. 2 and 25, which bracket the section. Both verses contain the same two Hebrew words: *'akal* (translated by the NIV as "enjoy" in verse 2 and "eat" in verse 25) and *nepesh* (translated by the NIV as "appetite" in verse 2 and "stomach" in verse 25).

Proverbs 14

SUBJECT: What is the mark of those who walk uprightly in the fear of the Lord?

COMPLEMENT: They show discernment in the way they live.

EXEGETICAL IDEA: The mark of those who walk uprightly in the fear of the Lord is discernment in the way they live.[7]

HOMILETICAL IDEA: The upright life is a life of discernment.

Proverbs 15

SUBJECT: Where does one see the difference between the wise and the wicked?

COMPLEMENT: In their speech (vv. 1–8), in their response to correction (vv. 9–12, 31–33), and in their disposition (vv. 13–30).[8]

EXEGETICAL IDEA: The difference between the wise and the wicked is evident in their speech, in their response to correction, and in their disposition.

HOMILETICAL IDEA: We can spot a wise person by their good attitude.

Proverbs 16

SUBJECT: How do kings and other wise people find success?

COMPLEMENT: By submitting to God's supreme control over their lives.

EXEGETICAL IDEA: Kings and wise people find success by submitting to God's supreme control over their lives.[9]

HOMILETICAL IDEA: Success comes to those who submit to God in every area of their lives.

---

7. The subject comes from the repeated emphasis on the fear of the Lord (vv. 2, 16, 26, 27), while the complement comes from vv. 8 and 15, where the prudent "give thought to their ways/ steps." The Hebrew term translated "give thought" is regularly translated as "discern." A sermon or lesson on this text will show how this discernment leads to virtues like truth (vv. 3, 7, 25), industry (vv. 4, 23), patience (v. 29), contentment (v. 30), and kindness (v. 31).

8. The "disposition" of the wise includes attitudes like cheerfulness (vv. 15, 30), love (v. 17), patience (v. 18), and purity (v. 26). Thus the sermon or lesson will need to develop at least some of these.

9. Notice that the idea of God's sovereignty or supreme control brackets this chapter. It is developed in the "Yahweh sayings" of vv. 1–9, reinforced in v. 20, and then summarized at the end of the chapter in v. 33. The sermon or lesson will look to the various sayings in this chapter for the specific ways in which the wise are to submit to God's supreme control over their lives.

Proverbs 17

SUBJECT: What is the difference between the impact of fools and wise people in a community?

COMPLEMENT: Fools create conflict, while wise people preserve unity.

EXEGETICAL IDEA: The difference between the impact of fools and wise people in a community is that fools create conflict, while wise people preserve unity.

HOMILETICAL IDEA: Fools create conflict in a community, while wise people preserve its unity.

Proverbs 18

SUBJECT: What effect does the speech of a fool and a wise person have on a community?

COMPLEMENT: The fool's speech plunders it, while the wise person's speech strengthens it.

EXEGETICAL IDEA: A fool's speech plunders a community, while a wise person's speech strengthens it.

HOMILETICAL IDEA: Foolish words tear down communities, while wise words build them up.

Proverbs 19

SUBJECT: Where can a man find true wealth?

COMPLEMENT: In relationships shaped by the fear of God.

EXEGETICAL IDEA: A man can find true wealth in relationships shaped by the fear of God.

HOMILETICAL IDEA: The place to find true wealth is in God-honoring relationships.[10]

Proverbs 20

SUBJECT: What does a righteous king do?

COMPLEMENT: He roots out evil and evildoers (vv. 8, 26).

---

10. This big idea takes into account the way the chapter alternates between integrity of speech and the relation of wealth and friends—as well as the fear of the Lord; see Paul E. Koptak, *Proverbs*, The NIV Application Commentary (Grand Rapids: Zondervan, 2003), 466. The sermon or lesson will look to the various sayings to define the characteristics of God-honoring relationships.

EXEGETICAL IDEA: A righteous king roots out evil and evildoers.

HOMILETICAL IDEA: A godly leader roots out evil.[11]

Proverbs 21

SUBJECT: How can the plans of a king succeed?

COMPLEMENT: Through a godly pursuit of righteousness and justice.

EXEGETICAL IDEA: The plans of a king can succeed through a godly pursuit of righteousness and justice.

HOMILETICAL IDEA: Your plans can succeed only when they reflect a godly pursuit of righteousness and justice.

Proverbs 22:1–16

SUBJECT: What does God's sovereignty over wealth demand?

COMPLEMENT: Prudence (v. 3), humility (v. 4), integrity (v. 5), child-training (v. 6), generosity (vv. 7–9), purity (vv. 10–12), diligence (v. 13), discipline (vv. 14–15), and justice (v. 16).

EXEGETICAL IDEA: God's sovereignty over wealth demands prudence, humility, integrity, child-training, generosity, purity, diligence, discipline, and justice.

HOMILETICAL IDEA: God's sovereignty over wealth compels us to handle it with integrity.

Proverbs 22:17–23:11[12]

SUBJECT: What is the right way to gain wealth?

COMPLEMENT: Through skill and not fraud.[13]

EXEGETICAL IDEA: The right way to gain wealth is through skill and not fraud.

HOMILETICAL IDEA: Wise people gain wealth through their skill, not fraud.[14]

11. Obviously there are many "positive" sayings in this chapter as well as negative ones. Part of rooting out evil is pursuing faithful love and standing for what is right.

12. This preaching unit is the first part of a collection known as "The Thirty Sayings of the Wise" (see 22:20). It is likely a creative adaptation of an Egyptian wisdom text—Instruction of Amenemope—under the inspiration of God's Spirit. See the NIV for the breakdown of this section in thirty sayings. There is too much material to preach in one sermon, so the breakdown of this section into preaching units follows the basic themes that are developed. The entire section could serve as a brief sermon series, perhaps in combination with 24:23–34—"Further Sayings of the Wise."

13. The complement comes from 22:29—the only "positive" saying in this section. The remaining ones (after the introduction to the thirty sayings in 22:17–21) are prohibitions.

14. Another potential homiletical idea is: One advances through competence and integrity, not cunning or careerism. See Koptak, *Proverbs*, 536.

Proverbs 23:12-24:2

SUBJECT: How can a wise son bring his parents joy?

COMPLEMENT: By developing a wise heart.

EXEGETICAL IDEA: A wise son can bring his parents joy by developing a wise heart.

HOMILETICAL IDEA: We can bring joy to our parents by developing wise hearts.

Proverbs 24:3-22

SUBJECT: How does wisdom protect the wise?

COMPLEMENT: It provides strength in difficult situations (vv. 2–12) and keeps them from destructive habits and people (vv. 13–22).

EXEGETICAL IDEA: Wisdom protects the wise by providing strength in difficult situations and keeping them from destructive habits and people.

HOMILETICAL IDEA: Wisdom gives us strength in distress and discernment in temptation.

Proverbs 24:23-34

SUBJECT: How does a wise person advance in life?

COMPLEMENT: Through hard work and honesty, not partiality or slander.

EXEGETICAL IDEA: A wise person advances in life through hard work and honesty, not partiality or slander.

HOMILETICAL IDEA: Our ticket to success is through hard work and honesty.

Proverbs 25:1-15

SUBJECT: What do princes need to do in order to be successful in the royal court?

COMPLEMENT: Relate to kings effectively (vv. 2–7), handle conflict carefully (vv. 8–10), and use words strategically (vv. 11–13).

EXEGETICAL IDEA: In order to be successful in the royal court, princes need to relate to kings effectively, handle conflict carefully, and use words strategically.

HOMILETICAL IDEA: True worship in the workplace requires skill in relating to powerful leaders effectively, handling conflict carefully, and using words strategically.

Proverbs 25:16-28

SUBJECT: How can princes honor God in a variety of social situations?

COMPLEMENT: By practicing social intelligence.

EXEGETICAL IDEA: Princes can honor God in a variety of social situations by practicing social intelligence.

HOMILETICAL IDEA: Greater social intelligence will lead to greater honor of God.[15]

Proverbs 26

SUBJECT: How can one practice shrewdness in relationships?

COMPLEMENT: By treating fools with caution (vv. 1–12), recognizing the traits of a sluggard (vv. 13–16),[16] guarding against troublemakers (vv. 17–22), and watching out for deceivers (vv. 23–28).

EXEGETICAL IDEA: One can practice shrewdness in relationships by treating fools with caution, recognizing the traits of a sluggard, guarding against trouble-makers, and watching out for deceivers.

HOMILETICAL IDEA: We will avoid severe damage to our lives if we guard against the dark side of human behavior.

Proverbs 27

SUBJECT: What do healthy, God-honoring friendships require?

COMPLEMENT: Discernment, commitment, and care.

EXEGETICAL IDEA: Healthy, God-honoring friendships require discernment, commitment, and care.

HOMILETICAL IDEA: Healthy friendships require careful handling.[17]

---

15. Once again, the idea of honoring God comes from the larger burden of the book—namely, that true wisdom is grounded in the fear of the Lord (see also Prov. 1:7; 9:10). The concept of practicing social intelligence is a way of summarizing a rather loose collection of sayings. Practic-ing social intelligence means understanding that boundaries are necessary (vv. 16–17), slander creates severe wounds (v. 18), unreliable people will let you down when you need them most (v. 19), telling a hurt heart to "be happy" is hurtful and harsh (v. 20), mercy is the best revenge on an enemy (vv. 21–22), gossip brings unexpected trouble (v. 23), it is difficult to live with a person who is always looking for a fight (v. 24), good news from those far away is refreshing (v. 25), righteous people who give into wickedness create a mess (v. 26), it is dishonorable to heap honor on yourself (v. 27), and a lack of self-control leads to self-destruction (v. 28). As noted, each one of these eleven sayings could be preached individually in a sermon series on social intelligence.

16. Sluggards find any and every excuse to put off work (v. 13), allow pleasure to prevent production (vv. 14–15), and ignore the wisdom of others (v. 16).

17. The notion of careful handling (or discernment, commitment, and care) must be fleshed out by developing seven specific insights discussed in this chapter. These insights include the

Proverbs 28:1-11

SUBJECT: Why is a righteous lifestyle the best way to live?

COMPLEMENT: Because the righteous will be as bold as a lion.

EXEGETICAL IDEA: A righteous lifestyle is the best way to live because the righteous will be as bold as a lion.[18]

HOMILETICAL IDEA: Righteousness is the best policy because the righteous enjoy lionlike confidence.

Proverbs 28:12-28

SUBJECT: What happens when the righteous triumph and the wicked lose power?

COMPLEMENT: Righteous people celebrate and thrive.

EXEGETICAL IDEA: When the righteous triumph and the wicked lose their power, righteous people celebrate and thrive.[19]

HOMILETICAL IDEA: People thrive when their leaders are righteous.

Proverbs 29:1-14

SUBJECT: What is the result of one's righteousness?

COMPLEMENT: It benefits the person (vv. 1–6) and those in one's community (vv. 7–14).

EXEGETICAL IDEA: One's righteousness benefits the person and those in one's community.

HOMILETICAL IDEA: Right makes might—for yourself and others.

Proverbs 29:15-28

SUBJECT: What is the value of correction and instruction?

---

following: praise needs to be handled with caution (vv. 2, 21), love offers rebuke instead of flattery (vv. 5–6, 9), home is where the help is (v. 8), tough times require loyalty (v. 10), true friends make a lasting impact (v. 17), more never satisfies desire (v. 20), and one's greatest assets need careful attention (vv. 23–27).

18. The remainder of the sayings in this preaching unit validate this idea. They provide several reasons why the righteous can be as bold as a lion: discernment brings stability (vv. 2, 7), oppression of the poor leads to ruin (vv. 3, 8), turning from instruction leaves you pathetic and helpless (vv. 4, 9), evildoers miss out on insight and inheritance (vv. 5, 10), and the righteous poor end up with more than the perverse rich (vv. 6, 11).

19. This idea comes from the first and last sayings in this preaching unit (vv. 12, 28). The sayings in between profile a righteous leader (vv. 13–27). Righteous leaders open their hearts to God (vv. 13–14), lead with integrity (vv. 15–18), work hard for what they have (vv. 19–22), and treat people right (vv. 23–27).

COMPLEMENT: It brings blessing and peace.

EXEGETICAL IDEA: The value of correction and instruction is that it brings blessing and peace.

HOMILETICAL IDEA: The road to blessing and peace goes through correction and instruction.

Proverbs 30:1-14

SUBJECT: How can one overcome the limitations of human understanding and inability to access God's limitless wisdom?

COMPLEMENT: By taking refuge in God's words.

EXEGETICAL IDEA: One can overcome the limitations of human understanding and our inability to access God's limitless wisdom by taking refuge in God's words.[20]

HOMILETICAL IDEA: We can overcome the massive gap between our understanding and God's wisdom by taking refuge in God's words.

Proverbs 30:15-33

SUBJECT: How can one live wisely for God's honor and one's good?

COMPLEMENT: By remembering that greed never satisfies (vv. 15–17), by treating God's gift of sex with wonder (vv. 18–20), by guarding against people who gain access to power (vv. 21–23), by learning how to overcome one's limitations (vv. 24–31), and by not stirring up anger (vv. 32–33).

EXEGETICAL IDEA: One can live wisely for God's honor and one's good by remembering that greed never satisfies, by treating God's gift of sex with wonder, by guarding against people who gain access to power, by learning how to overcome one's limitations, and by not stirring up anger.

HOMILETICAL IDEA: We can succeed in the life God gives us by paying attention to life's basic rules.[21]

20. This idea comes primarily from vv. 1–6. Verses 7–9 contribute to the argument by asking God to spare us from the sin and circumstances that would turn us away from him and his words. Then vv. 10–14 close the section with a warning. This warning consists of a picture of a corrupt generation—those who reject God's words.

21. Notice that the exegetical idea contains a multi-complement. The homiletical idea simply summarizes these as "life's basic rules." The sermon will work through each item in some detail. Haddon Robinson preached a well-known sermon on Prov. 30:24–28. His big idea was: We can learn wisdom by paying attention to four little creatures. Then he developed the lesson taught by each little creature: (1) the ant teaches us the value of preparing for the future, (2) the coney teaches us where to find security, (3) the locust teaches us to work in community, and (4) the lizard teaches us the incongruity of grace. See Haddon Robinson, "The Wisdom of

Proverbs 31:1-9

SUBJECT: What did King Lemuel's mother teach him about using his privilege?

COMPLEMENT: To serve people in need rather than to indulge his cravings.

EXEGETICAL IDEA: King Lemuel's mother taught him to use his privilege to serve people in need rather than to indulge his cravings.

HOMILETICAL IDEA: Godly moms teach their kids to use privilege to serve people in need rather than to satisfy their desires.[22]

Proverbs 31:10-31

SUBJECT: What characterizes women of strength?

COMPLEMENT: They model wisdom in every area of their lives.

EXEGETICAL IDEA: Women of strength model wisdom in every area of their lives.

HOMILETICAL IDEA: Mighty moms and other people of strength model wisdom in every area of their lives.[23]

Selected Proverbs on Conflict

SUBJECT: How does one handle conflict?

COMPLEMENT: Recognize how much God hates those who stir it up (6:16, 19), stop quarrels before they start (17:14), choose your battles wisely (26:17; 29:9), and choose forgiveness over revenge (24:29).

EXEGETICAL IDEA: One handles conflict by recognizing how much God hates those who stir it up, to stop quarrels before they start, to choose your battles wisely, and to choose forgiveness over revenge.

HOMILETICAL IDEA: We can handle conflict wisely by despising it, stopping it, avoiding it, and choosing to forgive.

Small Creatures," Preaching Today, https://www.preachingtoday.com/sermons/sermons/2007/july/wisdomofsmallcreatures.html.

22. This text may seem a bit pedantic on first reading, but it has much to say about how mothers can teach their children about using privilege for social justice rather than for self-indulgence. It makes a fine Mother's Day sermon as a surprising alternative to Prov. 31:10–31, the text many listeners expect to hear. You might even refer to King Lemuel's mother as "the other Proverbs 31 woman."

23. Preachers and teachers will need to explain what it means to model wisdom in every area of life. In this acrostic poem, it's clear that mighty moms (Hebrew 'eshet hayil, "a woman of strength") help their families flourish (vv. 13–19, 21–22, 27), care for the poor and needy (v. 20), and find success in the Lord rather than in outward appearance (v. 30). The decision to include "other people of strength" in the homiletical idea stems from the function of this poem at the end of the book of Proverbs. See "Difficult Passages/Verses" below for a discussion of this text.

Selected Proverbs on Speech

SUBJECT: Why do people need to use their words with care?

COMPLEMENT: Because they have the power to destroy or heal (12:18; 15:4).[24]

EXEGETICAL IDEA: People need to use their words with care because they have the power to destroy or heal.

HOMILETICAL IDEA: Words require care because they can destroy or heal.

Selected Proverbs on Wealth

SUBJECT: How can one handle material wealth wisely?

COMPLEMENT: Treat it as a gift of God rather than an idol (10:22; 30:8–9), recognize its limitations (11:4, 28; 15:16–17; 16:16; 17:1; 20:25), learn to protect and grow it (11:15; 17:18; 20:16; 21:13, 17, 20; 22:7, 16, 26; and 28:8), and practice generosity (11:24–26; 22:9; 28:22, 27).

EXEGETICAL IDEA: One handles material wealth wisely by treating it as a gift of God rather than an idol, to recognize its limitations, to learn to protect and grow it, and to practice generosity.

HOMILETICAL IDEA: Wise wealth management views wealth as a gift, recognizes its limitations, handles it well, and shares it generously.

Selected Proverbs on Decision-Making

SUBJECT: What is the source of wise decisions?

COMPLEMENT: Seeking wise counsel (11:14; 15:22; 20:18; 24:6) and submitting to God's plan for your life (3:5–6; 16:1, 3, 9, 33; 19:21; 30:5–6).

EXEGETICAL IDEA: The source of wise decisions is seeking wise counsel and submitting to God's plan for your life.

HOMILETICAL IDEA: You can make wise decisions when you seek wise counsel and submit to God's plan for your life.

Selected Proverbs on Parenting

SUBJECT: What gifts do wise parents give their children?

COMPLEMENT: The gift of direction (1:8; 22:16), the gift of discipline (13:24; 19:18; 22:15; 23:13–14; 29:15, 17), and the gift of a God-fearing example (14:26–27).

---

24. The sermon will develop various proverbs that fall into one of the two categories. Sayings that relate to "healing speech" include 12:25; 15:1, 23; 16:24; 24:26; 25:12, 15; and 27:5. Sayings that relate to "destroying speech" include 10:19; 12:19, 22; 13:3; 17:28; 18:8; 21:23; 26:20, 22; and 27:1–2.

EXEGETICAL IDEA: Wise parents give their children the gifts of direction, discipline, and a God-fearing example.

HOMILETICAL IDEA: The best gifts for parents to give children are direction, discipline, and devotion to God.

Difficult Passages/Verses

Proverbs 3:9-10

Sayings like this one can sound like support for the "prosperity gospel." This formulaic approach to life claims that if you honor God through the giving of your material resources, you will always overflow with financial blessings. This, of course, misses the fact that proverbial sayings are not promises (see "Cultural Perspectives and Application" below). It also ignores the fact that God's greatest blessings are not material ones (see 15:17; 22:1).

Proverbs 26:4-5

This passage stirred debate among ancient Jewish scholars about the authenticity of the book. How could verse 5 blatantly contradict what was just said in verse 4? The fact that this alleged contradiction occurs in side-by-side sayings provides the answer. The "contradiction" is intended! The point is: know your fool. There are times to keep silent and ignore a fool (v. 4), but there are other times when speaking up is the right approach (v. 5). The concern of verse 4 is protecting the wise from getting dragged into a foolish argument. The concern of verse 5 is protecting a fool from his or her own skewed wisdom.

Proverbs 31:10-31

This text has fallen out of favor with preachers, especially for use on Mother's Day. It's no wonder that female listeners say, "If I hear another sermon on the Proverbs 31 woman, I'm going to scream!" Perhaps the title of a book by Marcia Drake captures the way many woman feel about this text: *The Proverbs 31 Lady and Other Impossible Dreams*. The problem, though, is not with the text but with the way it has been misread and misused. Here are three facts to consider. First, Proverbs 31:10–31 is an alphabet poem that moves from *aleph* to *tav*—from A to Z—with the first word of each verse beginning with the next letter of the Hebrew alphabet (v. 10—*aleph*, v. 11—*bet*, etc.). Thus the argument does not move in linear fashion, from one paragraph to the next. Second, this poem is the ending to a book designed originally to prepare male princes to be wise kings. Therefore, the poem affirms that wisdom is for women as well as men. The Bible was ahead of its time in its high view and treatment of women. Third, this poem offers something for everyone. It provides a model of wisdom for men and women. The supermodel of wisdom happens to be a wife and mother who realizes everything that Proverbs has taught. Young men who proclaim that they are looking to marry "a Proverbs 31 woman" need to ask themselves if they are "a Proverbs 1 through 30 man." This poem, then, does not set an impossible standard; rather, it presents a woman as a supermodel of what wisdom looks like fleshed out in everyday life. She is an *'eshet hayil*, "a woman of might." It is wisdom, then, that makes a woman or a man of strength.

Cultural Perspectives and Application

Perhaps the most important perspective to adopt when preaching Proverbs is that proverbial sayings are not promises. They are not guaranteed formulas for success. This is not to water down the force of a proverbial saying but to understand its function. Proverbial sayings make observations about the way life works time after time after time. Thankfully, God has given us the books of Ecclesiastes and Job to keep us from misreading Proverbs. Job probes life's mysteries, while Ecclesiastes explores life's frustrations.

Also, given the competing invitations offered by Lady Wisdom and Madam Folly in chapters 1–9, it is worth asking whether the warnings against adultery refer to actual sexual sin or to the pursuit of a lifestyle represented by an adulterous woman. It seems that the answer is "both." It is difficult to understand Proverbs 5 as anything less than a warning against physical adultery and an exhortation to marital faithfulness. However, Proverbs 7 reads more like the personification of folly as an adulterous woman. There is no contradiction, though, between reading these chapters both ways. Wise people need to avoid the lure of sexual immorality as well as the lifestyle of folly that it personifies.

Finally, one of the most difficult teachings to apply in Proverbs is the use of the rod in disciplining children (13:24; 22:15; 23:13–14; 29:15). Preachers and teachers should rightly express concern about the physical abuse of children. They must also point out the harm caused by a failure to discipline children (13:24). Preachers and teachers will do well to tell listeners to use physical discipline sparingly and never to administer it when angry. Physical discipline must never turn into a beating.

---- **RECOMMENDED RESOURCES** ----

Fox, Michael V. *Proverbs 1–9*. Anchor Yale Bible. New Haven: Yale University Press, 2000.

————. *Proverbs 10–31*. Anchor Yale Bible. New Haven: Yale University Press, 2009.

Koptak, Paul E. *Proverbs*. The NIV Application Commentary. Grand Rapids: Zondervan, 2003.

Longman, Tremper, III. *Proverbs*. Baker Commentary on the Old Testament Wisdom and Psalms. Grand Rapids: Baker Academic, 2006.

Waltke, Bruce K. *The Book of Proverbs: Chapters 1–15*. The New International Commentary on the Old Testament. Grand Rapids: Eerdmans, 2004.

————. *The Book of Proverbs: Chapters 15–31*. The New International Commentary on the Old Testament. Grand Rapids: Eerdmans, 2005.

Ecclesiastes

CALVIN W. CHOI

The Big Idea of Ecclesiastes

Ecclesiastes is Solomon's memoir on his desperate search for meaning and significance in life, summarized in one painful and regretful phrase: "Vanity of vanities! All is vanity" (1:2 ESV). This phrase indicates his utter frustration at the futility of life and warns how misplaced pursuits in life can be meaningless. Solomon thereby realizes that a meaningful and significant life is possible only by living a life of deference to God.

SUBJECT: What is the message Solomon wants to convey to his audience?

COMPLEMENT: No matter how fast, how hard, and how much one attains what life offers under the sun—knowledge, wisdom, pleasure, career, happiness, work, wealth, honor, and fame—a life without a living and faithful relationship with God is meaningless and hopeless.

EXEGETICAL IDEA: Solomon wants to convey to his audience that no matter how fast, how hard, and how much one is attaining what life offers under the sun—knowledge, wisdom, pleasure, career, happiness, wealth, and fame—a life without a living and faithful relationship with God is meaningless and hopeless.

HOMILETICAL IDEA: Life under the sun is meaningless without the life of faith and obedience to God.

Selecting Preaching and Teaching Passages in Ecclesiastes

There is perhaps no book that resonates more powerfully with and relates more deeply to people's lives than Ecclesiastes in the way in which it confronts readers with the raw, real, and unfiltered reality of life. It covers almost all spheres of life from cradle to grave: youth, education, knowledge, wealth, entertainment, career, companionship, suffering, social justice, politics, retirement, and old age. Solomon invites readers to go on a quest with him as he takes them back to his life experiences so people can identify, process, and relate to his life journey.

Chapter 1 poses Solomon's dilemma of searching for meaningful life. Chapters 2–11 relay Solomon's discontent with his discoveries under the sun. Although the resolution to Solomon's dilemma for meaningful life is provided at the end of chapter 12, the challenge for some preachers and teachers might be to hold the suspense without mentioning or referencing too quickly the conclusion in 12:13–14. Instead, walk through the book chapter by chapter and wrestle with and fully appreciate Solomon's dilemma and frustration, which lead to that climactic discovery at the end. You will want to consider some of the secondary themes raised by Solomon in Ecclesiastes that will guide your text selection for preaching and teaching on this book.

Getting the Subject, Complement, Exegetical Idea, and Homiletical Idea

Ecclesiastes 1:1-11

SUBJECT: What do people gain after all their toil under the sun?

COMPLEMENT: Absolutely nothing.

EXEGETICAL IDEA: People gain absolutely nothing after all their toil under the sun.

HOMILETICAL IDEA: The sooner we realize life's vanity under the sun, the better prepared we are to embrace life.

Ecclesiastes 2:1-11

SUBJECT: Why can pleasure and success never bring satisfaction in life?

COMPLEMENT: Because all is meaningless when celebrated outside of God.

EXEGETICAL IDEA: Pleasure and success can never bring satisfaction in life because all is meaningless when celebrated outside of God.

HOMILETICAL IDEA: Every pleasure and success when rightly enjoyed glorifies God.

Ecclesiastes 3:1-15

SUBJECT: Why is life so frustrating and unpredictable?

COMPLEMENT: Because there is a divinely appointed time for everything.

EXEGETICAL IDEA: Life is so frustrating and unpredictable because there is a divinely appointed time for everything.

HOMILETICAL IDEA: Trust God for everything in life.

Ecclesiastes 3:16-4:3

SUBJECT: Why is it better to be dead than to be alive?

COMPLEMENT: Because at least when we are dead we don't have to experience injustice and oppression.

EXEGETICAL IDEA: It is better to be dead than to be alive because at least when we are dead we don't have to experience injustice and oppression.

HOMILETICAL IDEA: Death in Jesus is our first step into glory.

Ecclesiastes 5:1-7

SUBJECT: Why do the readers have to watch their steps when they worship?

COMPLEMENT: Because worshiping without obedience is meaningless.

EXEGETICAL IDEA: The readers have to watch their steps when they worship because worshiping without obedience is meaningless.

HOMILETICAL IDEA: Our obedience reflects our worship, and our worship determines the meaning of our life.

Ecclesiastes 6:1-12

SUBJECT: Why can't wealth, children, or longevity bring lasting contentment?

COMPLEMENT: Because life is transient, and in the end comes death.

EXEGETICAL IDEA: Wealth, children, or longevity cannot bring lasting contentment because life is transient, and in the end comes death.

HOMILETICAL IDEA: Only God is able to satisfy us eternally.

Ecclesiastes 7:1-14

SUBJECT: Why is grieving better than feasting?

COMPLEMENT: Because in brokenness people encounter God.

EXEGETICAL IDEA: Grieving is better than feasting because in brokenness people encounter God.

HOMILETICAL IDEA: There will be real feasting without grieving in heaven.

Ecclesiastes 8:2-9

SUBJECT: Why does the author instruct the reader to behave appropriately before the king?

COMPLEMENT: Because he failed to behave appropriately before the supreme king.

EXEGETICAL IDEA: The author instructs the reader to behave appropriately before the king because he failed to behave appropriately before the supreme king.

HOMILETICAL IDEA: Submit to your King.

Ecclesiastes 9:1-10

SUBJECT: Why should readers enjoy life today?

COMPLEMENT: For tomorrow comes death.

EXEGETICAL IDEA: The readers should enjoy life today, for tomorrow comes death.

HOMILETICAL IDEA: Jesus says tomorrow comes glory, so enjoy life today as his witness.

Ecclesiastes 10:1-7

SUBJECT: Why is it critical to make wise decisions?

COMPLEMENT: Because one foolish decision can ruin one's life and society.

EXEGETICAL IDEA: It is critical to make wise decisions because one foolish decision can ruin one's life and society.

HOMILETICAL IDEA: Run your choice by Christ, in Christ, and for Christ and you will never have regrets.

Ecclesiastes 11:1-10

SUBJECT: How does one overcome life's uncertainty?

COMPLEMENT: By knowing that life is fleeting, so don't miss an opportunity to bless and influence others positively by sowing seeds.

EXEGETICAL IDEA: One overcomes life's uncertainty by knowing that life is fleeting, so don't miss an opportunity to bless and influence others positively by sowing seeds.

HOMILETICAL IDEA: Reap what you will harvest.

Ecclesiastes 12:8-14

SUBJECT: What is the end of the matter?

COMPLEMENT: To fear God and keep his commandments, for this is the whole duty of people.

EXEGETICAL IDEA: The end of the matter is to fear God and keep his commandments, for this is the whole duty of people.

HOMILETICAL IDEA: Fear God and obey his commands.

Difficult Passages/Verses

While the traditional view endorses Solomon's authorship, it is true that many scholars think otherwise.[1] Yet even those who dismiss Solomonic authorship cannot deny the fact that the life experience mentioned in the book reflects Solomon's life. Regardless of the authorship, the fundamental message of the book and its impact are not affected or diminished.

As is often the case with poetic or wisdom literature, the challenge lies in deciphering and unlocking the figurative, metaphorical, sometimes ambiguous phrasing and seemingly contradictory passages or doctrines taught in the Bible. Ecclesiastes is no exception. It contains a number of difficult passages to interpret due to the lack of knowledge of context, difficulty in translating certain Hebrew words, and the figurative and cryptic nature of certain verses. For example, 7:17 says, "Be not overly wicked, neither be a fool" (ESV). Is it implying, then, that being moderately wicked is acceptable?

While it may be important to point out these linguistic difficulties, it is helpful to ensure that interpretation is viewed in light of the greater context and the author's intent and purpose and the overall message of the book. A study or review of literary devices in Wisdom literature will be helpful to clear up ambiguity that surrounds the passage.

---

1. For instance, Longman holds the view that the author is the narrator who compiled the monologue by Qohelet (a wise teacher). See Tremper Longman III, *The Book of Ecclesiastes* (Grand Rapids: Eerdmans, 1998), 9.

Cultural Perspectives and Application

What makes Ecclesiastes so relevant and applicable is that it doesn't take a long bridge to connect between the two worlds, the ancient and modern cultures. This is mainly because what the author wrestles with throughout the book very much reflects our own life experience and what we all wrestle with and desire universally as humankind—the emptiness, disappointment, and futility of life and the constant pursuit of a better, meaningful, and satisfying life.

The challenge, however, is to demonstrate how we can still identify with the author's search and struggle for meaning in different areas of life and yet show why such pursuit will be short-lived. Also, we must explain what that says about Solomon and us.

Another important consideration is to tie in the gospel, especially when dealing with the subjects of wisdom, death, and the afterlife. Ecclesiastes is a book that can be both evangelistic and apologetic in nature.

Some possible applications include the following:

- Be careful what you pursue, avoid fleeting pleasures and focus on eternal hope.
- Unless you have hope for eternity, you can never truly enjoy life under the sun.
- What God has given you as a gift can be a curse when used apart from God.
- What you already possess in God through Christ surpasses everything the world offers you.

RECOMMENDED RESOURCES

Eaton, Michael A. *Ecclesiastes*. Tyndale Old Testament Commentaries. Leicester, UK: InterVarsity, 1983.

Kidner, Derek. *The Message of Ecclesiastes*. Leicester, UK: InterVarsity, 1984.

Longman, Tremper, III. *The Book of Ecclesiastes*. The New International Commentary on the Old Testament. Grand Rapids: Eerdmans, 1997.

Song of Songs

PABLO A. JIMÉNEZ

The Big Idea of Song of Songs

There are several ways of interpreting the Song of Songs: allegorical, as a metaphor for the relationship between God and Israel or Jesus and the church; dramatic, as a play; and literal, as a poem about marital love.

SUBJECT: How is the Song of Songs an ode to marital love or an allegory about the church?

COMPLEMENT: The Song of Songs is a collection of poems that celebrates the beauty of marital love, and it can also be understood as a metaphor for the relationship between God and the people of God, between Jesus and the church.

EXEGETICAL IDEA: The Song of Songs is an ode to marital love and an allegory about the church in that its poems celebrate the beauty of marital love and that it can also be understood as a metaphor for the relationship between God and the people of God, between Jesus and the church.

HOMILETICAL IDEA: Marriage is a powerful metaphor to explain the relationship between God and humanity.

Selecting Preaching and Teaching Passages in Song of Songs

After the title (1:1), the Song of Songs presents several poems that reach their climax in a song about the power of love (8:5–14):

The Bride and the Women of Jerusalem (1:2–6)
The Bride and the Groom (1:7–2:17)

245

The Bride's Dream (3:1–5)

The Wedding Procession (3:6–5:1)

The Anxiety of Separation (5:2–6:3)

The Beauty of Love (6:4–8:4)

The Power of Love (8:5–14)

Getting the Subject, Complement, Exegetical Idea, and Homiletical Idea

Song of Songs 1:2-6

■ *The Bride and the Women of Jerusalem*

SUBJECT: Who is the main character of the book?

COMPLEMENT: A woman, whom we will call "the bride," who yearns for a man, whom we will call "the groom."

EXEGETICAL IDEA: The main character of the book is a woman, whom we will call "the bride," who yearns for a man, whom we will call "the groom."

HOMILETICAL IDEA: People of faith must seek the presence of God, as a bride in love seeks the company of a groom.

Song of Songs 1:7-2:17

■ *The Bride and the Groom*

SUBJECT: How does the author express marital love?

COMPLEMENT: As a bride and groom expressing their mutual admiration, using romantic and intimate language.

EXEGETICAL IDEA: The author expresses marital love as a bride and groom expressing their mutual admiration, using romantic and intimate language.

HOMILETICAL IDEA: Our relationship with God should be as intimate as the relationship between a couple in love.

Song of Songs 3:1-5

■ *The Bride's Dream*

SUBJECT: Why is the bride so anxious?

COMPLEMENT: She seeks the groom even while she sleeps.

EXEGETICAL IDEA: The bride is so anxious because she seeks the groom even while she sleeps.

HOMILETICAL IDEA: People of faith yearn for the presence of God, who loves them.

Song of Songs 3:6–5:1

■ *The Wedding Procession*

SUBJECT: What is the meaning of the vision?

COMPLEMENT: The groom sees a wedding procession and praises the beauty of the bride.

EXEGETICAL IDEA: The meaning of the vision is that the groom sees a wedding procession and praises the beauty of the bride.

HOMILETICAL IDEA: Just as marriage is a solemn covenant, we are united through a solemn covenant with God.

Song of Songs 5:2–6:3

■ *The Anxiety of Separation*

SUBJECT: Why does the bride reject the groom, only to seek him in the middle of the night?

COMPLEMENT: Because love is fickle, represented by rejection and desperation for the same husband.

EXEGETICAL IDEA: The bride rejects the groom, only to seek him in the middle of the night, because love is fickle, represented by rejection and desperation for the same husband.

HOMILETICAL IDEA: The people of God must work out their salvation with fear and trembling (cf. Phil. 2:12).

Song of Songs 6:4–8:4

■ *The Beauty of Love*

SUBJECT: Why is the tone here so joyful in comparison to the previous pericope?

COMPLEMENT: The bride and groom consummate and celebrate their love. (The bride is called "Shulammite" in 6:13. Shunem was a town in the southern border of Issachar [Josh. 19:18], opposite the town of Jezreel.)[1]

EXEGETICAL IDEA: The tone here is so joyful in comparison to the previous pericope because the bride and groom consummate and celebrate their love.

HOMILETICAL IDEA: Jesus loves the church as a husband loves his wife (cf. Eph. 5:25).

---

1. Nancy L. Lapp, "Shunem," in *Harper's Bible Dictionary*, ed. Paul J. Achtemeier et al. (San Francisco: Harper & Row, 1985), 948.

Song of Songs 8:5-14

▧ *The Power of Love*

SUBJECT: What does the Song of Songs teach readers about love?

COMPLEMENT: Love is a powerful and dangerous force.[2]

EXEGETICAL IDEA: The Song of Songs teaches readers that love is a powerful and dangerous force.

HOMILETICAL IDEA: Consider the cost of loving God above all other things.

Difficult Passages/Verses

Song of Songs 1:9

The text compares the bride to a mare. The comparison may refer to the Egyptian custom of sending a mare to distract the horse-driven enemy chariots. The implication is that the bride is as alluring as a mare in heat.[3]

Song of Songs 5:7

The torn cloak may be a reference to rape. This possible allusion to the sexual is disturbing. Interpreters should be cautious in the exposition of this text, for it is estimated that 25 percent of women have suffered some kind of sexual abuse.[4]

Cultural Perspectives and Application

Determining the social nature of the Song of Songs is a riddle. On the one hand, the main character of the poem is a poor woman who worked as a keeper of vineyards, which leads us to think about a rural context. On the other hand, the references to Jerusalem and King Solomon lead us to think about a king's court. In any case, the Song of Songs is a sophisticated writing that was composed in Jerusalem, in the king's court. The Song of Songs is a poem that celebrates human sexuality and marital love. Although it does not mention God, it can be understood as a metaphor for the relationship between God and his people, between Jesus and the church.

---

2. Renita J. Weems, "Song of Songs," in *The New Interpreter's Bible*, vol. 5, ed. Leander E. Keck (Nashville: Abingdon, 1997), 430.
3. Weems, "Song of Songs," 386–87.
4. Weems, "Song of Songs," 412.

RECOMMENDED RESOURCES

Pope, Marvin. *Song of Songs*. Anchor Bible. New York: Doubleday, 1977.

Weems, Renita J. "Song of Songs." In *The New Interpreter's Bible*, edited by Leander E. Keck, 5:361–431. Nashville: Abingdon, 1997.

Isaiah

ANDREW C. THOMPSON

The Big Idea of Isaiah

Isaiah the son of Amoz prophesied to Jerusalem and Judah during the time of the Southern Kingdom, under the kingships of Uzziah, Jotham, Ahaz, and Hezekiah (Isa. 1:1). As a prophet, he functioned as God's covenant enforcer. Isaiah reminded Judah of the Lord's faithfulness, accused them of unfaithfulness (particularly with regard to idolatry and injustice), recalled them to obedience, and foretold the consequences of repentance as well as rebellion.

His message and ministry addressed Judeans in his day, up to and through the Assyrian siege in 701 BC. He also spoke to future generations in exile, predicting their return and the glorious establishment of God's eternal kingdom. Thus while his words refer to events in his age and the near future, Isaiah also envisioned realities that are ushered in by the new covenant: the birth, ministry, death, and resurrection of Christ; the pouring out of the Spirit; the worldwide mission of the church; and the return of the Son of God in glory at the end of days. The scale and scope of his message is breathtaking.

SUBJECT: What did the Lord do to Judah and Jerusalem through the words of Isaiah?

COMPLEMENT: He rebuked the nation, called them to repentance, hardened their hearts, warned of disaster, forgave a contrite remnant, welcomed exiles back home, and said that he would establish his eternal kingdom.

EXEGETICAL IDEA: Through the words of Isaiah to Judah and Jerusalem, the Lord rebuked the nation, called them to repentance, hardened their hearts, warned of disaster, forgave a contrite remnant, welcomed exiles back home, and said that he would establish his eternal kingdom.

HOMILETICAL IDEA: Through the words of Isaiah, God calls to us.

Selecting Preaching and Teaching Passages in Isaiah

Passage selection in the Major Prophets is both easy and difficult. It is often easy to see where units of thought begin and end. Hints like introductory phrases ("Hear the word of the LORD," "In that day," etc.) or changes in tense or person mark most transitions. Chapter divisions are usually (but not always) reliable indicators, but many chapters will have more than one unit of thought.

The difficulty does not come in identifying preaching units but in planning for how to accommodate the massive number of passages in a preaching plan for Isaiah. As one of the Major Prophets, Isaiah's length poses a formidable preaching challenge. Sixty-six chapters, even at one per week, would take well over a year to preach. In addition, preachers will probably not just preach one chapter per sermon; there is simply too much happening in some chapters. The selection of passages below recognizes eighty-six preaching units. By following the natural divisions in the material, a series on Isaiah could last up to two years!

There are several options for preaching long prophetic books. First, preachers can just eat the elephant, one bite at a time. Start in chapter 1 and take it passage by passage. In some congregations, sermon series lasting two years or more are the norm. Breaks for Christmas and Easter, or for summer holidays, can relieve the monotony. Your parishioners will thank you for the reprieve!

Second, preachers can preach selective passages that represent the dominant themes of the book. This might shorten a book like Isaiah to somewhere between ten and fifteen weeks.

Third, preachers can preach one section of Isaiah in the same season each year. A fall series could cover Isaiah 1–6, and next fall Isaiah 9–11, and so forth. This is my preferred approach to longer books, because it covers all the material without dragging on for too long. Each time the series is picked back up, preachers can remind their congregation of the big idea of the book and where they left off last year. One should also keep in mind (especially in a growing church) that there will be many in the congregation who were not attending in prior years and who will be starting in the middle.

In any approach, another challenge will be to help congregations get a feel for the entire book without getting lost in the progress of passages. Isaiah is not organized as a narrative but is loosely and thematically grouped. Listeners will need regular reminders about where they are in the book and what Isaiah has said prior to a particular passage.

Getting the Subject, Complement, Exegetical Idea, and Homiletical Idea[1]

Isaiah 1:1-20

SUBJECT: What must Judah do on the brink of ruinous judgment?

COMPLEMENT: Judah must truly repent of their rebellion.

EXEGETICAL IDEA: Judah, on the brink of ruinous judgment, must truly repent of their rebellion.

HOMILETICAL IDEA: Without repentance, scarlet sins will not become white as snow.

Isaiah 1:21-31

SUBJECT: What would God do to Judah, whose best had become their worst?

COMPLEMENT: God would purify Jerusalem by purging it of corrupt leadership.

EXEGETICAL IDEA: Since Judah's best had become their worst, God would purify Jerusalem by purging it of corrupt leadership.

HOMILETICAL IDEA: When our best becomes our worst, we invite God's refining correction.

Isaiah 2:1-5

SUBJECT: What should Judah do because of God's future world-changing elevation of Zion in accordance with the Abrahamic promises?

COMPLEMENT: They should walk now in the light of the Lord.

---

1. A note on tense: Isaiah, like other Old Testament prophets, sometimes speaks of future events in the past or present tense. Sometimes he switches verb tenses within a single oracle. The exegetical ideas here attempt to adopt Isaiah's own tense selection as far as possible. The homiletical ideas, however, adopt a tense from the contemporary perspective. Even here, though, the phrasing is tricky: some events (like forgiving sins and bringing divine judgment) Isaiah speaks of as one event, whereas from our current perspective some aspects of those events are past (the resurrection), some are present (individual faith and repentance), and some are future (the return of Christ). Rather than seeing these as difficulties, the tense issue can be an opportunity for preachers to think through exactly *when* the things Isaiah talks about happen and what that means for the church today.

EXEGETICAL IDEA: Because of God's future world-changing elevation of Zion in accordance with the Abrahamic promises, Judah should walk now in the light of the Lord.

HOMILETICAL IDEA: Let us walk in the light of the Lord.

Isaiah 2:6–22

SUBJECT: What will the day of the Lord bring?

COMPLEMENT: It will bring the exaltation of the true God and the humiliation of people—even his own people—who seek after idols.

EXEGETICAL IDEA: The day of the Lord will bring the exaltation of the true God and the humiliation of people—even his own people—who seek after idols.

HOMILETICAL IDEA: There will come a day when God alone will be exalted.

Isaiah 3:1–15

SUBJECT: What will the Lord do for the sake of his oppressed people?

COMPLEMENT: He will remove corrupt leaders from Zion.

EXEGETICAL IDEA: The Lord, for the sake of his oppressed people, will remove corrupt leaders from Zion.

HOMILETICAL IDEA: In the kingdom of God, leaders are crucial.

Isaiah 3:16–4:1

SUBJECT: Why does the Lord warn the followers of corrupt systems?

COMPLEMENT: Because judgment will come to them too.

EXEGETICAL IDEA: The Lord warns the followers of corrupt systems because judgment will come to them too.

HOMILETICAL IDEA: In the kingdom of God, leaders are crucial, but followers are called.

Isaiah 4:2–6

SUBJECT: How will the judgments to come affect God's people?

COMPLEMENT: They will prepare the way for a perfect re-creation of God's people under the branch and by the Spirit.

EXEGETICAL IDEA: The judgments to come will prepare the way for a perfect re-creation of God's people under the branch and by the Spirit.

HOMILETICAL IDEA: The Father's anger did not bring total destruction but prepared his people for perfect communion in the Son and by the Spirit.

Isaiah 5:1-7

SUBJECT: What will the Lord do because of the rotten spiritual fruit borne by his people in response to his perfect care for them?

COMPLEMENT: He will bring ruin on them.

EXEGETICAL IDEA: Because of the rotten spiritual fruit borne by the Lord's people in response to his perfect care for them, he will bring ruin on them.

HOMILETICAL IDEA: Faith bears good fruit.

Isaiah 5:8-30

SUBJECT: Why is there woe to those who sin against the Lord?

COMPLEMENT: Because he will use natural disasters and a godless nation to bring inexorable punishment to Judah.

EXEGETICAL IDEA: Woe to those who sin against the Lord, because he will use natural disasters and a godless nation to bring inexorable punishment to Judah.

HOMILETICAL IDEA: Woe to those who claim the name of Christ but live in rebellion.

Isaiah 6:1-7

SUBJECT: What can provide the atonement for sin required by the presence of the Lord?

COMPLEMENT: The presence of the Lord.

EXEGETICAL IDEA: Only the presence of the Lord can provide the atonement for sin required by the presence of the Lord.

HOMILETICAL IDEA: The only remedy for the presence of God is the presence of God.

Isaiah 6:8-13

SUBJECT: What did God commission Isaiah to preach?

COMPLEMENT: A message to hard-hearted idolaters that idolatry would result in devastation, leaving only a holy remnant.

EXEGETICAL IDEA: God commissioned Isaiah to preach a message to hard-hearted idolaters that idolatry would result in a devastation, leaving only a holy remnant.

HOMILETICAL IDEA: We, the church, are a signpost.

Isaiah 7:1-9

SUBJECT: What did the Lord do when the Syrians and Israelites planned an attack on Judah?

COMPLEMENT: He sent Isaiah to call King Ahaz and his people to trust in him.

EXEGETICAL IDEA: When the Syrians and Israelites planned an attack on Judah, the Lord sent Isaiah to call King Ahaz and his people to trust in him.

HOMILETICAL IDEA: If we do not stand firm in faith, we will not stand at all.

Isaiah 7:10-25

SUBJECT: What did God do for Ahaz?

COMPLEMENT: He gave him a sign that he would be with Judah and destroy Syria and Israel by the hand of Assyria.

EXEGETICAL IDEA: God gave Ahaz a sign that he would be with Judah and destroy Syria and Israel by the hand of Assyria.

HOMILETICAL IDEA: In Christ, God has given us a sign—Immanuel—that he is with us.

Isaiah 8:1-15

SUBJECT: What did God's surprising solution to the problem of Syria do to Isaiah?

COMPLEMENT: It called him to fear only the Lord.

EXEGETICAL IDEA: God's surprising solution to the problem of Syria called Isaiah to fear only the Lord.

HOMILETICAL IDEA: Let the Lord alone be your fear.

Isaiah 8:16-22

SUBJECT: What did Isaiah do because the people would not listen to God's words but inquired of necromancers?

COMPLEMENT: He sealed up the sacred words of God among his followers.

EXEGETICAL IDEA: Because the people would not listen to God's words but inquired of necromancers, Isaiah sealed up the sacred words of God among his followers.

HOMILETICAL IDEA: God's Word is kept among God's people.

Isaiah 9:1-7

SUBJECT: What will the Divine King do?

COMPLEMENT: He will come, bringing light to the dark places of Israel and establishing an eternal kingdom.

EXEGETICAL IDEA: The Divine King will come, bringing light to the dark places of Israel and establishing an eternal kingdom.

HOMILETICAL IDEA: Our Divine King has come, bringing light to the dark places and establishing an eternal kingdom.

Isaiah 9:8-10:4

SUBJECT: What will the Lord do in response to Israel's persistent rebellion?

COMPLEMENT: He will bring persistent discipline leading to destruction.

EXEGETICAL IDEA: In response to Israel's persistent rebellion, the Lord will bring persistent discipline leading to destruction.

HOMILETICAL IDEA: Our God will bring as much correction as we need.

Isaiah 10:5-19

SUBJECT: How is Assyria mistaken?

COMPLEMENT: Although it thinks it is invincible, it is merely a tool in the Lord's hand to deliver a righteous remnant.

EXEGETICAL IDEA: Assyria is mistaken in that although it thinks it is invincible, it is merely a tool in the Lord's hand to deliver a righteous remnant.

HOMILETICAL IDEA: The powers that be are tools in God's good hands.

Isaiah 10:20-34

SUBJECT: How should Israel view the coming Assyrian invasion?

COMPLEMENT: As a way to trust that Assyria is in the Lord's hand and know that Assyria will not capture Jerusalem.

EXEGETICAL IDEA: Israel should view the coming Assyrian invasion as a way to trust that Assyria is in the Lord's hand and know that Assyria will not capture Jerusalem.

HOMILETICAL IDEA: God will not allow the final ruin of the faithful.

Isaiah 11

SUBJECT: What will become of the Davidic royal line?

COMPLEMENT: It will rule by the Spirit of the Lord, bringing worldwide peace and redemption.

EXEGETICAL IDEA: The Davidic royal line will rule by the Spirit of the Lord, bringing worldwide peace and redemption.

HOMILETICAL IDEA: By the Spirit, Christ is bringing his worldwide kingdom.

Isaiah 12

SUBJECT: How will God's people respond to his salvation?

COMPLEMENT: With songs of joyful gratitude.

EXEGETICAL IDEA: God's people will respond to his salvation with songs of joyful gratitude.

HOMILETICAL IDEA: Let us sing to the God who saves us!

Isaiah 13

SUBJECT: What will happen on the day of the Lord?

COMPLEMENT: It will come by the hand of Babylon, but Babylon itself will be finally broken.

EXEGETICAL IDEA: The day of the Lord will come by the hand of Babylon, but Babylon itself will be finally broken.

HOMILETICAL IDEA: The Father may use rebels for his purposes, but in the end Christ alone will reign.

Isaiah 14:1-23

SUBJECT: How will the fall of Babylon affect Israel?

COMPLEMENT: God will restore the remnant in such a glorious manner that they will taunt their former oppressors.

EXEGETICAL IDEA: At the fall of Babylon, God will restore the remnant in such a glorious manner that they will taunt their former oppressors.

HOMILETICAL IDEA: We will one day taunt those who taunt us today.

Isaiah 14:24-27

SUBJECT: What will the Lord's defeat of Assyria show?

COMPLEMENT: It will show that the Lord's hand cannot be turned back.

EXEGETICAL IDEA: The Lord's defeat of Assyria will show that his hand cannot be turned back.

HOMILETICAL IDEA: There is no one more powerful than the Lord.

Isaiah 14:28-32

SUBJECT: How should Israel respond to the taunts of the Philistines at the death of King Ahaz?

COMPLEMENT: They should know that they have a heritage but that Philistia will come to a final end.

EXEGETICAL IDEA: Though the Philistines taunt Israel at the death of King Ahaz, the Israelites should know that they have a heritage but that Philistia will come to a final end.

HOMILETICAL IDEA: Some people rise only to fall, but Christ's people fall only to rise.

Isaiah 15-16

SUBJECT: How should Israel respond to the Lord's destruction of Moab?

COMPLEMENT: They should mourn the destruction of the nation and welcome refugees into their land.

EXEGETICAL IDEA: Israel should respond to the Lord's destruction of Moab by mourning the destruction of the nation and welcoming refugees into their land.

HOMILETICAL IDEA: When God brings disaster, his people should mourn for those affected and invite them into the kingdom of Christ.

Isaiah 17

SUBJECT: What will Syria and Israel do when the Lord brings ruin on them?

COMPLEMENT: Israel will remember the Lord, and Syria will seek him.

EXEGETICAL IDEA: When the Lord brings ruin on Israel and Syria, Israel will remember the Lord, and Syria will seek him.

HOMILETICAL IDEA: Disaster calls God's people back and summons others to come with them.

Isaiah 18

SUBJECT: What will happen when the Lord summons disaster on Cush?

COMPLEMENT: They will bring tribute to the Lord on Mount Zion.

EXEGETICAL IDEA: When the Lord summons disaster on Cush, they will bring tribute to the Lord on Mount Zion.

HOMILETICAL IDEA: Our God can bring people to himself, even through disaster.

Isaiah 19:1-16

SUBJECT: What will the Lord do to Egypt?

COMPLEMENT: He will bring confusion on the wise and confound their wisdom to their own destruction.

EXEGETICAL IDEA: To Egypt the Lord will bring confusion on the wise and confound their wisdom to their own destruction.

HOMILETICAL IDEA: God can triumph over the strong at their point of strength.

Isaiah 19:17-25

SUBJECT: What is God's plan for the wicked empires of Egypt and Assyria?

COMPLEMENT: To make them his people, just as he did to Israel.

EXEGETICAL IDEA: For the wicked empires of Egypt and Assyria, God will make them his people, just as he did to Israel.

HOMILETICAL IDEA: God's design for the nations is to make them his people, just as he did to us.

Isaiah 20

SUBJECT: Why did the Lord command Isaiah to walk naked?

COMPLEMENT: It was to be a sign that Egypt and Cush, in whom many Judeans trusted, would be led into captivity.

EXEGETICAL IDEA: The Lord commanded Isaiah to walk naked as a sign that Egypt and Cush, in whom many Judeans trusted, would be led into captivity.

HOMILETICAL IDEA: Be careful where you place your faith.

Isaiah 21

SUBJECT: What is the fate of the nations that do not follow the Lord?

COMPLEMENT: It is darkness and defeat.

EXEGETICAL IDEA: The fate of the nations that do not follow the Lord is darkness and defeat.

HOMILETICAL IDEA: The fate of kingdoms in opposition to the kingdom of God is darkness and defeat.

Isaiah 22

SUBJECT: When Jerusalem refuses to repent and mourn over its sin, what will the Lord do?

COMPLEMENT: He will bring invaders who will sweep away even the honorable men.

EXEGETICAL IDEA: When Jerusalem refuses to repent and mourn over its sin, the Lord will bring invaders who will sweep away even the honorable men.

HOMILETICAL IDEA: Heed God's call to repentance!

Isaiah 23

SUBJECT: Why will Tyre be devastated?

COMPLEMENT: Because the Lord will humble the proud.

EXEGETICAL IDEA: Tyre will be devastated because the Lord will humble the proud.

HOMILETICAL IDEA: God will humble the proud.

Isaiah 24

SUBJECT: What will the Lord do in the end to the earth?

COMPLEMENT: He will bring devastation on the whole earth.

EXEGETICAL IDEA: In the end, the Lord will bring devastation on the whole earth.

HOMILETICAL IDEA: Christ's return will bring devastation on the whole earth.

Isaiah 25

SUBJECT: What will the Lord do in the end to the earth?

COMPLEMENT: He will destroy death and feast his people on rich food.

EXEGETICAL IDEA: In the end, the Lord will destroy death and feast his people on rich food.

HOMILETICAL IDEA: Christ's return will bring an end to death and eternal delight to his people.

Isaiah 26

SUBJECT: What will the Lord do for those who delight in him?

COMPLEMENT: He will care for them, giving them refuge in the midst of judgment.

EXEGETICAL IDEA: The Lord will care for those who delight in him, giving them refuge in the midst of judgment.

HOMILETICAL IDEA: Those who wait for the Lord in the path of his judgments will find refuge.

Isaiah 27

SUBJECT: What will happen on the day of the Lord?

COMPLEMENT: He will defeat evil, give life to his purified people, abandon the proud, and gather the lost from all nations.

EXEGETICAL IDEA: On the day of the Lord, he will defeat evil, give life to his purified people, abandon the proud, and gather the lost from all nations.

HOMILETICAL IDEA: In Christ, God has done and will do these things: defeat evil, give life to his people, abandon the proud, and gather the lost from all nations.

Isaiah 28:1-13

SUBJECT: What will the Lord do to the proud?

COMPLEMENT: He will cast them down with perfect and ironic judgment.

EXEGETICAL IDEA: The Lord will cast down the proud with perfect and ironic judgment.

HOMILETICAL IDEA: Those who will not hear will not understand.

Isaiah 28:14-29

SUBJECT: What does the Lord tell his people?

COMPLEMENT: He is the sure foundation and only refuge from his strange and unstoppable disaster.

EXEGETICAL IDEA: The Lord tells his people that he is the sure foundation and only refuge from his strange and unstoppable disaster.

HOMILETICAL IDEA: He who has ears, let him hear the Word of the Lord.

Isaiah 29

SUBJECT: Because Judah has abandoned living faith for dead tradition, what will the Lord do?

COMPLEMENT: He will execute wondrous reversals to remind them that he alone is God.

EXEGETICAL IDEA: Because Judah has abandoned living faith for dead tradition, the Lord will execute wondrous reversals to remind them that he alone is God.

HOMILETICAL IDEA: Because Christ is risen, we must abandon dead tradition for living faith.

Isaiah 30-31

SUBJECT: To whom should Israel turn?

COMPLEMENT: To the Lord, who exalts himself in judgment so that he might show mercy to those who run to him.

EXEGETICAL IDEA: Israel should turn to the Lord, who exalts himself in judgment so that he might show mercy to those who run to him.

HOMILETICAL IDEA: Turn to God, who exalts himself in judgment so that he might show us mercy.

Isaiah 32:1-8

SUBJECT: What will happen when the righteous King reigns?

COMPLEMENT: The might of humans will be cast down, but God's people will have godly leadership.

EXEGETICAL IDEA: When the righteous King reigns, the might of humans will be cast down, but God's people will have godly leadership.

HOMILETICAL IDEA: Those who follow King Jesus will find God's good order.

Isaiah 32:9–20

SUBJECT: What will happen when God pours out his Spirit?

COMPLEMENT: The destruction that complacent Judean women mourned will turn into joy and paradise.

EXEGETICAL IDEA: When God pours out his Spirit, the destruction that complacent Judean women mourned will turn into joy and paradise.

HOMILETICAL IDEA: The Spirit turns us from complacency and ruin to humble joy.

Isaiah 33

SUBJECT: Why is the fear of the Lord Zion's treasure?

COMPLEMENT: Because he will deliver them to safety forever.

EXEGETICAL IDEA: The fear of the Lord is Zion's treasure because he will deliver them to safety forever.

HOMILETICAL IDEA: The fear of the Lord is our treasure because he will deliver us to safety forever.

Isaiah 34

SUBJECT: What will the Lord do to the nations?

COMPLEMENT: He will turn the beautiful nations into a desert.

EXEGETICAL IDEA: The Lord will turn the beautiful nations into a desert.

HOMILETICAL IDEA: Christ's complete reign will mean ruin for rebels.

Isaiah 35

SUBJECT: How will the Lord bring the captives home?

COMPLEMENT: He will turn the desert into a paradise, with a holy road that leads captives back to Zion.

EXEGETICAL IDEA: The Lord will bring the captives home by turning the desert into a paradise, with a holy road that leads captives back to Zion.

HOMILETICAL IDEA: In Christ, the Father rescues us and brings us home by way of holiness.

Isaiah 36–37

SUBJECT: What did the Lord do in response to the prayers of his people?

COMPLEMENT: He miraculously delivered Jerusalem from Sennacherib of Assyria.

EXEGETICAL IDEA: In response to the prayers of his people, God miraculously delivered Jerusalem from Sennacherib of Assyria.

HOMILETICAL IDEA: The Lord hears our prayers and will rescue us from evil.

Isaiah 38-39

SUBJECT: What did King Hezekiah do in response to the grace of the Lord?

COMPLEMENT: He sought protection and quickly turned away from the Lord to a foreign alliance.

EXEGETICAL IDEA: King Hezekiah's response to the grace of the Lord was to seek protection and turn away from the Lord to a foreign alliance.

HOMILETICAL IDEA: Unlike Hezekiah, Christ our King trusted the Father so deeply that he did not shrink from death but gave himself up so that future generations would live.

Isaiah 40:1-11

SUBJECT: What should Israel do in exile?

COMPLEMENT: They should prepare the way for the Lord, who according to his Word will lead his people home.

EXEGETICAL IDEA: In exile, Israel should prepare the way for the Lord, who according to his Word will lead his people home.

HOMILETICAL IDEA: Jesus of Nazareth has come to lead his people home.

Isaiah 40:12-31

SUBJECT: Why can Judah take comfort?

COMPLEMENT: Because there is no one who compares in majesty with the Lord.

EXEGETICAL IDEA: Judah can take comfort because there is no one who compares in majesty to the Lord.

HOMILETICAL IDEA: We can take comfort because there is no one who compares in majesty to our God.

Isaiah 41:1-20

SUBJECT: Why does Israel not need to fear threats, unlike the nations?

COMPLEMENT: Because the Lord who controls those threats is with his people.

EXEGETICAL IDEA: Israel need not fear threats, unlike the nations, because the Lord who controls those threats is with his people.

HOMILETICAL IDEA: Unlike the world, believers need not fear threats, which can kill the body but not harm the soul.

Isaiah 41:21-29

SUBJECT: What are idols like?

COMPLEMENT: Idols, who cannot predict or control events, are powerless compared to the Sovereign One.

EXEGETICAL IDEA: Idols, who cannot predict or control events, are powerless compared to the Sovereign One.

HOMILETICAL IDEA: We worship the God who knows the end from the beginning.

Isaiah 42:1-17

SUBJECT: How will the Lord use his servant?

COMPLEMENT: To bring quiet justice to the nations and lead the blind home.

EXEGETICAL IDEA: The Lord will use his servant to bring quiet justice to the nations and lead the blind home.

HOMILETICAL IDEA: Christ brought quiet justice to the nations and is leading the blind home.

Isaiah 42:18-25

SUBJECT: Who is the blindest of all?

COMPLEMENT: Israel, the servant of the Lord.

EXEGETICAL IDEA: The blindest of all is Israel, the servant of the Lord.

HOMILETICAL IDEA: Though we are his people, we are not fit to do his work apart from Christ.

Isaiah 43:1-44:5

SUBJECT: What have Israel's chastisement, protection, and redemption accomplished?

COMPLEMENT: They have made Israel witnesses for the glory of the Lord, who redeemed them for his own sake.

EXEGETICAL IDEA: Israel's chastisement, protection, and redemption have made them witnesses for the glory of the Lord, who redeemed them for his own sake.

HOMILETICAL IDEA: Christ's rescue has made us witnesses to the one who redeemed us for his own sake.

Isaiah 44:6–28

SUBJECT: What must Israel do, unlike foolish idolaters?

COMPLEMENT: They must remember that the Lord is the one who has executed his purpose.

EXEGETICAL IDEA: Israel, unlike foolish idolaters, must remember that the Lord is the one who has executed his purpose.

HOMILETICAL IDEA: Remember that God alone is the one who has wrought his purposes in our lives.

Isaiah 45:1–13

SUBJECT: How will the Lord accomplish his purpose to restore Israel?

COMPLEMENT: Through the agency of the pagan ruler Cyrus.

EXEGETICAL IDEA: The Lord will accomplish his purpose to restore Israel through the agency of the pagan ruler Cyrus.

HOMILETICAL IDEA: Our God can use anyone to do his will.

Isaiah 45:14–25

SUBJECT: What does the Lord do for the nations?

COMPLEMENT: He invites the nations, who can see how he has executed his sovereign purposes, to come to him to be saved.

EXEGETICAL IDEA: The Lord invites the nations, who can see how he has executed his sovereign purposes, to come to him to be saved.

HOMILETICAL IDEA: God invites all people, who can see how he has executed his sovereign purposes in Christ, to come to him to be saved.

Isaiah 46

SUBJECT: What is the difference between the Lord and idols?

COMPLEMENT: People in Israel must carry their idols, but the Lord carries his people.

EXEGETICAL IDEA: The difference between the Lord and idols is that people in Israel must carry their idols but the Lord carries his people.

HOMILETICAL IDEA: People carry their idols, but the Father carries his people.

Isaiah 47

SUBJECT: What will happen to Babylon, the instrument in the Lord's hands to judge his people?

COMPLEMENT: It will itself be humbled in the end.

EXEGETICAL IDEA: Babylon, the instrument in the Lord's hands to judge his people, will itself be humbled in the end.

HOMILETICAL IDEA: God may use powerful agents to do his bidding, but in the end he will humble them.

Isaiah 48:1-11

SUBJECT: Why does the Lord continue to do new works in the midst of a stubborn people?

COMPLEMENT: For the sake of his own glory.

EXEGETICAL IDEA: The Lord continues to do new works in the midst of a stubborn people for the sake of his own glory.

HOMILETICAL IDEA: God deals with us patiently for the sake of his own glory.

Isaiah 48:12-22

SUBJECT: What does the Lord call Israel to do?

COMPLEMENT: To listen to his Word, which controls the world, so that they might have peace.

EXEGETICAL IDEA: The Lord calls Israel to listen to his Word, which controls the world, so that they might have peace.

HOMILETICAL IDEA: God calls us to listen to his word, which controls the world, so that we might have peace.

Isaiah 49:1-7

SUBJECT: What will happen to the servant of the Lord?

COMPLEMENT: Though despised, he will be honored by the world for the Lord's sake.

EXEGETICAL IDEA: The servant of the Lord, though despised, will be honored by the world for the Lord's sake.

HOMILETICAL IDEA: Christ, the servant of the Lord, though he was despised, will be honored by the world.

Isaiah 49:8–26

SUBJECT: Can the Lord forget his people?

COMPLEMENT: No; instead he will restore them and bring the nations to their feet.

EXEGETICAL IDEA: The Lord cannot forget his people but instead will restore them and bring the nations to their feet.

HOMILETICAL IDEA: In Christ, God cannot forget us.

Isaiah 50

SUBJECT: How is the servant distinct from Israel?

COMPLEMENT: Though Israel did not trust in the Lord when he called, the servant of the Lord listens and is sustained.

EXEGETICAL IDEA: The servant is distinct from Israel in that, though Israel did not trust in the Lord when he called, the servant of the Lord listens and is sustained.

HOMILETICAL IDEA: Though we have ignored God's voice, Christ obeyed the Father, and now we trust in him.

Isaiah 51

SUBJECT: What will Israel hear if they will listen to the Lord?

COMPLEMENT: They will find that God has taken the cup of wrath from their hands and given it to their tormentors.

EXEGETICAL IDEA: If Israel will listen to the Lord, they will find that God has taken the cup of wrath from their hands and given it to their tormentors.

HOMILETICAL IDEA: God is telling us good news, if we will listen.

Isaiah 52:1–12

SUBJECT: What will happen to Jerusalem and to the exiles?

COMPLEMENT: Jerusalem will be restored, and the Lord will summon his people to return from exile.

EXEGETICAL IDEA: Jerusalem will be restored, and the Lord will summon his people to return from exile.

HOMILETICAL IDEA: God is establishing his kingdom and calling people to enter.

Isaiah 52:13–53:12

SUBJECT: How has the servant of the Lord, humble and despised, done the will of God?

COMPLEMENT: By taking the sins of the nation on himself and will therefore be exalted after he pours out his soul unto death.

EXEGETICAL IDEA: The servant of the Lord, humble and despised, has done the will of God by taking the sins of the nation on himself and will therefore be exalted after he pours out his soul unto death.

HOMILETICAL IDEA: Jesus Christ, humble and despised, has done the will of God by taking the sins of the world on himself and was therefore exalted in resurrection from the dead.

Isaiah 54

SUBJECT: What will happen to Israel as the barren and estranged wife of the Lord?

COMPLEMENT: She will be restored in an eternal covenant with her God and will rear her children in peace.

EXEGETICAL IDEA: Israel, as the barren and estranged wife of the Lord, will be restored in an eternal covenant with her God and will rear her children in peace.

HOMILETICAL IDEA: The church, the bride of Christ, though she suffers, will live in eternal covenant with her husband.

Isaiah 55

SUBJECT: Why does the Lord offer abundant and free pardon to sinners?

COMPLEMENT: Because his ways are higher than Israel's.

EXEGETICAL IDEA: The Lord offers abundant and free pardon to sinners because his ways are higher than Israel's.

HOMILETICAL IDEA: God offers abundant and free pardon to sinners because his ways are higher than ours.

Isaiah 56:1-8

SUBJECT: What will the Lord do with faithful eunuchs and foreigners?

COMPLEMENT: He will gather them into his redeemed people.

EXEGETICAL IDEA: The Lord will gather faithful eunuchs and foreigners into his redeemed people.

HOMILETICAL IDEA: God gathers outcasts and brings them into his family.

Isaiah 56:9-57:21

SUBJECT: What is the difference between the fate of the unrepentant and that of the contrite?

COMPLEMENT: Though there is no peace for the unrepentant, the Lord will restore contrite sinners.

EXEGETICAL IDEA: The difference between the fate of the unrepentant and that of the contrite is that though there is no peace for the unrepentant, the Lord will restore contrite sinners.

HOMILETICAL IDEA: Though there is no peace for the unrepentant, in Christ God will restore contrite sinners.

Isaiah 58

SUBJECT: What does God call Israel to do?

COMPLEMENT: To abandon hypocritical fasting for true fasting that consists in doing justice and honoring the Lord.

EXEGETICAL IDEA: God calls Israel to abandon hypocritical fasting for true fasting that consists in doing justice and honoring the Lord.

HOMILETICAL IDEA: God calls us to abandon hypocritical fasting for true fasting that consists in doing justice and honoring the Lord.

Isaiah 59:1-15

SUBJECT: Why does Israel not find salvation?

COMPLEMENT: It is not because the Lord is unable to save but because their sins have separated them from him.

EXEGETICAL IDEA: Israel does not find salvation, not because the Lord is unable to save but because their sins have separated them from him.

HOMILETICAL IDEA: Consider the idea that pain could be discipline rather than abandonment.

Isaiah 59:16–21

SUBJECT: What will the Lord do now that Israel's grievous sins have separated it from its God and left him without anyone to intercede?

COMPLEMENT: He himself will bring salvation and put his Spirit in his people.

EXEGETICAL IDEA: Because Israel's grievous sins separated it from its God and left him without anyone to intercede, the Lord himself will bring salvation and put his Spirit in his people.

HOMILETICAL IDEA: Though our sins separate us from God, he himself rescues us, giving us his Spirit and his Word.

Isaiah 60

SUBJECT: What will the Lord do with his people and the nations?

COMPLEMENT: He will bring his people to a state of glory, and the nations will come to Jerusalem.

EXEGETICAL IDEA: The Lord will bring his people to a state of glory, and the nations will come to Jerusalem.

HOMILETICAL IDEA: The Lord will glorify his church, and people from every nation will worship him.

Isaiah 61

SUBJECT: What will happen because the Spirit of God is on the servant of the Lord?

COMPLEMENT: The servant will usher in the Lord's favor and his vengeance.

EXEGETICAL IDEA: Because the Spirit of God is on the servant of the Lord, the servant will usher in the Lord's favor and his vengeance.

HOMILETICAL IDEA: Because the Spirit of God rests on Christ, he alone brings God's favor and God's vengeance.

Isaiah 62

SUBJECT: What does Isaiah summon the faithful to do?

COMPLEMENT: To give God no rest until he makes Jerusalem the praise of the earth.

EXEGETICAL IDEA: Isaiah summons the faithful to give God no rest until he makes Jerusalem the praise of the earth.

HOMILETICAL IDEA: Let us pray without ceasing for the coming of the kingdom of God.

Isaiah 63:1-6

SUBJECT: What did the servant do, seeing that no one stood with him?

COMPLEMENT: He took it upon himself to execute vengeance on the nations.

EXEGETICAL IDEA: Because no one stood with him, the servant took it upon himself to execute vengeance on the nations.

HOMILETICAL IDEA: Christ alone is the one who will bring justice to the earth.

Isaiah 63:7–64:12

SUBJECT: In light of God's faithful care of his people, and their sinful response, what does Isaiah cry out to God?

COMPLEMENT: "Oh, that you would rend the heavens and come down" (64:1).

EXEGETICAL IDEA: In light of God's faithful care of his people, and their sinful response, Isaiah cries out, "Oh, that you would rend the heavens and come down!"

HOMILETICAL IDEA: Our Lord, come!

Isaiah 65:1-16

SUBJECT: What will the Lord do when he brings judgment?

COMPLEMENT: He will make a distinction between his true servants and the stubborn rebels.

EXEGETICAL IDEA: When he brings judgment, the Lord will make a distinction between his true servants and the stubborn rebels.

HOMILETICAL IDEA: Christ knows those who are truly his, and he is able to separate the true from the false.

Isaiah 65:17-25

SUBJECT: What will the new heavens and the new earth that God creates be like?

COMPLEMENT: They will be a place of life and peace.

EXEGETICAL IDEA: The new heavens and the new earth that God creates will be a place of life and peace.

HOMILETICAL IDEA: The new heavens and the new earth that God creates will be a place of life and peace.

Isaiah 66:1-14

SUBJECT: What will the Lord do for the humble remnant when he comes to establish his kingdom?

COMPLEMENT: He will deliver his faithful ones from their enemies and welcome them into his kingdom.

EXEGETICAL IDEA: When the Lord comes to establish his kingdom, he will deliver his faithful ones from their enemies and welcome them into his kingdom.

HOMILETICAL IDEA: As God ushers in his kingdom in Christ, he delivers his faithful ones from their enemies and welcomes them into his kingdom.

Isaiah 66:15-17

SUBJECT: What will the Lord do to the idolaters when he comes to establish his kingdom?

COMPLEMENT: He will bring judgment on them.

EXEGETICAL IDEA: When the Lord comes to establish his kingdom, he will bring judgment on the idolaters.

HOMILETICAL IDEA: As God consummates his kingdom in Christ, he will bring judgment on those who have refused his grace.

Isaiah 66:18-24

SUBJECT: What will the Lord do for the people of all nations when he comes to establish his kingdom?

COMPLEMENT: He will send his faithful ones to the nations to bring in those who have not known him.

EXEGETICAL IDEA: When the Lord comes to establish his kingdom, he will send his faithful ones to the nations to bring in those who have not known him.

HOMILETICAL IDEA: As God ushers in his kingdom in Christ, he sends his faithful ones to the nations to bring in those who have not known him.

Difficult Passages/Verses

Isaiah bristles with preaching challenges. Four of the most common deserve mention.

First, there are historical issues. It is often difficult to locate Isaiah's oracles in their original context. For instance, his prediction of the fall of Babylon in chapter 21 may refer to several instances of the defeat of that city. Though the most likely candidate is an event during the reign of Merodach-Baladan in 689 BC, uncertainty (and controversy) remains.[2]

However, even if the historical context is clear, preachers will find it challenging to make that context relevant to contemporary listeners, particularly if those listeners are not familiar with the Bible. The history of Israel is rich, intricate, and theologically loaded. It will raise complicated questions for the uninitiated: Why is Assyria invading Judah? Why are there two kingdoms in Israel? Why does the Lord pay more attention to these people than to Edomites or Egyptians? Preachers will have to find ways to explain that history without getting lost in it.

Second, there are literary challenges to preaching Isaiah's oracles. The prophet's words were effective in the ears of Hebrew speakers to a large degree because of his literary devices. Puns, alliteration, allusions, repetition of phrases, brutal irony, vivid images, and dramatic reversal all served to catch the ear and pierce the heart of rebellious Judeans. In Isaiah 5:7, God "looked for justice [*mishpat*], but behold, bloodshed [*mispah*]; for righteousness [*tsedaqah*], but behold, an outcry [*tsa'aqah*]!" (ESV). The puns Isaiah makes do not translate into English well, but this is a part of the oracle: like wild grapes appear to be good fruit but are not, the deeds of Judah appeared to them to be righteous but were not.

Preachers have the task of using their training and resources to understand those original devices. They have the added responsibility of helping listeners understand them as well. They can do this either by explaining those devices or by trying to emulate them in contemporary parlance. The danger of explaining a pun or other device, of course, is that you ruin the effect; the risk of trying to emulate these strange and confusing oracles is that you will preach strange and confusing sermons. Preachers must walk the tightrope between boredom and confusion to help congregations experience some of the subtle beauty of Isaiah's language.

Third, multiple passages seem in some way to refer to Christ. One must respect the original meaning of Isaiah's words while addressing how the advent of Christ has fulfilled and perhaps enhanced the meaning of Isaiah's words in ways that he himself did not understand. For example, when Isaiah speaks in chapter 7 of a virgin or young woman conceiving a child named Immanuel, that event (for Isaiah) was a sign to King Ahaz that as soon as the child had grown, Ahaz's enemies would be no more. Deliverance would come in a few short years. However, the New Testament writers see the virgin birth of Jesus of Nazareth as fulfilling this word from Isaiah. Preachers must help listeners

2. For discussion, see J. Alec Motyer, *The Prophecy of Isaiah* (Downers Grove, IL: Inter-Varsity, 1993), 172.

respect both contexts. If handled well, sermons from these passages will not upset their faith in God's ways but instead will deepen it. (See the recommended resources below for help on this complex issue.)

Finally, preachers of the prophetic corpus must reckon with prophetic monotony: though the prophets' oracles display an array of communicative *strategies*, their *content* is utterly unwavering. They remind Israel of God's covenant faithfulness, call Israel to covenant faithfulness in response, and herald the consequences of obedience and disobedience. The unceasing repetition of these themes reflects the hardened hearts of Israel and the persistence of the prophets. But preaching through dozens of oracles like this can try a congregation's patience.

The solution is for preachers to become deeply involved not just with what Isaiah said but also how he said it. How did he persuade? How did he charm, frighten, instill hope? If preachers can engage the Scriptures on the level of their rhetorical strategy, then their sermons will be able to display the same variety in faithfulness that Isaiah did.

Cultural Perspectives and Application

In order to apply prophetic material, it helps first to clarify one's approach to interpreting the prophets. Once that general approach is clear to preachers, it will give them clarity when facing issues of application.

My approach is to interpret the prophetic material in terms of its *covenant context*.[3] The prophets operate consciously under the terms of the covenants that God has made with Israel. Their accusations, warnings, and promises are not novel, nor are they invented by the prophets. The prophets merely repeat and reapply the terms of God's covenants that have already been established: the covenants with Noah, Abraham, Moses, and David.

The church is under the terms of the new covenant in Christ. That new covenant has deep connections with and significant differences from prior covenants. How preachers understand the similarities and differences will shape how they apply oracles under other covenants to a community under the new covenant.

For instance, the *covenant Lord* is the same Lord; God does not change. Any oracle in Isaiah that speaks of God's majesty or holiness can be applied directly to the church. However, there may be different *covenant demands* in view. Isaiah 58 commends Sabbath observance, while some view the Sabbath

3. The following is based on Andrew C. Thompson, "Community Oracles: A Model for Applying and Preaching the Old Testament Prophets," *Journal of the Evangelical Homiletics Society* 10, no. 1 (March 2010): 31–57.

as set aside by the coming of Christ. How has the Sabbath been fulfilled or abrogated by Christ? Answers to that question will guide the preacher in applying Isaiah's oracles.

More significantly, *covenant consequences* may not be the same. Isaiah may predict historical events that have already transpired (like the Assyrian invasion of Israel in the eighth century BC). Preachers can either point to the fulfillment of those events as confirmation of God's faithfulness or else point to parallel consequences that apply now to the church. The big ideas above generally take the latter approach.

One advantage of thinking through a framework like covenant contexts is that when preachers seek to apply Isaiah's words to contemporary Christians, they will avoid turning every passage into an individualistic moral. When God appears to Isaiah and calls him in chapter 6, when Isaiah walks naked in chapter 20, when Hezekiah is sick in chapter 38, when the servant of the Lord is sent to the nations in chapter 49—these are not patterns that repeat themselves in individual lives. They are covenant realities that apply corporately to God's people and then individually as people are members of that covenant community. In other words, it is not that we are each like Isaiah or like Hezekiah. Instead, we are (corporately) like the people to whom Isaiah preached.

Moving from the text to the covenant context, through that context to the church, and then to individuals is a longer pathway than individualistic interpretation. But it raises helpful questions and will eventually bear fruit in sermons that connect God's people more deeply to his character and promises.

With such a framework in mind, then, Isaiah will speak to believers as those in covenant with God in Christ. His words will address us as those who have been rescued by grace, who live under covenant demands from our Lord, and who have precious promises in that same Lord. Isaiah's words will also speak to unbelievers as those not within the covenant circle, calling them home with stern warnings and beautiful promises.

RECOMMENDED RESOURCES

Beale, G. K., and D. A. Carson. *Commentary on the New Testament Use of the Old Testament*. Grand Rapids: Baker Academic, 2007.

Motyer, J. Alec. *The Prophecy of Isaiah: An Introduction and Commentary*. Downers Grove, IL: InterVarsity, 1993.

Seitz, Christopher R. *Isaiah 1–39*. Interpretation. Louisville: Westminster John Knox, 2012.

Jeremiah

JULIAN R. GOTOBED

Jeremiah is a message of judgment directed at the kingdom of Judah in a time of social, political, and religious crisis, when the Babylonian Empire threatens the very existence of the nation. It offers a prospect of hope to Judah in the form of a small remnant surviving in exile.

SUBJECT: What is the message God gave the prophet Jeremiah to declare to Judah?

COMPLEMENT: God is working through the events in Jeremiah's generation to judge Judah for the people's disobedience, but God will preserve a remnant of the nation through exile in Babylon to continue the divine purpose.

EXEGETICAL IDEA: The message God gave the prophet Jeremiah to declare to Judah is that God is working through the events in Jeremiah's generation to judge Judah for the people's disobedience, but God will preserve a remnant of the nation through exile in Babylon to continue the divine purpose.

HOMILETICAL IDEA: God judges his people on account of their transgressions but always seeks a way for them to return to the fullness of divine fellowship.

Selecting Preaching and Teaching Passages in Jeremiah

Jeremiah is a sprawling literary composition describing his life and major historical episodes in seventh-century-BC Judah, punctuated by prophetic oracles and poetry. Its fifty-two chapters vary considerably in length. Chapter divisions do not always cohere with the flow of the text. Key subjects occur frequently. Although the preaching and teaching of Jeremiah lends itself more to a thematic approach to passage selection than chapter-by-chapter exposition, I have sought to be comprehensive and have therefore provided big ideas for each chapter and verse. For example, thematically one might engage the following passages:

The call of Jeremiah to proclaim the word of the Lord (1:1–19)
God pleads with Israel to repent (2:1–25)
Speaking truth to power is costly (6:1–12)
Israel and Judah have broken the covenant (11:1–17)
What does a real king look like? (21:11–22:19)
Beware false prophets and priests (23:1–22)
A letter to exiles: hope in the midst of despair (29:1–10)
Promise of a new covenant (31:31–34)
Judgment on the nations: Babylon (51:1–19)

Ernest Nicholson helpfully divides the chapters as follows:

Judgment on the nation (chaps. 1–25)
The word of God rejected (chaps. 26–36)
Jeremiah's ministry during the siege and fall of Jerusalem (chaps. 37–45)
Oracles against the nations [Conclusion] (chaps. 46–51 [52])[1]

Getting the Subject, Complement, Exegetical Idea, and Homiletical Idea

Jeremiah 1

SUBJECT: What was the Lord's purpose for Jeremiah?

COMPLEMENT: He would be a prophet who announced judgment on Judah for turning to false gods and breaking the covenant; he would be confident in the Lord's faithful presence with him when he experienced opposition.

EXEGETICAL IDEA: The Lord's purpose for Jeremiah was that he would be a prophet who announced judgment on Judah for turning to false gods and

1. Ernest W. Nicholson, *The Book of the Prophet Jeremiah: Chapters 1–25* (Cambridge: Cambridge University Press, 1973), 14–15.

breaking the covenant; he would be confident in the Lord's faithful presence with him when he experienced opposition.

HOMILETICAL IDEA: God empowers prophets to speak the truth and promises to sustain them with his presence.

Jeremiah 2

SUBJECT: What was the consequence of Israel pursuing false gods, seeking security with nations that cannot help, treating the poor unjustly, and protesting innocence when guilty of sin?

COMPLEMENT: The nation grieved the Lord, ruptured its special relationship with the Lord, and deservedly incurred judgment.

EXEGETICAL IDEA: The consequence of Israel pursuing false gods, seeking security with nations that cannot help, treating the poor unjustly, and protesting innocence when guilty of sin was that the nation grieved the Lord, ruptured its special relationship with the Lord, and deservedly incurred judgment.

HOMILETICAL IDEA: Rejecting God is self-destructive.

Jeremiah 3:1-5

SUBJECT: What hope existed for Israel to return to the Lord after repeatedly breaking the covenant and presuming on the Lord's generosity?

COMPLEMENT: The Lord had acted in judgment to persuade Israel to turn back in trust and obedience.

EXEGETICAL IDEA: Hope existed for Israel to return to the Lord after repeatedly breaking the covenant and presuming on the Lord's generosity because the Lord had acted in judgment to persuade Israel to turn back in trust and obedience.

HOMILETICAL IDEA: God seeks the return of everyone who has been alienated from fellowship with God.

Jeremiah 3:6-25

SUBJECT: How did the Lord appeal to Judah and Israel following their pursuit of false gods?

COMPLEMENT: They were to repent, and he would then raise up leaders of integrity and reunite both nations in the land of their ancestors.

EXEGETICAL IDEA: The Lord appealed to Judah and Israel following their pursuit of false gods to repent, and he would then raise up leaders of integrity and reunite both nations in the land of their ancestors.

HOMILETICAL IDEA: God appeals to us to turn away from substitutes for God and turn back to God to experience mercy and goodness.

Jeremiah 4:1–4

SUBJECT: How did the Lord appeal to Israel to return to him?

COMPLEMENT: If the people returned to him, the nations would want to be blessed like Israel, but if they did not amend their attitude and behavior, the Lord would judge Judah.

EXEGETICAL IDEA: The Lord appealed to Israel to return to him so that the nations would want to be blessed like Israel, but if they did not amend their attitude and behavior, the Lord would judge Judah.

HOMILETICAL IDEA: God seeks our return to divine fellowship to bless all peoples.

Jeremiah 4:5–31

SUBJECT: Why was Jeremiah's vision of invasion from the north deeply troubling to him?

COMPLEMENT: It confirmed judgment was certain because of Judah's rebellion and evil, but there was a glimmer of hope if the people returned to the Lord.

EXEGETICAL IDEA: Jeremiah's vision of invasion from the north was deeply troubling to him because it confirmed judgment was certain because of Judah's rebellion and evil, but there was a glimmer of hope if the people returned to the Lord.

HOMILETICAL IDEA: An authentic message of judgment and hope springs from a sorrowful heart and compassion for others.

Jeremiah 5:1–19

SUBJECT: Why was the absence of people in Jerusalem who acted justly and spoke the truth perplexing?

COMPLEMENT: It indicated that the population was corrupt and complacent, merited judgment, and depended on the Lord's goodness to survive coming troubles.

EXEGETICAL IDEA: The absence of people in Jerusalem who acted justly and spoke the truth was perplexing because it indicated that the population was corrupt and complacent, merited judgment, and depended on the Lord's goodness to survive coming troubles.

HOMILETICAL IDEA: People who deny truth and justice must expect judgment but can discover hope in the knowledge that God cares for them.

Jeremiah 5:20-31

SUBJECT: Why did people resist the Lord and stubbornly persist in practicing evil and exploiting the poor?

COMPLEMENT: They liked it, and the prophets and priests promoted false religion that reinforced distorted notions of the Lord and oppressive behavior in society.

EXEGETICAL IDEA: People resisted the Lord and stubbornly persisted in practicing evil and exploiting the poor because they liked it and the prophets and priests promoted false religion that reinforced distorted notions of the Lord and oppressive behavior in society.

HOMILETICAL IDEA: Bad ideas reinforced by bad religion embed evil and injustice in a community.

Jeremiah 6:1-15

SUBJECT: How did the people's rejection of the Lord's message of judgment that Jeremiah proclaimed affect the prophet?

COMPLEMENT: It disheartened him and caused him to try to contain the message within himself, which was exhausting.

EXEGETICAL IDEA: The people's rejection of the Lord's message of judgment that Jeremiah proclaimed disheartened the prophet and caused him to try to contain the message within himself, which was exhausting.

HOMILETICAL IDEA: Speaking God's truth is uncomfortable and costly.

Jeremiah 6:16-30

SUBJECT: What would happen to Judah as a result of ignoring the law of the Lord ("ancient paths") and the prophets ("sentinels" or "watchmen")?

COMPLEMENT: A nation to the north, from whom there is no escape, would march against Judah and defeat it.

EXEGETICAL IDEA: As a result of ignoring the law of the Lord ("ancient paths") and the prophets ("sentinels" or "watchmen"), a nation to the north, from whom there is no escape, would march against Judah and defeat it.

HOMILETICAL IDEA: Persistently ignoring God's guidance and correction for life together as a community of faith entails damaging consequences for everyone.

Jeremiah 7:1-15

SUBJECT: What is the message the Lord wanted Jeremiah to proclaim in the temple?

COMPLEMENT: The people must decide between insincere worship and exploiting the poor, leading to judgment, or true worship that abandons false gods and acts justly, leading to fellowship with the Lord.

EXEGETICAL IDEA: The message the Lord wanted Jeremiah to proclaim in the temple is that the people must decide between insincere worship and exploiting the poor, leading to judgment, or true worship that abandons false gods and acts justly, leading to fellowship with the Lord.

HOMILETICAL IDEA: Choose true worship over false worship and choose justice over oppression.

Jeremiah 7:16-8:17

SUBJECT: Why should Jeremiah not pray to the Lord for the people of Judah?

COMPLEMENT: The people have stubbornly persisted in worshiping other gods since their deliverance from Egypt and ignored prophets sent to call them back, so now the Lord planned to act in judgment.

EXEGETICAL IDEA: Jeremiah should not pray to the Lord for the people of Judah, as they have stubbornly persisted in worshiping other gods since their deliverance from Egypt and ignored the prophets sent to call them back, so now the Lord planned to act in judgment.

HOMILETICAL IDEA: Persistent disobedience exasperates God.

Jeremiah 8:18-9:3

SUBJECT: Why did Jeremiah mourn for his people?

COMPLEMENT: The pursuit of idols had alienated them from the Lord and corrupted their life together as a society.

EXEGETICAL IDEA: Jeremiah mourned for his people because the pursuit of idols had alienated them from the Lord and corrupted their life together as a society.

HOMILETICAL IDEA: Choosing a substitute for God disrupts our vertical relationship with God and distorts our horizontal relations with one another.

Jeremiah 9:4-11

SUBJECT: What was it about the society Jeremiah inhabited that caused him to experience and express deep sorrow?

COMPLEMENT: People routinely schemed, lied, and committed violence to exploit and oppress their neighbors, which the Lord condemned and judged.

EXEGETICAL IDEA: The society Jeremiah inhabited caused him to experience and express deep sorrow because people routinely schemed, lied, and committed violence to exploit and oppress their neighbors, which the Lord condemned and judged.

HOMILETICAL IDEA: Bad behavior that enables injustice offends God and should fill our hearts with sorrow and inspire us to speak truth to power for justice.

Jeremiah 9:12-26

SUBJECT: Why should people mourn at the judgment of the Lord?

COMPLEMENT: The experience of judgment to come, which is the consequence of a stubbornness of heart that refuses to turn aside from idols, would be severe.

EXEGETICAL IDEA: The people should mourn at the judgment of the Lord, which is the consequence of a stubbornness of heart that refuses to turn aside from idols, because the judgment to come would be severe.

HOMILETICAL IDEA: Lament is legitimate when called forth by a deep awareness of sin and disobedience toward God.

Jeremiah 10:1-16

SUBJECT: Why was Israel's adoption of idols problematic to the Lord?

COMPLEMENT: Israel denied the reality that these gods did not exist and could not act, unlike the Lord, who alone is God and created the cosmos and called Israel into a unique relationship.

EXEGETICAL IDEA: Israel's adoption of idols was problematic to the Lord because Israel denied the reality that these gods did not exist and could not act, unlike the Lord, who alone is God and created the cosmos and called Israel into a unique relationship.

HOMILETICAL IDEA: Acknowledge the true God, not a useless substitute for God.

Jeremiah 10:17-25

SUBJECT: What was the plight of the nation because its leadership had failed?

COMPLEMENT: It found itself cast adrift from the Lord, unable to control its destiny, soon to be driven into exile, and needing to recognize its dependency on the Lord for survival.

EXEGETICAL IDEA: The plight of the nation because its leadership had failed was that it found itself cast adrift from the Lord, soon to be driven into exile, unable to control its destiny, and needing to recognize its dependency on the Lord for survival.

HOMILETICAL IDEA: Leadership indifferent to God misdirects the people in its care.

Jeremiah 11:1-17

SUBJECT: What was the message the Lord wanted Jeremiah to proclaim to the cities of Judah?

COMPLEMENT: Israel and Judah had broken the covenant the Lord made with them; consequently judgment was inevitable and there was no escape from the disaster to come.

EXEGETICAL IDEA: The message the Lord wanted Jeremiah to proclaim to the cities of Jerusalem was that Israel and Judah had broken the covenant the Lord made with them; consequently judgment was inevitable and there was no escape from the disaster to come.

HOMILETICAL IDEA: We are accountable to God for how we live.

Jeremiah 11:18-23

SUBJECT: How did the Lord answer Jeremiah's cry for retribution on those who threatened his life because of his prophetic ministry?

COMPLEMENT: The Lord declared judgment on those who were antagonistic toward Jeremiah, and so vindicated him.

EXEGETICAL IDEA: The Lord answered Jeremiah's cry for retribution on those who threatened his life because of his prophetic ministry by declaring judgment on those who were antagonistic toward Jeremiah, and so vindicated him.

HOMILETICAL IDEA: God confirms the calling of faithful servants when they encounter hostility and opposition.

Jeremiah 12

SUBJECT: What did the Lord tell Jeremiah in response to the reality that the wicked rather than the faithful prospered and thought the Lord was indifferent to their behavior?

COMPLEMENT: Present difficulties were nothing compared to the coming judgment, and ultimately the Lord would show compassion to his people in the future.

EXEGETICAL IDEA: In response to the reality that the wicked rather than the faithful prospered and thought the Lord was indifferent to their behavior, the Lord told Jeremiah that present difficulties were nothing compared to the coming judgment, and ultimately the Lord would show compassion to his people in the future.

HOMILETICAL IDEA: God's compassion sustains the faithful in terrible times.

Jeremiah 13:1-14

SUBJECT: What did a soiled pair of shorts signify to Jeremiah's generation?

COMPLEMENT: Israel's refusal to listen to the Lord made them no more helpful to the Lord than a soiled pair of shorts was to a human being.

EXEGETICAL IDEA: A soiled pair of shorts signified to Jeremiah's generation that Israel's refusal to listen to the Lord made them no more helpful to the Lord than a soiled pair of shorts was to a human being.

HOMILETICAL IDEA: Listen to God to be useful in God's service.

Jeremiah 13:15-27

SUBJECT: What was going to happen to Judah if they did not listen and turn back to the Lord?

COMPLEMENT: They faced a future threat from the north; they would be humiliated and taken into exile.

EXEGETICAL IDEA: If Judah did not listen and turn back to the Lord, they faced a future threat from the north; they would be humiliated and taken into exile.

HOMILETICAL IDEA: The hope of those estranged from God lies in the goodness and love of God that perseveres in seeking their return.

Jeremiah 14:1-12

SUBJECT: How did the Lord respond to cries for help from the people of Judah in a time of drought that was endangering human life?

COMPLEMENT: The Lord lamented the evil of the people and intimated reluctance to heed their insincere worship.

EXEGETICAL IDEA: The Lord responded to cries for help from the people of Judah in a time of drought that was endangering human life by lamenting the evil of the people and intimating reluctance to heed their insincere worship.

HOMILETICAL IDEA: Insincere worship and the practice of evil in a community of faith alienate God.

Jeremiah 14:13-22

SUBJECT: What was the Lord's reply to the messages of false prophets who said no disaster would befall Judah?

COMPLEMENT: They were not sent by the Lord, they had no true knowledge of divine things, and events would ultimately prove they were wrong.

EXEGETICAL IDEA: The Lord's reply to the messages of false prophets who said no disaster would befall Judah was that they were not sent by the Lord, they had no true knowledge of divine things, and events would ultimately prove they were wrong.

HOMILETICAL IDEA: The passage of time exposes false claims made in the name of God.

Jeremiah 15:1-9

SUBJECT: How likely and extensive would be the judgment of the Lord on Judah announced by Jeremiah?

COMPLEMENT: It would be certain and comprehensive.

EXEGETICAL IDEA: The judgment of the Lord on Judah announced by Jeremiah would be certain and comprehensive.

HOMILETICAL IDEA: God's purpose is always decisive and all-encompassing.

Jeremiah 15:10-21

SUBJECT: How did the Lord demonstrate his trustworthiness to Jeremiah when the prophet complained about the treatment he received for proclaiming the message of the Lord?

COMPLEMENT: The Lord promised to sustain Jeremiah and deliver him from the hands of his enemies.

EXEGETICAL IDEA: The Lord demonstrated his trustworthiness to Jeremiah when the prophet complained about the treatment he received for proclaiming the message of the Lord by promising to sustain Jeremiah and deliver him from the hands of his enemies.

HOMILETICAL IDEA: God supports and rescues faithful servants when they do the right thing.

Jeremiah 16:1-13

SUBJECT: What would it cost Jeremiah to declare judgment on Judah?

COMPLEMENT: It would be best for him not to marry and have children because of the destruction and death to befall the nation.

EXEGETICAL IDEA: The cost to Jeremiah of declaring judgment on Judah was that it would be best for him not to marry and have children because of the destruction and death to befall the nation.

HOMILETICAL IDEA: The call to proclaim the Word of God in some contexts may require the messenger to think carefully before marrying and starting a family.

Jeremiah 16:14-21

SUBJECT: What hope was there for the nation after the Lord had taken Israel into exile?

COMPLEMENT: The Lord promised to restore Israel in the future to the land of its ancestors.

EXEGETICAL IDEA: The hope for Israel after the Lord had taken the nation into exile was that the Lord would restore Israel in the future to the land of its ancestors.

HOMILETICAL IDEA: The promise of God is a source of hope for the people of God.

Jeremiah 17

SUBJECT: How did Jeremiah account for persistent idolatry and disobedience on the part of Judah?

COMPLEMENT: Sin was etched in the depths of the human heart, which the Lord discerned and judged accordingly.

EXEGETICAL IDEA: Jeremiah accounted for persistent idolatry and disobedience on the part of Judah on the basis of sin being etched in the depth of the human heart, which the Lord discerned and judged accordingly.

HOMILETICAL IDEA: God discerns and takes seriously the fact of sin being embedded deep in the human heart, which causes us to disobey and distrust God.

Jeremiah 18:1-11

SUBJECT: What did observing a potter at work help show Jeremiah about the Lord?

COMPLEMENT: The Lord shaped the history of Israel and responded to events, like a potter who molded clay according to his purpose and changed his mind to create something new.

EXEGETICAL IDEA: Observing a potter at work helped show Jeremiah that the Lord shaped the history of Israel and responded to events, like a potter who molded clay according to his purpose and changed his mind to create something new.

HOMILETICAL IDEA: God acts flexibly according to divine purpose and character.

Jeremiah 18:12-23

SUBJECT: What effect did Jeremiah's denouncement of Judah's idolatry and abandoning the covenant ("ancient roads," v. 15 ESV) have on his contemporaries?

COMPLEMENT: They plotted to bring charges against the prophet to silence him.

EXEGETICAL IDEA: The effect of Jeremiah's denouncement of Judah's idolatry and abandoning the covenant ("ancient roads," v. 15 ESV) on his contemporaries was that they plotted to bring charges against the prophet to silence him.

HOMILETICAL IDEA: People committed to false notions of God and indifferent to injustice in society oppose those who point to the true God and campaign for justice.

Jeremiah 19

SUBJECT: What kind of disaster would the Lord bring on Jerusalem as judgment for the sacrifice of children to Baal?

COMPLEMENT: The Lord intended to break Judah much like Jeremiah shattered an earthenware jug so that nobody could remake it.

EXEGETICAL IDEA: The disaster the Lord intended to bring on Jerusalem as judgment for the sacrifice of children to Baal would break Judah much like Jeremiah shattered an earthenware jug so that nobody could remake it.

HOMILETICAL IDEA: God is not indifferent to terrible evil caused by human hands and holds the perpetrators to account.

Jeremiah 20

SUBJECT: What did it feel like for Jeremiah to be persecuted for proclaiming faithfully a message from the Lord?

COMPLEMENT: It produced a mixture of deep sorrow within and confidence in the Lord's presence to stand up to opposition from without.

EXEGETICAL IDEA: To be persecuted for proclaiming faithfully a message from the Lord produced in Jeremiah a mixture of deep sorrow within and confidence in the Lord's presence to stand up to opposition from without.

HOMILETICAL IDEA: Persecution for being true to God may drive us to despair, but knowledge of God's presence with us inspires hope.

Jeremiah 21:1–22:19

SUBJECT: What qualities were required of a king of Judah to rule the nation from within and protect it from enemies without?

COMPLEMENT: Execute justice without partiality and guide the people to worship the Lord alone or expect judgment.

EXEGETICAL IDEA: The qualities required of a king of Judah to rule the nation from within and protect it from enemies without were to execute justice without partiality and guide the people to worship the Lord alone or expect judgment.

HOMILETICAL IDEA: A wise leader acts justly and acknowledges God in all aspects of personal and community life.

Jeremiah 22:20–23:8

SUBJECT: What was the difference between good and bad leadership in Judah?

COMPLEMENT: Good leadership faithful to the Lord cared about people, whereas bad leadership unfaithful to the Lord was indifferent to people.

EXEGETICAL IDEA: The difference between good and bad leadership in Judah was that good leadership faithful to the Lord cared about people, whereas bad leadership unfaithful to the Lord was indifferent to people.

HOMILETICAL IDEA: The attitude of leaders to God and people in their care determines whether they are a help or hindrance to God's purposes.

Jeremiah 23:9–40

SUBJECT: What was the truth about the prophets that proclaimed a false hope of peace and prosperity?

COMPLEMENT: They never spoke for the Lord but instead declared their own thoughts, denied any threat to the nation, and encouraged the people to do evil.

EXEGETICAL IDEA: The truth about the prophets that proclaimed a false hope of peace and prosperity was that they never spoke for the Lord but instead declared their own thoughts, denied any threat to the nation, and encouraged the people to do evil.

HOMILETICAL IDEA: Persuading people to believe lies in the name of God ruins lives.

Jeremiah 24

SUBJECT: What did two baskets of figs, one good and one bad, signify following Babylon's victory?

COMPLEMENT: Good figs represented the Lord's favor and promise to return exiles in Babylon to Judah, and bad figs represented the Lord's judgment on Judeans in Judah and Egypt.

EXEGETICAL IDEA: Following Babylon's victory, two baskets of figs, one good and one bad, signified, respectively, the Lord's favor and promise to return exiles in Babylon to Judah, and the Lord's judgment on Judeans in Judah and Egypt.

HOMILETICAL IDEA: A community of faith must choose for or against God's purpose here and now.

Jeremiah 25

SUBJECT: What did Jeremiah's vision from the Lord of presenting a cup of wrath to all the rulers of all the nations signify?

COMPLEMENT: The Lord's sovereignty was comprehensive; every leader and every nation was accountable to the Lord and would be judged.

EXEGETICAL IDEA: Jeremiah's vision from the Lord of presenting a cup of wrath to all the rulers of all the nations signified that the Lord's sovereignty was comprehensive; every leader and every nation was accountable to the Lord and would be judged.

HOMILETICAL IDEA: All nations are accountable to God and judged by God.

Jeremiah 26

SUBJECT: What message did the Lord require Jeremiah to proclaim in public in the temple?

COMPLEMENT: Unless the people turned from their wickedness and once more lived together according to the law, the Lord would visit judgment on them.

EXEGETICAL IDEA: The message the Lord required Jeremiah to proclaim in public in the temple was that unless the people turned from their wickedness and once more lived together according to the law, the Lord would visit judgment on them.

HOMILETICAL IDEA: A message that calls a nation to repent and warns it of judgment is controversial and unpopular.

Jeremiah 27

SUBJECT: What did the yoke the Lord instructed Jeremiah to make and wear signify?

COMPLEMENT: The Lord, who created the earth and its peoples, had selected Babylon as his agent; all nations, including Judah, must accept Babylon's rule or face judgment.

EXEGETICAL IDEA: The yoke the Lord instructed Jeremiah to make and wear signified that the Lord, who created the earth and its peoples, had selected Babylon as his agent; all nations, including Judah, must accept Babylon's rule or face judgment.

HOMILETICAL IDEA: Discern and work with the agents God selects to accomplish the divine purpose in the world.

Jeremiah 28

SUBJECT: What was Jeremiah's retort to Hananiah's message to Zedekiah that the Lord would defeat Babylon and return the people and temple artifacts taken into exile?

COMPLEMENT: Hananiah had spoken falsely in the name of the Lord and would die for misleading the people.

EXEGETICAL IDEA: Jeremiah's retort to Hananiah's message to Zedekiah that the Lord would defeat Babylon and return the people and temple artifacts taken into exile was that Hananiah had spoken falsely in the name of the Lord and would die for misleading the people.

HOMILETICAL IDEA: God exposes false messages uttered in God's name.

Jeremiah 29:1-23

SUBJECT: What was Jeremiah's message to the exiles from Judah in Babylon?

COMPLEMENT: The Lord would return them to Judah, but in the meantime they must settle in Babylon and seek the well-being of the society they now live in.

EXEGETICAL IDEA: Jeremiah's message to the exiles in Babylon was that the Lord would return them to Judah, but in the meantime they must settle in Babylon and seek the well-being of the society they now live in.

HOMILETICAL IDEA: Work for the common good of the community you live in.

Jeremiah 29:24–30:24

SUBJECT: What hope was there for Judah and Israel, scattered among the nations on account of their sins?

COMPLEMENT: The Lord promised to restore the people to the land of their ancestors and heal their wounds, once judgment upon them was concluded.

EXEGETICAL IDEA: The hope for Judah and Israel, scattered among the nations for their sins, was that the Lord promised to restore the people to the land of their ancestors and heal their wounds, once judgment upon them was concluded.

HOMILETICAL IDEA: God looks beyond judgment to restoring relationship and making lives whole again.

Jeremiah 31

SUBJECT: How would the Lord transform his relationship with Israel after the people returned from exile?

COMPLEMENT: The Lord promised to make a new covenant through which people experienced forgiveness of sin and a new and intimate knowledge of the Lord.

EXEGETICAL IDEA: The Lord would transform his relationship with Israel after the people returned from exile by promising to make a new covenant through which people experienced forgiveness of sin and a new and intimate knowledge of the Lord.

HOMILETICAL IDEA: God promises to remake the human heart so we may know both divine forgiveness and fellowship.

Jeremiah 32

SUBJECT: Why did Jeremiah buy a field in Judah while Jerusalem was besieged by Babylon?

COMPLEMENT: It was a sign of hope that although the city must fall, the Lord would cause the people to return in the future and resume a settled way of life.

EXEGETICAL IDEA: Jeremiah bought a field in Judah while Jerusalem was besieged by Babylon as a sign of hope that although the city must fall, the Lord would cause the people to return in the future and resume a settled way of life.

HOMILETICAL IDEA: Symbols true to God's Word inspire hope.

Jeremiah 33

SUBJECT: How would the Lord help Judah and Jerusalem following defeat by Babylon and punishment of the people's disobedience?

COMPLEMENT: He would forgive and heal the people and raise up a descendent of David to perform justice and protect Jerusalem.

EXEGETICAL IDEA: Following defeat by Babylon and punishment of the people's rebellion, the Lord would help Judah and Jerusalem by forgiving and healing the people and raising up a descendent of David to perform justice and protect Jerusalem.

HOMILETICAL IDEA: God looks beyond judgment on disobedience to forgive, make whole, and advance justice.

Jeremiah 34

SUBJECT: How did the Lord view Zedekiah's making and breaking a covenant with the people of Judah to free all Hebrew slaves?

COMPLEMENT: The initial act of repentance was good, but its reversal was deeply unjust and affronted the Lord.

EXEGETICAL IDEA: The Lord viewed Zedekiah's making and breaking a covenant with the people of Judah to free all Hebrew slaves initially as an act of repentance that was good, but its reversal was deeply unjust and affronted the Lord.

HOMILETICAL IDEA: God judges liberty falsely offered and cruelly withdrawn.

Jeremiah 35

SUBJECT: What did the fidelity of the Rechabites to their vow not to drink wine teach Judah, which had been repeatedly unfaithful to the Lord?

COMPLEMENT: The Lord commended the loyalty of the Rechabites and promised to sustain the line of their descendants.

EXEGETICAL IDEA: The fidelity of the Rechabites to their vow not to drink wine taught Judah, which had been repeatedly unfaithful to the Lord, that the Lord commended the loyalty of the Rechabites and promised to sustain the line of their descendants.

HOMILETICAL IDEA: The Lord honors those who trust and obey him.

Jeremiah 36

SUBJECT: Why did King Jehoiakim burn Jeremiah's scroll, which declared Babylon would destroy Judah?

COMPLEMENT: The action symbolized the defiance of the king and the people toward the Lord's covenant claims on Judah and the corrective message announced by the prophet.

EXEGETICAL IDEA: King Jehoiakim burned Jeremiah's scroll, which declared Babylon would destroy Judah, to symbolize the defiance of the king and the people toward the Lord's covenant claims on Judah and the corrective message announced by the prophet.

HOMILETICAL IDEA: Rejection of God's Word does not invalidate its truth or diminish its resilience.

Jeremiah 37–38

SUBJECT: Why was Jeremiah consulted by King Zedekiah and, at various times, placed under house arrest, imprisoned in a cistern, and set free?

COMPLEMENT: His experience reflected varied responses to the Word of the Lord in his generation, including curiosity, hostile rejection, and positive reception.

EXEGETICAL IDEA: Jeremiah was consulted by King Zedekiah and, at various times, placed under house arrest, imprisoned in a cistern, and set free as a result of varied responses to the Word of the Lord in his generation, including curiosity, hostile rejection, and positive reception.

HOMILETICAL IDEA: God's Word evokes different responses in different people.

Jeremiah 39

SUBJECT: What did the Lord promise Jeremiah when the prophet's message about the fall of Jerusalem and King Zedekiah came to pass?

COMPLEMENT: The Lord would keep Jeremiah safe, which came about through the king of Babylon, who treated him with respect.

EXEGETICAL IDEA: The Lord promised Jeremiah when the prophet's message about the fall of Jerusalem and King Zedekiah came to pass that he would keep Jeremiah safe, which came about through the king of Babylon, who treated him with respect.

HOMILETICAL IDEA: God keeps his promises in surprising ways.

Jeremiah 40-41

SUBJECT: What characterized society in Judah under Babylon during the governorship of Gedaliah?

COMPLEMENT: Principal agents acted without reference to the Lord and in competition with one another, creating an environment marked by deception and violence.

EXEGETICAL IDEA: Society in Judah under Babylon during the governorship of Gedaliah was characterized by principal agents who acted without reference to the Lord and in competition with one another, creating an environment marked by deception and violence.

HOMILETICAL IDEA: A society where leaders operate without reference to God and in pursuit of singular causes quickly descends into violence and chaos.

Jeremiah 42

SUBJECT: Why did Jeremiah advise survivors in Judah to remain where they were and not flee to Egypt?

COMPLEMENT: Disaster awaited them in Egypt, but the Lord promised to help the people flourish under Babylonian rule.

EXEGETICAL IDEA: Jeremiah advised survivors in Judah to remain where they were and not flee to Egypt because disaster awaited them in Egypt, but the Lord promised to help the people flourish under Babylonian rule.

HOMILETICAL IDEA: God's wisdom is sometimes counterintuitive but represents the best strategy for flourishing as a community here and now.

Jeremiah 43

SUBJECT: What made Johanan's decision to flee to Egypt with the remnant from Judah to escape Babylon flawed?

COMPLEMENT: It was contrary to the will of the Lord and would be followed by judgment in the form of destruction by Babylon.

EXEGETICAL IDEA: Johanan's decision to flee to Egypt with the remnant from Judah to escape Babylon was flawed because it was contrary to the will of the Lord and would be followed by judgment in the form of destruction by Babylon.

HOMILETICAL IDEA: God's wisdom guides us to safe havens while human folly leads us into minefields.

Jeremiah 44

SUBJECT: What would be the consequence of persistent idolatry committed by Judeans living in Egypt?

COMPLEMENT: The Lord would punish them for their evil actions.

EXEGETICAL IDEA: The consequence of persistent idolatry committed by Judeans in Egypt would be that the Lord would punish them for their evil actions.

HOMILETICAL IDEA: Turning to substitutes for God results in disaster.

Jeremiah 45

SUBJECT: How did the Lord address Baruch's despair at Jeremiah's message of judgment against Judah?

COMPLEMENT: The Lord promised to preserve Baruch's life in the midst of the disaster visited upon Judah.

EXEGETICAL IDEA: The Lord addressed Baruch's despair at Jeremiah's message of judgment against Judah by promising to preserve his life in the midst of the disaster visited upon Judah.

HOMILETICAL IDEA: God sustains faithful messengers in turbulent times.

Jeremiah 46-52

SUBJECT: What was Jeremiah's message to Judah, neighboring peoples, and especially Babylon, which acted as the agent of the Lord against the nations?

COMPLEMENT: They were accountable to the Lord and must expect judgment as a result of their arrogance, idolatry, and unjust behavior.

EXEGETICAL IDEA: Jeremiah's message to Judah, neighboring peoples, and especially Babylon, which acted as the agent of the Lord against the nations, was that they were accountable to the Lord and must expect judgment as a result of their arrogance, idolatry, and unjust behavior.

HOMILETICAL IDEA: All nations everywhere are accountable to God and subject to judgment.

Difficult Passages/Verses

The purpose of Jeremiah is to announce a message of judgment on his own nation—namely, Judah—and foreign nations in close proximity to it. This primary theme is reiterated time and time again. Thankfully, it is not the only subject matter in the book. Hope makes an appearance on several occasions. Nonetheless, judgment is dominant from start to finish (see especially chaps. 1–25 and 46–51). The whole book, then, not merely a few isolated passages, is a challenge to the preacher or teacher! To help people understand Jeremiah, it is important to clarify what the prophet means by "judgment."

First, it refers to punishment for Judah abandoning its covenant obligation to the Lord. Second, judgment is conceived as a disciplinary measure designed to persuade Judah and Israel to abandon false gods and return in trust and obedience to the Lord. Both senses of judgment presuppose an acknowledgment that Judah is properly accountable to the Lord (as are all nations) and that how people live in relation to the Lord and in relation to one another is legitimately a matter of great concern to the Lord. Jeremiah makes clear that how we live before God and how we treat one another have consequences. God is not indifferent to injustice and holds us to account.

Jeremiah notes that judgment as a corrective to bring Judah back on track has not resulted in the desired outcome. He asks the question, Why, despite judgment designed to prompt it to return to God, did Judah not do so? Jeremiah attributes this resistance to a stubbornness deep in the human heart that chooses evil and resists returning to God. The prophet points to the need for a deeper transformation (31:31–34) because of the mysterious and self-deceiving nature of the human heart (17:9–10). Israel seems to be incapable of recalling the past (the exodus and what God has done), or at least interpreting it aright, or learning the lessons of more recent history. Judah suffers from a bad case of historic amnesia! Why do so many today also forget the past and believe lies in the present?

Ultimately, the human condition that so perplexes Jeremiah requires the gracious initiative and action of God to transform the human heart. Hope in Jeremiah is grounded in the faithful love and goodness of God that holds people to account but refuses to abandon a recalcitrant people and continuously seeks to find ways of enabling them to return to divine fellowship and pursue a quality of life in which they can truly flourish.

Cultural Perspectives and Application

In Western culture the name Jeremiah is associated with a disposition inclined toward doom and gloom. A Jeremiah is a person who sees in human experience and circumstances a glass half empty, never a glass half full. Hence, a Jeremiah perceives obstacles in life and struggles to recognize opportunities. Optimism is not the normal disposition of a Jeremiah. An attentive reading of Jeremiah in the Bible makes clear why such a negative characterization arose and persists. The prophet points remorselessly to reality as it is and questions false assumptions and misleading ideas. In and of itself, such a trait is a good thing; it guards against self-deception and surrendering to fantasy. Judgment begins with seeing things as they are, not as one might imagine them to be. Yet even though Jeremiah is primarily about judgment, it is not exclusively so. Passages about judgment (19:1–15; 46:1–51:64) need to be read alongside passages that point to hope and renewal (16:14–21; 31:1–34). The danger, otherwise, is that the preacher or teacher of Jeremiah assimilates and advocates a distorted vision of God.

Walter Brueggemann is correct that "the text requires very little explicit 'application'" in relation to the main themes in the book.[2] The message of Jeremiah makes clear that God holds *all* nations to account, including Judah. In effect, Jeremiah declares, "May God damn Judah!" No wonder the prophet elicited robust and hostile responses! How, when circumstances and events indicate that a nation is behaving in an unjust and evil fashion, do we preach a sermon against our own nation and the principal actors or leaders within it? Jeremiah indicates that it is necessary and inevitably costly to speak truth to power. Those who declare "May God damn _____" (fill in the blank) and dare to call their own nation to account are unlikely to be applauded by the tabloid press and social media.

RECOMMENDED RESOURCES

Adeyemo, Tokunboh, ed. *Africa Bible Commentary*. Grand Rapids: Zondervan, 2006.

Brueggemann, Walter. *A Commentary on Jeremiah: Exile and Home-coming*. 4th ed. Grand Rapids: Eerdmans, 1998.

Goldingay, John. *Jeremiah for Everyone*. London: SPCK, 2015.

---

2. Walter Brueggemann, *A Commentary on Jeremiah: Exile and Homecoming* (Grand Rapids: Eerdmans, 1998), 14.

Lamentations

CASEY C. BARTON

The Big Idea of Lamentations

The book of Lamentations is a series of five poetic prayers grieving the destruction of Jerusalem and the exile of God's people. These prayers give voice to the pain and tragedy God's people have experienced. The author focuses squarely on the destruction, memorializing and laying bare grief and suffering, and desiring that God see this suffering.[1]

SUBJECT: What is the prayer of Lamentations' author in the wake of Jerusalem's destruction and the people's exile?

COMPLEMENT: That God would see the destruction of his people and remember his promises to them.

EXEGETICAL IDEA: In the wake of Jerusalem's destruction and the people's exile, Lamentations' author prays that God would look upon the destruction of his people and remember his promises to them.

HOMILETICAL IDEA: When the ground beneath us collapses, we fall onto God's promises.

Selecting Preaching and Teaching Passages in Lamentations

Lamentations naturally falls into five preaching units divided by chapter. The first four chapters are alphabetic acrostics, highlighting the literary unity

---

1. Adele Berlin, *Lamentations: A Commentary* (Louisville: Westminster John Knox, 2002), 1.

of each poem. Chapter 5 maintains the style of lyric poetry without the alphabetic form. Adele Berlin notes that each poem observes the calamity of invasion and destruction from a different standpoint.[2]

Getting the Subject, Complement, Exegetical Idea, and Homiletical Idea

Lamentations 1

SUBJECT: What does the author pray to God in the wake of Jerusalem's destruction?

COMPLEMENT: For God to see and comfort his people in their calamity as they confess and repent of their sin.

EXEGETICAL IDEA: In the wake of Jerusalem's destruction, the author prays for God to see and comfort his people in their calamity as they confess and repent of their sin.

HOMILETICAL IDEA: In sin's calamity, we confess and pray for God's comfort.

Lamentations 2

SUBJECT: What does the author say to God's people in the wake of Jerusalem's destruction?

COMPLEMENT: He recounts the completeness of the destruction and despair of God's people and calls them to repent.

EXEGETICAL IDEA: The author recounts in the wake of Jerusalem's destruction the completeness of the destruction and despair of God's people and calls them to repent.

HOMILETICAL IDEA: In sin's ruin, we repent and pray for God's mercy.

Lamentations 3

SUBJECT: What does the one experiencing Jerusalem's destruction hope for his future?

COMPLEMENT: That even in God's righteous judgment, when he calls to the Lord for help, the Lord will respond out of his love by forgiving and putting the world right again.

EXEGETICAL IDEA: The one experiencing Jerusalem's destruction hopes for his future that even in God's righteous judgment, when he calls to the Lord

2. Berlin, *Lamentations*, 7.

for help, the Lord will respond out of his love by forgiving and putting the world right again.   .

HOMILETICAL IDEA: In sin's judgment, God's forgiveness and love will rise again.

Lamentations 4

SUBJECT: What does the author observe as he stands in the ruins of Jerusalem, taking account of the city's destruction?

COMPLEMENT: That the whole world has been turned upside down, but that this would soon end and God would make things right.

EXEGETICAL IDEA: As he stands in the ruins of Jerusalem, taking account of the city's destruction, the author observes that the whole world has been turned upside down, but that this would soon end and God would make things right.

HOMILETICAL IDEA: In sin's upside downness, God will right the world again.

Lamentations 5

SUBJECT: What is the author's final word in the aftermath of the fall of God's people?

COMPLEMENT: He cries out to God to remember and save them.

EXEGETICAL IDEA: The author's final word in the aftermath of the fall of God's people is to cry out to God to remember and save them.

HOMILETICAL IDEA: God is our hope for renewal.

Difficult Passages/Verses

Lamentations on the whole is a difficult text. Important considerations abound for the preacher.

Preaching a timely word to God's people today must take into account that the book of Lamentations is an occasional writing that laments the horrors of a specific event in the history of God's people: the destruction of Jerusalem and the people's exile. This event changes the course of faith and life for those who experienced it and everyone who will come after.[3] Homiletical work must not trivialize the gravity of the event, refusing to minimize the eventfulness or despair of the story.

3. Berlin, *Lamentations*, 1.

Additionally, Lamentations as *lyric poetry* should be taken into account throughout exegetical and homiletical work. F. W. Dobbs-Allsopp notes that this genre "is never a matter of boiling the lyric poem down to its essentials, but rather experiencing it for what it does as it does it."[4] Along with the text's idea, genre considerations must influence how the preacher identifies experiences created by the text and how she or he might craft the experience of the sermon.

Cultural Perspectives and Application

These poems lay naked the realities of tragedy and suffering in brutal and creative ways. They cut against a contemporary cultural preference for stories with a happy ending. Lamentations is not interested in offering a significant amount of hope. It is a natural tendency to move quickly away from grief, but that is not the purpose of this work. The author seeks to reveal the suffering of God's people and asks everyone, especially God, to look upon that suffering. To accomplish this purpose the author uses imagery that constitutes "some of the Bible's most violent and brutal pieces of writing . . . filled with horrifyingly dark and grizzly images of raw human pain and suffering."[5] The preacher must explore the root of this imagery and wrestle with how to preach it for God's people today.

Further, Lamentations presents an image of God as judge that many today are not comfortable with. Because we live on the other side of Christ's resurrection, it becomes easy to focus on the grace and love of God, forgetting God's judgment of sin. Lamentations is clear that the destruction before the people is the result of God's judgment of infidelity to the covenant. Today God's people rightly declare that there is no condemnation for those in Christ (Rom. 8:1), yet it is also true that there is time of putting the world to rights (Matt. 13:24–30). This can be a tricky road to walk.

While Lamentations is not full of good news, preaching the gospel must be. Preaching today takes place after Christ's cross, and in this context one must bring into the frame the grace of God in Christ, who is essentially the answer to these prayers. The preacher must be comfortable with the sadness of the world and be able to hold it in tension with the grace and hope given in Christ.

---

4. F. W. Dobbs-Allsopp, *Lamentations*, Interpretation (Louisville: Westminster John Knox, 2002), 13.

5. Dobbs-Allsopp, *Lamentations*, 2.

RECOMMENDED RESOURCES

Berlin, Adele. *Lamentations: A Commentary.* Louisville: Westminster John Knox, 2002.

Dobbs-Allsopp, F. W. *Lamentations.* Interpretation. Louisville: Westminster John Knox, 2002.

Goldingay, John. *Lamentations and Ezekiel for Everyone.* Louisville: Westminster John Knox, 2016.

Ezekiel

ANDREW C. THOMPSON

Ezekiel, the son of Buzi, a priest among the Judean exiles in Babylon, was commissioned as a prophet by the Lord just prior to the fall of Jerusalem and the end of Israel's hope as a nation.

Extreme times call for extreme measures. Ezekiel's task was to shake the exiles' confidence regarding their immediate future. God would not, as they believed, spare Jerusalem or return the exiles to their homeland in the near future. Instead, irrevocable destruction was decreed for their capital, and death and exile awaited those remaining in Israel. In order to subvert such a perverse but foundational belief, the Lord (through Ezekiel) employs extreme language and violent emotion. Ezekiel's messages are bizarre, foul, bloody, at times overtly erotic, and laden with pronouncements of inexorable doom.

However, after the fall of Jerusalem Ezekiel had the opposite task: to inspire shell-shocked Judeans to look to the Lord for a future restoration more glorious than any they had imagined. Thus the first half of the book is just as gruesome and dark as the second half is magnificent, defying the imagination.

SUBJECT: What does the Lord tell the Babylonian exiles through Ezekiel?

COMPLEMENT: That the present is worse than they can imagine, but the future would be better than they could hope for.

EXEGETICAL IDEA: The Lord tells the Babylonian exiles through Ezekiel that the present is worse than they can imagine, but the future would be better than they could hope for.

HOMILETICAL IDEA: The present is worse than we imagine, but the future is better than we can hope for.

Selecting Preaching and Teaching Passages in Ezekiel

See the discussion on selecting passages in the chapter on Isaiah in this volume. All the material in that section applies here as well.

Getting the Subject, Complement, Exegetical Idea, and Homiletical Idea[1]

Ezekiel 1:1-28a

SUBJECT: What happens to Ezekiel when the hand of the Lord is on him by the Chebar canal?

COMPLEMENT: He sees glorious visions of God on his throne.

EXEGETICAL IDEA: When the hand of the Lord is on Ezekiel by the Chebar canal, he sees glorious visions of God on his throne.

HOMILETICAL IDEA: Our God is glorious beyond imagination.

Ezekiel 1:28b-3:11

SUBJECT: How does the Lord commission Ezekiel?

COMPLEMENT: By putting his words in the prophet's mouth to fearlessly deliver to the rebellious house of Israel.

EXEGETICAL IDEA: The Lord commissions Ezekiel by putting his words in the prophet's mouth to fearlessly deliver to the rebellious house of Israel.

HOMILETICAL IDEA: God speaks to his people even when they are in rebellion.

Ezekiel 3:12-15

SUBJECT: What happens to Ezekiel after he is commissioned?

COMPLEMENT: He returns in bitterness and heat to his people.

---

1. The reader will note that, in many cases, what Ezekiel predicts as future for the exiles is already past for the church. In such cases it is often appropriate, when preaching, to find similar promises and warnings in our current new covenant context. The homiletical ideas in this section often indicate how this was done. Additionally, my own perspective on eschatology and Israel will be apparent in the homiletical ideas. Those with different views may make significant modifications.

EXEGETICAL IDEA: After he is commissioned, Ezekiel returns in bitterness and heat to his people.

HOMILETICAL IDEA: It's not always fun to be a spokesperson for God.

Ezekiel 3:16-21

SUBJECT: What is the implication of the fact that the Lord makes Ezekiel into a watchman for Israel?

COMPLEMENT: It makes him liable for the lives of the people, should he fail to deliver his message.

EXEGETICAL IDEA: The implication that the Lord makes Ezekiel into a watchman for Israel is that he is liable for the lives of the people, should he fail to deliver his message.

HOMILETICAL IDEA: Woe to us if we preach not the gospel!

Ezekiel 3:22-27

SUBJECT: What does the Lord do with Ezekiel?

COMPLEMENT: He binds Ezekiel to prevent him from associating with or interceding for Israel until the appointed time.

EXEGETICAL IDEA: The Lord binds Ezekiel to prevent him from associating with or interceding for Israel until the appointed time.

HOMILETICAL IDEA: One day it will be too late for repentance.

Ezekiel 4

SUBJECT: Why does the Lord make Ezekiel do such bizarre and unpleasant deeds before the exiles?

COMPLEMENT: So that they will understand the extent of sin and the resulting punishment of Jerusalem.

EXEGETICAL IDEA: The Lord makes Ezekiel do bizarre and unpleasant deeds so they will understand the extent of sin and the resulting punishment of Jerusalem.

HOMILETICAL IDEA: God gives clear warning of judgment to come.

Ezekiel 5

SUBJECT: What does Ezekiel's division of his own hair symbolize?

COMPLEMENT: It symbolizes the death and destruction of the Lord's covenant people in response to their unprecedented wickedness.

EXEGETICAL IDEA: Ezekiel's division of his own hair symbolizes the death and destruction of the Lord's covenant people in response to their unprecedented wickedness.

HOMILETICAL IDEA: In God's perfect justice, no rebel will be unaccounted for.

Ezekiel 6

SUBJECT: What does Ezekiel say would happen in the mountains and high places of Israel?

COMPLEMENT: The Lord will bring destruction to idolatrous shrines, death to idol worshipers, and shame to surviving exiles.

EXEGETICAL IDEA: Ezekiel says that in the mountains and high places of Israel, the Lord will bring destruction to idolatrous shrines, death to idol worshipers, and shame to surviving exiles.

HOMILETICAL IDEA: The Lord tolerates allegiance to no other gods.

Ezekiel 7

SUBJECT: What is the Lord's message to the land of Israel?

COMPLEMENT: The end of the nation has come, and after a hopeless defeat they will go into captivity.

EXEGETICAL IDEA: The Lord's message to the land of Israel is that the end of the nation has come, and after a hopeless defeat they will go into captivity.

HOMILETICAL IDEA: When God says it's time, then it's time.

Ezekiel 8

SUBJECT: What does Ezekiel see in his vision of the temple complex?

COMPLEMENT: He sees scene after scene of secret religious blasphemies.

EXEGETICAL IDEA: In his vision of the temple complex, Ezekiel sees scene after scene of secret religious blasphemies.

HOMILETICAL IDEA: God sees our secrets.

Ezekiel 9

SUBJECT: In Ezekiel's vision, what does the Lord do in response to the secret idolatry of Jerusalem?

COMPLEMENT: He orders the execution of the wicked and the protection of the faithful.

EXEGETICAL IDEA: In Ezekiel's vision, the Lord, in response to the secret idolatry of Jerusalem, orders the execution of the wicked and the protection of the faithful.

HOMILETICAL IDEA: God is able to justly punish and perfectly preserve.

Ezekiel 10

SUBJECT: What is the conclusion of Ezekiel's vision of the judgment of Jerusalem?

COMPLEMENT: The Lord scatters burning coals over the city and his presence departs from the temple.

EXEGETICAL IDEA: At the conclusion of Ezekiel's vision of the judgment of Jerusalem, the Lord scatters burning coals over the city and his presence departs from the temple.

HOMILETICAL IDEA: The presence and power of God are not unconditionally bound to a place or a people.

Ezekiel 11:1-13

SUBJECT: What is Ezekiel's message to the rebellious leaders in Jerusalem?

COMPLEMENT: They are not protected as they think, and they will be taken out of the city and slain, while the slain of the city will remain within.

EXEGETICAL IDEA: Ezekiel's message to the rebellious leaders in Jerusalem is that they are not protected as they think, and they will be taken out of the city and slain, while the slain of the city will remain within.

HOMILETICAL IDEA: The church is not a "sanctuary" for the violent.

Ezekiel 11:14-25

SUBJECT: What is the Lord's message for the exiled Israelites?

COMPLEMENT: He will bring them back from exile and purify their hearts so that they will purify the land.

EXEGETICAL IDEA: The Lord's message to the exiled Israelites is that he will bring them back from exile and purify their hearts so that they will purify the land.

HOMILETICAL IDEA: In God's eyes, present discipline does not indicate future disaster.

Ezekiel 12:1-20

SUBJECT: Why does Ezekiel move out of his settlement and live in fear?

COMPLEMENT: To be a sign of the exile of the prince of Israel and the terror of the people in Jerusalem.

EXEGETICAL IDEA: Ezekiel moves out of his settlement and lives in fear in order to be a sign of the exile of the prince of Israel and the terror of the people in Jerusalem.

HOMILETICAL IDEA: In God's eyes, present pleasure does not indicate future paradise.

Ezekiel 12:21-28

SUBJECT: What does the Lord say in response to the exiles' belief that his words are for the distant future?

COMPLEMENT: He says that he will fulfill his word in their own lifetime.

EXEGETICAL IDEA: In response to the exiles' belief that his words are for the distant future, the Lord says that he will fulfill his word in their own lifetime.

HOMILETICAL IDEA: God's kingdom is advancing now, and his Son is coming soon.

Ezekiel 13

SUBJECT: What will the Lord do in response to false prophets among the exiles?

COMPLEMENT: He will set himself against them and destroy their work.

EXEGETICAL IDEA: In response to false prophets among the exiles, the Lord will set himself against them and destroy their work.

HOMILETICAL IDEA: God sets himself against those who speak falsely in his name.

Ezekiel 14:1-11

SUBJECT: What is the Lord's reply to the inquiry of the idolatrous elders of Israel?

COMPLEMENT: He says that he will set his face against them and punish them so that Israel will know that he is the Lord.

EXEGETICAL IDEA: The Lord's reply to the inquiry of the idolatrous elders of Israel is that he says he will set his face against them and punish them so that Israel will know that he is the Lord.

HOMILETICAL IDEA: The Father calls for our undivided allegiance to Christ.

Ezekiel 14:12-23

SUBJECT: Can the presence of a few holy people save sinful Jerusalem from the Lord's judgment?

COMPLEMENT: No, the holy people can save only themselves.

EXEGETICAL IDEA: The presence of a few holy people cannot save Jerusalem from the Lord's judgment, because the holy people can save only themselves.

HOMILETICAL IDEA: No one can prevent God's judgment, but we can be rescued from it in Christ.

Ezekiel 15

SUBJECT: What is the character and fate of the inhabitants of Jerusalem?

COMPLEMENT: They are like the useless wood of a vine and will be consigned to the fire of destruction.

EXEGETICAL IDEA: The character and fate of the inhabitants of Jerusalem are like the useless wood of a vine and will be consigned to the fire of destruction.

HOMILETICAL IDEA: Apart from Christ, we bring nothing of worth to the Lord and are fit only for judgment.

Ezekiel 16:1-43

SUBJECT: To what does the Lord liken the idolatry of Jerusalem?

COMPLEMENT: The wickedness of the wife of the Lord, who commits unprecedented adultery with many lovers.

EXEGETICAL IDEA: The Lord likens the idolatry of Jerusalem to the wickedness of the wife of the Lord, who commits unprecedented adultery with many lovers.

HOMILETICAL IDEA: Christ loves his bride the church and insists that she be faithful.

Ezekiel 16:44-63

SUBJECT: Because Israel has become more corrupt than the surrounding nations, what will the Lord do?

COMPLEMENT: He will restore both it and the surrounding nations with an everlasting covenant—to their shameful remembrance.

EXEGETICAL IDEA: Because Israel has become more corrupt than the surrounding nations, he will restore both it and the surrounding nations with an everlasting covenant—to their shameful remembrance.

HOMILETICAL IDEA: God's covenant with us in Christ humbles us even as it rescues us.

Ezekiel 17

SUBJECT: What does the parable of the two eagles and the vine for Zedekiah and the future of Israel mean?

COMPLEMENT: That Zedekiah has turned to the king of Egypt and away from the Lord's command for submission to Babylon, he will be destroyed and the Lord will one day plant a new king in Israel.

EXEGETICAL IDEA: The parable of the two eagles and vine for Zedekiah and the future of Israel means that Zedekiah has turned to the king of Egypt and away from the Lord's command for submission to Babylon, he will be destroyed and the Lord will one day plant a new king in Israel.

HOMILETICAL IDEA: God uproots faithless leaders and has put his faithful Son on the throne.

Ezekiel 18

SUBJECT: What does the Lord say in response to the fatalistic worldview of the exiles?

COMPLEMENT: That they should turn from their wicked ways and live.

EXEGETICAL IDEA: In response to the fatalistic worldview of the exiles, the Lord tells them they should turn from their wicked ways and live.

HOMILETICAL IDEA: God calls us to turn from our wicked ways and live!

Ezekiel 19

SUBJECT: What does Ezekiel's satirical lamentation for the princes of Israel mean?

COMPLEMENT: That the Davidic kingship in Jerusalem has come to an end.

EXEGETICAL IDEA: Ezekiel's satirical lamentation for the princes of Israel means that the Davidic kingship in Jerusalem has come to an end.

HOMILETICAL IDEA: Only King Jesus, the faithful offspring of David, will sit on David's throne.

Ezekiel 20:1-31

SUBJECT: Why does the Lord refuse to be inquired of by the elders of Israel who come to Ezekiel?

COMPLEMENT: Because their entire history as a nation has been one of continual disobedience, in the face of which only his concern for his holy name has delayed judgment.

EXEGETICAL IDEA: The Lord refuses to be inquired of by the elders of Israel who come to Ezekiel because their entire history as a nation has been one of continual disobedience, in the face of which only his concern for his holy name has delayed judgment.

HOMILETICAL IDEA: Our wickedness runs far deeper than we know, and therefore our rescue in Christ is far grander than we imagine.

Ezekiel 20:32-44

SUBJECT: Why will Israel never be able to be like the other nations?

COMPLEMENT: Because of the unstoppable will of the Lord.

EXEGETICAL IDEA: Israel will never be able to be like the other nations because of the unstoppable will of the Lord.

HOMILETICAL IDEA: Christ *will* be king over us.

Ezekiel 20:45-21:7

SUBJECT: What message does Ezekiel preach against the land of Israel?

COMPLEMENT: The Negeb will burn and the sword of the Lord will be against Jerusalem.

EXEGETICAL IDEA: The message Ezekiel preaches against the land of Israel is that the Negeb will burn and the sword of the Lord will be against Jerusalem.

HOMILETICAL IDEA: The Lord will come to judge with flame and sword.

Ezekiel 21:8-17

SUBJECT: Why is the Lord bringing the sword against Jerusalem at the word of Ezekiel?

COMPLEMENT: Because his people have despised the wooden rod of discipline.

EXEGETICAL IDEA: The Lord is bringing the sword against Jerusalem at the word of Ezekiel because his people have despised the wooden rod of discipline.

HOMILETICAL IDEA: Do not despise the Lord's discipline.

Ezekiel 21:18-32

SUBJECT: How will the foretold destruction come to Judah?

COMPLEMENT: The Lord will guide the Babylonian king to Judah by pagan divination.

EXEGETICAL IDEA: The foretold destruction of Judah will come when the Lord guides the Babylonian king to Judah by pagan divination.

HOMILETICAL IDEA: Even those who do not know the Lord can be instruments in his hands.

Ezekiel 22:1-16

SUBJECT: Why can't Israel be strong on the day of judgment?

COMPLEMENT: Because of its violent injustice and persistent idolatry.

EXEGETICAL IDEA: Israel can't be strong on the day of judgment because of its violent injustice and persistent idolatry.

HOMILETICAL IDEA: Violent injustice and persistent idolatry rob us of our confidence that we are in Christ.

Ezekiel 22:17-22

SUBJECT: To what does the Lord liken the house of Israel?

COMPLEMENT: Dross that will be melted and drawn off in the furnace of Jerusalem.

EXEGETICAL IDEA: The Lord likens the house of Israel to dross that will be melted and drawn off in the furnace of Jerusalem.

HOMILETICAL IDEA: Silver and tin look the same, but they have different destinies.

Ezekiel 22:23-31

SUBJECT: What does the Lord say he sees when he looks for leaders who will intercede for the people and protect the land?

COMPLEMENT: He sees violence, oppression, and lies.

EXEGETICAL IDEA: The Lord says he looks for leaders who will intercede for the people and protect the land, but what he sees is violence, oppression, and lies.

HOMILETICAL IDEA: As Christ stood in the gap for us, leaders must stand in the gap for their people.

Ezekiel 23

SUBJECT: What does Ezekiel's sexually explicit story of Oholibah and her insatiable lust mean for Judah?

COMPLEMENT: That Judah's political alliances violate its covenant with the Lord, and it will be given over to the wrath and violence of those it has lusted after.

EXEGETICAL IDEA: Ezekiel's sexually explicit story of Oholibah and her insatiable lust means that Judah's political alliances violate its covenant with the Lord, and it will be given over to the wrath and violence of those it has lusted after.

HOMILETICAL IDEA: The Lord is faithful and asks for faithfulness in return.

Ezekiel 24:1-14

SUBJECT: How does the Lord respond to the Jerusalemites' belief that they were chosen cuts of finest meat, protected in a boiling pot?

COMPLEMENT: He tells them that they are bloody, unclean meat that has corrupted the pot, so that both the meat (the people) and the pot (Jerusalem) will be destroyed by the Lord's fire.

EXEGETICAL IDEA: The Lord responds to the Jerusalemites' belief they were chosen cuts of finest meat, protected in a boiling pot, by telling them that they are bloody, unclean meat that has corrupted the pot, so that both the meat (the people) and the pot (Jerusalem) will be destroyed by the Lord's fire.

HOMILETICAL IDEA: The Lord is cooking up something special, but it may not be what we think.

Ezekiel 24:15-27

SUBJECT: Why does the Lord command Ezekiel not to mourn the sudden death of his wife?

COMPLEMENT: To be a sign to the exiles that at the sudden fall of Jerusalem, even then they will not repent and mourn their sins appropriately.

EXEGETICAL IDEA: The Lord commands Ezekiel not to mourn the sudden death of his wife as a sign to the exiles that at the sudden fall of Jerusalem, even then they will not repent and mourn their sins appropriately.

HOMILETICAL IDEA: True repentance, not just sorrow, will lead to redemption.

Ezekiel 25:1-7

SUBJECT: What does the Lord say he will do in response to the Ammonites' clapping at the fall of Jerusalem.

COMPLEMENT: He will show them that he is the Lord by stretching out his hand against them.

EXEGETICAL IDEA: In response to the Ammonites' clapping at the fall of Jerusalem, the Lord will show them he is Lord by stretching out his hand against them.

HOMILETICAL IDEA: Don't clap for calamity, because his hands are bigger than ours.

Ezekiel 25:8-11

SUBJECT: What will the Lord do in response to Moab and the Ammonites saying that Israel is like all the other nations?

COMPLEMENT: He will show them that he is the Lord by making them forgotten among the nations.

EXEGETICAL IDEA: In response to Moab and the Ammonites saying that Israel is like all the other nations, the Lord will show them he is Lord by making them forgotten among the nations.

HOMILETICAL IDEA: Those who will not recognize God will not be recognized by God.

Ezekiel 25:12-17

SUBJECT: What will the Lord do in response to Edom and the Philistines taking vengeance on Judah when Jerusalem fell?

COMPLEMENT: He himself will take his vengeance on them.

EXEGETICAL IDEA: In response to Edom and the Philistines taking vengeance on Judah when Jerusalem fell, the Lord himself will take his vengeance on them.

HOMILETICAL IDEA: Vengeance is mine, says the Lord.

Ezekiel 26

SUBJECT: What will the Lord do to proud Tyre, the rich city by the sea?

COMPLEMENT: He will bring Nebuchadnezzar, king of Babylon, to destroy it completely.

EXEGETICAL IDEA: The Lord will bring Nebuchadnezzar, king of Babylon, to destroy proud Tyre, the rich city by the sea.

HOMILETICAL IDEA: Wealth and splendor will not shield anyone from the justice of God.

Ezekiel 27

SUBJECT: What does the destruction of Tyre, which contains within itself the glory of the nations, signify to the world?

COMPLEMENT: That the Lord will judge the nations.

EXEGETICAL IDEA: The destruction of Tyre, which contains within itself the glory of the nations, signifies to the world that the Lord will judge the nations.

HOMILETICAL IDEA: Christ at his coming will judge all the nations.

Ezekiel 28:1-19

SUBJECT: What does the ruin of the mighty prince of Tyre, who is exalted beyond mortal scale, signify to the world?

COMPLEMENT: That the Lord judges rulers, thrones, dominions, and authorities.

EXEGETICAL IDEA: The ruin of the mighty prince of Tyre, who is exalted beyond mortal scale, signifies that the Lord judges rulers, thrones, dominions, and authorities.

HOMILETICAL IDEA: Christ will judge rulers, thrones, dominions, and authorities.

Ezekiel 28:20-26

SUBJECT: How will Sidon and Israel know that the Lord is God?

COMPLEMENT: When God reveals his awful holiness to Sidon and his saving mercy to Israel.

EXEGETICAL IDEA: Sidon and Israel will know that the Lord is God when he reveals his awful holiness to Sidon and his saving mercy to Israel.

HOMILETICAL IDEA: God makes himself known in judgment and salvation.

Ezekiel 29

SUBJECT: What will the Lord do to Egypt in response to Pharaoh's pride and the false sense of strength that he has lent to Israel because he has allied with them?

COMPLEMENT: The Lord will destroy the land of Egypt by his servant Nebuchadnezzar and leave Egypt as a lowly kingdom forever.

EXEGETICAL IDEA: In response to Pharaoh's pride and the false sense of strength that he has lent to Israel because he has allied with them, the Lord will destroy the land of Egypt by his servant Nebuchadnezzar and leave Egypt as a lowly kingdom forever.

HOMILETICAL IDEA: There is no power and no plan that can prevent the judgment of our God.

Ezekiel 30

SUBJECT: What will the Lord do to proud Egypt and those that lean on it?

COMPLEMENT: He will break their strength.

EXEGETICAL IDEA: The Lord will break the strength of proud Egypt and of those that lean on it.

HOMILETICAL IDEA: The bigger they are, the harder they fall.

Ezekiel 31

SUBJECT: To what does the Lord compare Pharaoh, king of Egypt?

COMPLEMENT: Assyria, who in its greatness sealed its own doom.

EXEGETICAL IDEA: The Lord compares Pharaoh, king of Egypt, to Assyria, who in its greatness sealed its own doom.

HOMILETICAL IDEA: Humble yourselves under the mighty hand of God, that at the proper time he may exalt you.

Ezekiel 32:1-16

SUBJECT: What will the Lord's judgment of Egypt accomplish?

COMPLEMENT: The total removal of Egypt's power, bringing fear of the might of the Lord to the nations.

EXEGETICAL IDEA: The Lord's judgment of Egypt will accomplish the total removal of Egypt's power, bringing fear of the might of the Lord to the nations.

HOMILETICAL IDEA: God overthrows the powers of the earth to rouse us from our slumber.

Ezekiel 32:17-32

SUBJECT: What will be Pharaoh's comfort when he arrives in Sheol with his defeated horde?

COMPLEMENT: The presence of many other fallen empires whom the Lord has dispatched.

EXEGETICAL IDEA: Pharaoh will be comforted when he arrives in Sheol with his defeated horde by the presence of many other fallen empires whom the Lord has dispatched.

HOMILETICAL IDEA: The evil powers at present are just one more in a long line of enemies slated for destruction.

Ezekiel 33:1-20

SUBJECT: Why does the Lord again tell the people of Israel that Ezekiel is the watchman and that the Lord will judge each according to his ways?

COMPLEMENT: To reinforce the notion that he invites Israel to salvation in the midst of judgment.

EXEGETICAL IDEA: The Lord again tells the people of Israel that Ezekiel is the watchman and that the Lord will judge each according to his ways in order to reinforce the notion that he invites Israel to salvation in the midst of judgment.

HOMILETICAL IDEA: Turn back, turn back!

Ezekiel 33:21-29

SUBJECT: What does the Lord say to the inhabitants who remain in the land after the fall of Jerusalem?

COMPLEMENT: Because the promises to Abraham do not remove the requirements for holiness, even those who remain will die in their sins.

EXEGETICAL IDEA: The Lord says to the inhabitants who remain in the land after the fall of Jerusalem that because the promises to Abraham do not remove the requirements for holiness, even those who remain will die in their sins.

HOMILETICAL IDEA: Judgment delayed is not judgment avoided.

Ezekiel 33:30-33

SUBJECT: Why do the exiles come as God's people and listen to Ezekiel?

COMPLEMENT: Merely so that his words might give pleasure in listening.

EXEGETICAL IDEA: The exiles come as God's people and listen to Ezekiel merely so that his words might give pleasure in listening.

HOMILETICAL IDEA: Be doers of the Word and not hearers only.

Ezekiel 34:1-24

SUBJECT: What will the Lord do in response to the corrupt shepherds and strong sheep of the flock of Israel, who take advantage of the weak?

COMPLEMENT: He will remove the shepherds, care for the sheep in the person of a Davidic king, and judge between the strong and the weak.

EXEGETICAL IDEA: In response to the corrupt shepherds and strong sheep of the flock of Israel, who take advantage of the weak, the Lord will remove the shepherds, care for the sheep in the person of a Davidic king, and judge between the strong and the weak.

HOMILETICAL IDEA: The Lord shepherds us in the person of his Son Jesus Christ.

Ezekiel 34:25-31

SUBJECT: What is the covenant like that the Lord will make with Israel?

COMPLEMENT: It is a covenant of peace, whereby the Lord will be their God and they will be his people.

EXEGETICAL IDEA: The covenant that the Lord will make with Israel is a covenant of peace, whereby the Lord will be their God and they will be his people.

HOMILETICAL IDEA: We have a new covenant of peace in Christ.

Ezekiel 35

SUBJECT: How will the Lord judge Edom for its bloodthirst, anger, and rejoicing at the fall of Israel?

COMPLEMENT: The Lord decrees that blood will pursue them, anger will find them, and others will rejoice at their downfall.

EXEGETICAL IDEA: In response to Edom's bloodthirst, anger, and rejoicing at the fall of Israel, the Lord decrees that blood will pursue them, anger will find them, and others will rejoice at their downfall.

HOMILETICAL IDEA: With the same measure we use, it will be measured to us.

Ezekiel 36:1-15

SUBJECT: What does the Lord say to the mountains of Israel?

COMPLEMENT: He will judge those who despise them and bring redemption to them.

EXEGETICAL IDEA: The Lord says to the mountains of Israel that he will judge those who despise them and bring redemption to them.

HOMILETICAL IDEA: We have a Savior who will judge those who despise us and bring redemption to us.

Ezekiel 36:16-38

SUBJECT: What can Israel expect from the Lord, who acts for the sake of his holy name?

COMPLEMENT: He will not just restore them to the land but also cleanse them inside and out and grant them deep repentance.

EXEGETICAL IDEA: Israel can expect that the Lord, who acts for the sake of his holy name, will not just restore them to the land but also cleanse them inside and out and grant them deep repentance.

HOMILETICAL IDEA: Because our salvation is for the glory of God, it must bring deep changes within and without.

Ezekiel 37:1-14

SUBJECT: Is it too late for the redemption of the Israelites, who feel that their very bones have dried up in exile?

COMPLEMENT: No, for God can make even dry bones live and will breathe his Spirit into them to give them new life.

EXEGETICAL IDEA: It is not too late for the redemption of the Israelites, who feel that their very bones have dried up in exile, for God can make even dry bones live and will breathe his Spirit into them to give them new life.

HOMILETICAL IDEA: It is not too late to live.

Ezekiel 37:15-28

SUBJECT: What will the Lord's redemption of Israel mean for the two fallen kingdoms?

COMPLEMENT: He will restore the two divided peoples into one.

EXEGETICAL IDEA: The Lord's redemption of Israel means the two fallen kingdoms will be restored from two divided peoples into one.

HOMILETICAL IDEA: The gospel crosses lines and makes formerly divided people into one.

Ezekiel 38:1–39:24

SUBJECT: How will the Lord display his glory to the nations in the latter days, after Israel has been restored?

COMPLEMENT: He will summon and miraculously defeat the superarmy of Gog, prince of Magog.

EXEGETICAL IDEA: The Lord will display his glory to the nations in the latter days, after Israel has been restored, by summoning and miraculously defeating the superarmy of Gog, prince of Magog.

HOMILETICAL IDEA: On that day the nations will know that he is the Lord.

Ezekiel 39:25–29

SUBJECT: What does the Lord want Israel to know?

COMPLEMENT: That he has a plan for his glory and for their good.

EXEGETICAL IDEA: The Lord wants Israel to know that he has a plan for his glory and for their good.

HOMILETICAL IDEA: The Lord has a plan for his glory and for our good.

Ezekiel 40–42

SUBJECT: What does the Lord show Ezekiel in this vision?

COMPLEMENT: The future restored temple, where all is fully planned, perfectly proportioned, and ready for the Lord's presence.

EXEGETICAL IDEA: In this vision the Lord shows Ezekiel the future restored temple, where all is fully planned, perfectly proportioned, and ready for the Lord's presence.

HOMILETICAL IDEA: God builds the new-covenant temple as the perfect place for his presence.

Ezekiel 43:1–12

SUBJECT: What does Ezekiel see when he exited the east gate?

COMPLEMENT: He sees the Lord coming to dwell permanently in the temple.

EXEGETICAL IDEA: When Ezekiel exits the east gate, he sees the Lord coming to dwell permanently in the temple.

HOMILETICAL IDEA: God is with us forever.

Ezekiel 43:13-27

SUBJECT: What does Ezekiel learn regarding the new altar?

COMPLEMENT: He learns what to do in order to consecrate it so that the Lord will accept offerings on it.

EXEGETICAL IDEA: Ezekiel learns regarding the new altar what to do in order to consecrate it so that the Lord will accept offerings on it.

HOMILETICAL IDEA: In Christ, God provides the way for our sacrifices to be acceptable to him.

Ezekiel 44:1-14

SUBJECT: What are the restrictions placed on the formerly privileged people in the new temple?

COMPLEMENT: They include the following: the east gate is locked, the new prince may eat only in the gate, and the Levites are excluded from giving offerings.

EXEGETICAL IDEA: Restrictions placed on the formerly privileged people in the new temple include the following: the east gate is locked, the new prince may eat only in the gate, and the Levites are excluded from giving offerings.

HOMILETICAL IDEA: The new covenant has a higher standard of holiness.

Ezekiel 44:15-31

SUBJECT: Who will serve the Lord in the new temple?

COMPLEMENT: The Zadokite priests will serve the Lord in holiness.

EXEGETICAL IDEA: The Zadokite priests will serve the Lord in holiness in the new temple.

HOMILETICAL IDEA: God has instituted a new priesthood in his High Priest, Jesus Christ.

Ezekiel 45-46

SUBJECT: What will the land, the government, the economy, and the worship be like in the new temple?

COMPLEMENT: They will be ruled by justice so that everyone has enough.

EXEGETICAL IDEA: The land, the government, the economy, and the worship in the new temple will be ruled by justice so that everyone has enough.

HOMILETICAL IDEA: In God's economy, there is justice and plenty.

Ezekiel 47:1-12

SUBJECT: What flows from the temple?

COMPLEMENT: The miraculous river, giving life, food, and healing to the land.

EXEGETICAL IDEA: The miraculous river flows from the temple, giving life, food, and healing to the land.

HOMILETICAL IDEA: In the new creation, God's presence will grant abundant life and healing to the world.

Ezekiel 47:13-48:29

SUBJECT: How will the Lord divide the promised land when he restores Israel?

COMPLEMENT: Evenly among the tribes, the sojourners, the princes, the Levites, the priests, and the city dwellers.

EXEGETICAL IDEA: When the Lord restores Israel, he will divide the promised land evenly among the tribes, the sojourners, the princes, the Levites, the priests, and the city dwellers.

HOMILETICAL IDEA: The whole world will one day be ruled by the goodness and order of God.

Ezekiel 48:30-35

SUBJECT: What will the new city be like?

COMPLEMENT: It will be a perfect square, with gates for all God's people, and its name will signal the Lord's permanent presence.

EXEGETICAL IDEA: The new city will be a perfect square, with gates for all God's people, and its name will signal the Lord's permanent presence.

HOMILETICAL IDEA: In the age to come, all God's people will have permanent open access to him in Christ.

Difficult Passages/Verses

Once again, see my discussion in the chapter on Isaiah, which reviews four preaching challenges relevant to the Major Prophets and ways to meet those challenges. Here I mention two additional difficulties that pertain to the book of Ezekiel.

The first is that some passages are so bizarre or offensive that the shock of the content may threaten to overshadow the point of the passage. One thinks of, among other passages, Ezekiel lying on his side for over three hundred days and cooking his food over dung (chap. 4), or his parable of Israel and Judah as prostitute sisters (chap. 23), or his exhaustive (and exhausting) description of the new temple (chaps. 40–46). On nearly every page, Ezekiel goes over the top. Though commentaries will be of use in interpreting the meaning of this material, the challenge remains: How shall we preach it?

Preachers should remember that Ezekiel had an incredibly difficult task: to undermine nationalistic hopes that were rooted in hundreds of years of history, and then to call forth renewed hopes in the face of the collapse of the nation. The intensity of his language reflects the scale of his assignment. Preachers can help congregations by making this historical assignment clear. This is crisis ministry, and it uses crisis language.

Second, Ezekiel is a long work. Reading all the way through is like playing hard rock through loudspeakers at full volume for hours on end. It will wear down readers, and sermon series will wear down listeners. A week-by-week sermon series through Ezekiel could take years, and most of it will be deeply disturbing.

Preachers might instead consider using passages from Ezekiel in combination with other books, or at certain times of the year. Ezekiel will be a helpful resource when preachers feel the need to confront congregational values that are contrary to the gospel, but that parishioners are deeply committed to. In those cases, a "dose" of Ezekiel—one sermon or a short series—may shake parishioners out of their complacency. However, unless a preacher believes that the church as a whole is in dire crisis because of unfaithfulness and needs a radical reorientation, the entire book of Ezekiel may be too much to stomach in one pass.

In addition to these general challenges, specific passages in Ezekiel are emotionally and theologically troubling. Daniel Block makes a strong case that in chapter 13 Ezekiel resists his call and suffers for it.[2] Apparently, the task he received was so undesirable that he tried to refuse. In chapter 10 the glory of the Lord departs from the temple, which leaves readers wondering about the absence of our faithful God. And in chapter 24 Ezekiel's wife dies, but he is forbidden to mourn as a sign to the house of Israel. Such disturbing themes and passages must be pondered, not passed over or explained away. They reflect the troubled times in which Ezekiel ministered.

---

2. Daniel Block, *The Book of Ezekiel*, vol. 2, *Chapters 1–24*, New International Commentary on the Old Testament (Grand Rapids: Eerdmans, 1998), 126.

Cultural Perspectives and Application

I recommend that preachers interpret and apply the Old Testament prophetic material according to the *covenant context* of the biblical passage and the present-day congregation. See my explanation in this volume's chapter on Isaiah.

The book of Ezekiel contains oracles that predominantly address the impending fall of Jerusalem in 586 BC and the glorious restoration of the nation in the future. These are *covenant consequences*, most of which fall under the Mosaic covenant.

The destruction of Jerusalem is a *future* consequence for the exiles but *past* for us today. In this case, preachers can talk about the 586 BC collapse and remind listeners that God is faithful to his promises and warnings. More fruitfully, they can point to the future consequences of the new covenant in Christ. For although Christ gives us glorious promises, he also gives stern warnings for those who are ashamed of him (Mark 8:38) or who repeatedly refuse to obey (Matt. 18:15–20).

The restoration is, according to my own theological viewpoint, *future* for Ezekiel and *future* for the church. It is therefore appropriate to direct the church's attention to the coming glory of the consummated kingdom of God, the return of Christ, and the new creation. Stir up their hope!

In both cases, the application of Ezekiel's message to the church can be phrased in new-covenant terms (as I do in many cases above). Such phrasing can render the strange words and world of Ezekiel more familiar to contemporary ears.

Nevertheless, it is not enough to translate the basic message of Ezekiel; preachers must strive to preserve his intensity. Preaching from Ezekiel should be like his words: thunderous, frightening, overwhelming, and stirring. We may widen the range and intensity of our emotions in the pulpit; we may yell or weep or whisper; we may invent shocking contemporary images to parallel his own. We should pull out all the stops when we preach Ezekiel. Helping listeners to experience the power of his message will call for our best efforts as we construct sermons suited to the urgency of the book.

RECOMMENDED RESOURCES

Blenkinsopp, Joseph. *Ezekiel*. Interpretation. Louisville: Westminster John Knox, 1990.

Block, Daniel I. *The Book of Ezekiel*. 2 vols. The New International Commentary on the Old Testament. Grand Rapids: Eerdmans, 1997, 1998.

Duguid, Iain M. *Ezekiel*. The NIV Application Commentary. Grand Rapids: Zondervan, 1999.

Daniel

SCOTT A. WENIG

Named after its main character, the book of Daniel is composed of two parts. The first tells the story of the spiritual faithfulness of Daniel and his three friends Hananiah, Mishael, and Azariah (better known as Shadrach, Meshach, and Abednego) in a pagan, foreign culture following the forced relocation of the Hebrews during the Babylonian exile (605–586 BC). The second presents a number of complex visions given to Daniel that revolve around God's future restoration of his people in the midst of their oppression by a series of malevolent world empires.

SUBJECT: How does the sovereign God reveal his grace and purpose to his exiled people suffering under the oppression of foreign empires?

COMPLEMENT: Through the faithful witness of his devoted servants he shows his control of their lives, their future, and all of human history.

EXEGETICAL IDEA: The sovereign God reveals his grace and purpose to his exiled people suffering under the oppression of foreign empires through the faithful witness of his devoted servants to show his control of their lives, their future, and all of human history.

HOMILETICAL IDEA: Our sovereign and gracious God controls the history and future of humanity as well as our own individual destinies.

Selecting Preaching and Teaching Passages in Daniel

Most preachers and teachers could devote eleven or twelve weeks to Daniel. Some might be tempted to go through the narratives but then skip the prophetic texts because of their complex symbolism. However, to grasp the sovereign purpose of God in our lives and all of history, it's best to work through the entire book. Thus each of the narratives in the first half of Daniel can be covered in one sermon, while the apocalyptic sections can be completed in five or six messages.

Getting the Subject, Complement, Exegetical Idea, and Homiletical Idea

Daniel 1

SUBJECT: What happens when Daniel and his three friends are enculturated into Babylonian society but choose to avoid defiling themselves with King Nebuchadnezzar's food and wine?

COMPLEMENT: God blesses them and uses them at the highest level of that culture.

EXEGETICAL IDEA: When Daniel and his three friends are enculturated into Babylonian society but choose to avoid defiling themselves with Nebuchadnezzar's food and wine, God blesses them and uses them at the highest level of that culture.

HOMILETICAL IDEA: Christ calls us to engage the culture without being defiled by the culture so he can use us to impact the culture.

Daniel 2

SUBJECT: What happens when Nebuchadnezzar's disturbing dream of the great statue destroyed by a huge rock creates a deadly crisis at court?

COMPLEMENT: By graciously using Daniel to resolve the crisis, the sovereign God reveals that his kingdom will usurp all others.

EXEGETICAL IDEA: When Nebuchadnezzar's disturbing dream of the great statue destroyed by a huge rock creates a deadly crisis at court, the sovereign God graciously uses Daniel to resolve the crisis by revealing that his kingdom will usurp all others.

HOMILETICAL IDEA: God graciously reveals himself to be sovereign over our personal crises and human history as he extends his kingdom.

Daniel 3

SUBJECT: What happens when Shadrach, Meshach, and Abednego are thrown into the fiery furnace for refusing to bow to Nebuchadnezzar's statue?

COMPLEMENT: They are miraculously rescued by the preincarnate Son of God.

EXEGETICAL IDEA: When Shadrach, Meshach, and Abednego are thrown into the fiery furnace for refusing to bow to Nebuchadnezzar's statue, they are miraculously rescued by the preincarnate Son of God.

HOMILETICAL IDEA: Devotion to Christ might get us thrown into the furnace, but he'll meet us there for our good and his glory.

Daniel 4

SUBJECT: What happens when Nebuchadnezzar refuses Daniel's admonition to repent of his pride?

COMPLEMENT: He is humbled by the disease of lycanthropy but ultimately recognizes God as sovereign and is graciously restored to his throne.

EXEGETICAL IDEA: When Nebuchadnezzar refuses Daniel's admonition to repent of his pride, he is humbled by the disease of lycanthropy but ultimately recognizes God as sovereign and is graciously restored to his throne.

HOMILETICAL IDEA: God opposes the proud but gives grace to the humble.

Daniel 5

SUBJECT: What happens when King Belshazzar blasphemously challenges the sovereign God?

COMPLEMENT: Despite knowing of Nebuchadnezzar's repentance, he refuses to do the same and is consequently destroyed.

EXEGETICAL IDEA: When King Belshazzar blasphemously challenges the sovereign God, despite knowing of Nebuchadnezzar's repentance, he refuses to do the same and is consequently destroyed.

HOMILETICAL IDEA: In view of God's judgment, be teachable and repentant.

Daniel 6

SUBJECT: What happens when the aged Daniel is thrown into the lions' den for praying in violation of the law of the Medes and Persians?

COMPLEMENT: He is miraculously rescued by the living God, who is glorified throughout the Persian Empire.

EXEGETICAL IDEA: When the aged Daniel is thrown into the lions' den for praying in violation of the law of the Medes and Persians, he is miraculously rescued by the living God, who is glorified throughout the Persian Empire.

HOMILETICAL IDEA: Regardless of the situation, we can trust our Savior because he's the living God, who rescues and resurrects us for his glory.

Daniel 7

SUBJECT: What hope is there for God's people given that history is often filled with horrific empires?

COMPLEMENT: That in the end God's messianic kingdom will replace them all.

EXEGETICAL IDEA: Given that history is often filled with horrific empires, God's people have hope that in the end his messianic kingdom will replace them all.

HOMILETICAL IDEA: Because the world is infected with evil, expect suffering now but know that God's kingdom will triumph.

Daniel 8

SUBJECT: What happens when the evil Antiochus Epiphanes mysteriously comes to power out of the glory of Hellenistic civilization?

COMPLEMENT: He promotes himself as god and persecutes God's people.

EXEGETICAL IDEA: When the evil Antiochus Epiphanes mysteriously comes to power out of the glory of Hellenistic civilization, he promotes himself as god and persecutes God's people.

HOMILETICAL IDEA: Good things turn evil when they become our gods.

Daniel 9

SUBJECT: How does God respond to Daniel's confession of Israel's sin and prayer for their redemption?

COMPLEMENT: He sends Gabriel with the promise of the Messiah who will be sacrificed for their deliverance.

EXEGETICAL IDEA: God responds to Daniel's confession of Israel's sin and prayer for their redemption by sending Gabriel with the promise of the Messiah who will be sacrificed for their deliverance.

HOMILETICAL IDEA: We're deeply sinful, but God saves us through the sacrificial death of Christ.

Daniel 10-11

SUBJECT: How are God's people encouraged to respond to the mysterious vision about violent events and malevolent figures who consistently engage in conflict?

COMPLEMENT: They are to endure until the Lord eliminates all of this futile activity.

EXEGETICAL IDEA: God's people are to respond to the mysterious vision about violent events and malevolent figures who consistently engage in conflict by enduring until the Lord eliminates all of this futile activity.

HOMILETICAL IDEA: History is a long journey and a brutal battle, but we can endure because our Savior will eventually wipe away the sinful causes of suffering.

Daniel 12

SUBJECT: What can strengthen God's people to endure in the face of horrible suffering and confusion?

COMPLEMENT: The promise of his grace now and their resurrection then.

EXEGETICAL IDEA: God's people can be strengthened to endure horrible suffering and confusion by the promise of his grace now and their resurrection then.

HOMILETICAL IDEA: In the midst of misery, we find strength in God's grace now and hope in our resurrection then.

Difficult Passages/Verses

Daniel presents some unique interpretative challenges because of its literary composition. The six historical narratives that cover almost seventy years of Hebrew exile in Babylon are followed by the six chapters of apocalyptic material. Preachers and teachers must explicate what God was doing with his people during that difficult time in their history, as well as discern his promises for their future.

Chapter 2 is the most challenging of the narratives because of its length and layers of content. Preachers and teachers must tell the story, incorporating the key elements of God's gracious revelation of his plans for human history and how his sovereignty extends over believers and unbelievers alike. Moreover, they should limit their discussion of the statue (the world kingdoms) from

Nebuchadnezzar's dream and focus on "the stone cut without hands"—God's kingdom—and what that means for the lives of their listeners.

A second difficult narrative is the story of Belshazzar's destruction. This is a tale of God's judgment on the unrepentant—not a popular topic in today's society. So how do we go about communicating this? First, it's best to address the theme of judgment at the beginning of the message in a way that engenders interest rather than hostility. Second, it's important to demonstrate that Belshazzar knew of Nebuchadnezzar's repentance and yet still chose to blatantly challenge the God of Israel by drinking from the sacred vessels. If taught well, this narrative may awaken some sleepy consciences!

All the apocalyptic texts present interpretative challenges. Leveraging a good book on hermeneutics would be helpful for understanding these passages. Preachers must then try to show how the prophecies fit the ancient history of Israel. Finally, they should stress the theology of the visions: what they reveal about God, his work in human history, the nature of humanity, the mysterious way that evil manifests itself, and how God is working to bring about the redemption of his people.

For example, Daniel 7 presents a frightening spectacle of human history filled with suffering and oppression. While this is not a reality many in the contemporary West have experienced, numbers of Christians around the world do so on a daily basis. Preachers must not shy away from this uncomfortable truth but communicate God's sovereignty over these distressing developments. Moreover, this vision shows that at history's end there will be a climatic showdown between the antichrist and the son of man, Jesus. The former will be destroyed by the power of our Savior, who never leaves us or forsakes us and will take us home to his heavenly kingdom.

Daniel 9 is a challenging mix of narrative and apocalyptic literature. The chapter begins with Daniel's heartfelt confession of Israel's sin (vv. 1–19), followed by a visit from the angel Gabriel (vv. 20–23), who delivers the enigmatic prophecy of the "seventy sevens" (vv. 24–27). While entire books have been devoted to interpreting this strange vision, it appears to be messianic in nature (v. 26). Preachers should take care lest they miss the forest for the trees. The text communicates that despite the failures of his people, God is working in history for their redemption. This involves the sacrificial atonement of the anointed one (Jesus) and a long obedience on the part of the saints.[1]

Because of its seemingly interminable amount of strange historical details, the long apocalyptic section in chapters 10–11 is hard to interpret, difficult to

---

1. Dale Ralph Davis, *The Message of Daniel: His Kingdom Cannot Fail*, The Bible Speaks Today (Downers Grove, IL: InterVarsity, 2013), 138.

preach, and tempting to skip. Nonetheless, since it is part of God's inspired Word, we're called to this "so that the servant of God may be thoroughly equipped for every good work" (2 Tim. 3:17). How might we do so? First, take this text on its own terms. It was given to instruct the Jews about the difficulties they would face in the coming centuries under the oppressive rule of the Seleucids. Second, it shows that history is filled with egocentric maniacs committed to their own agendas rooted in terrible oppression.[2] Third, it shows that someday God will bring all this sinfully foolish behavior to an end. The application is one of faith and perspective. We should do our best to communicate that in this world we will have tribulation (John 16:33). Given that, we are to remain focused on Christ and not the causes of the tribulation, for they—or he—will be disposed of. Lord willing, that reality will "put steel in our bones, in case we have to face the final scourge of history."[3]

Cultural Perspectives and Application

Faithful application of the book of Daniel involves a number of components. A preeminent one involves the Christian's relationship to culture. Daniel and his friends were forced to learn a new language and new customs, engage a pagan educational system, and then serve in some ancient Near Eastern monarchies that had no concept of religious freedom. Yet they not only survived in that environment but also found themselves to be instruments of the Lord's grace, power, and glory (chaps. 1–3, 6). They did so by a combination of spiritual discipline, winsome behavior, and humble dependence on the God who saves. While different cultural contexts call for different responses of engagement, these stories and visions show us how God's people can navigate even the most challenging environments.

A second point of application revolves around trust in God. Time and again the book of Daniel emphasizes God's complete control of nations, people, and events and his insurmountable capacity to work through them for his glory and our good (cf. Rom. 8:28–30). Our listeners' faith and perhaps our own as preachers can be nurtured as we point out God's sovereign and yet tender care of his own people, even in the midst of suffering (chaps. 3, 6, 7, and 12).

A third application regards the practice of prayer, especially as seen in the life of Daniel. The crisis caused by Nebuchadnezzar's dream in chapter 2 was resolved only because Daniel and his friends corporately prayed, asking

---

2. For a contemporary manifestation of this, see Paul Johnson, *Modern Times: The World from the Twenties to the Nineties* (New York: HarperPerennial, 1992).
   3. Davis, *Message of Daniel*, 160.

God for his help and deliverance. Daniel's response to King Darius's decree of death for anyone praying to any other god was met with his thrice daily practice of prayer. His long, specific prayer of confession for Israel's sin and request for God's redemption in chapter 9 is a model that can be leveraged for the spiritual health of both individuals and churches.

A fourth area of application is one of theological perception. Daniel reveals a God who is not only omnipotent and omniscient but also mysterious in his dealings with believers and unbelievers alike. He allows his people to suffer grave persecution but also rescues them from angry kings, fiery furnaces, and hungry lions. He allows evil rulers to arise, seemingly abetted by malevolent spiritual forces, but promises to extend his kingdom over the whole earth. And he is not a God to be taken lightly or trifled with, as the notorious and blasphemous King Belshazzar of the Babylonians discovered to his own demise!

Finally, preachers must stress our need for endurance. The book of Daniel reveals that God's restoration of his people and the implementation of his kingdom is much more complex, nuanced, and further out in history than we often think. Thus we're called to stay focused on him through both the thick and the thin places of life. As Jesus himself said, those who endure to the end will be saved (Mark 13:7, 13).

RECOMMENDED RESOURCES

Davis, Dale Ralph. *The Message of Daniel: His Kingdom Cannot Fail.* The Bible Speaks Today. Downers Grove, IL: InterVarsity, 2013.

Wallace, Ronald. *The Message of Daniel: The Lord Is King.* The Bible Speaks Today. Downers Grove, IL: InterVarsity, 1979.

Widder, Wendy L. *Daniel.* The Story of God Bible Commentary. Grand Rapids: Zondervan, 2016.

Hosea

CHRIS RAPPAZINI

The Big Idea of Hosea

In a time of political upheaval and international uncertainty, the prophet Hosea (meaning "salvation") addresses Israel's rebelliousness and idolatry by prophesying the severe consequences they will reap, and also reveals the Lord's heart and mind, which offers love, mercy, and ultimately restoration to God's chosen people.

SUBJECT: What reprimand and hope does the prophet Hosea relay to the Northern Kingdom of Israel?

COMPLEMENT: They will be judged and exiled for breaking their covenant with the Lord through harlotry and idolatry, but God will eventually restore their relationship, for he is faithful to his kin.

EXEGETICAL IDEA: The reprimand and hope that the prophet Hosea relays to the Northern Kingdom of Israel is that they will be judged and exiled for breaking their covenant with the Lord through harlotry and idolatry, but God will eventually restore their relationship, for he is faithful to his kin.

HOMILETICAL IDEA: God's loving heart continually pursues your sinful heart.

Selecting Preaching and Teaching Passages in Hosea

The first theme, "Hosea's Family" (chaps. 1–3), reveals the condition of the Lord's relationship with Israel through Hosea's marriage to a harlot and his relationship with their offspring. Although this theme was the choice metaphor to portray Israel's adulterous nature and the people's idolatry, this was Hosea's reality.

The second theme, "God and His Family" (chaps. 4–14), lays out the Lord's charges against Israel like a prosecutor; however, its glimmer of reconciliation nullifies traditional judicial processes. The dissection of this unit enables readers to register the heartfelt cries of the Lord via Hosea. The goal is to draw out the passion and the genuine relational pain but also the Lord's hope for the future.

Getting the Subject, Complement, Exegetical Idea, and Homiletical Idea

Hosea 1-3

SUBJECT: Why does Hosea recount the suffering and sorrowful path of being betrayed by his wife?

COMPLEMENT: To reveal the Lord's own suffering and sorrow due to the idolatry of Israel, which results in severe consequences, and to reveal that one's love and mercy leads to restoration.

EXEGETICAL IDEA: Hosea recounts the suffering and sorrowful path of being betrayed by his wife to reveal the Lord's own suffering and sorrow due to the idolatry of Israel, which results in severe consequences, and also to reveal that one's love and mercy leads to restoration.

HOMILETICAL IDEA: Restoration can be messy, but it is necessary for a fresh relationship.

Hosea 4-11

SUBJECT: What does Hosea say is the consequence of Israel's hypocrisy and trusting in political alliances with other nations?

COMPLEMENT: The Lord is emotionally torn that his "son" has rebelled, but nonetheless his love for Israel remains.

EXEGETICAL IDEA: Hosea says the consequence of Israel's hypocrisy and trusting in political alliances with other nations is that the Lord is emotionally torn that his "son" has rebelled, but nonetheless his love for Israel remains.

HOMILETICAL IDEA: God's grace is bigger than sin's consequences.

Hosea 12-14

SUBJECT: Why does Hosea recall to his readers Israel's lies, rebellion, and selfishness?

COMPLEMENT: To illustrate that Israel has repetitively sinned against the Lord, but the Lord promises to forgive those who repent and turn to him.

EXEGETICAL IDEA: Hosea recalls to his readers Israel's lies, rebellion, and selfishness to illustrate that they have repetitively sinned against the Lord, but the Lord promises to forgive those who repent and turn to him.

HOMILETICAL IDEA: Some things never change, and thankfully God's love and promises *also* never change.

Difficult Passages/Verses

Hosea is littered with references to ancient Israel's rich past, ancient Near Eastern concepts, and significant geographical locations. These categories contain subjects ranging from Israel's history as a nation, surrounding nations' histories, the wilderness, Baalism, agricultural idioms, and the influence of Baal-Peor, Samaria, Gilgal, Shechem, Bethel, Mizpah, and Gilead. If the preacher or teacher dives into these topics, the listeners will experience a new depth and magnitude of *how* and *why* the Lord has related to his people and, possibly, still does in a like manner today.

One difficult theme is that of infidelity and its relation to men and women. Although God created men and women in his image, why does the beginning illustration in the book of Hosea portray Israel as an immoral woman? Was this done to enforce abusive patriarchy? Probably not, but surely men are sinners too and therefore are capable of infidelity. Why is masculinity oftentimes portrayed as the vehicle of Israel's moral compass?

Another sticky theme is God's choosing a preferred race, the people of Israel. Perhaps there needs to be some space in the sermons to unpack *how* God chose the people of Israel and *why* he decided to stick with them, even though they continually rebelled.

Last, what are the effects of expounding on God's judgment *before* his mercy? How do we preach something that runs against the grain of a "hyper-grace" Christianity and culture? It may seem odd to listeners that God allows evil and intense suffering to occur in both individuals and groups of people. But nonetheless, God's character is one of justice and grace. It is therefore vital to remind listeners that God's attributes and will do not change; rather, he is on a mission to prepare a way for the Messiah who is the embodiment of judgment, mercy, justice, and grace.

Cultural Perspectives and Application

What must we know about ancient Israel's lifestyle and mindset to better grasp Hosea? How did ancient Near Eastern politics operate, and what was its relationship to deities? What are the implications of the book of Hosea? By default, some modern-day preachers popularly summarize and apply the book of Hosea as "Confess with a contrite heart and be saved" or "Jesus is our forgiveness." However, it is important to keep in mind the context of the book.

Western Christianity is uncomfortable and poorly versed in God's judgment and quick to find and cleave to God's grace, individual rather than corporate application, and victory in Christ. Even though, on the basis of God himself, this is the outcome, much of the text in Hosea is devoted to delineating and naming God's pain, Israel's unfaithfulness, and impending discipline; therefore, we ought to properly expound on God's full range of emotions before quickly arriving at his unconditional grace.

When we take time to glean from Hosea as a *whole*, we find that its implications are multifaceted:

- Surrender to God and his discipline and redemption—or, in other words, his judgment (Hosea 2; 3; 5:13; 6:1–3).
- God is relational and seeks reconciliation with his rebellious people (2:18; 7:13–14; 11:1–11).
- God alone is our salvation (13:4; 14:1–3).

RECOMMENDED RESOURCES

Andersen, Francis I., and David Noel Freedman. *Hosea*. Anchor Bible. Garden City, NY: Doubleday, 1980.

McComiskey, Thomas Edward. "Hosea." In *The Minor Prophets*, edited by Thomas Edward McComiskey, 1–238. Grand Rapids: Baker Academic, 2009.

Stuart, Douglas. *Hosea–Jonah*. Word Biblical Commentary. Nashville: Thomas Nelson, 1987.

Joel

ANDREW C. THOMPSON

Aside from what we can glean from his writings, we know virtually nothing about the prophet Joel—not even the century in which he lived. However, we do know this: his oracles address disaster. Joel looks back on a recent locust infestation and looks ahead to warn Jerusalem of the impending day of the Lord. That day, disastrous though it may be, will accomplish important redemptive functions for God's people.

SUBJECT: What does God want to tell Israel and Jerusalem about the day of the Lord?

COMPLEMENT: That it is a coming disaster, which God will use to rescue his people.

EXEGETICAL IDEA: God wants to tell Israel and Jerusalem that the day of the Lord is a coming disaster that he will use to rescue his people.

HOMILETICAL IDEA: Disaster delivers us.

Selecting Preaching and Teaching Passages in Joel

The simplest approach for preaching through Joel is a three-week series that follows English chapter divisions, as shown here. It is possible, however, to preach a longer series by subdividing chapters 2 and 3.

Chapter 2 may be divided into three sections. Verses 1–17 call for repentance in light of an invading army that threatens final destruction. Verses 18–27 hold out the promise of God's gracious response to the people's genuine repentance. And verses 28–32 promise the gift of the Spirit before the final judgment.

Chapter 3 may be divided into two sections. Verses 1–16 promise that God will bring ultimate judgment on rebellious nations, while verses 17–21 foretell God's reinstatement of his people to paradise.

Getting the Subject, Complement, Exegetical Idea, and Homiletical Idea

Joel 1

SUBJECT: What should Israel do in response to the day of the Lord, when locusts will invade the land and consume the food supply?

COMPLEMENT: Israel should repent of their sins.

EXEGETICAL IDEA: In response to the day of the Lord, when locusts will invade the land and consume the food supply, Israel should repent of their sins.

HOMILETICAL IDEA: Disaster disciplines us.

Joel 2

SUBJECT: What should Israel do in anticipation of the future day of the Lord, when ultimate judgment comes?

COMPLEMENT: Israel should return to God in the hope of spiritual sustenance and ultimate rescue.

EXEGETICAL IDEA: In anticipation of the future day of the Lord, when ultimate judgment comes, Israel should return to God in the hope of spiritual sustenance and ultimate rescue.

HOMILETICAL IDEA: Disaster summons us.

Joel 3

SUBJECT: What should Israel do in anticipation of the future day of the Lord, when he comes to judge the multitude of nations and restore his people to paradise?

COMPLEMENT: Israel should hope in the rescue that God will provide when he comes.

EXEGETICAL IDEA: In anticipation of the future day of the Lord, when he comes to judge the multitude of nations and restore his people to paradise, Israel should hope in the rescue that God will provide.

HOMILETICAL IDEA: Disaster will rescue us.

Difficult Passages/Verses

Chapter 2 presents two major difficulties for preaching. First, the description of the invasion in verses 3–11 seems to waver between a literal locust infestation and a human horde of invaders. Joel appears to blend images intentionally, so that a recent locust blight serves as a metaphor for a future military invasion. The effect is an intermingling of two disasters, so that the occurrence of one reminds readers of the other. Though difficult to explain, the idea that current suffering reminds us of ultimate judgment holds tremendous pastoral value for disciples.[1]

Second, the famous passage about God pouring out his Spirit in Joel 2:28–32 (quoted in Acts 2:17–21) raises major theological issues. Preachers should, from their own theological perspectives, carefully think through how to address such questions as the relationship between Old and New Testaments, the gift of (and the gifts of) the Holy Spirit, and the relationship between Pentecost and parousia.

Cultural Perspectives and Application

Joel is about disaster of several sorts. Few of us enjoy thinking about this topic. But the book repays careful study, because it shows that the motif of the day of the Lord comes in various forms and plays several roles. The prophet shows us natural disasters, invading armies, cosmic upheaval, and divine judgment.

If we dig deeply into Joel, we will discover deep theological wisdom for the church. Our own disasters, in fact, can become a tool in the hands of our Father. If we have eyes to see and ears to hear, we can receive from disaster the gifts of rebuke, of discipline, of instruction—even of hope. In a culture that often seeks self-protection above all (and demands it from God), Joel sounds a contrary note for the good of God's people.

---

1. See, e.g., Luke 13:1–5.

────── RECOMMENDED RESOURCES ──────

Barton, John. *Joel and Obadiah*. The Old Testament Library. Louisville: Westminster John Knox, 2001.

Dillard, Raymond Bryan. "Joel." In *The Minor Prophets*, edited by
Thomas Edward McComiskey, 239–314. Grand Rapids: Baker
Academic, 2009.

Stuart, Douglas. *Hosea–Jonah*. Word Biblical Commentary. Waco:
Word, 1997.

Amos

JOEL C. GREGORY

The Big Idea of Amos

God intends to judge his own people when they engage in corrupt business, politics, and religious practices.

SUBJECT: What is the message of Amos to the northern tribes of God's disobedient and unrepentant people?

COMPLEMENT: God is preparing a menacing superpower to obliterate his chosen people Israel who have refused to repent after intercession, warning, and appeals.

EXEGETICAL IDEA: The message of Amos to the northern tribes of God's disobedient and unrepentant people is that God is preparing a menacing superpower to obliterate his chosen people Israel who have refused to repent after intercession, warning, and appeals.

HOMILETICAL IDEA: Repent while you still have the opportunity.

Selecting Preaching and Teaching Passages in Amos

I have divided up the preaching/teaching pericopes with some descriptions of their significance.

Earthquake Times (Amos 1:1-2)

Amos introduces the historical background of the book among the other eighth-century-BC prophets. There was an earthquake around 760 according

343

to excavations. He describes his name, home, and vocation during the middle of the eighth century. Amos showed up as a southerner in the north providing a sudden, shaking message of imminent judgment.

From Circumference to Center (Amos 1:3-2:5)

Amos uses a clever geographical/rhetorical device to surprise Israel with his message. He circumscribes Israel with messages of judgment on the injustice of their historical gentile neighbors encircling Israel. He would receive a hearty "Amen" for each oracle against Moabites, Edomites, and the like. He tightens the coil when he dooms Judah. The prophet finally hits his target with the judgment against Israel. Then the "Amens" stop.

When God's People Are Numbered among His Enemies (Amos 2:6-16)

After pronouncing doom on all Israel's historical enemies, Amos turns to Israel itself. Because of economic injustice, blatant sexual immorality, systemic exploitation, forgetfulness of God's past mercies, corruption of its own holy persons, and refusal to hear prophecy, the nation will perish in judgment that no one can escape.

Chosen for Responsibility (Amos 3)

God's elective favor of Israel had not been for a shallow exceptionalism rooted in corrupt practices but for special responsibility as his own people. God's gracious election does not bring exemption but rather higher expectation on his part. Just as there is cause and effect in nature, so also there is a cause-and-effect judgment on injustice. Amos calls on the pagan nations to act as witnesses to the unfaithfulness of his own people. God's spoiled, affluent, and unjust people will experience inescapable judgment.

Disturbed and Disturbing (Amos 4)

The luxury-laden women of the affluent capital will face judgment for their indulgent lives in the face of injustice. Their worship is worthless, and their liturgy only piles up their sins. God has acted in nature to warn them of imminent catastrophe. He has given them examples from their own history of his willingness to judge. The God of nature is storing up his judgment for a nation that was smaller than New Jersey.

Let Justice Roll Down like Water (Amos 5)

The prophetic cry of Amos epitomizing the book emerges in 5:24. This cry digests the book and epitomizes the prophecy. Amos cries out in the face of their rampant idolatry, injustice, heedless response to warnings, clueless hoping for God's intervention in the very teeth of their own corruption, and the impossibility of escape from God. Judgment is coming relentlessly.

At Ease in Zion (Amos 6)

Amos confronts a generation that is clueless about its luxury-laden, unjust lifestyle. He renders in glowing colors an indulgent society living the high life in the capital city. In an over-the-top narrative, he lampoons idle slackers who perfume themselves while they eat choice veal and drink wine from the temple bowls dedicated to God. Do they want to be first? They will be the first—the first to go into judgment. In unsparing sarcasm, Amos paints a picture of the idle affluent amid cringing need. Their great houses will collapse and their lifestyle will be reversed.

Intercession in Critical Times (Amos 7:1-9)

Amos reveals a compassion for the people he has confronted beyond what they could know. He stood before God for the people before he stood before the people for God. He had a hidden ministry of intercession. His singular prayers had delayed the judgment of God on Israel. Two times he averted national catastrophe through his prayers. In one of the biographical passages of Amos we see the heavy heart of the prophet interceding for the people even as he confronts the people with his prophetic word. We also see God as one who responds to the prayers of one praying preacher and relents from what he intended to do. This is both a mystery and a revelation.

High Noon at Bethel (Amos 7:10-17)

In the authentic presence of Amos, the king's inauthentic professional clergy, Amaziah, confronted reality. Amos had upset the religiopolitical balance at the king's personal religious shrine. In the professional religionist Amaziah there stands exposed the preacher to power who identifies the reign of God with the current ruler. Jeroboam II personified the co-opting of religion for his own purposes. Amos pronounced doom on this toxic combination of politics and religion. He famously announced his own independence from the professional prophetic guild. He did not graduate from their school. He was an agribusinessman, not a professional prophet. Amaziah cynically wants to give Amos a franchise in the south just to get him out of the king's sanctuary. Amos tells Amaziah where he can go with his money.

A Famine for the Word of God (Amos 8)

Israel is ripe for judgment. Its religious liturgy divorced from justice reveals a rotten core in the nation. They sit in the sanctuary plotting how to take what little the poor have. God promises an apocalyptic time coming on Israel. Ironically, those who do not want to hear a word from God will come to the point of famine for the word of God. They will seek the divine word with ravenous hunger but will not be able to find it. The entire edifice of their false, schismatic religion will be exposed for the empty thing that it is.

A Final Word of Hope (Amos 9:11-15)

Like a ray of sun cutting through clouds after the storm subsides, a word of hope slices through the thick layers of judgment. After judgment comes astonishing grace. God will reestablish his city. Even the gentiles will recognize the work of God. A striking fecundity will produce unprecedented growth in the vineyards. The cycle of sowing and reaping will collapse into the same time. A new security will mark God's people, who will be planted in their land, never to be moved again. The last word of Amos is a smashing word of hope out of nowhere. Judgment is a hallway Israel must pass through, not a room where they will live forever.

Getting the Subject, Complement, Exegetical Idea, and Homiletical Idea

Amos 1:1-2

SUBJECT: What characterizes the times and the man Amos?

COMPLEMENT: Amos's generation lived through a physical earthquake, but Amos, a nonprofessional prophet from another place, predicts a national earthquake of judgment.

EXEGETICAL IDEA: What characterizes the times and the man Amos is that his generation lived through a physical earthquake, but Amos, a nonprofessional prophet from another place, predicts a national earthquake of judgment.

HOMILETICAL IDEA: God can speak to us through an unlikely person a word that addresses his judgment on our own times.

Amos 1:3-2:5

SUBJECT: Why did Amos use the device of pronouncing judgment on the surrounding nations before confronting Israel itself?

COMPLEMENT: The same God who without favoritism judges unbelieving nations will be unsparing in his judgment of his own people.

EXEGETICAL IDEA: Amos used the device of pronouncing judgment on the surrounding nations before confronting Israel itself to show that the same God who without favoritism judges unbelieving nations will be unsparing in his judgment of his own people.

HOMILETICAL IDEA: The same God who judges nations around us will judge us by the same standards with greater intensity.

Amos 3

SUBJECT: Why does God choose his people?

COMPLEMENT: So that they will demonstrate a justice and righteousness that exceeds that of those around them.

EXEGETICAL IDEA: God chooses his people so that they will demonstrate a justice and righteousness that exceeds that of those around them.

HOMILETICAL IDEA: God's choice of us to be his own implies a stricter judgment rather than a milder tolerance.

Amos 4

SUBJECT: What is the result of Israel's living a selfish and heedless life while being God's chosen?

COMPLEMENT: Despite many warnings, Israel will face certain judgment.

EXEGETICAL IDEA: As a result of living a selfish and heedless life while being God's chosen, despite many warnings, Israel will face certain judgment.

HOMILETICAL IDEA: If you live a life of selfish, empty religiosity amid need, God's preliminary warnings will lead to ultimate judgment.

Amos 5

SUBJECT: What is the result of a corrupt lifestyle that ignores the disparities obvious to all and is unresponsive to God's warning?

COMPLEMENT: Amos reminds Israel that there is no way of escape from a selfish life.

EXEGETICAL IDEA: As a result of a corrupt lifestyle that ignores the disparities obvious to all and is unresponsive to God's warning, Amos reminds Israel that there is no way of escape from a selfish life.

HOMILETICAL IDEA: We can be empowered by God to seek justice in a corrupt world headed toward inevitable judgment.

Amos 6

SUBJECT: What is the result of an affluent, luxurious life amid crying need?

COMPLEMENT: Israel's desire to be the first in experiencing the best of all material things will lead to Israel being the first in judgment.

EXEGETICAL IDEA: The result of an affluent, luxurious life amid crying need is that Israel's desire to be the first in experiencing the best of all material things will lead to Israel being the first in judgment.

HOMILETICAL IDEA: We must forgo a life obsessed with comfort for a life rooted in doing the justice of God.

Amos 7:1-9

SUBJECT: What is the secret life of God's spokesperson?

COMPLEMENT: The proclaimer of God's message stands before God for the people as the proclaimer stands before the people for God.

EXEGETICAL IDEA: The secret life of God's spokesperson is that the proclaimer of God's message stands before God for the people as the proclaimer stands before the people for God.

HOMILETICAL IDEA: We need to beg God for mercy on others in the private place before we confront others in the public place.

Amos 7:10-17

SUBJECT: Who can God use to proclaim his word against corruption and injustice in religion and life?

COMPLEMENT: Unlikely people from unusual places.

EXEGETICAL IDEA: God can use unlikely people from unusual places to proclaim his word against corruption and injustice in religion and life.

HOMILETICAL IDEA: God can use us despite our unlikely background and personal history to speak his word in unexpected places.

Amos 8

SUBJECT: How does God deal with people who are deluded about their relationship with him?

COMPLEMENT: God uses metaphorical images and actual calamity to judge his people until they hunger for a word from beyond.

EXEGETICAL IDEA: God deals with people who are deluded about their relationship with him by using metaphorical images and actual calamity to judge his people until they hunger for a word from beyond.

HOMILETICAL IDEA: God may confront us at the very center of our selfish life with jarring warnings of the future to come.

Amos 9:11-15

SUBJECT: Is there any hope for the hopeless people of God?

COMPLEMENT: Yes, because beyond all expectation, God and God alone can bring a word of hope into a hopeless situation.

EXEGETICAL IDEA: There is hope for the hopeless people of God because beyond all expectation, God and God alone can bring a word of hope into a hopeless situation.

HOMILETICAL IDEA: When we feel there is no exit from despair because of our guilt, God may surprise us with a new message of hope.

Difficult Passages/Verses

The very idea of the judgment of God in history challenges the major elitist cultural understanding of God, even the notion of God's existence. Leo Tolstoy emphasized that the moment produces great men. Thomas Carlyle insisted that great men create great moments. Both males referred to males. For postmodern secular humans, the very idea that a righteous God will intervene in history to judge belongs to some benighted, remote past. The biblical God is a God of wrath. Wrath is the fluid love bleeds when you cut it. You cannot be an utterly good anybody and be angry at nothing, even as a human being. God's wrath is not human anger.

Amos 6 will trouble comfortable suburban people living affluent lives. It confronts all comfort built on an unjust exploitation of the weak and marginalized. Often churches in such communities have baptized the secular culture of consumption. Amos stands squarely against that.

Amos 7:1–9 presents the challenging relationship between prayer and God's intention. God intends to judge Israel with a locust plague and fire. Amos prays and God relents from what he intended to do. This demonstrates the dynamic tension between God's sovereign intention and human intercession. There remains an unexplainable theological mystery in Amos 7. God intends to do something. Amos prays. God delays. The idea that human prayer may cause God to relent is a fact, but not explainable to mere human minds that cannot grasp both human freedom and divine sovereignty.

Amos 9 suddenly surprises the reader with unanticipated hope on the other side of judgment. This is so shocking that some biblical critics wrongly believe it was added by another hand. A preacher can explore the relationship in Amos and other scriptures between judgment and hope. In Amos, as well as in Isaiah and Jeremiah, beyond immediate judgment is the bright sunrise of hope. Judgment is a hallway to pass through, not a room to live in.

Cultural Perspectives and Application

The highly resourced world today lives with numberless examples of heedless injustice. From migrant workers to coffee growers who receive a pittance for their labor, there is an endless surplus of examples of injustice for the preacher. The challenge is to name those close to home, under the very noses of the congregation. All prophetic preaching must be venue specific. A modern Amos has an abundance of targets, from opioid drug manufacturers who enjoy billionaire status to politicians who separate immigrant families.

Corrupt religion exposes itself in the cover-ups of clergy abuse, now numbered in the thousands. Mere religious professionals who live without a vital personal experience of God are capable of virtually any corrupt behavior. It is the brave proclaimer who addresses this in specific venues.

RECOMMENDED RESOURCES

Garland, D. David. *Amos: A Study Guide Commentary.* Grand Rapids: Zondervan, 1966.

Mays, James Luther. *Amos: A Commentary.* Philadelphia: Westminster, 1969.

Paul, Shalom M. *Amos: A Commentary on the Book of Amos.* Hermeneia. Minneapolis: Fortress, 1991.

Obadiah

MATTHEW D. KIM

Obadiah contains a prophecy of judgment concerning the nation of Edom (modern-day southwest Jordan) and God's eventual restoration of the nation of Judah.[1]

SUBJECT: What is the message that God wants the prophet Obadiah to give to Edom and Judah?

COMPLEMENT: Edom will be judged on the day of the Lord and destroyed for their violence to Jacob and their arrogance, but God will save a remnant from Judah because the kingdom belongs to him.

EXEGETICAL IDEA: The message that God wants the prophet Obadiah to give to Edom and Judah is that Edom will be judged on the day of the Lord and destroyed for their violence to Jacob and their arrogance, but God will save a remnant from Judah because the kingdom belongs to him.[2]

HOMILETICAL IDEA: We will all be judged on the day of Lord, for salvation belongs only to God.

---

1. A possible meaning of the name Obadiah is "worshiper of Yahweh." See Charles Swindoll, "Obadiah," Insight for Living Ministries, https://www.insight.org/resources/bible/the-minor-prophets/obadiah.
2. Charles Swindoll explains the main idea of Obadiah this way: "When people remove themselves from or place themselves in opposition to God's people, they can expect judgment, rather than restoration, at the end of life." See Swindoll, "Obadiah."

Selecting Preaching and Teaching Passages in Obadiah

Most preachers and teachers will address the book of Obadiah in one session since this shortest book of the Old Testament contains just twenty-one verses. However, since there are many prophetic details and much historical context in this book, one might choose to separate the book into two segments: verses 1–9 and verses 10–21. The first segment articulates God's displeasure with the Edomites. The second section foretells of God's judgment and Judah's impending restoration.

Getting the Subject, Complement, Exegetical Idea, and Homiletical Idea

See above.

Difficult Passages/Verses

Packed into this short prophetic book are a number of historical details, people, and places that require a preacher's or teacher's exploration, such as Teman (v. 9), the Negev (v. 19), Ephraim and Samaria (v. 19), Gilead (v. 19), Zarephath (v. 20), Canaan (v. 20), and Mount Zion (vv. 17, 21). It would be easy for preachers to gloss over these details. Instead, spend some time explaining this background.

The Edomites are descendants of Esau. Why is God so upset with Esau even though it appears that God blesses him richly in Genesis 33? In the Genesis narrative, Esau is the victim of Jacob's deception. So why does God favor Jacob over Esau/Edom? A proper understanding of the theology of God's favoritism/election would be beneficial to acknowledge and contemplate with listeners or students. In addition, what does it mean to preach judgment and grace at the same time? We must consider how to nuance this delicate theological balance for our particular listeners.

Cultural Perspectives and Application

How do we faithfully apply the book of Obadiah? What do we need to know about Jewish and Edomite cultures? The temptation in preaching the prophets, in this case a minor prophet, is for every sermon to sound the same and have the same application. A common default application might be "Repent and be restored." But we need to be more specific by considering the cultural contexts as well as naming God's displeasure with particular Edomite practices, forms of idolatry, and harmful attitudes.

There is clearly a behavioral aspect to this text. Our actions and attitudes have significant consequences and can bring about God's judgment. Yet is this the application of Obadiah? I'm not so sure.

Here are several possible applications: live humbly before God (v. 3), God is the one who humbles and exalts (v. 4), remember the day of the Lord and his judgment for our deeds (v. 15), recognize God's grace (v. 17), and remember that our salvation belongs to God (v. 21).

RECOMMENDED RESOURCES

Baker, David W. *Joel, Obadiah, Malachi*. The NIV Application Commentary. Grand Rapids: Zondervan Academic, 2006.

Block, Daniel I. *Obadiah: A Discourse Analysis of the Hebrew Bible*. Zondervan Exegetical Commentary on the Old Testament. Grand Rapids: Zondervan, 2015.

Jonah

MATTHEW D. KIM

The Big Idea of Jonah

Jonah is the story of God's command and call to Jonah to preach a message of repentance and forgiveness to the city of Nineveh in the nation of Assyria. One of the Minor Prophets, the book of Jonah captures Jonah's reluctant attitude to preach a message of repentance, an attitude clearly contrasted with God's merciful heart even for Israel's enemies.

SUBJECT: Why does God send Jonah to the Ninevites?[1]

COMPLEMENT: Because God shows compassion and mercy to anyone he wills, even Jonah's enemies, and he desires Jonah's obedience to share the good news with them so that they repent.

EXEGETICAL IDEA: God sends Jonah to the Ninevites because he shows compassion and mercy to anyone he wills, even Jonah's enemies, and he desires Jonah's obedience to share the good news with them so that they repent.

HOMILETICAL IDEA: Christians care about what God cares about.

Selecting Preaching and Teaching Passages in Jonah

The natural sermon text selections for Jonah are the four individual chapters, thus making Jonah a four-sermon series. However, depending on the

---

1. I discuss the same process of determining the big idea of Jonah in chap. 4 of *A Little Book for New Preachers: Why and How to Study Homiletics* (Downers Grove, IL: IVP Academic, 2020), 67–71.

preacher's purview, the entire story of Jonah could be preached in one or two sermons. Another option is to spend one to two weeks on Jonah's prayer alone, dissecting it for theological wisdom. For the purpose of this chapter, I will assume that the preacher will be preparing a sermon for each individual chapter.

Getting the Subject, Complement, Exegetical Idea, and Homiletical Idea

Jonah 1

SUBJECT: How does Jonah respond to God's command to preach a message of repentance to the Ninevites?

COMPLEMENT: He tries to flee from the Lord by getting on a boat to Tarshish but is thrown into the sea by pagan sailors and swallowed by a great fish.

EXEGETICAL IDEA: Jonah responds to God's command to preach a message of repentance to the Ninevites by trying to flee from the Lord by getting on a boat to Tarshish but is thrown into the sea by pagan sailors and swallowed by a great fish.

HOMILETICAL IDEA: When God calls us to share the good news with others, choose to obey.

Jonah 2

SUBJECT: What is Jonah's prayer to God as he waits in the stomach of the fish?

COMPLEMENT: He prays for God's help in his distress and acknowledges that God brings salvation to whomever he desires.

EXEGETICAL IDEA: As he waits in the stomach of the fish, Jonah prays for God's help in his distress and acknowledges that God brings salvation to whomever he desires.

HOMILETICAL IDEA: The Lord is our help in times of trouble, and he offers salvation to his people.

Jonah 3

SUBJECT: How does Jonah respond to God's second command to preach repentance to the city of Nineveh?

COMPLEMENT: Jonah obeys God, and God relents from his punishment and judgment.

EXEGETICAL IDEA: Jonah responds to God's second command to preach repentance to the city of Nineveh by obeying God, and God relents from his punishment and judgment.

HOMILETICAL IDEA: Tell everyone the gospel story and ask God to save them.

Jonah 4

SUBJECT: What is Jonah's response to God's mercy and compassion toward the Ninevites?

COMPLEMENT: He is angry with God even to the point of death.

EXEGETICAL IDEA: In response to God's mercy and compassion toward the Ninevites, Jonah is angry with God even to the point of death.

HOMILETICAL IDEA: Match God's mercy and compassion, because people are precious to God.

Difficult Passages/Verses

A first issue of importance is theological and regards the relationship between God's sovereignty and human responsibility.[2] Does God really give Jonah a choice to obey him? Did God press Jonah to the point of submission? Could God have used anyone else to serve as his prophet? Why Jonah and not someone else?

A second issue is the subject of life and death, which is, of course, quite common in the Old Testament. James Bruckner reminds us that life and death is a key theme throughout the book of Jonah. Each of the chapters in some way depicts this continuum (e.g., human physical life and death, spiritual life and death, life and death of animals, and life and death of plants).[3] What's perhaps more challenging to talk about is one's attitude with regard to the life and death of others—especially of our enemies. Jonah's callousness toward the Ninevites is perplexing because it requires some cultural digging into and awareness of the hostility between Jews and Assyrians. We will want to explain the cruel treatment of Israel at the hands of the Assyrians.

Third, particularly for our skeptical culture, Jonah will require some level of scientific investigation to explore his three-day stay inside the belly of the great fish. We cannot too quickly gloss over its biological significance. Even the somewhat astute listener will ask, "Is it physically possible to remain alive

2. Kim, *Little Book for New Preachers*, 50–51.

3. James Bruckner, *Jonah, Nahum, Habakkuk, Zephaniah*, The NIV Application Commentary (Grand Rapids: Zondervan, 2004), 18.

inside a fish for three days and three nights?" or "Was this a supernatural miracle?" Certain theological camps may argue that Jonah is fanciful literature and cannot possibly be a literal story with a literal fish.

Cultural Perspectives and Application

Jonah brings up a couple of different challenges with regard to cultural perspectives. First, it would be helpful to study the geographical, cultural, and religious backgrounds of Nineveh, Tarshish, and Assyria, as well as the variety of gods worshiped by the sailors in Jonah 1:5–7. Second, as mentioned above, Jonah's fear or hatred of the Assyrians, in this case the Ninevites, requires further exploration. The book informs us clearly that Jonah refuses to preach a message of repentance and forgiveness and was displeased greatly with God for his mercy and compassion. Although he finally acquiesces in 3:4, what held him back from doing so? Was it that Jonah was afraid of the Ninevites? Was it his ethnocentrism? Was it that he hated the Ninevites because of their recorded torture of the Israelites? It could be one or more of these cultural attitudes or even something different based on your study and conviction. Explain which perspective or perspectives you have landed on. Your interpretation here matters when it comes to applying the text faithfully.

As for application in Jonah, several come to mind. First, in what areas of life are we running away from God's will? Second is the question of our direct obedience to God in terms of preaching the good news. This is a universal responsibility for all believers in Christ. We are called by God to share the message of repentance, forgiveness, and salvation to all peoples. Third, related to this evangelistic heart, is that we are called to love others, especially our enemies. We might ask our listeners whom they have trouble loving. A fourth application, one for Westerners, pertains to desiring comfort (4:6) over listening to and obeying God. Jonah was angrier about losing his comfort from the vine dying than about people perishing without believing the good news. Fifth, what can we learn from Jonah's prayer in chapter 2? How does this prayer lead us to greater theological awareness for what the human heart desires and what God ultimately desires?

RECOMMENDED RESOURCES

Bruckner, James. *Jonah, Nahum, Habakkuk, Zephaniah*. The NIV Application Commentary. Grand Rapids: Zondervan, 2004.

Keller, Timothy. *The Prodigal Prophet: Jonah and the Mystery of God's Mercy*. New York: Viking, 2018.

Youngblood, Kevin J. *Jonah: A Discourse Analysis of the Hebrew Bible*. Exegetical Commentary on the Old Testament. Grand Rapids: Zondervan, 2015.

Micah

BRANDON R. CASH

The Big Idea of Micah

The context of Micah's prophetic ministry is the second half of the eighth century BC. The Assyrian Empire has taken control of much of the ancient Near East, and they are pressing in on Israel (Northern Kingdom) and Judah (Southern Kingdom). Micah proclaims that the looming invasion is God's judgment on his people. In the north, Israel will be crushed by Sargon II, king of Assyria, in 721 BC. In the south, Judah will be defeated by Sennacherib (Sargon II's son) in 701 BC. The attack on Israel is the end of the Northern Kingdom, and the cost to the Southern Kingdom is the loss of forty-six cities.[1] God's judgment is severe.

But there's another side to Micah's prophetic ministry. In addition to the proclamations of judgment are proclamations of salvation and reminders that God has made a promise to his people and is committed to keeping it. God will bring salvation through the forgiveness of sins and restoration through the establishment of a righteous king from the line of David. This is the backdrop for Micah's alternating message of judgment and salvation.

SUBJECT: How can God use Israel as the means of blessing to the nations when Israel is sinful?

COMPLEMENT: By judging Israel through the Assyrians and then saving a remnant of his people, forgiving their sins, and giving them a righteous king who will vanquish all threats and establish a kingdom of peace.

---

1. D. Winton Thomas, ed., *Documents from Old Testament Times* (New York: Harper & Row, 1958), 67.

EXEGETICAL IDEA: God can use Israel as the means of blessing to the nations, even though Israel is sinful, by judging Israel through the Assyrians and then saving a remnant of his people, forgiving their sins, and giving them a righteous king who will vanquish all threats and establish a kingdom of peace.

HOMILETICAL IDEA: The lengths to which God goes to save us are far greater than the lengths to which we go to sin against him.

Selecting Preaching and Teaching Passages in Micah

There are multiple ways to approach the book of Micah. Some divide the book into two sections (chaps. 1–5 and 6–7) because each section begins with the exhortation "hear." Others divide the book into three sections (chaps. 1–2, 3–5, and 6–7), wherein each section contains a pronouncement of judgment followed by blessing. And others divide the book into four sections (chaps. 1–3, 4–5, 6, and 7). While these divisions each have merit, they do not easily lend themselves to cohesive preaching units.

For the purposes of preaching Micah, I believe David Dorsey's chiastic structure is most appealing. He suggests the following structural arrangement:

A. Coming Defeat and Destruction (1:1–16)
  B. Corruption of the People (2:1–13)
    C. Corruption of the Leaders (3:1–12)
      D. Center—Glorious Future Restoration (4:1–5:15)
    C'. Corruption of the City and Its Leaders (6:1–16)
  B'. Corruption of the People (7:1–7)
A'. Future Reversal of Defeat and Destruction (7:8–20)[2]

This structure nicely divides the book into seven preaching units. Though the center section (4:1–5:15) is a large passage, the theme is consistent and it lends itself to one sermon. However, depending on your context and the length of your sermon series, you may choose to divide it into two or three sermons.

However, if you are preaching a series on the Minor Prophets and you need to take less time to get through Micah, this structure lends itself to a four-week series where the parallel passages are combined.

2. David A. Dorsey, *The Literary Structure of the Old Testament: A Commentary on Genesis–Malachi* (Grand Rapids: Baker, 1999), 296–300.

Getting the Subject, Complement, Exegetical Idea, and Homiletical Idea

Micah 1

SUBJECT: What are the consequences for Israel and Judah's sinful rebellion against God?

COMPLEMENT: God will come in judgment and they will be defeated, humiliated, and taken into exile.

EXEGETICAL IDEA: The consequences of Israel and Judah's sinful rebellion against God are that God will come in judgment and they will be defeated, humiliated, and taken captive.

HOMILETICAL IDEA: One day God will come to judge, and everyone will have to give an answer for their rebellious sins.

Micah 2

SUBJECT: What are the charges that God brings against the wealthy that make them worthy of judgment?

COMPLEMENT: Stealing property, taking advantage of the poor and weak, listening to false teaching, and wanton violence.

EXEGETICAL IDEA: The charges that God brings against the wealthy that make them worthy of judgment are stealing property, taking advantage of the poor and weak, listening to false teaching, and wanton violence.

HOMILETICAL IDEA: Where greed and exploitation are, there God's judgment will be also.

Micah 3

SUBJECT: What happens when rulers hate good and love evil, prophets lead people astray, priests teach for a price, and judges pervert justice?

COMPLEMENT: They experience God's judgment, they are stripped of their position, their land is devastated, and their community is destroyed.

EXEGETICAL IDEA: When rulers hate good and love evil, prophets lead people astray, priests teach for a price, and judges pervert justice, they experience God's judgment, they are stripped of their position, their land is devastated, and their community is destroyed.

HOMILETICAL IDEA: When leaders lose sight of God, they bring destruction on themselves and their community.

Micah 4:1–5:15

SUBJECT: What will happen when the Lord of all the earth establishes his king over his people in his kingdom?

COMPLEMENT: Everything will be as God intended it to be in his kingdom; the vulnerable will be cared for, justice will be the norm, and there will be peace in the land.

EXEGETICAL IDEA: When the Lord of all the earth establishes his king over his people in his kingdom, everything will be as God intended it to be; the vulnerable will be cared for, justice will be the norm, and there will be peace in the land.

HOMILETICAL IDEA: Be hopeful, for a day is coming when everything wrong will be made right.

Micah 6

SUBJECT: Why is it just for God to judge his people for their sins?

COMPLEMENT: Because he gave them the instruction they needed in order to live a life pleasing to him.

EXEGETICAL IDEA: It is just for God to judge his people for their sins because he gave them the instruction they needed in order to live a life pleasing to him.

HOMILETICAL IDEA: In his Word, and with his Spirit, God has given us all we need to live a life pleasing to him.

Micah 7:1–7

SUBJECT: Why is Micah in utter despair?

COMPLEMENT: Because as he looks at the state of his nation, he sees only problems: there is no righteousness, there is no justice, no one can trust their neighbor, and family members are enemies.

EXEGETICAL IDEA: Micah is in utter despair because as he looks at the state of his nation, he sees only problems: there is no righteousness, there is no justice, no one can trust their neighbor, and family members are enemies.

HOMILETICAL IDEA: It's okay to call evil evil, and to grieve over what we see.

Micah 7:8–20

SUBJECT: Why will salvation have the last word?

COMPLEMENT: Because God pardons iniquity, passes over transgression, delights in steadfast love, is characterized by compassion, and is faithful to his promises.

EXEGETICAL IDEA: Salvation has the last word because God pardons iniquity, passes over transgression, delights in steadfast love, is characterized by compassion, and is faithful to his promises.

HOMILETICAL IDEA: Salvation triumphs over judgment because of God's steadfast love.

Difficult Passages/Verses

The book of Micah is an incredibly powerful portrait of God. The prophet revels in God's sovereignty ("Lord of all the earth"), trembles at his might ("mountains will melt under him"), rejoices in his steadfast love and forgiveness, and extols his incomparability ("who is a God like you"). So on one level the book is easily comprehendible. However, on another level the beauty and message of Micah is missed because the eighth-century-BC imagery and allusions are unfamiliar to a twenty-first-century Christian. And Micah's oracles are replete with rich imagery. Spend the necessary time studying the images so that you can effectively show your listeners what they mean.

For example, it would be tempting to gloss over the list of cities found in 1:10–16. But if you take the time to look into it, you will discover that these were the cities that surrounded Micah's hometown of Moresheth-Gath. It's as if he was standing on a roof looking at the cities around him that were about to fall. This, along with the oracle in 7:1–7, helps drive home the personal nature of the book. Micah was not a dispassionate observer; this was personal. In addition to the geography, Micah makes a pun or play on words out of the name of each town.[3] Catching and understanding these sorts of connections will help you understand some of the more difficult verses in the book.

Cultural Perspectives and Application

As you preach through Micah, you'll want to keep in mind the stereotypical view of the "God of the Old Testament" that many of your listeners may have. Micah isn't shy about portraying God as judge, and he graphically describes the effects of God's judgment. Do people really deserve judgment? Are the sins

---

3. For a list of the cities and the plays on words, see Thomas J. Finley, *Joel, Obadiah and Micah* (Chicago: Moody, 1996), 126–27.

really *that* bad? How can a loving God do such things? These are the sorts of questions your people will be pondering as you work through the book, and so you'll need to show them why God's judgment is just. In order to do that, you'll need to spend time helping them understand how truly rebellious sin is.

Another issue you'll want to give heed to is the question of whether God will judge believers, and if so, how. For many it is easy to dismiss the threat of God's judgment because of the death, burial, and resurrection of Jesus. Certainly we are declared righteous by grace through faith alone. However, if we jump too fast to Jesus, we miss one of the main points of Micah— warning. Micah is included in the canon not just for eighth-century Israelites and Judeans. It is there for us too. God's requirements haven't changed; he still wants us to do justice, to love kindness, and to walk humbly with him. If we don't, there will be consequences.

With regard to relevancy, one of the most significant points of connection between then and now is the relationship between the wealthy and the poor. Those who have are always in a position to take advantage of those who have not. The issue isn't having; the issue is how we obtain it and what we do with it. Are we tightfisted or openhanded? As we close our fingers into a fist, we're pulling God's judgment toward us. We need to be constantly reminded of this truth, and Micah is a great opportunity to shepherd people in this area.

Finally, one of the reasons for Micah's popularity is Matthew's reference to Jesus as the fulfillment of Micah 5:2 (Jesus also alludes to Micah when he teaches on family strife in Matt. 10:35–36). While 5:2 might be the only specific reference cited in the New Testament, Micah is all over the ministry of Jesus. You don't need to go there every week, but don't be shy about allowing Micah to point people to the hope we have in King Jesus.

RECOMMENDED RESOURCES

Allen, Leslie C. *The Books of Joel, Obadiah, Jonah.* The New International Commentary on the Old Testament. Grand Rapids: Eerdmans, 1976.

Dorsey, David A. *The Literary Structure of the Old Testament: A Commentary on Genesis–Malachi.* Grand Rapids: Baker, 1999.

Walton, John H., ed. *Zondervan Illustrated Bible Backgrounds Commentary: Old Testament.* Grand Rapids: Zondervan, 2009.

Nahum

FRANCE B. BROWN JR.

The Big Idea of Nahum

More than a century after the spiritual revival that was sparked by the preaching of Jonah swept through Nineveh, the imperial capital of Assyria, Nahum prophesied God's judgment against the pagan city and promised restoration for God's covenant people Judah.

SUBJECT: What is God's message through the prophet Nahum to Nineveh and Judah?

COMPLEMENT: Because of its wickedness, Nineveh will suffer complete destruction and Judah will enjoy God's restoration.

EXEGETICAL IDEA: God's message through the prophet Nahum to Nineveh and Judah is that because of its wickedness, Nineveh will suffer complete destruction and Judah will enjoy God's restoration.[1]

HOMILETICAL IDEA: Recognize that God will destroy his enemies and deliver his people from sin.

---

1. As a judgment speech, the book of Nahum is a proclamation of God's judgment in response to sinful attitudes and actions. Specifically, it is a judgment speech against a foreign nation. This type of prophetic speech announces judgment against those who oppressed God's covenant people and encourages his people with the message of his perpetual faithfulness. These announcements feature proclamations related to past sin and future destruction. See William W. Klein, Craig L. Blomberg, and Robert L. Hubbard Jr., *Introduction to Biblical Interpretation*, 2nd ed. (Nashville: Thomas Nelson, 2004), 368–69.

Selecting Preaching and Teaching Passages in Nahum

The book of Nahum presents an intense, vivid, and forceful message of death, destruction, and devastation to the enemies of God while providing comfort and consolation to the people of God.[2] It falls into three major divisions: Nineveh's destruction declared (1:1–15), Nineveh's destruction described (2:1–13), and Nineveh's destruction deserved (3:1–19). The designation and range of sermon/lesson units vary as preachers or teachers utilize different exegetical and thematic markers to identify discrete material.[3] Four preaching or teaching units are presented in this chapter.

Getting the Subject, Complement, Exegetical Idea, and Homiletical Idea

Nahum 1

SUBJECT: What is the message that God wants Nahum to give to Nineveh and Judah?

COMPLEMENT: He is the all-powerful warrior God who will destroy his enemies and deliver his people.

EXEGETICAL IDEA: The message that God wants Nahum to give to Nineveh and Judah is that he is the all-powerful warrior God who will destroy his enemies and deliver his people.

HOMILETICAL IDEA: Be comforted to know that God is the all-powerful warrior who will destroy his enemies and deliver his people.

Nahum 2

SUBJECT: What is the message that God wants Nahum to give to Nineveh and Judah?

COMPLEMENT: He will restore Judah and cause the siege, defeat, and plunder of Nineveh.

EXEGETICAL IDEA: The message that God wants Nahum to give to Nineveh and Judah is that he will restore Judah and cause the siege, defeat, and plunder of Nineveh.

HOMILETICAL IDEA: Be confident in God who sovereignly brings about the restoration of his people and the destruction of his enemies.

2. The name Nahum means "comfort" or "consolation."
3. Some possible preaching/teaching units include 1:1–8; 1:9–15; 2:1–2; 2:3–13; 3:1–7; 3:8–15; 3:16–19.

Nahum 3:1-7

SUBJECT: What is the message that God wants Nahum to give to Nineveh and Judah?

COMPLEMENT: The reason that he will bring devastation, humiliation, and rejection to Nineveh is its rampant wickedness.

EXEGETICAL IDEA: The message that God wants Nahum to give to Nineveh and Judah is that he will bring devastation, humiliation, and rejection to Nineveh because of its rampant wickedness.[4]

HOMILETICAL IDEA: Wickedness draws God's wrath.

Nahum 3:8-19

SUBJECT: What is the message that God wants Nahum to give to Nineveh and Judah?

COMPLEMENT: Nineveh will suffer despair, devastation, and destruction because of its evil toward other nations.

EXEGETICAL IDEA: The message that God wants Nahum to give to Nineveh and Judah is that Nineveh will suffer despair, devastation, and destruction because of its evil toward other nations.[5]

HOMILETICAL IDEA: Rejoice that God will bring shame to the wicked because of their wickedness.

Difficult Passages/Verses

Notable interpretive challenges in Nahum involve the nature of its writing, the use of literary forms, and the meaning of terms. To begin with, the prophet's message is called a *massa*, which may be translated "oracle" or "burden" (1:1). An oracle refers to the proclamation of God delivered through his prophet. A burden refers to the weighty responsibility of the prophet in ministering the message of God's judgment or the devastating judgment that the Ninevites will suffer. At least three views are debated regarding the so-called acrostic form of 1:2–8. One view rejects the existence of an acrostic, the second view argues for a partial acrostic, and the third view contends that chapter 1 is a complete acrostic that has suffered textual

4. This passage is a "woe oracle," which expresses prophetic outrage and pronouncement of doom.
5. This passage is a "taunt song," which is a formalized mockery of an opponent intended to publicly humiliate and excoriate them.

corruption.[6] Additionally, there are several possible references to "gates of the river" in 2:6. They may be fortified bridges, city gates, sluice gates, wall breaches, or floodgates.[7]

Cultural Perspectives and Application

Nahum prophesied in the context of ferocious oppression. Assyria destroyed Israel and dominated Judah for more than a century. Assyria was a powerful, sadistic empire characterized by unmitigated cruelty, military ruthlessness, and idolatrous worship. They erected pillars of the severed heads of enemy soldiers, set up pyramids made of the corpses of conquered foes, flayed the skins of their enemies and spread them on city walls, cut off the hands and limbs of their enemies, and burned alive youth and women.

The following are possible applications: seek refuge in God (1:1–15), recognize God's power (1:1–8), and reject wickedness (3:1–7).

RECOMMENDED RESOURCES

Johnson, Elliott E. "Nahum." In *The Bible Knowledge Commentary: An Exposition of the Scriptures*, edited by J. F. Walvoord and R. B. Zuck, 1:1493–504. Wheaton: Victor, 1985.

Leggett, Donald A. "How to Preach from the Prophets." *Preaching* 8, no. 5 (March–April 1993): 25–32.

Longman, Tremper, III. "Nahum." In *The Minor Prophets*, edited by Thomas Edward McComiskey, 765–830. Grand Rapids: Baker Academic, 2009.

---

6. Tremper Longman III, "Nahum," in *The Minor Prophets*, ed. Thomas Edward McComiskey (Grand Rapids: Baker Academic, 2009), 773–75.

7. Elliott E. Johnson, "Nahum," in The *Bible Knowledge Commentary: An Exposition of the Scriptures*, ed. J. F. Walvoord and R. B. Zuck (Wheaton: Victor, 1985), 1:1500.

Habakkuk

HEATHER JOY ZIMMERMAN

The Big Idea of Habakkuk

Habakkuk is a prophetic book that proclaims God's sovereignty and goodness through dialogues between Habakkuk and the Lord amid the wickedness in Judah and the terrifying impending judgment through Babylon. Habakkuk concludes with an expression of trust and confidence in God's faithfulness.

SUBJECT: What is the message God instructs Habakkuk to give to Judah amid current and future violence, injustice, and judgment?

COMPLEMENT: Habakkuk and the people of Judah should righteously walk by faith because God will bring justice by judging Judah through Babylon and will hold Babylon accountable for its own wickedness.

EXEGETICAL IDEA: The message that God instructs Habakkuk to give to Judah amid current and future violence, injustice, and judgment is that Judah should righteously walk by faith because God will bring justice by judging Judah through Babylon and will hold Babylon accountable for its own wickedness.

HOMILETICAL IDEA: Persevere in faith in the face of violent injustice.

Selecting Preaching and Teaching Passages in Habakkuk

Habakkuk may be taught in a single message capturing the thrust of the book: in the face of violence and injustice, bring one's laments to God, praise his character, and resolve to remain faithful and trust God as one waits for him to bring justice.

Likewise, one could divide the book into three messages: Habakkuk 1:1–11; 1:12–2:20; 3:1–19. The first message (1:1–11) discusses the first dialogue cycle between Habakkuk and God, focusing on the theme of "Where is God in the face of violence and injustice?" The second message (1:12–2:20) explains the next two dialogue cycles between God and Habakkuk, emphasizing how God works his justice in ways one may not see or understand. The third message (3:1–19) walks through Habakkuk's psalm of confidence, proclaiming praise and trust in God in the midst of uncertain circumstances.

Getting the Subject, Complement, Exegetical Idea, and Homiletical Idea

Habakkuk 1:1-11

SUBJECT: How can God be good and just when he seems apathetic toward the wickedness of Judah?

COMPLEMENT: God will bring justice through judgment carried out by the Babylonians.

EXEGETICAL IDEA: God can be good and just when he seems apathetic toward the wickedness of Judah because God will bring justice through judgment carried out by the Babylonians.

HOMILETICAL IDEA: In the midst of hopeless violence and injustice, the God who sees injustice will bring justice in his perfect yet mysterious ways.

Habakkuk 1:12-2:20

SUBJECT: How can God's method for bringing justice be just when he uses the even more wicked Babylonians to judge Judah?

COMPLEMENT: It will involve the righteous living by their faithfulness and *all* the wicked (including those he uses to judge Judah) being brought to judgment.

EXEGETICAL IDEA: God's method for bringing justice can be just when he uses the even more wicked Babylonians to judge Judah because it will involve the righteous living by their faithfulness and *all* the wicked (including those he uses to judge Judah) being brought to judgment.

HOMILETICAL IDEA: When God's ways appear unclear, trust that he preserves the faithful and judges *all* who are violent or unjust.

Habakkuk 3

SUBJECT: How should Habakkuk respond to waiting on the Lord for justice?

COMPLEMENT: Through a psalm of trust and confidence.

EXEGETICAL IDEA: Habakkuk should respond to waiting on the Lord for justice through a psalm of trust and confidence.

HOMILETICAL IDEA: In the midst of the anguish and anxiety of waiting for justice, resolve to trust God.

Difficult Passages/Verses

While the big idea of Habakkuk is clear, many details throughout this short book require explanation. Provide a brief summary of the historical situation of Judah from the time of King Josiah through Babylonian captivity (609–538 BC). Explain the literary/theological genres of lament and woe oracles. Help listeners see how the speaker changes between God and Habakkuk throughout the book. Habakkuk 2:4 is challenging to preach in light of New Testament citations (Rom. 1:17; Gal. 3:11; Heb. 10:38).

Habakkuk is a great book for addressing theodicy, the problem of evil. As with Job, God gives Habakkuk space to be honest and vulnerable. God does not always directly answer Habakkuk's questions; God is the answer to Habakkuk's questions. Preach the tension throughout Habakkuk 3; it is not a "happy" song but a song of resolve even without resolution.

Cultural Perspectives and Application

We must first contextualize the setting of Habakkuk. Help the audience see the book through the lenses of the #MeToo movement, the violence that ravaged Aleppo, the horror of Ground Zero on 9/11. Allow space for people to enter the emotional intensity of Habakkuk so that they can find faith and healing even if they do not experience resolution here and now. In the midst of praying for justice (whether for ourselves or for those around us), Habakkuk 3 offers a model of a prayer of trust to pray as we wait for God to show up.

Here are several possible applications: cry out to God in the rawness of pain (1:2–4; 1:12–2:1); trust that God is doing more than one can see or understand (1:5); don't trust in one's own strength (1:12–17; 2:18–20); wait expectantly on the Lord (2:1); be confident in one's faith but open to how God may work (3:1–19).

--- **RECOMMENDED RESOURCES** ---

Bruce, F. F. "Habakkuk." In *The Minor Prophets*, edited by Thomas Edward McComiskey, 831–96. Grand Rapids: Baker Academic, 2009.

Bruckner, James. *Jonah, Nahum, Habakkuk, Zephaniah*. The NIV Application Commentary. Grand Rapids: Zondervan, 2004.

Goldingay, John, and Pamela J. Scalise. *Minor Prophets II*. New International Bible Commentary. Peabody, MA: Hendrickson, 2009.

Zephaniah

FRANCE B. BROWN JR.

The Big Idea of Zephaniah

During the pivotal period of the reign of King Josiah (640–609 BC), Zephaniah proclaims the day of the Lord when God provides universal restoration for the believing remnant after he judges Judah and gentile nations.[1]

SUBJECT: What is God's message through the prophet Zephaniah to Judah?

COMPLEMENT: Submit to God because the day of the Lord will bring judgment on the unrighteous and restoration to those who worship and serve him.

EXEGETICAL IDEA: God's message through the prophet Zephaniah to Judah is to submit to God because the day of the Lord will bring judgment on the unrighteous and restoration to those who worship and serve him.[2]

HOMILETICAL IDEA: Submit to God because the day of the Lord will bring judgment on the unrighteous and favor on those who worship and serve him.

---

1. Possible meanings of Zephaniah include: "Yahweh hides," "Yahweh has hidden," "Hidden in Yahweh," "Yahweh's watchman," or "Yahweh treasured."
2. The book of Zephaniah is composed of the two types of speeches that make up the preponderance of prophetic discourses: judgment and salvation. Judgment speeches are proclamations of God's judgment in response to sinful attitudes and actions. Salvation speeches refer to those proclamations that focus on God's deliverance of his people. Andreas J. Köstenberger and Richard Patterson, *Invitation to Biblical Interpretation: Exploring the Hermeneutical Triad of History, Literature, and Theology* (Grand Rapids: Kregel Academic, 2011), 321–37.

Selecting Preaching and Teaching Passages in Zephaniah

In fifty-three verses, this book presents a vivid and convincing picture of the day of the Lord and provides compelling descriptions of the major themes of prophecy. It is therefore referred to as a compendium of prophecy as well as the "Reader's Digest" of Old Testament prophetic speech. Zephaniah falls into two major divisions: the judgment of the day of the Lord (1:1–3:7) and the salvation of the day of the Lord (3:8–20). At least ten preaching/teaching units may be identified.[3] Four are presented in this chapter.

Getting the Subject, Complement, Exegetical Idea, and Homiletical Idea

Zephaniah 1:1-2:3

SUBJECT: What is the message that God wants Zephaniah to give to Judah?

COMPLEMENT: In order to avoid God's judgment they must submit to him.

EXEGETICAL IDEA: The message that God wants Zephaniah to give to Judah is that in order to avoid his judgment they must submit to him.[4]

HOMILETICAL IDEA: Submit to God in order to avoid his judgment.

Zephaniah 2:4-3:7

SUBJECT: What is the message that God wants Zephaniah to give to Judah?

COMPLEMENT: Judah and gentile nations will suffer God's judgment.

EXEGETICAL IDEA: The message that God wants Zephaniah to give to Judah is that Judah and gentile nations will suffer God's judgment.[5]

HOMILETICAL IDEA: Understand that the unrighteous will suffer God's judgment.

Zephaniah 3:8-13

SUBJECT: What is the message that God wants Zephaniah to give to Judah?

---

3. Possible preaching or teaching units: 1:1; 1:2–6; 1:7–13; 1:14–18; 2:1–3; 2:4–15; 3:1–7; 3:8; 3:9–13; 3:14–20.

4. The section 2:1–3 is a "repent summons" designed to move God's people to reject their evil ways and live in faithfulness to the covenant. They are delivered by way of warning, promise, and threat.

5. The section 2:4–15 contains judgment speeches against foreign nations, announcing judgment on those who oppressed God's covenant people and encouraging his people with the message of his perpetual faithfulness. The section 3:1–7 is a "woe oracle" expressing prophetic outrage and pronouncement of doom and destruction.

COMPLEMENT: The day of the Lord should inspire hope in the righteous because it brings about their restoration.

EXEGETICAL IDEA: The message that God wants Zephaniah to give to Judah is that the day of the Lord should inspire hope in the righteous because it brings about their restoration.

HOMILETICAL IDEA: Be comforted by God's eternal judgment of sin because it brings restoration to those who are faithful.

Zephaniah 3:14-20

SUBJECT: What is the message that God wants Zephaniah to give to Judah?

COMPLEMENT: The day of the Lord should inspire joy in the righteous because it brings about their restoration.

EXEGETICAL IDEA: The message that God wants Zephaniah to give to Judah is that the day of the Lord should inspire joy in the righteous because it brings about their restoration.

HOMILETICAL IDEA: Rejoice in God's eternal judgment of sin because it brings restoration to those who are faithful.

Difficult Passages/Verses

Interpretive challenges in the book of Zephaniah include the genealogy of the prophet, the exact timing of his prophecy, and the summary nature of the prophecy as well as subject references and structural elements within the prophecy. Specifically, was Zephaniah a descendant of King Hezekiah? At what point in Josiah's reign did Zephaniah minister—at the beginning, before, during, or after his religious reforms? How does Zephaniah's prophecy extend beyond its immediate historical context? Does "leap on the temple threshold" (1:9) refer to idolatrous worship, superstition, or violent looting? Does 3:8 conclude the previous section (3:1–7), introduce the section that follows (3:9–13), or does it serve both functions?

Cultural Perspectives and Application

Zephaniah prophesied in the context and climate of spiritual and social decadence. For more than fifty years prior to Josiah's reign, his immediate predecessors, King Manasseh (695–642 BC) and his son King Amon (642–640 BC), transfused rank idolatry and wickedness into the nation's religious and civic life. Judah engaged in evil practices such as the worship of pagan gods; worship of the sun, moon, and stars; child sacrifices; astrology; placing idols in the temple of God; rejection and violation of covenant prescriptions; social corruption; and socioeconomic oppression of the poor.

The following are possible applications: tell unbelievers about the judgment of God (2:4–3:7), beware of God's judgment (3:1–7), hope in God (3:8), stay faithful (3:8–13), and rejoice in the Lord (3:14–20).

RECOMMENDED RESOURCES

Chisholm, Robert B., Jr. *Interpreting the Minor Prophets*. Grand Rapids: Zondervan, 1990.

Constable, Thomas. "Notes on Zephaniah." https://planobiblechapel.org/tcon/notes/pdf/zephaniah.pdf.

Motyer, J. Alec. "Zephaniah." In *The Minor Prophets*, edited by Thomas Edward McComiskey, 897–962. Grand Rapids: Baker Academic, 2009.

Haggai

KENNETH LANGLEY

The Big Idea of Haggai

Judahites who returned to Jerusalem after the exile started rebuilding the temple but quit because of opposition (Ezra 4). Sixteen years have passed. Now the problem is not opposition but apathy, and God says it's time to get back to work. So he gives his messenger Haggai four oracles over four months in 520 BC: "Build my house!" (1:8).

SUBJECT: What is God's message through Haggai to the returned exiles?

COMPLEMENT: "It's time to reexamine your priorities and build the temple."

EXEGETICAL IDEA: God's message through Haggai to the returned exiles is, "It's time to reexamine your priorities and build the temple."[1]

HOMILETICAL IDEA: Reexamine your priorities and put God's "house" first.

Selecting Preaching and Teaching Passages in Haggai

Haggai's message came in four dated oracles:

    1:1–15: sixth month, day 1
    2:1–9: seventh month, day 21

---

1. Key statements in Haggai help us arrive at this exegetical idea. In 1:4 the Lord asks how they can be content with their fine houses when his is in ruins. Then four times he says, "Give careful thought to your ways" (1:5, 7; 2:15, 18); that is, get your priorities straight. "Build my house" (1:8).

2:10–19: ninth month, day 24

2:20–23: ninth month, day 24

One could preach four sermons, one on each of these. But the final passage, at least, may not seem the most promising sermon text. One sermon on the whole book works well because its message is sharply focused. Here's a plan for two sermons on Haggai.

Getting the Subject, Complement, Exegetical Idea, and Homiletical Idea

Haggai 1

Subject, complement, and ideas identified above for the whole book also work for a sermon on chapter 1. See the introductory paragraph and explanation of "key statements" in note 1. Consider having the congregation sing "Rise Up, O Church of God" or "God of Grace and God of Glory."

SUBJECT: What is God's message through Haggai to the returned exiles?

COMPLEMENT: "It's time to reexamine your priorities and build the temple."

EXEGETICAL IDEA: God's message through Haggai to the returned exiles is "It's time to reexamine your priorities and build the temple."

HOMILETICAL IDEA: Reexamine your priorities and put God's "house" first.

Haggai 2

Verse 4 is key: "Be strong . . . and work. For *I am with you*" (a silver thread running through the Bible). God will glorify his house, prosper their crops, and shake the world to establish his reign.

SUBJECT: How does God motivate the Judahites to get on with the work?

COMPLEMENT: He promises greater glory and prosperity to come and to be with them.

EXEGETICAL IDEA: God motivates the Judahites to get on with the work by promising greater glory and prosperity to come and to be with them.

HOMILETICAL IDEA: Be strong and do the work, for God is with us!

Difficult Passages/Verses

Haggai is uncomplicated. Difficulties arise less from interpretive puzzles than from misunderstood theology. Does the book say, "Scratch God's back and he'll scratch yours"? No, but God's gracious favor does entail covenant obligations. Are famine and drought always chastisement? No, but God can use them to get our attention. Does God promise to make Jehoiachin's grandson king? No, but Zerubbabel's governorship is part of God's plan to enthrone his Anointed. Does Haggai contradict earlier prophets who minimized the importance of the temple? No. Jeremiah and others said temple and cult without justice and integrity disgusted God. Now God wants to restore that powerful symbol of his presence with his chastened people.

The desire of nations in 2:7 is probably not Messiah but the silver and gold mentioned next. However, Messiah *did* fulfill the greater glory promise of verse 8 when he graced the second temple with his presence.

Cultural Perspectives and Application

Your congregation may not be guilty of the gross idolatry and injustice condemned by earlier prophets. Yet they may be preoccupied with their own affairs and apathetic about God's. Every generation needs Haggai's stirring call to reprioritize and be done with lesser things.

Prosperity is God's gift. We're more likely to enjoy it if we pursue the Giver. People needed this word in 520 BC, and they need it today. "Seek first his kingdom and his righteousness, and all these things will be given to you as well" (Matt. 6:33).

Some people may feel, like the old ones in Haggai 2:2–5, that the present falls far short of the good old days. Folks in dwindling mainline denominations, citizens in blighted communities, may need to focus less on the past than on the promise: greater glory awaits, God will shake the earth and establish Messiah's rule, and he is with us (Hag. 1:14; 2:4, 5).

RECOMMENDED RESOURCES

Achtemeier, Elizabeth. *Nahum–Malachi*. Interpretation. Louisville: Westminster John Knox, 1986.

———. *Preaching from the Minor Prophets*. Grand Rapids: Eerdmans, 1998.

Boda, Mark J. *Zechariah, Malachi*. The NIV Application Commentary. Grand Rapids: Zondervan, 2004.

Hill, Andrew. *Haggai, Zechariah, and Malachi*. Tyndale Old Testament Commentaries. Downers Grove, IL: InterVarsity, 2012.

Zechariah

GREGORY K. HOLLIFIELD

Zechariah (meaning "Yahweh remembers") is a prophecy of encouragement to the recently returned postexilic community, informing them of God's immediate and distant plans for Jerusalem, its enemies, and the coming Messiah.

SUBJECT: What was Zechariah's message, which he received from God both visually and audibly, to the Jewish exiles recently returned from Babylon?

COMPLEMENT: The Lord is returning in mercy to inhabit Jerusalem, where his temple will be rebuilt and the nations will assemble to worship him.

EXEGETICAL IDEA: Zechariah's message, which he received from God both visually and audibly, to the Jewish exiles recently returned from Babylonian captivity was that the Lord is returning in mercy to inhabit Jerusalem, where his temple will be rebuilt and the nations will assemble to worship him.

HOMILETICAL IDEA: The nations will one day worship the Lord in a fully restored Jerusalem.

Selecting Preaching and Teaching Passages in Zechariah

The book of Zechariah divides naturally into three sections. Section one consists of eight visions (chaps. 1–6). Section two contains four answers to a question about fasting (chaps. 7–8). Section three concludes with two major undated oracles (chaps. 9–14). With such clear divisions one might jump to the conclusion that the book should be preached in fourteen separate sermons. Upon closer examination, however, one will detect a chiastic structure in section one—with visions 1 and 8, visions 2–3 and 6–7, and visions 4 and 5 corresponding to one another. This first section could therefore be preached in as few as three sermons, if not one (because all eight visions were given in a single night and would have had an aggregate effect on Zechariah and his early audience).

The ethical and religious exhortations pertaining to fasting in section two could be divided into four sermons or taken as a whole. A single sermon on these two chapters would decry empty ritualism (here, fasting without obedience [7:4–14]) and instead encourage the showing of mercy and justice as the way to please God (8:14–17).

The book's two concluding undated oracles, given their length and immediate and more distant orientations, suggest at least two sermons. Nevertheless, the numerous christological prophecies in this section could as effectively be drawn together into one thematic sermon.

Getting the Subject, Complement, Exegetical Idea, and Homiletical Idea

Zechariah 1:1-6

SUBJECT: What did the Lord tell Zechariah to tell the people?

COMPLEMENT: Return to me so that I may return to you—unlike your fathers who turned away from my word and suffered the consequences.

EXEGETICAL IDEA: The Lord told Zechariah to tell the people: Return to me so that I may return to you—unlike your fathers who turned away from my word and suffered the consequences.

HOMILETICAL IDEA: The Lord invites us to return to him now before the consequences of future disobedience overtake us.

Zechariah 1:7-17

■ *Vision 1*

SUBJECT: What did Zechariah's vision of a man riding a red horse signify?

COMPLEMENT: The earth appeared to be at rest, but the Lord who was returning to Jerusalem was jealous and angry with the nations and would restore his cities' fortunes.

EXEGETICAL IDEA: Zechariah's vision of a man riding a red horse signified that although the earth appeared to be at rest, the Lord who was returning to

Jerusalem was jealous and angry with the nations and would restore his cities' fortunes.

HOMILETICAL IDEA: Our jealous and angry Lord will return to bless his own.

Zechariah 1:18-21

▨ *Vision 2*

SUBJECT: What did Zechariah's vision of four horns and smiths signify?

COMPLEMENT: The nations that attacked and scattered Judah, Israel, and Jerusalem would experience terrifying defeat.

EXEGETICAL IDEA: Zechariah's vision of four horns and smiths signified that the nations that attacked Judah, Israel, and Jerusalem would experience terrifying defeat.

HOMILETICAL IDEA: Those who abuse God's own are destined for defeat.

Zechariah 2

▨ *Vision 3*

SUBJECT: What did Zechariah's vision of a man with a measuring line signify?

COMPLEMENT: Jerusalem would be inhabited by a multitude returned from Babylon and beyond and would be protected by its God in its midst.

EXEGETICAL IDEA: Zechariah's vision of a man with a measuring line signified that Jerusalem would be inhabited by a multitude returned from Babylon and beyond, and would be protected by its God in its midst.

HOMILETICAL IDEA: Our God who dwells among us is our source of protection and prosperity.

Zechariah 3

▨ *Vision 4*

SUBJECT: What did Zechariah's vision of Joshua the high priest signify?

COMPLEMENT: The Lord was cleansing and restoring the priesthood in the person of Joshua in anticipation of the coming Branch, who would signal the removal of iniquity and the restoration of contentment.

EXEGETICAL IDEA: Zechariah's vision of Joshua the high priest signified that the Lord was cleansing the priesthood in anticipation of the coming Branch, who would signal the removal of iniquity and the restoration of contentment.

HOMILETICAL IDEA: The Lord cleanses us sinners to serve as his priests, introducing others to our great High Priest (see 1 Pet. 2:9).

Zechariah 4

Vision 5

SUBJECT: What did Zechariah's vision of a golden lampstand signify?

COMPLEMENT: The Lord had anointed Zerubbabel and Joshua for leading in the restoration of Jerusalem and the temple, and nothing would stop them.

EXEGETICAL IDEA: Zechariah's vision of a golden lampstand signified that the Lord had anointed Zerubbabel and Joshua for leading in the restoration of Jerusalem and the temple, and nothing would stop them.

HOMILETICAL IDEA: The Lord anoints for effectual leadership whom he chooses.

Zechariah 5:1-4

Vision 6

SUBJECT: What did Zechariah's vision of a flying scroll signify?

COMPLEMENT: A curse was going out against the thief and the one who swore falsely by the Lord's name, to purge them and their houses from the land.

EXEGETICAL IDEA: Zechariah's vision of a flying scroll signified that a curse was going out against the thief and the one who swore falsely by the Lord's name, to purge them and their houses from the land.

HOMILETICAL IDEA: There is no room for the one who wrongs his neighbor or God in that place where God dwells (see 1 Cor. 6:9–10).

Zechariah 5:5-11

Vision 7

SUBJECT: What did Zechariah's vision of a woman in a basket signify?

COMPLEMENT: Wickedness would be removed from the land and relocated to its own house in Shinar (Babylon).

EXEGETICAL IDEA: Zechariah's vision of a woman in a basket signified that wickedness would be removed from the land and relocated to its own house in Shinar.

HOMILETICAL IDEA: Wickedness has no home in the place where God resides (see 2 Cor. 6:16–18).

Zechariah 6

Vision 8

SUBJECT: What did Zechariah's vision of four chariots signify?

COMPLEMENT: With God's Spirit at rest and the earth subdued under his watchful eye, Joshua could be crowned as his princely priest, the Branch, who would rebuild the temple and rule in peace.

EXEGETICAL IDEA: Zechariah's vision of four chariots signified that with God's Spirit at rest and the earth subdued under his watchful eye, Joshua could be crowned as his princely priest, the Branch, who would rebuild the temple and rule in peace.

HOMILETICAL IDEA: God's princely priest, the Branch, will rule in peace when God's Spirit is finally at rest.

Zechariah 7:1-7

■ *Question and Answer 1*

SUBJECT: Should we who have returned from exile continue observing the fasts that commemorate Jerusalem's destruction?[1]

COMPLEMENT: You observed those fasts, just like your former feasts, for your own purposes.

EXEGETICAL IDEA: To the postexilic community's question of whether they should continue observing the fasts that commemorated Jerusalem's destruction, the Lord answered: You observed those fasts, just like your former feasts, for your own purposes.

HOMILETICAL IDEA: Whether we fast or feast, we should do all to God's glory (see 1 Cor. 10:31; Rom. 14).

Zechariah 7:8-14

■ *Answer 2*

SUBJECT: Should we who have returned from exile continue observing the fasts that commemorate Jerusalem's destruction?

COMPLEMENT: Act with justice and merciful love—unlike your fathers who didn't and were therefore dispersed abroad.

EXEGETICAL IDEA: To the postexilic community's question of whether they should continue observing the fasts that commemorated Jerusalem's destruction, the Lord answered: Act with justice and merciful love—unlike your fathers who didn't and were therefore dispersed abroad.

---

1. Typically we would refrain from using "we" in the subject question, complement, and exegetical idea. However, since we're speaking from the perspective of Jewish exiles, this is permissible.

HOMILETICAL IDEA: The Lord desires from us justice and mercy, not mere rituals (see Mic. 6:1–8).

Zechariah 8:1-17

■ *Answer 3*

SUBJECT: Should we who have returned from exile continue observing the fasts that commemorate Jerusalem's destruction?

COMPLEMENT: Prosperity shall be restored to all Jerusalem and the house of Judah (thereby removing the reason for your fasts), so practice justice.

EXEGETICAL IDEA: To the postexilic community's question of whether they should continue observing the fasts that commemorated Jerusalem's destruction, the Lord answered: Prosperity shall be restored to all Jerusalem and the house of Judah (thereby removing the reason for your fasts), so practice justice.

HOMILETICAL IDEA: Those to whom the Lord has done good should do good to all.

Zechariah 8:18-23

■ *Answer 4*

SUBJECT: Should we who have returned from exile continue observing the fasts that commemorate Jerusalem's destruction?

COMPLEMENT: Your fasts shall become feasts, and the Lord's favor toward you who love truth and peace shall draw in the nations.

EXEGETICAL IDEA: To the postexilic community's question of whether they should continue observing the fasts that commemorated Jerusalem's destruction, the Lord answered: Your fasts shall become feasts, and the Lord's favor toward you who love truth and peace shall draw in the nations.

HOMILETICAL IDEA: God favors us in order to draw others to himself.

Zechariah 9-11

■ *Oracle 1*

SUBJECT: What was the message of Zechariah's first major undated oracle?

COMPLEMENT: The enemies of a reunited Israel would be judged, Israel's king and land restored (chaps. 9–10), and Israel itself punished for rejecting the shepherding care of the Lord (chap. 11).

EXEGETICAL IDEA: The message of Zechariah's first major undated oracle was that the enemies of a reunited Israel would be judged, Israel's king and land restored, and Israel itself punished for rejecting the shepherding care of the Lord.

HOMILETICAL IDEA: All who reject the true Shepherd will eventually suffer the consequences of their decision.

Zechariah 12-14

■ *Oracle 2*

SUBJECT: What was the message of Zechariah's second major undated oracle?

COMPLEMENT: The Lord will finally deliver Israel, having repented of its earlier rejection of him (chaps. 12–13), and establish his universal kingdom with his throne in Jerusalem (chap. 14).

EXEGETICAL IDEA: The message of Zechariah's second major undated oracle was that the Lord will finally deliver Israel, having repented of its earlier rejection of him, and establish his universal kingdom with his throne in Jerusalem.

HOMILETICAL IDEA: The day is coming when God's people will be finally at rest and the earth will be fully his own.

Difficult Passages/Verses

Commentators across the ages agree that the book of Zechariah is one of the Bible's most difficult books to interpret. Obscurity abounds on every page. The first section (chaps. 1–6) consists of strange visions and oracles that sometimes seem disconnected. The second section (chaps. 7–8) opens with a strange question whose significance (see 2 Kings 25) the modern reader is likely to miss and concludes with a handful of divine replies. Once again, the connection between the people's question and God's answers isn't always clear. The third section (chaps. 9–14) presents a "kaleidoscope of divine threats and promises regarding the future of Jerusalem, the nations, and the cosmos, but often having no clearly identifiable historical referents."[2]

The reader must constantly bear in mind that the prophet's primary focus was on the restoration of Jerusalem, its temple (attended by God's presence),

---

2. William J. Webb, "Zechariah, Book of," in *Dictionary for Theological Interpretation of the Bible*, ed. Kevin J. Vanhoozer (Grand Rapids: Baker Academic, 2005), 862.

and its people. Zechariah sought to remind his original audience that they found themselves in their difficult circumstances because of their forefathers' disobedience; nevertheless, the Lord had not forgotten them or his covenant with them. The Lord himself was returning to them, restoring their former glory, and expected their faithful obedience. All of this talk of a restored (or new) Jerusalem, descriptions of what Zechariah saw in certain of his visions (such as four horses and their riders), the mention of one called "the Branch," and numerous messianic predictions (especially in the book's final section) can cause the reader to overlook or underappreciate the book's historical setting and its significance for that first generation of Jews who had returned from Babylonian exile and dispersion.

The repetitious manner in which the book's key themes are presented may obscure the nuanced ways Zechariah restates those themes and how he applies them. For example, the horsemen's report that the earth appeared "at rest" in 1:11 belied the reality of God's then-present anger toward those nations that had taken undue advantage of his people, but their report that God's Spirit was "at rest" in the north country in 6:8 was a true statement of how God then felt. His wrath toward Babylon was appeased.

The chiastic presentation of the eight visions in section one creates its own set of difficulties. While it is possible to analyze each vision separately (as above), the outer visions (1 and 8) clearly bear some correspondence to each other, as do visions 2 and 3 with visions 6 and 7, leaving visions 4 and 5 together as the central focal point. How were these paired visions meant to correspond exactly? Were visions 4 and 5 meant to elevate Joshua and Zerubbabel equally, thus portending the coming of two messiahs (as some Jewish scholars believed)? If not, how does one explain vision 8, which sets forth Joshua as a princely priest typifying one messiah? These are only three questions that might be asked of this section.

The location of Israel's enemies named in 9:1–8, as well as their roles in Israel's history, will be unfamiliar to many readers. Time should be taken to identify these enemies on a map, to summarize their mistreatment of God's people, and to tell how they met their own demise.

Zechariah's second major oracle (chaps. 12–14) looks to the distant future, naturally raising questions of an eschatological nature. The preacher will want to avoid becoming bogged down in unnecessary speculation here and concentrate instead on the clear message of God's final victory and eternal rule.

Cultural Perspectives and Application

The Lord disciplines his wayward children, but how do we respond to this form of his loving care? Do we allow feelings of guilt to defeat us or resentment to constrain us so that we don't return humbly to his side and service? Or do we confess our sin, accept his forgiveness, thank him for turning us from our own destructive ways, and again follow him? It was at this decisive crossroads where the recently returned exiles sat, and it was here where God placed Zechariah as a signpost pointing to a brighter future for those who would submit to their God.

Zechariah's message to the dejected returnees was this: The Lord remembers. The Lord returns. The Lord restores. No matter how things may appear, he hasn't forgotten his covenant. He is returning to his people. He will make all things right again. How often do we forget that? How badly do we need Zechariah to remind us?

Jerusalem's final restoration is the world's ultimate salvation. Their long-awaited Branch has borne the sins of all humankind. He came first to be rejected by Israel (6:12; 11:12–13; 12:10); he is returning to rule over all (2:11; 6:15; 8:23; 14:16, 20–21).

Some of Zechariah's lessons are as follows:

- The rebuilding of God's house is an indispensable condition of a better era (1:16).[3]
- The Lord is watching the earth and remains God over all nations (1:11–15; 2:11; 4:10; 6:5–8; 8:20–23; 9:1–8; 14:13–21).
- Satan is the chief adversary of God's people (3:1).
- It's not by power, or by might, but by his Spirit that the Lord's work is done (4:6).
- Religious rituals are no substitute for justice, mercy, truth, and righteousness (8:16–17).
- The rejected Branch is the returning King who will usher in a new day (14:6–9).
- God's promises of a restored temple, priest, king, and people, a rejected shepherd, and a universal sovereign in an eschatological future all find fulfillment in Jesus Christ.

---

3. George L. Robinson, *The Twelve Minor Prophets* (Grand Rapids: Baker, 1984), 153–55.

───── **RECOMMENDED RESOURCES** ─────

Baldwin, Joyce G. *Haggai, Zechariah, Malachi*. Tyndale Old Testament Commentaries. Downers Grove, IL: InterVarsity, 1972.

Fee, Gordon D., and Douglas Stuart. *How to Read the Bible Book by Book*. Grand Rapids: Zondervan, 2002.

Malachi

TIMOTHY BUSHFIELD

The Big Idea of Malachi

The book of Malachi (meaning "my messenger") is written to God's covenant people not in a time of crisis but in a time of spiritual decline. It is a series of disputations or arguments initiated by God as he brings accusations against his people, for they have wandered from the covenant and neglected the full experience of life with their God.

SUBJECT: What does the overall message of the book of Malachi teach about the relationship between God and his people in the postexilic community?

COMPLEMENT: In a time of spiritual decay, God confronts the people's wandering ways while inviting them back into their covenant relationship with their God.

EXEGETICAL IDEA: The overall message of the book of Malachi teaches about the relationship between God and his people in the postexilic community when, during a time of spiritual decay, God confronts the people's wandering ways while inviting them back into their covenantal relationship with their God.

HOMILETICAL IDEA: God confronts us to care for us as he calls us back to himself.

Selecting Preaching and Teaching Passages in Malachi

Malachi consists of six disputations that are clearly evident in the text. An initial week of introduction to the book would provide necessary historical and biblical context. Following this, allocating one week to each disputation yields six additional weeks of study. One final week emerges from chapter 4. By reserving or revisiting 3:16 during this final week, an opportunity for congregational response can be included, as the text points to the promised Messiah. Following the structure of the text itself in this way, the book of Malachi can be preached effectively across eight weeks.

Getting the Subject, Complement, Exegetical Idea, and Homiletical Idea

Malachi 1:1

SUBJECT: What is the purpose of the book of Malachi?

COMPLEMENT: For God to send his messenger to call his people back into a restored relationship with him during a time of spiritual decline.

EXEGETICAL IDEA: The purpose of the book of Malachi is for God to send his messenger to call his people back into a restored relationship with him during a time of spiritual decline.

HOMILETICAL IDEA: Hard words are coming, but God loves us too much to let us wander too far.

Malachi 1:2–5

SUBJECT: What does God establish first as he confronts his people?

COMPLEMENT: That God loves them and has chosen to work among them and through them, not because of their merit, but because of his grace.

EXEGETICAL IDEA: What God establishes first as he confronts his people is that God loves them and has chosen to work among them and through them, not because of their merit, but because of his grace.

HOMILETICAL IDEA: Return to the Lord, for his love isn't based on our goodness but on his grace.[1]

Malachi 1:6–2:9

SUBJECT: What does this second disputation reveal about God's honor among his people?

COMPLEMENT: That the priests were showing contempt for God by allowing blemished animals to be used for sacrifices in worship.

---

1. See "Difficult Passages/Verses" for a discussion of how the terms "love" and "hate" are used covenantally rather than emotionally in Malachi and throughout Scripture.

EXEGETICAL IDEA: The second disputation reveals about God's honor among his people that the priests were showing contempt for God by allowing blemished animals to be used for sacrifices in worship.

HOMILETICAL IDEA: God is great so worship accordingly.

Malachi 2:10-16[2]

SUBJECT: What does this third disputation teach about God's character?

COMPLEMENT: That God is a faithful, covenant-making God, and his people are to reflect this in their own relationships—especially in marriage.

EXEGETICAL IDEA: This third disputation teaches that God is a faithful, covenant-making God, and his people are to reflect this faithfulness in their own relationships—especially in marriage.

HOMILETICAL IDEA: God is faithful, so marriage is to be a reflection of his faithfulness.

Malachi 2:17-3:5

SUBJECT: What does the fourth disputation reveal about God's justice?

COMPLEMENT: While withheld for a season, it will certainly come, and God's own people will not be exempt from the justice for which they clamor.

EXEGETICAL IDEA: The fourth disputation reveals that God's justice, while withheld for a season, will certainly come, and God's own people will not be exempt from the justice for which they clamor.

HOMILETICAL IDEA: God is just and his justice is coming, and we are not exempt.

Malachi 3:6-12

SUBJECT: What does this fifth disputation convey about returning to the Lord?

COMPLEMENT: It involves every aspect of life, including bringing a whole tithe to the Lord instead of robbing God by withholding it.

EXEGETICAL IDEA: The fifth disputation conveys about returning to the Lord that it involves every aspect of life, including bringing a whole tithe to the Lord instead of robbing God by withholding it.

---

2. Malachi 2:16 is one of the most difficult Hebrew verses to translate in the whole Bible. There is significant interpretive variety among the various translations.

HOMILETICAL IDEA: God is unchanging, so our entire lives are to be oriented around his grace, including our finances.

Malachi 3:13-15, 17-18

SUBJECT: What does this final disputation reveal?

COMPLEMENT: That seeing evil prosper, they had lost hope in God's redeeming purposes, even though God had promised a future day when he will act and vindicate his people as his treasured possession.

EXEGETICAL IDEA: This final disputation reveals that the people see evil prosper and they lost hope in God's redeeming purposes, even though God had promised a future day when he will act and vindicate his people as his treasured possession.

HOMILETICAL IDEA: God is good, so we hope for God's future because the present will soon be past.

Malachi 3:16 and 4:1-6

SUBJECT: What does the conclusion to the book of Malachi reveal about God's ultimate redeeming purposes?

COMPLEMENT: With messianic allusion, God invites his people to recommit to their covenant life with him, promising that the great day of healing and vindication will indeed come.

EXEGETICAL IDEA: The conclusion of the book of Malachi reveals about God's ultimate redeeming purposes that with messianic allusion God invites his people to recommit to their covenant life with him, promising that the great day of healing and vindication will indeed come.

HOMILETICAL IDEA: Return to the Lord, for healing and vindication are found only in Jesus's name.

Difficult Passages/Verses

In Malachi 1:2–3, as God reminds his people of their chosen status as God's covenant people, the text says that he loved Jacob but "Esau I have hated." The idea that God hates someone needs to be unpacked by explaining the covenantal framework for these ideas as opposed to the emotional connotations they carry to today's modern ears.

You will also encounter a wide variety of translations for Malachi 2:16. This is some of the most difficult Hebrew in the whole Bible. Read multiple translations of this verse to grasp the various interpretive options, and preach with humility by not speaking with more conviction than the clarity of the text allows.

Cultural Perspectives and Application

Malachi is a refreshingly practical book. As you teach through this book, draw attention to God's expectation that outward behavior should be a reflection of one's inward heart condition. Whether Malachi is addressing worship, tithing, sacrifices, or marriage, the text highlights a pragmatic expression of faith as we make meaningful decisions that outwardly reflect our inward relationship with God.

There are also numerous references throughout the book where God's people don't see his justice or his influence or his blessing around them. This is clearly something with which contemporary hearers can identify. The prophet emphasizes that a promised day of healing and vindication is coming, even when life today seems hopeless. While Jesus has indeed already come, we do continue to wait for his glorious return, and we can share in this posture of hopeful, expectant waiting.

RECOMMENDED RESOURCES

Baker, David W. *Joel, Obadiah, Malachi.* The NIV Application Commentary. Grand Rapids: Zondervan, 2006.

Clendenin, Ray E. *Haggai, Malachi.* The New American Commentary. Nashville: Broadman & Holman, 2004.

Hugenberger, Gordon P. *Marriage as Covenant: Biblical Law and Ethics as Developed from Malachi.* Grand Rapids: Baker, 1994.

Stuart, Douglas. "Malachi." In *The Minor Prophets*, edited by Thomas Edward McComiskey, 1245–396. Grand Rapids: Baker Academic, 2009.

THE NEW TESTAMENT

Matthew

SCOTT A. WENIG

The Big Idea of Matthew

Matthew's Gospel is a biographical account of the birth, ministry, death, and resurrection of Jesus originally written for Hebrew Christians. It demonstrates that Jesus is God's promised Messiah who serves as Savior, King, and Lord over both Israel and the world. After an opening genealogy that identifies Jesus as the son of David and Abraham (1:1–17), Matthew highlights his unusual birth, baptism by John, and satanic temptation to show that he has come to save people from their sins. Jesus began his public ministry by teaching on the kingdom of God and effected supernatural healings, feedings, and exorcisms to prove that the kingdom had arrived in his person. His ministry culminated with a mock trial by the Jewish leaders, who handed him over to the Roman authorities for sentencing. This resulted in his horrible death by crucifixion but was followed three days later by his promised resurrection from the dead. The former atoned for the sins of humanity, while the latter demonstrated his deity and lordship. Those who choose to follow Jesus as King are to take his message of salvation to the larger world, making disciples from every tribe, tongue, and nationality.

SUBJECT: How are God's promises of a Messiah who provides salvation for Jews and gentiles alike fulfilled in Jesus?

COMPLEMENT: By means of his Jewish lineage, ministry to both Jews and gentiles, atoning death on the cross, and physical resurrection from the dead, through which Jesus inaugurated God's kingdom.

EXEGETICAL IDEA: God's promises of a Messiah who provides salvation for Jews and gentiles alike are fulfilled in Jesus by means of his Jewish lineage, ministry to both Jews and gentiles, atoning death on the cross, and physical resurrection from the dead, through which Jesus inaugurated God's kingdom.

HOMILETICAL IDEA: God's promised Messiah is King Jesus, who by his death for sin and resurrection from the dead provides salvation for all kinds of people.

Selecting Preaching and Teaching Passages in Matthew

An expository series on all or most of the twenty-eight chapters of Matthew's Gospel could last several months and is one way to preach the book. If preachers and teachers opt for this approach, the following outlines show the themes of each major section.

Outline 1

    I. The Genealogy and Birth of Jesus the Messiah (chaps. 1–2)

   II. Jesus's Proclamation of God's Kingdom (chaps. 3–4)

  III. The Lifestyle of Those Who Belong to the Kingdom (chaps. 5–7)

   IV. The Expansion of the Kingdom (chaps. 8–10)

    V. Growing Opposition to the Kingdom (chaps. 11–12)

   VI. Parables on the Nature of the Kingdom (chap. 13)

  VII. Miracles of the King in the Face of Growing Opposition (chaps. 14–17)

 VIII. The Demands on Those Who Belong to the Kingdom (chaps. 18–22)

   IX. Fraudulent Religion and the Call to Faithful Kingdom Living (chaps. 23–25)

    X. The Passion, Crucifixion, and Resurrection of the King and His Call for Kingdom Expansion (chaps. 26–28)

Outline 2

    I. The Identity of Jesus the Messiah and the Ethos of His Mission (chaps. 1–7)

   II. Jesus's Messianic Mission to Israel in the Face of Opposition (chaps. 8–12)

  III. The Growth and Spread of Jesus's Messianic Mission Illustrated by Parables (chap. 13)

   IV. Jesus's Ministry of Healing, Feeding, and Teaching in the Face of Condemnation and Rejection (chaps. 14–18)

V. The Messianic Mission of Jesus Moves toward Its Climax (chaps. 19–25)

VI. Jesus Is Rejected as the Messiah and Brutally Suffers unto Death (chaps. 26–27)

VII. Jesus's Resurrection from the Dead Validates Him as the Messiah and Empowers His Call to Make Disciples of All Nations (chap. 28)

For those pastors and teachers who feel less confident about devoting a year to Matthew's Gospel, going through different sections at different times may be a better approach. For example, a sermon series on the identity, birth, and initial ministry of Jesus, covering chapters 1–4, might begin after Thanksgiving and continue through January. This could then be followed by a second series on the Sermon on the Mount (chaps. 5–7). A year later, a third series could focus on Jesus's parables of the kingdom (chaps. 13, 18, 24, and 25). A fourth series might commence sometime in the following year, covering the nature and expansion of Jesus's messianic ministry (chaps. 8–22). A fifth and final series, expositing all of chapters 26–28, could then be preached through the Lenten season, culminating after Easter with a message on the Great Commission.

However one chooses to preach this Gospel, the fact that Matthew has a diverse literary makeup presents some exciting options for teaching. Because it contains a genealogy, a significant amount of narrative, a large number of parables, and the didactic section known as the Sermon on the Mount, preachers and teachers can approach it in various ways. In view of its literary diversity, eleven texts with their corresponding exegetical and homiletical ideas are provided below. Each of the four genres is utilized in these examples, which include some introductory comments on each type.

Getting the Subject, Complement, Exegetical Idea, and Homiletical Idea

GENEALOGIES

Genealogies trace the descent of an individual or group from an earlier time, linking them to God's people and his work in prior generations. Consistent with his Hebrew heritage, Matthew provides the genealogy of Jesus to demonstrate his familial link with Abraham, the father of God's people, and more specifically to David, from whom would come Israel's Messiah. Matthew also proves that God's plans in history will be fulfilled in his time and way (thus the threefold fourteen generations) and that Jesus is the Savior of all kinds of people: Jews and gentiles, men and women, and commoners and kings, as well as adulterers, fornicators, liars, spies, idolaters, and those who sought to live for God.

Matthew 1:1-17

SUBJECT: What does Matthew's genealogy of Christ reveal about the plans and purposes of God as he has worked in Hebrew history?

COMPLEMENT: They have come to fruition in Jesus the Messiah, the Son of David, so that all kinds of people may be blessed with salvation.

EXEGETICAL IDEA: Matthew's genealogy of Christ reveals that the plans and purposes of God as he has worked in Hebrew history have come to fruition in Jesus the Messiah, the Son of David, so that all kinds of people may be blessed with salvation.

HOMILETICAL IDEA: God has a plan to bless humanity with salvation in Christ, and his plans always come to pass.

DIDACTIC LITERATURE

Didactic literature provides both theological instruction and guidelines for godly living. In the Sermon on the Mount, Jesus reveals the nature of God's kingdom and how his disciples are to live out its values. As Jesus notes, only those whose hearts have been touched by God's grace can live in the way of the kingdom. His grace moves us beyond outward conformity to religious and moral obligations to love God and others with all of our hearts. This is the narrow gate built on Jesus and his word that leads to salvation and helps us navigate the storms of life.

Matthew 6:19-34

SUBJECT: What characterizes those who seek to be totally devoted to God and his kingdom?

COMPLEMENT: A focus on God and his values rather than on material concerns as they store up treasure in heaven, trusting him to provide for their daily needs.

EXEGETICAL IDEA: Those who seek to be totally devoted to God and his kingdom are characterized by a focus on God and his values rather than on material concerns as they store up treasure in heaven, trusting him to provide for their daily needs.

HOMILETICAL IDEA: Those who center their lives on Jesus and his kingdom will be adequately taken care of now and amazingly rewarded then.

Matthew 7:1–5

SUBJECT: How are those who follow Jesus to act in relation to others?

COMPLEMENT: By being reluctant to condemn others while living in a self-critical fashion.

EXEGETICAL IDEA: Those who follow Jesus are to act in relation to others by being reluctant to condemn and living in a self-critical fashion.

HOMILETICAL IDEA: Those who follow Jesus go easy on others but are hard on themselves.

Matthew 7:24–27

SUBJECT: What is the difference between those who build their lives on Jesus and his words and those who do not?

COMPLEMENT: The former will withstand the storms of life and judgment, while the latter will be laid to waste.

EXEGETICAL IDEA: The difference between those who build their lives on Jesus and his words and those who do not is that the former will withstand the storms of life and judgment, while the latter will be laid to waste.

HOMILETICAL IDEA: Building our lives on Jesus and his words provides a sure foundation for life now and judgment then.

THE PARABLES

The stories Jesus told, known as parables, are among some of the most famous pieces of literature in the history of Western civilization. A parable can be a figure of speech (e.g., a city set on a hill), a similitude (e.g., the kingdom of God is like a farmer who . . .) or a story (e.g., the parable of the sower). Jesus employed all three forms in his teaching in order to communicate the mysteries of God's kingdom. Matthew consistently presents Jesus's parables as explanations and illustrations of the nature, values, and ultimate arrival of this kingdom. They were designed not only to reveal theological truth and provocative insights but also to call forth a response from the hearers.[1] Given our visually oriented, media-driven society of the early twenty-first century,

1. Gordon D. Fee and Douglas Stuart, *How to Read the Bible for All Its Worth*, 3rd ed. (Grand Rapids: Zondervan, 2003), 152.

preaching and teaching these stories can help us understand and communicate
what Jesus's inauguration of the kingdom means for us and our listeners.

Matthew 13:24–30, 36–43

SUBJECT: How does God's kingdom function in the midst of a fallen world
marked by evil?

COMPLEMENT: It coexists with evil and grows until the end of the age, when
Jesus will eradicate evil and allow his righteousness to reign.

EXEGETICAL IDEA: In the midst of a fallen world marked by evil, God's kingdom
coexists with evil and grows until the end of the age, when Jesus will eradicate evil and allow his righteousness to reign.

HOMILETICAL IDEA: As we live in the midst of the world's weeds, Jesus calls us
to plant wheat and to wait in hope for his harvest.

Matthew 18:15–35

SUBJECT: How are the followers of the King to treat those who sin against
them?

COMPLEMENT: They are to forgive others their sins because the King has forgiven their innumerable sins against him.

EXEGETICAL IDEA: The followers of the King are to treat those who sin against
them by forgiving others their sins because the King has forgiven their innumerable sins against him.

HOMILETICAL IDEA: Since God's kingdom is grounded in his forgiveness, his followers learn to forgive others.

Matthew 25:14–30

SUBJECT: How is saving faith demonstrated by those who claim to follow
Jesus as King?

COMPLEMENT: By risking the resources he has entrusted to them in order to
advance his kingdom.

EXEGETICAL IDEA: Saving faith is demonstrated by those who claim to follow
Jesus as King by risking the resources he has entrusted to them in order to
advance his kingdom.

HOMILETICAL IDEA: Risking our resources proves our profession.

THE NARRATIVES

The Gospels are historically accurate and factually based biographies about Jesus's life, teaching, and ministry. As biographies they contain numerous narratives focused on Jesus that include the following: setting, characters, plot, point of view, a flow of time, and various details.[2] The Gospel authors often arranged their material topically in order to communicate theological truth to their original readers. Thus the Gospels are examples of theological history, not necessarily narratives in the manner used by modern historians. Gospel narratives are biographical in the sense that they are always Christocentric; they are singularly focused on Jesus and his redemptive work in bringing about God's kingdom.

Matthew's Gospel revolves around Jesus's inauguration of God's kingdom, by which he means God's rule and reign in the lives of people and, in the fullness of time, over all creation. While the kingdom was not consummated during Jesus's lifetime, it spread by means of his ministry in Judea, Galilee, and beyond. We cannot accurately read or interpret the narratives of Matthew's Gospel or understand Jesus's redemptive mission without an understanding of the kingdom.[3] This should be our frame of reference as we read, preach, and teach these narratives.

Matthew 15:21-28

SUBJECT: What happens when Jesus tests the Canaanite woman's faith in him and the disciples' love for those outside the boundaries of Israel?

COMPLEMENT: The Canaanite woman perseveres and responds with "mega-faith," while the disciples shrink in their compassion for those they regard as "dogs."

EXEGETICAL IDEA: When Jesus tests the Canaanite woman's faith in him and the disciples' love for those outside the boundaries of Israel, the Canaanite woman perseveres and responds with "mega-faith," while the disciples shrink in their compassion for those they regard as "dogs."

HOMILETICAL IDEA: When Jesus gives us the endurance test, let's respond in faith; when Jesus gives us the relationship test, let's respond in love.[4]

---

2. For an insightful discussion of each of these elements, see Jeffrey D. Arthurs, *Preaching with Variety: How to Re-create the Dynamics of Biblical Genres* (Grand Rapids: Kregel, 2007), 68–82.

3. Fee and Stuart, *How to Read the Bible*, 145.

4. John Ortberg, *Everybody's Normal Till You Get to Know Them* (Grand Rapids: Zondervan, 2003), 185–203.

Matthew 19:16-29

SUBJECT: What keeps the rich young ruler from joining Jesus and gaining eternal life?

COMPLEMENT: Despite his religious outlook, he won't forsake his financial fortune for God's grace.

EXEGETICAL IDEA: The rich young ruler is kept from joining Jesus and gaining eternal life despite his religious outlook because he won't forsake his financial fortune for God's grace.

HOMILETICAL IDEA: Let's rely on God's grace daily so that we can follow Jesus fully and steward our wealth wisely.

Matthew 27:32-56

SUBJECT: What happens historically and spiritually as Jesus hangs on the cross?

COMPLEMENT 1: He is abused by all kinds of sinners, forsaken by the Father, and handed over to death.

COMPLEMENT 2: His suffering pays the price for sin and brings salvation to all who believe in him.

EXEGETICAL IDEA: Historically and spiritually, as Jesus hangs on the cross, he is abused by all kinds of sinners, forsaken by the Father, and handed over to death, and his suffering pays the price for sin and brings salvation to all who believe in him.

HOMILETICAL IDEA: Jesus's worst day is our best day if we trust in what he did for us on the cross.

Matthew 28:16-20

SUBJECT: What are the final instructions given by the resurrected Jesus to his eleven disciples?

COMPLEMENT: By relying on the promises of his divine authority and personal presence, they are to make more disciples from all nations for the kingdom of God.

EXEGETICAL IDEA: The final instructions given by the resurrected Jesus to his eleven disciples are that, by relying on the promises of his divine authority and personal presence, they are to make more disciples from all nations for the kingdom of God.

HOMILETICAL IDEA: Those who follow the resurrected Jesus are called to the ministry of disciple-making, trusting in his power and presence as they extend his kingdom to all nations.

Difficult Passages/Verses

As preachers and teachers of Matthew recognize, this Gospel is both a joy and a challenge to preach. One of the initial difficulties, as noted above, lies in its sheer size (twenty-eight chapters). In addition, various sections and even specific verses demand some concentrated attention because of their inherent difficulty. Foremost among these is the Sermon on the Mount. Jesus's message shocks us with its revolutionary ideals and seemingly impossible demands. Innumerable teachers and pastors have pondered and fretted about how to communicate these chapters. One helpful approach is to see the sermon as an expression of God's grace to his fallen creatures, entangled by the sins of the world and the flesh and under attack by the devil. Moreover, if we view Jesus's message as containing promises for the life to come as well as reversing the often oppressive structures of every society and then promoting psychological and emotional health, our task as preachers and teachers becomes a bit clearer, if not easier.[5]

A second difficulty presented by Matthew concerns the genealogy and birth narratives of Jesus. The former has been addressed above; the latter concerns us here. The stories about Joseph's hesitation to wed Mary upon finding out about her pregnancy and the arrival of the magi are both straightforward narratives about God's mysterious work in providing redemption for all kinds of people, including gentile astrologers. The greater challenge comes with the magi's interaction with Herod and his subsequent "Slaughter of the Innocents" (Matt. 2). Three observations follow. First, this section should be addressed in a straightforward manner that focuses on the fallen nature of our world and the horrific potential of human depravity. Herod and his destruction of the Hebrew children illustrate those unfortunate realities. Second, this narrative reveals that the Gospel creates enmity. Jesus is born to bring salvation—certainly good news—and yet a man known as "the Great" erupts in violent opposition. We need to face the fact that Jesus and the advent of his kingdom sometimes create conflict, division, and persecution. Third, these narratives prove that God's sovereign plan will come to fruition. Even in the face of ethnic cleansing and genocide, Jesus could not be killed until his time had come (Matt. 26–27). This allows us to preach hope even in the most distressing of times.

5. Philip Yancey, *The Jesus I Never Knew* (Grand Rapids: Zondervan, 1995), 105–44.

Some further homiletical challenges presented by this Gospel revolve around specific encounters Jesus has with different people. One of these is the narrative of the Canaanite woman begging Jesus to heal her demon-possessed daughter (15:21–28). At first glance this is a distressing passage because Jesus seems distant and hard-hearted in the face of her suffering. He initially ignores her request just as the disciples encourage him to "send her away." Jesus then appears to stiff-arm her by stating he was sent only to the people of Israel, all the while seeing the plight of her desperately ill daughter. The encounter then evolves into something of a debate between Jesus and the woman over her worthiness to be given his help since she is a gentile "dog." Finally, the narrative concludes with Jesus praising her "mega-faith" and subsequently healing her daughter. What to make of all this? Kenneth Bailey has done yeoman's work in getting behind the historical, cultural, and implied details of the narrative to provide a straightforward understanding of what Jesus was doing in this encounter with both the woman *and* the disciples.[6] The exegetical work and homiletical idea presented in the prior section reflect Matthew's intent in this pericope, as interpreted by Bailey. While challenging on the surface, it possesses homiletical power and encouragement for faithful living as a disciple of Jesus.

Another homiletical challenge, especially for contemporary North American audiences, lies in the rich young ruler's request of Jesus to gain eternal life (19:16–29). The conflict at the heart of this encounter is the young man's desire to hold on to his wealth in the face of Jesus's exhortation to give it away and join his apostolic band. He leaves with his wealth intact, provoking Jesus to note that it's difficult for the rich to enter the kingdom of God. Given that he says this twice (vv. 23 and 24), it seems clear that Jesus is making a definitive comment about the relationship between money and salvation. And in view of proverbial Jewish piety that the rich were blessed by God, Peter speaks for all the disciples when he asks, "If that guy can't get in, then who can?" This pericope forces those of us in the contemporary Western world to confront our relationship with money. We live in the most affluent civilization the world has ever seen, and money is one of its core values. Moreover, money has significant power in our lives. As preachers and teachers of God's Word, we must address this personal, emotional, and spiritual reality head-on, just as Jesus did! Then we should move to the crux of his teaching that salvation is impossible for us, "but with God all things are possible" (v. 26). Salvation comes only by God's gracious work in our lives, and if that transpires, money then becomes a tool

---

6. Kenneth E. Bailey, *Jesus through Middle Eastern Eyes: Cultural Studies in the Gospels* (Downers Grove, IL: IVP Academic, 2008), 217–26.

for kingdom advancement rather than a measure of self-worth or the be-all and end-all of our earthly existence. While difficult at first glance, this provocative narrative can be effectively leveraged to teach about the power of money, God's grace, and his providential care for us as we sacrificially follow him (vv. 27–29).

Jesus's teaching on forgiveness is often lauded even by nonbelievers, but if we take it seriously it creates some significant dilemmas for preachers and teachers. For starters, Jesus makes it crystal clear that there is a conditional element to forgiveness: if we don't forgive others, our heavenly Father will not forgive us (6:14–15; 18:35). Given his authority as the Son of God, it's unwise to dance around these statements or rationalize them away by appealing to the doctrine of justification by faith. While Jesus certainly does not mean that we earn forgiveness or salvation by our willingness to forgive others, genuinely penitential people who are honest about the enormity of their own debt to God will seek, by his grace, to have a forgiving spirit toward others. This approach forces us as communicators to imitate our Lord and speak about the condition of the human heart. A heart genuinely touched by God's forgiveness and grace cannot, in the long run, remain hardened toward other sinners, even those who have done horrific things. Despite some erroneous thinking to the contrary, forgiveness does not by necessity imply relational reconciliation. Instead, forgiveness means to open our hearts so as to let others off the hook. The error of the unforgiving servant in Jesus's parable of Matthew 18 was his inability to do exactly that. As preachers and teachers, we want to drive home to ourselves and our listeners the necessity of seeing the depth of our sin and the enormity of God's grace. If that can be clearly communicated, hearts can be touched by the Holy Spirit, forgiveness given and received, and God's kingdom advanced.

Jesus's lengthy diatribe against the Jewish religious leaders in Matthew 23 can appear to contemporary Christians as irrelevant, unnecessarily intolerant, or simply an example of Jesus having a bad day. This creates an inherent temptation to skip this text and move on to his teaching about the second coming in chapter 24. But to minimize or ignore Christ's harsh criticisms of the religious leaders does a disservice to our listeners. First, this section portrays Christ in the mode of the Hebrew prophets, thereby completing his promise to fulfill everything in the Old Testament (5:17–20). Second, Christ's critique of false religion implores us to examine ourselves and our own practice of the Gospel or lack thereof. Third, this section demonstrates the reality that Jesus came to bring new wine for new wineskins (9:16–17). His angry and pointed rebuke in this text demonstrates that he was finished with the complex and irrelevant religious traditions developed by the Jewish leaders over the prior decades and that a fresh start centered in him as Savior and Lord was the only way forward spiritually and morally. Thus there is a direct link between Jesus's spirited denunciation recorded here and his "Sermon on the End of the World" given in chapters 24 and 25.

Some final comments must be made about the difficulty of preaching on the passages in Matthew 11 and 25 that describe judgment and hell. In the former, Jesus vividly denounces the cities of Chorazin, Bethsaida, and Capernaum for their unwillingness to repent in view of his miracles. The latter chapter contains Jesus's parable of the talents and parable of the sheep and goats, both of which end with dire warnings of darkness, weeping and gnashing of teeth, and eternal punishment (25:30, 46). No one likes the idea of judgment or hell, yet Jesus speaks on these themes more than anyone else in Scripture. Therefore, they need to be taught on, albeit with wisdom and sensitivity. To accomplish this I suggest expositing the main themes of these texts and then applying the excellent observations that Timothy Keller makes when teaching on these topics.[7] This approach may not overcome the skeptical unbelief of some in our audience, but it might go a long ways toward increasing the reverential awe of the resurrected, sovereign, and glorified Christ.

Cultural Perspectives and Application

Faithful application of Matthew involves a number of components. A preeminent one involves clearly understanding the nature of God's kingdom that Jesus came to inaugurate (4:17, 23). This kingdom, centered in Christ and his redemptive work, arrived in his person and ministry but not fully. It won't be consummated until his second coming, but it is mysteriously spreading throughout human history to promote God's rule and reign in the lives of people (13:1–52). While inclusive of the church, the kingdom is larger than the church and demands everything from those who are part of it (Matt. 5–7). It is rooted in the righteousness of God, and its inhabitants are to shine as lights in the darkness (5:14–16). Moreover, the kingdom of God is spread by zealous evangelistic activity and reflected in a vibrant social concern of compassionate ministry to the least of these (25:31–45; 28:18–20). At a practical level, the reality of God's kingdom as proclaimed by Jesus allows preachers and teachers to promote hands-on ministry by all believers both inside and outside the walls of the church.

A second point of application involves the lifestyle demanded of those who claim to be part of God's kingdom. As noted above, this is most clearly

---

7. Timothy Keller, *The Reason for God: Belief in an Age of Skepticism* (New York: Penguin, 2008), 70–86.

reflected in Jesus's Sermon on the Mount. While the specific application of this teaching has been and will continue to be debated by church leaders and teachers, there is no question that every disciple is to take these admonitions to heart and, by God's grace, live them out on a daily basis. Christians are to be people of humility and peace, known for their good character, healthy relationships, and love of others rather than for their wealth, status, achievements, and religiosity. To quote one famous expositor, God's people are to comprise a "Christian counter-culture."[8] While it takes time to move a group or church in this direction, a preacher or teacher committed to the exposition and application of Matthew 5–7 will be used by God to create such a culture.

A third application involves Jesus's call to faithfulness in light of his second coming. Our default mode as humans, even as Christians, is to lose our spiritual fervor and become lax in our devotion. The content of Matthew 24 and 25, known by some as the Sermon on the End of the World, can be leveraged by preachers and teachers to promote spiritual renewal and recommitment. In a time when many are fearful about world events or being "left behind," faithful expositors can demonstrate that Christ's followers are called to be vigilant in both their relationship to him and their ministry to others (24:42–25:46). Given that the timing of the Lord's return is unknown to all but the Father (24:36), faithful stewardship for Christ's kingdom through the ups and downs of life is what matters in the end (25:21–23).

A fourth area of application is Christ's atonement for sin. While not discounting the enormous importance of Jesus's resurrection and his Great Commission (see below), it is theologically significant that Matthew devotes a very large portion of the final section of his Gospel to Christ's passion and death (129 verses out of 141 in chaps. 26 and 27). In an age rife with conflicting messages about the nature of humanity, Matthew's extensive focus on Christ's death points to our sinfulness as well as our innate value to God. Any worthwhile exposition of this great Gospel will, sooner or later, point to this great truth.

A fifth application of Matthew's Gospel revolves around Christ's call to take the good news of the kingdom to the world. This call was initiated in chapters 10 and 11, where Jesus sends out the Twelve to minister to "the lost sheep of Israel." This was a mission of hope and help centered in healing and proclamation, and yet they are told to expect tribulation and persecution. Moreover, as Matthew builds his narrative, we see that Jesus himself encounters growing opposition as he moves toward Jerusalem (chap. 21 and

---

8. John R. W. Stott, *Christian Counter-Culture: The Message of the Sermon on the Mount*, The Bible Speaks Today (Downers Grove, IL: InterVarsity, 1978).

following). After his passion, death, and resurrection, Jesus issues his Great Commission to make disciples of all nations (chap. 28). How are we to preach these texts in a way that instructs, encourages, and motivates without inducing either fear or guilt? First, we must recognize that the specifics of these commands to the original disciples are not applicable to the vast majority of our listeners. They were Christ's apostles, and we are not; they were being trained for a lifetime of evangelistic activity, and we are not; they were young men with the ability to live on little and travel a lot, and we are not. Yet Jesus's call on his followers to engage in evangelistic activity is transcultural and must be clearly exposited and applied to our various congregational settings. This might be done by encouraging our listeners to build relationships at home, at school, in the neighborhood, and at work with those who do not yet know Jesus. That first step can then be supplemented with an encouragement to pray for those we befriend, that the Spirit might touch their hearts. Next, we can encourage our congregants to live in love, even when faced with pressure or opposition. Finally, we can teach our people to share the good news at appropriate times and places with those they have befriended. None of this will be easy, and it will take time. Nonetheless, Christ's call on all his followers to gospel ministry and mission is nonnegotiable.

RECOMMENDED RESOURCES

Bruner, Frederick Dale. *Matthew*, vol. 1, *The Christbook: Matthew 1–12*. Waco: Word, 1987.

———. *Matthew*, vol. 2, *The Churchbook: Matthew 13–28*. Dallas: Word, 1990.

Stott, John R. W. *Christian Counter-Culture: The Message of the Sermon on the Mount*. The Bible Speaks Today. Downers Grove, IL: InterVarsity, 1978.

Wilkins, Michael J. *Matthew*. The NIV Application Commentary. Grand Rapids: Zondervan, 2004.

Mark

PATRICIA M. BATTEN

The Gospel of Mark, based on the eyewitness account of the apostle Peter, is an invitation to hear and respond to the good news of Jesus Christ, the Son of God.

SUBJECT: What does Mark's Gospel demonstrate about the identity of Jesus?

COMPLEMENT: He is the Messiah, the Son of God, who ushers in God's kingdom and demands a response.

EXEGETICAL IDEA: Mark's gospel demonstrates that Jesus is the Messiah, the Son of God, who ushers in God's kingdom and demands a response.

HOMILETICAL IDEA: Jesus is the Messiah, the Son of God, who invites us to respond to him.

Pastors and preachers will benefit from reading Mark's Gospel as one single, unified story.[1] As such, it is difficult to outline the Gospel and determine an overarching structure. Most scholars recognize Mark 8:29 as an important division in the Gospel when Peter recognizes Jesus as Messiah and Jesus explains his mission. After this point, the story moves away from Galilee and

---

1. A helpful tool for studying the Gospel is David Rhoads, Joanna Dewey, and Donald Michie, *Mark as Story: An Introduction to the Narrative of a Gospel*, 3rd ed. (Minneapolis: Fortress, 2012).

into Jerusalem. Many commentators divide the book geographically into three sections: Galilee, *toward* Jerusalem, and *in* Jerusalem. New Testament scholar R. T. France finds the geographical division artificial and prefers to think of Mark's structure in terms of a drama in three acts.[2]

We shall use France's structure (with some minor tweaks) of a drama in three acts:

Prologue (1:1–13)[3]

Act I: Galilee (1:14–8:21)

Act II: On the Way to Jerusalem (8:22–10:52)

Act III: Jerusalem (11:1–16:8)

Although only sixteen chapters, the book of Mark can be divided into nearly fifty preaching and teaching passages. Some passages have more than one possible subject, and some passages overlap with others.

Getting the Subject, Complement, Exegetical Idea, and Homiletical Idea

Mark 1:1-8

SUBJECT: How does Mark say John prepares the people for the coming of Jesus the Messiah, the Son of God, the one who will baptize with the Holy Spirit?

COMPLEMENT: By preaching a baptism of repentance for the forgiveness of sins.

2. R. T. France writes:
> All this suggests that Mark's simple outline of an extensive ministry in and around Galilee followed by a lengthy and carefully marked journey southwards culminating in a single climactic visit to Jerusalem owes more to his dramatic reshaping of the story than to a naive recording of events just as they happened. We shall consider later whether this "Galilee and Jerusalem" schema may properly be understood to have symbolic significance for Mark; but even as a purely geographical datum it looks like a structure deliberately imposed on the story. (*The Gospel of Mark: A Commentary on the Greek Text*, The New International Greek Testament Commentary [Grand Rapids: Eerdmans, 2002], 12)

That is why I find it appropriate to read Mark as a drama in three acts. This is not meant to suggest either that Mark designed it for "performance" in three sections or that it is possible to discern clear breaks between the "acts." It is an observation about how I discern the development of the plot, not about any indication Mark may have given of how he planned the structure of his text.

3. Some commentators end the prologue with verse 15, thus forming an inclusio with the phrase "good news" in 1:1 and 1:15. Other commentators prefer ending with verse 13 to mark the distinction between the big picture, God doing something new—take note of words largely unique to the prologue, such as "*Holy Spirit*" and "*wilderness*"—and Jesus actually beginning ministry on the ground in verse 14.

EXEGETICAL IDEA: Mark says that John prepares the people for the coming of Jesus the Messiah, the Son of God, the one who will baptize with the Holy Spirit, by preaching a baptism of repentance for the forgiveness of sins.

HOMILETICAL IDEA: A fresh start begins with a repentant mind and heart.

Mark 1:9-13

SUBJECT: Who is Jesus, whom the Spirit thrusts into the wilderness to confront the powers of evil?

COMPLEMENT: He is King ("You are my Son" [cf. Ps. 2]), beloved of God ("whom I love"), the suffering servant who brings justice ("with you I am well pleased"), filled with God's reconciling Spirit ("torn open" [cf. Isa. 64:1]);[4] Jesus is God who will confront and defeat all the powers of evil.

EXEGETICAL IDEA: Jesus, whom the Spirit thrusts into the wilderness to confront the powers of evil, is King, beloved of God, the suffering servant who brings justice, filled with God's reconciling Spirit; Jesus is God who will confront and defeat all the powers of evil.

HOMILETICAL IDEA: Jesus is perfectly equipped by God to defeat sin and Satan.

Mark 1:14-20

SUBJECT: How does Mark say that Simon, Andrew, James, and John respond to the news that the kingdom of God is near?

COMPLEMENT: They repent and believe the good news and follow Jesus.

EXEGETICAL IDEA: Mark says that Simon, Andrew, James, and John respond to the news that the kingdom of God is near by repenting, believing the good news, and following Jesus.

HOMILETICAL IDEA: Answer the kingdom call in your life and make him Lord of all.

Mark 1:21-39

SUBJECT: What do Jesus's teaching, exorcism, and healing on the Sabbath indicate?

COMPLEMENT: That Jesus has the power and authority to bring in Sabbath rest (the kingdom).

---

4. The verb "to tear open" also occurs in Isa. 64:1, where the prophet calls on God to rend the heavens and come down and rebuild a desolated kingdom. Isaiah 64 is an anguished plea for God to forgive the sins of the people of Judah, secure its prosperity, and establish justice in the world. R. J. Kernaghan, *Mark*, The IVP New Testament Commentary (Downers Grove, IL: InterVarsity, 2007), 35.

EXEGETICAL IDEA: Jesus's teaching, exorcism, and healing on the Sabbath indicate that Jesus has the power and authority to bring in Sabbath rest (the kingdom).

HOMILETICAL IDEA: When Christ reigns in our lives, the rule of Satan is routed and the kingdom takes root.

Mark 1:40-45

SUBJECT: How does Mark say Jesus responds to the man's faithful request to be made clean?

COMPLEMENT: By healing him in compassion and anger and telling him to go quietly to the priest to be declared clean.

EXEGETICAL IDEA: Mark says Jesus responds to the man's faithful request to be made clean by healing him in compassion and anger and telling him to go quietly to the priest to be declared clean.

HOMILETICAL IDEA: God's touch is present in the outer reaches.

Mark 2:1-12

SUBJECT: Why does Mark say Jesus heals the paralytic?

COMPLEMENT: To show that he is the one with the authority to forgive sins (he is God).

EXEGETICAL IDEA: Mark says Jesus heals the paralytic to show that he is the one with the authority to forgive sins (he is God).

HOMILETICAL IDEA: When Jesus says "forgiven," we are transformed.

Mark 2:13-17

SUBJECT: Who does Jesus say he has come to call?

COMPLEMENT: Sinners who know they are sick, as opposed to the righteous who don't believe they are sick.

EXEGETICAL IDEA: Jesus says that he has come to call sinners who know they are sick, as opposed to the righteous who don't believe they are sick.

HOMILETICAL IDEA: God's kingdom is full of surprises because it's filled with forgiven sinners.

Mark 2:18-22

SUBJECT: Why don't the disciples fast like the other religious renewal movements do?

COMPLEMENT: Because the start of a new relationship is a time to feast, not fast.

EXEGETICAL IDEA: The disciples don't fast like the other religious renewal movements because the start of a new relationship is a time to feast, not fast.

HOMILETICAL IDEA: Either your religion is about rules or it's about a relationship—and a new relationship is a reason to rejoice!

Mark 2:23–3:6

SUBJECT: How does Jesus answer the Pharisees when they question him about picking grain and healing on the Sabbath?

COMPLEMENT: By telling them that as Lord of the Sabbath, he knows that the Sabbath was made to benefit people (to do good and save life), not break people.

EXEGETICAL IDEA: When the Pharisees question Jesus about picking grain and healing on the Sabbath, Jesus responds by telling them that as Lord of the Sabbath, he knows that the Sabbath was made to benefit people, not break people.

HOMILETICAL IDEA: Every day is a day to do good and save life (Mark 3:4; Matt. 12:12; Luke 6:9).

Mark 3:7–35

SUBJECT: Who does Jesus say is his family?

COMPLEMENT: Whoever does the will of God.

EXEGETICAL IDEA: Jesus says his family is whoever does the will of God.

HOMILETICAL IDEA: Family members follow the will of God.

Mark 4:1–25

SUBJECT: Why is how listeners hear the word important?

COMPLEMENT: Because listeners are in danger of losing it.

EXEGETICAL IDEA: How listeners hear the word is important because listeners are in danger of losing it.

HOMILETICAL IDEA: Use God's Word in your life or lose it.

Mark 4:26–34

SUBJECT: What does Jesus say about God's kingdom?

COMPLEMENT: God is at work to make it grow far beyond what the disciples can do or imagine.

EXEGETICAL IDEA: Jesus says that God is at work to make his kingdom grow far beyond what the disciples can do or imagine.

HOMILETICAL IDEA: Build God's kingdom and know that God is at work.

Mark 4:35–41

SUBJECT: What do the disciples fear?

COMPLEMENT: That they have given their lives to a doomed king and kingdom.

EXEGETICAL IDEA: The disciples fear that they have given their lives to a doomed king and kingdom.

HOMILETICAL IDEA: We can trust that God's kingdom will be victorious through Jesus, who has been given all authority.

Mark 5:1–20

SUBJECT: What does the healing of the demoniac demonstrate?

COMPLEMENT: That Jesus has authority over evil and he cares for those who are held hostage to it.

EXEGETICAL IDEA: The healing of the demoniac demonstrates that Jesus has authority over evil and he cares for those who are held hostage to it.

HOMILETICAL IDEA: We can plead with Jesus to stay and touch those who are bound by evil.

Mark 5:21–43

SUBJECT: What happens when a fearful Jairus and the woman with the issue of blood approach Jesus with faith in a desperate situation?

COMPLEMENT: God's saving power is unleashed.

EXEGETICAL IDEA: When a fearful Jairus and the woman with the issue of blood approach Jesus with faith in a desperate situation, God's saving power is unleashed.

HOMILETICAL IDEA: God's power is unleashed when we forget fear and trust that he is at work in a desperate situation.

Mark 6:1–6a

SUBJECT: Why do the people of Jesus's hometown who are amazed at his teaching take offense at him?

COMPLEMENT: Because they don't believe that God can do amazing things through an ordinary man (a poor local carpenter).

EXEGETICAL IDEA: The people of Jesus's hometown who are amazed at his teaching took offense at him because they don't believe that God can do amazing things through an ordinary man (a poor local carpenter).

HOMILETICAL IDEA: Believe that God works the extraordinary through the ordinary.

Mark 6:6b-13

SUBJECT: How does Jesus send out his disciples?

COMPLEMENT: In faith, as shepherds, with power and authority and a message of repentance.

EXEGETICAL IDEA: Jesus sends out his disciples in faith, as shepherds, with power and authority and a message of repentance.

HOMILETICAL IDEA: Bring your staff and you'll remember the sheep.

Mark 6:14-44

SUBJECT: What is Jesus teaching his disciples through the miracle of the loaves and fish?

COMPLEMENT: That he is the true king, a shepherd of a new Israel, opposed to Herod, and that his disciples must be shepherds who act in faith to shepherd the flock.

EXEGETICAL IDEA: Jesus is teaching his disciples through the miracle of the loaves and fish that he is the true king, a shepherd of a new Israel, opposed to Herod, and that his disciples must be shepherds who act in faith to shepherd the flock.

HOMILETICAL IDEA: When we trust that Jesus is king we'll act in faith, even when we have little to give.

Mark 6:45-56

■ Option 1

SUBJECT: What is the aftermath of the miracle of the loaves?

COMPLEMENT: Jesus needs to pray because people, including his disciples, misunderstand his mission and identity.

EXEGETICAL IDEA: The aftermath of the miracle of the loaves is that Jesus needs to pray because people, including his disciples, misunderstand his mission and identity.

HOMILETICAL IDEA: Don't let the meal crowd out the cook/Maker.

Option 2

SUBJECT: How do the disciples respond to Jesus's revelation?

COMPLEMENT: With hard hearts filled with fear and exhaustion, missing Jesus's revelation.

EXEGETICAL IDEA: The disciples respond to Jesus's revelation with hard hearts filled with fear and exhaustion, missing Jesus's revelation.

HOMILETICAL IDEA: We miss a work of God in our midst when we operate in fear instead of faith.

Mark 7:1-23

SUBJECT: How does Jesus respond to the Pharisees and scribes who criticize him for allowing his disciples to break with the traditions (purity laws) of the elders?

COMPLEMENT: By chastising them for letting go of the commands of God and emphasizing a religion of ritual (outside) rather than a religion of the heart (inside).

EXEGETICAL IDEA: Jesus responds to the Pharisees and scribes who criticize him for allowing his disciples to break with the traditions (purity laws) of the elders by chastising them for letting go of the commands of God and emphasizing a religion of ritual (outside) rather than a religion of the heart (inside).

HOMILETICAL IDEA: Only a change of heart will change our heart condition.

Mark 7:24-30

SUBJECT: How does Jesus respond to an unclean outsider who begs for the healing of her demon-possessed daughter?

COMPLEMENT: With an insult designed to test her faith and teach his disciples that even outsiders (unclean) have access to God's mercy when they admit (as Jews and gentiles alike should) that they don't deserve it.

EXEGETICAL IDEA: Jesus responds to an unclean outsider who begs for the healing of her demon-possessed daughter with an insult designed to test her faith and teach his disciples that even outsiders (unclean) have access to God's mercy when they admit (as Jews and gentiles alike should) that they don't deserve it.

HOMILETICAL IDEA: Keep great faith because God has mercy on outsiders (the undeserving).

Mark 7:31-37

SUBJECT: Why does Mark say that Jesus travels to foreign territory where he heals a deaf and mute man, resulting in the proclamation of Jesus in that region?

COMPLEMENT: As a fulfillment of the prophecies of Isaiah (29:17–18; 35:6) that outsiders shall be included in God's kingdom.

EXEGETICAL IDEA: Mark says that Jesus travels to foreign territory where he heals a deaf and mute man, resulting in the proclamation of Jesus in that region, as a fulfillment of the prophecies of Isaiah (29:17–18; 35:6) that outsiders shall be included in God's kingdom.

HOMILETICAL IDEA: God's kingdom is open to all who recognize him as king.

Mark 8:1-13

SUBJECT: Why are the disciples not anxious to feed the four thousand, while the Pharisees demand a miraculous sign?

COMPLEMENT: Because the disciples don't believe that they, as a predominantly gentile crowd, should receive anything from God, while the Pharisees demand a sign that demonstrates why gentiles should receive blessing from God.

EXEGETICAL IDEA: The disciples are not anxious to feed the four thousand because they don't believe that they, as a predominantly gentile crowd, should receive anything from God, and the Pharisees demand a sign that demonstrates why gentiles should receive blessing from God.

HOMILETICAL IDEA: God's kingdom crosses racial, ethnic, and cultural boundaries.

Mark 8:14-21

SUBJECT: What do the disciples need to understand about the yeast of the Pharisees and Herod?

COMPLEMENT: That their sin of not embracing gentiles and of not recognizing Jesus as king will infiltrate their thinking if they aren't careful (a double-minded response to God's Word and hypocrisy).

EXEGETICAL IDEA: What the disciples need to understand about the yeast of the Pharisees and Herod is that their sin of not embracing gentiles and of not recognizing Jesus as king will infiltrate their thinking if they aren't careful.

HOMILETICAL IDEA: A seemingly small sin can lead to rejecting Christ.

Mark 8:22-26

SUBJECT: Why does Jesus perform a two-stage miracle in order for the blind man's sight to be fully recovered?

COMPLEMENT: To demonstrate that who, how, and what the disciples see is of crucial importance in the kingdom of God (how one sees Jesus and how one sees other people).

EXEGETICAL IDEA: Jesus performs a two-stage miracle in order for the blind man's sight to be fully recovered to demonstrate that who, how, and what the disciples see is of crucial importance in the kingdom of God (how one sees Jesus and how one sees other people).

HOMILETICAL IDEA: Look for God's perspective in every situation.

Mark 8:27-30

SUBJECT: Who does Peter say Jesus is?

COMPLEMENT: The Christ.

EXEGETICAL IDEA: Peter says that Jesus is the Christ.

HOMILETICAL IDEA: Every person must wrestle with and answer the question of who Jesus is.

Mark 8:31-9:1

SUBJECT: What is required of disciples of the suffering, rejected, murdered, and risen Christ?

COMPLEMENT: They must deny themselves, take up their cross, and follow Jesus.

EXEGETICAL IDEA: Disciples of the suffering, rejected, murdered, and risen Christ must deny themselves, take up their cross, and follow Jesus.

HOMILETICAL IDEA: Following Jesus means sacrifice.

▦ *Mark 8:33*

SUBJECT: How does Peter act in the role of Satan?

COMPLEMENT: By tempting Jesus to avoid what God wants him to do and be.

EXEGETICAL IDEA: Peter acts in the role of Satan by tempting Jesus to avoid what God wants him to do and be.

HOMILETICAL IDEA: Jesus's death is crucial to God's plan.

Mark 9:1-13

SUBJECT: What happens when Jesus appears with Moses and Elijah as he is transfigured before Peter, James, and John and the voice of God is heard?

COMPLEMENT: A new covenant is revealed consisting of the good news of the kingdom of God in the person of Jesus Christ, the Son of God.

EXEGETICAL IDEA: When Jesus appears with Moses and Elijah as he is transfigured before Peter, James, and John and the voice of God is heard, a new covenant is revealed consisting of the good news of the kingdom of God in the person of Jesus Christ, the Son of God.

HOMILETICAL IDEA: If you want a relationship with God, listen to his Son.

Mark 9:14-32

SUBJECT: Why are the disciples unable to heal the boy with the evil spirit?

COMPLEMENT: Because they are not aligned with God's will through prayer and they have stopped trusting in Jesus's power.

EXEGETICAL IDEA: The disciples are unable to heal the boy with the evil spirit because they are not aligned with God's will through prayer and they have stopped trusting in Jesus's power.

HOMILETICAL IDEA: When we pray, we align ourselves with God's will and God's Word and we're ready to make a difference in other people's lives.

Mark 9:33-37

SUBJECT: Who does Jesus say is the greatest?

COMPLEMENT: The one who serves and does not desire and work to be first in this life, thereby welcoming God.

EXEGETICAL IDEA: Jesus says the greatest is the one who serves and does not desire and work to be first in this life, thereby welcoming God.

HOMILETICAL IDEA: Welcome God by being great and serving.

Mark 9:38-50

SUBJECT: How are Jesus's followers to use their power and position?

COMPLEMENT: By serving all people without turning any away from Jesus.

EXEGETICAL IDEA: Jesus's followers are to use their power and position by serving all people without turning any away from Jesus.

HOMILETICAL IDEA: Don't turn people away from Jesus by the way you use your power and position.

Mark 10:1-12

SUBJECT: How does Jesus respond to the Pharisees' test regarding divorce?

COMPLEMENT: By appealing to Genesis 1 to show the value of women and Genesis 2 to show how marriage is like a new creation that cannot easily be undone.

EXEGETICAL IDEA: Jesus responds to the Pharisees' test regarding divorce by appealing to Genesis 1 to show the value of women and Genesis 2 to show how marriage is like a new creation that cannot easily be undone.

HOMILETICAL IDEA: When we see that everyone is valued by God, then we see that we receive God when we receive our spouse to serve them.

Mark 10:13-45

SUBJECT: What does Jesus reveal by his interaction with little children, the rich young man, and James and John?

COMPLEMENT: That the world's values are turned upside down in God's kingdom.

EXEGETICAL IDEA: Jesus reveals by his interaction with little children, the rich young man, and James and John that the world's values are turned upside down in God's kingdom.

HOMILETICAL IDEA: Jesus's death and resurrection change the way we think about everyone and the way we see life.

Mark 10:46-52

SUBJECT: How does Jesus say the blind man who begged for mercy is healed?

COMPLEMENT: By faith.

EXEGETICAL IDEA: Jesus says the blind man who begged for mercy is healed by faith.

HOMILETICAL IDEA: Seeing in God's kingdom (a kingdom perspective) means that we know our need for mercy and that we trust Jesus to give us the mercy we need.

Mark 11:1–26

SUBJECT: How does Jesus, a king like no one before him who is misunderstood and ignored, say the dysfunctional system of religion that bears no fruit will be removed?

COMPLEMENT: By trusting God in prayer.

EXEGETICAL IDEA: Jesus, a king like no one before him who is misunderstood and ignored, says the dysfunctional system of religion that bears no fruit will be removed by trusting God in prayer.

HOMILETICAL IDEA: Trust Jesus the king when he says that change can and does take place when we trust God in prayer.

Mark 11:1–11

SUBJECT: How does Jesus enter Jerusalem?

COMPLEMENT: As a king like no other before him who is misunderstood and ignored.

EXEGETICAL IDEA: Jesus enters Jerusalem as king like no other before him who is misunderstood and ignored.

HOMILETICAL IDEA: Make sure you understand Jesus.

Mark 11:27–12:12

SUBJECT: How does Jesus respond to those who question his authority?

COMPLEMENT: By telling a parable in which he is God's beloved cornerstone who is rejected by the Jewish leaders who use worship of God for their own ends.

EXEGETICAL IDEA: Jesus responds to those who question his authority by telling a parable in which he is God's beloved cornerstone who is rejected by Jewish leaders who use worship to their own ends.

HOMILETICAL IDEA: God builds his church on Jesus for those who know that worship belongs to God alone.

Mark 12:13–17

SUBJECT: How does Jesus turn the trap of the Pharisees and Herodians back on them?

COMPLEMENT: By using a coin with Caesar's image to show them they have committed the greatest offense by not giving God the worship he deserves.

EXEGETICAL IDEA: Jesus turns the trap of the Pharisees and Herodians back on them by using a coin with Caesar's image to show them they have committed the greatest offense by not giving God the worship he deserves.

HOMILETICAL IDEA: Before you question anyone else about their devotion to God, make sure yours is properly aligned, because God alone deserves our worship.

Mark 12:18-34

SUBJECT: What do people who are close to the kingdom of God know that those who are "badly mistaken" do not know?

COMPLEMENT: At the center of worship is a relationship with God that lasts for eternity and manifests itself on earth in love for others.

EXEGETICAL IDEA: People who are close to the kingdom of God know that those who are "badly mistaken" do not know that at the center of worship is a relationship with God that lasts for eternity and manifests itself on earth in love for others.

HOMILETICAL IDEA: When we have a relationship with God now we have one with him forever.

Mark 12:35-37

SUBJECT: Why does Jesus quote Psalm 110:1 to refute the law teachers' faulty understanding of Scripture?

COMPLEMENT: To show his hearers that the Messiah is Lord.

EXEGETICAL IDEA: Jesus quotes Psalm 110:1 to refute the law teachers' faulty understanding of Scripture to show his hearers that the Messiah is Lord.

HOMILETICAL IDEA: Jesus, the Messiah, is Lord!

Mark 12:38-44

SUBJECT: How does Jesus respond to teachers of the law who bend God's law for their own benefit and abuse others in the process?

COMPLEMENT: By issuing a severe warning of punishment.

EXEGETICAL IDEA: Jesus responds to teachers of the law who bend God's law for their own benefit and abuse others in the process by issuing a severe warning of punishment.

HOMILETICAL IDEA: Use people and position for God's glory, not your own.

Mark 13

SUBJECT: How are the disciples, in response to deceivers regarding end times and persecution, supposed to live?

COMPLEMENT: By staying on task, remaining watchful, and preaching the gospel.

EXEGETICAL IDEA: The disciples, in response to deceivers regarding end times and persecution, are supposed to live by staying on task, remaining watchful, and preaching the gospel.

HOMILETICAL IDEA: Stay focused on proclaiming the good news of Jesus!

Mark 14:1-52

SUBJECT: What does Mark say lies between the extreme loyalty of the woman with the alabaster jar and the extreme betrayal of Judas?

COMPLEMENT: The denial and desertion of the disciples.

EXEGETICAL IDEA: Mark says what lies between the extreme loyalty of the woman with the alabaster jar and the extreme betrayal of Judas is the denial and desertion of the disciples.

HOMILETICAL IDEA: We can deny, desert, or be disloyal to Jesus and his mission, but only loyalty to him and his mission is commended.

Mark 14:1-11

SUBJECT: How does Jesus commend the loyalty of a woman who knows where Jesus is headed and responds in worship?

COMPLEMENT: By assuring her and the crowd that her story of loyalty will never be forgotten.

EXEGETICAL IDEA: Jesus commends the loyalty of a woman who knows where Jesus is headed and responds in worship by assuring her and the crowd that her story of loyalty will never be forgotten.

HOMILETICAL IDEA: Jesus demands our devotion—break the jar and pour your worship on him, the only one who conquers death and gives life.

Mark 14:12-26

SUBJECT: How does Mark say Jesus institutes a new covenant?

COMPLEMENT: Through an insider's act of betrayal, resulting in Jesus's death but ending in his resurrection.

EXEGETICAL IDEA: Mark says Jesus institutes a new covenant through an insider's act of betrayal, resulting in Jesus's death but ending in his resurrection.

HOMILETICAL IDEA: The death and resurrection of Jesus transform the old into something brand new.

Mark 14:53-65

SUBJECT: Why do the high priest and members of the Sanhedrin believe Jesus must die?

COMPLEMENT: Because he greatly offends them by his claim to be the Messiah, by invoking the divine name, and by asserting that the chief priests and elders will be judged (sitting at the right hand of the Mighty One in Ps. 110:1; "son of man" and "clouds of heaven" in Dan. 7:13).

EXEGETICAL IDEA: The high priest and members of the Sanhedrin believe Jesus must die because he greatly offends them by his claim to be the Messiah, by invoking the divine name, and by asserting that the chief priests and elders will be judged.

HOMILETICAL IDEA: We can't see Jesus and his agenda when we can't see beyond ourselves and our own agendas.

Mark 14:66-72

SUBJECT: How does Peter respond to his own denial of Jesus?

COMPLEMENT: By breaking down and weeping.

EXEGETICAL IDEA: Peter responds to his own denial of Jesus by breaking down and weeping.

HOMILETICAL IDEA: God builds his kingdom on the tears of broken men and women who have hurt Christ.

Mark 15:1-15:32

SUBJECT: Who does Mark say was innocent in Jesus's death?

COMPLEMENT: No one.

EXEGETICAL IDEA: Mark says no one was innocent in Jesus's death.

HOMILETICAL IDEA: We all played a role in the death of Jesus.

Mark 15:21-41

SUBJECT: What does Mark report happens at the death of Jesus?

COMPLEMENT: Darkness blankets the land, the curtain of the temple tears in half, and the centurion confesses Jesus as the Son of God while the women watch from a distance.

EXEGETICAL IDEA: Mark reports that at the death of Jesus darkness blankets the land, the curtain of the temple tears in half, and the centurion confesses Jesus as the Son of God while the women watch from a distance.

HOMILETICAL IDEA: God's judgment fell on Jesus while the most unlikely perceived God was at work.

Mark 15:42–16:8

SUBJECT: How do the women respond to the scene at the empty tomb?

COMPLEMENT: By fleeing, trembling in fear and confusion.

EXEGETICAL IDEA: The women respond to the scene at the empty tomb by fleeing, trembling in fear and confusion.

HOMILETICAL IDEA: The empty tomb demands our response.

Difficult Passages/Verses

Mark is a short Gospel, but it's not an easy one to unpack, beginning with the prologue. Mark brings up broad, sweeping themes that are interwoven throughout the rest of the story.

Many of the passages in Mark leave the reader confused. Answers don't come easily. He often uses scenes with Jesus as "enacted parables" that force the reader to think deeply about who Jesus is and what is important to him.

Chapter 13 is challenging because it deals with end times and the fall of Jerusalem. Scholars are not in agreement as to which passages refer to which events. The preacher can quickly become bogged down in the details.

Cultural Perspectives and Application

A modern audience needs to understand how parables work. Preachers need to help audiences see the deep prejudices held by the disciples against gentiles in particular. The disciples and the Jewish people of Jesus's day thought the kingdom belonged to them and them alone.

Preachers are also wise to point out how God's kingdom includes the most unexpected people (women, children, gentiles) and how the most unexpected people have insight into God's kingdom while Jesus's closest followers struggle to see who Jesus truly is.

Ultimately, the Gospel of Mark forces one to decide for oneself who Jesus is.

─── **RECOMMENDED RESOURCES** ───

France, R. T. *The Gospel of Mark: A Commentary on the Greek Text*. The New International Greek Testament Commentary. Grand Rapids: Eerdmans, 2002.

Kernaghan, R. J. *Mark*. The IVP New Testament Commentary. Downers Grove, IL: InterVarsity, 2007.

Rhoads, David, Joanna Dewey, and Donald Michie. *Mark as Story: An Introduction to the Narrative of a Gospel*. 3rd ed. Minneapolis: Fortress, 2012.

Luke

JULIAN R. GOTOBED

The Big Idea of Luke

Luke, the first volume in a two-part work, portrays the birth, life, ministry, death, resurrection, and ascension of Jesus of Nazareth and his significance for Israel. Acts, the second volume, tells the story of the community gathered around the risen Jesus and witnesses to his significance for all peoples everywhere.

SUBJECT: What was the significance of Jesus of Nazareth for the people of Israel?

COMPLEMENT: He was the fulfillment of God's promise in the Old Testament to redeem his people Israel, proclaiming and demonstrating the inbreaking of God's rule through his life, ministry, teaching, death, resurrection, and ascension.

EXEGETICAL IDEA: The significance of Jesus of Nazareth for the people of Israel was that he was the fulfillment of God's promise in the Old Testament to redeem his people Israel, proclaiming and demonstrating the inbreaking of God's rule through his life, ministry, teaching, death, resurrection, and ascension.

HOMILETICAL IDEA: In Jesus, God keeps the promise he made in the past to make a way to redeem people in the present.

Selecting Preaching and Teaching Passages in Luke

Preachers in denominations that follow a lectionary or three-year plan of Bible readings used in public worship through the Christian year (Advent to Christ the King) will find texts selected for them in the year dedicated to Luke and in annual seasons (e.g., Advent) when passages from Luke are typically included. Some denominations follow a basic outline of the Christian year (e.g., Advent-Christmas, Lent-Easter, Ascension-Pentecost). Passages from Luke can be selected that correspond to the key moment in the life of Jesus being celebrated at any given point in the Christian year. The Christian year is patterned on the life of Jesus, and Luke is especially suited to the shape of the Christian year.

The preacher accustomed to greater freedom in text selection and planning sermon series can draw on the structure of Luke's account:

Introduction (1:1–4)

Infancy and Childhood (1:5–2:52)

Jesus's Preparation for Ministry (3:1–4:13)

Jesus in Galilee (4:14–9:50)

Journey to Jerusalem (9:51–19:28)

Jesus in Jerusalem (19:29–21:38)

The Passion (22:1–23:56)

The Resurrection (24:1–53)[1]

Getting the Subject, Complement, Exegetical Idea, and Homiletical Idea

Luke 1:1–4

SUBJECT: Why did the author of the Gospel according to Luke write a carefully researched and ordered account about Jesus of Nazareth?

COMPLEMENT: To confirm the truth and accuracy of the message that Theophilus, the recipient, had received previously.

EXEGETICAL IDEA: The author of the Gospel according to Luke wrote a carefully researched and ordered account about Jesus of Nazareth to confirm the truth and accuracy of the message that Theophilus, the recipient, had received previously.

---

1. Fred B. Craddock, *Luke*, Interpretation (Louisville: Westminster John Knox, 2009), ix–xi.

HOMILETICAL IDEA: Luke confirms faithful accounts of Christian witness to Jesus in every generation.

Luke 1:5-25

SUBJECT: Who would the son promised by God to Zechariah and his wife, Elizabeth, grow to become?

COMPLEMENT: A prophet full of the Holy Spirit who proclaimed God's message to Israel and caused many to turn back to God.

EXEGETICAL IDEA: The son promised by God to Zechariah and his wife, Elizabeth, would grow to become a prophet full of the Holy Spirit who proclaimed God's message to Israel and caused many to turn back to God.

HOMILETICAL IDEA: A person full of the Holy Spirit who declares God's message enables others to return to God.

Luke 1:26-45

SUBJECT: What did Mary do when she learned she was to conceive, as a virgin and by the Holy Spirit, a child who would grow to serve God?

COMPLEMENT: She offered her life to God, confident that the promise would be fulfilled.

EXEGETICAL IDEA: When Mary learned she was to conceive, as a virgin and by the Holy Spirit, a child who would grow to serve God, she offered her life to God, confident that the promise would be fulfilled.

HOMILETICAL IDEA: The character of true service to God is trust and obedience in response to God's Word and the Holy Spirit.

Luke 1:46-80

SUBJECT: How do Mary and Zechariah respond to the news of having a child (Mary having Jesus and Zechariah having John, respectively)?

COMPLEMENT: By Mary responding with initial belief and praise while Zechariah responds with initial disbelief and eventual praise.

EXEGETICAL IDEA: Mary and Zechariah respond to the news of having a child (Mary having Jesus and Zechariah having John, respectively) by Mary responding with initial belief and praise while Zechariah responds with initial disbelief and eventual praise.

HOMILETICAL IDEA: Put your full trust in God and give him praise.

Luke 2

SUBJECT: Why was the birth of Jesus important?

COMPLEMENT: He was the Messiah promised according to God's sovereign purpose in the Old Testament, who would be God's agent of salvation for Israel and, ultimately, for all peoples everywhere.

EXEGETICAL IDEA: The birth of Jesus was important since he was the Messiah promised according to God's sovereign purpose in the Old Testament, who would be God's agent of salvation for Israel and, ultimately, for all peoples everywhere.

HOMILETICAL IDEA: Jesus is Savior of all peoples everywhere.

Luke 3:1-20

SUBJECT: What was the message of John the Baptist?

COMPLEMENT: God's salvation of Israel promised in Isaiah had drawn near in the Messiah, so people should turn to God for forgiveness, be baptized, and live a life worthy of God.

EXEGETICAL IDEA: The message of John the Baptist was that God's salvation of Israel promised in Isaiah had drawn near in the Messiah, so people should turn to God for forgiveness, be baptized, and live a life worthy of God.

HOMILETICAL IDEA: Turn back to God, be baptized, and reform your life accordingly.

Luke 3:21-4:13

SUBJECT: How did Jesus, empowered by the Holy Spirit in his baptism, subsequently resist several enticements to disobey God?

COMPLEMENT: He discerned the false ideas in the enticements presented to him with the aid of the Old Testament.

EXEGETICAL IDEA: Jesus, empowered by the Holy Spirit in his baptism, subsequently resisted several enticements to disobey God because he discerned the false ideas in the enticements presented to him with the aid of the Old Testament.

HOMILETICAL IDEA: Depend on the Holy Spirit, who empowers us, and be attentive to Scripture, which guides us, to choose aright for God.

Luke 4:14-44

SUBJECT: Why was Jesus driven from Nazareth by his audience after he claimed that Isaiah had been fulfilled in their hearing?

COMPLEMENT: He reminded them that Israel had previously rejected prophets and God had demonstrated compassion to gentiles in such moments.

EXEGETICAL IDEA: Jesus was driven from Nazareth by his audience after he claimed that Isaiah had been fulfilled in their hearing because he reminded them that Israel had previously rejected prophets and God had demonstrated compassion to gentiles in such moments.

HOMILETICAL IDEA: Jesus announces good news of redemption and confronts us with hard truths we don't want to admit.

Luke 5

SUBJECT: How did Simon become a disciple of Jesus?

COMPLEMENT: He trusted and obeyed him, acknowledged his own unworthiness, changed his way of life, and followed Jesus to share in his work of drawing people to God.

EXEGETICAL IDEA: Simon became a disciple of Jesus by trusting and obeying him, acknowledging his own unworthiness, changing his way of life, and following Jesus to share in his work of drawing people to God.

HOMILETICAL IDEA: To follow Jesus, trust in God, imitate the pattern of Jesus's life, and draw others to God.

Luke 6-7

SUBJECT: How did Jesus interact with the people he encountered in his ministry?

COMPLEMENT: He shared the goodness and challenge of God, relevant to their particular life stories, to connect them with God and change how they saw self, others, and God.

EXEGETICAL IDEA: Jesus interacted with the people he encountered in his ministry by sharing the goodness and challenge of God, relevant to their particular life stories, to connect them with God and change how they saw self, others, and God.

HOMILETICAL IDEA: To meet Jesus is to see ourselves, others, and God differently, and to be transformed.

Luke 8:1-21

SUBJECT: How did Jesus use parables to teach the kingdom of God?

COMPLEMENT: He drew on experiences in daily life to subvert distorted notions of God and religion, and also to convey new redemptive possibilities of God's power and presence.

EXEGETICAL IDEA: Jesus used parables to teach the kingdom of God by drawing on experiences in daily life to subvert distorted notions of God and religion, and also to convey new redemptive possibilities of God's power and presence.

HOMILETICAL IDEA: The stories Jesus told subvert and remake our vision of God and our relationship with God.

Luke 8:22-56

SUBJECT: What difference did Jesus make to the people he encountered?

COMPLEMENT: He liberated them from physical danger, demonic evil, crippling sickness, and death, and so gave cause to celebrate and witness with discretion to the goodness of God.

EXEGETICAL IDEA: Jesus made a difference to the people he encountered by liberating them from physical danger, demonic evil, crippling sickness, and death, and so gave cause to celebrate and witness with discretion to the goodness of God.

HOMILETICAL IDEA: When God in Jesus makes broken lives whole, celebrate joyfully and tell others soberly and wisely what God has done.

Luke 9:1-20

SUBJECT: Who did Peter conclude that Jesus was in light of his proclamation of the kingdom of God, the concern he caused Herod, and his feeding of a hungry crowd?

COMPLEMENT: The Messiah promised by God to Israel in the Old Testament.

EXEGETICAL IDEA: Peter concluded that Jesus—in light of his proclamation of the kingdom of God, the concern he caused Herod, and his feeding of a hungry crowd—was the Messiah promised by God to Israel in the Old Testament.

HOMILETICAL IDEA: Jesus is God's anointed servant who brings God's redeeming power into our lives.

Luke 9:21-27

SUBJECT: What was entailed in following Jesus, who anticipated rejection, suffering and death, and being raised from the dead?

COMPLEMENT: The likelihood of experiencing suffering and death in the knowledge of final vindication.

EXEGETICAL IDEA: Following Jesus, who anticipated rejection, suffering and death, and being raised from the dead, entailed the likelihood of experiencing suffering and death in the knowledge of final vindication.

HOMILETICAL IDEA: Following Jesus can be costly, but loyalty will be vindicated.

Luke 9:28-62

SUBJECT: What did the transfiguration of Jesus show about his identity?

COMPLEMENT: That he was Lord and the Son of God.

EXEGETICAL IDEA: The transfiguration of Jesus confirmed his identity as Lord and the Son of God.

HOMILETICAL IDEA: By virtue of who Jesus is, he has the first and final claim over our lives.

Luke 10:1-24

SUBJECT: What did Jesus commission his followers to do?

COMPLEMENT: To announce the kingdom of God and accept the hospitality offered when the message was received, but to move on to new territory when it was rejected.

EXEGETICAL IDEA: Jesus commissioned his followers to announce the kingdom of God and accept the hospitality offered when the message was received, but to move on to new territory when it was rejected.

HOMILETICAL IDEA: Followers of Jesus are called to proclaim the good news of the kingdom of God, no matter what.

Luke 10:25-42

SUBJECT: What did Jesus teach about loving one's neighbor?

COMPLEMENT: It required one to show intentional goodwill toward people different from oneself even if it meant taking risks, overcoming social conventions, and offering practical assistance and long-term care.

EXEGETICAL IDEA: Jesus taught about loving one's neighbor that it required one to show intentional goodwill toward people different from oneself even if it meant taking risks, overcoming social conventions, and offering practical assistance and long-term care.

HOMILETICAL IDEA: Show no partiality in being compassionate to others.

Luke 11:1-13

SUBJECT: What did Jesus teach his disciples about prayer?

COMPLEMENT: To pray was to worship God, desire God's kingdom, ask God for essentials to live and forgiveness of sins, and resist temptation; he taught persistence in prayer.

EXEGETICAL IDEA: Jesus taught his disciples that to pray was to worship God, desire God's kingdom, ask God for essentials to live and forgiveness of sins, and resist temptation; he taught persistence in prayer.

HOMILETICAL IDEA: In prayer we orient our lives to God and persist in the endeavor.

Luke 11:14-54

SUBJECT: Why did crowds, Pharisees, and lawyers question Jesus's authority and teaching?

COMPLEMENT: They failed to discern the divine source of his authority to cast out evil and prioritized external appearances at the expense of inward disposition of heart.

EXEGETICAL IDEA: Crowds, Pharisees, and lawyers questioned Jesus's authority and teaching because they failed to discern the divine source of his authority to cast out evil and prioritized external appearances at the expense of inward disposition of heart.

HOMILETICAL IDEA: False notions of God and piety are threatened by God's truth and power in Jesus.

Luke 12:1-12

SUBJECT: Why should followers of Jesus not be afraid of confessing faith in him when persecuted and threatened with death?

COMPLEMENT: Jesus promised the Spirit would enable their witness and, ultimately, they would be vindicated by God.

EXEGETICAL IDEA: Followers of Jesus should not be afraid of confessing faith in him when persecuted and threatened with death, since Jesus promised the

Spirit would enable their witness and, ultimately, they would be vindicated by God.

HOMILETICAL IDEA: Fear not in the face of opposition to Jesus, because the Spirit helps us witness and God will vindicate us in the end.

Luke 12:13-21

SUBJECT: What did Jesus teach about accumulating material wealth before all else?

COMPLEMENT: It resulted in a false confidence in human plans and possessions that obscured accountability to God.

EXEGETICAL IDEA: Jesus taught that accumulating material wealth before all else resulted in a false confidence in human plans and possessions that obscured accountability to God.

HOMILETICAL IDEA: Putting stuff first distorts our vision of God and has harmful consequences for us.

Luke 12:22-48

SUBJECT: What did Jesus say are the appropriate attitudes, respectively, to worry and watchfulness?

COMPLEMENT: Not to worry (since it adds nothing of quality or longevity to life) and instead trust God, and be watchful or diligent in discipleship, ready to give a satisfactory account to Jesus.

EXEGETICAL IDEA: Jesus said the appropriate attitudes, respectively, to worry and watchfulness are not to worry (since it adds nothing of quality or longevity to life) and instead trust God, and be watchful or diligent in discipleship, ready to give a satisfactory account to Jesus.

HOMILETICAL IDEA: Don't worry, trust God, and be watchful to serve Jesus.

Luke 12:49-59

SUBJECT: What was the impact of Jesus on his contemporaries?

COMPLEMENT: He divided opinion, even in families; people choose for or against him.

EXEGETICAL IDEA: The impact of Jesus on his contemporaries was that he divided opinion, even in families; people choose for or against him.

HOMILETICAL IDEA: Nobody can sit on the fence about Jesus.

Luke 13:1-9

SUBJECT: Why was repentance central to the message of Jesus?

COMPLEMENT: Failure to repent had fatal consequences that were best avoided.

EXEGETICAL IDEA: Repentance was central to the message of Jesus, because failure to repent had fatal consequences that were best avoided.

HOMILETICAL IDEA: Turning back to God is not optional if we truly want life to the full.

Luke 13:10-17

SUBJECT: Why was it right for Jesus to heal a crippled woman on the Sabbath?

COMPLEMENT: To make a person whole truly honored God.

EXEGETICAL IDEA: It was right for Jesus to heal a crippled woman on the Sabbath because to make a person whole truly honored God.

HOMILETICAL IDEA: Improving a person's quality of life is part of true worship.

Luke 13:18-21

SUBJECT: What is the kingdom of God like?

COMPLEMENT: A mustard seed or yeast, seemingly slight and insignificant, but charged with life so that it grows to become vast and impressive.

EXEGETICAL IDEA: The kingdom of God is like a mustard seed or yeast, seemingly slight and insignificant, but charged with life so that it grows to become vast and impressive.

HOMILETICAL IDEA: The kingdom of God is hidden from view, but present, active, and important for all peoples everywhere.

Luke 13:22-30

SUBJECT: Who were the ones who would be saved?

COMPLEMENT: Those who accepted the costly demands of following Jesus and cooperated with the kingdom of God.

EXEGETICAL IDEA: The ones who would be saved were those who accepted the costly demands of following Jesus and cooperated with the kingdom of God.

HOMILETICAL IDEA: To be saved, follow Jesus and work with the kingdom of God.

Luke 13:31-35

SUBJECT: Why did Jesus grieve over Jerusalem?

COMPLEMENT: The city had a history of rejecting and killing prophets sent by God to declare the Word of the Lord, and Jesus anticipated he too would be rejected and killed for the same reason.

EXEGETICAL IDEA: Jesus grieved over Jerusalem because the city had a history of rejecting and killing prophets sent by God to declare the Word of the Lord, and Jesus anticipated he too would be rejected and killed for the same reason.

HOMILETICAL IDEA: Speaking God's truth to power entails the risk of rejection, suffering, and death.

Luke 14:1-6

SUBJECT: Why did Jesus ask a Pharisee if it was lawful to heal a person on the Sabbath?

COMPLEMENT: To expose the inhumanity of an interpretation that prevented healing on the Sabbath but permitted the rescue of an animal or a person from a pit.

EXEGETICAL IDEA: Jesus asked a Pharisee if it was lawful to heal a person on the Sabbath to expose the inhumanity of an interpretation that prevented healing on the Sabbath but permitted the rescue of an animal or a person from a pit.

HOMILETICAL IDEA: God delights to heal and make people whole.

Luke 14:7-24

SUBJECT: What did Jesus teach about humility and hospitality?

COMPLEMENT: That one should not presume to be more important than anyone else, because in God's eyes others might be worthy of more honor.

EXEGETICAL IDEA: Jesus taught about humility and hospitality that one should not presume to be more important than anyone else, because in God's eyes others might be worthy of more honor.

HOMILETICAL IDEA: There is no place for pride before God; rather, be humble in order that you might be surprised by God's goodness and generosity.

Luke 14:25-35

SUBJECT: Why was it important to consider the consequence of becoming a follower of Jesus before doing so?

COMPLEMENT: Following Jesus as his disciple was costly; it entailed being willing to give up material security and to die for his sake.

EXEGETICAL IDEA: It was important to consider the consequences of becoming a follower of Jesus before choosing to do so because following Jesus as his disciple was costly; it entailed being willing to give up material security and to die for his sake.

HOMILETICAL IDEA: Think carefully before deciding to follow Jesus, because it can lead to death.

Luke 15

SUBJECT: How did Jesus challenge religious teachers' condemnation of his mixing with tax collectors and sinners, viewed as outcasts from society and alienated from God?

COMPLEMENT: He taught that God cared deeply for them and intentionally sought to find and recover them.

EXEGETICAL IDEA: Jesus challenged religious teachers' condemnation of his mixing with tax collectors and sinners, viewed as outcasts from society and alienated from God, by teaching that God cared deeply for them and intentionally seeking to find and recover them.

HOMILETICAL IDEA: Human judgment is challenged by God's love and transformed into compassion that shares the good news.

Luke 16:1-13

SUBJECT: Why did Jesus commend a steward dismissed for mismanaging his master's resources and who acted in his own interest?

COMPLEMENT: He was shrewd in canceling the commission due to him from his master's creditors to secure their help in the future.

EXEGETICAL IDEA: Jesus commended a steward dismissed for mismanaging his master's resources and who acted in his own interest because he was shrewd in canceling the commission due to him from his master's creditors to secure their help in the future.

HOMILETICAL IDEA: Be prudent in difficult situations to make wise and strategic decisions to prepare for the future.

Luke 16:14-31

SUBJECT: How did Jesus challenge complacent attitudes to money?

COMPLEMENT: He taught that wealth should be used to alleviate poverty and the decision to do so must be based on the Old Testament, not on an arbitrary requirement for a supernatural sign.

EXEGETICAL IDEA: Jesus challenged complacent attitudes to money when he taught that wealth should be used to alleviate poverty and the decision to do so must be based on the Old Testament, not on an arbitrary requirement for a supernatural sign.

HOMILETICAL IDEA: Use wealth to alleviate poverty as required in Scripture, and don't make excuses by demanding a supernatural sign for confirmation.

Luke 17

SUBJECT: What did Jesus's teaching about the last things affirm?

COMPLEMENT: The kingdom was already present and God's intervention in the future would be sudden and unexpected, so people should not try to predict it; the important thing is to remain faithful to God.

EXEGETICAL IDEA: Jesus's teaching about the last things affirmed that the kingdom was already present and God's intervention in the future would be sudden and unexpected, so people should not try to predict it; the important thing is to remain faithful to God.

HOMILETICAL IDEA: Don't waste time trying to predict God's future action; rather, focus on following Jesus faithfully in the present.

Luke 18:1-19:27

SUBJECT: How did Jesus's words and deeds about the kingdom of God subvert widespread notions of divine-human relations?

COMPLEMENT: He showed that God cared for the vulnerable, social outcasts, and sinners, and rejected spiritualities of blessing based on human merit.

EXEGETICAL IDEA: Jesus's words and deeds about the kingdom of God subverted widespread notions of divine-human relations in that he showed God cared for the vulnerable, social outcasts, and sinners, and rejected spiritualities of blessing based on human merit.

HOMILETICAL IDEA: Jesus subverts merit-based ideas of spirituality and proclaims God's unmerited but freely given goodness that changes lives.

Luke 19:28-22:6

SUBJECT: Why did Jesus's entry to Jerusalem and teaching in the temple provoke resistance from the priests and Pharisees?

COMPLEMENT: He subverted their teaching, challenged economic exploitation within the temple, and foretold the destruction of the temple and Jerusalem.

EXEGETICAL IDEA: Jesus's entry to Jerusalem and teaching in the temple provoked resistance from the priests and Pharisees because he subverted their teaching, challenged economic exploitation within the temple, and foretold the destruction of the temple and Jerusalem.

HOMILETICAL IDEA: The good news of Jesus challenges flawed ideas of God, human spirituality, religious institutions, and societies, and so elicits opposition.

Luke 22:7-23:25

SUBJECT: What did the last hours of Jesus at supper and in betrayal, arrest, and trial show about his life and ministry?

COMPLEMENT: They served the purpose of God to redeem Israel in the making of a new covenant through his death.

EXEGETICAL IDEA: The last hours of Jesus at supper and in betrayal, arrest, and trial showed that his life and ministry served the purpose of God to redeem Israel in the making of a new covenant through his death.

HOMILETICAL IDEA: Events that appear insignificant now may serve God's purpose in ways grasped only with the benefit of hindsight.

Luke 23:26-49

SUBJECT: What did Jesus ask God to do for those who crucified him?

COMPLEMENT: Forgive them, because they did not understand what they had done.

EXEGETICAL IDEA: Jesus asked God to forgive those who crucified him, because they did not understand what they had done.

HOMILETICAL IDEA: Forgiving enemies is at the heart of following Jesus.

Luke 24:1-12

SUBJECT: What was the explanation for the empty tomb?

COMPLEMENT: Jesus had risen from the dead.

EXEGETICAL IDEA: The explanation for the empty tomb was that Jesus had risen from the dead.

HOMILETICAL IDEA: Jesus is alive!

Luke 24:13-53

SUBJECT: How did Jesus confirm he had risen from the dead?

COMPLEMENT: He appeared to two disciples on the road to Emmaus, to Simon, and to a gathering of his disciples.

EXEGETICAL IDEA: Jesus confirmed he had risen from the dead by appearing to two disciples on the road to Emmaus, to Simon, and to a gathering of his disciples.

HOMILETICAL IDEA: Jesus encounters people to show he is alive.

Difficult Passages/Verses

Difficulties in preaching from Luke arise in several ways. Luke is one of four biographical portraits of Jesus in the New Testament. Luke shares a core of material about Jesus with Matthew that most scholars believe is derived from Mark. Luke and Matthew share a chunk of material that is found in both their accounts but not in Mark. In addition, Luke and Matthew include material about Jesus that is peculiar to each of their Gospels. The Gospels narrate different versions of the same episodes. A sermon is not the place to engage in complex discussions about the textual relationships between the Synoptic Gospels, but many in a congregational worship service or Bible study will be familiar with the alternative versions of the same episode. Questions about such differences can arise in their thought processes while listening to a sermon or Bible teaching. It is important in preaching and teaching from Luke not to gloss over or ignore the challenges posed by alternative accounts in Mark and Matthew (and John!).

Two themes in Luke merit particular comment. First, forgiveness is a theme in Luke's account of Jesus's ministry (which is shared with Mark and Matthew) and is an especially prominent requirement of discipleship. Interestingly, although Jesus on the cross petitions God the Father to forgive the sins of the people who crucified him (without demanding repentance), nowhere in Luke is the death of Jesus on the cross connected with the forgiveness of sins for humanity. There is no doctrine of atonement in Luke. A key challenge, therefore, is to guard against reading a doctrine of atonement into Luke, yet at the same time it is vital to unpack the example and teaching of Jesus to practice forgiveness.

Second, Luke stresses the importance of the Holy Spirit in the conception, baptism, and ministry of Jesus. The Holy Spirit is also seen to be vital in the life and witness of his followers. It is important to recognize in Luke that the

Holy Spirit and the Word of God in Scripture are held together. The Spirit is not viewed in isolation from Scripture. God's initiative in and through the Spirit recorded in the infancy narratives is interpreted with reference to the Old Testament. In his baptism Jesus is empowered by the Spirit and led out into the wilderness. His struggle with the devil occurs in the context of life in the Spirit lived with reference to Scripture (i.e., the Old Testament).

Cultural Perspectives and Application

Perhaps the greatest obstacle to the preacher or teacher communicating the message of Luke (or any of the canonical Gospels) clearly and effectively within and beyond Christian communities in a Western context in the twenty-first century is a sense of familiarity. Jesus is central to Christian faith and practice, so we think we know him and there is little more to discover. Hence, the potential to be surprised and challenged can appear limited. The Jesus we read about in Luke repeatedly found ways of getting the attention of his audience and disturbing their settled notions of God and what it means to live in relationship with God and others. F. F. Bruce notes, "It is all too easy to believe in a Jesus who is largely a construction of our own imagination—an inoffensive person whom no one would really trouble to crucify."[2] Once we penetrate behind the facade of the Jesus we are familiar with, we may find he is more puzzling and uncomfortable than we realized.

Two practical obstacles to understanding Jesus in Luke stem from the layout of English translations of the Bible. First, it is important to acknowledge that the division of books of the Bible into chapter and verse is a simple and elegant means of navigating our way around Scripture. But these artificial arrangements do not always assist the reader or listener attending to Scripture to grasp and follow the flow of the text. Second, many stories and episodes in Luke (as indeed all four Gospel accounts) appear under titles that obscure rather than illuminate a passage (e.g., the parable of the dishonest manager). Such titles function as a convenient shorthand to identify what we are about to read or hear. At the same time, they interpret the passage for the reader or hearer in ways that may either illuminate or obscure its meaning.

Jesus in Luke exemplifies and embodies the searching love of God (4:14–8:6) that seeks after the sinner alienated from divine fellowship (15:1–32). Such love is costly and leads to a cross but moves forward in hope inspired by God's

2. F. F. Bruce, *The Hard Sayings of Jesus*, The Jesus Library (London: Hodder & Stoughton, 1983), 15.

promise of resurrection (9:21–27). Such a life is the one God calls the disciple of Jesus to embrace.

RECOMMENDED RESOURCES

Adeyemo, Tokunboh, ed. *Africa Bible Commentary*. Grand Rapids: Zondervan, 2006.

Craddock, Fred B. *Luke*. Interpretation. Louisville: Westminster John Knox, 1990.

Trites, Allison A. *The Gospel of Luke*. Cornerstone Biblical Commentary. Carol Stream, IL: Tyndale, 2006.

John

MARY S. HULST

The Big Idea of John

John is an unusual Gospel in that 92 percent of what is found in John is not found in the other three Gospels, which gives us better insight into who Jesus is than if we had only Matthew, Mark, and Luke. John utilizes various themes throughout his Gospel, such as light and darkness, blindness and sight, grace and truth, and rejecting or receiving. Because he wants to emphasize these themes, John takes the time to tell long, detailed stories (e.g., in chaps. 3, 4, 9, and 11). John expresses his hope for those who hear his message when he says, "These things are written that you may believe that Jesus is the Messiah, the Son of God, and that by believing you may have life in his name" (20:31).

SUBJECT: Why did John write his Gospel?

COMPLEMENT: To reveal that Jesus is the Son of God—fully human, fully divine—and that whoever believes in him will have life in his name.

EXEGETICAL IDEA: John wrote his Gospel to reveal that Jesus is the Son of God—fully human, fully divine—and that whoever believes in him will have life in his name.

HOMILETICAL IDEA: John wrote his Gospel so that we will believe that Jesus is the Son of God and in believing have life in his name.

Selecting Preaching and Teaching Passages in John

To best help the preacher, at least one passage from each chapter of John has been selected for this volume. Most often the passage selected is a story not found in one of the other Gospels.

John uses strong themes in his Gospel and sets them out already in the prologue. A preacher could use the themes presented in the prologue to develop multiple series. For example, John describes Jesus as being "full of grace and truth." A series on the stories in which Jesus both extends grace and brings truth would be interesting. In John 5, for example, Jesus heals the man by the pool (grace), but he also warns him to stop sinning (truth). In John 6 Jesus feeds the five thousand (grace), but he also warns them against thinking this is all about bread and not about God (truth). He spares the woman caught in adultery (which begs the question: Where was the man who was caught in adultery?) by speaking truth to her accusers, granting grace to her, and then also extending truth to her: "Go and sin no more."

John also engages with themes of light and darkness, including stories that take place at certain times of day: Nicodemus, who wants to remain hidden, comes at night (John 3). Jesus meets the woman at the well at noon (John 4). In John 19, Joseph and Nicodemus race to get Jesus buried before the sun goes down (a significant moment for a man who previously wanted to be hidden by the dark!). Light and darkness are also at play when it comes to who is really able to see: the man born blind can see, but the Pharisees who can see are spiritually blind. In what stories in the Gospel of John does light shine in the darkness and the darkness does not overcome it (cf. 1:5)?

Another important theme is the concept of the hour, as in "my hour has not yet come" (2:4) and "an hour is coming, and is now here" (5:25 ESV). The term arises first in John 2 but comes up again in John 4, 5, 7, 8, 12, 13, 16, 17, and 19. Jesus is communicating a sense of both the fulfillment of time (he is here) and the waiting for fulfillment (he is not yet glorified). Walking through these passages during the season of Lent in anticipation of Holy Week would make for a rich sermon series.

Commentators often divide the book into the "Book of Signs" (chaps. 1–12) and the "Book of Glory" (chaps. 13–21), or "Jesus's Public Ministry" and "Jesus's Personal Glorification." Organizing a series around the two halves of the book (perhaps the first half during Epiphany and the second half during Lent) would make good sense.

For passages not covered below, refer to one of the excellent commentaries referenced at the end of the chapter.

Getting the Subject, Complement, Exegetical Idea, and Homiletical Idea

John 1:1-18

SUBJECT: Who does John say that Jesus is?

COMPLEMENT: The Word of God made flesh.

EXEGETICAL IDEA: John says that Jesus is the Word of God made flesh.

HOMILETICAL IDEA: John names Jesus as the Word made flesh, full of grace and truth, the one who was at the beginning of all things. (See "Cultural Perspectives and Application" below.)

John 2:1-12

SUBJECT: Why does John say that the disciples put their faith in Jesus?

COMPLEMENT: Because Jesus revealed his glory in the miracle of turning water into wine.

EXEGETICAL IDEA: John says that the disciples put their faith in Jesus because Jesus revealed his glory in the miracle of turning water into wine.

HOMILETICAL IDEA: Jesus's provision of wine fulfills prophesy and provides a picture for when he returns. (See "Difficult Passages/Verses" below.)

John 3:1-21

SUBJECT: Why does John say that God sent Jesus into the world?

COMPLEMENT: Because God loves the world and wants all who believe in Jesus to have eternal life.

EXEGETICAL IDEA: John says that God sent Jesus into the world because God loves the world and wants all who believe in Jesus to have eternal life.

HOMILETICAL IDEA: God loves us and wants us to have eternal life through Jesus: "for God so loved the world" (3:16) includes us!

John 3:22-30

SUBJECT: How does John say that the joy of John the Baptist is fulfilled?

COMPLEMENT: He prepared the way for the bridegroom.

EXEGETICAL IDEA: John says that the joy of John the Baptist is fulfilled because he prepared the way for the bridegroom.

HOMILETICAL IDEA: John the Baptist reminds us that we all point to Jesus—"He must increase, but I must decrease"—and in this our joy will be fulfilled.

John 4:1–42

SUBJECT: Why does John say that Jesus had a conversation with a Samaritan woman, breaking all social norms?

COMPLEMENT: To reveal to her that he is the Messiah.

EXEGETICAL IDEA: John says that Jesus had a conversation with a Samaritan woman, breaking all social norms, in order to reveal to her that he is the Messiah.

HOMILETICAL IDEA: Social norms will not limit Jesus: he will speak to whomever he needs to speak to and use whomever he wants to use to share the good news—including us! (See "Difficult Passages/Verses" below.)

John 5:1–18

SUBJECT: Why does John say that Jesus healed on the Sabbath?

COMPLEMENT: Because his Father is still working, so Jesus is working too, for he and the Father are one.

EXEGETICAL IDEA: John says that Jesus healed on the Sabbath because his Father is still working, so Jesus is working too, for he and the Father are one.

HOMILETICAL IDEA: Jesus aligns himself with God as one who continues to make things new, even on the Sabbath.

John 6:16–21

SUBJECT: Why does John say that the disciples do not need to be afraid even in the storm?

COMPLEMENT: Because Jesus is there with them.

EXEGETICAL IDEA: John says that the disciples do not need to be afraid even in the storm, because Jesus is there with them.

HOMILETICAL IDEA: Even in the storm Jesus is with us and we do not need to be afraid.

John 6:22–50

SUBJECT: What does John say is the true bread from heaven?

COMPLEMENT: Jesus, who comes down from heaven and gives life to the world.

EXEGETICAL IDEA: John says that the true bread from heaven is Jesus, who comes down from heaven and gives life to the world.

HOMILETICAL IDEA: Jesus is the true bread of life, enough for today (such as manna or daily bread), but also enough for our forever. (See "Difficult Passages/Verses" below.)

John 7:10-31

SUBJECT: Who does John say Jesus reveals himself to be?

COMPLEMENT: He is not an impostor, but is the Messiah sent by God, who is true.

EXEGETICAL IDEA: John says that Jesus reveals himself as not an impostor but as the Messiah sent by God, who is true.

HOMILETICAL IDEA: We believe Jesus is the Messiah sent by the one true God, even when he doesn't say or do what we want.

John 8:31-59

SUBJECT: How does John say that all people are set free from sin?

COMPLEMENT: By the Son who sets them free.

EXEGETICAL IDEA: John says that all people are set free from sin by the Son who sets them free.

HOMILETICAL IDEA: "Everyone who sins is a slave to sin" is the whole reason Jesus came, and it is his joy to set us free.

John 9

SUBJECT: Why does John say that the man was born blind?

COMPLEMENT: Not as a result of personal sin but so that Jesus could reveal God's glory in him.

EXEGETICAL IDEA: John says that the man was born blind not as a result of personal sin but so that Jesus could reveal God's glory in him.

HOMILETICAL IDEA: Nothing disqualifies us from being used by God to reveal his glory and point more people to him. (See "Cultural Perspectives and Application" below.)

John 10:1-21

SUBJECT: What does John say that Jesus the good shepherd does?

COMPLEMENT: He lays down his life for his sheep.

EXEGETICAL IDEA: John says that Jesus the good shepherd lays down his life for his sheep.

HOMILETICAL IDEA: Jesus cares for us with the tender, attentive love of a shepherd for his sheep—sheep who have no idea most of the time what the shepherd is doing for them!

John 11:1-44

SUBJECT: Why does John say that Jesus raised Lazarus?

COMPLEMENT: To reveal the glory of God and to reveal himself as the resurrection and the life.

EXEGETICAL IDEA: John says that Jesus raised Lazarus to reveal the glory of God and to reveal himself as the resurrection and the life.

HOMILETICAL IDEA: Even death itself cannot win when the Messiah is present, because he himself is resurrection and life. (It is also important to note that Jesus grieves, even though he knows that this is not how Lazarus's story ends. Christians are free to grieve, even though we know that death does not win.)

John 12:1-8

SUBJECT: Why does John say that Mary anointed Jesus?

COMPLEMENT: To prepare him for burial.

EXEGETICAL IDEA: John says that Mary anointed Jesus to prepare him for burial.

HOMILETICAL IDEA: Jesus welcomes the gift of anointing as a way to prepare for what is yet to come—he knows what is next for him.

John 12:12-19

SUBJECT: Why does John say that the crowds praised Jesus?

COMPLEMENT: Because they had seen or heard about the signs he had done.

EXEGETICAL IDEA: John says that the crowds praised Jesus because they had seen or heard about the signs he had done.

HOMILETICAL IDEA: When we see and hear what Jesus has done, we cannot help but praise him.

John 12:20-36

SUBJECT: What hour does John say has come?

COMPLEMENT: The hour for Jesus the Son of Man to be glorified and the ruler of this world to be driven out.

EXEGETICAL IDEA: John says that the hour has come for Jesus the Son of Man to be glorified and the ruler of this world to be driven out.

HOMILETICAL IDEA: Counter to the world's ideas of glory, the glorification of Jesus comes through death, just like a kernel of wheat only bears fruit once it dies, and when he is glorified the ruler of this world will be driven out.

John 13:1-20

SUBJECT: Why does John say that Jesus washed the disciples' feet?

COMPLEMENT: To show them how to love and serve one another.

EXEGETICAL IDEA: John says that Jesus washed the disciples' feet to show them how to love and serve one another.

HOMILETICAL IDEA: Jesus's act of service is a model of love and service for us so let's "wash the feet" of our friends, family, and church members.

John 14:1-7

SUBJECT: How does John say that the disciples can get to the Father?

COMPLEMENT: Only through Jesus, the way, the truth, and the life.

EXEGETICAL IDEA: John says that the disciples can get to the Father only through Jesus, the way, the truth, and the life.

HOMILETICAL IDEA: Even though we may chafe at that exclusivity, Jesus offers the warm invitation that the way to a relationship with the Father is available only through him. (See "Difficult Passages/Verses" below.)

John 15:1-11

SUBJECT: How does John say that Jesus's followers will bear fruit?

COMPLEMENT: Only by abiding in Jesus, the vine.

EXEGETICAL IDEA: John says that Jesus's followers will bear fruit only by abiding in Jesus, the vine.

HOMILETICAL IDEA: Jesus wants us to have joy and bear fruit to glorify God, and the only way we can do that is by abiding in his love.

John 15:12-17

SUBJECT: What does Jesus say is the greatest act of love?

COMPLEMENT: To lay down one's life for one's friends.

EXEGETICAL IDEA: Jesus says the greatest act of love is to lay down one's life for one's friends.

HOMILETICAL IDEA: Jesus calls us his friends, and he lays his life down for us.

John 16:25-33

SUBJECT: How does John say that Jesus's followers will find peace in a world that hates them?

COMPLEMENT: By remembering Jesus has conquered the world.

EXEGETICAL IDEA: John says that Jesus's followers will find peace in a world that hates them by remembering that Jesus has conquered the world.

HOMILETICAL IDEA: Even when we are persecuted for our faith, we will find peace in remembering Jesus has conquered the world.

John 17

SUBJECT: Why does John say that Jesus prays for his followers?

COMPLEMENT: Because he wants them to be one as he and the Father are one, so that the world will see their unity as a witness to God.

EXEGETICAL IDEA: John says that Jesus prays for his followers because he wants them to be one as he and the Father are one, so that the world will see their unity as a witness to God.

HOMILETICAL IDEA: Jesus prays for us to be united as a witness to a broken world.

John 18:15-18, 25-27 (Background Passage: John 13:36-38)

SUBJECT: What does John describe Peter as doing?

COMPLEMENT: Denying Jesus and fulfilling Jesus's prophecy that he would do so.

EXEGETICAL IDEA: John describes Peter as denying Jesus and fulfilling Jesus's prophecy that he would do so.

HOMILETICAL IDEA: Peter was one of Jesus's closest friends, but Jesus knows that under the right circumstances even those who profess to love him will deny him, including us.

John 18:28-19:16

SUBJECT: Who does John say listens to Jesus's voice?

COMPLEMENT: Everyone who belongs to the truth.

EXEGETICAL IDEA: John says that everyone who listens to Jesus's voice belongs to the truth.

HOMILETICAL IDEA: Listening to Jesus's voice will attach us more and more to truth, to the point where we long for the truth and belong to the truth.

John 19:38-42

SUBJECT: Who does John say buried Jesus?

COMPLEMENT: Josephus and Nicodemus, two wealthy Pharisees, in the light before the sun had set.

EXEGETICAL IDEA: John says that Jesus was buried by Josephus and Nicodemus, two wealthy Pharisees, in the light before the sun had set.

HOMILETICAL IDEA: The death of Jesus moves Josephus and Nicodemus to spend lavishly on the burial of Jesus, despite what it may cost them socially as Pharisees to take these actions in broad daylight. (See "Cultural Perspectives and Application" below.)

John 20:1-10

SUBJECT: Why does John say that the disciple (probably John himself) believed?

COMPLEMENT: Because he saw the linen wrappings lying there and the cloth that had been on Jesus's head was rolled up.

EXEGETICAL IDEA: John says that the disciple (probably John himself) believed because he saw the linen wrappings lying there and the cloth that had been on Jesus's head was rolled up.

HOMILETICAL IDEA: We can be moved, like the disciple was, to believe in God's amazing power as evidenced in the empty tomb.

John 20:24-29

SUBJECT: Who does Jesus say are the ones who are blessed?

COMPLEMENT: Those who have not seen and yet believe.

EXEGETICAL IDEA: Jesus says the ones who are blessed are those who have not seen and yet believe.

HOMILETICAL IDEA: Jesus blesses those (like us!) who have not seen and yet believe.

John 21

SUBJECT: What does John say it looks like to love Jesus?

COMPLEMENT: To feed his sheep.

EXEGETICAL IDEA: John says that to love Jesus is to feed his sheep.

HOMILETICAL IDEA: Jesus not only restores his relationship with Peter; he also restores him with a purpose, which is also what Jesus does for us.

Difficult Passages/Verses

John 2

Why is Jesus rude to his mother? "Woman, . . . my hour has not yet come" (v. 4) may sound rude to us but look at Mary's response: "Do whatever he tells you" (v. 5). Mary does not appear at all bothered by Jesus's words to her. In this passage, Mary gives the impression that she understands who Jesus is and what he's doing. Mary knows that Jesus no longer answers to her.

John wants us to be clear that Jesus is not merely doing something that his mom asked him to do. If Jesus does anything, it will be because God the Father directs him to do it. Jesus essentially says, "I don't answer to you, Mom. I take my orders from someone else now," and Mary says, "I understand. God's will be done." That's the point of this exchange. Jesus is obedient to one being, and that's his heavenly Father.

Also, why is water turned into wine the first miracle, and why do the disciples put their faith in Jesus because of it? Jesus's miraculous provision of wine is a fulfillment of a prophesy in Amos 9:13–15. Really good wine produced really quickly is a sign that the kingdom of God is on its way, that this is the Son of God, that the Messiah is in the house. And that's why the disciples believe! Because God has shown up, right there, in the middle of a wedding in the little village of Cana.

The sign here is also the foretaste of all Jesus's miracles, because they all move people ahead to the new heavens and the new earth. When Jesus heals someone, it's a fast forward to the restoration of all things that will come when he returns. When Jesus comes back, all blind people will see and all lame people will dance and all people who can't eat gluten will have pizza and beer.

John 4

Why does Jesus speak at length with a Samaritan woman? The radical way in which Jesus interacts with this person cannot be overstated. She is a female, a Samaritan, a woman who has been taken advantage of by many men, and all of these traits mean that Jesus should not speak to her, let alone drink from one of her containers. He breaks every social rule and makes the disciples feel incredibly awkward. But the woman becomes the first evangelist, going into her town and inviting everyone to come and see Jesus: "Could this be the Messiah?" (v. 29). To understand the impact of this passage, the preacher must engage with the issues of race and gender and how Jesus upends contemporary social norms, treating this woman as a valued theological conversation partner and proclaimer of the gospel.

John 6

Why does Jesus talk so much about bread? The people considered Moses to be the bringer of manna, as if there were a storehouse of bread in heaven and Moses could ask God to bring it whenever he wanted. If Moses could do that, the crowd wants to know, why can't Jesus? The crowd is saying, "Come on, Jesus, show us what you got." But Jesus doesn't play that game, because the game is shortsighted. Jesus is playing the long game. Jesus is playing the eternity game. Jesus knows that if he gives the crowd what they want, they'll never ask for what they need. They'll just keep asking for more. If he gives them bread, they'll want money. If he gives them money, they'll want sex. If he gives them sex, they'll want power. They will keep asking for more, and the things they will ask for will never satisfy them. Which is why he says this: I am the bread of life. I have come down from heaven. The Father has sent me to you, and everyone he sends my way I will welcome with open arms. Because you don't need a snack, you need me. You need hope. You need purpose. You need life. I am the bread of life.

John 14

Does Jesus really mean it when he says, "No one comes to the Father except through me" (v. 6)? The exclusivity of Christ is a challenge in a religiously pluralistic world. Perhaps C. S. Lewis can help:

> Here is another thing that used to puzzle me. Is it not frightfully unfair that this new life should be confined to people who have heard of Christ and been able to believe in Him? But the truth is God has not told us what His arrangements about the other people are. We do know that no [one] can be saved except through Christ; we do not know that only those who know Him can be saved through Him. But in the meantime, if you are worried about people outside, the most unreasonable thing you can do is to remain outside yourself. Christians are Christ's body, the organism through which He works. Every addition to that body enables Him to do more. If you want to help those outside you must add your own little cell to the body of Christ who alone can help them.[1]

1. C. S. Lewis, *Mere Christianity* (New York: HarperOne, 2001), 64.

Cultural Perspectives and Application

The author of the Gospel of John was John, the son of Zebedee, the brother of James and one of the twelve disciples of Jesus. He was probably the disciple who was called the beloved disciple, as it was John who was asked by Jesus to care for Jesus's mother, Mary, when Jesus was on the cross. John may have been the youngest of all the disciples, as his Gospel is written later than the others and it seems that he outlived the other disciples as well.

John wrote his Gospel to Christians, and to Jewish Christians in particular. He mentions Jewish customs and festivals more than anyone else, and he encourages Christians to keep believing even when people tell them that they shouldn't.

From the first verse, John addresses a heresy that the church has been dealing with ever since Jesus ascended. There were people who said that Jesus was a good person but not the Son of God. Jesus was unusual but not divine. They said that he was human, but with a special measure of God's spirit. Yet John begins his Gospel not with the birth of Jesus, as do Matthew and Luke, and not with the baptism, as does Mark, but with the beginning of time itself: "In the beginning." John is declaring, "Jesus was God, back at the beginning, participating in creation. He wasn't created at the beginning; he was before all things." (John also clarifies that John the Baptist is the one who foretells the Messiah but is not the Messiah himself.)

From the prologue onward, John also plays with the themes of light and darkness. In John 1 the light shines in the darkness and the darkness does not overcome it. In John 3 Nicodemus comes to Jesus at night because he is afraid and doesn't want to be seen, but John also shows that Nicodemus isn't ready to see who Jesus really is. In John 4 the Samaritan woman meets Jesus at high noon, and she is able to see clearly that he is the Messiah. In John 8 Jesus declares that he is the light of the world. In John 9 a blind man is healed and can see literally and spiritually. In John 19 two formerly secret followers of Jesus prepare his body and bury him in daylight before the sun sets.

The identity of Jesus is debated throughout this Gospel: Is he the Messiah or isn't he? John wants his readers to see the truth (truth is another strong theme in John) and answer the question with a definite yes. As John states it so clearly after he writes of the postresurrection appearances: "These [things] are written that you may believe that Jesus is the Messiah, the Son of God, and that by believing you may have life in his name" (20:31). John wants his readers to see.

John's Gospel calls us to pay attention to who Jesus really is, not who we would like him to be. How is Jesus revealing himself and his glory to us?

How can we know? How can we see? Where is Jesus calling us to move from darkness into light? What's at stake if we miss him, or reject him, or fail to see him? In the Gospel of John, receiving Jesus or rejecting him is a matter of life or death.

RECOMMENDED RESOURCES

Bruner, Dale. *The Gospel of John: A Commentary.* Grand Rapids: Eerdmans, 2012.

Card, Michael. *John: The Gospel of Wisdom.* Downers Grove, IL: InterVarsity, 2014.

Keener, Craig. *The Gospel of John: A Commentary.* 2 vols. Peabody, MA: Hendrickson, 2003.

Acts

BRANDON R. CASH

The Big Idea of Acts

In the book of Acts, Luke seeks to show that God's great plan of salvation has come to fulfillment in the life, death, resurrection, and ascension of Jesus the Messiah, and continues to unfold as the Spirit-filled church takes the message of salvation from Jerusalem to Judea to Samaria and to the ends of the earth.

SUBJECT: Why could the early church be confident that there was a new people of God, made up of Jews and gentiles alike, who were being empowered by the Holy Spirit to bear witness to the resurrected Lord Jesus in Jerusalem, Judea, and Samaria and to the ends of the earth in the midst of persecution, obstacles, and seemingly insurmountable odds?

COMPLEMENT: Because of the signs and wonders performed by the Spirit-filled apostles and the increasing number of Spirit-filled converts from Jerusalem to Rome.

EXEGETICAL IDEA: The early church could be confident that there was a new people of God, made up of Jews and gentiles alike, who were being empowered by the Holy Spirit to bear witness to the resurrected Lord Jesus in Jerusalem, Judea, and Samaria and to the ends of the earth in the midst of persecution, obstacles, and seemingly insurmountable odds because of the signs and wonders performed by the Spirit-filled apostles and the increasing number of Spirit-filled converts from Jerusalem to Rome.

HOMILETICAL IDEA: The Holy Spirit empowers us, unites us, and sends us with the message of salvation that is open to all.

Selecting Preaching and Teaching Passages in Acts

Preaching twenty-eight chapters of historical narrative can be a daunting task, not just for preachers but for congregations as well. In order to keep Luke's focus our focus and not get bogged down in unnecessary detail, I recommend crafting sermons around the natural breaks in the stories. Often this will mean preaching a chapter, sometimes it will mean focusing on a paragraph (e.g., 2:42–47), and sometimes it will mean panning out and covering more than two chapters (e.g., 21:15–23:35). I've found that a helpful way to think about it is to liken Acts to a movie that has moved from the theater to television; it is one big story, but, so that networks can collect their advertising dollars, they build in commercial breaks. Generally speaking, the producers do an admirable job of finding the natural breaks. On occasion they get it wrong and viewers are frustrated because a scene was cut short. Our job as preachers is to pay attention to the clues in the text and figure out where the natural breaks are; cutting a story short can frustrate our listeners.

Fortunately, Luke has done us a favor and has given us some clear signals as to where we can "cut to commercial." For example, Luke often ends a section with a summary statement. In the following example, notice that the distance between summary statements is fairly small:

- 2:41: "So those who received his word were baptized, and there were added that day about three thousand souls."[1]
- 2:47: "And the Lord added to their number day by day those who were being saved."
- 5:42: "And every day, in the temple and from house to house, they did not cease teaching and preaching that the Christ is Jesus."
- 6:7: "And the word of God continued to increase, and the number of disciples multiplied greatly in Jerusalem, and a great many of the priests became obedient to the faith."

However, in the next four examples, the units are quite large:

- 8:40: "But Philip found himself at Azotus, and as he passed through he preached the gospel to all the towns until he came to Caesarea."
- 9:31: "So the church throughout all Judea and Galilee and Samaria had peace and was being built up. And walking in the fear of the Lord and in the comfort of the Holy Spirit, it multiplied."

1. Scripture quotations in this chapter are from the ESV.

- 12:24: "But the word of God increased and multiplied."
- 13:52: "And the disciples were filled with joy and with the Holy Spirit."

I've tried to divide the preaching units according to where I perceive Luke's natural breaks to be. Many of them are quite clear; some of them are not. If you decide to break one of the larger units into two smaller units, be sure to make the break where there is an appropriate subject/complement in both units. I have divided the twenty-eight chapters into thirty-four preaching units.

Getting the Subject, Complement, Exegetical Idea, and Homiletical Idea

Acts 1:1-14

SUBJECT: How were Jesus's disciples to carry out the mission he entrusted to them?

COMPLEMENT: In accordance with God's time line through the power of the Holy Spirit.

EXEGETICAL IDEA: Jesus's disciples were to carry out the mission that he entrusted to them in accordance with God's time line through the power of the Holy Spirit.

HOMILETICAL IDEA: Jesus empowers us to carry out his plans in his time.

Acts 1:15-26

SUBJECT: How were the disciples to replace Judas so that there were twelve apostles to lead God's mission?

COMPLEMENT: Through prayer and the casting of lots as they choose from among those who had followed Jesus since his baptism.

EXEGETICAL IDEA: The disciples were to replace Judas, so that there were twelve apostles to lead God's mission, through prayer and the casting of lots as they choose from among those who had followed Jesus since his baptism.

HOMILETICAL IDEA: We can trust that God has already prepared the leaders we need to achieve what he wants.

Acts 2:1-41

SUBJECT: What happened when Jesus's disciples were filled with the Holy Spirit on the day of Pentecost?

COMPLEMENT: The Scriptures were fulfilled; the crucified, risen, and exalted Christ was proclaimed; and three thousand people were saved and baptized.

EXEGETICAL IDEA: When Jesus's disciples were filled with the Holy Spirit on the day of Pentecost, the Scriptures were fulfilled; the crucified, risen, and exalted Christ was proclaimed; and three thousand people were saved and baptized.

HOMILETICAL IDEA: God fills us with his Spirit so that Christ can be powerfully and persuasively proclaimed.

Acts 2:42-47

SUBJECT: What happened when Jesus's disciples devoted themselves to the apostles' teaching, fellowship, shared meals, and prayers?

COMPLEMENT: They were unified, their witness was strengthened, their material needs were met, God received praise, and more people were saved.

EXEGETICAL IDEA: When Jesus's disciples devoted themselves to the apostles' teaching, fellowship, shared meals, and prayers, they were unified, their witness was strengthened, their material needs were met, God received praise, and people were saved.

HOMILETICAL IDEA: When we pursue God and healthy relationships with one another, our missional reach grows.

Acts 3

SUBJECT: How did God confirm that the disciples had been empowered to carry on the ministry of Jesus?

COMPLEMENT: The healing of the lame man in the name of Jesus and the offer of forgiveness of sins to the Jews of Jerusalem.

EXEGETICAL IDEA: God confirmed that the disciples had been empowered to carry on the ministry of Jesus through the healing of the lame in the name of Jesus and the offer of forgiveness of sins to the Jews in Jerusalem.

HOMILETICAL IDEA: God's mission is carried out as we minister in the name of Jesus.

Acts 4:1-31

SUBJECT: What happened when the disciples boldly proclaimed Jesus as the Messiah and Savior?

COMPLEMENT: They faced opposition and arrest and were empowered to continue boldly proclaiming the truth.

EXEGETICAL IDEA: When the disciples boldly proclaimed Jesus as the Messiah and Savior, they faced opposition and arrest and were empowered to continue boldly proclaiming the truth.

HOMILETICAL IDEA: God gives us what we need to boldly proclaim what he wants.

Acts 4:32–5:11

SUBJECT: How did God provide for the needy and protect the unity of his church?

COMPLEMENT: Through the gracious generosity of others and the exposure and expulsion of liars.

EXEGETICAL IDEA: God provided for the needy and protected the unity of his church through the gracious generosity of others and the exposure and expulsion of liars.

HOMILETICAL IDEA: God powerfully protects and graciously provides for his church.

Acts 5:12–42

SUBJECT: What happened when the disciples defied the local authorities and continued to joyfully and boldly proclaim Jesus?

COMPLEMENT: They were arrested and divinely delivered so that they could continue to bear witness to the risen Jesus.

EXEGETICAL IDEA: When the disciples defied the local authorities and continued to joyfully and boldly proclaim Jesus, they were arrested and divinely delivered so that they could continue to bear witness to the risen Jesus.

HOMILETICAL IDEA: When our testimony brings trouble, we can boldly and joyfully proclaim Jesus because God is with us.

Acts 6:1–7

SUBJECT: How did the apostles wisely handle the complexities of growth so that they could continue focusing on their primary responsibilities of prayer and the ministry of the word?

COMPLEMENT: By appointing new leaders to focus on new responsibilities that were necessary for the unity of the church.

EXEGETICAL IDEA: The apostles wisely handled the complexities of growth so that they could continue focusing on their primary responsibilities of prayer and the ministry of the word by appointing new leaders to focus on new responsibilities that were necessary for the unity of the church.

HOMILETICAL IDEA: Shared ministry protects the unity of the church and the ministry of the word.

Acts 6:8–8:3

SUBJECT: When the Jewish religious leaders tried to stop Stephen's Spirit-empowered ministry by arresting him, trying him, and stoning him, how did he respond?

COMPLEMENT: He uncompromisingly proclaimed Jesus and asked God to forgive those who were murdering him.

EXEGETICAL IDEA: When the Jewish religious leaders tried to stop Stephen's Spirit-empowered ministry by arresting him, trying him, and stoning him, he uncompromisingly proclaimed Jesus and asked God to forgive those who were murdering him.

HOMILETICAL IDEA: The Spirit empowers us to be firm with the gospel and to forgive our enemies.

Acts 8:4–25

SUBJECT: How did the gospel break through ethnic barriers and reach the hostile culture of Samaria?

COMPLEMENT: God empowered his disciples and gave his Spirit.

EXEGETICAL IDEA: The gospel broke through ethnic barriers and reached the hostile culture of Samaria as God empowered his disciples and gave his Spirit.

HOMILETICAL IDEA: Hostility can become hospitality through the power of the gospel.

Acts 8:26–40

SUBJECT: How did the gospel reach an Ethiopian eunuch?

COMPLEMENT: God sovereignly prepared the way for an obedient Philip to share it.

EXEGETICAL IDEA: The gospel reached an Ethiopian eunuch as God sovereignly prepared the way for Philip to share it.

HOMILETICAL IDEA: God puts us in the right place at the right time to be his witness.

Acts 9:1–31

SUBJECT: How did Saul, a zealous persecutor of the church, become a passionate disciple of Jesus and be welcomed into the new people of God?

COMPLEMENT: Jesus revealed himself to Saul, and his plans for Saul to Ananias, through visions.

EXEGETICAL IDEA: Saul, a zealous persecutor of the church, became a passionate disciple of Jesus and was welcomed into the new people of God because Jesus revealed himself to Saul, and his plans for Saul to Ananias, through visions.

HOMILETICAL IDEA: God is able to turn the worst enemies into the staunchest allies.

Acts 9:32-43

SUBJECT: Why did God work through Peter to heal Aeneas and raise Tabitha from the dead?

COMPLEMENT: To authenticate Peter's preaching of the gospel.

EXEGETICAL IDEA: God worked through Peter to heal Aeneas and raise Tabitha from the dead to authenticate Peter's preaching of the gospel.

HOMILETICAL IDEA: God's power works through us to authenticate his message.

Acts 10:1-11:18

SUBJECT: How did God reveal that salvation is available to all peoples?

COMPLEMENT: Through visions to Cornelius and Peter and the gifting of his Holy Spirit to the gentiles.

EXEGETICAL IDEA: God revealed that salvation is available to all peoples through visions to Cornelius and Peter and the gifting of the Holy Spirit to the gentiles.

HOMILETICAL IDEA: There is no "them" in God's family.

Acts 11:19-30

SUBJECT: How did God empower his disciples to carry out his mission farther and farther away from Jerusalem?

COMPLEMENT: Through the preaching of the word, ministry partnerships, and the solidarity of churches.

EXEGETICAL IDEA: God empowered his disciples to carry out his mission farther and farther away from Jerusalem through the preaching of the word, ministry partnerships, and the solidarity of churches.

HOMILETICAL IDEA: God uses preaching and partnerships to reach the world.

Acts 12

SUBJECT: How was powerful Herod's attempt to prevent God's Word from spreading thwarted?

COMPLEMENT: God miraculously delivered Peter and judged Herod.

EXEGETICAL IDEA: Powerful Herod's attempt to prevent God's Word from spreading was thwarted as God miraculously delivered Peter and judged Herod.

HOMILETICAL IDEA: The most powerful leaders on earth can't stop the spread of heaven.

Acts 13

SUBJECT: What happened when Paul and Barnabas were sent on their first missionary journey to those who were receptive to their message?

COMPLEMENT: The Holy Spirit empowered them through the church in Antioch who sent them, and the Jews opposed them while the gentiles joyfully received the word of the Lord.

EXEGETICAL IDEA: When Paul and Barnabas were sent on their first missionary journey to those who were receptive to their message, the Holy Spirit empowered them through the church in Antioch who sent them, and the Jews opposed them while the gentiles joyfully received the word of the Lord.

HOMILETICAL IDEA: God sends us to all, but only some accept the delivery.

Acts 14

SUBJECT: How did Paul and his team respond to increasingly hostile opposition?

COMPLEMENT: By pointing people to God with relentless persistence.

EXEGETICAL IDEA: Paul and his team responded to increasingly hostile opposition by pointing people to God with relentless persistence.

HOMILETICAL IDEA: Faithfulness is our concern, but fruitfulness is up to God.

Acts 15:1-33

SUBJECT: What did the early church determine about whether gentiles needed to become Jews in order to be Christians?

COMPLEMENT: Faith in Jesus and the grace of God are what make all people Christians, and this was confirmed by the gift of the Holy Spirit to the gentiles.

EXEGETICAL IDEA: The early church determined that gentiles didn't need to become Jews in order to be Christians because faith in Jesus and the grace of God are what make all people Christians, and this was confirmed by the gift of the Holy Spirit to the gentiles.

HOMILETICAL IDEA: The grace we receive is the grace we're to give.

Acts 15:35–16:5

SUBJECT: What happened when the mission was threatened because of an irreconcilable difference over strategy between Paul and Barnabas?

COMPLEMENT: God provided a new partnership for Paul to carry out his mission.

EXEGETICAL IDEA: When the mission was threatened because of an irreconcilable difference over strategy between Paul and Barnabas, God provided a new partnership for Paul to carry out his mission.

HOMILETICAL IDEA: Sometimes we have to divide in order to conquer.

Acts 16:6–40

SUBJECT: What happened when the mission moved from Asia Minor to Europe as increasing persecution and difficulties prevented the spread of the gospel?

COMPLEMENT: God sustained Paul and Silas through social, cultural, demonic, political, and legal difficulties.

EXEGETICAL IDEA: When the mission moved from Asia Minor to Europe as increasing persecution and difficulties prevented the spread of the gospel, God sustained Paul and Silas through social, cultural, demonic, political, and legal difficulties.

HOMILETICAL IDEA: The power of darkness is no match for the power of God.

Acts 17:1–15

SUBJECT: How did the word of the Lord reach the upper socioeconomic and educated class of people?

COMPLEMENT: God worked through Paul's reasoned and persuasive preaching.

EXEGETICAL IDEA: The word of the Lord reached the upper socioeconomic and educated class of people as God worked through Paul's reasoned and persuasive preaching.

HOMILETICAL IDEA: The gospel isn't just true; it's also reasonable.

Acts 17:16–34

SUBJECT: How did Paul engage the brightest philosophical minds in Greece?

COMPLEMENT: By speaking truth about God, human beings, the world, and the gospel.

EXEGETICAL IDEA: Paul engaged the brightest philosophical minds in Greece by speaking truth about God, human beings, the world, and the gospel.

HOMILETICAL IDEA: A culturally relevant portrait of God is a powerful apologetic.

Acts 18:1-23

SUBJECT: How did God encourage Paul after he arrived in Corinth alone?

COMPLEMENT: By giving him three specific and encouraging signs (18:2, 8, 9).

EXEGETICAL IDEA: God encouraged Paul after he arrived in Corinth alone by giving him three specific and encouraging signs.

HOMILETICAL IDEA: God gives us the encouragement we need to persevere in his task.

Acts 18:24-20:1

SUBJECT: How does Luke reveal Paul as a model missionary in Paul's last mission work in Ephesus before he was arrested?

COMPLEMENT: He was one who, empowered by the Holy Spirit, corrected inadequate theology, preached boldly, and overcame opposition, and whose ministry continues to impact society at large.[2]

EXEGETICAL IDEA: Luke reveals Paul as a model missionary in Paul's last mission work in Ephesus before he was arrested in that he was one who, empowered by the Holy Spirit, corrected inadequate theology, preached boldly, and overcame opposition, and whose ministry continues to impact society at large.

HOMILETICAL IDEA: Our mission is daunting, but the impact is lasting through the power of the Holy Spirit.

Acts 20:2-38

SUBJECT: How did Paul encourage those he had loved and raised in Christ as his arrest drew near?

COMPLEMENT: By commending them to God and the word of his grace, which was able to build them up and sustain them.

EXEGETICAL IDEA: Paul encouraged those he had loved and raised in Christ as his arrest drew near by commending them to God and the word of his grace, which was able to build them up and sustain them.

HOMILETICAL IDEA: The best that we can do for those we love is to point them to the God who loves them even more.

2. Eckhard Schnabel, *Acts*, Zondervan Exegetical Commentary on the New Testament (Grand Rapids: Zondervan, 2012), 773.

Acts 21:1-14

SUBJECT: How did Paul respond when he found out that arrest and imprisonment awaited him in Jerusalem?

COMPLEMENT: With a resolute willingness to suffer for the name of Jesus.

EXEGETICAL IDEA: When Paul found out that arrest and imprisonment awaited him in Jerusalem, he responded with a resolute willingness to suffer for the name of Jesus.

HOMILETICAL IDEA: Knowing that God's mission will not be stopped, when ministry means sacrifice we can boldly press on.

Acts 21:15-26

SUBJECT: Why did Paul submit to the request of the leaders of the Jerusalem church to publicly show his observance of the law?

COMPLEMENT: In order to preserve the unity of the church.

EXEGETICAL IDEA: Paul submitted to the request of the leaders of the Jerusalem church to publicly show his observance of the law in order to preserve the unity of the church.

HOMILETICAL IDEA: For the sake of the gospel, unity trumps individual freedoms.

Acts 21:27-23:35

SUBJECT: How did God use Paul's arrest in Jerusalem to accomplish his plans?

COMPLEMENT: It became an opportunity for Paul to preach the gospel to the Jews living in Jerusalem.

EXEGETICAL IDEA: God used Paul's arrest in Jerusalem to accomplish his plans as it became an opportunity for Paul to preach the gospel to the Jews living in Jerusalem.

HOMILETICAL IDEA: Because God is ultimately in control, our greatest opposition can become our greatest opportunity.

Acts 24

SUBJECT: How did Paul respond to unjust treatment and imprisonment at Caesarea?

COMPLEMENT: By taking the opportunity to preach the gospel to a Roman governor, Felix.

EXEGETICAL IDEA: Paul responded to unjust treatment and imprisonment at Caesarea by taking the opportunity to preach the gospel to a Roman governor, Felix.

HOMILETICAL IDEA: If we're looking for a way to share the gospel, God will open unexpected doors.

Acts 25-26

SUBJECT: What did Paul, in his final speech, want people to know about God and Jesus?

COMPLEMENT: That God raises people from the dead, controls history, and offers salvation to all, and that Jesus is the risen Christ.

EXEGETICAL IDEA: Paul, in his final speech, wanted people to know that God raises people from the dead, controls history, and offers salvation to all, and that Jesus is the risen Christ.

HOMILETICAL IDEA: With confidence and clarity we can tell people about God and what he has done through Jesus.

Acts 27:1-28:16

SUBJECT: What did Paul's tumultuous voyage to Rome reveal about God?

COMPLEMENT: God is sovereign over nature, faithful to his promises, and committed to his missionaries and the message they proclaim.

EXEGETICAL IDEA: Paul's tumultuous voyage to Rome revealed that God is sovereign over nature, faithful to his promises, and committed to his missionaries and the message they proclaim.

HOMILETICAL IDEA: The more we experience God's faithfulness, the more joyfully committed we'll be to his mission.

Acts 28:17-31

SUBJECT: Why could the disciples of Jesus be confident that their witness would reach the ends of the earth?

COMPLEMENT: God fulfilled his promise to Paul that he would safely reach Rome, the heart of the Roman Empire, where he could proclaim the kingdom of God and teach about the Lord Jesus Christ with all boldness and without hindrance.

EXEGETICAL IDEA: Disciples of Jesus could be confident that their witness would reach the ends of the earth because God fulfilled his promise to Paul that he would safely reach Rome, the heart of the Roman Empire, where he could proclaim the kingdom of God and teach about the Lord Jesus Christ with all boldness and without hindrance.

HOMILETICAL IDEA: As long as we're willing, God will empower us to be his witnesses.

Difficult Passages/Verses

Acts contains many difficult passages, as any good commentary will point out. The major interpretive issue that leads to many of these difficulties is deciding whether Acts is generally *prescriptive* or *descriptive*. Is Luke primarily concerned with telling us what happened or with telling us what happens. Obviously, there are elements of both. However, in light of Luke's purpose I tend toward the view that Acts is primarily *descriptive*.

For example, let's look at the portrayal of tongues in Acts. If we take Acts to be *prescriptive*, then one could argue that unless one speaks in tongues, one is not filled with the Spirit (though this is problematic in light of Acts 8, where the Spirit is given and there is no record of tongues spoken). If, however, we take Acts to be *descriptive*, then tongues is an authenticating sign given in a particular setting. In each of the three instances where tongues are mentioned, a different group of people is confirmed as part of the new covenant people of God: in Acts 2, on Pentecost, it's the apostles and disciples in the upper room; in Acts 10 it's the gentiles; in Acts 19 it's John's disciples.[3]

Additionally, there is the issue of what role our theological convictions (analogy of faith) should play in our interpretation of the text. While it is impossible to come to Acts with total objectivity, we do want to give the text priority to the extent that we are able. Whether one is Calvinist or Arminian, dispensational or covenantal, charismatic or Pentecostal, aim for the message of the text.

In order to tackle some of the theological issues that arise in Acts, it is acceptable, preferred even, to preach a few sermons on some of the more difficult and controversial issues, such as the role of miraculous gifts in the church today. This will free you to preach the main point of a passage without getting sidetracked on tangential issues.

---

3. I am not arguing here for cessationism; my point is simply that in Acts tongues seem to serve a specific authenticating purpose with regard to the identification of groups of people as being fully received into the new people of God.

Cultural Perspectives and Application

At the heart of Acts is the presence of the Holy Spirit. The Spirit is empowering God's people, uniting God's people, and sending God's people. In order for people to understand the significance of this, a preacher will want to help them understand how vicious the ethnic issues were between the Jews and the Samaritans and between the Jews and the gentiles. As miraculous as the healings, deliverances, and resurrections were, perhaps the greatest miracle was that Jews and gentiles were one people in Christ. This is a timely and relevant message for our culture today!

Another key point of application (and a corrective to certain pervasive perspectives in our culture today) is that the Holy Spirit is not given for personal gains. In fact, when that request is made, the person is just about struck dead (8:18–24). God's Spirit is concerned with God's priorities. People are empowered for mission, not for magic or fame or fulfillment.

In addition to empowering the church for mission, the Holy Spirit brings unity to the church. The story of Ananias and Sapphira (5:1–11) is terrifying. What was at stake was the unity of the early church. The Jerusalem Council (Acts 15) and Paul's return to Jerusalem in Acts 21 are two other stories that are focused on unity. A united church has the opportunity to be an inviting counterculture to the fractured and contentious world around us.

Finally, one of the key themes that runs through the book of Acts is encouragement. It seems that Barnabas's main function in the story is to highlight the power of encouragement. And Paul, as he made his various journeys, went out of his way to visit with his brothers and sisters in various cities in order to encourage them. Following Jesus is a team sport, and the best teammates are encouragers. Don't let the opportunity to highlight that message escape.

RECOMMENDED RESOURCES

Bock, Darrell L. *A Theology of Luke and Acts: God's Promised Program, Realized for All Nations*. Biblical Theology of the New Testament. Grand Rapids: Zondervan, 2012.

Schnabel, Eckhard J. *Acts*. Zondervan Exegetical Commentary on the New Testament. Grand Rapids: Zondervan, 2012.

Thompson, Alan J. *The Acts of the Risen Lord Jesus: Luke's Account of God's Unfolding Plan*. New Studies in Biblical Theology. Downers Grove, IL: InterVarsity, 2011.

Romans

CALVIN W. CHOI

The Big Idea of Romans

The central theme of Romans is the righteousness of God (1:16–17). Paul spends the rest of the book defining and elaborating on that theme and explaining how the righteousness of God in Christ can be obtained (chaps. 1–11) and experienced in the life of the believers (chaps. 12–16).

SUBJECT: What is the gospel Paul wants the Romans to believe?

COMPLEMENT: God's redemptive work is planned, accomplished, and applied on the believers' faith by grace, whereby God's righteousness is imputed through Christ by faith so that the elect believers, in response, will live a life led by love and humble obedience to Christ.

EXEGETICAL IDEA: The gospel Paul wants the Romans to believe is that God's redemptive work planned, accomplished, and applied on the believers' faith by grace, whereby God's righteousness is imputed through Christ by faith so that the elect believers, in response, will live a life led by love and humble obedience to Christ.

HOMILETICAL IDEA: Sound doctrine results in sound living in Christ.

Selecting Preaching and Teaching Passages in Romans

The whole gamut of Christian doctrine is treated in Romans. For this reason, it has a wealth of homiletic material.

The book of Romans is often divided into three sections. In the first section (chaps. 1–8) Paul elaborates why God's justification through faith in Christ is indicative for the salvation of Jews and gentiles. Terms such as *justification* and *righteousness of God* play a key role in understanding Paul's gospel framework. In the second section (chaps. 9–11) Paul expounds further the righteousness of God in Christ in light of God's mysterious and ongoing redemptive work between Israel and gentiles. In the final section (chaps. 12–16) Paul demonstrates the fruit of the righteousness of God in the life of the believer.

Romans is saturated with key Christian doctrines, and every chapter is also replete with relevant and practical life applications. While the book can be preached thematically, expository preaching is most preferred. The key is not to rush through the book but to have major portions of Scripture divided well. It is almost impossible to cover a chapter in one sitting.

Getting the Subject, Complement, Exegetical Idea, and Homiletical Idea

Romans 1:1–7

SUBJECT: Where does Paul find the believers' identity and calling?

COMPLEMENT: Rooted in the gospel of Christ.

EXEGETICAL IDEA: Paul finds the believers' identity and calling rooted in the gospel of Christ.

HOMILETICAL IDEA: We are called to belong, be loved, and be his saints.

Romans 2:1–16

SUBJECT: What makes God's judgment righteous?

COMPLEMENT: No human righteousness can measure up to God's holiness.

EXEGETICAL IDEA: God's judgment is righteous because no human righteousness can measure up to God's holiness.

HOMILETICAL IDEA: Unless we come to grips with our own sinfulness, we will never come to grips with his amazing grace.

Romans 2:17–3:20

SUBJECT: What is Paul's message to the Jews?

COMPLEMENT: No one is righteous and exempt from God's judgment.

EXEGETICAL IDEA: Paul's message to the Jews is that no one is righteous and exempt from God's judgment.

HOMILETICAL IDEA: Except Christ, all other ground is sinking sand.

Romans 4:1-17

SUBJECT: Why is Paul concerned about the Jews' view of salvation?

COMPLEMENT: Jews believed that there is one way of salvation for them and another for the gentiles.

EXEGETICAL IDEA: Paul is concerned about the Jews' view of salvation because they believed that there is one way of salvation for them and another for the gentiles.

HOMILETICAL IDEA: God's righteousness through Christ is the only way to be saved.

Romans 5:1-2

SUBJECT: What do the Roman believers have as a result of justification by faith in Christ?

COMPLEMENT: Peace and access to his presence.

EXEGETICAL IDEA: The Roman believers have, as a result of justification by faith in Christ, peace and access to his presence.

HOMILETICAL IDEA: Are you part of Paul's "we"?

Romans 6:1-11

SUBJECT: How are the Roman believers united to Christ?

COMPLEMENT: In his death and resurrection.

EXEGETICAL IDEA: The Roman believers are united to Christ in his death and resurrection.

HOMILETICAL IDEA: We are under new management in Christ.

Romans 7:1-6

SUBJECT: What is the role of the law for the believer?

COMPLEMENT: The law is not a prerequisite to salvation but a motivation for sanctification.

EXEGETICAL IDEA: For the believer, the role of the law is not a prerequisite to salvation but a motivation for sanctification.

HOMILETICAL IDEA: Law convicts and directs us to Christ our redeemer.

Romans 8:1-4

SUBJECT: Why are those who are in Christ never condemned?

COMPLEMENT: Because the triune God—the Father, the Son, the Holy Spirit—has fulfilled the work of salvation.

EXEGETICAL IDEA: Those who are in Christ are never condemned because the triune God—the Father, the Son, the Holy Spirit—has fulfilled the work of salvation.

HOMILETICAL IDEA: Redemption is arranged by the Father, accomplished by the Son, and applied by the Holy Spirit.

Romans 9:1-5

SUBJECT: Why does Paul have such longing for his fellow countrymen?

COMPLEMENT: Because he wants them to recognize Jesus as their Messiah.

EXEGETICAL IDEA: Paul has such longing for his fellow countrymen because he wants them to recognize Jesus as their Messiah.

HOMILETICAL IDEA: We have great pain for the lost souls.

Romans 10:14-21

SUBJECT: Why is there no excuse for the Jews not to believe the gospel?

COMPLEMENT: Because God has sent preachers to preach the good news generation after generation so that they can respond in faith, not rebellion.

EXEGETICAL IDEA: There is no excuse for the Jews not to believe the gospel because God has sent preachers to preach the good news generation after generation so that they can respond in faith, not rebellion.

HOMILETICAL IDEA: There's no excuse for not believing and sharing the good news of Christ.

Romans 11:1-5

SUBJECT: Is God through with Israel?

COMPLEMENT: No—there is a remnant chosen by God's sovereign will.

EXEGETICAL IDEA: God is not through with Israel because there is a remnant chosen by God's sovereign will.

HOMILETICAL IDEA: By grace God has chosen us to respond in faith.

Romans 12:17-21

SUBJECT: How are believers to respond when nonbelievers persecute them?

COMPLEMENT: By not getting even but rather doing good for the sake of witnessing.

EXEGETICAL IDEA: Believers are to respond when nonbelievers persecute them by not getting even but rather doing good for the sake of witnessing.

HOMILETICAL IDEA: "Vengeance is mine," says God, "you pay back with the gospel."

Romans 13:1-7

SUBJECT: How are believers to respond to government authority?

COMPLEMENT: By submitting as good citizens because God has authorized leaders—whom God will hold accountable—to carry out justice.

EXEGETICAL IDEA: Believers are to respond to government authority by submitting as good citizens because God has authorized leaders—whom God will hold accountable—to carry out justice.

HOMILETICAL IDEA: Submit and pray for leaders, for God will hold them accountable.

Romans 14:1-4

SUBJECT: Why are believers called not to pass judgment on other believers?

COMPLEMENT: Because the Lord is their judge.

EXEGETICAL IDEA: Believers are called not to pass judgment on other believers because the Lord is their judge.

HOMILETICAL IDEA: Don't judge lest you be judged.

Romans 15:1-7

SUBJECT: Why does Paul say it is important to stay united?

COMPLEMENT: To promote Christ's love, selflessness, and humility by putting others first.

EXEGETICAL IDEA: Paul says it is important to stay united in order to promote Christ's love, selflessness, and humility by putting others first.

HOMILETICAL IDEA: Let's be a "Jesus first, others second, me third" church for God's glory.

Romans 16:1-16

SUBJECT: Why does Paul list these names at the end?

COMPLEMENT: To show that what made his ministry possible was God's grace manifested through the collective body of these faithful and humble servants around him.

EXEGETICAL IDEA: Paul lists these names at the end to show that what made his ministry possible was God's grace manifested through the collective body of faithful and humble servants around him.

HOMILETICAL IDEA: God uses the ordinary to do the extraordinary for his kingdom.

Difficult Passages/Verses

To Paul, the gospel is not a New Testament phenomenon but finds its trace in the Old Testament. Paul shows how the gospel was already effected in the Old Testament through God's sovereign grace and election. The doctrines of God's sovereignty and election are the two undergirding doctrines that some preachers and teachers might find difficult to embrace. Take time to explain and explore how these doctrines are key and consistent throughout Scripture.

Scholars are divided on whether the person mentioned in 7:13–25 is Paul himself or some other believer. Regardless, it is clear that the believer's battle with sin continues even after conversion. We must constantly flee from sin and remain in Christ.

Paul contrasts extensively the roles of the law and the gospel, and it will be helpful to study Paul's use of the law in his other epistles.

Many might think we know the gospel enough. Romans is a book that proves us wrong. Paul invites us to realize how limited and shallow our understanding is, and how profound, how deep, and how unbelievable God's grace is—we will never fully know, in this life at least.

Cultural Perspectives and Application

In an age of cultural pluralism where different "gospels" were preached and taught in Rome, as it is now, Romans presents the true gospel with clarity and conviction and declutters our parochial and individualistic understanding of the gospel.

To Paul, the gospel is not so much about the love of God as our current culture tends to emphasize. To be sure, the love of God is part of it. But the gospel is the righteousness of God through which we are made right with God. Paul is not too quick to use the words "love of God" until he demonstrates how that love is manifested in God's act of justification.

Romans is a book that confronts us all, including skeptics and atheists, and unashamedly declares no one righteous. Nevertheless, it doesn't leave us there but calls us to a righteous God who provides the means of salvation through his beloved Son, Jesus Christ.

No other book deals with Christian doctrine more systematically and effectively than Romans. In an age of pragmatism, Romans teaches why sound doctrine is essential to sound Christian living.

Some applications include the following: a life of freedom in Christ is not the absence of obedience but a life of obedience to Christ (6:15–23); the more we realize how sinful we are, the more we realize how amazing God's grace is for us (7:1–12); and how we can emulate God in choosing to be merciful and compassionate toward others who may not "deserve" such grace (9:14–18).

RECOMMENDED RESOURCES

Moo, Douglas J. *The Epistle to the Romans*. The New International Commentary on the New Testament. Grand Rapids: Eerdmans, 1996.

Morris, Leon. *The Epistle to the Romans*. The Pillar New Testament Commentary. Grand Rapids: Eerdmans, 1988.

1 Corinthians

JOEL C. GREGORY

The Big Idea of 1 Corinthians

God's troubled but triumphant church can and will move toward maturity in Christ through corrective measures empowered by the Spirit and revealed in the Word.

SUBJECT: What is the apostle Paul's message to the Corinthian church?

COMPLEMENT: In the face of doctrinal and behavioral challenges, the willing church can find a way forward to Christian maturity.

EXEGETICAL IDEA: The apostle Paul's message to the Corinthian church is that in the face of doctrinal and behavioral challenges, the willing church can find a way forward to Christian maturity.

HOMILETICAL IDEA: The triumphant church moves toward maturity.

Selecting Preaching and Teaching Passages in 1 Corinthians

To go through the entire letter of 1 Corinthians pericope by pericope for a preaching or teaching series would be quite lengthy. Therefore, I would recommend preaching the first four chapters of the letter in one sermon regarding disunity in the church and then preach/teach each whole chapter for the remaining portions of the letter. I acknowledge that it's a lot of material to cover if you go through an entire chapter at a time, but Paul's instructions are straightforward and the main overarching principles will be able to be presented to your listeners.

482

Getting the Subject, Complement, Exegetical Idea, and Homiletical Idea

1 Corinthians 1-4

SUBJECT: What do divisions in the Corinthian church reveal?

COMPLEMENT: A fundamental misunderstanding of the most basic facts of the Christian experience.

EXEGETICAL IDEA: The divisions in the Corinthian church reveal a fundamental misunderstanding of the most basic facts of the Christian experience.

HOMILETICAL IDEA: When a church is divided, it demonstrates a basic misunderstanding of the cross and Christian wisdom.

1 Corinthians 5

SUBJECT: How does Paul tell the Corinthian church to handle the case of unthinkable immorality?

COMPLEMENT: In a way that cuts off all relationship with the offender and prays that restoration will be the result.

EXEGETICAL IDEA: Paul tells the Corinthian church to handle the case of unthinkable immorality in a way that cuts off all relationship with the offender and prays that restoration will be the result.

HOMILETICAL IDEA: The church today needs to recover biblical discipline lest the church itself be polluted and at the same time offend even the outside world.

1 Corinthians 6

SUBJECT: How does Paul tell the Corinthian Christians to settle grievances with one another?

COMPLEMENT: Inside the church by Christian arbitration, rather than dragging one another into public civil court and shaming the cause of Christ.

EXEGETICAL IDEA: Paul tells the Corinthian Christians to settle grievances with one another inside the church by Christian arbitration, rather than dragging one another into public civil court and shaming the cause of Christ.

HOMILETICAL IDEA: You should so relate to the body of Christ that matters between members should be settled inside the church rather than in public civil litigation.

1 Corinthians 7

SUBJECT: What does Paul tell the Corinthian church are the principles of marriage and singleness for Christians?

COMPLEMENT: It is best for Christians to remain as they are when they come to Christ, but if they lack self-control, it is best to marry only Christians.

EXEGETICAL IDEA: Regarding marriage and singleness for Christians, Paul tells the Corinthian church that it is best for Christians to remain as they are when they come to Christ, but if they lack self-control it is best to marry only Christians.

HOMILETICAL IDEA: If you have the gift of celibacy, you may stay single for the sake of Christian service; those without that gift should marry other Christians.

1 Corinthians 8

SUBJECT: How does Paul say a mature Christian should behave when confronted with the choice of participating in an act that causes a weaker Christian spiritual trauma?

COMPLEMENT: He or she should exercise the discretion to give up the right to do anything that would harm the other.

EXEGETICAL IDEA: Paul says a mature Christian, when confronted with the choice of participating in an act that causes a weaker Christian trauma, should exercise the discretion to give up the right to do anything that would harm the other.

HOMILETICAL IDEA: Our freedom as Christians is limited by its impact on a weaker Christian observing our behavior.

1 Corinthians 9

SUBJECT: How does Paul instruct the Corinthian church that a disciplined Christian should serve?

COMPLEMENT: As one who forgoes rights and privileges in the effort to edify the struggling believer and win those outside the faith, as Paul himself did.

EXEGETICAL IDEA: Paul instructs the Corinthian church that a disciplined Christian should serve as one who forgoes rights and privileges in the effort to edify the struggling believer and win those outside the faith, as Paul himself did.

HOMILETICAL IDEA: We can afford to give up our privileges in order to be servants building up the body of Christ.

1 Corinthians 10

SUBJECT: What does Paul tell the Corinthian church is the goal in all Christian behavior?

COMPLEMENT: To live a life that does only those things that glorify God.

EXEGETICAL IDEA: Paul tells the Corinthian church that the goal in all Christian behavior is to live a life that does only those things that glorify God.

HOMILETICAL IDEA: Your life should defer to others in every way that brings about the glory of God.

1 Corinthians 11

SUBJECT: What does Paul tell the Corinthian church is the governing principle for conduct when the church gathers?

COMPLEMENT: Members of the body should attire themselves in an appropriate way for the culture without giving offense and should be sensitive to the needs of all members.

EXEGETICAL IDEA: Paul tells the Corinthian church that the governing principle for conduct when the church gathers is that members of the body should attire themselves in an appropriate way for the culture without giving offense and should be sensitive to the needs of all members.

HOMILETICAL IDEA: We can live with the sensitivity to dress ourselves and conduct ourselves with appropriate deference to the needs of all in the church gathering.

1 Corinthians 12

SUBJECT: What does Paul instruct the Corinthian church as to the nature of spiritual gifts and office in the church?

COMPLEMENT: God sovereignly gifts all believers for the building up of the church and no believer has no gift or all the gifts.

EXEGETICAL IDEA: As to the nature of spiritual gifts and office in the church, Paul instructs the Corinthian church that God sovereignly gifts all believers for the building up of the church and no believer has no gift or all the gifts.

HOMILETICAL IDEA: God has given you at least one gift for the building up of the body of Christ, but you do not have all the gifts.

1 Corinthians 13

SUBJECT: What does Paul tell the Corinthian church is the defining nature of Christian love?

COMPLEMENT: It is not an emotion but rather is always seeking the highest good of the other person.

EXEGETICAL IDEA: Paul tells the Corinthian church that the defining nature of Christian love is that it is not an emotion but rather is always seeking the highest good of the other person.

HOMILETICAL IDEA: We can demonstrate our Christian love by always seeking the highest good of the other person, regardless of emotions or circumstances.

1 Corinthians 14

SUBJECT: How does Paul instruct the Corinthians regarding the nature of orderly worship?

COMPLEMENT: Spiritual gifts are to be exercised with the mindset of promoting order and peace among God's people.

EXEGETICAL IDEA: Paul instructs the Corinthians regarding the nature of orderly worship that spiritual gifts are to be exercised with the mindset of promoting order and peace among God's people.

HOMILETICAL IDEA: Use your spiritual gift in the gathering of God's people so that you will reflect biblical order and self-control.

1 Corinthians 15

SUBJECT: What does Paul tell the Corinthian church regarding the resurrected body of the believer?

COMPLEMENT: It can be explained only by the power of God, who will give each believer a body fitted for eternal life.

EXEGETICAL IDEA: Paul tells the Corinthian church regarding the resurrected body of the believer that it can be explained only by the power of God, who will give each believer a body fitted for eternal life.

HOMILETICAL IDEA: At the resurrection we will be given bodies fitted for eternity just as God has given us bodies fitted for time.

1 Corinthians 16

SUBJECT: What does Paul tell the Corinthians is God's will for stewardship of life and time?

COMPLEMENT: God intends people who believe in the resurrection to give in a timely and proportionate way.

EXEGETICAL IDEA: Paul tells the Corinthians God's will for stewardship of life and time is that God intends people who believe in the resurrection to give in a timely and proportionate way.

HOMILETICAL IDEA: Manage your money and minutes well.

Difficult Passages/Verses

First Corinthians 7 presents several challenges. What is the nature of platonic, celibate cohabitation? It may be that some believers assumed a false discipline of denying each other sexual fulfillment, thinking this would please God. Paul addresses that clearly in the negative. There is also a mystery in Paul's reference to "the present distress" (7:26 ESV). This refers to some trial, persecution, or situation related to the church at large or the Corinthian church.

First Corinthians 15 must be understood against the backdrop of the Greek view of the immortality of the soul. The Greek word for body is *sōma*, and the word for tomb is *sēma*. The Greeks had a saying, "*Sōma sēma*." The goal in death was to get the good soul out of the bad body. The Christian view of bodily resurrection was foolishness to the Greeks. It required nothing less than the power of God to bring it about.

Cultural Perspectives and Application

No letter of Paul touches with such fullness the spectrum of church problems that existed in principle both then and now. Divisions over leadership, the treatment of immorality in church discipline, nagging questions about marriage, doubtful areas of conduct, the use of spiritual gifts, and the possibility of bodily resurrection are just as animated today as they were then.

As an example, consider the consumption of alcohol. There are entire Christian denominations that are defined either by abstinence or moderate use of alcohol. One application of Paul's principles is simple: if you are in the presence of anyone who is troubled or could stumble by the use of alcohol, even though it gives you no problem, refuse to drink it in their presence.

RECOMMENDED RESOURCES

Blomberg, Craig L. *1 Corinthians*. The NIV Application Commentary. Grand Rapids: Zondervan, 1995.

Garland, David E. *1 Corinthians*. Baker Exegetical Commentary on the New Testament. Grand Rapids: Baker Academic, 2003.

Vang, Preben. *1 Corinthians*. Teach the Text Commentary Series. Grand Rapids: Baker Books, 2014.

2 Corinthians

CASEY C. BARTON

The Big Idea of 2 Corinthians

Within the corpus of Paul's letters, 2 Corinthians may be the most deeply personal and painful. The apostle writes to a church that he established and that he loves. After his departure Paul's opponents moved in and led the church astray by criticizing Paul specifically as one whose life, ministry, speech, and suffering were weak and inauthentic, thereby invalidating his gospel. As a result, a significant number of the church abandoned Paul and the gospel he had preached in favor of a version of faith that reinforced the surrounding culture rather than calling for life transformation out of it. By the time 2 Corinthians was composed and delivered, a majority of those who had abandoned Paul's gospel had repented through the heart-wrenching ministry of Paul from afar and Titus in their presence. Paul writes this letter out of a broken heart with three specific goals: to defend his ministry as an apostle of Jesus Christ precisely because of God's power shown through his weakness, to encourage the repentant Corinthians in their return to faith, and to call his opponents and those still following them to repentance before his arrival. Here Paul writes with emotion, pain, and unvarnished honesty as he seeks to bring this church back to the gospel.[1]

SUBJECT: Why does Paul write this second letter to the Corinthian church?

---

1. See Scott J. Hafemann, *2 Corinthians*, The NIV Application Commentary (Grand Rapids: Zondervan, 2000), 19–36; Ernest Best, *Second Corinthians*, Interpretation (Louisville: Westminster John Knox, 1987), 1–6.

COMPLEMENT: To defend his apostolic ministry of God's power shown through weakness, calling his opponents to repentance and the repentant to faithfulness in Christ.

EXEGETICAL IDEA: Paul writes this second letter to the Corinthian church to defend his apostolic ministry of God's power shown through weakness, calling his opponents to repentance and the repentant to faithfulness in Christ.

HOMILETICAL IDEA: The gospel is God's power through human weakness, for the repentant and for the rebellious.

Selecting Preaching and Teaching Passages in 2 Corinthians

In his book *2 Corinthians*, Scott Hafemann outlines the book broadly along the textual lines of Paul's main arguments. After a customary greeting and prologue (1:1–11), Paul recounts his history with the Corinthians (1:12–2:11) and then launches into the body of his apologetic for his ministry and its application to the church. His argument proceeds in an apologetic for his own apostolic authority out of weakness (2:12–7:1), an application of his apologetic to the repentant (7:2–9:15), and an application of his apologetic to the rebellious (10:1–13:14).[2] Within this broader outline the preacher must delineate units of Paul's thought as she or he seeks to understand Paul in his context and for the present congregation.

Getting the Subject, Complement, Exegetical Idea, and Homiletical Idea

2 Corinthians 1:1-11

SUBJECT: For what does the apostle Paul praise God at the beginning of this letter to the Corinthians?

COMPLEMENT: That through his participation in the suffering of Christ he has experienced the comfort of God who raises the dead.

EXEGETICAL IDEA: The apostle Paul praises God at the beginning of this letter to the Corinthians that through his participation in the suffering of Christ he has experienced the comfort of God who raises the dead.

HOMILETICAL IDEA: Suffering in Christ is met with the comfort of God.

2 Corinthians 1:12-2:11

SUBJECT: Why does Paul say that he changed his plans to visit the Corinthians?

2. Hafemann, *2 Corinthians*, 37–39.

COMPLEMENT: To spare the church the pain of judgment, allowing them the opportunity to forgive the one who had repented of causing Paul's grief and the church's division.

EXEGETICAL IDEA: Paul says he changed his plans to visit the Corinthians in order to spare the church the pain of judgment, allowing them the opportunity to forgive the one who had repented of causing Paul's grief and the church's division.

HOMILETICAL IDEA: Together in Christ we forgive hurt and heal division.

2 Corinthians 2:12-3:3

SUBJECT: How does Paul defend his sufficiency as a minister of the gospel, even in the reality of his anxiety over Titus and the Corinthians?

COMPLEMENT: By explaining that he has been conquered by Christ and commissioned by God for the task, evidenced by the Spirit written on the Corinthians' hearts.

EXEGETICAL IDEA: Paul defends his sufficiency as a minister of the gospel, even in the reality of his anxiety over Titus and the Corinthians, by explaining that he has been conquered by Christ and commissioned by God for the task, evidenced by the Spirit written on the Corinthians' hearts.

HOMILETICAL IDEA: God's calling and Christ's conquering are the sufficiency for the gospel's work.

2 Corinthians 3:4-18

SUBJECT: Why does Paul say he has confidence in his sufficiency as a minister of God's new covenant?

COMPLEMENT: Because God's Spirit is the one who gloriously transforms from death to life, emboldening his proclamation.

EXEGETICAL IDEA: Paul says he has confidence in his sufficiency as a minister of God's new covenant because God's Spirit is the one who gloriously transforms from death to life, emboldening his proclamation.

HOMILETICAL IDEA: The Spirit transforms life gloriously, so we proclaim life confidently.

2 Corinthians 4:1-15

SUBJECT: How does Paul describe his ministry of the new covenant?

COMPLEMENT: As God's power shown through weak vessels enduring affliction, for the grace of many and the glory of God.

EXEGETICAL IDEA: Paul describes his ministry of the new covenant as God's power shown through weak vessels enduring affliction, for the grace of many and the glory of God.

HOMILETICAL IDEA: God's power through our fragility extends his grace and brings him glory.

2 Corinthians 4:16-5:10

SUBJECT: Why does Paul say he is able to endure the afflictions of his ministry?

COMPLEMENT: Because the hope beyond death is life eternal in Christ.

EXEGETICAL IDEA: Paul says that he is able to endure the afflictions of his ministry because the hope beyond death is life eternal in Christ.

HOMILETICAL IDEA: We endure the present because the hope beyond death is life with Christ.

2 Corinthians 5:11-6:2

SUBJECT: What does Paul urge the Corinthians to do as those who have received the death and resurrection of Jesus?

COMPLEMENT: To be reconciled to God and live as the new creatures God has made them to be in this day of salvation.

EXEGETICAL IDEA: Paul urges the Corinthians as those who have received the death and resurrection of Jesus to be reconciled to God and live as the new creatures God has made them to be in this day of salvation.

HOMILETICAL IDEA: Now is the time to be the new creature God has made you in Christ.

2 Corinthians 6:3-13

SUBJECT: What does Paul present as evidence for the legitimacy of his ministry in calling the Corinthians to repentance for rejecting his gospel?

COMPLEMENT: His endurance through hardships, grace, dire circumstances, and God's deliverance, for them, as a servant of God.

EXEGETICAL IDEA: As evidence for the legitimacy of his ministry in calling the Corinthians to repentance for rejecting his gospel, Paul presents his endurance through hardships, grace, dire circumstances, and God's deliverance, for them, as a servant of God.

HOMILETICAL IDEA: God's servants endure all they can for those they lovingly serve.

2 Corinthians 6:14–7:1

SUBJECT: Why does Paul command the Corinthians to separate themselves from those who have led them astray?

COMPLEMENT: Because the church as God's temple is to be pure, now as through all of God's history.

EXEGETICAL IDEA: Paul commands the Corinthians to separate themselves from those who have led them astray because the church as God's temple is to be pure, now as through all of God's history.

HOMILETICAL IDEA: Do everything you must to keep your faith pure.

2 Corinthians 7:2–16

SUBJECT: Why does Paul say that he rejoices over the Corinthians?

COMPLEMENT: Because his call to repentance led to repentance, restoring his confidence in the majority who had repented.

EXEGETICAL IDEA: Paul says that he rejoices over the Corinthians because his call to repentance led to repentance, restoring his confidence in the majority who had repented.

HOMILETICAL IDEA: Joy is the end of the painful process of repentance.

2 Corinthians 8:1–15

SUBJECT: Why does Paul call the Corinthians to give generously to the churches that are in need?

COMPLEMENT: Because generous giving to the needs of others is a mark of genuine love in the likeness of Christ.

EXEGETICAL IDEA: Paul calls the Corinthians to give generously to the churches that are in need because generous giving to the needs of others is a mark of genuine love in the likeness of Christ.

HOMILETICAL IDEA: Love genuinely by giving generously to meet the needs of others.

2 Corinthians 8:16–9:15

SUBJECT: How does Paul say the collection must be taken in Corinth?

COMPLEMENT: With integrity, uncoerced, and with generosity toward those in need, all in response to God's grace.

EXEGETICAL IDEA: Paul says the collection in Corinth must be taken with integrity, uncoerced, and with generosity toward those in need, all in response to God's grace.

HOMILETICAL IDEA: Give with joy and generosity for others' needs and God's glory.

2 Corinthians 10

SUBJECT: How does Paul assert his apostolic authority to his opponents in Corinth?

COMPLEMENT: By pointing to the fruit of his ministry in the Corinthians' faith, which itself is the commendation of God.

EXEGETICAL IDEA: Paul asserts his apostolic authority to his opponents in Corinth by pointing to the fruit of his ministry in the Corinthians' faith, which itself is the commendation of God.

HOMILETICAL IDEA: Authority for ministry is rooted only in the commendation of God's call.

2 Corinthians 11

SUBJECT: How does Paul call the remaining unrepentant Corinthians who sided with Paul's opponents to reject the "super-apostles" who boast of their own strength?

COMPLEMENT: By resorting to the foolishness of boasting himself, but only in his weakness and suffering on behalf of the gospel.

EXEGETICAL IDEA: Paul calls the remaining unrepentant Corinthians who sided with Paul's opponents to reject the "super-apostles" who boast of their own strength by resorting to the foolishness of boasting himself, but only in his weakness and suffering on behalf of the gospel.

HOMILETICAL IDEA: The foolishness of godly weakness overpowers the appeal of human strength.

2 Corinthians 12:1-13

SUBJECT: In what does Paul find authority for his apostolic message?

COMPLEMENT: Not his spiritual experiences but only the strength of Christ shown through his weakness.

EXEGETICAL IDEA: Paul finds authority for his apostolic message not in his spiritual experiences but only in the strength of Christ shown through his weakness.

HOMILETICAL IDEA: We elevate only Christ's strength to proclaim Christ's glory.

2 Corinthians 12:14–13:14

SUBJECT: What does Paul say is his desire for the Corinthians as he prepares to visit the church for a third time?

COMPLEMENT: Repentance and restoration in the grace of Christ, love of God, and fellowship of the Spirit.

EXEGETICAL IDEA: Paul's desire for the Corinthians as he prepares to visit the church for a third time is their repentance and restoration in the grace of Christ, love of God, and fellowship of the Spirit.

HOMILETICAL IDEA: The grace of God provides for repentance and restoration.

Difficult Passages/Verses

There are passages of Scripture that, over time, are lifted from their literary and cultural context and through casual usage take on an interpretation and life of their own. They become pithy aphorisms that may or may not reflect the original intent of the author. As they are repeated in this way, the preacher may, through familiarity with the text divorced from its context, be moved toward a shallow proclamation. Even if the preacher is careful with context and exegesis, the popular though less than biblical understanding of a verse may still hold sway in the preacher's audience. Such is the case with a number of verses in 2 Corinthians.

For instance, in chapter 3 Paul writes of the glory of God coming through his gospel proclamation: "And we all, with unveiled face, beholding the glory of the Lord, are being transformed into the same image from one degree of glory to another" (v. 18 ESV). Often this verse is cited as a general principle of one's identity in Christ. However, it is important to consider the context in which Paul is defending his own ministry as an apostle, grounding his sufficiency for such a ministry in God's action and grace. The text does have to do with transformation in Christ. Yet the context makes this declaration larger than the personal experience of the individual believer.

The command in chapter 6, "Do not be unequally yoked with unbelievers" (v. 14 ESV), has been cited in countless youth groups and church ministries as a prohibition for a believer to have a dating or marriage relationship with an unbeliever. This usage is so ubiquitous it is presented largely without question or critical engagement. However, Paul's admonition here is much bigger than a romantic relational ethic. In fact, the context of Paul's words does not necessarily indicate that he has this in mind at all. Rather, his concern is for the Corinthians to extricate themselves from those who have led them astray. His call is to purity of faith shown through rejection of the false gospel and its proponents. There may be application here that relates to relationships of all kinds, but to accept Paul's words as centrally about dating or marriage relationships is to make Paul say something he is not saying here.[3]

Other verses that the church has at times separated from context and run in danger of individualizing or potentially missing Paul's meaning include 5:17: "Therefore, if anyone is in Christ, he is a new creation. The old has passed away; behold, the new has come" (ESV). The context of this statement as a defense of Paul's ministry and a call away from cultural religious norms to the weakness and suffering of Christ can become lost in the popular usage of the words to affirm one's individual identity in Christ. Chapter 10's statement that Christ takes every thought captive (v. 5) becomes a general prescriptive for disciples today, separate from the context of Paul's describing God's commendation of his apostolic authority and readiness to punish the disobedience of his opponents (v. 6). The preacher must take care to consider these texts within their larger literary and historical context.

Cultural Perspectives and Application

Hafemann observes that 2 Corinthians is "widely recognized as the most difficult to understand among Paul's letters."[4] The letter is dense with the pain, emotion, and brokenness of both Paul and the church. Interpretation requires an immersion in its specific occasional nature with Paul addressing a unique situation. The saturation in first-century life requires study in order to understand Paul's words and the culture lying behind them. These background issues are interconnected and provide hermeneutical connections for preaching 2 Corinthians today.

Paul's situation finds the Corinthians have been led astray by a group of "super-apostles" (11:5; 12:11) who have taken the church back into alignment with worldly values instead of Christlike sacrifice. It becomes apparent that this has been an ongoing hardship for Paul and the church, with their rebellion

---

3. Best discusses this dynamic with reference to idolatry (*Second Corinthians*, 65–68). Hafemann's discussion on being *yoked together* is helpful (*2 Corinthians*, 289–304).
4. Hafemann, *2 Corinthians*, 19.

against his gospel occurring shortly after he left them. Second Corinthians is at least Paul's fourth letter to the church and arrives after his tearful, severe writing and his painful visit mentioned in chapter 2. The church's rejection of Paul as a weak and ultimately poor example of the gospel because of his weakness and suffering has been heartbreaking. While many in the church have repented by the time Paul writes this correspondence, the path has been severe on both sides. Paul views the rejection of the gospel he's given as ultimately a rejection of Christ.

The eruption and acceptance of the competing message of Paul's opponents in part centers on the cultural milieu in Corinth at the time. First-century religion in Corinth focused on multiple deities that exuded strength and provided material success and social standing to their followers. Religion was a means of reinforcing and appropriating a culture that worshiped wealth and social mobility as central to one's life in the world. The panoply of deities promised this through rituals of sacrifice. This was in complete opposition to the gospel of sacrifice and self-emptying viewed most completely in Christ's death and resurrection, and displayed in the suffering and sacrifice of Paul as the messenger of this different kind of religion. Paul's gospel called for life change, emptying oneself, giving away as opposed to accumulating, and indeed suffering. It is easy to imagine that skillful and entertaining orators promising health, wealth, prominence, and escape from suffering must not have had a difficult time persuading the Corinthian believers back into a pursuit of everything their world valued.

While the letter is occasional, there are significant parallels to the state of Western culture today. The pursuit of wealth as the mark of social success, the focus on achievement and social standing, and the desire to minimize one's own pain and suffering in the present moment—all of these ring true for the Western church in the twenty-first century. It is not outlandish to say that these strong currents of social influence have led the church and its people on a quest that takes as its script something other than Paul's gospel and Christ's example of self-emptying for the sake of others. There are opponents to the gospel in this day just as there were in Paul's, whether they be actual people preaching openly another gospel, false teachers proclaiming a gospel of prosperity and presenting themselves as within the church, or merely the cultural currents that tempt us away from God. Even while being a letter that addresses a specific moment in time, Paul's words address the church in *this* moment in time as well. It will be the preacher's calling to apply Paul's words first to himself or herself and then to the people of God, inviting them always back to the true gospel.

RECOMMENDED RESOURCES

Best, Ernest. *Second Corinthians*. Interpretation. Louisville: Westminster John Knox, 1987.

Hafemann, Scott J. *2 Corinthians*. The NIV Application Commentary. Grand Rapids: Zondervan, 2000.

Keener, Craig S. "Second Corinthians." In *The IVP Bible Background Commentary: New Testament*, 498–522. Downers Grove, IL: InterVarsity, 1993.

Galatians

PAUL A. HOFFMAN

The Big Idea of Galatians

Galatians is a rejoinder polemic. Hence, it is "three-sided—*Paul*, to the *Galatians*, against the *agitators*."[1] Paul writes to rebut a heretical version of the gospel (1:7) infecting the Galatian churches propagated by false teachers he calls "agitators" (5:12). Concomitantly, Paul defends his apostleship and gospel as divine in origin (1:11–2:10).

This letter unfolds through two overlapping trajectories: Paul counterattacks the agitators—who have sought to discredit his message and ministry—while expressing exasperation toward the Galatians for entertaining such blatantly false teachings.

Why all the fuss? The stakes are astronomically high. The agitators insist that to be saved, the gentile Christians must believe in Jesus *and* be circumcised. Thus the Galatians must choose between two competing paradigms: grace + circumcision (observing the law) = justification; or grace + 0 = justification.[2] Put succinctly, "a person is not justified by the works of the law, but by faith in Jesus Christ" (2:16). Consequently, Christians are "adopted"

---

1. Gordon D. Fee and Douglas Stuart, *How to Read the Bible Book by Book* (Grand Rapids: Zondervan, 2002), 341.

2. Justification can be defined as "God's powerful, cosmic and universal action in effecting a change in the situation between sinful humanity and God, by which God is able to acquit and vindicate believers, setting them in a right and faithful relation to himself." A. E. McGrath, "Justification," in *Dictionary of Paul and His Letters*, ed. Gerald F. Hawthorne, Ralph P. Martin, and Daniel G. Reid (Downers Grove, IL: InterVarsity, 1993), 518.

$(4:5)^3$ and thus become "children of God" (3:26) who've been "set free" (5:1) to "live by the Spirit" (5:25).

SUBJECT: Why does Paul assert the agitators are wrong to insist gentile Christians must get circumcised (observe the law) for God to justify them?

COMPLEMENT: The true gospel is that all people, including gentiles, are justified and adopted by faith in Jesus Christ alone.

EXEGETICAL IDEA: Paul asserts the agitators are wrong to insist gentile Christians must get circumcised (observe the law) for God to justify them because the true gospel is that all people, including gentiles, are justified and adopted by faith in Jesus Christ alone.

HOMILETICAL IDEA: The true gospel is that all people are justified and adopted by faith in Jesus Christ alone.

Selecting Preaching and Teaching Passages in Galatians

There is no universally accepted outline for Galatians. However, Gordon Fee provides a helpful nine-part framework, which I appropriate below.[4] The preacher or teacher is free to construct a longer nine-part series as I've presented here or may choose to cover broader themes in a six-part series working through an entire chapter at a time.

Getting the Subject, Complement, Exegetical Idea, and Homiletical Idea

Galatians 1:1–5

SUBJECT: How does Paul define the gospel?

COMPLEMENT: Jesus Christ died for sin to rescue the Galatians from this evil age according to God's will and for his glory.

EXEGETICAL IDEA: Paul defines the gospel as Jesus Christ dying for sin to rescue the Galatians from this evil age according to God's will and for his glory.

HOMILETICAL IDEA: Jesus Christ died for our sins to rescue us from this evil age according to God's will and for his glory.

---

3. The NIV provides this text note on 4:5: "The Greek word for *adoption to sonship* is a legal term referring to the full legal standing of an adopted male heir in Roman culture." *The Holy Bible*, New International Version (Grand Rapids: Zondervan, 2011), 1063.

4. See Fee and Stuart, *How to Read the Bible Book by Book*, 343–46.

Galatians 1:6-10

SUBJECT: Why does Paul curse the agitators (false teachers)?

COMPLEMENT: Because they preach a perverted gospel.

EXEGETICAL IDEA: Paul curses the agitators because they preach a perverted gospel.

HOMILETICAL IDEA: Ban those who preach a perverted gospel.

Galatians 1:11-2:14

SUBJECT: How does Paul validate his ministry to the Galatians?

COMPLEMENT: By insisting that he received his gospel message and apostleship directly from God.

EXEGETICAL IDEA: Paul validates his ministry to the Galatians by insisting that he received his gospel message and apostleship directly from God.

HOMILETICAL IDEA: Jesus Christ calls, equips, and sends his servants to preach his gospel.

Galatians 2:15-21

SUBJECT: What is Paul's argument in rebuking Peter's hypocrisy?[5]

COMPLEMENT: That "a person is not justified by the works of the law, but by faith in Jesus Christ" (2:16).

EXEGETICAL IDEA: Paul rebukes Peter's hypocrisy by arguing that "a person is not justified by the works of the law, but by faith in Jesus Christ" (2:16).

HOMILETICAL IDEA: We are not justified by the works of the law, but by faith in Jesus Christ.

Galatians 3:1-4:7

SUBJECT: Under what conditions did the Galatians receive the Holy Spirit and adoption?

COMPLEMENT: Through faith in Jesus Christ and not obedience to the law.

EXEGETICAL IDEA: The Galatians received the Holy Spirit and adoption through faith in Jesus Christ and not obedience to the law.

---

5. Richard N. Longenecker states this text "is not only the hinge between what has gone before and what follows but actually the central affirmation of the letter." *Galatians*, Word Biblical Commentary (Waco: Word, 1990), 83.

HOMILETICAL IDEA: We receive the Holy Spirit and adoption through faith in Jesus Christ and not obedience to the law.

Galatians 4:8–20

SUBJECT: Why does Paul fear for the Galatians?

COMPLEMENT: Because they have (apparently) abandoned the gospel, evidenced by their hostility toward him and "relapse into slavery"[6] under the law.

EXEGETICAL IDEA: Paul fears for the Galatians because they have abandoned the gospel, evidenced by their hostility toward him and "relapse into slavery" under the law.

HOMILETICAL IDEA: Abandoning the gospel leads to hostility and slavery.

Galatians 4:21–5:12

SUBJECT: Why does Paul refer to the story of Hagar and Sarah?

COMPLEMENT: To prove that freedom in Christ is better than slavery to the law.

EXEGETICAL IDEA: Paul refers to the story of Hagar and Sarah to prove that freedom in Christ is better than slavery to the law.

HOMILETICAL IDEA: If Christ has set you free, keep choosing freedom!

Galatians 5:13–6:10

SUBJECT: Why did Christ free the Galatians from their sinful nature?

COMPLEMENT: So they could live by the Spirit and love one another.

EXEGETICAL IDEA: Christ freed the Galatians from their sinful nature so they could live by the Spirit and love one another.

HOMILETICAL IDEA: Christ freed you from your sinful nature to live by the Spirit and love one another.

Galatians 6:11–18

SUBJECT: Why does Paul boast in the cross and not in circumcision?

COMPLEMENT: The cross is the only thing that makes him a new creation, free from the law and the sinful nature.

---

6. Ronald Y. Fung, *The Epistle to the Galatians*, The New International Commentary on the New Testament (Grand Rapids: Eerdmans, 1988), vii.

EXEGETICAL IDEA: Paul boasts in the cross and not in circumcision because the cross is the only thing that makes him a new creation, free from the law and the sinful nature.

HOMILETICAL IDEA: Boast in the cross—it's the only thing that makes you a new creation.

Difficult Passages/Verses

The following texts are potentially confusing and hence call for careful exegesis and precise explanation.

Galatians 1:8–9

"Let him be eternally condemned!"[7] Is Paul actually asking God to send false teachers to hell?

Galatians 2:16; 3:2, 5, 10

What is the meaning of "works of the law"? Does it refer to a legalistic, works-righteousness approach to salvation—the classic Protestant reformers' interpretation? Or, as some of the "new perspective" advocates (e.g., E. P. Sanders, N. T. Wright) assert, is Paul denouncing nationalist or ethnic privilege? In this view, the apostle is "not opposing salvation-by-works, but rather racial and ethnic exclusivity."[8]

Galatians 3:24

The communicator will want to explain the statement "the law was our guardian until Christ came."

Galatians 3:27

The communicator will want to explain the phrase "baptized into Christ."

Galatians 3:28

"Nor is there male and female, for you are all one in Christ Jesus." Is Paul arguing the gospel abolishes all sex or gender differences?

Galatians 5:12

"I wish they would go the whole way and emasculate themselves!" How can a Spirit-inspired text express such a harsh desire—namely, that people would cut off their own genitals?

---

7. This quotation is from the 1984 edition of the NIV.
8. Timothy Keller, *Galatians for You* (Charlotte: The Good Book Company, 2013), 195.

Galatians 5:19-21

How does one tactfully define "debauchery" and "orgies"?

Cultural Perspectives and Application

Galatians highlights the ethnic and cultural tensions Jews and gentiles experienced in the first century. It is hard to overemphasize the challenges that arose when a flood of gentiles joined a nascent movement spearheaded by Jewish Christians. Integration was messy, especially when certain teachers demanded that gentile converts get circumcised to become "official Christians." Even the apostle Peter, known for being strong-willed, faltered under pressure and started separating himself from gentile believers (2:11–14). Consequently, these tensions are a major theme running through the New Testament, including Acts 15, Romans 9–11, Ephesians 2, and so on. The expositor is wise to elucidate these underpinnings, which modern people are likely not attuned to.

This epistle poses numerous applications:

- *The doctrine of justification by faith.* Galatians presents evangelistic and revivalist thrusts because it describes how individuals are "not justified by the works of the law, but by faith in Jesus Christ" (2:16). Church historian Stuart Piggin asserts, "Preaching for revival stresses justification by faith alone as the antidote to self-sufficiency, and the blood of Christ as the antibiotic that kills guilt, the stain of sin."[9]
- *The true gospel.* The true, apostolic gospel must be defended against heresy (5:1–6). There is a need for polemics in the church. As the apostle staked his life and ministry on the true gospel, we can do no less (2:20; 5:11).
- *The doctrine of adoption.* Our primary identity as Christians is as "children of God" (3:23–29). J. I. Packer contends, "If you want to judge how well a person understands Christianity, find out how much he makes of the thought of being God's child, and having God as his Father. . . . Our understanding of Christianity cannot be better than our grasp of adoption."[10]

---

9. Stuart Piggin, *Firestorm of the Lord: The History of and Prospects for Revival in the Church and the World* (Carlisle, UK: Paternoster, 2000), 7.

10. J. I. Packer, *Knowing God*, 20th anniversary ed. (Downers Grove, IL: InterVarsity, 1993), 201–2.

- *The basis for Christian unity* (3:23–29). The gospel transcends the importance of one's ethnicity, class, and sex: "In this new community, distinctions are not eliminated as much as they have become irrelevant for determining who can be 'in Christ' because now believers are children of God through faith rather than the law."[11]
- *Freedom in Christ* (5:1–12). Jesus sets us free from the "yoke of slavery" that comes from works-righteousness.
- *The Spirit-led life and community* (5:13–6:10). Paul paints a compelling Christian social ethic.

RECOMMENDED RESOURCES

Fee, Gordon D., and Douglas Stuart. *How to Read the Bible Book by Book*. Grand Rapids: Zondervan, 2002.

Keller, Timothy. *Galatians for You*. Charlotte: The Good Book Company, 2013.

Longenecker, Richard N. *Galatians*. Word Biblical Commentary. Waco: Word, 1982.

11. Michelle Lee-Barnewall, *Neither Complementarian nor Egalitarian: A Kingdom Corrective to the Evangelical Gender Debate* (Grand Rapids: Baker Academic, 2016), 86.

Ephesians

SID BUZZELL

The Big Idea of Ephesians

Ephesians, where Paul spells out the glories and responsibilities of Christian redemption, has received the highest praise from New Testament scholars, who refer to it as the crown of Pauline theology and rank it as one of the most influential documents ever written.[1]

SUBJECT: What does Paul say in Ephesians about why and how believers should live?

COMPLEMENT: Because God has taken such astounding measures to redeem believers for his own glory, believers should diligently live the new life he instructs them to live.

EXEGETICAL IDEA: Paul says in Ephesians that because God has taken such astounding measures to redeem believers for his own glory, believers should diligently live the new life he instructs them to live.

HOMILETICAL IDEA: As our understanding of God's investment to redeem us for his own glory grows, so must our diligent commitment to live by the instructions he has provided.

Selecting Preaching and Teaching Passages in Ephesians

Ephesians divides thematically into two sections. In chapters 1–3 Paul lays a theological foundation praising God for his intimate involvement in human

---

1. Klyne Snodgrass, *Ephesians*, The NIV Application Commentary (Grand Rapids: Zondervan, 1996), 17.

redemption and establishing the church. Then, on the basis of his theological presentation in the first three chapters, he offers a number of specific ways believers should live in light of God's marvelous plan of redemption. There are six preaching segments in chapters 1–3 and eight in chapters 4–6.

Getting the Subject, Complement, Exegetical Idea, and Homiletical Idea

Ephesians 1:1-14

SUBJECT: Why does Paul offer elaborate praise to God?

COMPLEMENT: Because God the Father, Son, and Holy Spirit participate fully in human redemption.

EXEGETICAL IDEA: Paul offers elaborate praise to God because God the Father, Son, and Holy Spirit participate fully in human redemption.

HOMILETICAL IDEA: We should praise and worship God the Father, Son, and Spirit for their full participation in our redemption.

Ephesians 1:15-23

SUBJECT: What does Paul ask God for when he prays for his readers?

COMPLEMENT: That the Holy Spirit will enable them to know the full extent of God's blessing on them as believers.

EXEGETICAL IDEA: When Paul prays for his readers, he asks God that the Holy Spirit will enable them to know the full extent of God's blessing on them as believers.

HOMILETICAL IDEA: Asking God's Holy Spirit to help us grasp the depths of God's blessings in Christ is an essential component in our prayers.

Ephesians 2:1-10

SUBJECT: How does Paul describe the process whereby one who did not believe in Christ as Savior becomes saved?

COMPLEMENT: By his grace through faith God makes people who were dead in sin alive in Christ and equips them to serve him.

EXEGETICAL IDEA: Paul describes the process whereby one who did not believe in Christ as Savior becomes saved as one in which by his grace through faith God makes people who were dead in sin alive in Christ and equips them to serve him.

HOMILETICAL IDEA: God graciously gives us the gift of life, honor, and purpose by his grace through faith, because we are unable to earn it by our own effort.

Ephesians 2:11-22

SUBJECT: How does Paul say that God created peace between Jews and gentiles and built them into the dwelling where he lives by his Spirit?

COMPLEMENT: By giving both Jews and gentiles access to himself when he set aside the law's commandments and regulations by Christ's crucifixion and established peace between them.

EXEGETICAL IDEA: Paul says that God created peace between Jews and gentiles and built them into the dwelling where he lives by his Spirit by giving both Jews and gentiles access to himself when he set aside the law's commandments and regulations by Christ's crucifixion and established peace between them.

HOMILETICAL IDEA: God invites all people to join together as members of his own household by receiving his gift of salvation made available through Christ's crucifixion.

Ephesians 3:1-13

SUBJECT: How does Paul define his ministry to the gentiles?

COMPLEMENT: It is one in which God has called him to tell gentiles about the boundless riches of Christ and join with Jewish believers in one body to reveal God's manifold wisdom to the heavenly authorities through the church.

EXEGETICAL IDEA: Paul defines his ministry to the gentiles as one in which God has called him to tell gentiles about the boundless riches of Christ and join with Jewish believers in one body to reveal God's manifold wisdom to the heavenly authorities through the church.

HOMILETICAL IDEA: God gathers believers from all nations and invites them into the one body of Christ to demonstrate God's profound wisdom to the rulers and authorities in the heavenly realms.

Ephesians 3:14-21

SUBJECT: What does Paul pray for the Ephesians?

COMPLEMENT: That God will give them inner strength so that Christ can dwell in their hearts and that they can comprehend the incomprehensible dimensions of Christ's love and trust that God has the power to answer that prayer.

EXEGETICAL IDEA: Paul prays for the Ephesians that God will give them inner strength so that Christ can dwell in their hearts and that they can comprehend the incomprehensible dimensions of Christ's love and trust that God has the power to answer that prayer.

HOMILETICAL IDEA: We must ask God to strengthen us so that Christ can dwell in our heart and we can comprehend the full extent of his love.

Ephesians 4:1-6

SUBJECT: Why does Paul urge the Ephesians to preserve the unity of the Spirit in the bond of peace?

COMPLEMENT: Because they had been called to the unity that is inherent in their life as Christians.

EXEGETICAL IDEA: Paul urges the Ephesians to preserve the unity of the Spirit in the bond of peace because they had been called to the unity that is inherent in their life as Christians.

HOMILETICAL IDEA: We walk worthy of our calling as Christians only when we walk in unity.

Ephesians 4:7-16

SUBJECT: What does Paul say is the role of gifted Christian leaders that God gave to the church?

COMPLEMENT: To equip saints for maturity and ministry so they can contribute to the church's health and growth.

EXEGETICAL IDEA: Paul says the role of gifted Christian leaders that God gave to the church is to equip saints for maturity and ministry so they can contribute to the church's health and growth.

HOMILETICAL IDEA: Christ has given gifted leaders to the church to equip each of us to contribute to the church's health and growth.

Ephesians 4:17-24

SUBJECT: What does Paul insist the Ephesians do?

COMPLEMENT: Stop living like gentiles, put off their old self, renew their mental attitude, and put on the new self that is created to be like God.

EXEGETICAL IDEA: Paul insists that the Ephesians stop living like gentiles, put off their old self, renew their mental attitude, and put on the new self that is created to be like God.

HOMILETICAL IDEA: God insists that we Christians stop living like non-Christians, renew our thinking, and start to live the new life he has enabled us to live.

Ephesians 4:25-5:2

SUBJECT: What does Paul want the Ephesians to do as a result of their new life?

COMPLEMENT: To maintain and strengthen unity with others in the body of Christ when it is fractured.

EXEGETICAL IDEA: Paul wants the Ephesians, as a result of their new life, to maintain and strengthen unity with others in the body of Christ when it is fractured.

HOMILETICAL IDEA: God provides specific instructions for healing and strengthening the unity of the Spirit when it becomes strained or fractured.

Ephesians 5:3-14

SUBJECT: Why does Paul insist that the Ephesians put off the old life and put on the new life?

COMPLEMENT: Because the old life's activities do not please God and arouse his wrath.

EXEGETICAL IDEA: Paul insists that the Ephesians put off the old life and put on the new life because the old life's activities do not please God and arouse his wrath.

HOMILETICAL IDEA: Abandon your old life and adopt the new life Christ provides because the old life's activities do not please God and arouse his wrath.

Ephesians 5:15-20

SUBJECT: What instructions does Paul give the Ephesians for pursuing wise living?

COMPLEMENT: He encourages them to understand God's will, to be filled in the Spirit, to worship in song, and give thanks to God for everything.

EXEGETICAL IDEA: The instructions Paul gives the Ephesians for pursuing wise living involve encouraging them to understand God's will, to be filled in the Spirit, to worship in song, and give thanks to God for everything.

HOMILETICAL IDEA: Because the new life in Christ is superior to the old way of life, aggressively pursue the new life God offers us in Christ.

Ephesians 5:21–6:9

SUBJECT: Why does Paul teach the Ephesians that submission to Christ contributes to the believer's new life in Christ?

COMPLEMENT: Because it honors Christ and benefits those who participate in it.

EXEGETICAL IDEA: Paul teaches the Ephesians that submission to Christ contributes to the believer's new life in Christ because it honors him and benefits those who participate in it.

HOMILETICAL IDEA: Practice submission to Christ because submission honors God and benefits all who participate in it.

Ephesians 6:10–24

SUBJECT: How does Paul state that Christians find the strength needed to stand against the devil's schemes and live the Christian life?

COMPLEMENT: By putting on God's whole armor and by praying consistently.

EXEGETICAL IDEA: Paul states that Christians find the strength needed to stand against the devil's schemes and live the Christian life by putting on God's whole armor and by praying consistently.

HOMILETICAL IDEA: We Christians find the strength we need to stand against the devil and live the life God offers us by putting on God's full armor and by constantly praying for ourselves and for one another.

Difficult Passages/Verses

Ephesians 1:3–14

This long sentence is notoriously difficult to outline. Peter O'Brien writes, "Although there have been many efforts to determine the form and structure of the paragraph, no general agreement has been reached."[2] Invest time to develop a sense of logical connections between its ideas. One thematic approach is to divide it between the Father's (vv. 3–6), the Son's (vv. 6–13), and the Spirit's (vv. 13–14) participation in salvation.

The repeated references to the fact that God chose and predestined our salvation according to *his own* plan, purpose, and will may raise questions about God's sovereignty and human will. Address this issue and point out that Paul's emphasis in this passage is God's sovereign involvement in our redemption and that the debates about election are not the focus. Klyne

---

2. Peter T. O'Brien, *The Letter to the Ephesians*, The Pillar New Testament Commentary (Grand Rapids: Eerdmans, 1999), 90.

Snodgrass wisely counsels in reference to this passage that because they detract from its primary focus, "most of the debates about election should be politely set aside."[3]

Ephesians 4:8

Paul paraphrases Psalm 68:18 here but changes its focus. Acquaint yourself with the psalm and with what Paul is doing with it to explain the differences. Paul refers to Christ's resurrection and ascension as his victory over the principalities and powers, and states that as a triumphant victor it is his right to give gifts to those who follow him (cf. 4:11–16).

Ephesians 4:9

This verse states that Jesus descended to "the lower, earthly regions." Although church tradition teaches that he descended into hell, Peter O'Brien, Snodgrass, and Andrew Lincoln interpret the statement as a reference to Jesus's incarnation.[4]

Ephesians 5:21

There is some discussion about whether this verse concludes the preceding pericope (5:15–20) or introduces the following one (5:22–6:9). It may be best to see it as a transition statement that ties the two together.

Ephesians 5:22–6:9

This passage will require more than the "normal" amount of study because of some interpretive questions.

- Be clear on your view of submission and headship because commentaries differ on how to define the terms.
- Clarify how Paul compares the relationships between the husband as "head of the wife" and Christ as "head of the church" (5:23), and how he compares the concepts of the church's submission to Christ and a wife's submission to her husband (5:24).
- Decide how to present each conclusion here: Is each a question for dialogue, a conclusion for discussion, or a conviction for debate?
- Both Snodgrass and Lincoln state that our current cultural norms suggest a different application of this passage than Paul was teaching

---

3. Snodgrass, *Ephesians*, 59.

4. O'Brien, *Letter to the Ephesians*, 296; Snodgrass, *Ephesians*, 202; Andrew T. Lincoln, *Ephesians*, Word Biblical Commentary (Dallas: Word, 1990), 247.

to his readers.[5] But we must be ready to explain these differences and explain why it is legitimate to "update" the applications here and not in some other passages.

Ephesians 5:31–32

Paul's quotation of Genesis 2:24 has the appearance that he is referring to marriage between a husband and a wife. But in 5:32 he states that he is speaking about Christ and the church. Take time to sort through Paul's language here and be clear about what he is saying.

Ephesians 5:32

Lincoln connects Paul's use of "mystery" in 5:32 with his uses in 1:9; 3:3, 6, 9. "Both the OT passage and the marriage relationship of which he speaks are connected with mystery, but their connection is that they point to the secret now revealed, that of the relationship between Christ and the church."[6] It may take some meditative study for this theologically important connection between the church's marriage to Christ and the marriage between a man and a woman to form in your mind.

Cultural Perspectives and Application

There is some evidence that Ephesians was written as a circular letter intended for churches in western Asia Minor, but with Ephesus as the primary church addressed. Walter Elwell and Robert Yarbrough inform us that "Ephesus was the center of worship of the pagan goddess Artemis (Diana)." In addition, they state, "If religious life was dominated by emperor worship, idolatry, and the black arts of occultism and spiritism, moral life was typical of a Greco-Roman city: A large brothel stood at one of the major intersections."[7]

We can sense Paul's urgency when he encourages his readers to abandon their old way of life and embrace their new life in Christ (4:17–24). His instructions to put on God's full armor to defeat the devil's schemes (6:10–20) had immediate identification with his readers. Most of Ephesians' teachings have universal application. However, Paul's instructions to husbands and wives and to masters and slaves (5:22–6:9) require some additional thinking for specific application in today's cultures.

---

5. Snodgrass, *Ephesians*, 313–16; Lincoln, *Ephesians*, 392–93.

6. Lincoln, *Ephesians*, 381.

7. Walter Elwell and Robert Yarbrough, *Encountering the New Testament* (Grand Rapids: Baker Books, 1998), 308–9.

In chapters 1–3 Paul attempts to sufficiently impress his reader with God's complete participation in our salvation with the intention that we would take seriously his instructions in chapters 4–6 about how to live the new life God offers us in Christ.

RECOMMENDED RESOURCES

Lincoln, Andrew T. *Ephesians*. Word Biblical Commentary. Dallas: Word, 1990.

O'Brien, Peter T. *The Letter to the Ephesians*. The Pillar New Testament Commentary. Grand Rapids: Eerdmans, 1999.

Snodgrass, Klyne. *Ephesians*. The NIV Application Commentary. Grand Rapids: Zondervan, 1996.

Philippians

SCOTT M. GIBSON

Paul is thankful to God for the Philippian Christians. They have invested in his life and ministry because he has invested in their lives. The letter is a response to the gift sent to Paul in prison by the hand of Epaphroditus from the Philippian church. In the letter, Paul expresses his partnership with them in Christ, that they share in ministry and they share in becoming like Christ, even through Paul's example. They can even rejoice in the middle of suffering—from the culture and from tensions within the church.

SUBJECT: Why does Paul write to the Philippian Christians?

COMPLEMENT: To let them know of his thanks to God for them and to encourage them as they struggle—externally from living their faith in a culture of opposition, and internally to live for Christ faithfully as a church with one another.

EXEGETICAL IDEA: Paul writes to the Philippian Christians to let them know of his thanks to God for them and to encourage them as they struggle—externally from living their faith in a culture of opposition, and internally to live for Christ faithfully as a church with one another.

HOMILETICAL IDEA: Thankfully, because of Christ Christians can live faithfully in the culture and in the church.

Selecting Preaching and Teaching Passages in Philippians

Below the letter is divided into a fourteen-week series. Some commentaries section the letter into as many as sixteen segments. Careful preachers will want to assess the units of thought as they prepare to preach, laying out a series for their listeners.[1]

Getting the Subject, Complement, Exegetical Idea, and Homiletical Idea

Philippians 1:1-2

SUBJECT: What do Paul and Timothy desire the Philippian church to have as they greet them at the beginning of their letter?

COMPLEMENT: Grace and peace from God and Christ Jesus.

EXEGETICAL IDEA: Paul and Timothy desire the Philippian church to have grace and peace from God and Christ Jesus as they greet them at the beginning of their letter.

HOMILETICAL IDEA: Good beginnings start with grace and peace.

Philippians 1:3-11

SUBJECT: Why is Paul grateful with joy to God for the Philippian church, and what does he pray for them?

COMPLEMENT: For their faithful partnership in the gospel, and that they will grow in knowledge, discernment, and blamelessness in Christ so that they may glorify God in their lives.

EXEGETICAL IDEA: Paul is grateful with joy to God for the Philippian church for their faithful partnership in the gospel, and he prays that they will grow in knowledge, discernment, and blamelessness in Christ so that they may glorify God in their lives.

HOMILETICAL IDEA: Thank God that he does what he does in us and we do what we do—for him.

Philippians 1:12-26

SUBJECT: What does Paul say is the result of his being imprisoned for Christ?

COMPLEMENT: The gospel is being preached with courage and Christ will be exalted in Paul's body, for to him to live is Christ and to die is gain.

EXEGETICAL IDEA: Paul says the result of his being imprisoned for Christ is that the gospel is being preached with courage and Christ will be exalted in Paul's body, for to him to live is Christ and to die is gain.

HOMILETICAL IDEA: Living is Christ and dying is gain.

1. Some of this material was previously published on the website of PreachingToday.com (https://www.preachingtoday.com). Used by permission.

Philippians 1:27-30

SUBJECT: How does Paul instruct the Philippian Christians to live their lives in light of his commitment to Christ and to them and his imprisonment?

COMPLEMENT: By conducting themselves in a manner worthy of the gospel of Christ, not being afraid of opposition and confident that God will save them, even though they too will suffer because of the gospel.

EXEGETICAL IDEA: Paul instructs the Philippian Christians to live their lives in light of his commitment to Christ and to them and his imprisonment by conducting themselves in a manner worthy of the gospel of Christ, not being afraid of opposition and confident that God will save them, even though they too will suffer because of the gospel.

HOMILETICAL IDEA: Suitable saints may suffer and struggle, but this is a sign of salvation.

Philippians 2:1-11

SUBJECT: How does Paul tell the Philippian Christians to conduct themselves with one another as a church?

COMPLEMENT: They are to be like-minded and humble like Jesus Christ, who humbled himself even to death on the cross and is exalted to the highest place as Lord, who will humble all in heaven and on earth to the glory of God the Father.

EXEGETICAL IDEA: Paul tells the Philippian Christians to conduct themselves with one another as a church in a way that they are like-minded and humble like Jesus Christ, who humbled himself even to death on the cross and is exalted to the highest place as Lord, who will humble all in heaven and on earth to the glory of God the Father.

HOMILETICAL IDEA: Christ shows us how to be humble when we stumble and bumble.

Philippians 2:12-18

SUBJECT: What does Paul mean when he tells the Philippian Christians to work out their salvation with fear and trembling as they trust God to work in them for his good will and purpose?

COMPLEMENT: That they are to do everything without complaining so that they can be pure children of God in the midst of a depraved generation and therefore live lives that shine, enabling Paul to boast and rejoice in what God is doing in and through them.

EXEGETICAL IDEA: When Paul tells the Philippian Christians to work out their salvation with fear and trembling as they trust God to work in them for his good will and purpose, he means that they are to do everything without complaining so that they can be pure children of God in the midst of a depraved generation and therefore live lives that shine, enabling Paul to boast and rejoice in what God is doing in and through them.

HOMILETICAL IDEA: Carefully live your life so you can carefully shine your light.

Philippians 2:19-30

SUBJECT: What does Paul want to do with Timothy and Epaphroditus?

COMPLEMENT: He wants to send Timothy, his son in the faith, to report on the Philippians' welfare in hopes of his own coming to them, and he intends to send back to them Epaphroditus, his brother and fellow worker in the faith, who almost died for the work of Christ, and whom he wants the Philippians to honor upon his return.

EXEGETICAL IDEA: What Paul wants to do with Timothy and Epaphroditus is to send Timothy, his son in the faith, to report on the Philippians' welfare in hopes of his own coming to them, and he intends to send back to them Epaphroditus, his brother and fellow worker in the faith, who almost died for the work of Christ, and whom he wants the Philippians to honor upon his return.

HOMILETICAL IDEA: Christians care for one another like family.

Philippians 3:1-11

SUBJECT: Why does Paul tell the Philippian Christians to rejoice in the Lord in the midst of people who twist the truth and are confident in who they are?

COMPLEMENT: Because it is a safeguard for them as they encounter opposition, and what matters is not an impressive résumé but knowing Christ and the power of his resurrection.

EXEGETICAL IDEA: Paul tells the Philippian Christians to rejoice in the Lord in the midst of people who twist the truth and are confident in who they are because it is a safeguard for them as they encounter opposition, and what matters is not an impressive résumé but knowing Christ and the power of his resurrection.

HOMILETICAL IDEA: There's no comparison: we can be content only when we have Christ written all over our résumé.

Philippians 3:12-4:1

SUBJECT: What does Paul say in light of his desire to know Christ and the power of his resurrection?

COMPLEMENT: That he has not obtained it perfectly but he presses on to do so, and he wants the Philippian Christians to live maturely by following his and others' example, awaiting the return of Christ and standing firm in the Lord as Paul's brothers and sisters.

EXEGETICAL IDEA: Paul says in light of his desire to know Christ and the power of his resurrection that he has not obtained it perfectly but he presses on to do so and he wants the Philippian Christians to live maturely by following his and others' example, awaiting the return of Christ and standing firm in the Lord as Paul's brothers and sisters.

HOMILETICAL IDEA: Mature models move forward in faith while standing firmly in Christ.

Philippians 4:2-3

SUBJECT: Why does Paul beg Euodia and Syntyche to make peace with each other with Syzygus's help?[2]

COMPLEMENT: Because they helped Paul and Clement and others in the cause of the gospel, and such discord doesn't befit those whose names are written in the Book of Life.

EXEGETICAL IDEA: Paul begs Euodia and Syntyche to make peace with each other with Syzygus's help because they helped Paul and Clement and others in the cause of the gospel, and such discord doesn't befit those whose names are written in the Book of Life.

HOMILETICAL IDEA: Make peace with one another, for fighting doesn't fit those who are fit for heaven.

Philippians 4:4-7

SUBJECT: What does Paul instruct the Philippian Christians to do in light of their circumstances?

COMPLEMENT: To rejoice in the Lord always, to not be anxious about anything but instead to pray and petition with thanksgiving, which leads to God's

2. In some Bible versions the name Syzygus in 4:3 is translated as "companion."

peace that transcends all understanding and guards their hearts and minds in Christ Jesus.

EXEGETICAL IDEA: Paul instructs the Philippian Christians in light of their circumstances to rejoice in the Lord always, to not be anxious about anything but to pray and petition with thanksgiving, which leads to God's peace that transcends all understanding and guards their hearts and minds in Christ Jesus.

HOMILETICAL IDEA: In difficult times, rejoice, pray, and give thanks as God grants us peace and guards our lives in Christ Jesus.

Philippians 4:8-9

SUBJECT: How does Paul instruct the Philippian Christians about the virtues of Christian thinking?

COMPLEMENT: That that which is praiseworthy is to occupy their thinking, and in their doing they are to model themselves after Paul and God's peace will be with them.

EXEGETICAL IDEA: Paul instructs the Philippian Christians about the virtues of Christian thinking so that which is praiseworthy will occupy their thinking, and in their doing they are to model themselves after Paul and God's peace will be with them.

HOMILETICAL IDEA: Good thinking leads to good doing.

Philippians 4:10-20

SUBJECT: Why does Paul rejoice in light of the generosity extended to him by the Philippian church, the only church that cared for him in Thessalonica and now in prison?

COMPLEMENT: Because despite his circumstances he is content because of Christ's strength, and he recognizes their gifts as offerings pleasing to God.

EXEGETICAL IDEA: Paul rejoices in light of the generosity extended to him by the Philippian church, the only church that cared for him in Thessalonica and now in prison, because despite his circumstances he is content because of Christ's strength, and he recognizes their gifts as offerings pleasing to God.

HOMILETICAL IDEA: Contentment in Christ is a generous gift that glorifies God.

Philippians 4:21-23

SUBJECT: How does Paul encourage the Philippian Christians in the conclusion of his letter?

COMPLEMENT: With greetings from other Christians who are with him in prison and a benediction that they be sustained by the grace of the Lord Jesus Christ.

EXEGETICAL IDEA: Paul encourages the Philippian Christians in the conclusion of his letter with greetings from other Christians who are with him in prison and a benediction that they be sustained by the grace of the Lord Jesus Christ.

HOMILETICAL IDEA: Saints encourage one another because saints are sustained by grace.

Difficult Passages/Verses

The following are texts that pose potential challenges in either exegesis, explanation, or sermon development.

Philippians 2:1-11

Becoming familiar with the types of letters in the ancient world will be helpful here. Both a letter of friendship and a letter of moral exhortation seem to be at work in this passage, in which the story of Christ and Paul's story come together.

In addition, this passage (particularly vv. 5–11) has a literary form that bears notice. Some scholars have described this portion as a christological hymn. Whether Paul adopted an early Christian hymn or wrote it himself, Paul gives his readers a splendid summation of who Christ is.

Philippians 4:2-3

Here is a passage that on occasion is skipped by some preachers. It is passed over either because there is tension in the preacher's congregation or because the passage deals with women in ministry, so the preacher wants to go to the next verse! Both avoidances are unsustainable. Every church faces controversy that needs to be dealt with. As for women in the church, this passage concerns two coworkers of Paul who had a falling-out. They, as Paul notes, "have contended at my side." He simply wants them to bury the hatchet and reflect the sacrificial love he wrote about earlier in the letter. This small scene is a case study of what Paul is getting at—to be like Christ, to have his mind.

Cultural Perspectives and Application

Philippi was a Roman city built and fortified by Philip, the father of Alexander the Great, in 358–357 BCE, founded on Roman law, culture, and practice.

Eight miles from the sea, Philippi became a strategic stopping place for the Roman army. The city was rebuilt as a military outpost (42 BCE) and was made a colony with the highest recognition outside Italy, having strong links to Rome.

Paul's encounter with the Philippian church is found in Acts 16:11–39. There he found no synagogue in the city, which had a small Jewish population, and on the Sabbath he met a group of worshiping women outside the city. He preached Christ, and Lydia, a leading businesswoman, was converted and the church was established.

The challenge in preaching Philippians is not to pass over the rich theological and practical instruction that this letter provides for one's congregation. Since it is a letter, theology is made practical, personal, and accessible. With careful study of the text, the ancient context, and the pastor's present church or teaching context, connections can be made with listeners to encourage them to become the people God has called them to be with one another and with those found in the nooks and crannies of their everyday lives.

Regarding application of this letter of Paul to the Philippians, G. Campbell Morgan notes, "The application of this message to the Church today is that the measure of the Church's authority is the measure of her conformity to the mind of Christ."[3] Good words that remind readers that Christ is Lord from head to toe, from brain to boot.

RECOMMENDED RESOURCES

Garland, David E. "Philippians." In *Ephesians–Philemon*, edited by Tremper Longman III and David E. Garland, 175–262. The Expositor's Bible Commentary. Grand Rapids: Zondervan, 2006.

Hawthorne, Gerald F., and Ralph P. Martin. *Philippians*. Revised ed. Word Biblical Commentary. Grand Rapids: Zondervan, 2018.

Martin, Ralph P. *Philippians*. Tyndale New Testament Commentaries. Downers Grove, IL: IVP Academic, 2015.

3. G. Campbell Morgan, *Living Messages of the Books of the Bible: Matthew to Revelation* (New York: Revell, 1912), 203.

Colossians

FRANCE B. BROWN JR.

The Big Idea of Colossians

Composed of ninety-five verses organized into four chapters, the Epistle to the Colossians is one of the most Christ-centered books in all Scripture, emphasizing the supremacy of Christ (his person) and the sufficiency of his death and resurrection for salvation and spiritual transcendence (his provision).

SUBJECT: What is the message that God wants Paul to share with the Colossians?

COMPLEMENT: In the midst of false teaching they should respond to the supremacy and sufficiency of Christ by clinging to him in worshipful submission.

EXEGETICAL IDEA: The message that God wants Paul to share with the Colossians is that in the midst of false teaching they should respond to the supremacy and sufficiency of Christ by clinging to him in worshipful submission.

HOMILETICAL IDEA: Respond to the supremacy and sufficiency of Christ by clinging to him in worshipful submission.

Selecting Preaching and Teaching Passages in Colossians

Colossians can be divided into two major sections. The first is a polemic against false teaching related to Christ's supremacy and sufficiency (chaps. 1–2). The second features instructions for responsive Christian living to Christ's supremacy and sufficiency (chaps. 3–4).

Technically, preaching/teaching through an epistle calls for developing sermons/lessons according to the individual paragraphs that comprise the epistle. For Colossians, this allows for at least twenty units.[1] For the purposes of this chapter, however, six units are presented.

Getting the Subject, Complement, Exegetical Idea, and Homiletical Idea

Colossians 1:1–14

SUBJECT: Why is Paul thankful for the Colossians?

COMPLEMENT: God is responsible for their demonstrated faith, love, and hope.

EXEGETICAL IDEA: Paul is thankful for the Colossians because God is responsible for their demonstrated faith, love, and hope.

HOMILETICAL IDEA: Rely on God and live exemplary Christian lives.

Colossians 1:15–23

SUBJECT: What does Paul tell the Colossians about Jesus Christ?

COMPLEMENT: He is preeminent because he is the sovereign creator and redeemer.

EXEGETICAL IDEA: Paul tells the Colossians that Jesus Christ is preeminent because he is the sovereign creator and redeemer.

HOMILETICAL IDEA: Jesus is preeminent because he is the sovereign creator and redeemer.

Colossians 1:24–29

SUBJECT: What does Paul tell the Colossians is the purpose of his reconciliation ministry?

COMPLEMENT: To present, by God's power, everyone fully mature in Christ.

EXEGETICAL IDEA: Paul tells the Colossians that the purpose of his reconciliation ministry is to present, by God's power, everyone fully mature in Christ.

HOMILETICAL IDEA: The goal of ministry is life-transformation by the power of God.

Colossians 2

SUBJECT: What does Paul encourage the Colossians, Laodiceans, and others who have not met him to do?

---

1. Possible preaching/teaching units: 1:1–2; 1:3–8; 1:9–14; 1:15–20; 1:21–23; 1:24–29; 2:1–5; 2:6–7; 2:8–15; 2:16–19; 2:20–23; 3:1–4; 3:5–11; 3:12–17; 3:18–21; 3:22–4:1; 4:2–4; 4:5–6; 4:7–9; 4:10–18.

COMPLEMENT: Cling to Christ and reject the false teachers.

EXEGETICAL IDEA: Paul encourages the Colossians, Laodiceans, and others who have not met him to cling to Christ and reject the false teachers.

HOMILETICAL IDEA: Cling to Christ and reject false teachers.

Colossians 3:1–4:1

SUBJECT: What does Paul want the Colossians to know as a result of their union with Christ?

COMPLEMENT: That they should reject unrighteousness and practice righteousness.

EXEGETICAL IDEA: Paul wants the Colossians to know, as a result of their union with Christ, that they should reject unrighteousness and practice righteousness.

HOMILETICAL IDEA: Given our union with Christ, we should reject unrighteousness and practice righteousness.

Colossians 4:2–18

SUBJECT: How does Paul instruct the Colossian believers in their life of faith?

COMPLEMENT: They should be encouraged and be intentionally Christian in their relationships with God, others, and themselves.

EXEGETICAL IDEA: Paul instructs the Colossian believers in their life of faith that they should be encouraged and be intentionally Christian in their relationships with God, others, and themselves.

HOMILETICAL IDEA: Be encouraged in the faith and be intentionally Christian in relationships.

Difficult Passages/Verses

Three major interpretive challenges are found in the first chapter of Colossians. The first issue is the subject of the verb "was pleased" (*eudokēsen*) in 1:19. Some possibilities include Christ, God, or "all the fullness" (*pan to plērōma*). The second issue is the meaning of "all the fullness." Colossians 1:22–23 has been used to support both Arminian and Calvinistic views in various ways. Charles C. Bing presents five views: warning of loss of salvation, warning of hypothetical loss of salvation, warning of false salvation, warning to emphasize God's promises, and warning about the believer's evaluation at the judgment seat of Christ.[2] The phrase "lacking in Christ's afflictions" in 1:24 is interpreted in at least four ways: corporate quota of the church, similarity between Paul's and Christ's suffering, residual suffering for believers, and Christ's suffering through Paul.

Cultural Perspectives and Application

The "Colossian heresy" or false teaching that distorted and minimized the person and work of Christ was a fusion of Hellenistic philosophy and Jewish legalism. It emphasized cosmic higher knowledge, Judaistic rituals, angelic veneration, asceticism, and philosophic authority. To be sure, false ideas continue to threaten the contemporary church as acceptance of all religious and cultural views is extolled as the highest virtue of social pluralism. Thankfully, the book of Colossians provides instruction that empowers the church to reject false teaching and embrace the Lord Jesus.

The following are possible applications: praise the Lord (1:15–20), embrace the benefits of the faith (2:8–12), beware of impostors (2:16–23), live life from an eternal perspective (3:1–4), make one's home God's house (3:18–4:1), and follow in the footsteps of the faithful (4:7–18).

RECOMMENDED RESOURCES

O'Brien, Peter T. *Colossians, Philemon.* Word Biblical Commentary. Waco: Word, 1982.

Pao, David W. *Colossians and Philemon.* Zondervan Exegetical Commentary on the New Testament. Grand Rapids: Zondervan, 2012.

Wiersbe, Warren W. "Colossians." In *The Bible Exposition Commentary,* 2:101–54. Wheaton: Victor, 1996.

---

2. Charles C. Bing, "The Warning in Colossians 1:21–23," *Bibliotheca Sacra* 164 (January–March 2007): 74–88.

1 Thessalonians

HEATHER JOY ZIMMERMAN

The Big Idea of 1 Thessalonians

First Thessalonians is a letter from Paul, Silvanus, and Timothy to the church in Thessalonica to encourage the young church in the face of adversity and exhort the believers in holiness.

SUBJECT: Why does God want Paul, Silvanus, and Timothy to write to the church in Thessalonica?

COMPLEMENT: To encourage the Thessalonian believers and instruct them in holy living.

EXEGETICAL IDEA: God wants Paul, Silvanus, and Timothy to write to the church in Thessalonica to encourage the Thessalonian believers and instruct them in holy living.

HOMILETICAL IDEA: Let your life be defined by Christlike community and holiness.

Selecting Preaching and Teaching Passages in 1 Thessalonians

Preachers and teachers may proclaim the book of 1 Thessalonians effectively in five to eight sessions: 1:1–10 expresses the apostles' thanksgiving; 2:1–3:13 demonstrates the apostles' deep affection for the Thessalonians through narrative; 4:1–12 addresses Christian ethical living (in two sections: 4:1–8 on sexual ethics, 4:9–12 on work ethic); 4:13–5:11 vividly portrays our Christian hope (4:14–17 offers hope in death and 5:1–11 offers hope in life); and 5:12–28 appeals for the ideal Christian community.

Getting the Subject, Complement, Exegetical Idea, and Homiletical Idea

1 Thessalonians 1

SUBJECT: What are the reasons that Paul, Silvanus, and Timothy thank God for the Thessalonian believers?

COMPLEMENT: Their faith, love, hope, election, imitation, perseverance, and witness.

EXEGETICAL IDEA: Paul, Silvanus, and Timothy thank God for the Thessalonians' faith, love, hope, election, imitation, perseverance, and witness.

HOMILETICAL IDEA: Live a faith worthy of thanksgiving. (Or: Thank others for their faithfulness.)

1 Thessalonians 2-3

SUBJECT: How do Paul, Silvanus, and Timothy express their affection for the Thessalonians, despite affliction and satanic opposition?

COMPLEMENT: They minister out of a heart of authenticity, diligence, gentleness, joy, persistence, prayer, rejoicing, and thanksgiving.

EXEGETICAL IDEA: Paul, Silvanus, and Timothy express their affection for the Thessalonians, despite affliction and satanic opposition, by ministering out of a heart of authenticity, diligence, gentleness, joy, persistence, prayer, and thanksgiving.

HOMILETICAL IDEA: Disciple out of a heart of authenticity, diligence, gentleness, joy, persistence, prayer, and thanksgiving.

1 Thessalonians 4:1-12

SUBJECT: How should the Thessalonians live out the will of God, which is their sanctification?

COMPLEMENT: By refraining from sexual immorality and practicing spiritual sibling love through a quiet, diligent life.

EXEGETICAL IDEA: The Thessalonians are to live out the will of God, which is their sanctification, by refraining from sexual immorality and practicing spiritual sibling love through a quiet, diligent life.

HOMILETICAL IDEA: Let your sex life and your daily life be defined by holiness.

1 Thessalonians 4:13-18

SUBJECT: Why should the Thessalonians have hope in their grief over Christians who have already died?

COMPLEMENT: Because Christ's resurrection assures their resurrection, Jesus is coming back, the already dead will not be disadvantaged, and all believers will forever be with Jesus after he returns.

EXEGETICAL IDEA: The Thessalonians should have hope in their grief over Christians who have already died because Christ's resurrection assures their resurrection, Jesus is coming back, the already dead will not be disadvantaged, and all believers will forever be with Jesus after he returns.

HOMILETICAL IDEA: Jesus's resurrection and return give us hope in death.

1 Thessalonians 5:1-11

SUBJECT: How should the Thessalonians live in anticipation of the day of the Lord?

COMPLEMENT: As "children of light" (v. 5) who are alert and sober-minded, putting on faith, hope, and love and encouraging one another with eschatological hope.

EXEGETICAL IDEA: The Thessalonians should live in anticipation of the day of the Lord as "children of light" (v. 5) who are alert and sober-minded, putting on faith, hope, and love and encouraging one another with eschatological hope.

HOMILETICAL IDEA: Jesus's resurrection and return give us hope in life as we live as children of light.

1 Thessalonians 5:12-28

SUBJECT: How should the Thessalonian believers live as the family of God?

COMPLEMENT: By respecting their leaders, other believers, outsiders, and God with holiness and love.

EXEGETICAL IDEA: The Thessalonians should live as the family of God by respecting their leaders, other believers, outsiders, and God with holiness and love.

HOMILETICAL IDEA: Choose love and holiness in all your relationships.

Difficult Passages/Verses

Set this book in context by describing Paul, Silvanus, and Timothy and how Thessalonica fits into Paul's missionary journeys. Be sure to define holiness/sanctification.

Several passages in 1 Thessalonians prove challenging. First, 2:14–16 has been misconstrued as anti-Semitic. Second, scholars debate whether the "vessel" in 4:4 refers to one's wife, one's body, or a euphemism for the male sex organ. And third, 4:1–8 not only challenges our current societal norms for sex but it challenged the norms of Thessalonian society as well, since the Greco-Roman culture "simply did not think of sexual promiscuity or indulgence as 'wrongdoing.'"[1]

Preach and teach 4:9–12 without encouraging Western individualistic self-sufficiency. First Thessalonians 4:13–18 should be taught within a theology of suffering that neither sentimentalizes our hope nor stigmatizes grief. Preachers and teachers must decide if they are going to connect 4:13–5:12 to an eschatological systematic theological framework. However, this text should not be taught as eschatological messages of fear or threats. Be careful not to lose the passage's focus on hope. When teaching 5:1–12, explain the Old Testament referents of the "day of the Lord."

Cultural Perspectives and Application

How do we faithfully apply the book of 1 Thessalonians? What do we need to know about the Thessalonian culture? First, Westerners often miss the communal ethos of this book. Be sure to highlight the following as you teach: the multiple authors, the familial imagery ("brothers," "sisters," "father," "nursing mother"), and the frequency of first-person plural pronouns. Second, recognize that in 1 Thessalonians most references to suffering are references to persecution. This does not negate applications to other forms of suffering; however, do not miss the original context.

As an epistle, this book is full of exhortations, but these are each rooted in truths about the Thessalonians' identity as believers and the identity of their Lord God. Potential applications include the following: encourage others in their faith (1:1–11), disciple others with an affectionate and persistent heart (2:1–3:13), pursue sexual purity (4:1–8), develop a godly work ethic (4:9–12),

---

1. Gordon G. Fee, *The First and Second Letters to the Thessalonians*, The New International Commentary on the New Testament (Grand Rapids: Eerdmans, 2009), 150.

grieve with hope (4:13–18), be alert and sober-minded (5:1–11), and pursue holiness in every relationship (5:12–28).

RECOMMENDED RESOURCES

Fee, Gordon G. *The First and Second Letters to the Thessalonians.* The New International Commentary on the New Testament. Grand Rapids: Eerdmans, 2009.

Green, Gene L. *The Letters to the Thessalonians.* The Pillar New Testament Commentary. Grand Rapids: Eerdmans, 2002.

Shogren, Gary S. *1 and 2 Thessalonians.* Zondervan Exegetical Commentary on the New Testament. Grand Rapids: Zondervan, 2012.

---

2 Thessalonians

HEATHER JOY ZIMMERMAN

The Big Idea of 2 Thessalonians

Second Thessalonians is a follow-up letter from Paul, Silvanus, and Timothy to the church in Thessalonica to address concerns in the church and to offer hope during persecution.

SUBJECT: What is the message that God wants Paul, Silvanus, and Timothy to share with the Thessalonian church?

COMPLEMENT: That while they await the Lord's justice toward their persecutors, the Thessalonians should rely on the Lord's sustaining grace, resist false messages of fear about the future, work diligently, discipline discerningly, and stand firm in their hope.

EXEGETICAL IDEA: The message that God wants Paul, Silvanus, and Timothy to share with the Thessalonian church is that while they await the Lord's justice toward their persecutors, the Thessalonians should rely on the Lord's sustaining grace, resist false messages of fear about the future, work diligently, discipline discerningly, and stand firm in their hope.

HOMILETICAL IDEA: As you wait for Jesus's return, rest in hope, resist false messages of fear, revitalize your work ethic, and rebuke other believers with loving discernment.

Selecting Preaching and Teaching Passages in 2 Thessalonians

Preachers and teachers often proclaim 2 Thessalonians in three messages, one per chapter. However, Michael W. Holmes's fourfold division is quite helpful:

- 1:1–12 offers assurance for persecuted believers.
- 2:1–12 discusses the day of the Lord.
- 2:13–3:5 provides assurance and urges perseverance.
- 3:6–18 articulates a Christian work ethic and models church discipline.[1]

Getting the Subject, Complement, Exegetical Idea, and Homiletical Idea

2 Thessalonians 1

SUBJECT: Why should the Thessalonian believers be encouraged in the face of persecution?

COMPLEMENT: Because God will bring justice, sustain them, and be glorified through their faithfulness.

EXEGETICAL IDEA: The Thessalonian believers should be encouraged in the face of persecution because God will bring justice, sustain them, and be glorified through their faithfulness.

HOMILETICAL IDEA: Trust that the God who brings justice will sustain you until you see his justice.

2 Thessalonians 2:1-12

SUBJECT: Why should the Thessalonians have confidence that the day of the Lord has not already come?

COMPLEMENT: Because it will follow the rebellion and the revelation of the man of lawlessness.

EXEGETICAL IDEA: The Thessalonians should have confidence that the day of the Lord has not already come because it will follow the rebellion and the revelation of the man of lawlessness.

HOMILETICAL IDEA: Love the truth when facing future uncertainty.

2 Thessalonians 2:13-3:5

SUBJECT: How should the Thessalonian believers persevere in the faith?

COMPLEMENT: With confidence in their calling and by holding firm to their tradition, hope, and the faithful sustaining power of the Lord.

---

1. Michael W. Holmes, *1 and 2 Thessalonians*, The NIV Application Commentary (Grand Rapids: Zondervan, 1998).

EXEGETICAL IDEA: The Thessalonian believers should persevere in the faith with confidence in their calling and by holding firm to their tradition, hope, and the faithful sustaining power of the Lord.

HOMILETICAL IDEA: Stand firm in your calling and in the Lord's faithfulness.

2 Thessalonians 3:6-18

SUBJECT: How should the Thessalonians respond to idleness?

COMPLEMENT: By imitating the apostles' example through avoiding the idle busybody, practicing a quiet work ethic, and implementing church discipline.

EXEGETICAL IDEA: The Thessalonians should respond to idleness by imitating the apostles' example through avoiding the idle busybody, practicing a quiet work ethic, and implementing church discipline.

HOMILETICAL IDEA: Work like your work matters and demonstrate discerning (church) discipline.

Difficult Passages/Verses

Explain the setting of 2 Thessalonians: identify Paul, Silvanus, and Timothy; place Thessalonica within Paul's missionary journeys; explain the relationship of this letter to 1 Thessalonians.

Perhaps the most challenging text is 2 Thessalonians 2:1–12. Explain how this passage should shape our eschatology without producing what the apostles were preaching against: fear of or obsession with date setting or antichrist identity guessing. Amid speculation and fears, believers must be those who "love the truth" (2:10) and trust that God will reveal the future events in their time.

Utilize 3:6–13 to preach a "theology of work."[2] Recognize the challenges of explaining church discipline in 3:14–15 in light of the few specifics the text provides.

Cultural Perspectives and Application

How do we faithfully apply the book of 2 Thessalonians? First, we need to understand the extent of persecution the believers in Thessalonica faced. Second, we need to recognize how Paul wrote 2:1–12 to counter false speculation rather than to provide a list for identifying the antichrist. Third, we need to

---

2. For additional resources, go to https://www.theologyofwork.org.

recognize that 3:6–13 was not written to construct an economic system or condemn a welfare system. It was written into a communal culture and to reinforce the Christian work ethic laid out in 1 Thessalonians 4:9–12.

While 2 Thessalonians was written to a specific church, there are numerous applications for today, including the following: encourage and advocate for persecuted Christians (1:1–12); trust God to bring those who harm you to justice (1:5–12); always submit speculations to Scripture (2:1–12); remember your calling in Christ (2:13–14); rely on the Lord to sustain your faith (3:1–5); work like your work matters (3:6–12); practice well-thought church discipline (3:13–15).

RECOMMENDED RESOURCES

Fee, Gordon G. *The First and Second Letters to the Thessalonians*. The New International Commentary on the New Testament. Grand Rapids: Eerdmans, 2009.

Green, Gene L. *The Letters to the Thessalonians*. The Pillar New Testament Commentary. Grand Rapids: Eerdmans, 2002.

Holmes, Michael W. *1 and 2 Thessalonians*. The NIV Application Commentary. Grand Rapids: Zondervan, 1998.

1 Timothy

CHRIS RAPPAZINI

The Big Idea of 1 Timothy

In 1 Timothy, Paul offers Timothy advice on how to protect himself and others from false teachings (1:3–7, 19–20; 4:1–3, 7, 16; 6:3–6, 20). His antidote to false teachers is sound ecclesiology. Other topics do appear in this short letter, but Paul is clear that he writes to Timothy for the purpose of establishing proper conduct in the household of God (3:15).

SUBJECT: What is Paul's advice to Timothy concerning false teaching in Ephesus?

COMPLEMENT: Establish proper theology and right conduct within the household of God.

EXEGETICAL IDEA: Paul's advice to Timothy concerning false teaching in Ephesus is to establish proper theology and right conduct within the household of God.

HOMILETICAL IDEA: What we believe shapes how we live.

Selecting Preaching and Teaching Passages in 1 Timothy

Many preachers and teachers would work through 1 Timothy a few verses at a time. However, it may be beneficial to divide the book into four sections. Each section would have one to four units that could be preached each week, resulting in an eleven-week series. Several of the units could be combined or expanded if a longer or shorter series is needed.

Getting the Subject, Complement, Exegetical Idea, and Homiletical Idea

1 Timothy 1:1-11

SUBJECT: How does Paul task Timothy to combat the false teachers who are promoting lies, stirring up controversies, and causing some to leave the faith at the church in Ephesus?

COMPLEMENT: In love with a pure heart, a good conscience, and a sincere faith.

EXEGETICAL IDEA: Paul tasks Timothy to combat the false teachers—who are promoting lies, stirring up controversies, and causing some to leave the faith at the church in Ephesus—in love with a pure heart, a good conscience, and a sincere faith.

HOMILETICAL IDEA: Correct false teaching while having the correct motives.

1 Timothy 1:12-20

SUBJECT: Why does Paul share details about his sinful life with Timothy?

COMPLEMENT: To demonstrate God's grace and mercy as an example of his patience and willingness to use the worst of sinners for his glory.

EXEGETICAL IDEA: Paul shares details about his sinful life with Timothy to demonstrate God's grace and mercy as an example of his patience and willingness to use the worst of sinners for his glory.

HOMILETICAL IDEA: Your past can be used for God's glory.

1 Timothy 2:1-7

SUBJECT: Why does Paul tell Timothy he should lead people in praying for everyone, especially those in authority?

COMPLEMENT: Because when there is peace in the land, there are greater opportunities for the gospel to spread and people to be saved.

EXEGETICAL IDEA: Paul tells Timothy he should lead people in praying for everyone, especially those in authority, because when there is peace in the land, there are greater opportunities for the gospel to spread and people to be saved.

HOMILETICAL IDEA: Pray for peace in our land and salvation in people's lives.

1 Timothy 2:8-15

SUBJECT: How does Paul tell Timothy that men and women should behave in worship?

COMPLEMENT: Men ought to pray for one another instead of angrily disputing one another, and women ought to care for one another instead of causing conflict among one another.

EXEGETICAL IDEA: Paul tells Timothy that in worship men ought to pray for one another instead of angrily disputing one another, and women ought to care for one another instead of causing conflict among one another.

HOMILETICAL IDEA: Worship God on the inside and out.

1 Timothy 3:1-13

SUBJECT: Who does Paul tell Timothy should be the ones in leadership at the church in Ephesus?

COMPLEMENT: Men and women who live lives above reproach, have a noble character, and demonstrate a strong faith in Christ Jesus.

EXEGETICAL IDEA: Paul tells Timothy the ones in leadership at the church in Ephesus should be men and women who live lives above reproach, have a noble character, and demonstrate a strong faith in Christ Jesus.

HOMILETICAL IDEA: Appoint godly leaders who live godly lives.

1 Timothy 3:14-16

SUBJECT: Why is Paul writing to Timothy regarding instructions about how people ought to conduct themselves within the church?

COMPLEMENT: Because the church of the risen Lord, Jesus Christ, is the pillar and foundation of truth.

EXEGETICAL IDEA: Paul writes to Timothy regarding instructions about how people ought to conduct themselves within the church because the church of the risen Lord, Jesus Christ, is the pillar and foundation of truth.

HOMILETICAL IDEA: Live godly lives for Jesus Christ, the living God.

1 Timothy 4

SUBJECT: How does Paul tell Timothy to correct the poor theology of the false teachers who are teaching the Ephesians to abstain from certain foods and marriage, among other regulations?

COMPLEMENT: By pointing out falsehoods, putting his hope in the living God, and living as an example of a true Christ-follower despite his young age.

EXEGETICAL IDEA: Paul tells Timothy to correct the poor theology of the false teachers who are teaching the Ephesians to abstain from certain foods and marriage, among other regulations, by pointing out falsehoods, putting his hope in the living God, and living as an example of a true Christ-follower despite his young age.

HOMILETICAL IDEA: Point out false teaching with both the right words and the right actions.

1 Timothy 5:1-16

SUBJECT: How does Paul instruct Timothy to teach the church how to care for relatives and widows?

COMPLEMENT: To treat one another as family so the leaders of the church can focus on those who need extra help.

EXEGETICAL IDEA: Paul instructs Timothy to teach the church how to care for relatives and widows by treating one another as family so the leaders of the church can focus on those who need extra help.

HOMILETICAL IDEA: Treat one another as family.

1 Timothy 5:17-25

SUBJECT: How does Paul instruct Timothy to treat the elders of the church?

COMPLEMENT: With respect and honor without favoritism but to publicly rebuke those who habitually live in sin, because an elder's lifestyle is on display for all to see.

EXEGETICAL IDEA: Paul instructs Timothy to treat the elders of the church with respect and honor without favoritism but to publicly rebuke those who habitually live in sin, because an elder's lifestyle is on display for all to see.

HOMILETICAL IDEA: Watch your lifestyle because God and others are watching you.

1 Timothy 6:1-2

SUBJECT: How does Paul tell Timothy those under the yoke of slavery are to treat their masters?

COMPLEMENT: With full respect, as they serve more than just their masters, are strategically placed there to be witnesses for God, and are not to associate with the vicious slave rebellions.

EXEGETICAL IDEA: Paul tells Timothy that those under the yoke of slavery are to treat their masters with full respect, as they serve more than just their masters, are strategically placed there to be witnesses for God, and are not to associate with the vicious slave rebellions.

HOMILETICAL IDEA: Persuade, don't repulse, people into God's family with your faithful service.

1 Timothy 6:3–21

SUBJECT: How does Paul tell Timothy he is to teach against the corrupt teachers and their greed?

COMPLEMENT: By instructing the Ephesian Christians to become rich in their good works and become content with all the Lord has provided for them.

EXEGETICAL IDEA: Paul tells Timothy he is to teach against the corrupt teachers and their greed by instructing the Ephesian Christians to become rich in their good works and become content with all the Lord has provided for them.

HOMILETICAL IDEA: Be committed to being content.

Difficult Passages/Verses

This short letter contains several passages that in many ways go against the grain of our culture. For this reason, the passages concerning homosexuality (1:8–11), men and women in the church (chaps. 2–3), and master-servant relationships (6:1–2) should be handled with the utmost grace and care. Paul offers Timothy sound advice early on in the letter, saying, "The goal of our instruction is love from a pure heart and a good conscience and a sincere faith" (1:5 NASB).

Other passages are difficult because of their theological implications. The idea that Paul "handed" anyone over to Satan (1:20) requires serious explanation. Paul explains that God desires that everyone be saved (2:3–4), but not everyone is saved. This raises a large conversation and usually stokes a debate between Calvinism and Arminianism. The expositor must handle such passages with detailed care. The qualifications for elders, specifically concerning gender, divorce, alcohol, and money (3:2, 3, 8; 5:17), also require significant explanation.

A list of difficult passages and topics:

- law/homosexuality (1:8–11)[1]
- "handed over to Satan" (1:20)
- God's desire that all come to faith (2:3–4)
- women in the church (2:9–15)[2]
- qualifications of church leaders (3:2, 3, 8)
- honor/money in ministry (5:17)
- master-slave relationship (6:1–2)

Cultural Perspectives and Application

Some of the most helpful historical and cultural information comes from Scripture itself. Ephesus appears in Acts on several occasions. It is a large city with a well-established pagan religion to the goddess Artemis (Acts 19:11–27). Even though Ephesus already had a deep-rooted religion, Paul remained there longer than he would usually remain in a city and established a substantial church (Acts 18:23; 19:1).[3]

The letter of 1 Timothy may be applied today by considering the universal, timeless truths concerning ecclesiology. The church ought to be known for its integrity, good works, and service to the poor and marginalized, which draw people toward the love of Christ. There will never be a time that the church is not confronted with false teaching and false teachers who lead true believers astray. Paul's advice for the young pastor at Ephesus—to establish proper beliefs and right conduct in the household of God—will always be helpful advice until Jesus's return.

---

1. *The Master's Seminary Journal* 28, no. 2 (Fall 2017), contains four very helpful articles that address the biblical approach to homosexuality.

2. Here are some resources that may be helpful on the topic of women in the church: Sarah Sumner, *Men and Women in the Church: Building Consensus on Christian Leadership* (Downers Grove, IL: InterVarsity, 2003); Kathy Keller, *Jesus, Justice and Gender Roles: A Case for Gender Roles in Ministry* (Grand Rapids: Zondervan, 2012); John Piper and Wayne Grudem, *Recovering Biblical Manhood and Womanhood* (Wheaton: Crossway, 2006); Stanley N. Gundry, ed., *Two Views on Women in Ministry* (Grand Rapids: Zondervan, 2005).

3. Philip H. Towner, *The Letters of Timothy and Titus*, The New International Commentary on the New Testament (Grand Rapids: Eerdmans, 2006), 37–52. Towner offers a detailed and comprehensive survey of the historical and cultural context.

RECOMMENDED RESOURCES

Mounce, William D. *Pastoral Epistles*. Word Biblical Commentary. Nashville: Thomas Nelson, 2000.

Towner, Philip H. *The Letters to Timothy and Titus*. The New International Commentary on the New Testament. Grand Rapids: Eerdmans, 2006.

Yarbrough, Robert W. *The Letters to Timothy and Titus*. The Pillar New Testament Commentary. Grand Rapids: Eerdmans, 2018.

See also recommendations for 2 Timothy and Titus.

2 Timothy

CHRIS RAPPAZINI

The Big Idea of 2 Timothy

The Second Letter to Timothy is Paul's final letter. Paul is imprisoned in Rome, and he senses his life on earth is nearing its end. He wants Timothy to visit so he can pass on his ideas about ministry and missionary plans.

SUBJECT: What is Paul's concluding charge to Timothy in his final letter?

COMPLEMENT: Although many have fallen and will fall away from right preaching and living because of persecutions that arise, believers are to remain faithful in proclaiming the gospel and living rightly.

EXEGETICAL IDEA: Paul's concluding charge to Timothy in his final letter is that although many have fallen and will fall away from right preaching and living because of persecutions that arise, believers are to remain faithful in proclaiming the gospel and living rightly.

HOMILETICAL IDEA: Following Jesus is risky but so worth it.

Selecting Preaching and Teaching Passages in 2 Timothy

This letter can easily be divided up and preached in sections with the goal of going through one verse at a time. Given the brevity of the book, being only four chapters, it is possible to preach through the entire book section by section. Being a letter, picking and choosing certain verses or sections to preach and teach would not give a proper and true understanding of it.

There are two large sections in this letter: (1) Paul challenges Timothy to rest assured in his calling, and (2) Paul challenges Timothy to deal with the corrupt leaders in Ephesus. Paul concludes with his last requests and words of wisdom.

Getting the Subject, Complement, Exegetical Idea, and Homiletical Idea

2 Timothy 1

SUBJECT: Why does Paul tell Timothy he should not be ashamed to testify about the Lord?

COMPLEMENT: Because Timothy has been loyal to God since his upbringing and the Holy Spirit empowers believers through love and self-discipline to be advocates for the risen Jesus, even when others turn away.

EXEGETICAL IDEA: Paul tells Timothy he should not be ashamed to testify about the Lord because Timothy has been loyal to God since his upbringing and the Holy Spirit empowers believers through love and self-discipline to be advocates for the risen Jesus, even when others turn away.

HOMILETICAL IDEA: Do not be ashamed of the Lord's work in your life.

2 Timothy 2:1-13

SUBJECT: What does Paul tell Timothy is a result of being strong in the grace of Jesus?

COMPLEMENT: Obtaining a source of power to endure during excruciating environments, sacrificial seasons, and commitments to something bigger than oneself for the purpose of salvation, which Jesus has brought into this world through his death and resurrection.

EXEGETICAL IDEA: Paul tells Timothy that a result of being strong in the grace of Jesus is obtaining a source of power to endure during excruciating environments, sacrificial seasons, and commitments to something bigger than oneself for the purpose of salvation, which Jesus has brought into this world through his death and resurrection.

HOMILETICAL IDEA: The grace of Jesus is our source of power to endure all things.

2 Timothy 2:14-3:9

SUBJECT: How does Paul challenge Timothy to confront the false teachers in Ephesus who teach that the resurrection of the saints has already occurred?

COMPLEMENT: By avoiding quarrels, godless chatter, evil desires, and foolish arguments, and instead presenting oneself as one approved by God who rightly handles the Scriptures and preaches the gospel of Jesus's death and resurrection.

EXEGETICAL IDEA: Paul challenges Timothy to confront the false teachers in Ephesus who teach that the resurrection of the saints has already occurred by avoiding quarrels, godless chatter, evil desires, and foolish arguments, and instead presenting oneself as one approved by God who rightly handles the Scriptures and preaches the gospel of Jesus's death and resurrection.

HOMILETICAL IDEA: Choose your words carefully and your actions caringly.

2 Timothy 3:10–17

SUBJECT: Why does Paul tell Timothy of his way of life as well as his trials and sufferings?

COMPLEMENT: As a reminder that godly people will face persecution, and that the God-breathed, holy Scriptures can equip people for the life and work God has called them to.

EXEGETICAL IDEA: Paul tells Timothy of his way of life as well as his trials and sufferings as a reminder that godly people will face persecution, and that the God-breathed, holy Scriptures can equip people for the life and work God has called them to.

HOMILETICAL IDEA: Perseverance of the faith comes through reliance on the Scriptures.

2 Timothy 4:1–5

SUBJECT: What is Paul's final charge to Timothy as he looks ahead to the future?

COMPLEMENT: To be prepared at all times to preach the truth, since a time will come when people will substitute sound doctrine for soft, shallow teachings.

EXEGETICAL IDEA: Paul's final charge to Timothy, as he looks ahead to the future, is to be prepared at all times to preach the truth, since a time will come when people will substitute sound doctrine for soft, shallow teachings.

HOMILETICAL IDEA: In every season, preach the Word.

2 Timothy 4:6–8

SUBJECT: How does Paul view the end of his time on earth?

COMPLEMENT: With great satisfaction that he suffered for the Lord and with anticipation for his crown of righteousness.

EXEGETICAL IDEA: Paul views the end of his time on earth with great satisfaction that he suffered for the Lord and with anticipation for his crown of righteousness.

HOMILETICAL IDEA: Rewards await the faithful followers.

2 Timothy 4:9–22

SUBJECT: What are Paul's personal remarks to Timothy as he concludes his letter?

COMPLEMENT: His requests for particular items, a warning to stay away from Alexander, and an acknowledgment that even though many have deserted him, the Lord has remained with him and gives him the strength he needs each day.

EXEGETICAL IDEA: Paul's personal remarks to Timothy as he concludes his letter include his requests for particular items, a warning to stay away from Alexander, and an acknowledgment that even though many have deserted him, the Lord has remained with him and gives him the strength he needs each day.

HOMILETICAL IDEA: Even if you are standing alone, God is by your side.

Difficult Passages/Verses

One of the first challenges with this short letter is determining the exact date when it was written. It is uncertain how much time has passed since Paul wrote 1 Timothy. He could be writing from his house arrest in Rome (Acts 28), or he could be writing from a later Roman imprisonment after his release from house arrest (2 Tim. 4:13–15).

Another interpretative challenge may be determining who exactly are all the people Paul lists throughout his letter and what their relation to him is. However, the sheer fact of the unknown reminds the reader that this was a personal letter from Paul to his "dear son" Timothy, who would have known exactly who Paul was talking about.

Cultural Perspectives and Application

Paul's Second Letter to Timothy is a reminder to all Christians that a life of worship and ministry to the Lord Jesus Christ is often, if not always, marked with consistent resistance and persecution. Paul's hardships can be felt throughout his letter. His chains, loneliness, betrayals, accusations, and living conditions are just a few of the persecutions he is left to endure. Nonetheless, Paul reminds Christians everywhere to stand firm in the faith until the Lord calls us home.

Following Jesus and standing up for the truths of Scripture involves sacrificing safety and inviting tension. Challenging times are not a symbol that God has abandoned Christians. Instead, those tough and demanding seasons are when a Christian's faith is solidified and reliance on Jesus's love and comfort becomes the most genuine and tangible.

RECOMMENDED RESOURCES

Fee, Gordon D. *1 and 2 Timothy, Titus*. New International Biblical Commentary. Peabody, MA: Hendrickson, 1992.

Knight, George W., III. *The Pastoral Epistles*. The New International Greek Testament Commentary. Grand Rapids: Eerdmans, 1992.

Marshall, I. Howard. *Pastoral Epistles*. The International Critical Commentary. New York: T&T Clark, 1999.

See also recommendations for 1 Timothy and Titus.

Titus

SCOTT M. GIBSON

Titus, a Greek convert to Christianity, was led to Christ by Paul, who referred to him as "Titus, my true son in our common faith" (1:4). Titus accompanied Paul to various cities, including Corinth (2 Cor. 8:16–9:5; 12:19–21), and was commissioned to go to Dalmatia (2 Tim. 4:10) among other duties assigned by the apostle, including going to Crete, where Titus was serving on receipt of this letter from Paul.

Titus was sent to Crete to complete a challenging assignment, as stated in 1:5: "The reason I left you in Crete was that you might put in order what was left unfinished and appoint elders in every town, as I directed you," Paul writes. Titus was to establish the church in the midst of a pagan culture while contending with false teachers, teaching them about grace, and doing good.

SUBJECT: Why does Paul write his letter to Titus?

COMPLEMENT: To ask Titus to straighten out an uncompleted situation, appoint elders, teach sound doctrine to a young church, and disciple the church to embrace grace and godliness, to live godly lives in the midst of a difficult pagan culture, and to avoid controversies and people who incite them, all the while doing good to the glory of God.

EXEGETICAL IDEA: Paul writes his letter to Titus to ask him to straighten out an uncompleted situation, appoint elders, teach sound doctrine to a young church, and disciple the church to embrace grace and godliness, to live godly lives in the midst of a difficult pagan culture, and to avoid controversies and people who incite them, all the while doing good to the glory of God.

HOMILETICAL IDEA: Even in a tough cultural climate, we can be embraced by grace and sound teaching that leads to godly living.

Selecting Preaching and Teaching Passages in Titus

This brief letter is divided into a five-week series, which can be expanded. Some commentaries section the letter into as many as eight segments. The careful preacher will want to assess the units of thought as he or she prepares to preach, laying out a series for his or her listeners.

Getting the Subject, Complement, Exegetical Idea, and Homiletical Idea

Titus 1:1-4

SUBJECT: What does Paul say in his greeting to Titus about himself and about God?

COMPLEMENT: He describes himself as a servant of God, an apostle for the purpose of the faith of the elect, that they may know God and eternal life given by God, who does not lie, who fulfills his promises, even choosing and commanding Paul to preach Christ who brings grace and peace.

EXEGETICAL IDEA: In his greeting to Titus, Paul describes himself as a servant of God, an apostle for the purpose of the faith of the elect, that they may know God and eternal life given by God, who does not lie, who fulfills his promises, even choosing and commanding Paul to preach Christ who brings grace and peace.

HOMILETICAL IDEA: A trustworthy God makes his messengers trustworthy, giving salvation, which is grace and peace.

Titus 1:5-16

SUBJECT: What did Paul say is the reason he left Titus on the island of Crete?

COMPLEMENT: To straighten out an unfinished task, appointing elders and recognizing the opposition from Judaizers and the corrupt Cretan culture.

EXEGETICAL IDEA: Paul left Titus on the island of Crete to straighten out an unfinished task, appointing elders and recognizing the opposition from Judaizers and the corrupt Cretan culture.

HOMILETICAL IDEA: Get this straight: beware of the lies of corrupt teaching and culture.

Titus 2

SUBJECT: What is the result of teaching sound doctrine with straightforwardness and courage to the various groups in the church at Crete?

COMPLEMENT: Older and younger men, older and younger women, and slaves will reflect the doctrines in their lives by recognizing God's grace in Christ that enables them to turn from ungodliness as they await the second coming of Christ, eager to do the good they are called to do.

EXEGETICAL IDEA: The result of teaching sound doctrine with straightforwardness and courage to the various groups in the church at Crete is that older and younger men, older and younger women, and slaves will reflect the doctrines in their lives by recognizing God's grace in Christ that enables them to turn from ungodliness as they await the second coming of Christ, eager to do the good they are called to do.

HOMILETICAL IDEA: Bold teaching and bold embracing lead to bold living and longing.

Titus 3:1-11

SUBJECT: Why does Paul want Titus to remind the Cretan church to do good by showing humility to all people?

COMPLEMENT: Because every one of them was self-absorbed before Christ came into their lives; Christ saved them not because they deserved it but because of his mercy, which was poured out on them by the Holy Spirit; and Paul wants the church not to forget where they came from.

EXEGETICAL IDEA: Paul wants Titus to remind the Cretan church to do good by showing humility to all people because every one of them was self-absorbed before Christ came into their lives; Christ saved them not because they deserved it but because of his mercy, which was poured out on them by the Holy Spirit; and Paul wants the church not to forget where they came from.

HOMILETICAL IDEA: Humility gives perspective on what it means to do good.

Titus 3:12-15

SUBJECT: What is Paul's final charge for Titus?

COMPLEMENT: To instruct people to live productive lives by doing good and helping those who need help—and grace will be with them all.

EXEGETICAL IDEA: Paul's final charge for Titus is to instruct people to live productive lives by doing good and helping those who need help—and grace will be with them all.

HOMILETICAL IDEA: A productive life does good by helping those who need help, giving grace to all.

Difficult Passages/Verses

Titus 2:9–10 may be difficult for twenty-first-century sensibilities to grasp. Some commentaries appear to ignore the similarities and differences of the nuances of ancient slavery and more recent expressions of it. This inhumane and depraved institution has prevailed in the ancient world and across time. One out of every three persons in Rome was a slave during this period. Slavery resulted from capture in war, crime, kidnapping, piracy, debt, need for support, selling oneself, being sold as a child, and birth to slave parents.[1]

That slaves appear in this list of people whom Paul exhorts in chapter 2 does not ignore the horrific social institution that slavery is, yet Paul is making the point that they all—older and younger men and women, including slaves—are to embrace sound doctrine and make this teaching about God attractive (2:1, 10) because of the grace given them all by Christ to do good.

Cultural Perspectives and Application

One does not want to overlook the impact that one sees on the Cretan church from false teachers and from the wider culture. As for the false teachers, Paul acknowledges that the Judaizers, "the circumcision group" whom he describes as "rebellious" in relationship to orthodox doctrine, are having a negative impact on "whole households" (1:10–11). The letter emphasizes the importance of good teaching that will make a church strong for good living.

The other factor, Cretan culture in general, is pictured realistically in Paul's quote from the island's poet, Epimenides, who wrote, "Cretans are always liars, evil brutes, lazy gluttons" (1:12). Cretans had the inglorious reputation for being liars. One of the Greek words for lying, *kretizein*, characterized the culture. The island even became a haven for pirates and robbers. This cultural penchant for untruth surely had an impact on life in the local church, and Paul wrote Titus to address it.

---

1. David Platt, Daniel L. Akin, and Tony Merida, *Christ-Centered Exposition Exalting Jesus in 1 and 2 Timothy and Titus* (Nashville: B&H Academic, 2013), 267–68.

In addition, an awareness of the widespread nature of slavery in this age will give the expositor perspective, recognizing that many slaves were among the first to convert to Christianity. See discussion in the chapter on Philemon.

The distance between Cretans of the first century and readers of this letter in the twenty-first century may not be as distant as one might think. False teachers continue to twist Scripture, and popular culture manipulates the church. Paul's spotlight on grace and doing good is applicable now more than ever.

RECOMMENDED RESOURCES

Guthrie, Donald. *The Pastoral Epistles: An Introduction and Commentary*. Tyndale New Testament Commentaries. Grand Rapids: Eerdmans, 1957.

Köstenberger, Andreas. "Titus." In *Ephesians–Philemon*, edited by Tremper Longman III and David E. Garland, 601–26. The Expositor's Bible Commentary. Grand Rapids: Zondervan, 2006.

Liefeld, Walter L. *1 and 2 Timothy, Titus*. The NIV Application Commentary. Grand Rapids: Zondervan, 1999.

Platt, David, Daniel L. Akin, and Tony Merida. *Christ-Centered Exposition Exalting Jesus in 1 and 2 Timothy and Titus*. Nashville: B&H Academic, 2013.

Philemon

PAUL A. HOFFMAN

The Big Idea of Philemon

Philemon is one of the four prison epistles and the shortest of the apostle Paul's writings. It is addressed first to Philemon, a gentile Christian and slaveowner in Colossae, and second to the church that meets in his home. The letter is an impassioned and personal plea in which Paul asks his friend Philemon to receive Onesimus back, not as a runaway slave, but as a "dear brother . . . in the Lord" (v. 16). In God's sovereignty, Onesimus fled to Rome, where he met Paul (who previously led Philemon to faith) and became a Christian. While sending Onesimus back to Philemon (a dangerous move for a runaway), Paul argues that the gospel has changed the nature of their relationship: their mutual bond in Christ now transcends their sociocultural identities of slave and master. This letter illustrates how the gospel can transform our real, and sometimes difficult, relationships.

SUBJECT: Why does Paul write to his friend Philemon?

COMPLEMENT: To appeal to Philemon—"on the basis of love" (v. 9)—to receive the returning Onesimus, not as a runaway slave, but rather as a "dear brother . . . in the Lord" (v. 16).

EXEGETICAL IDEA: Paul writes to his friend Philemon to appeal to him—on the basis of love—to receive the returning Onesimus, not as a runaway slave, but rather as a dear brother in the Lord.

HOMILETICAL IDEA: Jesus Christ transforms our identity and relationships.

Selecting Preaching and Teaching Passages in Philemon

Because Philemon is only twenty-five verses long (about 335 words in the original Greek), it can be preached or taught in one sitting. It is possible, however, to divide the book into two coherent sections: (1) the greeting (vv. 1–3) and thanksgiving and prayer (vv. 4–7), and (2) Paul's appeal (vv. 8–21), along with the final appeal, greetings, and benediction (vv. 22–25).

Difficult Passages/Verses

The issue of slavery cannot be avoided when one preaches or teaches this letter. Given the United States' ugly history with slavery and the recent increase in human trafficking across the globe, the communicator would be wise to approach Philemon with humility, sensitivity, and moral clarity.

Slavery in the first century does not precisely correlate with more contemporary forms. In Paul's milieu, slavery was more widespread: "Estimates are that 85–90 percent of the inhabitants of Rome and peninsula Italy were slaves or of slave origin." Furthermore, slaves "were granted many rights" and "could expect to be set free at least by the time they reached age thirty," and many slaves "were trusted household servants, teachers, librarians, accountants and estate managers."[1]

But that is not to say such slavery is acceptable. While the New Testament neither directly condemns nor condones this practice, it was, and remains, morally abhorrent. Paul subtly undermines slavery when he requests that Philemon redefine the relationship: to forgive Onesimus and embrace him as a brother rather than a seditious slave because of his newfound identity in Christ. Thus Paul's "focus is upon transforming personal relationships within the system."[2] Paul's critique of slavery is more indirect than direct, more relational than institutional (and possibly more effective for that reason; cf. Col. 4:9).

Cultural Perspectives and Application

Once the matter of slavery is appropriately handled, there are few historical or cultural matters the communicator needs to address.

---

1. A. A. Rupprecht, "Slave, Slavery," in *Dictionary of Paul and His Letters*, ed. Gerald Hawthorne, Ralph P. Martin, and Daniel G. Reid (Downers Grove, IL: InterVarsity, 1993), 881.
2. Peter T. O'Brien, "Philemon," in *New Bible Commentary: 21st Century Edition*, ed. G. J. Wenham et al. (Downers Grove, IL: InterVarsity, 1994), 1317.

This letter offers multiple application points:

- The gospel defines our identity: humans see a slave; God sees a beloved son and "useful" (v. 11) brother.
- The gospel transforms our relationships: the love of Christ motivates Christians to forgive one another and seek reconciliation when relationships are broken (cf. Matt. 5:23–24; 18:15–17). Christians will also act as peacemakers and reconcilers: Paul initiates the restoration process between Philemon and Onesimus (cf. Matt. 5:9; 2 Cor. 5:11–21).
- The sweetness of God's sovereignty: Paul led Philemon to Christ; his slave runs away to Rome, one of the largest cities in the ancient world, and yet somehow meets the imprisoned Paul and becomes a Christian; Paul returns the transformed Onesimus to his friend.

--- **RECOMMENDED RESOURCES** ---

Moo, Douglas J. *The Letters to the Colossians and Philemon*. The Pillar New Testament Commentary. Grand Rapids: Eerdmans, 2008.

O'Brien, Peter T. *Colossians, Philemon*. Word Biblical Commentary. Waco: Word, 1982.

Wright, N. T. *Colossians and Philemon*. Tyndale New Testament Commentaries. Downers Grove, IL: IVP Academic, 2015.

Hebrews

PABLO A. JIMÉNEZ

The Big Idea of Hebrews

Hebrews, rather than a letter, is an expository sermon on Psalm 110 that explains the work of Jesus Christ. Besides references to this psalm, Hebrews includes several references and brief comments about other passages of Scripture. All of these references and comments are subordinate to the central theme of the sermon.

Hebrews has a relevant message for the Christian church today. The epistle calls us to take our faith seriously, to deepen our knowledge of the Holy Scriptures, to show solidarity with other believers, to live our faith without fear, and to fight for the transformation of society in light of the values of the kingdom of God.

SUBJECT: What is the central message of Hebrews?

COMPLEMENT: Jesus is the high priest of the new covenant who encourages believers who suffer under Roman rule.

EXEGETICAL IDEA: The central message of Hebrews is that Jesus is the high priest of the new covenant who encourages believers who suffer under Roman rule.

HOMILETICAL IDEA: Jesus is the only mediator between God and humanity and the leader of our salvation.

Selecting Preaching and Teaching Passages in Hebrews

The Epistle to the Hebrews begins with a brief prologue that does not resemble the rest of the New Testament epistles. The body of the letter is divided into five sections, each of which in turn deals with two topics. In four of the five sections there is a text that serves as a bridge between one theme and the other. The document ends with a conclusion similar to other New Testament letters.

Prologue (1:1–4)

The Superiority of the Son (1:5–2:18)

Christ Is Our High Priest (3:1–5:10)

Characteristics of the High Priesthood of Christ (5:11–10:39)

Perseverance (11:1–12:13)

Orientation for the Christian life (12:14–13:19)

Conclusion (13:20–25)

Getting the Subject, Complement, Exegetical Idea, and Homiletical Idea

Hebrews 1:1-4

▣ *Prologue*

SUBJECT: Why are the first verses of Hebrews different from the introductions in most epistles of the New Testament?

COMPLEMENT: Because the main theme of the prologue is the intervention of God in human history as he takes the initiative in the process of salvation through divine intervention in the person of Jesus Christ.

EXEGETICAL IDEA: The first verses of Hebrews are different from the introductions in most epistles of the New Testament because the main theme of the prologue is the intervention of God in human history as he takes the initiative in the process of salvation through divine intervention in the person of Jesus Christ.

HOMILETICAL IDEA: Jesus is the prophet par excellence through whom God has spoken.

Hebrews 1:5-2:18

▣ *The Superiority of the Son*

SUBJECT: Why does the author affirm that Jesus is superior to the angels?

COMPLEMENT: Because of the coronation of the Son as king and his solidarity with humanity achieved through suffering; therefore they should not "neglect so great a salvation" (2:3 NASB).

EXEGETICAL IDEA: The author affirms that Jesus is superior to the angels because of the coronation of the Son as king and his solidarity with humanity achieved through suffering; therefore they should not "neglect so great a salvation" (2:3 NASB).

HOMILETICAL IDEA: God has made salvation possible through the suffering of Jesus, the one who is superior to angels.

Hebrews 3:1–5:10

▨ Christ Is Our High Priest

SUBJECT: Why does Hebrews affirm Jesus's superiority over all major figures of the Old Testament?

COMPLEMENT: Because Christ is our faithful, compassionate high priest who is superior to Moses and Joshua.

EXEGETICAL IDEA: Hebrews affirms Jesus's superiority over all major figures of the Old Testament because Christ is our faithful, compassionate high priest who is superior to Moses and Joshua.

HOMILETICAL IDEA: In Jesus we have a faithful, compassionate high priest who can identify with humanity and lead us to salvation.

Hebrews 5:11–10:39

▨ Characteristics of the High Priesthood of Christ

SUBJECT: Why does Hebrews affirm that Jesus is the high priest according to the order of Melchizedek?

COMPLEMENT: Because Jesus is the perfect high priest who offered the perfect sacrifice for the salvation of humanity.

EXEGETICAL IDEA: Hebrews affirms that Jesus is the high priest according to the order of Melchizedek because Jesus is the perfect high priest who offered the perfect sacrifice for the salvation of humanity.

HOMILETICAL IDEA: Jesus is the perfect high priest who offered the perfect sacrifice—himself—and who made salvation possible "once for all" (9:26).

Hebrews 11:1–12:13

▨ Perseverance

SUBJECT: What is the connection between the discourse about faith in chapter 11 and the metaphor of the race in chapter 12?

COMPLEMENT: The heroes mentioned in chapter 11 form the "cloud of witnesses" (12:1) that surrounds the believers who struggle to finish the race in spite of so much opposition.

EXEGETICAL IDEA: The connection between the discourse about faith in chapter 11 and the metaphor of the race in chapter 12 is that the heroes mentioned in chapter 11 form the "cloud of witnesses" (12:1) that surrounds the believers who struggle to finish the race in spite of so much opposition.

HOMILETICAL IDEA: Following the example of the heroes of faith who have preceded us, Christians strive to follow Jesus, who is the goal of our salvation.

Hebrews 12:14–13:19

Orientation for the Christian Life

SUBJECT: What are the practical implications of Hebrews for the church?

COMPLEMENT: The church is called to holiness and obedience and to solidarity with the world and suffering parts of the church.

EXEGETICAL IDEA: The practical implications of Hebrews for the church are that the church is called to holiness and obedience and to solidarity with the world and suffering parts of the church.

HOMILETICAL IDEA: As Jesus suffered for humanity, we share in his sufferings by pursuing holiness and obedience.

Hebrews 13:20–25

Conclusion

SUBJECT: What is the theological meaning of the long blessing that closes Hebrews?

COMPLEMENT: Jesus, who is "the great shepherd of the sheep" (13:20 ESV), blesses those who recognize him as Lord and Savior.

EXEGETICAL IDEA: The theological meaning of the long blessing that closes Hebrews is that Jesus, who is "the great shepherd of the sheep" (13:20 ESV), blesses those who recognize him as Lord and Savior.

HOMILETICAL IDEA: God blesses the church, empowering Christians for life in holiness.

Difficult Passages/Verses

Hebrews 2:10

This text affirms that the exaltation of Jesus implies the exaltation of humanity. Through his solidarity with humanity, Jesus has opened the way through which we can reach the glorification promised in Psalm 8:4–6. The new element of the message of Hebrews is found in 2:10. The phrase "it was fitting" translates a Greek verb that implies that something belongs to, or is linked to the nature of, or is characteristic of something. The verse contains several relative pronouns that indicate the subject of the sentence. In this case, the subject is "the one" who causes and organizes the universe. That creator is the God and Father of Jesus Christ. The phrase "all things" is a collective term that refers to the cosmos or the universe. The goal toward which the Son of God is directed is "glory"—that is, salvation understood as the glorification of the believer.

In this verse, we find one of the christological titles that appears only in the Epistle to the Hebrews: "founder." This word, which also appears in 12:2, can be translated as "captain," "leader," or "prince." Literally, it means "the first to perform an action." The term is used in the Septuagint (Lev. 21:10) in reference to the consecration of the high priest. Hebrews 2:10 ends with an interesting phrase: "perfect [yourself] through what he suffered." The word "perfect" here means "to lead to the fullness of character, to consummate, to lead to maturity."

Hebrews 9:23-28

This section implies that Jesus's death accomplished what the old covenant could only announce. Through his perfect sacrifice, Jesus bridged the distance that separated humanity from God, leading humanity to heaven and ushering it forever into the intimacy of God.

Hebrews affirms that the sacrifice of Jesus Christ provides the final solution to the problem of sin. On the one hand, this gives a solemn meaning to the present. "Today" is the day of salvation (cf. 4:7–9). On the other hand, the author's emphasis on the effectiveness of the sacrifice of Jesus Christ explains why "if we deliberately keep on sinning after we received the knowledge of the truth, no sacrifice for sins is left" for humanity. Jesus died only once and forever. To repeat Jesus's sacrifice would be to deny the effectiveness of his death on the cross.

Hebrews 11:1-2

Chapter 11 begins with a brief prologue that defines the term "faith." Faith is the "confidence of what we hope for and assurance about what we do not see"

(v. 1). Note that this verse is constructed poetically, using a parallelism that evokes the Psalms and Proverbs. The definition has two very similar clauses. The first affirms that faith is the certainty or security of our Christian hope. The second emphasizes the idea, indicating that faith is the conviction or assurance that those spiritual realities are true, although they cannot be seen with human eyes.

Hebrews 13:12-13

The phrase "outside the camp" (v. 13) comes from the time when Israel worshiped God in the tabernacle, not in the temple in Jerusalem. After the construction of the temple, the priests took the body of the immolated goat out of the city. Specifically, they burned it near the garbage dump in the Hinnom Valley, which is south of the city of Jerusalem.

Crucified people were also considered "unclean," according to Deuteronomy 21:23. Therefore, Jewish leaders did not allow the Roman military to crucify people within the city of Jerusalem. In order to avoid contaminating the Holy City, crucifixions occurred on the outskirts of the city.

Jesus died outside the gate of the city of Jerusalem, just as the animal sacrificed by the high priest on the day of purification was burned "outside the camp" (see John 19:20; Acts 7:58). On this basis, Hebrews challenges us to go "outside the camp." The text urges the audience to identify both with the death of Jesus Christ and with his suffering. Believers should not be locked in the holy place, hidden from the attacks of the world. On the contrary, God wants us to testify to our faith there, in the world, in front of those who murdered Jesus.

Cultural Perspectives and Application

This epistle is called "To the Hebrews" because it deals with issues related to the Old Testament, such as the Jewish high priesthood, sacrifices, and the order of worship in the temple. The traditional hypothesis is that Hebrews was written to a Christian congregation of Jewish background. At first glance, the use of Jewish biblical interpretation techniques (such as the Midrash) and the complicated exposition based on worship in the temple of Jerusalem seem to confirm this idea. However, most modern scholars claim that Hebrews was originally written for a group of Christians of Greek background—that is, for a congregation of gentile Christians who were pagans before converting to the gospel of Jesus Christ. They support their ideas with verses such as Hebrews 2:3, which suggests that both the addressees and the author did not listen to the gospel from Jesus of Nazareth but came to faith because of the preaching of the apostles.

Hebrews was originally written in Greek, in an elegant style. This leads us to conclude that its author was a person of great literary ability and that, in the same way, the people who heard it for the first time also had the ability to understand this elevated literary style. In fact, many experts claim that the literary style of the letter recalls preaching in the synagogues where the Jews of Greek background gathered to worship. Providing such historical context will enable listeners to more fully appreciate the Letter to the Hebrews.

RECOMMENDED RESOURCES

Bruce, F. F. *The Epistle to the Hebrews*. The New International Commentary on the New Testament. Grand Rapids: Eerdmans, 1964.

Johnsson, William G. *Hebrews*. Knox Preaching Guides. Atlanta: John Knox, 1980.

Lindars, Barnabas. *The Theology of the Letter to the Hebrews*. Cambridge: Cambridge University Press, 1991.

James

JOEL C. GREGORY

James, the younger half-brother of the Lord Jesus, first pastor of the Jerusalem church, and martyr, writes scattered Christians a reminder that faith must be made visible in deeds.

SUBJECT: Why does James address the diaspora of Christians about authentic faith?

COMPLEMENT: Because invisible personal faith must become visible in concrete deeds that validate the reality of faith.

EXEGETICAL IDEA: James addresses the diaspora of Christians about authentic faith because invisible personal faith must become visible in concrete deeds that validate the reality of faith.

HOMILETICAL IDEA: Real faith has real deeds.

Selecting Preaching and Teaching Passages in James

The book of James is rather straightforward in terms of text selection. I've stuck with entire chapters for the most part except for combining portions of chapters 4 and 5. One is also welcome to go by the subject headings in various Bible translations to engage with less verses per sermon/Bible lesson.

Getting the Subject, Complement, Exegetical Idea, and Homiletical Idea

James 1

SUBJECT: What does James say is the divine purpose in life's testing times?

COMPLEMENT: God uses trials to produce persevering faith that demonstrates itself in believing prayer and consistent Christian conduct.

EXEGETICAL IDEA: James says the divine purpose in life's testing times is that God uses trials to produce persevering faith that demonstrates itself in believing prayer and consistent Christian conduct.

HOMILETICAL IDEA: Tough times are tested by prayer and practice.

James 2

SUBJECT: How does James articulate the criterion by which genuine faith is to be judged?

COMPLEMENT: Genuine faith exhibits itself by visible deeds of practical helpfulness in an attitude of impartiality that gives precedence to the poor.

EXEGETICAL IDEA: James articulates the criterion by which genuine faith is to be judged is that genuine faith exhibits itself by visible deeds of practical helpfulness in an attitude of impartiality that gives precedence to the poor.

HOMILETICAL IDEA: Tangible, visible Christian outward behavior gives the only validation of inward, invisible faith.

James 3

SUBJECT: What does James say is the nature of human speech and how can the confessing Christian deal with it?

COMPLEMENT: It cannot be controlled by human power and must be subjected to divine wisdom.

EXEGETICAL IDEA: James says that human speech cannot be controlled by human power, and the confessing Christian must subject it to divine wisdom.

HOMILETICAL IDEA: Only the power of God can give you the wisdom to control your tongue.

James 4:1-5:6

SUBJECT: What does James say characterizes earthly wisdom versus heavenly wisdom?

COMPLEMENT: Unbridled lust, and humble dependence on God in the present and future.

EXEGETICAL IDEA: James says unbridled lust characterizes earthly wisdom, while humble dependence on God in the present and future marks heavenly wisdom.

HOMILETICAL IDEA: You inevitably demonstrate your inward spiritual condition in either uncontrolled desire or humble dependence on God in the present and future.

James 5:7-20

SUBJECT: Why does James exhort believers to consider nature, biblical heroes (Job and Elijah), and their own personal conditions as a witness to the genuineness of their faith?

COMPLEMENT: Because the Christian life that lasts demonstrates steadfast endurance above all and exhibits an appropriate Christian response in all of life's circumstances.

EXEGETICAL IDEA: James exhorts believers to consider nature, biblical heroes (Job and Elijah), and their own personal conditions as a witness to the genuineness of their faith because the Christian life that lasts demonstrates steadfast endurance above all and exhibits an appropriate Christian response in all of life's circumstances.

HOMILETICAL IDEA: You can persevere in your Christian life, demonstrating patience and a Godward orientation in every circumstance.

Difficult Passages/Verses

The famed historical difficulty in James is found in 2:14–26. Luther famously called James an "epistle of straw" because of a basic misunderstanding of the two ways the word "justified" may be used and the two ways "works" may be used. When Paul uses the word "works," he means conforming to the Jewish law in order to be saved by our own merits. When James uses the word "works," he signifies winsome deeds of caring for others that reveal saving faith. When Paul uses the word "justified," he refers to our belief in the substitutionary death of Christ by which we are pronounced "not guilty" in the presence of God. When James uses the word "justified" in James 2, he uses it in the sense of being "validated" or "shown to be righteous." In that sense, Abraham was "shown to be righteous" when he offered his son Isaac (Gen. 22). Rahab was "validated" as righteous when she hid the spies (Heb.

11:31). This can be explained by the English use of the word "rest." If I need to relax for a few minutes at work, I may say, "Let me rest." It is altogether different in the cemetery when we lay someone to "rest."

Cultural Perspectives and Application

We face an ever more privatized and subjective concept of the Christian faith in today's church. Mere creedal confession shares the same creed as the demons (James 2:19). At least the demons tremble, while complacent church members are at ease with their empty faith. The great tension in the contemporary church rests in holding a warm, saving faith and engaging in outward social action that demonstrates the reality of the saving faith. On the one hand, churches devoted only to social action run out of steam because there is no emphasis on saving faith. On the other hand, Christians that privatize their faith as a personal creed but have no social conscience contradict the faith.

RECOMMENDED RESOURCES

McCartney, Dan G. *James*. Baker Exegetical Commentary on the New Testament. Grand Rapids: Baker Academic, 2009.

Ropes, James Hardy. *A Critical and Exegetical Commentary on the Epistle of James*. Edinburgh: T&T Clark, 1916.

Vaughan, Curtis. *James: A Study Guide*. Grand Rapids: Zondervan, 1969.

1 Peter

ALISON GERBER

The Big Idea of 1 Peter

First Peter is a letter of encouragement and instruction by Peter to gentile Christians across Asia Minor who are suffering for their faith.

SUBJECT: What does Peter want the gentile Christians in Asia Minor to do in the face of suffering?

COMPLEMENT: To praise God for their salvation; to find their identity, encouragement, and example for holy living in Christ; and to look forward to their glorious future.

EXEGETICAL IDEA: Peter wants the gentile Christians in Asia Minor, in the face of suffering, to praise God for their salvation; to find their identity, encouragement, and example for holy living in Christ; and to look forward to their glorious future.

HOMILETICAL IDEA: As we suffer, we will find everything we need in Christ.

Selecting Preaching and Teaching Passages in 1 Peter

First Peter can be broken into four parts: greeting (1:1–2), thanksgiving (1:3–12), body (1:13–5:11), and closing (5:12–14). The body of the letter has three movements: 1:13–2:10; 2:11–4:11; and 4:12–5:11. These are demarcated by the greeting "dear friends" in 2:11 and 4:12. Each of these passages is long and full of worthy content for multiple sermons. Therefore, consider breaking each movement into at least two parts, since each contains at least two distinguishable themes.

Getting the Subject, Complement, Exegetical Idea, and Homiletical Idea

1 Peter 1:1-12

SUBJECT: Why, according to Peter, can the gentile Christians praise God in the midst of their suffering?

COMPLEMENT: Because of the salvation they have, which was planned by God, given in a new birth, secured in heaven, confirmed by their suffering, wondered about by the prophets, and watched by the angels.

EXEGETICAL IDEA: According to Peter, the gentile Christians can praise God in the midst of their suffering because of the salvation they have, which was planned by God, given in a new birth, secured in heaven, confirmed by their suffering, wondered about by the prophets, and watched by the angels.

HOMILETICAL IDEA: Even Christians who suffer can praise God, because they have a marvelous and sure salvation.

1 Peter 1:13-2:3

SUBJECT: How does Peter expect the gentile Christians to live now that they have been redeemed?

COMPLEMENT: By anticipating Jesus's return, by being holy, by loving one another deeply, and by craving more of God's Word.

EXEGETICAL IDEA: Peter expects the gentile Christians to live, now that they have been redeemed, by anticipating Jesus's return, by being holy, by loving one another deeply, and by craving more of God's Word.

HOMILETICAL IDEA: God gave you a new life, so live it in a new way.

1 Peter 2:4-10

SUBJECT: According to Peter, who are the gentile Christians?

COMPLEMENT: They are living stones (as Christ is the Living Stone), a temple (as Christ is the cornerstone of the temple), a people of honor (as Christ honors them), and a people belonging to God.

EXEGETICAL IDEA: According to Peter, the gentile Christians are living stones (as Christ is the Living Stone), a temple (as Christ is the cornerstone of the temple), a people of honor (as Christ honors them), and a people belonging to God.

HOMILETICAL IDEA: Our identity is found with Christ, and our belonging is found with God.

1 Peter 2:11–3:12

SUBJECT: How does Peter instruct gentile Christians to live among their unbelieving neighbors?

COMPLEMENT: With honorable conduct, submitting to those in authority over them, that their unbelieving neighbors might one day honor God.

EXEGETICAL IDEA: Peter instructs the gentile Christians to live among their unbelieving neighbors with honorable conduct, submitting to those in authority over them, that their unbelieving neighbors might one day honor God.

HOMILETICAL IDEA: Live honorably in the world around you, that one day the world around you might honor God.

1 Peter 3:13–4:11

SUBJECT: How does Peter instruct the gentile Christians to respond to unjust suffering?

COMPLEMENT: By remembering Christ's suffering and triumph as both their encouragement and their example for how to live through this time.

EXEGETICAL IDEA: Peter instructs the gentile Christians to respond to unjust suffering by remembering Christ's suffering and triumph as both their encouragement and their example for how to live through this time.

HOMILETICAL IDEA: When suffering, let Christ lead you through.

1 Peter 4:12–19

SUBJECT: How does Peter console the gentiles who suffer for being Christian and doing good?

COMPLEMENT: By encouraging them to remember that there is glory in suffering: glory in being united with Christ, glory in being called Christian, glory at the final judgment.

EXEGETICAL IDEA: Peter consoles the gentiles who suffer for being Christian and doing good by encouraging them to remember that there is glory in suffering: glory in being united with Christ, glory in being called Christian, glory at the final judgment.

HOMILETICAL IDEA: Take heart when you suffer for doing good; inside that suffering there is glory to be found.

1 Peter 5:1-13

SUBJECT: How do Peter's final instructions encourage the gentile elders and youth to endure as believers?

COMPLEMENT: By being humble before God, watching out for the devil, remembering those who are suffering around the world, looking forward to the future, and standing firm in grace.

EXEGETICAL IDEA: Peter's final instructions encourage the gentile elders and youth to endure as believers by being humble before God, watching out for the devil, remembering those who are suffering around the world, looking forward to the future, and standing firm in grace.

HOMILETICAL IDEA: To endure in the faith, remember God, remember the devil, remember the global church, remember the future, remember God's grace.

Difficult Passages/Verses

The most complicated passage in 1 Peter is 3:19–20, where Jesus is preaching to the spirits. There are multiple interpretations of these verses, including (1) that Jesus in his preincarnate state preached through Noah, (2) that after his crucifixion Jesus proclaimed God's victory to the imprisoned fallen angels that had tempted humans before the flood, and (3) that after his crucifixion Jesus proclaimed God's victory to those who had perished at the time of the flood.

To present a full explanation of all the interpretive options of this text in a sermon will overwhelm listeners and distract them from the main point of the passage. A brief mention of two possible readings of the text is enough to show the meaning is unclear. Instead, focus on what Peter is attempting to do with these verses. Peter is displaying Jesus triumphantly proclaiming God's victory, despite remaining incomplete, to spirits who do not believe. Peter intends such an image to be an encouragement and an example for gentile Christians, who themselves are surrounded by opposition and waiting for God's victory.

Cultural Perspectives and Application

Slaves and Women

First Peter has been used to justify slavery in the United States. It has also been used to tell battered women to stay married to their abusive husbands.

Is Peter proslavery and against the safety of women? Or has something gone awry in our understanding and application of this text?

The first-century church had little power to eradicate slavery or change the status of women. With that in mind, Peter is teaching powerless people how to live within a broken system. Remember that what Peter is not teaching in this moment is God's ultimate design for our human systems, or what we should do if we have the power to effect change.

When we view the Bible as a whole, we learn how God values all human beings and that his ultimate design for humanity includes both the eradication of slavery (consider Onesimus) and the safety of women (consider Ruth, Rahab, and others). And for some readers of 1 Peter, our situation is different from those in the first century—we do have the power to effect change to bring those systems more in line with God's design.

In preaching 1 Peter 2:11–3:12, preachers may need to state these facts in order to correct grievous mishandlings of this passage. Preach explicitly that the presence of slavery in this text does not mean God endorses slavery. Preach explicitly that God does not endorse a man hurting his wife. It is quite possible that at least one of the women in your church is a battered wife and confused about what to do. Take this moment as an opportunity to tell her how to find safe shelter. Preach that Christians can effect change.

Persecution and Suffering

The original audience of 1 Peter was facing all kinds of suffering because of their faith. They lived in fear of shaming, threats, physical attacks, fines, imprisonment, mob violence, and execution. Many Christians continue to be persecuted in similar ways today.

In the Western church, however, this is not our experience. To pretend that the occasional bullying we face in the West is persecution is disrespectful to the truly persecuted church. So how do we apply 1 Peter to the nonpersecuted church?

Though some churches may evade persecution, it is downright impossible that there is a church that will evade suffering. And to those who suffer—for any reason—1 Peter contains buckets full of guidance and hope. First Peter is especially applicable to those who find themselves suffering because they are doing good, because they refuse to sin. To the young person who chooses not to engage in premarital sex, but struggles with loneliness, preach 1 Peter. To the business owner who is honest with his or her financial dealings but remains poor, preach 1 Peter. To the couple who struggle with a difficult marriage but refuse divorce, 1 Peter has a message for them too. First Peter exalts Christ. And as they suffer, he is who they need.

─────────────── **RECOMMENDED RESOURCES** ───────────────

Jobes, Karen H. *1 Peter*. Baker Exegetical Commentary on the New
   Testament. Grand Rapids: Baker Academic, 2005.
Marshall, I. Howard. *1 Peter*. IVP New Testament Commentary.
   Downers Grove, IL: InterVarsity, 1991.

2 Peter

GREGORY K. HOLLIFIELD

The second letter attributed to Simon Peter, one of Jesus's Twelve, served to remind an unnamed but specific group of believers to grow in the faith as a hedge against false teaching and falling away.

SUBJECT: What does Peter remind his readers of to keep them from falling away under the influence of certain false teachers who lead licentious lives while denying Christ's return?

COMPLEMENT: Growth in godliness, grounded in a sure faith in the trustworthiness of God's Word, will spare one from judgment when Christ returns.

EXEGETICAL IDEA: Peter, to keep his readers from falling away under the influence of certain false teachers who lead licentious lives while denying Christ's return, reminds them that growth in godliness, grounded in a sure faith in the trustworthiness of God's Word, will spare one from judgment when Christ returns.

HOMILETICAL IDEA: Growth in godliness now will spare us from judgment later.

Selecting Preaching and Teaching Passages in 2 Peter

Peter opens his second letter praying that *grace* and peace might be *multiplied* to his readers in the *knowledge* of God and of our *Lord Jesus* (1:2). He concludes by urging his readers to "*grow* in the *grace* and *knowledge* of our

Lord and Savior Jesus Christ" (3:18 emphasis added). The theme of 2 Peter is obvious!

Between his opening and conclusion, Peter identifies the addends that sum up spiritual growth (1:5–11) and attests to the powerful return of Christ on the basis of his personal experience of Christ's transfiguration and the more sure, Spirit-inspired prophetic word (1:16–21). Afterward, he explains why spiritual growth and confidence in Christ's return are necessary by describing the gross depravity, utter emptiness, and imminent destruction of certain false teachers who would creep in and pose a dire threat to those "who are *barely* escaping from those who live in error" (2:18 ESV, emphasis added)—those whose weakened state leaves them at considerable risk (2:1–22). Peter then lays bare the reason for these false teachers' licentiousness and inevitable judgment—their denial of Christ's return, stemming from a mistaken view of time and God's patience (3:1–10). Only those who grow and persevere in godliness will escape the coming conflagration (3:11–18).

At a minimum, this epistle's exposition will require three sermons: the first on how to grow spiritually, the second on the ways and end of false teachers, and the third on a proper perspective on Christ's return. A fuller treatment might include two sermons from chapter 1 (1:1–11; 1:12–21), three sermons from chapter 2 (2:1–10a; 2:10b–16; 2:17–22), and two sermons from chapter 3 (3:1–10; 3:11–18).

Getting the Subject, Complement, Exegetical Idea, and Homiletical Idea

2 Peter 1

SUBJECT: How does Peter say his readership would confirm their election and entrance into Christ's eternal kingdom?

COMPLEMENT: By growing in the knowledge of Jesus and not losing confidence in his promised return.

EXEGETICAL IDEA: Peter says that his readership would confirm their election and entrance into Christ's eternal kingdom by growing in the knowledge of Jesus and not losing confidence in his promised return.

HOMILETICAL IDEA: Heaven is assured to growing believers.

2 Peter 2

SUBJECT: Why does Peter insist that his readers grow in the knowledge of Jesus and not lose confidence in his return?

COMPLEMENT: Because of the emergence of false teachers—sensual, greedy, and blasphemous—who threatened to destroy those whom they deceive.

EXEGETICAL IDEA: Peter insists that his readers grow in the knowledge of Jesus and not lose confidence in his return because of the emergence of false teachers—sensual, greedy, and blasphemous—who threatened to destroy those whom they deceive.

HOMILETICAL IDEA: False teaching especially threatens the spiritually immature.

2 Peter 3

SUBJECT: What does Peter say was the false teachers' misunderstanding that resulted in their scoffing and licentiousness but, when correctly understood, would lead to his readers' holiness and readiness for Jesus's return?

COMPLEMENT: God's view of time and his patience.

EXEGETICAL IDEA: Peter says the false teachers' misunderstanding that resulted in their scoffing and licentiousness but, when correctly understood, would lead to his readers' holiness and readiness for Jesus's return, was God's view of time and his patience.

HOMILETICAL IDEA: God's view of time and great patience are why Jesus hasn't returned yet.

Difficult Passages/Verses

It's easy to miss an author's meaning in a long sentence (1:3–4), and to get bogged down when preaching through a list of items (1:5–7). Clarity and concision will require the preacher to pay careful attention when working through these verses.

Peter takes for granted his readers' familiarity with several historical referents—Jesus's transfiguration, the angels who sinned, Noah, the destruction of Sodom and Gomorrah, and, not least of all, Balaam and his talking donkey (1:16–2:16)! Today's preacher would be wise not to assume an audience's familiarity with these events while, at the same time, not spending so much time explaining them that hearers miss Peter's train of thought.

Talk of Jesus's return may spark hearers' interest, blank stares, or rolled eyes, depending on what they've heard before. Pastoral sensitivity must be exercised here.

Cultural Perspectives and Application

Eschatology informs ethics. Like Peter, preachers should underscore the trustworthiness of God's promises, the inevitable consequences for denying them, and the impetus they provide for growth and holiness.

RECOMMENDED RESOURCES

Jobes, Karen H. *Letters to the Church: A Survey of Hebrews and the General Epistles*. Grand Rapids: Zondervan, 2011.

1 John

JOEL C. GREGORY

The Big Idea of 1 John

First John identifies love for other Christians, habitual obedience, and the faithful confession that Jesus is the Christ as the marks of the authentic Christian.

SUBJECT: What does John say are the marks of a true Christian?

COMPLEMENT: A life dominated by consistent obedience, a confession that Jesus of Nazareth is the Son of God, and love for other Christians.

EXEGETICAL IDEA: John says the marks of a true Christian are a life dominated by consistent obedience, a confession that Jesus of Nazareth is the Son of God, and love for other Christians.

HOMILETICAL IDEA: Christians consistently confess Christ.

Selecting Preaching and Teaching Passages in 1 John

I have chosen to preach/teach the letter of 1 John thematically rather than going verse by verse in four sermons/lessons. You are, of course, welcome to take a different approach by going chapter by chapter or section heading by section heading. Some of the thematic elements are repeated in different chapters which led me to take a thematic approach.

Getting the Subject, Complement, Exegetical Idea, and Homiletical Idea

1 John 1:1-4

SUBJECT: How does John say his readers should have certainty that the man Jesus is the Christ, the Son of God?

COMPLEMENT: Through the faithful witness of the apostle, who gives evidence based on empirical observation.

EXEGETICAL IDEA: John says his readers are to have certainty that the man Jesus is the Christ, the Son of God, through the faithful witness of the apostle, who gives evidence based on empirical observation.

HOMILETICAL IDEA: You can live in fellowship with God and one another in fullness of joy because your faith rests on eyewitness evidence.

1 John 2:3-6; 3:7-9, 24

SUBJECT: What does John say is the evidence that a person has had a genuine conversion experience?

COMPLEMENT: A life of habitual obedience.

EXEGETICAL IDEA: John says that the evidence that a person has had a genuine conversion experience is a life of habitual obedience.

HOMILETICAL IDEA: You can examine yourself for a life of consistent obedience as one of three evidences of the presence of authentic Christian experience.

1 John 2:10-11; 3:10-16; 4:7-11

SUBJECT: What does John say is demonstrated by a life of habitual love versus a life of habitual hatred?

COMPLEMENT: A life of habitual love demonstrates the move from spiritual darkness to light, just as a life of habitual hatred demonstrates the absence of any relationship to God, who is love.

EXEGETICAL IDEA: John says a life of habitual love demonstrates the move from spiritual darkness to light, just as a life of habitual hatred demonstrates the absence of any relationship to God, who is love.

HOMILETICAL IDEA: Your concrete expression of love gives you the very best evidence that you have experienced the transformation of life that comes from God through Christ.

1 John 2:22; 4:1-6; 5:1

SUBJECT: What does John say is the relation of the Christian confession to the reality of the Christian experience?

COMPLEMENT: The confession that the man Jesus is Christ, the Son of God, necessarily demonstrates the reality of Christian experience.

EXEGETICAL IDEA: John says the confession that the man Jesus is Christ, the Son of God, necessarily demonstrates the reality of Christian experience.

HOMILETICAL IDEA: The genuine Christian maintains the confession that the man Jesus of Nazareth is the Christ, the promised Son of God, in the face of all that life brings.

Difficult Passages/Verses

The major difficulty with 1 John is the apparent contradiction between the necessary confession that all believers still sin (1:8–10) and the flat statement that the person begotten of God does not sin (3:9). This contradiction is only apparent. The tense of the verb in chapter 1 depicts someone who slips into sin like slipping on ice. It is not a habit of life. The tense of the verb in 3:9 suggests someone who lives a life of habitual sin as the signature of life and the dominant motif of the day. It suggests a durable career in sin, not an occasional unintentional slip. The person who delights in sin as the dominant characteristic of life gives evidence of no conversion.

Cultural Perspectives and Application

Mere confession of a creed in no way demonstrates the certainty of Christian life. The confession of Christ must be accompanied by a life of habitual obedience and love for brothers and sisters in Christ. The faith that fizzles before the finish had a fatal flaw from the first. Unregenerate church members may include those who merely mouth the words of the Christian confession but do not demonstrate obedience as the theme of their lives and love for the brothers and sisters as their behavior.

The belief that Jesus of Nazareth was a gifted humanitarian and great moral philosopher, but a mere human, has characterized the Unitarian movement and other marginal belief systems near the Christian faith. Robust, historical Christianity insists he is nothing less than God incarnate, one of the Holy Trinity.

─────── **RECOMMENDED RESOURCES** ───────

Johnson, Thomas Floyd. *First, Second, and Third John.* Peabody, MA: Hendrickson, 1993.

Vaughan, Curtis. *1, 2, 3 John: A Study Guide.* Grand Rapids: Zondervan, 1970.

Yarbrough, Robert W. *1–3 John.* Baker Exegetical Commentary on the New Testament. Grand Rapids: Baker Academic, 2008.

2 John

DAVID A. CURRIE

The Big Idea of 2 John

Second John is a letter to a congregation providing encouragement to remain faithful to the truth in love and to be watchful for false teachers. The feel and tone are similar to Paul's letter to the Philippians. Second John develops many of the same themes—for example, love, truth, the "new commandment," and false teaching—more fully.

SUBJECT: How does John say the recipients of his letter obey Christ's foundational command to love one another?

COMPLEMENT: By watching that they are continuing to walk and abide in the truth of Christ's teaching, believing that he has come in the flesh, so that they may not lose what they have worked for, but have the full reward of having the Father and the Son, unlike deceivers who deny this and thus should not be received or greeted.

EXEGETICAL IDEA: John says the recipients of his letter can obey Christ's foundational command to love one another by watching that they are continuing to walk and abide in the truth of Christ's teaching, believing that he has come in the flesh, so that they may not lose what they have worked for, but have the full reward of having the Father and the Son, unlike deceivers who deny this and thus should not be received or greeted.

HOMILETICAL IDEA: True love walks in the truth of Christ's teaching and watches for those who would wickedly weasel us onto any other way.

Selecting Preaching and Teaching Passages in 2 John

Most preachers and teachers could cover 2 John, at only thirteen verses, in one session. There is a natural break between encouragement in verses 1–6 and warning in verses 7–11 for two sessions with a more singular thematic focus.

Difficult Passages/Verses

Who is "the elder" and why is he usually identified with the apostle John? Who is "the elect lady": an image of a congregation as a whole (see parallel with v. 13: "your elect sister"), or the female leader (Greek *kyria*, feminine of *kyrios*, "Lord") of the congregation (v. 1: "her children")? How does the antichrist in verse 7 relate to the same designation in 1 John 2:18, 22; 4:3 and "the lawless one" in 2 Thessalonians 2:1–10 and "the beast" in Revelation 13?

Unpack what is meant in verse 5 by a "new commandment" (Greek *entolēn kainēn*—"new" in terms of quality, not time) by pointing to the parallel construction in 1 John 2:7–8 and how both passages echo John 13:34, where Jesus says, "A new commandment I give to you, that you love one another" (ESV).

Cultural Perspectives and Application

The warning in verse 11 that anyone who greets a false teacher "takes part in his wicked works" (ESV) sounds overly harsh to modern ears. Explain how expressions of hospitality in general had far more significance in the ancient world and that the Greek word for "greet" in verses 10–11 has highly positive connotations, from the same root as "rejoice," implying approval, not merely a passing nod or "Hello."

Many today separate or even oppose truth and love, or obedience and love, but 2 John strongly argues that they are all inextricably bound together, so the choice is never, "Should I do the truthful/obedient thing or the loving thing in this situation?" Love is not a passing feeling but a way of life that believers walk or abide in, based on obeying the commandments of Jesus and affirming the truth of his teaching. While the specific false teaching of denying "the coming Jesus Christ in the flesh" (v. 7 ESV), reflecting then popular Gnostic dualistic thinking, no longer is a main concern, what contemporary perspectives might those you are preaching to or teaching unwittingly welcome that are equally contrary to who Jesus is and what he taught and commanded?

Verse 3 could be used as the closing benediction in a worship service when preaching on 2 John.

RECOMMENDED RESOURCES

Bateman, Herbert W., IV, and Aaron C. Peer. *John's Letters: An Exegetical Guide for Preaching and Teaching*. Big Greek Idea. Grand Rapids: Kregel Academic, 2018.

Smalley, Stephen S. *1, 2, 3 John*. Word Biblical Commentary. Waco: Word, 1984.

Witherington, Ben, III. *Letters and Homilies for Hellenized Christians: A Socio-Rhetorical Commentary on Titus, 1–2 Timothy, and 1–3 John*, vol. 1. Downers Grove, IL: IVP Academic, 2006.

3 John

DAVID A. CURRIE

The Big Idea of 3 John

Third John is a letter written to an individual ("beloved" and "you" are singular, referring to Gaius) to encourage him and instruct him about dealing with an opponent who is causing division in the church by not submitting to the author's authority. The approach is similar to the Pastoral Epistles addressed to Timothy and Titus.

SUBJECT: How does John say Gaius can attain a testimony as beloved from friends and strangers?

COMPLEMENT: By walking in the truth, by welcoming and supporting those going to the nations in the name of God, and by not imitating evil like Diotrephes, whom the elder is coming to set straight, but doing good as someone who is from God like Demetrius.

EXEGETICAL IDEA: John says Gaius can attain a testimony as beloved from friends and strangers by walking in the truth, by welcoming and supporting those going to the nations in the name of God, and by not imitating evil like Diotrephes, whom the elder is coming to set straight, but doing good as someone who is from God like Demetrius.

HOMILETICAL IDEA: If you want a reputation as a beloved leader, walk in God's truth, welcome God's servants, and warn God's people to acknowledge God's apostles.

Selecting Preaching and Teaching Passages in 3 John

Third John is short enough to be covered in a single session, but the repeated address, "beloved" (vv. 2, 5, 11), divides the material into three sections that could structure a sermon or teaching as a whole or divide into three separate units.

Difficult Passages/Verses

Who is "the elder" and why is he usually identified with the apostle John? Who is Gaius and what is his relationship with the elder? Was he a protégé who was sent by the elder to deal with division in this church? Was he a local leader? What is the relationship between the elder and those who have "gone out for the sake of the name" (v. 7)?[1] Why might they have been known to him and unknown to Gaius? What was their relationship with the gentiles?

When the elder indicates that he has "written something to the church" (v. 9), what might he be alluding to? First John? Second John? A lost letter? Who is Diotrephes and what might have been his relationship to the church that Gaius is associated with? What of Demetrius and his relationship (perhaps the one who delivered the letter for the elder)?

Why is 3 John the only book in the New Testament that does not mention Jesus explicitly? Is Jesus alluded to implicitly in "for the sake of the name" (v. 7), "workers for the truth" (v. 8), or "from the truth itself" (v. 12)?

Cultural Perspectives and Application

Verse 2 has been misapplied by some as a promise to be claimed guaranteeing health and wealth. This is not a special promise to all believers for all time but a standard expression of blessing that usually followed the greeting in letters in the ancient world. The equivalent today would be "Dear Gaius, hope all is well . . ."

Third John provides some tantalizing hints about how mission and ministry were carried out in the early church. Verses 7–8 seem to reflect a similar pattern to the missionary journeys of Paul and of teams sent out from Paul to the gentiles (literally "the nations," *ethnikōn*) and supported by both the sending church and those churches that provided hospitality and resources along the way. Highlighting a congregation's mission relationships, or initiating some if there are none, would be a good contemporary application to encourage

---

1. Scripture quotations in this chapter are from the ESV.

believers to "be fellow workers for the truth" (v. 8). Today's church leaders who feel their authority being questioned or rejected can draw comfort that even the apostle John experienced something similar, and should imitate his counsel to Gaius to resist fighting fire with fire ("Do not imitate evil," v. 11) and to seek out likeminded trustworthy colleagues (like Demetrius).

RECOMMENDED RESOURCES

See recommended resources for 2 John.

Jude

KENNETH LANGLEY

The Big Idea of Jude

Jude might be the most neglected book in the New Testament. The author's harsh tone and citation of nonbiblical sources have been off-putting for many preachers. But his message is one we and our congregants need. Arrogant, licentious influencers in the church still pose a threat, using grace as an excuse for undermining biblical standards of sexuality.

SUBJECT: How does Jude instruct the church when troubled by godless influencers in its midst?

COMPLEMENT: To beware of them and to contend for the faith by mercifully ministering to one another and trusting God to keep his people.

EXEGETICAL IDEA: Jude instructs the church, when troubled by godless influencers in its midst, to beware of them and to contend for the faith by mercifully ministering to one another and trusting God to keep his people.

HOMILETICAL IDEA: When professing Christians cheapen grace and say that anything goes, the church must keep the faith and trust God to keep his people faithful.

This idea views the doxology as essential to the letter's message. Depending on circumstances (e.g., if the congregation is hearing a series on sexuality), a preacher might consider being more specific in the wording of the big idea, including something about licentiousness or the erosion of God's standards for sex.

Selecting Preaching and Teaching Passages in Jude

Jude can be preached in one sermon if we don't get bogged down in its problematic paragraphs. Its structure is straightforward: What? Contend for the faith (vv. 1–3). Why? Arrogant, licentious, godless men pretending to be Christians threaten the church (vv. 4–19). How? Keep ourselves in God's love (vv. 20–21), being merciful to those who struggle (vv. 22–23) and trusting God's power to keep us (vv. 24–25). Or consider two sermons: "Contend for the Faith—Why?" (vv. 1–19) and "Contend for the Faith—How?" (vv. 20–25). Either way, the preacher or worship leader will want to use the well-loved doxology of verses 24–25.

Difficult Passages/Verses

Jude's description of the godless presents at least two challenges for preachers. First, his tone is harsh. He says he would have rather written a warm, happy letter (v. 3), but the threat to his flock is so serious he can't afford to play nice. Preaching Jude, a preacher will have to decide what vocabulary and delivery best communicate the urgency of contending for the faith in our day. And note: "the faith" for Jude is not his readers' believing but the objective, nonnegotiable content of the gospel. This, Jude implies, includes the lordship of Christ and a concept of grace that involves sanctification.

Second, Jude quotes noncanonical literature familiar to his congregation but not to ours. The preacher can concisely summarize the point of Jude's citations and note that we too sometimes cite nonbiblical literature without implying that what we quote is inspired.

Cultural Perspectives and Application

How do we apply Jude's letter to our own congregation? Here are four possibilities:

- Work with the key word "keep." Jude begins and ends his letter saying we're *kept by God* (vv. 1, 24), but urges us to *keep ourselves* in God's love. Jesus said we remain in his love by obeying him.
- The threat in Jude is not primarily doctrinal but the arrogant, licentious character of the godless. They take grace to mean anything goes and so deny the lordship of Jesus. Where in our own day do we

see influential professed Christians endorsing sexual perversion (and greed, though sexual sin dominates in Jude's portrait)?

- How can we minister to believers who are influenced in varying degrees (vv. 22–23) by the ungodly in the church?
- Verses 24–25 are not exhortation, but preachers can tease out the practical implications of this wonderful doxology.

RECOMMENDED RESOURCES

Helm, David R. *1 and 2 Peter and Jude.* Wheaton: Crossway, 2008.

Lucas, Dick, and Christopher Green. *The Message of 2 Peter and Jude.* Downers Grove, IL: InterVarsity, 1995.

Moo, Douglas J. *2 Peter and Jude.* The NIV Application Commentary. Grand Rapids: Zondervan, 1996.

Revelation

DAVID L. MATHEWSON

The Big Idea of Revelation

The book of Revelation (from "Apocalypse," meaning an unveiling or uncovering) records a vision given by God to John that addresses the situation of seven churches in Asia Minor (AD 90s) struggling to live out their faithful witness in the context of the first-century pagan Roman Empire. After an introduction (1:1–8) and initial commissioning vision (1:9–20), the risen Christ addresses the seven churches (chaps. 2–3) and then gives John a vision to write down for the churches (4:1–22:5). The book ends with concluding instructions to John and the readers on how the book is to be received (22:6–21).

SUBJECT: Why does John say Christians in Asia Minor are to refuse to compromise with Rome but maintain allegiance to God and follow the Lamb in obedience no matter what consequences it brings?

COMPLEMENT: Because God will return to judge the world and save his people.

EXEGETICAL IDEA: John says Christians in Asia Minor are to refuse to compromise with Rome but maintain allegiance to God and follow the Lamb in obedience no matter what consequences it brings because God will return to judge the world and save his people.

HOMILETICAL IDEA: Our motivation for refusing to compromise our allegiance to God and the Lamb in this present world is our future reward when the righteous Judge returns.

Selecting Preaching and Teaching Passages in Revelation

With the book of Revelation, the preacher will probably want to steer away from preaching verses or small paragraphs. Revelation tells a story, and the listeners need to get a sense of the whole. While it is possible to preach or teach through the entire book in a series over the course of a year or longer, given the length and complexity of the book the preacher may wish to select major representative sections from Revelation to focus on while still being aware of the surrounding context. This could cover roughly sixteen weeks. This will give listeners a broad cross section of the kind of material in Revelation, as well as touch on all the dominant themes and concerns of the book. To avoid getting bogged down in too many of the minute details of the vision, the expositor should probably aim to cover entire chapters or larger sections, starting with chapter 1. The expositor might then choose to spend time on each of the seven messages in chapters 2–3, since they are discrete messages to specific churches and their problems. Then the rest of the book could be covered in larger representative chunks (e.g., chaps. 4–5, 6, 7, 10–11, 12–13, 17–18, 19, 20, 21–22). Alternatively, if the expositor wants to treat Revelation in a little more detail, he or she could cover chapters 1–11 in about fifteen weeks and then in several months or even a year come back to chapters 12–22 for another fifteen weeks.

Getting the Subject, Complement, Exegetical Idea, and Homiletical Idea

Revelation 1

SUBJECT: Why does John say that Christ is qualified to examine and address the seven churches in Asia Minor?

COMPLEMENT: Because through his resurrection and defeat of death he is the exalted Son of Man and Lord over the entire universe.

EXEGETICAL IDEA: John says that Christ is qualified to examine and address the seven churches in Asia Minor because through his resurrection and defeat of death he is the exalted Son of Man and Lord over the entire universe.

HOMILETICAL IDEA: Christ is Lord over his church because through his resurrection he is the exalted Lord over all things.

Revelation 2-3

SUBJECT: Why does John warn the churches to repent of their compromise or give them encouragement to persevere in the midst of suffering?

COMPLEMENT: So that they will maintain their faithful witness to the world and receive their future reward.

EXEGETICAL IDEA: John warns the churches to repent of their compromise or gives them encouragement to persevere in the midst of suffering so that they will maintain their faithful witness to the world and receive their future reward.

HOMILETICAL IDEA: The church that refuses to compromise will be a faithful witness and receive a future reward.

Revelation 4-5

SUBJECT: Why does John say that all of heaven worships God and the Lamb?

COMPLEMENT: Because God is the sovereign creator of all things and through the Lamb has redeemed all things.

EXEGETICAL IDEA: John says that all of heaven worships God and the Lamb because God is the sovereign creator of all things and through the Lamb has redeemed all things.

HOMILETICAL IDEA: We are drawn to worship God and the Lamb because they are the creator of all things and the redeemer of all things.

Revelation 6

SUBJECT: How does John encourage God's people to respond to the suffering they encounter in an evil and unjust world?

COMPLEMENT: By waiting patiently until God vindicates his people by pouring out his wrath in judgment on their enemies.

EXEGETICAL IDEA: John encourages God's people to respond to the suffering they encounter in an evil and unjust world by waiting patiently until God vindicates them by pouring out his wrath in judgment on their enemies.

HOMILETICAL IDEA: God's people can face suffering with patience in an unjust world because of the assurance that God will one day vindicate them.

Revelation 7

SUBJECT: What does John say will happen if the church is victorious by remaining faithful in the midst of the pagan empire?

COMPLEMENT: They will joyfully stand before the throne and receive the reward of their future salvation.

EXEGETICAL IDEA: John says that if the church is victorious by remaining faithful in the midst of the pagan empire, they will joyfully stand before the throne and receive the reward of their future salvation.

HOMILETICAL IDEA: The reward for standing firm in the presence of an evil world is one day standing victorious in the presence of God.

Revelation 11

SUBJECT: What does John say is the role of the church during the time God pours out his preliminary judgments on the world?

COMPLEMENT: To maintain its faithful witness in the face of persecution until God vindicates his people.

EXEGETICAL IDEA: John says that the role of the church during the time God pours out his preliminary judgments on the world is to maintain its faithful witness in the face of persecution until God vindicates his people.

HOMILETICAL IDEA: While we wait for God's justice, we as God's people faithfully witness to the reality of God's kingdom no matter what consequences we face.

Revelation 12-13

SUBJECT: Why does John tell God's people to stand firm in the face of opposition and persecution by human authorities?

COMPLEMENT: Because they know that its true source is Satan's attempt to thwart God's purposes and to destroy God's people, which will fail.

EXEGETICAL IDEA: John tells God's people to stand firm in the face of opposition and persecution by human authorities because they know that its true source is Satan's attempt to thwart God's purposes and to destroy God's people, which will fail.

HOMILETICAL IDEA: God's people can stand firm in the face of opposition knowing that their battle is against a defeated foe.

Revelation 14

SUBJECT: What does John say is the effect of God's judgment on those who hear the gospel?

COMPLEMENT: Salvation for those who respond to the gospel in obedience but punishment for those who reject it.

EXEGETICAL IDEA: John says that the effect of God's judgment on those who hear the gospel is salvation for those who respond in obedience but punishment for those who reject it.

HOMILETICAL IDEA: God's judgment is good news for those who respond to the gospel in obedience but bad news for those who reject it.

Revelation 17-18

SUBJECT: Why does John say Christians are to refuse to associate with Babylon/Rome and all that it offers?

COMPLEMENT: Because despite appearances it is unjust and evil, and God is going to destroy it in judgment.

EXEGETICAL IDEA: John says Christians are to refuse to associate with Babylon/Rome and all that it offers because despite appearances it is unjust and evil, and God is going to destroy it in judgment.

HOMILETICAL IDEA: God's people should reject Babylon because one day God will reject it and those belonging to it.

Revelation 19

SUBJECT: Why does John explain that believers can have confidence that God will one day eliminate all evil and injustice?

COMPLEMENT: Because God's judgment is an expression of his own holy, just, and true character.

EXEGETICAL IDEA: John explains that believers can have confidence that God will one day eliminate all evil and injustice because God's judgment is an expression of his holy, true, and just character.

HOMILETICAL IDEA: We can have confidence that God will one day eliminate all evil and injustice because God's character is holy, true, and just.

Revelation 20

SUBJECT: What does John say God will do for his people when he returns in the future to judge the dragon?

COMPLEMENT: He will vindicate his people, showing that their sacrifice and suffering in this life was not in vain.

EXEGETICAL IDEA: John says that when God returns in the future to judge the dragon, he will vindicate his people, showing that their sacrifice and suffering in this life was not in vain.

HOMILETICAL IDEA: One day when God returns to judge the church's chief enemy, he will not forget the sacrifice of his faithful people.

Revelation 21:1–22:5

SUBJECT: What does John say is the ultimate reward for the people of God who refuse to compromise with the pagan empire?

COMPLEMENT: Life in the New Jerusalem in a New Creation void of all evil, where God and the Lamb live in their midst.

EXEGETICAL IDEA: John says that the ultimate reward for the people of God who refuse to compromise with the pagan empire is life in the New Jerusalem in a New Creation void of all evil, where God and the Lamb live in their midst.

HOMILETICAL IDEA: One day God will reward his faithful people not with an escape to heaven but with a New Creation where God himself lives with us.

Revelation 22:6–21

SUBJECT: How does John encourage the readers of Revelation to respond to the message of the book?

COMPLEMENT: In worship and obedience, because Christ will soon return to reward those who obey and judge those who refuse to obey.

EXEGETICAL IDEA: John encourages the readers of Revelation to respond to the message of the book in worship and obedience, because Christ will soon return to reward those who obey and judge those who refuse to obey.

HOMILETICAL IDEA: The expected return of Christ to reward and judge should motivate God's people to holy living.

Difficult Passages/Verses

Perhaps the biggest barrier to understanding Revelation is coming to grips with the kind of literature it is. Most of the misunderstanding surrounding Revelation stems from a failure to realize what kind of a book it is. Revelation actually consists of three literary forms that would have been familiar to a first-century audience, however much they are unfamiliar to us today.[1]

1. See Richard Bauckham, *The Theology of the Book of Revelation* (Cambridge: Cambridge University Press, 1993), chap. 1, for a helpful description of the three genres of Revelation and hermeneutical implications.

First, Revelation is an apocalypse. The term "apocalypse" refers to a type of literature in existence in the first century that records a seer/prophet's vision. An apocalypse consists of visions of the heavenly world, and also of events in the readers' own day and in the future. It is not primarily meant to predict the future, but to unveil the true nature of things. It helps readers to see their situation in a new light so that they will act accordingly. As an apocalypse, Revelation communicates through symbols and metaphors, not literally (see below).

Second, Revelation is a prophecy. The primary purpose of prophecy is not so much to predict the future as to console and to exhort or warn God's people. For those in Asia Minor tempted to compromise their faith, Revelation is a warning for them of the consequences of failing to remain faithful.

Third, Revelation is a letter. Therefore, it is meant to address the needs of the seven historical churches in Asia Minor and so must have communicated information that the readers would have understood and that would have addressed the crisis they faced (it was not hidden for a later twenty-first-century audience). So an important principle for the expositor to remember is that any interpretation of Revelation that John could never have intended, and his first-century readers could never have understood, is probably to be rejected (nuclear war, helicopters, computer chips, etc.). As with any other book in the New Testament, the preacher will want to spend time exploring the original historical-cultural context of the book and ask what the original author (John) most likely intended to communicate to his first-century readers (the seven churches in Asia Minor).

The most crucial issue that the expositor will need to deal with is the pervasive symbolism in the book. The visions of Revelation are communicated not literally but in highly symbolic or metaphorical language. The visions refer to real persons, places, and events, but they are described not literally but metaphorically. John sees a Lamb with seven horns and eyes, but what is important is what this refers to metaphorically: Jesus Christ who was sacrificed for our sins, but who is all powerful and sees all things. John sees two witnesses, but the two witnesses symbolize the entire witnessing church. John sees a new Jerusalem coming down out of heaven, but because he refers to it as the bride, the wife of the Lamb (21:9–10), the new Jerusalem refers not so much to a literal city as to the people of God themselves. The source of most of John's metaphors is the Old Testament, particularly the prophetic literature (Isaiah, Ezekiel, Daniel, Zechariah). Therefore, many of John's metaphors can be understood only when interpreted in light of their usage and context in the Old Testament. Here, if ever, the preacher needs to rely on good up-to-date commentaries to help in understanding Revelation's symbolism.

Another issue relates to the temporal context of Revelation's vision. Does John's vision refer to events that are already past, that happened in the first century (preterist view), or is his vision exclusively future, referring to events that will take place just prior to and during the second coming of Christ (futurist view)? Or is it just symbolic of the overall struggle between God and his kingdom versus Satan and his rule that will characterize the entire church age until Christ returns, a struggle that could find expression at different times throughout history (idealist view)? Most likely the preacher will find a combination of these approaches. Revelation is addressing the first-century church in the Roman Empire to help them make sense of their situation. But John also sees the future wrap-up of history at the second coming of Christ (esp. chaps. 19–22). Until then, the symbols have a way of transcending the first-century situation to address similar situations with timeless principles until Christ returns. Therefore, Revelation temporally is a combination of references to the present of the first readers and the future, as well as the time in between.

There are still numerous passages that may create difficulties for the interpreter. The seven messages to the churches in chapters 2–3 can be difficult for the preacher because of numerous historical-cultural references that the first-century readers would have assumed but are sticking points for the modern expositor. For example, when the church in Pergamum is promised a "white stone" (2:17) if they repent and overcome, it is not clear to us what John has in mind. Suggestions are that the white stone in the ancient world was a vote of acquittal, or was used for admission into a banquet or festival. At this point the expositor may not need to decide on the precise background but recognize that it is metaphorical for entrance into heaven as a reward for faithfulness.

With other passages, understanding the cultural background is even more critical. In 3:15–16 the church of Laodicea is told to be either "hot" or "cold," but instead they are "lukewarm." This has commonly been taken as a reference to spiritual temperature. Jesus wants people to either take a stand for him (spiritually hot) or against him (spiritually cold), but instead Laodicean Christians are wishy-washy and middle-of-the-road (spiritually lukewarm). Yet given the historical background of these terms in the context of Laodicea, this is precisely *not* what John meant. Hot and cold were both positive metaphors for John and his first readers; hot and cold were both good things. The "hot" referred to the hot water springs of nearby Hierapolis, which were good for healing. The "cold" referred to the cold water supply of nearby Colossae, which was refreshing for drink. And hot and cold drinks were desirable at banquets. Instead, Laodicea's own water supply was tepid and questionable for drinking. Lukewarm water was also used to induce vomiting.

Consequently, lukewarm here means "useless" and "worthless," precisely the state of the Laodicean church. Lukewarm does not mean uncommitted, middle-of-the-road Christianity. When reading the rest of the message, one sees that the Laodicean church had completely rejected Christ and were proud of their own accomplishments and wealth, so that they did not need Christ any longer. The preacher should avoid using the message of lukewarm Christians as a warning against middle-of-the-road or uncommitted Christianity, but use it instead as a warning against the danger of outright rejection of Christ due to complacency and self-sufficiency.

A special challenge for the expositor is the series of seven judgment plagues. In chapter 6 the first four seal judgments are identified as horses of different colors. But what is being referred to? For first-century readers, it is likely that they would have identified them as judgments on the Roman Empire, and subsequently on all world empires until the arrival of the second coming to bring about the final judgment at the day of the Lord. Conquest, conflict, death, economic disparity, famine, and so on are all results of a people that pursues conquest, status, and economic prosperity at any cost. These plagues can be seen as similar to Paul's teaching in Romans 1:18–32: the pouring out of God's wrath on an ungodly world consists of God "handing them over" to their desires; likewise, God's judgment on unjust nations, empires, and people can be seen in God handing them over to the consequences of their own thirst for power and prosperity.

Something similar could be said about the trumpet judgments in chapters 8–9. How does one preach the trumpet judgments? Here the expositor will want to avoid speculating about what exactly these plagues refer to and will look like. Rather, he or she should emphasize that God is calling us to repentance and faithful obedience through anticipations of the final end-time judgment in the form of these preliminary judgments. The main point is not what these judgments will look like but the certainty of God's judgments and the unreliability of all that this world offers as an alternative to the worship and allegiance that is due only to God.

Another challenging text is the vision of the two witnesses in chapter 11. Who are these two witnesses? Are they two literal individuals who will emerge in the future, or do they refer to something else? First, the preacher should recall the symbolic nature of John's visions: they refer to actual persons and events but describe them metaphorically rather than literally. The key seems to be that John identifies the two witnesses as two lampstands (11:4). Back in 1:20 the lampstands have already been identified by Jesus himself as the church. Therefore, it is likely that the two lampstands symbolize the entire witnessing church throughout the entire church age. This would be similar to

Uncle Sam symbolizing the entire US government rather than a literal person living in the nation's capital. That there are only two witnesses may reflect the fact that only two churches in chapters 2–3 are faithful. This vision, then, is not just a future prediction but a call for the church to maintain its faithful witness until Christ returns, even in the face of suffering and opposition. The result will be vindication and reward when Christ returns (11:11–12). The preacher should refrain from getting bogged down in the details of fire coming out of the mouth of the two witnesses (11:5) or how the entire world can see them (11:10). The main point is the effective witness of the church, even in the face of suffering and death.

A perennially difficult text to handle is Revelation 13:18 with its reference to the cryptic number 666. Here if anywhere the preacher needs to resist the temptation to speculate about what this might refer to, recalling the symbolic nature of Revelation and that, whatever it is, the first readers must have been able to make sense of it. Two likely options are that it referred in some way to the name Nero, a particularly evil emperor that John wanted his readers to recall as the embodiment of evil and anti-godly values, or that it expresses falling short of the perfect number 777, indicating imperfection, sin, and evil. In any case, chapters 12–13 together unveil the true source of the church's persecution and struggle. Ultimately, the source is Satan (chap. 12) and his two beastly representatives (chap. 13), who likely represent those responsible in the first century, or any age, for promoting allegiance to Satan and anything that would substitute for true worship of God. The 666, the mark of the beast, is worn on the right hand or forehead (13:16). A mark symbolizes ownership and allegiance. To receive the mark of the beast means to belong to or be loyal to that which opposes God and his kingdom. The issue that the preacher will want to emphasize, then, is not the identity of the beast or the number 666 but competing allegiances. One cannot serve God and the world at the same time. God's people cannot give God the exclusive obedience and worship he deserves while giving allegiance and obedience to any person or institution that would challenge our allegiance to God and Jesus Christ.

Probably the most popular but problematic text in Revelation is the millennium passage in 20:4–6.[2] This vision of Satan being bound for a thousand years while the saints come to life and reign for a thousand years (hence, the millennium) has been interpreted in a variety of ways. Some have interpreted

---

2. For a discussion of five types of premillennialism, showing that not all premillennialists are created equal, see Sung Wook Chung and David L. Mathewson, *Models of Premillennialism* (Eugene, OR: Cascade Books, 2018).

this to mean that the thousand years is symbolic of the entire period of church history between the first and second comings of Christ (amillennialism). Others have seen it as a reference to a future golden age that the church itself will usher in through its evangelizing and through the work of the Holy Spirit. After that period of time Christ will return (postmillennialism). Another view is to see it as a future period of time that will come about only with the return of Christ to set up his reign on earth (premillennialism).

In preaching this passage it would probably be better to steer away from these debates and focus on the function of the millennium in this chapter. The millennium is a reward for the faithful people of God who have suffered at the hands of Satan during their time on earth. In the context of Satan's judgment, the millennium is a reversal of all that the people suffered on earth. Satan ruled over them and persecuted them, even putting some to death. Now in a profound reversal the saints come to life and they reign. A sermon on Revelation 20 should emphasize that the millennium will be God's last word on whether all the suffering and sacrifice were worth it. God will one day reward and vindicate his people, and it will more than compensate for anything they sacrificed here on earth.

Cultural Perspectives and Application

There are a number of areas of application that the modern-day expositor will want to emphasize in preaching through Revelation. First, and perhaps most obvious, is the assurance and hope Revelation gives. In a world that is full of evil, violence, injustice, and pain, Revelation provides a message of hope that Jesus will one day return to fix everything that is wrong with this world. But Revelation does not offer an escape from this world to float around in heaven on clouds. The book ends with God and the Lamb dwelling with their people on a new *earth* (21:1–22:5). The hope of God's people is physical and earthly, albeit an earth renewed and transformed, stripped of all the effects of sin and everything that makes life on this earth miserable. A future physical and earthly hope is worth sacrificing the things of this earth for.

A second important area of application is faithful obedience. The book of Revelation is not meant to give us information to speculate as to the time of Christ's return, how close we are to the end, or to construct a time line of end-time events. It was written to call the seven churches in Asia Minor to repent and maintain their faithful witness. In the same way, the last book of the Bible is a call to the church today to maintain its faithful witness to the truth of God's Word and the reality of his kingdom on earth in a world that rejects and contests God's truth and kingdom. The church is to be a kingdom of priests (1:5–6) that witnesses to and models the values of God's kingdom in the present. This requires faithful obedience to God's Word. It requires that we follow the Lamb wherever he goes (14:4), no matter the consequences it brings. Revelation is first and foremost a call to unqualified obedience to Christ in faithful endurance and discipleship.

Related to this, a third area of application revolves around the theme of worship. Revelation is primarily a book of worship and calls on God's people to give God and the Lamb the exclusive worship and allegiance that only they deserve. To worship anyone or anything else is idolatry. In a world, much like the first century, that offers competing claims and alternative objects of worship, Revelation calls on us to resist all such claims and to worship God and the Lamb. Revelation reorients us to what stands at the center of all reality—the throne of the sovereign God and the redeemer Lamb (chaps. 4–5) who alone are worthy of our worship.

A fourth area of application should be a warning against complacency. Five of the seven churches in chapters 2–3 had become complacent and were compromising to some degree with their pagan surroundings. For many Christians, the book of Revelation will not be a comfort in times of persecution but a wake-up call to get us out of our complacency in this world. Revelation calls on God's people not to become too comfortable with what this world has to offer and compromise our faithful witness to the gospel as the distinctive people of God. Persecution may never be an issue for many Christians, especially living in North America, but compromise with the world will always be a danger that must be resisted. Revelation is a call to resist all such dangers to compromise and become complacent, lest we find ourselves on the wrong side of God's judgments in the future.

A final area of application is to expose injustice, idolatry, and evil in this world and even in our own lives. One of the main functions of Revelation is to expose the true nature of the dominant empire in John's day: Rome (chaps. 17–18). John's apocalypse exposes first-century Rome for what it truly was—evil, idolatrous, ungodly, and violent—so that God's people would refuse to participate in it. In the same way, Revelation continues to expose empires and entities today that are also ungodly, violent, evil, and unjust. And it calls on us to resist and stand against them with the truth of God's Word. Revelation's vision also exposes areas in our own lives where we may be the source of injustice, violence, or oppression in the lives of others. It roots out areas where we may be complicit in evil and ungodliness.

RECOMMENDED RESOURCES

Bauckham, Richard J. *The Theology of the Book of Revelation.* Cambridge: Cambridge University Press, 1993.

Gorman, Michael J. *Reading Revelation Responsibly: Uncivil Worship and Witness.* Eugene, OR: Cascade Books, 2011.

Paul, Ian. *Revelation.* Tyndale New Testament Commentaries. Downers Grove, IL: IVP Academic, 2018.

Conclusion

SCOTT M. GIBSON

This book is intended to be a handbook, a companion, a guide in helping you teach and preach God's Word. It does not replace good, hard work as one studies in preparation for teaching and preaching. Each biblical book is divided into preachable and teachable units, but you may want to combine these units or compress them as you work your way through a book. We ask that you do your homework. Do not rely solely on the work of the authors in this volume. Check them. Make sure that what they have determined as the idea of the text is indeed the idea of the text. Those who have been schooled in the ancient languages of biblical Hebrew and Greek have the responsibility to use these tools as they study each passage.

On another front, the homiletical ideas may not be phrased the way you would word them. You have every right to change them to make them yours. When you do, make sure that the homiletical idea you develop does not alter the meaning of the biblical passage. Be sure that your idea reflects the intention of the exegetical idea—but make the homiletical idea yours.

As for suggested sermon series, you may want to lengthen or shorten a series. Take a look at your teaching and preaching context to determine what biblical books and passages to preach on. You want to meet your listeners where they are so that through your teaching and preaching you may move them toward maturity in Christ.[1]

---

1. For help in determining sermon planning, see Scott M. Gibson, *Preaching with a Plan: Sermon Strategies for Growing Mature Believers* (Grand Rapids: Baker Books, 2012).

This handbook does not commend any particular sermon structure for each idea suggested. Your task is to determine the best way to communicate the idea from each biblical text, all the while making sure that the listeners know, see, and understand the idea you are communicating. Sometimes sermon structures can be more confusing than clear. Remember, you want to get across to your listeners the homiletical idea—and show how it is supported by the passage. You want your listeners to remember the homiletical idea. All teachers and preachers would be helped if they remembered this: clarity is key in sermon structure and in teaching.[2]

We hope that this companion will be a resource to which you will return again and again as you preach and teach. Know that it has been prepared with you in mind. Our hope is to help you—and to aid those to whom you speak.

All the contributors to this volume are men and women who are committed to the authority of God's Word and trust its effectual work in the lives of those to whom we teach and preach. As the apostle Paul urged Timothy, his son in the faith, we urge the same: "Do your best to present yourself to God as one approved, a worker who does not need to be ashamed and who correctly handles the word of truth" (2 Tim. 2:15).

Thank you for investing yourself and your listeners in good, clear biblical preaching and teaching!

---

2. For help in sermon structure, see Haddon W. Robinson, *Biblical Preaching: The Development and Delivery of Expository Messages*, 3rd ed. (Grand Rapids: Baker Academic, 2014); Keith Willhite and Scott M. Gibson, eds., *The Big Idea of Biblical Preaching: Connecting the Bible to People* (Grand Rapids: Baker, 1998).

Contributors

Casey C. Barton (PhD, University of Toronto) is ordained to word and sacrament in the Evangelical Covenant Church and currently preaches and teaches in California's Central Valley.

Patricia M. Batten (DMin, Gordon-Conwell Theological Seminary) is associate director of the Haddon W. Robinson Center for Preaching and ranked adjunct assistant professor of preaching at Gordon-Conwell Theological Seminary.

France B. Brown Jr. (PhD candidate, Midwestern Baptist Theological Seminary) is Ernest L. Mays assistant professor of expository preaching and biblical teaching at College of Biblical Studies, Houston.

Timothy Bushfield (PhD candidate, London School of Theology) is senior pastor of Community Church of East Gloucester, Gloucester, Massachusetts.

Sid Buzzell (PhD, Michigan State University) is dean of the school of theology, academic vice president, and professor of biblical exposition and leadership at Colorado Christian University.

Brandon R. Cash (PhD, Biola University) is chair of Christian ministry and leadership and assistant professor of preaching and hermeneutics at Talbot School of Theology, Biola University.

Calvin W. Choi (PhD, London School of Theology) is senior pastor of Watertown Evangelical Church, Watertown, Massachusetts.

David A. Currie (PhD, University of St. Andrews) is professor of pastoral theology and dean of the doctor of ministry program at Gordon-Conwell Theological Seminary.

J. Kent Edwards (PhD, Biola University) is professor of preaching and leadership at Talbot School of Theology, Biola University.

Bruce W. Fong (PhD, University of Aberdeen) is dean and professor of pastoral ministries at Dallas Theological Seminary, Houston.

Alison Gerber (MDiv, Gordon-Conwell Theological Seminary) is senior pastor of Second Congregational Church, Peabody, Massachusetts.

Scott M. Gibson (DPhil, University of Oxford) is professor of preaching and holder of the David E. Garland Chair of Preaching and director of the PhD program in preaching at George W. Truett Theological Seminary, Baylor University.

Julian R. Gotobed (PhD, Boston University) is director of practical theology and mission at Westcott House, Cambridge, England.

Joel C. Gregory (PhD, Baylor University) is professor of preaching and holder of the George W. Truett endowed chair in preaching and evangelism at George W. Truett Theological Seminary, Baylor University.

Paul A. Hoffman (PhD, University of Manchester) is senior pastor of Evangelical Friends Church, Newport, Rhode Island.

Gregory K. Hollifield (PhD, Mid-America Baptist Theological Seminary) is associate dean of assessment and reporting and adjunct faculty at Memphis College of Urban and Theological Studies.

Mary S. Hulst (PhD, University of Illinois) is university pastor and adjunct professor at Calvin University.

Pablo A. Jiménez (DMin, Columbia Theological Seminary) is associate dean of the Latino and global ministries program and associate professor of preaching at Gordon-Conwell Theological Seminary.

Matthew D. Kim (PhD, University of Edinburgh) is the George F. Bennett Professor of Preaching and Practical Theology, director of the Haddon W. Robinson Center for Preaching, and director of Mentored Ministry at Gordon-Conwell Theological Seminary.

Kenneth Langley (DMin, Denver Seminary) is adjunct professor of preaching at Trinity Evangelical Divinity School and senior pastor of Christ Community Church, Zion, Illinois.

David L. Mathewson (PhD, University of Aberdeen) is associate professor of New Testament at Denver Seminary.

Steven D. Mathewson (DMin, Gordon-Conwell Theological Seminary) is director of the doctor of ministry program at Western Seminary and senior pastor of CrossLife Evangelical Free Church, Libertyville, Illinois.

Chris Rappazini (PhD, Gonzaga University) is associate professor and program head in pastoral studies at Moody Bible Institute and Moody Theological Seminary.

Ken Shigematsu (DMin, San Francisco Theological Seminary) is pastor of Tenth Church, Vancouver, British Columbia.

Andrew C. Thompson (PhD, London School of Theology) is pastor of Union City Church, Brunswick, Georgia.

Scott A. Wenig (PhD, University of Colorado Boulder) is professor of applied theology and the Haddon W. Robinson chair of biblical preaching at Denver Seminary.

Nathaniel M. Wright (PhD, London School of Theology) is a deacon ordinand in the Anglican diocese of Christ Our Hope.

Heather Joy Zimmerman (PhD candidate, Wheaton College) is a doctoral student in Old Testament and Homiletics at Wheaton College Graduate School.

Subject Index

Scripture Index